THREE THOUSAND YEARS
of
EDUCATIONAL WISDOM

THREE THOUSAND YEARS *of* EDUCATIONAL WISDOM

Selections from Great Documents

EDITED AND COMMENTED UPON

BY ROBERT ULICH
HARVARD UNIVERSITY

SECOND EDITION, ENLARGED, WITH
NEW CHAPTERS ON JOHN DEWEY AND
THE JUDAIC TRADITION

HARVARD UNIVERSITY PRESS

CAMBRIDGE, MASSACHUSETTS

LONDON, ENGLAND

PREFACE

WE ARE fumbling around in education because we know so little about the future and do not bother to know enough about the past. Education is not only one of the greatest human enterprises in immediate planning, with parents, teachers, "educators," school administrators, and college presidents as its leaders. It is also a long-enduring process of cultural self-evolution. This process expresses itself through the minds of men who are interested in, and capable of, looking deeper into the nature, the needs, and the aspirations of human beings than are most people.

As long as the daily planning, doing, and structuring in education are constantly nourished by the wellsprings of the total cultural evolution, education and civilization are in a state of health; when the contact is cut they are sick and a crisis occurs.

We live now in such a crisis. The degree of futile busy-ness constantly increases in proportion to the loss of a feeling for cultural depth and continuity.

This book is an attempt to help in the rebuilding of the lost contact between the surface and the depth of civilization. One could also say it is an attempt at general education; the term "general education" being understood not in the sense of education in generalities, but in the sense of placing ideas of general human significance behind the often chopped up and atomistic activities of life.

Therefore, if in this book large extracts of the educational writings of such men as Confucius, Plato, Aristotle, the medieval theologians, Luther, Erasmus, Rousseau, Pestalozzi and others are offered, it is not for the sake of these men—they do not need it. It is for our sake. For this reason I also dare hope that the book will be read not only by teachers and students of education, but by all those for whom the values of civilization are not just given facts, but incessant demands upon our emotions, our reason, and our purposes.

The shortcomings of any book like this are obvious. All selection is, to a degree, arbitrary. The number of authors worthy of being mentioned could easily be doubled. Furthermore, why select exactly these and not other parts of the authors who are included?

Even more important: extracts are distortions unless they are used as invitations.

Those readers who want to be reminded more fully of the lives and ideas of the authors included here (from Plato on), before delving more deeply into the original sources, may easily refer to my *History of Educational Thought*, New York: American Book Company, 1950. For this book the present anthology was originally intended as a companion-piece.

ROBERT ULICH

ACKNOWLEDGMENTS

DURING the preparation of this anthology I received aid from the William F. Milton Fund (Harvard University) for which I am very grateful.

I also wish to express my gratitude for the coöperation of Dr. Mary Ewen Ulich, Dr. Hedwig Schleiffer, and Dr. Israel Scheffler.

My thanks are due to the following publishers who have so generously permitted me the use of copyrighted material:

American Book Company, New York, for passages from F. C. Prescott's *Alexander Hamilton and Thomas Jefferson;* F. I. Carpenter's *Ralph Waldo Emerson;* F. L. Mott and C. E. Jorgenson's *Benjamin Franklin;* and F. V. N. Painter's *Great Pedagogical Essays: Plato to Spencer.*

D. Appleton-Century Company, New York, for passages from Froebel's *The Education of Man,* translated by W. N. Hailmann; and Montaigne's *The Education of Children,* translated by L. E. Rector.

Bardeen's Inc., Syracuse, for passages from Froebel's *Autobiography,* translated and annotated by Emilie Michaelis and H. Keatley Moore.

Cambridge University Press, England, and The Macmillan Company, New York, for passages from *The Philosophical Works of Descartes,* translated by Elizabeth Haldane and G. R. T. Ross.

The Catholic University of America Press, Washington, for passages from *Aeneae Silvii De Liberorum Educatione,* translated by Brother Joel Stanislaus Nelson.

Columbia University Press, New York, for passages from *The Education of a Christian Prince* by Desiderius Erasmus, translated by Lester K. Born.

Concordia Publishing House, Saint Louis, for passages from F. V. N. Painter's *Luther on Education.*

Harvard University Press, for passages from Plato, Plutarch, Aristotle, Quintilian and St. Augustine, in the Loeb Classical Library.

D. C. Heath and Company, Boston, for passages from Pestalozzi's *Leonard and Gertrude,* translated and abridged by Eva Channing; and Herbart's *Science of Education,* translated by Henry M. and Emmie Felkin.

vii

ACKNOWLEDGMENTS

Houghton Mifflin Company, Boston, for passages from *Lectures and Biographical Essays*, by Ralph Waldo Emerson.

McGraw-Hill Book Company, New York, for passages from *St. Ignatius and the Ratio Studiorum*, edited by Edward A. Fitzpatrick.

The Macmillan Company, New York, for passages from *The Ascetic Works of St. Basil*, translated by W. K. L. Clarke.

Oxford University Press, London and New York, for passages from *The Sacred Books of the East*, edited by F. Max Müller.

Charles Scribner's Sons, New York, for passages from *The Ante-Nicene Fathers*, Alexander Roberts and James Donaldson, editors; and *A Selected Library of Nicene and Post-Nicene Fathers of the Christian Church*, under the editorial supervision of Philip Schaff and Henry Wace.

The University Press of Liverpool, for a passage from Comenius' *The Way of Light*, translated by E. T. Campagnac.

Yale University Press for passages from Frederick Morgan Padelford's *Essays on the Study and Use of Poetry by Plutarch and Basil the Great.*

The Soncino Press, London, for passages from *Baba Bathra*, translated by Maurice Simon and Israel W. Slotki.

Hebrew Publishing Company, New York, for passages from the book by Moses ben Maimon, *Book of Mishnah Torah Yod Ha-Hazakah*, translated by Rabbi Simon Glazer.

Pardes Publishing House, New York, for passages from Moses Maimonides, *The Guide for the Perplexed*, translated by M. Friedländer.

Behrman House, Inc., New York, for passages from *The Memoirs of Glückel von Hameln*, translated by Marvin Lowenthal.

The Jewish Publication Society of America, Philadelphia, for passages from Moses Hayyim Luzzatto's *Mesillat Yesharim. The Path of the Upright*, translated by Mordecai M. Kaplan.

The Macmillan Company, New York, for permission to reprint John Dewey's essay "From Absolutism to Experimentalism" from *Contemporary American Philosophy, Volume II*, edited by George P. Adams and William P. Montague.

R. U.

THE HARVARD UNIVERSITY PRESS also takes pleasure in gratefully acknowledging substantial gifts from Friends of the Harvard University Press.

CONTENTS

ix

CONTENTS

x

ASIA

INDIA

Whenever a people's culture has been fully nourished by its religious tradition, education has not been a separate branch of activity. It has been a part of total life with its daily tasks, social contacts, rituals, and its beliefs about God, man, and the universe. For this reason one cannot find in ancient cultures special books on the subject of education; rather one has to search for it in the sacred texts which explain the religious and moral law to the faithful.

Such sacred texts of the Indians were the Vedas and Upanishads, which took shape during the first millennium B.C., the Gitas, particularly the Bhagavad Gita, the origin of which goes back probably to the fourth century B.C., and the Ordinances of Manu. These were formulated probably around 500 A.D. and contain the moral and legal code of the Brahmans.

In order to understand the educational ideas found in these books, one has to keep in mind that for the pious Hindu, as well as for the Buddhist, life in all its appearances is an effluence of the Divine Essence. To return into its peace, or the Nirvana, is the meaning of all reincarnations. Yet, traveling the path toward Nirvana is not an act of self-extinction, as those familiar with certain Christian forms of asceticism may easily surmise. Rather it is an act of wise self-interest which comes from the realization of the true character of the human soul and its intrinsic unity with the World Spirit.

The Ordinances of Manu say:

"Learn the Dharma which is followed by the learned and good, by those ever free from spite and passions, and which is acknowledged by the mind.

"Selfishness is not praiseworthy, yet unselfishness exists not here; for the study of the Vedas is for selfish ends, and the practice of rites according to the Vedas. . . .

"Yet, one rightly occupied in those acts goes to the world of the immortals, and gets all his desires here as hoped for."

This combination of self-realization and other-worldliness is the reason why old Indian education, though extremely metaphysical and devotional in character, is nevertheless not sacrificial. It demands the joyful fulfillment of one's specific destiny, duty, and mission, or of one's *Dharma*. This fulfillment can come only through the natural maturing of a person in the various stages of development: childhood, adolescence, adulthood, and responsibility for the family and the community. Without having proved oneself in these stages of life, one cannot become a saint, because saintliness is a consummation, not a jump. Therefore education for the Brahman is "Science of Life" to the same degree as it is applied theology. The Brahman teacher, the "Guru," is not the schoolmaster, but the friend and

3

guide of mankind; he is the "destroyer of darkness." According to one of the Vedas "Gur" means "darkness," and "Ru" means "destruction."

Since nature and humanity are reflections of divine will, the Indian is inclined to believe in a hierarchical and static society which man must not try to change arbitrarily. When the order of society is disturbed it can be restored only through man's return to the divine sources of life. Change of mind is the only effective form of revolution. "Satyagraha," the movement of nonviolent disobedience to unjust laws, of which the modern western world has heard so much in connection with the work of Mahatma Gandhi, means in literal translation: "Insistence on Truth."

The following selections are taken from the sources listed: I. *The Song Celestial. Bhagavad-Gîtâ. (From the Mahâbhârata,)* Being a discourse between Arjuna, Prince of India, and The Supreme Being under the Form of Krishna. Translated from the Sanskrit Text by Edwin Arnold and published in Boston by Roberts Brothers in 1885. The selection is from Chapter III, pages 37-45.

II. *The Satapatha-Brâhmana, According to the Text of the Madhyandina School.* Translated by Julius Eggeling. Part V. Book XI. XI. Kânda, 5 Adhyâya, 6 Brâhmana, 2. Seventh Brâhmana. The Study of the Veda. The selection is taken from *The Sacred Books of the East,* edited by F. Max Müller, Volume XLIV (Oxford: At the Clarendon Press, 1900), pages 99-100.

III. *The Khândogya-Upanishad.* Translated by F. Max Müller. (The Upanishad, Part I.) Eighth Prapâthaka. First Khanda. Second, Third, Fourth, Fifth Khanda. The selection is taken from *The Sacred Books of the East,* edited by F. Max Müller, Volume I (Oxford: At the Clarendon Press, 1879), page 125 and following pages.

IV. *Hitopadeśa.* A New Literal Translation from the Sanskrit Text of Professor F. Johnson. For the Use of Students. By Frederic Pincott, published in London by W. H. Allen and Co., in 1880. The selection is taken from page 1.

V. *The Ordinances of Manu.* Translated from the Sanskrit and introduced by Arthur Coke Burnell. Completed and Edited by Edward W. Hopkins. Lecture II. Published in London by Trübner and Co., in 1884. The selections are from pages 16 ff. and 42 ff.

In this section on India, and the following one on China, the numerous parentheses and footnotes found in the scholarly translations have been omitted.

BHAGAVAD-GÎTÂ

(The Bhagavad-Gîtâ represents a discourse between Arjuna, Prince of India, and the Supreme Being under the form of the God Krishna. Krishna in the guise of a charioteer appears to Prince Arjuna while a battle is impending between his army and that of the enemy. The conversation is going on in a chariot between the opposing armies, after Arjuna has expressed doubts as to his right to fight his Indian brothers.)

4

INDIA

ARJUNA:

Thou whom all mortals praise, Janârdana! [1]
If meditation be a nobler thing
Than action, wherefore, then, great Keśava! [1]
Dost thou impel me to this dreadful fight?
Now am I by thy doubtful speech disturbed!
Tell me one thing, and tell me certainly;
By what road shall I find the better end?

KRISHNA:

I told thee blameless Lord! there be two paths
Shown to this world; two schools of wisdom. First
The Sânkhya's, which doth save in way of works
Prescribed by reason; next, the Yôg, which bids
Attain by meditation, spiritually:
Yet these are one! No man shall 'scape from act
By shunning action; nay, and none shall come
By mere renouncements unto perfectness.
Nay, and no jot of time, at any time,
Rests any actionless; his nature's law
Compels him, even unwilling, into act;
For thought is act in fancy. He who sits
Suppressing all the instruments of flesh,
Yet in his idle heart thinking on them,
Plays the inept and guilty hypocrite:
But he who, with strong body serving mind,
Gives up his mortal powers to worthy work,
Not seeking gain, Arjuna! such an one
Is honorable. Do thine allotted task!
Work is more excellent than idleness;
The body's life proceeds not, lacking work.
There is a task of holiness to do,
Unlike world-binding toil, which bindeth not
The faithful soul; such earthly duty do
Free from desire, and thou shalt well perform
Thy heavenly purpose. Spake Prajâpati—
In the beginning, when all men were made,
And, with mankind, the sacrifice—"Do this!
Work! sacrifice! Increase and multiply
With sacrifice! This shall be Kamadûk,

[1] Appellative for the God Krishna.

5

Your 'Cow of Plenty,' giving back her milk
Of all abundance. Worship the gods thereby;
The gods shall yield ye grace. Those meats ye crave
The gods will grant to Labor, when it pays
Tithes in the altar-flame. But if one eats
Fruits of the earth, rendering to kindly Heaven
No gift of toil, that thief steals from his world."

Who eat of food after their sacrifice
Are quit of fault, but they that spread a feast
All for themselves, eat sin and drink of sin.
By food the living live; food comes of rain,
And rain comes by the pious sacrifice,
And sacrifice is paid with tithes of toil;
Thus action is of Brahmâ, who is One,
The Only, All-pervading; at all times
Present in sacrifice. He that abstains
To help the rolling wheels of this great world,
Glutting his idle sense, lives a lost life,
Shameful and vain. Existing for himself,
Self-concentrated, serving self alone,
No part hath he in aught; nothing achieved,
Nought wrought or unwrought toucheth him; no hope
Of help for all the living things of earth
Depends from him. Therefore, thy task prescribed
With spirit unattached gladly perform,
Since in performance of plain duty man
Mounts to his highest bliss. By works alone
Janak, and ancient saints reached blessedness!
Moreover, for the upholding of thy kind,
Action thou should'st embrace. What the wise choose
The unwise people take; what best men do
The multitude will follow. Look on me,
Thou Son of Prithâ! in the three wide worlds
I am not bound to any toil, no height
Awaits to scale, no gift remains to gain,
Yet I act here! and, if I acted not—
Earnest and watchful—those that look to me
For guidance, sinking back to sloth again
Because I slumbered, would decline from good,
And I should break earth's order and commit
Her offspring unto ruin, Bharata!

6

Even as the unknowing toil, wedded to sense,
So let the enlightened toil, sense-freed, but set
To bring the world deliverance, and its bliss;
Not sowing in those simple, busy hearts
Seed of despair. Yea! let each play his part
In all he finds to do, with unyoked soul.
All things are everywhere by Nature wrought
In interaction of the qualities.
The fool, cheated by self, thinks, "This I did"
And "That I wrought;" but—ah, thou strong-armed Prince!—
A better-lessoned mind, knowing the play
Of visible things within the world of sense,
And how the qualities must qualify,
Standeth aloof even from his acts. Th' untaught
Live mixed with them, knowing not Nature's way
Of highest aims unwitting, slow and dull.
Those make thou not to stumble, having the light;
But all thy dues discharging, for My sake,
With meditation centred inwardly,
Seeking no profit, satisfied, serene,
Heedless of issue—fight! They who shall keep
My ordinance thus, the wise and willing hearts,
Have quittance from all issue of their acts;
But those who disregard my ordinance,
Thinking they know, know nought, and fall to loss,
Confused and foolish. 'Sooth, the instructed one
Doth of his kind, following what fits him most;
And lower creatures of their kind; in vain
Contending 'gainst the law. Needs must it be
The objects of the sense will stir the sense
To like and dislike, yet th' enlightened man
Yields not to these, knowing them enemies.
Finally, this is better, that one do
His own task as he may, even though he fail,
Than take tasks not his own, though they seem good.
To die performing duty is no ill;
But who seeks other roads shall wander still.

Arjuna:
Yet tell me, Teacher! by what force doth man
Go to his ill, unwilling; as if one
Pushed him that evil path?

7

KRISHNA:

Kama it is!

Passion it is! born of the Darknesses,
Which pusheth him. Mighty of appetite,
Sinful, and strong is this!—man's enemy!
As smoke blots the white fire, as clinging rust
Mars the bright mirror, as the womb surrounds
The babe unborn, so is the world of things
Foiled, soiled, enclosed in this desire of flesh.
The wise fall, caught in it; the unresting foe
It is of wisdom, wearing countless forms,
Fair but deceitful, subtle as a flame.
Sense, mind, and reason—these, O Kunti's son!
Are booty for it; in its play with these
It maddens man, beguiling, blinding him.
Therefore, thou noblest child of Bharata!
Govern thy heart! Constrain th' entangled sense!
Resist the false, soft sinfulness which saps
Knowledge and judgment! Yea, the world is strong,
But what discerns it stronger, and the mind
Strongest; and high o'er all the ruling Soul.
Wherefore, perceiving Him who reigns supreme,
Put forth full force of Soul in thy own soul!
Fight! vanquish foes and doubts, dear Hero! slay
What haunts thee in fond shapes, and would betray!

THE SATAPATHA-BRÂHMANA

1. Now, then, the praise of the study of the scriptures. The study
and teaching of the Veda are a source of pleasure to him, he becomes ready-minded, and independent of others, and day by day
he acquires wealth. He sleeps peacefully; he is the best physician
for himself; and peculiar to him are restraint of the senses, delight
in the one thing, growth of intelligence, fame, and the task of perfecting the people. The growing intelligence gives rise to four
duties attaching to the Brâhmana—Brâhmanical descent, a befitting
deportment, fame, and the perfecting of the people; and the people
that are being perfected guard the Brâhmana by four duties—by
showing him respect, and liberality, and by granting him security
against oppression, and security against capital punishment.

2. And, truly, whatever may be the toils here between heaven
and earth, the study of the scriptures is their last stage, their goal,

limit, for him who, knowing this, studies his lesson: therefore one's daily lesson should be studied.

3. And, verily, whatever portion of the sacred poetry, khandas, he studies for his lesson with that sacrificial rite, offering is made by him who, knowing this, studies his lesson: therefore one's daily lesson should be studied.

4. And, verily, if he studies his lesson, even though lying on a soft couch, anointed, adorned and completely satisfied, he is burned with holy fire up to the tips of his nails, whosoever, knowing this, studies his lesson: therefore one's daily lesson should be studied.

KHÂNDOGYA-UPANISHAD

1. There is this city of Brahman the body, and in it the palace, the small lotus of the heart, and in it that small ether. Now what exists within that small ether, that is to be sought for, that is to be understood.

2. And if they should say to him: 'Now with regard to that city of Brahman, and the palace in it, i.e. the small lotus of the heart, and the small ether within the heart, what is there within it that deserves to be sought for, or that is to be understood?'

3. Then he should say: 'As large as this ether, all space, is, so large is that ether within the heart. Both heaven and earth are contained within it, both fire and air, both sun and moon, both lightning and stars; and whatever there is of him, the Self, here in the world, and whatever is not, i.e. whatever has been or will be, all that is contained within it.'

4. And if they should say to him: 'If everything that exists is contained in that city of Brahman, all beings and all desires, whatever can be imagined or desired, then what is left of it, when old age reaches it and scatters it, or when it falls to pieces?'

5. Then he should say: 'By the old age of the body, that the ether, or Brahman within, it does not age; by the death of the body, that, the ether, or Brahman within it, is not killed. That, the Brahman, is the true Brahma-city, not the body. In it all desires are contained. It is the Self, free from sin, free from old age, from death and grief, from hunger and thirst, which desires nothing but what it ought to desire, and imagines nothing but what it ought to imagine. Now as here on earth people follow as they are commanded, and depend on the object which they are attached to, be it a country or a piece of land.

6. 'And as here on earth, whatever has been acquired by exertion,

perishes, so perishes whatever is acquired for the next world by sacrifices and other good actions performed on earth. Those who depart from hence without having discovered the Self and those true desires, for them there is no freedom in all the worlds. But those who depart from hence, after having discovered the Self and those true desires, for them there is freedom in all the worlds.

HITOPADEŚA. INTRODUCTION

1. May there be success, for the good, in what is to be accomplished, through the favour of that Dhûrjati,[1] on whose brow there is a digit of the Moon, like a streak of foam of the Jâhnavî.[2]

2. This Hitopadeśa,[3] attended to, gives skill in Sanskrit speaking, variety of expression universally, and the knowledge of policy.

3. A wise man should think of knowledge and wealth as though he were undecaying and immortal; he should practise virtue as though seized in the hairs of the head by Death.

4. Among all things knowledge, they say, is truly the best thing; from, at all times, its unstealableness, its unpurchaseableness, and its indestructibility.

5. Knowledge truly unites a man with a king difficult of access, as a descending river unites with the ocean; hence results exceeding prosperity.

6. Knowledge gives prudence, from prudence one attains fitness for work, from fitness one attains wealth, from wealth the power of doing good; thence arises happiness.

7. Arms and literature are both kinds of knowledge, they are the two kinds of knowledge conducive to celebrity; the first leads to ridicule in old age, the second is honoured always.

8. Since the pattern impressed on a new earthen vessel cannot become otherwise than it is at the time of manufacture, therefore, by the artifice of fables, the moral guidance of youths is here set forth.

9. The Acquisition of Friends, the Separation of Friends, War, and Peace,—having been abstracted from the Panchatantra and another book,—is written here.

[1] The god Siva.
[2] The river Ganges.
[3] Meaning "friendly advice."

THE ORDINANCES OF MANU. LECTURE II

SOURCES OF THIS SYSTEM AND THE COUNTRIES WHERE IT OBTAINS; ON THE FIRST CONDITION OF LIFE OF A BRAHMAN, OR THAT OF A STUDENT. 1. Learn the *dharma* which is followed by the learned and good, by those ever free from spite and passions, and which is acknowledged by the mind:

2. Selfishness is not praiseworthy, yet unselfishness exists not here; for the study of the Vedas is for selfish ends, and the practice of rites according to the Vedas.

3. Selfishness certainly has its root in the hope of a reward; sacrifices have their origin in selfishness; all vows and prohibitive rules are said to arise from a hope of reward.

4. Any act of an unselfish man is never at any time seen here; for whatever one does, that is the act of selfishness.

5. Yet one rightly occupied in those acts goes to the world of the immortals, and gets all his desires here as hoped for.

6. The entire Veda is the root of law, so also tradition and the practice of those that know it; also the custom of the good, as well as satisfaction of one's self.

7. Whatsoever *dharma* was proclaimed by Manu for any one, that is all directed in the Veda; he was possessed of all knowledge.

8. So a learned man, having viewed by the eye of knowledge all this complete system as according to the authority of revelation, should certainly be firm in his own *dharma.*

9. For a man performing the *dharma* declared by revelation and tradition obtains fame here, and after his death extreme happiness.

10. Now the Veda is to be understood as "revelation," but the law-treatises *dharma-çāstra* as "tradition"; these two are irrefutable in all matters, for by these two virtue arose.

11. A Brahman who, from adherence to rationalism, shall despise these two sources, he, an infidel blamer of the Vedas, is to be banished by the just.

12. The Veda, tradition, good custom, and what is pleasing to one's self, that the wise have plainly declared to be the fourfold definition of *dharma.*

13. A knowledge of *dharma* is ordained for men not given up to wealth and pleasure; of those who would know *dharma*, the Veda is the supreme authority.

225. A teacher is the image of Brahma; a father is the image of Prajāpati; a mother is the image of the earth; one's own brother is the image of one's self.

226. So a teacher, a father, a mother, and an elder brother, are not to be disrespectfully treated, especially by a Brahman, even though injured.

227. The pain that a father and mother endure in producing human beings, of that acquittance cannot be made even by hundreds of years.

228. One should ever do what is pleasing to them and to a teacher always; for these three being satisfied, all austerity is accomplished.

229. Obedience to these three is called the highest austerity; except permitted by them, one should not perform other religious duties.

230. For they themselves are the three worlds, they are also the three orders; they are the three Vedas, and they also are called the three fires.

232. A householder not neglectful to those three will conquer the three worlds; like a god, illuminated by his own body, he rejoices in the sky.

233. By devotion to his mother he obtains this world; by devotion to his father, the middle world; but by obedience to his Guru, the Brahma-world.

234. All religious duties are fulfilled by him by whom those three persons are respected; but of him by whom those are not respected, all acts are fruitless.

235. As long as those three live, so long let him do no other religious duty; he should, devoted to their desires, ever do obedience to just those three.

236. Whatever act he may do with a view to a future state, by mind, word, or deed, and without derogation to them, let him tell them that.

237. By acting thus toward those three, the obligation of a man is indeed completed; that is plainly the highest religious duty; other duty is called subordinate religious duty.

238. A faithful man may receive pure knowledge even from a low-caste man; the highest virtue from the lowest, a jewel of a woman even from a bad family.

239. Ambrosia can be extracted even from poison; elegant speech, even from a child; good conduct, even from an enemy; gold, even from impurity.

240. From all are to be accepted, women, gems, knowledge, duty, purity, good speech, and the various arts.

241. In time of distress learning the Veda from one not a Brah-

man is enjoined, and attendance and obedience to him as to a Guru as long as the study lasts.

242. But if the Guru be not a Brahman, the pupil should not live all his life with him, nor even with a Brahman who has not thoroughly studied the Veda, if he desire the best way.

243. But if he desire to live all his life in the family of his Guru, attentive he should serve him till he is released from his body.

244. Now the Brahman who obeys his Guru till the end of his body goes straight to the eternal abode of Brahma.

245. Let not one who knows his duty offer anything earlier to his Guru, but when, dismissed by his Guru, he is about to bathe on his return home, let him, as he best can, present property to his Guru.

246. A field, gold, a cow, a horse, an umbrella, shoes, a seat, grain and vegetables, clothes—such let him offer to his Guru as a mark of affection.

247. But, truly, after his teacher is dead, let him serve as he would his Guru the Guru's son endowed with good qualities, the Guru's wife, or Sapinda.

248. If these do not exist, let him perfect his own body, occupying his Guru's place, seat, and occupations, and practising attendance on the fires.

249. The Brahman who thus uninterrupted passes his student-ship, goes to the highest place, and is not born here again.

CHINA

In old Chinese thought on education we find a difference in emphasis which has continued throughout the whole history of education.

Essentially the difference lies between the type of thinker who is more interested in institutions and morality, and the more mystical type. For the first, represented in China by Confucius, education is primarily a means of preserving society; for the second, represented by Lao-Tse, education is more of a contemplative nature. The first lays emphasis on learning and knowledge, the second on a certain state of mind without which any external achievement would be useless. For the one the Divine reflects itself in order, structure, and proportion; for the other it is the profound, the hidden and yet creative. The Confucius type lays stress on the good citizen, the Lao-Tse type on the spirit which *makes* a good man.

But in great minds, such as Confucius and Lao-Tse, the two attitudes do not exclude each other; when reading them we must always keep in mind that the totality is in each though it may be mirrored in varying shapes.

Sources of the following selections are: I. *The Sacred Books of the East,* edited by F. Max Müller. Volume XXXIX: *The Sacred Books of China, The Texts of Taoism,* Translated by James Legge, Part I, The Tao Teh King. (London: Oxford University Press, 1891). The selections are found on page 47 and following pages.

II. *The Sacred Books of the East,* edited by F. Max Müller. Volume XXVIII: *The Sacred Books of China, The Texts of Confucianism,* Translated by James Legge, Part IV, The Li Ki, XI-XLVI. (Oxford: At the Clarendon Press, 1885). The selection is found on page 82.

III. *The Life and Teachings of Confucius,* by James Legge. London: N. Trübner and Co., 1867. The selection is on page 124 and following pages.

IV. *Dschuang Dsi. (Chuang Tzu.) Das Wahre Buch vom Südlichen Blütenland. Nau Hua Dschenging.* Verdeutscht und erläutert von Richard Wilhelm. It was published in Jena by Eugen Diederichs in 1923. The selection is found on page 143 and following pages. The English translation is by the present editor.

14

LAO-TSE LIVED 6TH CENTURY B.C.

THE TÂO TEH KING. PART I

Ch. *1*. 1. The Tâo[1] that can be trodden is not the enduring and unchanging Tâo. The name that can be named is not the enduring and unchanging name.

2. Conceived of as having no name, it is the Originator of heaven and earth; conceived of as having a name, it is the Mother of all things.

.   .   .   .   .

4. Under these two aspects, it is really the same; but as development takes place, it receives the different names. Together we call them the Mystery. Where the Mystery is the deepest is the gate of all that is subtle and wonderful.

2. 1. All in the world know the beauty of the beautiful, and in doing this they have the idea of what ugliness is; they all know the skill of the skilful, and in doing this they have the idea of what the want of skill is.

2. So it is that existence and non-existence give birth the one to the idea of the other; that difficulty and ease produce the one the idea of the other; that length and shortness fashion out the one the figure of the other; that the ideas of height and lowness arise from the contrast of the one with the other; that the musical notes and tones become harmonious through the relation of one with another; and that being before and behind give the idea of one following another.

3. Therefore the sage manages affairs without doing anything, and conveys his instructions without the use of speech.

4. All things spring up, and there is not one which declines to show itself; they grow, and there is no claim made for their ownership; they go through their processes, and there is no expectation of

---

[1] The concept of Tâo, on which the philosophy of Lao-Tse and the school of Tâoism are based has no equivalent in the western languages. The primary meaning is "the Way." Then it signifies the eternally creative, though always hidden source of life—something not unsimilar to Rousseau's "Nature." But it is also similar to, though not at all identical with, the Greek-Christian concept of "Logos" or "Spirit." "He who knows the Tâo" is the man who is capable of identifying his Self, his thinking, and his action with the divine force beyond and within the Universe.

a reward for the results. The work is accomplished, and there is no resting in it as an achievement.

The work is done, but how no one can see;
'Tis this that makes the power not cease to be.

30. 1. He who would assist a lord of men in harmony with the Tâo will not assert his mastery in the kingdom by force of arms. Such a course is sure to meet with its proper return.

2. Wherever a host is stationed, briars and thorns spring up. In the sequence of great armies there are sure to be bad years.

3. A skilful commander strikes a decisive blow, and stops. He does not dare by continuing his operations to assert and complete his mastery. He will strike the blow, but will be on his guard against being vain or boastful or arrogant in consequence of it. He strikes it as a matter of necessity; he strikes it, but not from a wish for mastery.

4. When things have attained their strong maturity they become old. This may be said to be not in accordance with the Tâo: and what is not in accordance with it soon comes to an end.

33. 1. He who knows other men is discerning; he who knows himself is intelligent. He who overcomes others is strong; he who overcomes himself is mighty. He who is satisfied with his lot is rich; he who goes on acting with energy has a firm will.

2. He who does not fail in the requirements of his position, continues long; he who dies and yet does not perish, has longevity.

41. 1. Scholars of the highest class, when they hear about the Tâo, earnestly carry it into practice. Scholars of the middle class, when they have heard about it, seem now to keep it and now to lose it. Scholars of the lowest class, when they have heard about it, laugh greatly at it. If it were not thus laughed at, it would not be fit to be the Tâo.

47. 1. Without going outside his door, one understands all that takes place under the sky; without looking out from his window, one sees the Tâo of Heaven. The farther that one goes out from himself, the less he knows.

2. Therefore the sages got their knowledge without travelling; gave their right names to things without seeing them; and accomplished their ends without any purpose of doing so.

48. 1. He who devotes himself to learning seeks from day to day to increase his knowledge; he who devotes himself to the Tâo seeks from day to day to diminish his doing.

2. He diminishes it and again diminishes it, till he arrives at do-

ing nothing on purpose. Having arrived at this point of non-action there is nothing which he does not do.

3. He who gets as his own all under heaven does so by giving himself no trouble with that end. If one take trouble with that end, he is not equal to getting as his own all under heaven.

49. 1. The sage has no invariable mind of his own; he makes the mind of the people his mind.

2. To those who are good to me, I am good; and to those who are not good to me, I am also good;—and thus all get to be good. To those who are sincere with me, I am sincere; and to those who are not sincere with me, I am also sincere;—and thus all get to be sincere.

3. The sage has in the world an appearance of indecision, and keeps his mind in a state of indifference to all. The people all keep their eyes and ears directed to him, and he deals with them all as his children.

51. 1. All things are produced by the Tâo, and nourished by its outflowing operation. They receive their forms according to the nature of each, and are completed according to the circumstances of their condition. Therefore all things without exception honour the Tâo, and exalt its outflowing operation.

2. This honouring of the Tâo and exalting of its operation is not the result of any ordination, but always a spontaneous tribute.

3. Thus it is that the Tâo produces all things, nourishes them, brings them to their full growth, nurses them, completes them, matures them, maintains them, and overspreads them.

4. It produces them and makes no claim to the possession of them; it carries them through their processes and does not vaunt its ability in doing so; it brings them to maturity and exercises no control over them;—this is called its mysterious operation.

57. 1. A state may be ruled by measures of correction; weapons of war may be used with crafty dexterity; but the kingdom is made one's own only by freedom from action and purpose.

2. How do I know that it is so? By these facts;—In the kingdom the multiplication of prohibitive enactments increases the poverty of the people; the more implements to add to their profit that the people have, the greater disorder is there in the state and clan; the more acts of crafty dexterity that men possess, the more do strange contrivances appear; the more display there is of legislation, the more thieves and robbers there are.

3. Therefore a sage has said, 'I will do nothing of purpose, and

the people will be transformed of themselves; I will be fond of keeping still, and the people will of themselves become correct. I will take no trouble about it, and the people will of themselves become rich; I will manifest no ambition, and the people will of themselves attain to the primitive simplicity.'

77. 1. May not the Way or Tâo of Heaven be compared to the method of bending a bow? The part of the bow which was high is brought low, and what was low is raised up. So Heaven diminishes where there is superabundance, and supplements where there is deficiency.

2. It is the Way of Heaven to diminish superabundance, and to supplement deficiency. It is not so with the way of man. He takes away from those who have not enough to add to his own superabundance.

3. Who can take his own superabundance and therewith serve all under heaven? Only he who is in possession of the Tâo!

4. Therefore the ruling sage acts without claiming the results as his; he achieves his merit and does not rest arrogantly in it:—he does not wish to display his superiority.

78. 1. There is nothing in the world more soft and weak than water, and yet for attacking things that are firm and strong there is nothing that can take precedence of it;—for there is nothing so effectual for which it can be changed.

2. Every one in the world knows that the soft overcomes the hard, and the weak the strong, but no one is able to carry it out in practice.

4. Words that are strictly true seem to be paradoxical.

79. 1. When a reconciliation is effected between two parties after a great animosity, there is sure to be a grudge remaining in the mind of the one who was wrong. And how can this be beneficial to the other?

2. Therefore to guard against this, the sage keeps the left-hand portion of the record of the engagement, and does not insist on the speedy fulfilment of it by the other party. So, he who has the attributes of the Tâo regards only the conditions of the engagement, while he who has not those attributes regards only the conditions favourable to himself.

3. In the Way of Heaven, there is no partiality of love; it is always on the side of the good man.

CONFUCIUS c. 550–478 B.C.

BOOK XVI. -HSIO KI, OR, RECORD ON THE SUBJECT OF EDUCATION

1. When a ruler is concerned that his measures should be in accordance with law, and seeks for the assistance of the good and upright, this is sufficient to secure him a considerable reputation, but not to move the multitudes.

When he cultivates the society of the worthy, and tries to embody the views of those who are remote from the court, this is sufficient to move the multitudes, but not to transform the people.

If he wish to transform the people and to perfect their manners and customs, must he not start from the lessons of the school?

2. The jade uncut will not form a vessel for use; and if men do not learn, they do not know the way in which they should go. On this account the ancient kings, when establishing states and governing the people, made instruction and schools a primary object;—as it is said in the Charge to Yüeh, 'The thoughts from first to last should be fixed on learning.'

3. However fine the viands be, if one do not eat, he does not know their taste; however perfect the course may be, if one do not learn it, he does not know its goodness. Therefore when he learns, one knows his own deficiencies; when he teaches, he knows the difficulties of learning. After he knows his deficiencies, one is able to turn round and examine himself; after he knows the difficulties, he is able to stimulate himself to effort. Hence it is said, 'Teaching and learning help each other'; as it is said in the Charge to Yüeh, 'Teaching is the half of learning.'

4. According to the system of ancient teaching, for the families of a hamlet there was the village school; for a neighborhood there was the hsiang; for the larger districts there was the hsü; and in the capitals there was the college.

5. Every year some entered the college, and every second year there was a comparative examination. In the first year it was seen whether they could read the texts intelligently, and what was the meaning of each; in the third year, whether they were reverently attentive to their work, and what companionship was most pleasant to them; in the fifth year, how they extended their studies and

sought the company of their teachers; in the seventh year, how they could discuss the subjects of their studies and select their friends. They were now said to have made some small attainments. In the ninth year, when they knew the different classes of subjects and had gained a general intelligence, were firmly established and would not fall back, they were said to have made grand attainments. After this the training was sufficient to transform the people, and to change anything bad in manners and customs. Those who lived near at hand submitted with delight, and those who were far off thought of the teaching with longing desire. Such was the method of the Great learning; as is said in the Record, 'The little ant continually exercises the art of amassing.'

6. At the commencement of the teaching in the Great college, the masters in their skin caps presented the offerings of vegetables to the ancient sages, to show their pupils the principle of reverence for them; and made them sing at the same time the first three pieces of the Minor Odes of the Kingdom, as their first lesson in the duties of officers. When they entered the college, the drum was beaten and the satchels were produced, that they might begin their work reverently. The cane and the thorns were there to secure in them a proper awe. It was not till the time for the summer sacrifice was divined for, that the testing examination was held;—to give composure to their minds. They were continually under inspection, but not spoken to,—to keep their minds undisturbed. They listened, but they did not ask questions; and they could not transgress the order of study imposed on them. These seven things were the chief regulations in the teaching. As it is expressed in the Record, 'In all learning, for him who would be an officer the first thing is the knowledge of business; for scholars the first thing is the directing of the mind.'

7. In the system of teaching at the Great college, every season had its appropriate subject; and when the pupils withdrew and gave up their lessons for the day, they were required to continue their study at home.

8. If a student do not learn at college to play in tune, he cannot quietly enjoy his lutes; if he do not learn extensively the figures of poetry, he cannot quietly enjoy the odes; if he do not learn the varieties of dress, he cannot quietly take part in the different ceremonies; if he do not acquire the various accomplishments, he cannot take delight in learning.

9. Therefore a student of talents and virtue pursues his studies, withdrawn in college from all besides, and devoted to their culti-

vation, or occupied with them when retired from it, and enjoying himself. Having attained to this, he rests quietly in his studies and seeks the company of his teachers; he finds pleasure in his friends, and has all confidence in their course. Although he should be separated from his teachers and helpers, he will not act contrary to the course;—as it is said in the Charge to Yüeh, 'Maintain a reverent humility, and strive to be constantly earnest. In such a case the cultivation will surely come.'

10. According to the system of teaching now-a-days, the masters hum over the tablets which they see before them, multiplying their questions. They speak of the learners' making rapid advances, and pay no regard to their reposing in what they have acquired. In what they lay on their learners they are not sincere, nor do they put forth all their ability in teaching them. What they inculcate is contrary to what is right, and the learners are disappointed in what they seek for. In such a case, the latter are distressed by their studies and hate their masters; they are embittered by the difficulties, and do not find any advantage from their labour. They may seem to finish their work, but they quickly give up its lessons. That no results are seen from their instructions:—is it not owing to these defects?

11. The rules aimed at in the Great college were the prevention of evil before it was manifested; the timeliness of instruction just when it was required; the suitability of the lessons in adaptation to circumstances; and the good influence of example to parties observing one another. It was from these four things that the teaching was so effectual and flourishing.

12. Prohibition of evil after it has been manifested meets with opposition, and is not successful. Instruction given after the time for it is past is done with toil, and carried out with difficulty. The communication of lessons in an undiscriminating manner and without suitability produces injury and disorder, and fails in its object. Learning alone and without friends makes one feel solitary and uncultivated, with but little information. Friendships of festivity lead to opposition to one's master. Friendships with the dissolute lead to the neglect of one's learning. These six things all tend to make teaching vain.

13. When a superior man knows the causes which make instruction successful, and those which make it of no effect, he can become a teacher of others. Thus in his teaching, he leads and does not drag; he strengthens and does not discourage; he opens the way but does not conduct to the end without the learner's own efforts. Leading and not dragging produces harmony. Strengthening and not

discouraging makes attainment easy. Opening the way and not conducting to the end makes the learner thoughtful. He who produces such harmony, easy attainment, and thoughtfulness may be pronounced a skilful teacher.

14. Among learners there are four defects with which the teacher must make himself acquainted. Some err in the multitude of their studies; some, in their fewness; some, in the feeling of ease with which they proceed; and some, in the readiness with which they stop. These four defects arise from the difference of their minds. When a teacher knows the character of his mind, he can save the learner from the defect to which he is liable. Teaching should be directed to develop that in which the pupil excels, and correct the defects to which he is prone.

15. The good singer makes men able to continue his notes, and so the good teacher makes them able to carry out his ideas. His words are brief, but far-reaching; unpretentious, but deep; with few illustrations, but instructive. In this way he may be said to perpetuate his ideas.

16. When a man of talents and virtue knows the difficulty on the one hand and the facility on the other in the attainment of learning, and knows also the good and bad qualities of his pupils, he can vary his methods of teaching. When he can vary his methods of teaching, he can be a master indeed. When he can be a teacher indeed, he can be the Head of an official department. When he can be such a Head, he can be the Ruler of a state. Hence it is from the teacher indeed that one learns to be a ruler, and the choice of a teacher demands the greatest care; as it is said in the Record, 'The three kings and the four dynasties were what they were by their teachers.'

17. In pursuing the course of learning, the difficulty is in securing the proper reverence for the master. When that is done, the course which he inculcates is regarded with honour. When that is done, the people know how to respect learning. Thus it is that there are two among his subjects whom the ruler does not treat as subjects. When one is personating his ancestor he does not treat him as such, nor does he treat his master as such. According to the rules of the Great college, the master, though communicating anything to the son of Heaven, did not stand with his face to the north. This was the way in which honour was done to him.

18. The skilful learner, while the master seems indifferent, yet makes double the attainments of another, and in the sequel ascribes the merit to the master. The unskilful learner, while the master is diligent with him, yet makes only half the attainments of the for-

mer, and in the sequel is dissatisfied with the master. The skilful questioner is like a workman addressing himself to deal with a hard tree. First he attacks the easy parts, and then the knotty. After a long time, the pupil and the master talk together, and the subject is explained. The unskilful questioner takes the opposite course. The master who skilfully waits to be questioned, may be compared to a bell when it is struck. Struck with a small hammer, it gives a small sound. Struck with a great one, it gives a great sound. But let it be struck leisurely and properly, and it gives out all the sound of which it is capable. He who is not skilful in replying to questions is the opposite of this. This all describes the method of making progress in learning.

19. He who gives only the learning supplied by his memory in conversations is not fit to be a master. Is it not necessary that he should hear the questions of his pupils? Yes, but if they are not able to put questions, he should put subjects before them. If he do so, and then they do not show any knowledge of the subjects, he may let them alone.

20. The son of a good founder is sure to learn how to make a fur-robe. The son of a good maker of bows is sure to learn how to make a sieve. Those who first yoke a young horse place it behind, with the carriage going on in front of it. The superior man who examines these cases can by them instruct himself in the method of learning.

21. The ancients in prosecuting their learning compared different things and traced the analogies between them. The drum has no special relation to any of the musical notes; but without it they cannot be harmonized. Water has no particular relation to any of the five colours; but without it they cannot be displayed. Learning has no particular relation to any of the five senses; but without it they cannot be regulated. A teacher has no special relation to the five degrees of mourning; but without his help they cannot be worn as they ought to be.

22. A wise man has said, 'The Great virtue need not be confined to one office; Great power of method need not be restricted to the production of one article; Great truth need not be limited to the confirmation of oaths; Great seasonableness accomplishes all things, and each in its proper time.' By examining these four cases, we are taught to direct our aims to what is fundamental.

When the three sovereigns sacrificed to the waters, they did so first to the rivers and then to the seas; first to the source and then to its result. This was what is called 'Paying attention to the root.'

THE ANALECTS, BOOK II, CHAPTERS IX-XVII

IX. The Master said, "I have talked with Hwuy for a whole day, and he has not made any objections *to anything I said;*—as if he were stupid. He has retired, and I have examined his conduct when away from me, and found him able to illustrate *my teachings.* Hwuy! He is not stupid."

X. The Master said, 1. "See what a man does.

2. "Mark his motives.

3. "Examine in what things he rests.

4. "How can a man conceal his character!

5. "How can a man conceal his character!"

XI. The Master said, "If a man keeps cherishing his old knowledge so as continually to be acquiring new, he may be a teacher of others."

XII. The Master said, "The accomplished scholar is not an utensil."

XIII. Tsze-kung asked what constituted the superior man. The Master said, "He acts before he speaks, and afterwards speaks according to his actions."

XIV. The Master said, "The superior man is catholic and no partizan. The mean man is a partizan and not catholic."

XV. The Master said, "Learning without thought is labour lost; thought without learning is perilous."

XVI. The Master said, "The study of strange doctrines is injurious indeed!"

XVII. The Master said, "Yew, shall I teach you what knowledge is? When you know a thing, to hold that you know it; and when you do not know a thing, to allow that you do not know it;—this is knowledge."

BOOK VII. CHAPTERS III AND VIII

III. The Master said, "The leaving virtue without proper cultivation; the not thoroughly discussing what is learned; not being able to move towards righteousness of which a knowledge is gained; and not being able to change what is not good:—these are the things which occasion me solicitude."

VIII. The Master said, "I do not open up the truth to one who is not eager *to get knowledge,* nor help out any one who is not anxious to explain himself. When I have presented one corner of a subject to any one, and he cannot from it learn the other three, I do not repeat my lesson."

CHINA

BOOK XIII. CHAPTER XXVIII

XXVIII. Tsze-loo asked saying, "What qualities must a man possess to entitle him to be called a scholar?" The Master said, "He must be thus,—earnest, urgent, and bland:—among his friends, earnest and urgent; among his brethren, bland."

BOOK XIV. CHAPTER III

III. The Master said, "The scholar who cherishes the love of comfort, is not fit to be deemed a scholar."

BOOK XV. CHAPTERS XXXVIII-XL

XXXVIII. The Master said, "There being instruction, there will be no distinction of classes."

XXXIX. The Master said, "Those whose courses are different cannot lay plans for one another."

XL. The Master said, "In language it is simply required that it convey the meaning."

BOOK XIX.[1] CHAPTERS IV-VII, XII, XIII

IV. Tsze-hea said, "Even in inferior studies and employments there is something worth being looked at, but if it be attempted to carry them out to what is remote, there is a danger of their proving inapplicable. Therefore, the superior man does not practise them."

V. Tsze-hea said, "He, who from day to day recognizes what he has not yet, and from month to month does not forget what he has attained to, may be said indeed to love to learn."

VI. Tsze-hea said, "There are learning extensively, and having a firm and sincere aim; inquiring with earnestness, and reflecting with self-application:—virtue is in such a course."

VII. Tsze-hea said, "Mechanics have their shops to dwell in, in order to accomplish their works. The superior man learns, in order to reach to the utmost of his principles."

XII. 1. Tsze-yew said, "The disciples and followers of Tsze-hea, in sprinkling and sweeping the ground, in answering and replying, in advancing and receding, are sufficiently accomplished. But these are only the branches *of learning*, and they are left ignorant of what is essential.—How can they be acknowledged as sufficiently taught?"

---

[1] "Confucius does not appear personally in this book at all. . . . The disciples deliver their sentiments very much after the manner of the Master, and yet we can discern a falling off from him." Legge.

2. Tsze-hea heard of the remark and said, "Alas! Yen Yew is wrong. According to the way of the superior man *in teaching,* what departments are there which he considers of prime importance, and therefore *first* delivers? what are there which he considers of secondary importance, and so allows himself to be idle about? *But* as in the case of plants, which are assorted according to their classes, *so he deals with his disciples.* How can the way of a superior man be such as to make fools of *any* of them? Is it not the sage alone, who can unite in one the beginning and the consummation *of learning?*"

XIII. Tsze-hea said, "The officer, *having discharged all his duties,* should devote his leisure to learning. The student, having completed his learning, should apply himself to be an officer."

THE GREAT LEARNING (THE TEXT OF CONFUCIUS)

1. What the Great Learning teaches, is—to illustrate illustrious virtue; to renovate the people; and to rest in the highest excellence.

2. The point where to rest being known, the object of pursuit is then determined; and, that being determined, a calm unperturbedness may be attained. To that calmness there will succeed a tranquil repose. In that repose there may be careful deliberation, and that deliberation will be followed by the attainment *of the desired end.*

3. Things have their root and their completion. Affairs have their end and their beginning. To know what is first and what is last will lead near to what is taught in *the Great Learning.*

4. The ancients who wished to illustrate illustrious virtue throughout the empire, first ordered well their own States. Wishing to order well their States, they first regulated their families. Wishing to regulate their families, they first cultivated their persons. Wishing to cultivate their persons, they first rectified their hearts. Wishing to rectify their hearts, they first sought to be sincere in their thoughts. Wishing to be sincere in their thoughts, they first extended to the utmost their knowledge. Such extension of knowledge lay in the investigation of things.

5. Things being investigated, knowledge became complete. Their knowledge being complete, their thoughts were sincere. Their thoughts being sincere, their hearts were then rectified. Their hearts being rectified, their persons were cultivated. Their persons being cultivated, their families were regulated. Their families being regu-

CHINA

lated, their States were rightly governed. Their States being rightly governed, the whole empire was made tranquil and happy.

6. From the emperor down to the mass of the people, all must consider the cultivation of the person the root of *everything besides*.

7. It cannot be, when the root is neglected, that what should spring from it will be well ordered. It never has been the case that what was of great importance has been slightly cared for, and, at the same time, that what was of slight importance has been greatly cared for.

CHUANG TZU

THE WOOD CARVER

A wood carver made a post to hang bells on. When the post was finished, all people admired it as a miraculous work of art.

Also the Prince of Lu looked at it and asked the carver: "What is your secret?"

The carver answered: "I am a simple artisan and do not know of secrets. There is only one thing to be considered. When I was about to make the post, I was on my guard not to allow my energy to be diverted by any other idea. I fasted in order to bring my mind to balance. When I had fasted for three days, I did not dare any longer think of reward and honor; after five days I no longer dared think of praise or blame; after seven days I had forgotten my body and my limbs. At this time I did not even think of His Majesty's court. In this way I identified myself completely with my art, and all temptations of the outer world had vanished. After that I went into the forest and looked at the natural shape and growth of the trees. When I happened to see the right one, the post for the bells stood ready before my eyes, and I could go to work. Otherwise I would have failed. And the people hold my work divine because my innermost nature became merged with the nature of the material."

GREEK-ROMAN ANTIQUITY

PLATO c. 428–c. 348 B.C.

IT IS one of the astounding facts in the history of culture that the first coherent treatise on government and education which we possess in Western civilization, namely Plato's *Republic*, is at the same time the most profound. Plato's penetrating mind has revealed the problems with which mankind has struggled, consciously or unconsciously, ever since it has had an organized society and education. How can we have an élite which does not use its position for establishing false privileges? What is the relation between stability and change? How can justice prevail not only within the country, but also in its relation to other countries?

What is, with respect to education, the proper emotional foundation which has to be laid before and with the beginning of formal intellectual training? How can the active and the contemplative life be interconnected in such a way that education results in a full and wise personality? What is the responsibility of the community to the nurture and culture of its youth?

It would be wrong to say that Plato has sufficiently answered the problems he himself has raised. Sometimes he leaves us in the dilemma, e.g. with respect to justice and truth in the affairs of the state; sometimes he gives entirely artificial answers, e.g., with respect to depriving the "guardians of the State" of natural family life; and some of his answers are dangerous, e.g., his insistence on censorship and the enforced maintenance of tradition.

Yet, Plato's work proves that the profoundness and stimulation radiating from a great mind are not shown by the degree of consensus, but by the radicalness of inquiry which forces us away from easy commonplace answers into the depth of a problem.

The following selections are taken from Plato's *Republic* in Paul Shorey's translation, two volumes, published in 1930-1935 by the Harvard University Press in the Loeb Classical Library.

THE REPUBLIC, BOOK II

XVI. [Socrates] "Then may we not confidently lay it down in the case of man too, that if he is to be in some sort gentle to friends and familiars he must be by nature a lover of wisdom and of learning?" "Let us so assume," he [Glaucon] replied. "The love of wisdom, then, and high spirit and quickness and strength will be combined for us in the nature of him who is to be a good and true guardian of the state." "By all means," he said. "Such, then," I said, "would be

31

the basis of his character. But the rearing of these men and their education, how shall we manage that? And will the consideration of this topic advance us in any way towards discerning what is the object of our entire inquiry—the origin of justice and injustice in a state—our aim must be to omit nothing of a sufficient discussion, and yet not to draw it out to tiresome length?" . . .

XVII. "What, then, is our education? Or is it hard to find a better than that which long time has discovered? Which is, I suppose, gymnastics for the body and for the soul music." "It is." "And shall we not begin education in music earlier than in gymnastics?" "Of course." "And under music you include tales, do you not?" "I do." "And tales are of two species, the one true and the other false?" . . . "Shall we, then, thus lightly suffer our children to listen to any chance stories fashioned by any chance teachers and so to take into their minds opinions for the most part contrary to those that we shall think it desirable for them to hold when they are grown up?" "By no manner of means will we allow it." "We must begin, then, it seems, by a censorship over our storymakers, and what they do well we must pass and what not, reject. And the stories on the accepted list we will induce nurses and mothers to tell to the children and so shape their souls by these stories far rather than their bodies by their hands. But most of the stories they now tell we must reject." "What sort of stories?" he said. . . . "There is, first of all," I said, "the greatest lie about the things of greatest concernment, which was no pretty invention of him who told how Uranus did what Hesiod says he did to Cronos, and how Cronos in turn took his revenge; and then there are the doings and sufferings of Cronos at the hands of his son. Even if they were true I should not think that they ought to be thus lightly told to thoughtless young persons. But the best way would be to bury them in silence, and if there were some necessity for relating them, that only a very small audience should be admitted under pledge of secrecy and after sacrificing, not a pig, but some huge and unprocurable victim, to the end that as few as possible should have heard these tales." . . . "Neither must we admit at all," said I, "that gods war with gods and plot against one another and contend—for it is not true either—if we wish our future guardians to deem nothing more shameful than lightly to fall out with one another. . . . For the young are not able to distinguish what is and what is not allegory, but whatever opinions are taken into the mind at that age are wont to prove indelible and unalterable. For which reason, maybe, we should do our utmost that the

32

PLATO

first stories that they hear should be so composed as to bring the fairest lessons of virtue to their ears."

.   .   .   .   .

I. "Concerning the gods then," said I, "this is the sort of thing that we must allow or not allow them to hear from childhood up, if they are to honour the gods and their fathers and mothers, and not to hold their friendship with one another in light esteem." "That was our view and I believe it right." "What then of this? If they are to be brave, must we not extend our prescription to include also the sayings that will make them least likely to fear death? Or do you suppose that anyone could ever become brave who had that dread in his heart?" "No indeed, I do not," he replied. "And again if he believes in the reality of the underworld and its terrors, do you think that any man will be fearless of death and in battle will prefer death to defeat and slavery?" "By no means." "Then it seems we must exercise supervision also, in the matter of such tales as these, over those who undertake to supply them and request them not to dispraise in this undiscriminating fashion the life in Hades but rather praise it, since what they now tell us is neither true nor edifying to men who are destined to be warriors." . . . "And shall we also do away with the wailings and lamentations of men of repute?" "That necessarily follows," he said, "from the other." . . . "Then if anyone represents men of worth as overpowered by laughter we must not accept it, much less if gods." "Much indeed," he replied. "Then we must not accept from Homer such sayings as these either about the gods:

Quenchless then was the laughter that rose from the blessed immortals
When they beheld Hephaestus officiously puffing and panting.

—we must not accept it on your view" . . . "But further we must surely prize truth most highly. For if we were right in what we were just saying and falsehood is in very deed useless to gods, but to men useful as a remedy or form of medicine, it is obvious that such a thing must be assigned to physicians, and laymen should have nothing to do with it." "Obviously," he replied. "The rulers then of the city may, if anybody, fitly lie on account of enemies or citizens for the benefit of tne state; no others may have anything to do with it, but for a layman to lie to rulers of that kind we shall affirm to be as great a sin, nay a greater, than it is for a patient not to tell his physician or an athlete his trainer the truth about his bodily condition, or for a man to deceive the pilot about the ship and the sailors as to the real condition of himself or a fellow-sailor, and how they fare." "Most true," he replied. "If then the ruler catches anybody else in the city lying, any of the craftsmen

Whether a prophet or healer of sickness or joiner of timbers,

he will chastise him for introducing a practice as subversive and destructive of a state as it is of a ship." "He will," he said, "if deed follows upon word." "Again, will our lads not need the virtue of self-control?" "Of course." . . .

VIII. "If, then, we are to maintain our original principle, that our guardians, released from all other crafts, are to be expert craftsmen of civic liberty, and pursue nothing else that does not conduce to this, it would not be fitting for these to do nor yet to imitate anything else. But if they imitate they should from childhood up imitate what is appropriate to them—men, that is, who are brave, sober, pious, free and all things of that kind; but things unbecoming the free man they should neither do nor be clever at imitating, nor yet any other shameful thing, lest from the imitation they imbibe the reality. Or have you not observed that imitations, if continued from youth far into life, settle down into habits and (second) nature in the body, the speech, and the thought?" "Yes, indeed," said he. "We will not then allow our charges, whom we expect to prove good men, being men, to play the parts of women and imitate a woman young or old wrangling with her husband, defying heaven, loudly boasting, fortunate in her own conceit, or involved in misfortune and possessed by grief and lamentation—still less a woman that is sick, in love, or in labour." "Most certainly not," he replied. "Nor may they imitate slaves, female and male, doing the offices of slaves." "No, not that either." . . . "If a man, then, it seems, who was capable by his cunning of assuming every kind of shape and imitating all things should arrive in our city, bringing with himself the poems which he wished to exhibit, we should fall down and worship him as a holy and wondrous and delightful creature, but should say to him that there is no man of that kind among us in our city, nor is it lawful for such a man to arise among us, and we should send him away to another city, after pouring myrrh down over his head and crowning him with fillets of wool, but we ourselves, for our souls' good, should continue to employ the more austere and less delightful poet and tale-teller, who would imitate the diction of the good man and would

34

tell his tale in the patterns which we prescribed in the beginning, when we set out to educate our soldiers." "We certainly should do that if it rested with us." "And now, my friend," said I, "we may say that we have completely finished the part of music that concerns speeches and tales. For we have set forth what is to be said and how it is to be said." "I think so too," he replied.

X. "After this, then," said I, "comes the manner of song and tunes?" . . . "You certainly . . . have a sufficient understanding of this—that the song is composed of three things, the words, the tune, and the rhythm?" "Yes," said he, "that much." "And so far as it is words, it surely in no manner differs from words not sung in the requirement of conformity to the patterns and manner that we have prescribed?" "True," he said. "And again, the music and the rhythm must follow the speech." "Of course." "But we said we did not require dirges and lamentations in words." "We do not." "What, then, are the dirge-like modes of music? Tell me, for you are a musician." "The mixed Lydian," he said, "and the tense or higher Lydian, and similar modes." "These, then," said I, "we must do away with. For they are useless even to women who are to make the best of themselves, let alone to men." "Assuredly." "But again, drunkenness is a thing most unbefitting guardians, and so is softness and sloth." "Yes." "What, then, are the soft and convivial modes?" "There are certain Ionian and also Lydian modes that are called lax." "Will you make any use of them for warriors?" "None at all," he said . . .

XL. . . . "Good speech, then, good accord, and good grace, and good rhythm wait upon a good disposition, not that weakness of head which we euphemistically style goodness of heart, but the truly good and fair disposition of the character and the mind." "By all means," he said. "And must not our youth pursue these everywhere if they are to do what it is truly theirs to do?" "They must indeed." "And there is surely much of these qualities in painting and in all similar craftsmanship—weaving is full of them and embroidery and architecture and likewise the manufacture of household furnishings and thereto the natural bodies of animals and plants as well. For in all these there is grace or gracelessness. And gracelessness and evil rhythm and disharmony are akin to evil speaking and the evil temper, but the opposites are the symbols and the kin of the opposites, the sober and good disposition." "Entirely so," he said.

XII. "Is it, then, only the poets that we must supervise and compel to embody in their poems the semblance of the good character or else not write poetry among us, or must we keep watch over the other craftsmen, and forbid them to represent the evil disposition,

35

the licentious, the illiberal, the graceless, either in the likeness of living creatures or in buildings or in any other product of their art, on penalty, if unable to obey, of being forbidden to practise their art among us, that our guardians may not be bred among symbols of evil, as it were in a pasturage of poisonous herbs, lest grazing freely and cropping from many such day by day they little by little and all unawares accumulate and build up a huge mass of evil in their own souls. But we must look for those craftsmen who by the happy gift of nature are capable of following the trail of true beauty and grace, that our young men, dwelling as it were in a salubrious region, may receive benefit from all things about them, whence the influence that emanates from works of beauty may waft itself to eye or ear like a breeze that brings from wholesome places health, and so from earliest childhood insensibly guide them to likeness, to friendship, to harmony with beautiful reason." "Yes," he said, "that would be far the best education for them." "And is it not for this reason, Glaucon," said I, "that education in music is most sovereign, because more than anything else rhythm and harmony find their way to the inmost soul and take strongest hold upon it, bringing with them and imparting grace, if one is rightly trained, and otherwise the contrary? . . . "Then, by heaven, am I not right in saying that by the same token we shall never be true musicians, either—neither we nor the guardians that we have undertaken to educate—until we are able to recognize the forms of soberness, courage, liberality, and high-mindedness and all their kindred and their opposites, too, in all the combinations that contain and convey them, and to apprehend them and their images wherever found, disregarding them neither in trifles nor in great things, but believing the knowledge of them to belong to the same art and discipline?" "The conclusion is inevitable," he said. "Then," said I, "when there is a coincidence of a beautiful disposition in the soul and corresponding and harmonious beauties of the same type in the bodily form—is not this the fairest spectacle for one who is capable of its contemplation?" "Far the fairest." "And surely the fairest is the most lovable." "Of course." "The true musician, then, would love by preference persons of this sort; but if there were disharmony he would not love this." "No," he said, "not if there was a defect in the soul; but if it were in the body he would bear with it and still be willing to bestow his love." . . .

XIII. "After music our youth are to be educated by gymnastics?" "Certainly." . . . "For I, for my part, do not believe that a sound body by its excellence makes the soul good, but on the contrary that

36

a good soul by its virtue renders the body the best that is possible. What is your opinion?" "I think so too." "Then if we should sufficiently train the mind and turn over to it the minutiae of the care of the body, and content ourselves with merely indicating the norms or patterns, not to make a long story of it, we should be acting rightly?" "By all means." "From intoxication we said that they must abstain. For a guardian is surely the last person in the world to whom it is allowable to get drunk and not know where on earth he is." "Yes," he said, "it would be absurd that a guardian should need a guard." "What next about their food? These men are athletes in the greatest of contests, are they not?" "Yes." "Is, then, the bodily habit of the athletes we see about us suitable for such?" "Perhaps." "Nay," said I, "that is a drowsy habit and precarious for health. Don't you observe that they sleep away their lives, and that if they depart ever so little from their prescribed regimen these athletes are liable to great and violent diseases?" "I do." "Then," said I, "we need some more ingenious form of training for our athletes of war, since these must be as it were sleepless hounds, and have the keenest possible perceptions of sight and hearing, and in their campaigns undergo many changes in their drinking water, their food, and in exposure to the heat of the sun and to storms, without disturbance of their health." "I think so." "Would not, then, the best gymnastics be akin to the music that we were just now describing?" "What do you mean?" "It would be a simple and flexible gymnastic, and especially so in the training for war." . . .

XIV. "Will you be able to find a surer proof of an evil and shameful state of education in a city than the necessity of first-rate physicians and judges, not only for the base and mechanical, but for those who claim to have been bred in the fashion of free men? Do you not think it disgraceful and a notable mark of bad breeding to have to make use of a justice imported from others, who thus become your masters and judges, from lack of such qualities in yourself?" "The most shameful thing in the world." . . .

XX. "Well then, as I was just saying, we must look for those who are the best guardians of the indwelling conviction that what they have to do is what they at any time believe to be best for the state. Then we must observe them from childhood up and propose for them tasks in which one would be most likely to forget this principle or be deceived, and he whose memory is sure and who cannot be beguiled we must accept and the other kind we must cross off from our list. Is not that so?" "Yes." "And again we must subject them to toils and pains and competitions in which we have to watch for the same traits." "Right," he said. "Then," said I, "must we not institute a third kind of competitive test with regard to sorcery and observe them in that? Just as men conduct colts to noises and uproar to see if they are liable to take fright, so we must bring these lads while young into fears and again pass them into pleasures, testing them much more carefully than men do gold in the fire, to see if the man remains immune to such witchcraft and preserves his composure throughout, a good guardian of himself and the culture which he has received, maintaining the true rhythm and harmony of his being in all those conditions, and the character that would make him most useful to himself and to the state. And he who as boy, lad, and man endures the test and issues from it unspoiled we must establish as ruler over our city and its guardian, and bestow rewards upon him in life, and in death the allotment of the supreme honours of burial-rites and other memorials. But the man of the other type we must reject. . . .

XXI. . . . While all of you in the city are brothers, we will say in our tale, yet God in fashioning those of you who are fitted to hold rule mingled gold in their generation, for which reason they are the most precious—but in the helpers silver, and iron and brass in the farmers and other craftsmen. And as you are all akin, though for the most part you will breed after your kinds, it may sometimes happen that a golden father would beget a silver son and that a golden off-spring would come from a silver sire and that the rest would in like manner be born of one another. So that the first and chief injunction that the god lays upon the rulers is that of nothing else are they to be such careful guardians and so intently observant as of the inter-mixture of these metals in the souls of their offspring, and if sons are born to them with an infusion of brass or iron they shall by no means give way to pity in their treatment of them, but shall assign to each the status due to his nature and thrust them out among the artizans or the farmers. And again, if from these there is born a son with un-expected gold or silver in his composition they shall honour such and bid them go up higher, some to the office of guardian, some to the assistanceship, alleging that there is an oracle that the state shall then be overthrown when the man of iron or brass is its guardian. Do you see any way of getting them to believe this tale?" "No, not these themselves," he said, "but I do, their sons and successors and the rest of mankind who come after." . . .

"But let us arm these sons of earth and conduct them under the leadership of their rulers. And when they have arrived they must look out for the fairest site in the city for their encampment, a posi-

38

tion from which they could best hold down rebellion against the laws from within and repel aggression from without as of a wolf against the fold. And after they have encamped and sacrificed to the proper gods they must make their lairs, must they not?" "Yes," he said. "And these must be of a character to keep out the cold in winter and be sufficient in summer?" "Of course. For I presume you are speaking of their houses." "Yes," said I, "the houses of soldiers not of money-makers." "What distinction do you intend by that?" he said. "I will try to tell you," I said. "It is surely the most monstrous and shameful thing in the world for shepherds to breed the dogs who are to help them with their flocks in such wise and of such a nature that from indiscipline or hunger or some other evil condition the dogs themselves shall attack the sheep and injure them and be likened to wolves instead of dogs." "A terrible thing, indeed," he said. "Must we not then guard by every means in our power against our helpers treating the citizens in any such way and, because they are the stronger, converting themselves from benign assistants into savage masters?" "We must," he said. "And would they not have been provided with the chief safeguard if their education has really been a good one?" "But it surely has," he said. . . . "In addition, moreover, to such an education a thoughtful man would affirm that their houses and the possessions provided for them ought to be such as not to interfere with the best performance of their own work as guardians and not to incite them to wrong the other citizens." "He will rightly affirm that." "Consider then," said I, "whether, if that is to be their character, their habitations and ways of life must not be something after this fashion. In the first place, none must possess any private property save the indispensable. Secondly, none must have any habitation or treasure-house which is not open for all to enter at will. Their food, in such quantities as are needful for athletes of war sober and brave, they must receive as an agreed stipend from the other citizens as the wages of their guardianship, so measured that there shall be neither superfluity at the end of the year nor any lack. And resorting to a common mess like soldiers on campaign they will live together. Gold and silver, we will tell them, they have of the divine quality from the gods always in their souls, and they have no need of the metal of men nor does holiness suffer them to mingle and contaminate that heavenly possession with the acquisition of mortal gold, since many impious deeds have been done about the coin of the multitude, while that which dwells within them is unsullied. But for these only of all the dwellers in the city it is not lawful to handle gold and silver and to touch them nor yet to come under the same roof with them, nor to hang them as ornaments on their limbs nor to drink from silver and gold. So living they would save themselves and save their city. But whenever they shall acquire for themselves land of their own and houses and coin, they will be householders and farmers instead of guardians, and will be transformed from the helpers of their fellow-citizens to their enemies and masters, and so in hating and being hated, plotting and being plotted against they will pass their days fearing far more and rather the townsmen within than the foemen without—and then even then laying the course of near shipwreck for themselves and the state. For all these reasons," said I, "let us declare that such must be the provision for our guardians in lodging and other respects and so legislate. Shall we not?" "By all means," said Glaucon.

BOOK IV

I. And Adeimantus broke in and said, "What will be your defence, Socrates, if anyone objects that you are not making these men very happy, and that through their own fault? For the city really belongs to them and yet they get no enjoyment out of it as ordinary men do by owning lands and building fine big houses and providing them with suitable furniture and winning the favour of the gods by private sacrifices and entertaining guests and enjoying too those possessions which you just now spoke of, gold and silver and all that is customary for those who are expecting to be happy? But they seem, one might say, to be established in idleness in the city, exactly like hired mercenaries, with nothing to do but keep guard." "Yes," said I, "and what is more, they serve for board-wages and do not even receive pay in addition to their food as others do, so that they will not even be able to take a journey on their own account, if they wish to, or make presents to their mistresses, or spend money in other directions according to their desires like the men who are thought to be happy. These and many similar counts of the indictment you are omitting." "Well," said he, "assume these counts too." "What then will be our apology you ask?" "Yes." "By following the same path I think we shall find what to reply. For we shall say that while it would not surprise us if these men thus living prove to be the most happy, yet the object on which we fixed our eyes in the establishment of our state was not the exceptional happiness of any one class but the greatest possible happiness of the city as a whole. For we thought that in a state so constituted we should be most likely to discover justice as we should injustice in the worst governed state, and that when we had made these out we could pass judgement on the issue of our long inquiry. Our first task then, we take it, is to mould the model of a happy state—we are not isolating a small class in it and postulating their happiness, but that of the city as a whole. . . . But guardians of laws and of the city who are not what they pretend to be, but only seem, destroy utterly, I would have you note, the entire state, and on the other hand, they alone are decisive of its good government and happiness. If then we are forming true guardians and keepers of our liberties, men least likely to harm the commonwealth, but the proponent of the other ideal is thinking of farmers and 'happy' feasters as it were in a festival and not in a civic community, he would have something else in mind than a state. Consider, then, whether our aim in establishing the guardians is the greatest possible happiness among them or whether that is something we must look to see develop in the city as a whole, but these helpers and guardians are to be constrained and persuaded to do what will make them the best craftsmen in their own work, and similarly all the rest. And so, as the entire city develops and is ordered well, each class is to be left to the share of happiness that its nature comports." . . .

And so long as your city is governed soberly in the order just laid down, it will be the greatest of cities. I do not mean greatest in repute, but in reality, even though it have only a thousand defenders. For a city of this size that is really one you will not easily discover either among Greeks or barbarians—but of those that seem so you will find many and many times the size of this. Or do you think otherwise?" "No, indeed I don't," said he.

III. "Would not this, then, be the best rule and measure for our governors of the proper size of the city and of the territory that they should mark off for a city of that size and seek no more?" "What is the measure?" "I think," said I, "that they should let it grow so long as in its growth it consents to remain a unity, but no further." "Excellent," he said. "Then is not this still another injunction that we should lay upon our guardians, to keep guard in every way that the city shall not be too small, nor great only in seeming, but that it shall be a sufficient city and one?" "That behest will perhaps be an easy one for them," he said. "And still easier, haply," I said, "is this that we mentioned before when we said that if a degenerate offspring was born to the guardians he must be sent away to the other classes, and likewise if a superior to the others he must be enrolled among the guardians; and the support of all this was that the other citizens too must be sent to the task for which their natures were fitted, one man to one work, in order that each of them fulfilling his own function may be not many men, but one, and so the entire city may come to be not a multiplicity but a unity." "Why yes," he said, "this is even more trifling than that." "These are not, my good Adeimantus, as one might suppose, numerous and difficult injunctions that we are imposing upon them, but they are all easy, provided they guard, as the saying is, the one great thing—or instead of great let us call it sufficient." "What is that?" he said. "Their education and nurture," I replied. "For if a right education makes of them reasonable men they will easily discover everything of this kind—and other principles that we now pass over, as that the possession of wives and marriage, and the procreation of children and all that sort of thing should be made as far as possible the proverbial goods of friends that are common." "Yes, that would be the best way," he said. "And, moreover," said I, "the state, if it once starts well, proceeds as it were in a cycle of growth. I mean that a sound nurture and education if kept up creates good natures in the state, and sound natures in turn receiving an education of this sort develop into better men than their predecessors both for other purposes and for the production of offspring as among animals also." "It is probable," he said. "To put it briefly, then," said I, "it is to this that the overseers of our state must cleave and be watchful against its insensible corruption. They must throughout be watchful against innovation in music and gymnastics counter to the established order, and to the best of their power guard against them, fearing when anyone says that that song is most regarded among men

which hovers newest on the singer's lips,

lest haply it be supposed that the poet means not new songs but a new way of song and is commending this. But we must not praise that sort of thing nor conceive it to be the poet's meaning. For a change to a new type of music is something to beware of as a hazard of all our fortunes. For the modes of music are never disturbed without unsettling of the most fundamental political and social conventions, as Damon affirms and as I am convinced." "Set me too down in the number of the convinced," said Adeimantus.

IV. "It is here, then," I said, "in music, as it seems, that our guardians must build their guard-house and post of watch." "It is certain," he said, "that this is the kind of lawlessness that easily insinuates itself unobserved." "Yes," said I, "because it is supposed to be only a form of play and to work no harm." "Nor does it work any," he said, "except that by gradual infiltration it softly overflows upon the char-

42

acter and pursuits of men and from these issues forth grown greater
to attack their business dealings, and from these relations it proceeds
against the laws and the constitution with wanton licence, Socrates,
till finally it overthrows all things public and private." "Well," said
I, "are these things so?" "I think so," he said. "Then, as we were
saying in the beginning, our youth must join in a more law-abiding
play, since, if play grows lawless and the children likewise, it is
impossible that they should grow up to be men of serious temper
and lawful spirit." "Of course," he said. "And so we may reason that
when children in their earliest play are imbued with the spirit of
law and order through their music . . .—this spirit waits upon them
in all things and fosters their growth, and restores and sets up again
whatever was overthrown in the other type of state." "True, indeed," he said. "Then such men rediscover for themselves those
seemingly trifling conventions which their predecessors abolished
altogether." "Of what sort?" "Such things as the becoming silence
of the young in the presence of their elders; the giving place to them
and rising up before them, and dutiful service of parents, and the cut
of the hair and the garments and the fashion of the footgear, and
in general the deportment of the body and everything of the kind.
Don't you think so?" "I do." "Yet to enact them into laws would, I
think, be silly. For such laws are not obeyed nor would they last,
being enacted only in words and on paper." "How could they?" "At
any rate, Adeimantus," I said, "the direction of the education from
whence one starts is likely to determine the quality of what follows.
Does not like ever summon like?" "Surely." "And the final outcome,
I presume, we would say is one complete and vigorous product of
good or the reverse." "Of course," said he. "For my part, then," I
said, "for these reasons I would not go on to try to legislate on such
matters." "With good reason," said he. "But what, in heaven's
name," said I, "about business matters, the deals that men make with
one another in the agora—and, if you please, contracts with workmen and actions for foul language and assault, the filing of declara-
tions, the impanelling of juries, the payment and exaction of any
dues that may be needful in markets or harbours and in general
market, police or harbour regulations and the like, can we bring ourselves to legislate about these?" "Nay, 'twould not be fitting," he
said, "to dictate to good and honourable men. For most of the enactments that are needed about these things they will easily, I presume, discover." "Yes, my friend, provided God grants them the
preservation of the principles of law that we have already discussed." "Failing that," said he, "they will pass their lives multiply-

43

ing such petty laws and amending them in the expectation of attaining what is best." . . .

V. . . . "What part of legislation, then," he said, "is still left for us?" And I replied, "For us nothing, but for the Apollo of Delphi, the chief, the fairest and the first of enactments." "What are they?" he said. "The founding of temples, and sacrifices, and other forms of worship of gods, daemons, and heroes; and likewise the burial of the dead and the services we must render to the dwellers in the world beyond to keep them gracious. For of such matters we neither know anything nor in the founding of our city if we are wise shall we entrust them to any other or make use of any other interpreter than the God of our fathers. For this God surely is in such matters for all mankind the interpreter of the religion of their fathers who from his seat in the middle and at the very navel of the earth delivers his interpretation." "Excellently said," he replied; "and that is what we must do." . . .

VI. . . . "Then it is by virtue of its smallest class and minutest part of itself, and the wisdom that resides therein, in the part which takes the lead and rules, that a city established on principles of nature would be wise as a whole. And as it appears these are by nature the fewest, the class to which it pertains to partake of the knowledge which alone of all forms of knowledge deserves the name of wisdom." "Most true," he said. "This one of our four, then, we have, I know not how, discovered, the thing itself and its place in the state." "I certainly think," said he, "that it has been discovered sufficiently." . . .

X. "Listen then," said I, "and learn if there is anything in what I say. For what we laid down in the beginning as a universal requirement when we were founding our city, this I think, or some form of this, is justice. And what we did lay down, and often said, if you recall, was that each one man must perform one social service in the state for which his nature was best adapted." "Yes, we said that." "And again that to do one's own business and not to be a busybody is justice, is a saying that we have heard from many and have very often repeated ourselves." "We have." "This, then," I said, "my friend, if taken in a certain sense appears to be justice, this principle of doing one's own business. Do you know whence I infer this?" "No, but tell me," he said. "I think that this is the remaining virtue in the state after our consideration of soberness, courage, and intelligence, a quality which made it possible for them all to grow up in the body politic and which when they have sprung up preserves

44

them as long as it is present. And I hardly need to remind you that we said that justice would be the residue after we had found the other three." "That is an unavoidable conclusion," he said. "But moreover," said I, "if we were required to decide what it is whose indwelling presence will contribute most to making our city good, it would be a difficult decision whether it was the unanimity of rulers and ruled or the conservation in the minds of the soldiers of the convictions produced by law as to what things are or are not to be feared, or the watchful intelligence that resides in the guardians, or whether this is the chief cause of its goodness, the principle embodied in child, woman, slave, free, artisan, ruler, and ruled, that each performed his one task as one man and was not a versatile busybody." "Hard to decide indeed," he said. "A thing, then, that in its contribution to the excellence of a state vies with and rivals its wisdom, its soberness, its bravery, is this principle of everyone in it doing his own task." "It is indeed," he said. "And is not justice the name you would have to give to the principle that rivals these as conducing to the virtue of state?" "By all means," "Consider it in this wise too if so you will be convinced. Will you not assign the conduct of lawsuits in your state to the rulers?" "Of course." "Will not this be the chief aim of their decisions, that no one shall have what belongs to others or be deprived of his own?" "Nothing else but this." "On the assumption that this is just?" "Yes." "From this point of view too, then, the having and doing of one's own and what belongs to oneself would admittedly be justice." "That is so." "Consider now whether you agree with me. A carpenter undertaking to do the work of a cobbler or a cobbler of a carpenter or their interchange of one another's tools or honours or even the attempt of the same man to do both—the confounding of all other functions would not, think you, greatly injure a state, would it?" "Not much," he said. "But when I fancy one who is by nature an artisan or some kind of money-maker tempted and incited by wealth or command of votes or bodily strength or some similar advantage tries to enter into the class of the soldiers or one of the soldiers into the class of counsellors and guardians, for which he is not fitted, and these interchange their tools and their honours or when the same man undertakes all these functions at once, then, I take it, you too believe that this kind of substitution and meddlesomeness is the ruin of a state." "By all means." "The interference with one another's business, then, of three existent classes and the substitution of the one for the other is the greatest injury to a state and would most rightly be designated

45

as the thing which chiefly works it harm." "Precisely so." "And the thing that works the greatest harm to one's own state, will you not pronounce to be injustice?" "Of course." "This, then, is injustice. . . .

BOOK VII

I. "Next," said I, "compare our nature in respect of education and its lack to such an experience as this. Picture men dwelling in a sort of subterranean cavern with a long entrance open to the light on its entire width. Conceive them as having their legs and necks fettered from childhood, so that they remain in the same spot, able to look forward only, and prevented by the fetters from turning their heads. Picture further the light from a fire burning higher up and at a distance behind them, and between the fire and the prisoners and above them a road along which a low wall has been built, as the exhibitors of puppet-shows have partitions before the men themselves, above which they show the puppets." "All that I see," he said. "See also, then, men carrying past the wall implements of all kinds that rise above the wall, and human images and shapes of animals as well, wrought in stone and wood and every material, some of these bearers presumably speaking and others silent." "A strange image you speak of," he said, "and strange prisoners." "Like to us," I said; "for, to begin with, tell me do you think that these men would have seen anything of themselves or of one another except the shadows cast from the fire on the wall of the cave that fronted them?" "How could they," he said, "if they were compelled to hold their heads unmoved through life?" "And again, would not the same be true of the objects carried past them?" "Surely." "If then they were able to talk to one another, do you not think that they would suppose that in naming the things that they saw they were naming the passing objects?" "Necessarily." "And if their prison had an echo from the wall opposite them, when one of the passers-by uttered a sound, do you think that they would suppose anything else than the passing shadow to be the speaker?" "By Zeus, I do not," said he. "Then in every way such prisoners would deem reality to be nothing else than the shadows of the artificial objects." "Quite inevitably," he said. "Consider, then, what would be the manner of the release and healing from these bonds and this folly if in the course of nature something of this sort should happen to them: When one was freed from his fetters and compelled to stand up suddenly and turn his head around and walk and to lift up his eyes to the light, and in doing all this felt pain and, because of the dazzle

46

and glitter of the light, was unable to discern the objects whose shadows he formerly saw, what do you suppose would be his answer if someone told him that what he had seen before was all a cheat and an illusion, but that now, being nearer to reality and turned toward more real things, he saw more truly? And if also one should point out to him each of the passing objects and constrain him by questions to say what it is, do you not think that he would be at a loss and that he would regard what he formerly saw as more real than the things now pointed out to him?" "Far more real," he said.

II. "And if he were compelled to look at the light itself, would not that pain his eyes, and would he not turn away and flee to those things which he is able to discern and regard them as in very deed more clear and exact than the objects pointed out?" "It is so," he said. "And if," said I, "someone should drag him thence by force up the ascent which is rough and steep, and not let him go before he had drawn him out into the light of the sun, do you not think that he would find it painful to be so haled along, and would chafe at it, and when he came out into the light, that his eyes would be filled with its beams so that he would not be able to see even one of the things that we call real?" "Why, no, not immediately," he said. "Then there would be need of habituation, I take it, to enable him to see the things higher up. And at first he would most easily discern the shadows and after that, the likeness or reflections in water of men and other things, and later, the things themselves, and from these he would go on to contemplate the appearances in the heavens and heaven itself, more easily by night, looking at the light of the stars and the moon, than by day the sun and the sun's light." "Of course." "And so, finally, I suppose, he would be able to look upon the sun itself and see its true nature, not by reflections in water or phantasms of it in an alien setting, but in and by itself in its own place." "Necessarily," he said. "And at this point he would infer and conclude that this it is that provides the seasons and the courses of the year and presides over all things in the visible region, and is in some sort the cause of all these things that they had seen." "Obviously," he said, "that would be the next step." "Well then, if he recalled to mind his first habitation and what passed for wisdom there, and his fellow-bondsmen, do you not think that he would count himself happy in the change and pity them?" "He would indeed." "And if there had been honours and commendations among them which they bestowed on one another and prizes for the man who is quickest to make out the shadows as they pass and best able to remember their customary precedences, sequences and co-existences, and so most successful in guessing at what was to come, do you think he would be very keen about such rewards, and that he would envy and emulate those who were honoured by these prisoners and lorded it among them, or that he would feel with Homer and greatly prefer while living on earth to be serf of another, a landless man, and endure anything rather than opine with them and live that life?" "Yes," he said, "I think that he would choose to endure anything rather than such a life." "And consider this also," said I, "if such a one should go down again and take his old place would he not get his eyes full of darkness, thus suddenly coming out of the sunlight?" "He would indeed." "Now if he should be required to contend with these perpetual prisoners in "evaluating" these shadows while his vision was still dim and before his eyes were accustomed to the dark—and this time required for habituation would not be very short—would he not provoke laughter, and would it not be said of him that he had returned from his journey aloft with his eyes ruined and that it was not worth while even to attempt the ascent? And if it were possible to lay hands on and to kill the man who tried to release them and lead them up, would they not kill him?" "They certainly would," he said.

III. "This image then, dear Glaucon, we must apply as a whole to all that has been said, likening the region revealed through sight to the habitation of the prison, and the light of the fire in it to the power of the sun. And if you assume that the ascent and the contemplation of the things above is the soul's ascension to the intelligible region, you will not miss my surmise, since that is what you desire to hear. But God knows whether it is true. But, at any rate, my dream as it appears to me is that in the region of the known the last thing to be seen and hardly seen is the idea of good, and that when seen it must needs point us to the conclusion that this is indeed the cause for all things of all that is right and beautiful, giving birth in the visible world to light, and the author of light, and itself in the intelligible world being the authentic source of truth and reason, and that anyone who is to act wisely in private or public must have caught sight of this." "I concur," he said, "so far as I am able." "Come then," I said, "and join me in this further thought, and do not be surprised that those who have attained to this height are not willing to occupy themselves with the affairs of men, but their souls ever feel the upward urge and the yearning for that sojourn above. For this, I take it, is likely if in this point too the likeness of our image holds." "Yes, it is likely." "And again, do you think it at all strange," said I, "if a man returning from divine contemplations to

48

the petty miseries of men cuts a sorry figure and appears most ridiculous, if, while still blinking through the gloom, and before he has become sufficiently accustomed to the environing darkness, he is compelled in courtrooms or elsewhere to contend about the shadows of justice or the images that cast the shadows and to wrangle in debate about the notions of these things in the minds of those who have never seen justice itself?" "It would be by no means strange," he said. "But a sensible man," I said, "would remember that there are two distinct disturbances of the eyes arising from two causes, according as the shift is from light· to darkness or from darkness to light, and, believing that the same thing happens to the soul too, whenever he saw a soul perturbed and unable to discern something, he would not laugh unthinkingly, but would observe whether coming from a brighter life its vision was obscured by the unfamiliar darkness, or whether the passage from the deeper dark of ignorance into a more luminous world and the greater brightness had dazzled its vision. And so he would deem the one happy in its experience and way of life and pity the other, and if it pleased him to laugh at it, his laughter would be less laughable than that at the expense of the soul that had come down from the light above." "That is a very fair statement," he said.

IV. "Then, if this is true, our view of these matters must be this, that education is not in reality what some people proclaim it to be in their professions. What they aver is that they can put true knowledge into a soul that does not possess it, as if they were inserting vision into blind eyes." "They do indeed," he said. "But our present argument indicates," said I, "that the true analogy for this indwelling power in the soul and the instrument whereby each of us apprehends is that of an eye that could not be converted to the light from the darkness except by turning the whole body. Even so this organ of knowledge must be turned around from the world of becoming together with the entire soul, like the scene-shifting periact in the theatre, until the soul is able to endure the contemplation of essence and the brightest region of being. And this, we say, is the good, do we not?" "Yes." "Of this very thing, then" I said, "there might be an art, an art of the speediest and most effective shifting or conversion of the soul, not an art of producing vision in it, but on the assumption that it possesses vision but does not rightly direct it and does not look where it should, an art of bringing this about." "Yes, that seems likely," he said. "Then the other so-called virtues of the soul do seem akin to those of the body. For it is true that where they do not pre-exist, they are afterwards created by

49

habit and practice. But the excellence of thought, it seems, is certainly of a more divine quality, a thing that never loses its potency, but, according to the direction of its conversion, becomes useful and beneficent, or, again, useless and harmful. Have you never observed in those who are popularly spoken of as bad, but smart men, how keen is the vision of the little soul, how quick it is to discern the things that interest it, a proof that it is not a poor vision which it has, but one forcibly enlisted in the service of evil, so that the sharper its sight the more mischief it accomplishes?" "I certainly have," he said. "Observe then," said I, "that this part of such a soul, if it had been hammered from childhood, and had thus been struck free of the leaden weights, so to speak, of our birth and becoming, which attaching themselves to it by food and similar pleasures and gluttonies turn downwards the vision of the soul—if, I say, freed from these, it had suffered a conversion towards the things that are real and true, that same faculty of the same men would have been most keen in its vision of the higher things, just as it is for the things toward which it is now turned." "It is likely," he said. "Well, then," said I, "is not this also likely and a necessary consequence of what has been said, that neither could men who are uneducated and inexperienced in truth ever adequately preside over a state, nor could those who had been permitted to linger on to the end in the pursuit of culture —the one because they have no single aim and purpose in life to which all their actions, public and private, must be directed, and the others, because they will not voluntarily engage in action, believing that while still living they have been transported to the Islands of the Blest." "True," he said. "It is the duty of us, the founders, then," said I, "to compel the best natures to attain the knowledge which we pronounced the greatest, and to win to the vision of the good, to scale that ascent, and when they have reached the heights and taken an adequate view, we must not allow what is now permitted." "What is that?" "That they should linger there," I said, "and refuse to go down again among those bondsmen and share their labours and honours, whether they are of less or of greater worth." "Do you mean to say that we must do them this wrong, and compel them to live an inferior life when the better is in their power?"

. . . . .

VI. "Would you, then, have us proceed to consider how such men may be produced in a state and how they may be led upward to the light even as some are fabled to have ascended from Hades to the gods?" "Of course I would." "So this, it seems, would not be the whirling of the shell in the children's game, but a conversion and turning about of the soul from a day whose light is darkness to the veritable day—that ascension to reality of our parable which we will affirm to be true philosophy." "By all means." "Must we not, then, consider what studies have the power to effect this?" "Of course." "What, then, Glaucon, would be the study that would draw the soul away from the world of becoming to the world of being? A thought strikes me while I speak: Did we not say that these men in youth must be athletes of war?" "We did." "Then the study for which we are seeking must have this additional qualification." "What one?" "That it be not useless to soldiers." "Why, yes, it must," he said, "if that is possible." "But in our previous account they were educated in gymnastics and music." "They were," he said. "And gymnastics, I take it, is devoted to that which grows and perishes; for it presides over the growth and decay of the body." "Obviously." "Then this cannot be the study that we seek." "No." "Is it, then, music, so far as we have already described it?" "Nay, that," he said, "was the counterpart of gymnastics, if you remember. It educated the guardians through habits, imparting by the melody a certain harmony of spirit that is not science, and by the rhythm measure and grace, and also qualities akin to these in the words of tales that are fables and those that are more nearly true. But it included no study that tended to any such good as you are now seeking." "Your recollection is most exact," I said; "for in fact it had nothing of the kind. But in heaven's name, Glaucon, what study could there be of that kind? For all the arts were in our opinion base and mechanical." "Surely; and yet what other study is left apart from music, gymnastics and the arts?" "Come," said I, "if we are unable to discover anything outside of these, let us take something that applies to all alike." "What?" "Why, for example, this common thing that all arts and forms of thought and all sciences employ, and which is among the first things that everybody must learn." "What?" he said. "This trifling matter," I said, "of distinguishing one and two and three. I mean, in sum, number and calculation. Is it not true of them that every art and science must necessarily partake of them?" "Indeed it is," he said. "The art of war too?" said I. "Most necessarily," he said. "Certainly, then," said I, "Palamedes in the play is always making Agamemnon appear a most ridiculous general. Have you not noticed that he affirms that by the invention of number he marshalled the troops in the army at Troy in ranks and companies and enumerated the ships and everything else as if before that they had not been counted, and Agamemnon apparently did not know how

51

many feet he had if he couldn't count? And yet what sort of a general do you think he would be in that case?" "A very queer one in my opinion," he said, "if that was true."

VII. "Shall we not, then," I said, "set down as a study requisite for a soldier the ability to reckon and number?" "Most certainly, if he is to know anything whatever of the ordering of his troops—or rather if he is to be a man at all." "Do you observe then," said I, "in this study what I do?" "What?" "It seems likely that it is one of those studies which we are seeking that naturally conduce to the awakening of thought, but that no one makes the right use of it, though it really does tend to draw the mind to essence and reality." "What do you mean?" he said. "I will try," I said, "to show you at least my opinion. Do you keep watch and observe the things I distinguish in my mind as being or not being conducive to our purpose, and either concur or dissent, in order that here too we may see more clearly whether my surmise is right." "Point them out," he said. "I do point them out," I said, "if you can discern that some reports of our perceptions do not provoke thought to reconsideration because the judgement of them by sensation seems adequate, while others always invite the intellect to reflection because the sensation yields nothing that can be trusted."

. . . . .

VIII. "This, then, is just what I was trying to explain a little while ago when I said that some things are provocative of thought and some are not, defining as provocative things that impinge upon the senses together with their opposites, while those that do not I said do not tend to awaken reflection." "Well, now I understand," he said, "and agree." "To which class, then, do you think number and the one belong?" "I cannot conceive," he said. "Well, reason it out from what has already been said. For, if unity is adequately seen by itself or apprehended by some other sensation, it would not tend to draw the mind to the apprehension of essence. . . . But if some contradiction is always seen coincidentally with it, so that it no more appears to be one than the opposite, there would forthwith be need of something to judge between them, and it would compel the soul to be at a loss and to inquire, by arousing thought in itself, and to ask, whatever then is the one as such, and thus the study of unity will be one of the studies that guide and convert the soul to the contemplation of true being." "But surely," he said, "the visual perception of it does especially involve this. For we see the same thing at once as one and as an indefinite plurality." "Then if this is true of the one," I said, "the same holds of all number, does it not?" "Of

52

course." "But, further, reckoning and the science of arithmetic are wholly concerned with number." "They are, indeed." "And the qualities of number appear to lead to the apprehension of truth." "Beyond anything," he said. "Then, as it seems, these would be among the studies that we are seeking. For a soldier must learn them in order to marshal his troops, and a philosopher, because he must rise out of the region of generation and lay hold on essence or he can never become a true reckoner." "It is so," he said. "And our guardian is soldier and philosopher in one." "Of course." "It is befitting, then, Glaucon, that this branch of learning should be prescribed by our law and that we should induce those who are to share the highest functions of state to enter upon that study of calculation and take hold of it, not as amateurs, but to follow it up until they attain to the contemplation of the nature of number, by pure thought, not for the purpose of buying and selling, as if they were preparing to be merchants or hucksters, but for the uses of war and for facilitating the conversion of the soul itself from the world of generation to essence and truth." "Excellently said," he replied. "And, further," I said, "it occurs to me, now that the study of reckoning has been mentioned, that there is something fine in it, and that it is useful for our purpose in many ways, provided it is pursued for the sake of knowledge and not for huckstering." "In what respect?" he said. "Why, in respect of the very point of which we were speaking, that it strongly directs the soul upward and compels it to discourse about pure numbers, never acquiescing if anyone proffers to it in the discussion numbers attached to visible and tangible bodies. For you are doubtless aware that experts in this study, if anyone attempts to cut up the 'one' in argument, laugh at him and refuse to allow it; but if *you* mince it up, *they* multiply, always on guard lest the one should appear to be not one but a multiplicity of parts." "Most true," he replied. "Suppose now, Glaucon, someone were to ask them, 'My good friends, what numbers are these you are talking about, in which the one is such as you postulate, each unity equal to every other without the slightest difference and admitting no division into parts?' What do you think would be their answer?" "This, I think—that they are speaking of units which can only be conceived by thought, and which it is not possible to deal with in any other way." "You see, then, my friend," said I, "that this branch of study really seems to be indispensable for us, since it plainly compels the soul to employ pure thought with a view to truth itself." "It most emphatically does." "Again, have you ever noticed this, that natural reckoners are by nature quick in virtually all their studies? And the slow, if they are trained and drilled in this, even if no other benefit results, all improve and become quicker than they were?" "It is so," he said. "And, further, as I believe, studies that demand more toil in the learning and practice than this we shall not discover easily nor find many of them." "You will not, in fact." "Then, for all these reasons, we must not neglect this study, but must use it in the education of the best endowed natures." "I agree," he said.

IX. "Assuming this one point to be established," I said, "let us in the second place consider whether the study that comes next is suited to our purpose." "What is that? Do you mean geometry," he said. "Precisely that," said I. "So much of it," he said, "as applies to the conduct of war is obviously suitable. For in dealing with encampments and the occupation of strong places and the bringing of troops into column and line and all the other formations of an army in actual battle and on the march, an officer who had studied geometry would be a very different person from what he would be if he had not." "But still," I said, "for such purposes a slight modicum of geometry and calculation would suffice. What we have to consider is whether the greater and more advanced part of it tends to facilitate the apprehension of the idea of good. That tendency, we affirm, is to be found in all studies that force the soul to turn its vision round to the region where dwells the most blessed part of reality, which it is imperative that it should behold." "You are right," he said. "Then if it compels the soul to contemplate essence, it is suitable; if genesis, it is not." "So we affirm." "This at least," said I, "will not be disputed by those who have even a slight acquaintance with geometry, that this science is in direct contradiction with the language employed in it by its adepts." "How so?" he said. "Their language is most ludicrous, though they cannot help it, for they speak as if they were doing something and as if all their words were directed towards action. For all their talk is of squaring and applying and adding and the like, whereas in fact the real object of the entire study is pure knowledge." "That is absolutely true," he said. "And must we not agree on a further point?" "What?" "That it is the knowledge of that which always is, and not of a something which at some time comes into being and passes away." "That is readily admitted," he said, "for geometry is the knowledge of the eternally existent." "Then my good friend, it would tend to draw the soul to truth, and would be productive of a philosophic attitude of mind, directing upward the faculties that now wrongly are turned earthward." "Nothing is surer," he said. "Then nothing is surer," said I, "than that we must require that the men of your Fair City shall

54

never neglect geometry, for even the by-products of such study are not slight." "What are they?" said he. "What you mentioned," said I, "its uses in war, and also we are aware that for the better reception of all studies there will be an immeasurable difference between the student who has been imbued with geometry and the one who has not." "Immense indeed, by Zeus," he said. "Shall we, then, lay this down as a second branch of study for our lads?" "Let us do so," he said.

X. "Shall we set down astronomy as a third, or do you dissent?" "I certainly agree," he said; "for quickness of perception about the seasons and the course of the months and the years is serviceable, not only to agriculture and navigation, but still more to the military art." "I am amused," said I, "at your apparent fear lest the multitude may suppose you to be recommending useless studies. It is indeed no trifling task, but very difficult to realize that there is in every soul an organ or instrument of knowledge that is purified and kindled afresh by such studies when it has been destroyed and blinded by our ordinary pursuits, a faculty whose preservation outweighs ten thousand eyes; for by it only is reality beheld. . . . For I, for my part, am unable to suppose that any other study turns the soul's gaze upward than that which deals with being and the invisible. But if anyone tries to learn about the things of sense, whether gaping up or blinking down, I would never say that he really learns—for nothing of the kind admits of true knowledge—nor would I say that his soul looks up, but down, even though he study floating on his back on sea or land."

XI. "A fair retort," he said; "your rebuke is deserved. But how, then, did you mean that astronomy ought to be taught contrary to the present fashion if it is to be learned in a way to conduce to our purpose?" "Thus," said I: "these sparks that paint the sky, since they are decorations on a visible surface, we must regard to be sure, as the fairest and most exact of material things; but we must recognize that they fall far short of the truth, the movements, namely, of real speed and real slowness in true number and in all true figures both in relation to one another and as vehicles of the things they carry and contain. These can be apprehended only by reason and thought, but not by sight; or do you think otherwise?" "By no means," he said. "Then," said I, "we must use the blazonry of the heavens as patterns to aid in the study of those realities, just as one would do who chanced upon diagrams drawn with special care and elaboration by Daedalus or some other craftsman or painter. For anyone acquainted with geometry who saw such designs would admit the beauty of the workmanship, but would think it absurd to examine them seriously in the expectation of finding in them the absolute truth with regard to equals or doubles or any other ratio." "How could it be otherwise than absurd?" he said. "Do you not think," said I, "that one who was an astronomer in very truth would feel in the same way when he turned his eyes upon the movements of the stars? He will be willing to concede that the artisan of heaven fashioned it and all that it contains in the best possible manner for such a fabric; but when it comes to the proportions of day and night, and of their relation to the month, and that of the month to the year, and of the other stars to these and one another, do you not suppose that he will regard as a very strange fellow the man who believes that these things go on for ever without change or the least deviation—though they possess bodies and are visible objects—and that his unremitting quest is the realities of these things?" "I at least do think so," he said, "now that I hear it from you." "It is by means of problems, then," said I, "as in the study of geometry, that we will pursue astronomy too, and we will let be the things in the heavens, if we are to have a part in the true science of astronomy and so convert to right use from uselessness that natural indwelling intelligence of the soul." "You enjoin a task," he said, "that will multiply the labour of our present study of astronomy many times." "And I fancy," I said, "that our other injunctions will be of the same kind if we are of any use as lawgivers."

XII. "However, what suitable studies have you to suggest?" "Nothing," he said, "thus off-hand." "Yet, surely," said I, "motion in general provides not one but many forms or species, according to my opinion. To enumerate them all will perhaps be the task of a wise man, but even to us two of them are apparent." "What are they?" "In addition to astronomy, its counterpart," I replied. "What is that?" "We may venture to suppose," I said, "that as the eyes are framed for astronomy so the ears are framed for the movements of harmony; and these are in some sort kindred sciences, as the Pythagoreans affirm and we admit, do we not, Glaucon?" . . . Their method exactly corresponds to that of the astronomer; for the numbers they seek are those found in these heard concords, but they do not ascend to generalized problems and the consideration which numbers are inherently concordant and which not and why in each case." "A superhuman task," he said. "Say, rather, useful" said I, "for the investigation of the beautiful and the good, but if otherwise pursued, useless." "That is likely," he said.

XIII. "And what is more," I said, "I take it that if the investigation

56

of all these studies goes far enough to bring out their community and kinship with one another, and to infer their affinities, then to busy ourselves with them contributes to our desired end, and the labour taken is not lost; but otherwise it is vain." "I too so surmise," said he; "but it is a huge task of which you speak, Socrates." "Are you talking about the prelude," I said, "or what? Or do we not know that all this is but the preamble of the law itself, the prelude of the strain that we have to apprehend? For you surely do not suppose that experts in these matters are reasoners and dialecticians?" "No, by Zeus," he said, "except a very few whom I have met." "But have you ever supposed," I said, "that men who could not render and exact an account of opinions in discussion would ever know anything of the things we say must be known?" "*No* is surely the answer to that too." "This, then, at last, Glaucon," I said, "is the very law which dialectics recites, the strain which it executes, of which, though it belongs to the intelligible, we may see an imitation in the progress of the faculty of vision, as we described its endeavour to look at living things themselves and the stars themselves and finally at the very sun. In like manner, when anyone by dialectics attempts through discourse of reason and apart from all perceptions of sense to find his way to the very essence of each thing and does not desist till he apprehends by thought itself the nature of the good in itself, he arrives at the limit of the intelligible, as the other in our parable came to the goal of the visible." "By all means," he said. "What, then, will you not call this progress of thought dialectic?" "Surely." "And the release from bonds," I said, "and the conversion from the shadows to the images that cast them and to the light and the ascent from the subterranean cavern to the world above, and there the persisting inability to look directly at animals and plants and the light of the sun, but the ability to see the phantasms created by God in water and shadows of objects that are real and not merely, as before, the shadows of images cast through a light which compared with the sun, is as unreal as they—all this procedure of the arts and sciences that we have described indicates their power to lead the best part of the soul up to the contemplation of what is best among realities, as in our parable the clearest organ in the body was turned to the contemplation of what is brightest in the corporeal and visible region." . . .

XIV. "And is not this true of the good likewise—that the man who is unable to define in his discourse and distinguish and abstract from all other things the aspect or idea of the good, and who cannot, as it were in battle, running the gauntlet of all tests, and striving to examine everything by essential reality and not by opinion, hold on his way through all this without tripping in his reasoning—the man who lacks this power, you will say, does not really know the good itself or any particular good; but if he apprehends any adumbration of it, his contact with it is by opinion, not by knowledge; and dreaming and dozing through his present life, before he awakens here he will arrive at the house of Hades and fall asleep for ever?" "Yes, by Zeus," said he, "all this I will stoutly affirm." "But, surely," said I, "if you should ever nurture in fact your children whom you are now nurturing and educating in word, you would not suffer them, I presume, to hold rule in the state, and determine the greatest matters, being themselves as irrational as the lines so called in geometry." "Why, no," he said. "Then you will provide by law that they shall give special heed to the discipline that will enable them to ask and answer questions in the most scientific manner?" "I will so legislate," he said, "in conjunction with you." "Do you agree, then," said I, "that we have set dialectics above all other studies to be as it were the coping-stone—and that no other higher kind of study could rightly be placed above it, but that our discussion of studies is now complete?" "I do," he said.

XV. "The distribution, then, remains," said I, "to whom we are to assign these studies and in what way." "Clearly," he said. "Do you remember, then, the kind of man we chose in our former selection of rulers?" "Of course," he said. "In most respects, then," said I, "you must suppose that we have to choose those same natures. The most stable, the most brave and enterprising are to be preferred, and, so far as practicable, the most comely. But in addition we must now require that they not only be virile and vigorous in temper, but that they possess also the gifts of nature suitable to this type of education." "What qualities are you distinguishing?" "They must have, my friend, to begin with, a certain keenness for study, and must not learn with difficulty. For souls are much more likely to flinch and faint in severe studies than in gymnastics, because the toil touches them more nearly, being peculiar to them and not shared with the body." "True," he said. "And we must demand a good memory and doggedness and industry in every sense of the word. Otherwise how do you suppose anyone will consent both to undergo all the toils of the body and to complete so great a course of study and discipline?" "No one could," he said, "unless most happily endowed." "Our present mistake," said I, "and the disesteem that has in consequence fallen upon philosophy are, as I said before, caused by the unfitness of her associates and wooers. They

58

should not have been bastards but true scions." "What do you mean?" he said. "In the first place," I said, "the aspirant to philosophy must not limp in his industry, in the one half of him loving, in the other shunning, toil. This happens when anyone is a lover of gymnastics and hunting and all the labours of the body, yet is not fond of learning or of listening or inquiring, but in all such matters hates work. And he too is lame whose industry is one-sided in the reverse way." "Most true," he said. "Likewise in respect of truth," I said, "we shall regard as maimed in precisely the same way the soul that hates the voluntary lie and is troubled by it in its own self and greatly angered by it in others, but cheerfully accepts the involuntary falsehood and is not distressed when convicted of lack of knowledge, but wallows in the mud of ignorance as insensitively as a pig." "By all means," he said. . . .

XVI. "Now, all this study of reckoning and geometry and all the preliminary studies that are indispensable preparation for dialectics must be presented to them while still young, not in the form of compulsory instruction." "Why so?" "Because," said I, "a free soul ought not to pursue any study slavishly; for while bodily labours performed under constraint do not harm the body, nothing that is learned under compulsion stays with the mind." "True," he said. "Do not, then, my friend, keep children to their studies by compulsion but by play. That will also better enable you to discern the natural capacities of each." "There is reason in that," he said. "And do you not remember," I said, "that we also declared that we must conduct the children to war on horseback to be spectators, and wherever it may be safe, bring them to the front and give them a taste of blood as we do with whelps?" "I do remember." "And those who as time goes on show the most facility in all these toils and studies and alarms are to be selected and enrolled on a list." "At what age?" he said. "When they are released from their prescribed gymnastics. For that period, whether it be two or three years, incapacitates them for other occupations. For great fatigue and much sleep are the foes of study, and moreover one of our tests of them, and not the least will be their behaviour in their physical exercises." "Surely it is," he said. "After this period," I said, "those who are given preference from the twenty-year class will receive greater honours than the others, and they will be required to gather the studies which they disconnectedly pursued as children in their former education into a comprehensive survey of their affinities with one another and with the nature of things." "That, at any rate," he said, "is the only instruction that abides with those who receive it." "And it is also," said I, "the chief test of the dialectical nature and its opposite. For he who can view things in their connexion is a dialectician; he who cannot, is not." "I concur," he said. "With these qualities in mind," I said, "it will be your task to make a selection of those who manifest them best from the group who are steadfast in their studies and in war and in all lawful requirements, and when they have passed the thirtieth year to promote them, by a second selection from those preferred in the first, to still greater honours, and to prove and test them by the power of dialectic to see which of them is able to disregard the eyes and other senses and go on to being itself in company with truth. And at this point, my friend, the greatest care is requisite." "How so?" he said. "Do you not note," said I, "how great is the harm caused by our present treatment of dialectics?" "What is that?" he said. "Its practitioners are infected with lawlessness." "They are indeed." . . .

XVII. "Then that we may not have to pity thus your thirty-year-old disciples, must you not take every precaution when you introduce them to the study of dialectics?" "Yes, indeed," he said. "And is it not one chief safeguard not to suffer them to taste of it while young? For I fancy you have not failed to observe that lads, when they first get a taste of disputation, misuse it as a form of sport, always employing it contentiously, and, imitating confuters, they themselves confute others. They delight like puppies in pulling about and tearing with words all who approach them." "Exceedingly so," he said. "And when they have themselves confuted many and been confuted by many, they quickly fall into a violent distrust of all that they formerly held true; and the outcome is that they themselves and the whole business of philosophy are discredited with other men." "Most true," he said. "But an older man will not share this craze," said I, "but will rather choose to imitate the one who consents to examine truth dialectically than the one who makes a jest and a sport of mere contradiction, and so he will himself be more reasonable and moderate, and bring credit rather than discredit upon his pursuit." "Right," he said. "And were not all our preceding statements made with a view to this precaution— our requirement that those permitted to take part in such discussions must have orderly and stable natures, instead of the present practice of admitting to it any chance and unsuitable applicant?" "By all means," he said.

XVIII. Is it enough, then, to devote to the continuous and strenuous study of dialectics undisturbed by anything else, as in the corresponding discipline in bodily exercises, twice as many years as

were allotted to that?" "Do you mean six or four?" he said. "Well,"
I said, "set it down as five. For after that you will have to send them
down into the cave again, and compel them to hold commands in
war and the other offices suitable to youth, so that they may not fall
short of the other type in experience either. And in these offices,
too, they are to be tested to see whether they will remain steadfast
under diverse solicitations or whether they will flinch and swerve."
"How much time do you allow for that?" he said. "Fifteen years,"
said I, "and at the age of fifty those who have survived the tests and
approved themselves altogether the best in every task and form of
knowledge must be brought at last to the goal. We shall require
them to turn upwards the vision of their souls and fix their gaze on
that which sheds light on all, and when they have thus beheld the
good itself they shall use it as a pattern for the right ordering of the
state and the citizens and themselves throughout the remainder of
their lives, each in his turn, devoting the greater part of their time
to the study of philosophy, but when the turn comes for each, toiling in the service of the state and holding office for the city's sake,
regarding the task not as a fine thing but a necessity; and so, when
each generation has educated others like themselves to take their
place as guardians of the state, they shall depart to the Islands of
the Blest and there dwell. And the state shall establish public
memorials and sacrifices for them as to divinities if the Pythian
oracle approves or, if not, as to divine and godlike men." . . . "And
on the women too, Glaucon," said I; "for you must not suppose that
my words apply to the men more than to all women who arise
among them endowed with the requisite qualities." . . .

ARISTOTLE 384-322 B.C.

ARISTOTLE's wisdom results to a large degree from observation, but observation applied by a mind not less capable of discovering the eternal principles of Truth in the flux of facts and things than the more intuitional mind of Plato.

In addition, the urge for logical structure and classification is stronger in Aristotle than in Plato. Aristotle has always been the master of the system makers, such as Thomas Aquinas, the great rationalizer of the Catholic faith, whereas Plato has been the master of the men of intuition.

Aristotle is the first giant orderer of the universe of thought. If one considers how germinal the knowledge of his time was in comparison with ours then one can appreciate the creativeness of his mind. For it is no exaggeration to say that he laid the basis of our scholarly vocabulary in the whole broad field of the humanities, and that from his work issued the development of the higher curriculum as was customary from the times of the university of Alexandria up to the beginning of the 19th century; even the essential categories of natural philosophy have sprung from his mind.

Those of his works which deal with the permanent problems of humanity, with politics, ethics, esthetics, and the art of thinking, are today as basic as they were in his period, whereas most of his statements about nature are now obsolete. Yet, even here his conceptions about shape and form, and about a goal-directed vitality in all things growing, are still great topics for the modern thinker. And certainly he would have shaken hands gladly with Copernicus and Galileo when they discovered that his views about astronomy and physics were erroneous.

The selections from Aristotle's *Politics* are from H. Rackham's translation, published by the Harvard University Press in 1932, in the Loeb Classical Library. The selections from the *Nicomachean Ethics* are also from H. Rackham's translation, published in 1939, in the Loeb Classical Library.

POLITICS, BOOK VII

XV. When the children have been born, the particular mode of rearing adopted must be deemed an important determining influence in regard to their power of body. It appears from examining the other animals, and is also shown by the foreign races that make it their aim to keep up the military habit of body, that a diet giving an abundance of milk is most suited to the bodies of children, and

62

one that allows rather little wine because of the diseases that it causes. Moreover it is advantageous to subject them to as many movements as are practicable with children of that age. To prevent the limbs from being distorted owing to softness, some races even now employ certain mechanical appliances that keep the bodies of infants from being twisted. And it is also advantageous to accustom them at once from early childhood to cold, for this is most useful both for health and with a view to military service. Hence among many non-Greek races it is customary in the case of some peoples to wash the children at birth by dipping them in a cold river, and with others, for instance the Celts, to give them scanty covering. For it is better to inure them at the very start to everything possible, but to inure them gradually; and the bodily habit of children is naturally wellfitted by warmth to be trained to bear cold. In the earliest period of life then it is expedient to employ this or a similar method of nursing; and the next period to this, up to the age of five, which is not well to direct as yet to any study nor to compulsory labours, in order that they may not hinder the growth, should nevertheless be allowed enough movement to avoid bodily inactivity; and this exercise should be obtained by means of various pursuits, particularly play. But even the games must not be unfit for freemen, nor laborious, nor undisciplined. Also the question of the kind of tales and stories that should be told to children of this age must be attended to by the officials called Children's Tutors. For all such amusements should prepare the way for their later pursuits; hence most children's games should be imitations of the serious occupations of later life. The legislators in the *Laws* forbid allowing children to have paroxysms of crying, but this prohibition is a mistake; violent crying contributes to growth, for it serves in a way as exercise for the body, since holding the breath is the strength-giving factor in hard labour, and this takes place also with children when they stretch themselves in crying. The Tutors must supervise the children's pastimes, and in particular must see that they associate as little as possible with slaves. For children of this age, and up to seven years old, must necessarily be reared at home; so it is reasonable to suppose that even at this age they may acquire a taint of illiberality from what they hear and see. The lawgiver ought therefore to banish indecent talk, as much as anything else, out of the state altogether (for light talk about anything disgraceful soon passes into action)—so most of all from among the young, so that they may not say nor hear anything of the sort; and anybody found saying or doing any of the things prohibited, if he is of free station but not yet promoted to reclining at the public meals, must be punished with marks of dishonour and with beating, and an older offender must be punished with marks of dishonour degrading to a free man, because of his slavish behaviour. And since we banish any talk of this kind, clearly we must also banish the seeing of either pictures or representations that are indecent. The officials must therefore be careful that there may be no sculpture or painting that represents indecent actions, except in the temples of a certain class of gods to whom the law allows even scurrility; but in regard to these the law permits men still of suitable age to worship the gods both on their own behalf and on behalf of the children and women. But the younger ones must not be allowed in the audience at lampoons and at comedy, before they reach the age at which they will now have the right to recline at table in company and to drink deeply, and at which their education will render all of them immune to the harmful effects of such things. For the present therefore we have merely mentioned these matters in passing, but later we must stop to settle them more definitely, first discussing fully whether legislation prohibiting the attendance of the young is desirable or not, and how such prohibition should be put in force; but on the present occasion we have touched on the question only in the manner necessary. For perhaps the tragic actor Theodorus used to put the matter not badly: he had never once allowed anybody to produce his part before him, not even one of the poor actors, as he said that audiences are attracted by what they hear first; and this happens alike in regard to our dealings with people and to our dealings with things—all that comes first we like better. On this account we ought to make all base things unfamiliar to the young, and especially those that involve either depravity or malignity.

But when the five years from two to seven have passed, the children must now become spectators at the lessons which they will themselves have to learn. And there are two ages corresponding to which education should be divided—there must be a break after the period from seven to puberty, and again after that from puberty to twenty-one. For those who divide the ages by periods of seven years are generally speaking not wrong, and it is proper to follow the division of nature, for all art and education aim at filling up nature's deficiencies. First therefore we must consider whether some regulation in regard to the boys ought to be instituted, next whether it is advantageous for their supervision to be conducted on a public footing or in a private manner as is done at present in most

64

states, and thirdly of what particular nature this supervision ought to be.

BOOK VIII

I. Now nobody would dispute that the education of the young requires the special attention of the lawgiver. Indeed the neglect of this in states is injurious to their constitutions; for education ought to be adapted to the particular form of constitution, since the particular character belonging to each constitution both guards the constitution generally and originally establishes it—for instance the democratic spirit promotes democracy and the oligarchic spirit oligarchy; and the best spirit always causes a better constitution. Moreover in regard to all the faculties and crafts certain forms of preliminary education and training in their various operations are necessary, so that manifestly this is also requisite in regard to the actions of virtue. And inasmuch as the end for the whole state is one, it is manifest that education also must necessarily be one and the same for all and that the superintendence of this must be public, and not on private lines, in the way in which at present each man superintends the education of his own children, teaching them privately, and whatever special branch of knowledge he thinks fit. But matters of public interest ought to be under public supervision; at the same time also we ought not to think that any of the citizens belongs to himself, but that all belong to the state, for each is a part of the state, and it is natural for the superintendence of the several parts to have regard to the superintendence of the whole. And one might praise the Spartans in respect of this, for they pay the greatest attention to the training of their children, and conduct it on a public system.

It is clear then that there should be legislation about education and that it should be conducted on a public system. But consideration must be given to the question, what constitutes education and what is the proper way to be educated. At present there are differences of opinion as to the proper tasks to be set; for all peoples do not agree as to the things that the young ought to learn, either with a view to virtue or with a view to the best life, nor is it clear whether their studies should be regulated more with regard to intellect or with regard to character. And confusing questions arise out of the education that actually prevails, and it is not at all clear whether the pupils should practise pursuits that are practically useful, or morally edifying, or higher accomplishments—for all these views have won the support of some judges; and nothing is agreed as regards the exercise conducive to virtue, for, to start with, all men do not honour the same virtue, so that they naturally hold different opinions in regard to training in virtue.

II. It is therefore not difficult to see that the young must be taught those useful arts that are indispensably necessary; but it is clear that they should not be taught all the useful arts, those pursuits that are liberal being kept distinct from those that are illiberal, and that they must participate in such among the useful arts as will not render the person who participates in them vulgar. A task and also an art or a science must be deemed vulgar if it renders the body or soul or mind of free men useless for the employments and actions of virtue. Hence we entitle vulgar all such arts as deteriorate the condition of the body, and also the industries that earn wages; for they make the mind preoccupied and degraded. And even with the liberal sciences, although it is not illiberal to take part in some of them up to a point, to devote oneself to them too assiduously and carefully is liable to have the injurious result specified. Also it makes much difference what object one has in view in a pursuit or study; if one follows it for the sake of oneself or one's friends, or on moral ground, it is not illiberal, but the man who follows the same pursuit because of other people would often appear to be acting in a menial and servile manner.

The branches of study at present established fall into both classes, as was said before. There are perhaps four customary subjects of education, reading and writing, gymnastics, music, and fourth, with some people, drawing; reading and writing and drawing being taught as being useful for the purposes of life and very serviceable, and gymnastics as contributing to manly courage; but as to music, here one might raise a question. For at present most people take part in it for the sake of pleasure; but those who originally included it in education did so because, as has often been said, nature itself seeks to be able not only to engage rightly in business but also to occupy leisure nobly; for—to speak about it yet again—this is the first principle of all things. For if although both business and leisure are necessary, yet leisure is more desirable and more fully an end than business, we must inquire what is the proper occupation of leisure. For assuredly it should not be employed in play, since it would follow that play is our end in life. But if this is impossible, and sports should rather be employed in our times of business (for a man who is at work needs rest, and rest is the object of play, while business is accompanied by toil and exertion), it

66

follows that in introducing sports we must watch the right opportunity for their employment, since we are applying them to serve as medicine; for the activity of play is a relaxation of the soul, and serves as recreation because of its pleasantness. But leisure seems itself to contain pleasure and happiness and felicity of life. And this is not possessed by the busy but by the leisured; for the busy man busies himself for the sake of some end as not being in his possession, but happiness is an end achieved, which all men think is accompanied by pleasure and not by pain. But all men do not go on to define this pleasure in the same way, but according to their various natures and to their own characters, and the pleasure with which the best man thinks that happiness is conjoined is the best pleasure and the one arising from the noblest sources. So that it is clear that some subjects must be learnt and acquired merely with a view to the pleasure in their pursuit, and that these studies and these branches of learning are ends in themselves, while the forms of learning related to business are studied as necessary and as means to other things. Hence our predecessors included music in education not as a necessity (for there is nothing necessary about it), nor as useful (in the way in which reading and writing are useful for business and for household management and for acquiring learning and for many pursuits of civil life, while drawing also seems to be useful in making us better judges of the works of artists), nor yet again as we pursue gymnastics, for the sake of health and strength (for we do not see either of these things produced as a result of music); it remains therefore that it is useful as a pastime in leisure, which is evidently the purpose for which people actually introduce it, for they rank it as a form of pastime that they think proper for free men. For this reason Homer wrote thus:

> But him alone
> 'Tis meet to summon to the festal banquet;

and after these words he speaks of certain others

> Who call the bard that he may gladden all.

And also in other verses Odysseus says that this is the best pastime, when, as men are enjoying good cheer.

> The banqueters, seated in order due
> Throughout the hall, may hear a minstrel sing.

III. It is clear therefore that there is a form of education in which boys should be trained not because it is useful or necessary but as being liberal and noble; though whether there is one such subject

67

of education or several, and what these are and how they are to be pursued, must be discussed later, but as it is we have made this much progress on the way, that we have some testimony even from the ancients, derived from the courses of education which they founded—for the point is proved by music. And it is also clear that some of the useful subjects as well ought to be studied by the young not only because of their utility, like the study of reading and writing, but also because they may lead on to many other branches of knowledge; and similarly they should study drawing not in order that they may not go wrong in their private purchases and may avoid being cheated in buying and selling furniture, but rather because this study makes a man observant of bodily beauty; and to seek for utility everywhere is entirely unsuited to men that are great-souled and free. And since it is plain that education by habit must come before education by reason, and training of the body before training of the mind, it is clear from these considerations that the boys must be handed over to the care of the wrestling-master and the trainer; for the latter imparts a certain quality to the habit of the body and the former to its actions.

Now at the present time some of the states reputed to pay the greatest attention to children produce in them an athletic habit to the detriment of their bodily form and growth, while the Spartans although they have avoided this error yet make their boys animal in nature by their laborious exercises, in the belief that this is most contributory to manly courage. Yet, as has often been said, it is not right to regulate education with a view to one virtue only, or to this one most of all; indeed they do not even investigate the question whether this virtue is to be had in view at all. For neither in the lower animals nor in the case of foreign races do we see that courage goes with the wildest, but rather with the gentler and lion-like temperaments. And there are many foreign races inclined to murder and cannibalism, for example among the tribes of the Black Sea the Achaeans and Heniochi, and others of the mainland races, some in the same degree as those named and some more, which although piratical have got no share of manly courage. And again we know that even the Spartans, although so long as they persisted by themselves in their laborious exercises they surpassed all other peoples, now fall behind others both in gymnastic and in military contests; for they used not to excel because they exercised their young men in this fashion but only because they trained and their adversaries did not. Consequently honour and not animal ferocity should play the first part; for it is not a wolf nor one of the other wild animals that will venture upon any noble hazard, but rather a good man. But those who let boys pursue these hard exercises too much and turn them out untrained in necessary things in real truth render them vulgar, making them available for statesmanship to use for one task only, and even for this task training them worse than others do, as our argument proves. And we must not judge them from their former achievements but from the facts of to-day; for they have rivals in their education now, but they used to have none before.

IV. It is therefore agreed that we should employ gymnastic training, and how we should employ it. For until puberty we should apply lighter exercises, forbidding hard diet and severe exertions, in order that nothing may hinder the growth; for there is no small proof that too severe training can produce this result in the fact that in the list of Olympic victors one would only find two or three persons who have won both as men and as boys, because when people go into training in youth the severe exercises rob them of their strength. But when they have spent three years after puberty upon their other studies, then it is suitable to occupy the next period of life with laborious exercises and strict training diet; for it is wrong to work hard with the mind and the body at the same time, for it is the nature of the two different sorts of exertion to produce opposite effects, bodily toil impeding the development of the mind and mental toil that of the body.

· · · ·

NICOMACHEAN ETHICS BOOK I

I. Every art and every investigation, and likewise every practical pursuit or undertaking, seems to aim at some good: hence it has been well said that the Good is That at which all things aim. . . . But as there are numerous pursuits and arts and sciences, it follows that their ends are correspondingly numerous: for instance, the end of the science of medicine is health, that of the art of shipbuilding a vessel, that of strategy victory, that of domestic economy wealth. Now in cases where several such pursuits are subordinate to some single faculty . . . the ends of the master arts are things more to be desired than all those of the arts subordinate to them; since the latter ends are only pursued for the sake of the former . . .

II. If therefore among the ends at which our actions aim there be one which we wish for its own sake, while we wish the others only for the sake of this . . . it is clear that this one ultimate End must be the Good, and indeed the Supreme Good. Will not then a knowledge of this Supreme Good be also of great practical importance for the conduct of life? Will it not better enable us to attain what is fitting, like archers having a target to aim at? If this be so, we ought to make an attempt to determine at all events in outline what exactly this Supreme Good is, and of which of the theoretical or practical sciences it is the object.

Now it would be agreed that it must be the object of the most authoritative of the sciences—some science which is pre-eminently a master-craft. But such is manifestly the science of Politics; for it is this that ordains which of the sciences are to exist in states, and what branches of knowledge the different classes of the citizens are to learn, and up to what point; and we observe that even the most highly esteemed of the faculties, such as strategy, domestic economy, oratory, are subordinate to the political science. Inasmuch then as the rest of the sciences are employed by this one, and as it moreover lays down laws as to what people shall do and what things they shall refrain from doing, the end of this science must include the ends of all the others. Therefore, the Good of man must be the end of the science of Politics. For even though it be the case that the Good is the same for the individual and for the state, nevertheless, the good of the state is manifestly a greater and more perfect good, both to attain and to preserve. To secure the good of one person only is better than nothing; but to secure the good of a nation or a state is a nobler and more divine achievement.

This then being its aim, our investigation is in a sense the study of Politics.

III. Now our treatment of this science will be adequate, if it achieves that amount of precision which belongs to its subject matter. The same exactness must not be expected in all departments of philosophy alike, any more than in all the products of the arts and crafts. The subjects studied by political science are Moral Nobility and Justice; but these conceptions involve much difference of opinion and uncertainty, so that they are sometimes believed to be mere conventions and to have no real existence in the nature of things. And a similar uncertainty surrounds the conception of the Good, because it frequently occurs that good things have harmful consequences: people have before now been ruined by wealth, and in other cases courage has cost men their lives. We must therefore be content if, in dealing with subjects and starting from premises thus uncertain, we succeed in presenting a broad outline of the truth: when our subjects and our premises are merely generalities,

70

it is enough if we arrive at generally valid conclusions. Accordingly we may ask the student also to accept the various views we put forward in the same spirit; for it is the mark of an educated mind to expect that amount of exactness in each kind which the nature of the particular subject admits. It is equally unreasonable to accept merely probable conclusions from a mathematician and to demand strict demonstration from an orator.

Again, each man judges correctly those matters with which he is acquainted; it is of these that he is a competent critic. To criticize a particular subject, therefore, a man must have been trained in that subject: to be a good critic generally, he must have had an all-round education. Hence the young are not fit to be students of Political Science. For they have no experience of life and conduct, and it is these that supply the premises and subject matter of this branch of philosophy. And moreover they are led by their feelings; so that they will study the subject to no purpose or advantage, since the end of this science is not knowledge but action. And it makes no difference whether they are young in years or immature in character: the defect is not a question of time, it is because their life and its various aims are guided by feeling; for to such persons their knowledge is of no use, any more than it is to persons of defective self-restraint. But Moral Science may be of great value to those who guide their desires and actions by principle.

Let so much suffice by way of introduction as to the student of the subject, the spirit in which our conclusions are to be received, and the object that we set before us.

IV. To resume, inasmuch as all studies and undertakings are directed to the attainment of some good, let us discuss what it is that we pronounce to be the aim of Politics, that is, what is the highest of all the goods that action can achieve. As far as the name goes, we may almost say that the great majority of mankind are agreed about this; for both the multitude and persons of refinement speak of it as Happiness, and conceive 'the good life' or 'doing well' to be the same thing as 'being happy.' But what constitutes happiness is a matter of dispute; and the popular account of it is not the same as that given by the philosophers. Ordinary people identify it with some obvious and visible good, such as pleasure or wealth or honour—some say one thing and some another, indeed very often the same man says different things at different times: when he falls sick he thinks health is happiness, when he is poor, wealth. At other times, feeling conscious of their own ignorance, men admire those who propound something grand and above their heads; and it has been held by some thinkers that beside the many good things we have mentioned, there exists another Good, that is good in itself, and stands to all those goods as the cause of their being good.

Now perhaps it would be a somewhat fruitless task to review all the different opinions that are held. It will suffice to examine those that are most widely prevalent, or that seem to have some argument in their favour.

And we must not overlook the distinction between arguments that start from first principles and those that lead to first principles. It was a good practice of Plato to raise this question, and to enquire whether the right procedure was to start from or to lead up to the first principles, as in a race-course one may run from the judges to the far end of the track or reversely. Now no doubt it is proper to start from the known. But 'the known' has two meanings—'what is known to us,' which is one thing, and 'what is knowable in itself,' which is another. Perhaps then for us at all events it is proper to start from what is known to us. This is why in order to be a competent student of the Right and Just, and in short of the topics of Politics in general, the pupil is bound to have been well trained in his habits. For the starting-point or first principle is the fact that a thing is so; if this be satisfactorily ascertained, there will be no need also to know the reason why it is so. And the man of good moral training knows first principles already, or can easily acquire them. As for the person who neither knows nor can learn, let him hear the words of Hesiod:

> Best is the man who can himself advise;
> He too is good who hearkens to the wise;
> But who, himself being witless, will not heed
> Another's wisdom, is worthless indeed.

V. But let us continue from the point where we digressed. To judge from men's lives, the more or less reasoned conceptions of the Good or Happiness that seem to prevail among them are the following. On the one hand the generality of men and the most vulgar identify the Good with pleasure, and accordingly are content with the Life of Enjoyment—for there are three specially prominent Lives, the one just mentioned, the Life of Politics, and thirdly, the Life of Contemplation. The generality of mankind then show themselves to be utterly slavish, by preferring what is only a life for cattle; but they get a hearing for their view as reasonable because many persons of high position share the feeling of Sardanapallus.[1]

[1] Sardanapallus was a mythical Assyrian king; two versions of his epitaph are recorded by Athenaeus (336, 530), one containing the words: 'Eat, drink, play, since all else is not worth a snap of the fingers.'

72

Men of refinement, on the other hand, and men of action think that the Good is honour—for this may be said to be the end of the Life of Politics. But honour after all seems too superficial to be the Good for which we are seeking; since it appears to depend on those who confer it more than on him upon whom it is conferred, whereas we instinctively feel that the Good must be something proper to its possessor and not easy to be taken away from him. Moreover men's motive in pursuing honour seems to be to assure themselves of their own merit; at least they seek to be honoured by men of judgement and by people who know them, that is, they desire to be honoured on the ground of virtue. It is clear therefore that in the opinion at all events of men of action, virtue is a greater good than honour; and one might perhaps accordingly suppose that virtue rather than honour is the end of the Political Life. But even virtue proves on examination to be too incomplete to be the End; since it appears possible to possess it while you are asleep, or without putting it into practice throughout the whole of your life; and also for the virtuous man to suffer the greatest misery and misfortune—though no one would pronounce a man living a life of misery to be happy, unless for the sake of maintaining a paradox. . . .

The third type of life is the Life of Contemplation, which we shall consider in the sequel. . . .

VII. We may now return to the Good which is the object of our search, and try to find out what exactly it can be. For good appears to be one thing in one pursuit or art and another in another: it is different in medicine from what it is in strategy, and so on with the rest of the arts. What definition of the Good then will hold true in all the arts? Perhaps we may define it as that for the sake of which everything else is done. This applies to something different in each different art—to health in the case of medicine, to victory in that of strategy, to a house in architecture, and to something else in each of the other arts; but in every pursuit or undertaking it describes the end of that pursuit or undertaking, since in all of them it is for the sake of the end that everything else is done. Hence if there be something which is the end of all the things done by human action, this will be the practicable Good—or if there be several such ends, the sum of these will be the Good. . . .

Now there do appear to be several ends at which our actions aim; but as we choose some of them—for instance wealth, or flutes, and instruments generally—as a means to something else, it is clear that not all of them are final ends; whereas the Supreme Good seems to be something final. Consequently if there be some one thing which alone is a final end, this thing—or if there be several final ends, the one among them which is the most final—will be the Good which we are seeking. . . . Now happiness above all else appears to be absolutely final in this sense, since we always choose it for its own sake and never as a means to something else; whereas honour, pleasure, intelligence, and excellence in its various forms, we choose indeed for their own sakes (since we should be glad to have each of them although no extraneous advantage resulted from it), but we also choose them for the sake of happiness, in the belief that they will be a means to our securing it. But no one chooses happiness for the sake of honour, pleasure, etc., nor as a means to anything whatever other than itself.

.   .   .   .   .

Happiness, therefore, being found to be something final and self-sufficient, is the End at which all actions aim.

To say however that the Supreme Good is happiness will probably appear a truism; we still require a more explicit account of what constitutes happiness. Perhaps then we may arrive at this by ascertaining what is man's function. For the goodness or efficiency of a flute-player or sculptor or craftsman of any sort, and in general of anybody who has some function or business to perform, is thought to reside in that function; and similarly it may he held that the good of man resides in the function of man, if he has a function.

Are we then to suppose that, while the carpenter and the shoe-maker have definite functions or businesses belonging to them, man as such has none, and is not designed by nature to fulfil any function? Must we not rather assume that, just as the eye, the hand, the foot and each of the various members of the body manifestly has a certain function of its own, so a human being also has a certain function over and above all the functions of his particular members? What then precisely can this function be? The mere act of living appears to be shared even by plants, whereas we are looking for the function peculiar to man; we must therefore set aside the vital activity of nutrition and growth. Next in the scale will come some form of sentient life; but this too appears to be shared by horses, oxen, and animals generally. There remains therefore what may be called the practical life of the rational part of man. (This part has two divisions, one rational as obedient to principle, the other as possessing principle and exercising intelligence.) Rational life again has two meanings; let us assume that we are here concerned with the active exercise of the rational faculty, since this

74

seems to be the more proper sense of the term. If then the function of man is the active exercise of the soul's faculties in conformity with rational principle . . . if this is so, and if we declare that the function of man is a certain form of life, and define that form of life as the exercise of the soul's faculties and activities in association with rational principle, and say that the function of a good man is to perform these activities well and rightly, and if a function is well performed when it is performed in accordance with its own proper excellence—from these premises it follows that the Good of man is the active exercise of his soul's faculties in conformity with excellence or virtue, or if there be several human excellences or virtues, in conformity with the best and most perfect among them. Moreover this activity must occupy a complete lifetime; for one swallow does not make spring, nor does one fine day; and similarly one day or a brief period of happiness does not make a man supremely blessed and happy. . . .

VIII. . . . Now with those who pronounce happiness to be virtue, or some particular virtue, our definition is in agreement; for 'activity in conformity with virtue' involves virtue. But no doubt it makes a great difference whether we conceive the Supreme Good to depend on possessing virtue or on displaying it—on disposition, or on the manifestation of a disposition in action. For a man may possess the disposition without its producing any good result, as for instance when he is asleep, or has ceased to function from some other cause; but virtue in active exercise cannot be inoperative—it will of necessity act, and act well. And just as at the Olympic games the wreaths of victory are not bestowed upon the handsomest and strongest persons present, but on men who enter for the competitions—since it is among these that the winners are found. —so it is those who *act* rightly who carry off the prizes and good things of life.

And further, the life of active virtue is essentially pleasant. . . . But whereas the mass of mankind take pleasure in things that conflict with one another, because they are not pleasant of their own nature, things pleasant by nature are pleasant to lovers of what is noble, and so always are actions in conformity with virtue, so that they are pleasant essentially as well as pleasant to lovers of the noble. Therefore their life has no need of pleasure as a sort of ornamental appendage, but contains its pleasure in itself. For there is the further consideration that the man who does not enjoy doing noble actions is not a good man at all: no one would call a man just if he did not like acting justly, nor liberal if he did not like doing liberal things, and similarly with the other virtues. But if so, actions in conformity with virtue must be essentially pleasant.

But they are also of course both good and noble, and each in the highest degree, if the good man judges them rightly; and his judgement is as we have said. It follows therefore that happiness is at once the best, the noblest, and the pleasantest of things: these qualities are not separated as the inscription at Delos makes out—

> Justice is noblest, and health is best,
> But the heart's desire is the pleasantest—,

for the best activities possess them all; and it is the best activities, or one activity which is the best of all, in which according to our definition happiness consists. . . .

X. . . . since none of man's functions possess the quality of permanence so fully as the activities in conformity with virtue: they appear to be more lasting even than our knowledge of particular sciences. And among these activities themselves those which are highest in the scale of values are the more lasting, because they most fully and continuously occupy the lives of the supremely happy: for this appears to be the reason why we do not forget them.

The happy man therefore will possess the element of stability in question, and will remain happy all his life; since he will be always or at least most often employed in doing and contemplating the things that are in conformity with virtue. And he will bear changes of fortunes most nobly, and with perfect propriety in every way, being as he is 'good in very truth' and 'four-square without reproach.'

But the accidents of fortune are many and vary in degree of magnitude; and although small pieces of good luck, as also of misfortune, clearly do not change the whole course of life, yet great and repeated successes will render life more blissful, since both of their own nature they help to embellish it, and also they can be nobly and virtuously utilized; while great and frequent reverses can crush and mar our bliss both by the pain they cause and by the hindrance they offer to many activities. Yet nevertheless even in adversity nobility shines through, when a man endures repeated and severe misfortune with patience, not owing to insensibility but from generosity and greatness of soul. And if, as we said, a man's life is determined by his activities, no supremely happy man can ever become miserable. For he will never do hateful or base actions, since we hold that the truly good and wise man will bear all kinds of

76

fortune in a seemly way, and will always act in the noblest manner that the circumstances allow; even as a good general makes the most effective use of the forces at his disposal, and a good shoemaker makes the finest shoe possible out of the leather supplied him, and so on with all the other crafts and professions. And this being so, the happy man can never become miserable; though it is true he will not be supremely blessed if he encounters the misfortunes of a Priam. . . .

May not we then confidently pronounce that man happy who realizes complete goodness in action, and is adequately furnished with external goods? Or should we add, that he must also be destined to go on living not for any casual period but throughout a complete lifetime in the same manner, and to die accordingly, because the future is hidden from us, and we conceive happiness as an end, something utterly and absolutely final and complete? If this is so, we shall pronounce those of the living who possess and are destined to go on possessing the good things we have specified to be supremely blessed, though on the human scale of bliss.

So much for a discussion of this question. . . .

XIII. But inasmuch as happiness is a certain activity of soul in conformity with perfect goodness, it is necessary to examine the nature of goodness. For this will probably assist us in our investigation of the nature of happiness. Also, the true statesman seems to be one who has made a special study of goodness, since his aim is to make the citizens good and law-abiding men—witness the lawgivers of Crete and Sparta, and the other great legislators of history; but if the study of goodness falls within the province of Political Science, it is clear that in investigating goodness we shall be keeping to the plan which we adopted at the outset.

Now the goodness that we have to consider is clearly human goodness, since the good or happiness which we set out to seek was human good and human happiness. But human goodness means in our view excellence of soul, not excellence of body; also our definition of happiness is an activity of the soul. Now if this is so, clearly it behoves the statesman to have some acquaintance with psychology, just as the physician who is to heal the eye or the other parts of the body must know their anatomy. Indeed a foundation of science is even more requisite for the statesman, inasmuch as politics is a higher and more honourable art than medicine; but physicians of the better class devote much attention to the study of the human body. The student of politics therefore as well as the psychologist must study the nature of the soul, though he will do

77

so as an aid to politics, and only so far as is requisite for the objects of enquiry that he has in view: to pursue the subject in further detail would doubtless be more laborious than is necessary for his purpose. . . .

BOOK II

I. Virtue being, as we have seen, of two kinds, intellectual and moral, intellectual virtue is for the most part both produced and increased by instruction, and therefore requires experience and time; whereas moral or ethical virtue is the product of habit (*ethos*), and has indeed derived its name, with a slight variation of form, from that word. And therefore it is clear that none of the moral virtues is engendered in us by nature, for no natural property can be altered by habit. . . .

Moreover, the faculties given us by nature are bestowed on us first in a potential form; we exhibit their actual exercise afterwards. This is clearly so with our senses: we did not acquire the faculty of sight or hearing by repeatedly seeing or repeatedly listening, but the other way about—because we had the senses we began to use them, we did not get them by using them. The virtues on the other hand we acquire by first having actually practised them, just as we do the arts. We learn an art or craft by doing the things that we shall have to do when we have learnt it: for instance, men become builders by building houses, harpers by playing on the harp. Similarly we become just by doing just acts, temperate by doing temperate acts, brave by doing brave acts. This truth is attested by the experience of states: lawgivers make the citizens good by training them in habits of right action—this is the aim of all legislation, and if it fails to do this it is a failure; this is what distinguishes a good form of constitution from a bad one. Again, the actions from or through which any virtue is produced are the same as those through which it also is destroyed—just as is the case with skill in the arts, for both the good harpers and the bad ones are produced by harping, and similarly with builders and all the other craftsmen: as you will become a good builder from building well, so you will become a bad one from building badly. Were this not so, there would be no need for teachers of the arts, but everybody would be born a good or bad craftsman as the case might be. The same then is true of the virtues. It is by taking part in transactions with our fellow-men that some of us become just and others unjust; by acting in dangerous situations and forming a habit of fear or of confidence we become

78

courageous or cowardly. And the same holds good of our dispositions with regard to the appetites, and anger; some men become temperate and gentle, others profligate and irascible, by actually comporting themselves in one way or the other in relation to those passions. In a word, our moral dispositions are formed as a result of the corresponding activities. Hence it is incumbent on us to control the character of our activities, since on the quality of these depends the quality of our dispositions. It is therefore not of small moment whether we are trained from childhood in one set of habits or another; on the contrary it is of very great, or rather of supreme, importance.

II. As then our present study, unlike the other branches of philosophy, has a practical aim (for we are not investigating the nature of virtue for the sake of knowing what it is, but in order that we may become good, without which result our investigation would be of no use), we have consequently to carry our enquiry into the region of conduct, and to ask how we are to act rightly; since our actions, as we have said, determine the quality of our dispositions.

Now the formula 'to act in conformity with right principle' is common ground, and may be assumed as the basis of our discussion. (We shall speak about this formula later, and consider both the definition of right principle and its relation to the other virtues.)

But let it be granted to begin with that the whole theory of conduct is bound to be an outline only and not an exact system, in accordance with the rule we laid down at the beginning, that philosophical theories must only be required to correspond to their subject matter; and matters of conduct and expediency have nothing fixed or invariable about them, any more than have matters of health. And if this is true of the general theory of ethics, still less is exact precision possible in dealing with particular cases of conduct; for these come under no science or professional tradition, but the agents themselves have to consider what is suited to the circumstances on each occasion, just as is the case with the art of medicine or of navigation. But although the discussion now proceeding is thus necessarily inexact, we must do our best to help it out.

First of all then we have to observe, that moral qualities are so constituted as to be destroyed by excess and by deficiency—as we see is the case with bodily strength and health (for one is forced to explain what is invisible by means of visible illustrations). Strength is destroyed both by excessive and by deficient exercises, and similarly health is destroyed both by too much and by too little food and drink; while they are produced, increased and preserved by suitable quantities. The same therefore is true of Temperance, Courage, and the other virtues. The man who runs away from everything in fear and never endures anything becomes a coward; the man who fears nothing whatsoever but encounters everything becomes rash. Similarly he that indulges in every pleasure and refrains from none turns out a profligate, and he that shuns all pleasure, as boorish persons do, becomes what may be called insensible. Thus Temperance and Courage are destroyed by excess and deficiency, and preserved by the observance of the mean.

But not only are the virtues both generated and fostered on the one hand, and destroyed on the other, from and by the same actions, but they will also find their full exercise in the same actions. This is clearly the case with the other more visible qualities, such as bodily strength: for strength is produced by taking much food and undergoing much exertion, while also it is the strong man who will be able to eat most food and endure most exertion. The same holds good with the virtues. We become temperate by abstaining from pleasures, and at the same time we are best able to abstain from pleasures when we have become temperate. And so with Courage: we become brave by training ourselves to despise and endure terrors, and we shall be best able to endure terrors when we have become brave.

III. An index of our dispositions is afforded by the pleasure or pain that accompanies our actions. A man is temperate if he abstains from bodily pleasures and finds this abstinence itself enjoyable, profligate if he feels it irksome; he is brave if he faces danger with pleasure or at all events without pain, cowardly if he does so with pain.

In fact pleasures and pains are the things with which moral virtue is concerned. . . .

VI. . . . Virtue then is a settled disposition of the mind determining the choice of actions and emotions, consisting essentially in the observance of the mean relative to us, this being determined by principle, that is, as the prudent man would determine it.

And it is a mean state between two vices, one of excess and one of defect. Furthermore, it is a mean state in that whereas the vices either fall short of or exceed what is right in feelings and in actions, virtue ascertains and adopts the mean. Hence while in respect of its substance and the definition that states what it really is in essence virtue is the observance of the mean, in point of excellence and rightness it is an extreme.

Not every action or emotion however admits of the observance of a due mean. Indeed the very names of some directly imply evil, for instance malice, shamelessness, envy, and, of actions, adultery, theft, murder. All these and similar actions and feelings are blamed as being bad in themselves; it is not the excess or deficiency of them that we blame. It is impossible therefore ever to go right in regard to them—one must always be wrong; nor does right or wrong in their case depend on the circumstances, for instance, whether one commits adultery with the right woman, at the right time, and in the right manner; the mere commission of any of them is wrong. One might as well suppose there could be a due mean and excess and deficiency in acts of injustice or cowardice or profligacy, which would imply that one could have a medium amount of excess and of deficiency, an excessive amount of excess and a deficient amount of deficiency. But just as there can be no excess or deficiency in temperance and justice, because the mean is in a sense an extreme, so there can be no observance of the mean nor excess nor deficiency in the corresponding vicious acts mentioned above, but however they are committed, they are wrong; since, to put it in general terms, there is no such thing as observing a mean in excess or deficiency, nor as exceeding or falling short in the observance of a mean. . . .

VII. Thus much then is clear, that it is the middle disposition in each department of conduct that is to be praised, but that one should lean sometimes to the side of excess and sometimes to that of deficiency, since this is the easiest way of hitting the mean and the right course.

BOOK X

VI. Having now discussed the various kinds of Virtue, of Friendship and of Pleasure, it remains for us to treat in outline of Happiness, inasmuch as we count this to be the End of human life. But it will shorten the discussion if we recapitulate what has been said already.

Now we stated that happiness is not a certain disposition of character; since if it were it might be possessed by a man who passed the whole of his life asleep, living the life of a vegetable, or by one who was plunged in the deepest misfortune. If then we reject this as unsatisfactory, and feel bound to class happiness rather as some form of activity, as has been said in the earlier part of this treatise, and if activities are of two kinds, some merely necessary means and desirable only for the sake of something else, others desirable in themselves, it is clear that happiness is to be classed among activities desirable in themselves, and not among those desirable as a means to something else; since happiness lacks nothing, and is self-sufficient.

But those activities are desirable in themselves which do not aim at any result beyond the mere exercise of the activity. Now this is felt to be the nature of actions in conformity with virtue; for to do noble and virtuous deeds is a thing desirable for its own sake.

But agreeable amusements also are desirable for their own sake; we do not pursue them as a means to something else, for as a matter of fact they are more often harmful than beneficial, causing men to neglect their health and their estates. Yet persons whom the world counts happy usually have recourse to such pastimes; and this is why adepts in such pastimes stand in high favour with princes, because they make themselves agreeable in supplying what their patrons desire, and what they want is amusement. So it is supposed that amusements are a component part of happiness, because princes and potentates devote their leisure to them.

But (i) perhaps princes and potentates are not good evidence. Virtue and intelligence, which are the sources of man's higher activities, do not depend on the possession of power; and if these persons, having no taste for pure and liberal pleasure, have recourse to the pleasures of the body, we must not on that account suppose that bodily pleasures are the more desirable. Children imagine that the things they themselves value are actually the best; it is not surprising therefore that, as children and grown men have different standards of value, so also should the worthless and the virtuous. Therefore, as has repeatedly been said, those things are actually valuable and pleasant which appear so to the good man; but each man thinks that activity most desirable which suits his particular disposition, and therefore the good man thinks virtuous activity most desirable. It follows therefore that happiness is not to be found in amusements.

(ii) Indeed it would be strange that amusement should be our End—that we should toil and moil all our life long in order that we may amuse ourselves. For virtually every object we adopt is pursued as a means to something else, excepting happiness, which is an end in itself; to make amusement the object of our serious pursuits and our work seems foolish and childish to excess: Anacharsis's motto, Play in order that you may work, is felt to be the right rule. For amusement is a form of rest; but we need rest because we are

82

not able to go on working without a break, and therefore it is not an end, since we take it as a means to further activity.

(iii) And the life that conforms with virtue is thought to be a happy life; but virtuous life involves serious purpose, and does not consist in amusement.

(iv) Also we pronounce serious things to be superior to things that are funny and amusing; and the nobler a faculty or a person is, the more serious, we think, are their activities; therefore, the activity of the nobler faculty or person is itself superior, and therefore more productive of happiness.

(v) Also anybody can enjoy the pleasures of the body, a slave no less than the noblest of mankind; but no one allows a slave any measure of happiness, any more than a life of his own. Therefore happiness does not consist in pastimes and amusements, but in activities in accordance with virtue, as has been said already.

VII. But if happiness consists in activity in accordance with virtue, it is reasonable that it should be activity in accordance with the highest virtue; and this will be the virtue of the best part of us. Whether then this be the intellect, or whatever else it be that is thought to rule and lead us by nature, and to have cognizance of what is noble and divine, either as being itself also actually divine, or as being relatively the divinest part of us, it is the activity of this part of us in accordance with the virtue proper to it that will constitute perfect happiness; and it has been stated already that this activity is the activity of contemplation.

And that happiness consists in contemplation may be accepted as agreeing both with the results already reached and with the truth. For contemplation is at once the highest form of activity (since the intellect is the highest thing in us, and the objects with which the intellect deals are the highest things that can be known), and also it is the most continuous, for we can reflect more continuously than we can carry on any form of action. And again we suppose that happiness must contain an element of pleasure; now activity in accordance with wisdom is admittedly the most pleasant of the activities in accordance with virtue: at all events it is held that philosophy or the pursuit of wisdom contains pleasures of marvellous purity and permanence, and it is reasonable to suppose that the enjoyment of knowledge is a still pleasanter occupation than the pursuit of it. Also the activity of contemplation will be found to possess in the highest degree the quality that is termed self-sufficiency; for while it is true that the wise man equally with the just

83

man and the rest requires the necessaries of life, yet, these being adequately supplied, whereas the just man needs other persons towards whom or with whose aid he may act justly, and so likewise do the temperate man and the brave man and the others, the wise man on the contrary can also contemplate by himself, and the more so the wiser he is; no doubt he will study better with the aid of fellow-workers, but still he is the most self-sufficient of men. Also the activity of contemplation may he held to be the only activity that is loved for its own sake: it produces no result beyond the actual act of contemplation, whereas from practical pursuits we look to secure some advantage, greater or smaller, beyond the action itself. Also happiness is thought to involve leisure; for we do business in order that we may have leisure, and carry on war in order that we may have peace. Now the practical virtues are exercised in politics or in warfare; but the pursuits of politics and war seem to be unleisured—those of war indeed entirely so, for no one desires to be at war for the sake of being at war, nor deliberately takes steps to cause a war: a man would be thought an utterly bloodthirsty character if he declared war on a friendly state for the sake of causing battles and massacres. But the activity of the politician also is unleisured, and aims at securing something beyond the mere participation in politics—positions of authority and honour, or, if the happiness of the politician himself and of his fellow-citizens, this happiness conceived as something distinct from political activity (indeed we are clearly investigating it as so distinct). If then among practical pursuits displaying the virtues, politics and war stand out pre-eminent in nobility and grandeur, and yet they are unleisured, and directed to some further end, not chosen for their own sakes: whereas the activity of the intellect is felt to excel in serious worth, consisting as it does in contemplation, and to aim at no end beyond itself, and also to contain a pleasure peculiar to itself, and therefore augmenting its activity: and if accordingly the attributes of this activity are found to be self-sufficiency, leisuredness, such freedom from fatigue as is possible for man, and all the other attributes of blessedness: it follows that it is the activity of the intellect that constitutes complete human happiness—provided it be granted a complete span of life, for nothing that belongs to happiness can be incomplete.

Such a life as this however will be higher than the human level: not in virtue of his humanity will a man achieve it, but in virtue of something within him that is divine; and by as much as this something is superior to his composite nature, by so much is its activity superior to the exercise of the other forms of virtue. If then the intellect is something divine in comparison with man, so is the life of the intellect divine in comparison with human life. Nor ought we to obey those who enjoin that a man should have man's thoughts and a mortal the thoughts of mortality, but we ought so far as possible to achieve immortality, and do all that man may to live in accordance with the highest thing in him; for though this be small in bulk, in power and value it far surpasses all the rest.

It may even be held that this is the true self of each, inasmuch as it is the dominant and better part and therefore it would be a strange thing if a man should choose to live not his own life but the life of some other than himself.

Moreover what was said before will apply here also: that which is best and most pleasant for each creature is that which is proper to the nature of each; accordingly the life of the intellect is the best and the pleasantest life for man, inasmuch as the intellect more than anything else is man; therefore this life will be the happiest.

VIII. The life of moral virtue, on the other hand, is happy only in a secondary degree. For the moral activities are purely human: Justice, I mean, Courage and the other virtues we display in our intercourse with our fellows, when we observe what is due to each in contracts and services and in our various actions, and in our emotions also; and all of these things seem to be purely human affairs. And some moral actions are thought to be the outcome of the physical constitution, and moral virtue is thought to have a close affinity in many respects with the passions. Moreover, Prudence is intimately connected with Moral Virtue, and this with Prudence, inasmuch as the first principles which Prudence employs are determined by the Moral Virtues, and the right standard for the Moral Virtues is determined by Prudence. But these being also connected with the passions are related to our composite nature; now the virtues of our composite nature are purely human; so therefore also is the life that manifests these virtues, and the happiness that belongs to it. Whereas the happiness that belongs to the intellect is separate: so much may be said about it here, for a full discussion of the matter is beyond the scope of our present purpose. And such happiness would appear to need but little external equipment, or less than the happiness based on moral virtue. Both, it may be granted, require the mere necessaries of life, and that in an equal degree (though the politician does as a matter of fact take more trouble about bodily requirements and so forth than the philosopher); for in this respect there may be little difference between them. But for the purpose of their special activities their requirements will differ widely. The liberal man will need wealth in order to do liberal actions, and so indeed will the just man in order to discharge his obligations (since mere intentions are invisible, and even the unjust pretend to wish to act justly); and the brave man will need strength if he is to perform any action displaying his virtue; and the temperate man opportunity for indulgence: otherwise how can he, or the possessor of any other virtue, show that he is virtuous? It is disputed also whether purpose or performance is the more important factor in virtue, as it is alleged to depend on both; now the perfection of virtue will clearly consist in both; but the performance of virtuous actions requires much outward equipment, and the more so the greater and more noble the actions are. But the student, so far as the pursuit of his activity is concerned, needs no external apparatus: on the contrary, worldly goods may almost be said to be a hindrance to contemplation; though it is true that, being a man and living in the society of others, he chooses to engage in virtuous action, and so will need external goods to carry on his life as a human being.

The following considerations also will show that perfect happiness is some form of contemplative activity. The gods, as we conceive them, enjoy supreme felicity and happiness. But what sort of actions can we attribute to them? Just actions? but will it not seem ridiculous to think of them as making contracts, restoring deposits and the like? Then brave actions—enduring terrors and running risks for the nobility of so doing? Or liberal actions? but to whom will they give? Besides, it would be absurd to suppose that they actually have a coinage or currency of some sort! And temperate actions—what will these mean in their case? surely it would be derogatory to praise them for not having evil desires! If we go through the list we shall find that all forms of virtuous conduct seem trifling and unworthy of the gods. Yet nevertheless they have always been conceived as, at all events, living, and therefore living actively, for we cannot suppose they are always asleep like Endymion. But for a living being, if we eliminate action, and *a fortiori* creative action, what remains save contemplation? It follows that the activity of God, which is transcendent in blessedness, is the activity of contemplation; and therefore among human activities that which is most akin to the divine activity of contemplation will be the greatest source of happiness.

A further confirmation is that the lower animals cannot partake of happiness, because they are completely devoid of the contemplative activity. The whole of the life of the gods is blessed, and that of man is so in so far as it contains some likeness to the divine activity; but none of the other animals possess happiness, because they are entirely incapable of contemplation. Happiness therefore is co-extensive in its range with contemplation: the more a class of beings possesses the faculty of contemplation, the more it enjoys happiness, not as an accidental concomitant of contemplation but as inherent in it, since contemplation is valuable in itself. It follows that happiness is some form of contemplation.

But the philosopher being a man will also need external well-being, since man's nature is not self-sufficient for the activity of contemplation, but he must also have bodily health and a supply of food and other requirements. Yet if supreme blessedness is not possible without external goods, it must not be supposed that happiness will demand many or great possessions; for self-sufficiency does not depend on excessive abundance, nor does moral conduct, and it is possible to perform noble deeds even without being ruler of land and sea: one can do virtuous acts with quite moderate resources. This may be clearly observed in experience: private citizens do not seem to be less but more given to doing virtuous actions than princes and potentates. It is sufficient then if moderate resources are forthcoming; for a life of virtuous activity will be essentially a happy life.

Solon also doubtless gave a good description of happiness, when he said that in his opinion those men were happy who, being moderately equipped with external goods, had performed noble exploits and had lived temperately; for it is possible for a man of but moderate possessions to do what is right. Anaxagoras again does not seem to have conceived the happy man as rich or powerful, since he says that he would not be surprised if he were to appear a strange sort of person in the eyes of the many; for most men judge by externals, which are all that they can perceive. So our theories seem to be in agreement with the opinions of the wise.

Such arguments then carry some degree of conviction; but it is by the practical experience of life and conduct that the truth is really tested, since it is there that the final decision lies. We must therefore examine the conclusions we have advanced by bringing them to the test of the facts of life. If they are in harmony with the facts, we may accept them; if found to disagree, we must deem them mere theories.

And it seems likely that the man who pursues intellectual activity, and who cultivates his intellect and keeps that in the best condition, is also the man most beloved of the gods. For if, as is generally believed, the gods exercise some superintendence over human affairs, then it will be reasonable to suppose that they take pleasure in that part of man which is best and most akin to themselves, namely the intellect, and that they recompense with their favours those men who esteem and honour this most, because these care for the things dear to themselves, and act rightly and nobly. Now it is clear that all these attributes belong most of all to the wise man. He therefore is most beloved by the gods; and if so, he is naturally most happy. Here is another proof that the wise man is the happiest.

IX. If then we have sufficiently discussed in their outlines the subjects of Happiness and of Virtue in its various forms, and also Friendship and Pleasure, may we assume that the investigation we proposed is now complete? Perhaps however, as we maintain, in the practical sciences the end is not to attain a theoretic knowledge of the various subjects, but rather to carry out our theories in action. If so, to know what virtue is is not enough; we must endeavour to possess and to practise it, or in some other manner actually ourselves to become good.

Now if discourses on ethics were sufficient in themselves to make men virtuous, 'large fees and many' (as Theognis says) 'would they win,' quite rightly, and to provide such discourses would be all that is wanted. But as it is, we see that although theories have power to stimulate and encourage generous youths, and, given an inborn nobility of character and a genuine love of what is noble, can make them susceptible to the influence of virtue, yet they are powerless to stimulate the mass of mankind to moral nobility. For it is the nature of the many to be amenable to fear but not to a sense of honour, and to abstain from evil not because of its baseness but because of the penalties it entails; since, living as they do by passion, they pursue the pleasures akin to their nature, and the things that will procure those pleasures, and avoid the opposite pains, but have not even a notion of what is noble and truly pleasant, having never tasted true pleasure. What theory then can reform the natures of men like these? To dislodge by argument habits long firmly rooted in their characters is difficult if not impossible. We may doubtless think ourselves fortunate if we attain some measure of virtue when all the things believed to make men virtuous are ours.

Now some thinkers hold that virtue is a gift of nature; others think we become good by habit, others that we can be taught to be good. Natural endowment is obviously not under our control; it is bestowed on those who are fortunate, in the true sense, by some divine dispensation. Again, theory and teaching are not, I fear, equally efficacious in all cases: the soil must have been previously tilled if it is to foster the seed, the mind of the pupil must have been prepared by the cultivation of habits, so as to like and dislike aright. For he that lives at the dictates of passion will not hear nor understand the reasoning of one who tries to dissuade him; but if so, how can you change his mind by argument?

And, speaking generally, passion seems not to be amenable to reason, but only to force.

We must therefore by some means secure that the character shall have at the outset a natural affinity for virtue, loving what is noble and hating what is base. And it is difficult to obtain a right education in virtue from youth up without being brought up under right laws; for to live temperately and hardily is not pleasant to most men, especially when young; hence the nurture and exercises of the young should be regulated by law, since temperance and hardiness will not be painful when they have become habitual. But doubtless it is not enough for people to receive the right nurture and discipline in youth; they must also practise the lessons they have learnt, and confirm them by habit, when they are grown up. Accordingly we shall need laws to regulate the discipline of adults as well, and in fact the whole life of the people generally; for the many are more amenable to compulsion and punishment than to reason and to moral ideals. Hence some persons hold, that while it is proper for the lawgiver to encourage and exhort men to virtue on moral grounds, in the expectation that those who have had a virtuous moral upbringing will respond, yet he is bound to impose chastisement and penalties on the disobedient and ill-conditioned, and to banish the incorrigible out of the state altogether. For (they argue) although the virtuous man, who guides his life by moral ideals, will be obedient to reason, the base, whose desires are fixed on pleasure, must be chastised by pain, like a beast of burden. This indeed is the ground for the view that the pains and penalties for transgressors should be such as are most opposed to their favourite pleasures. . . .

PLUTARCH c. 46–120 A.D.

IT HAPPENS sometimes that authors become more known through a work of minor quality than through their better achievements, and that lesser men achieve more fame than greater but more abstruse minds.

Compared with hundreds of men of letters Plutarch is of second rank. However, through his *Parallel Lives* he set an example of biographical and inspirational essays on great heroes widely read in the classical schools of Europe up to our modern times, and in his *Moralia* he transmitted to posterity the mellowed thought of late Antiquity about almost everything which could interest a person with a desire for instructive entertainment: from useful advice about a good and healthy life to the description of strange phenomena in the world of nature.

In the *Moralia* Plutarch deals also with education, putting much emphasis on good breeding, good habits, and an all-round liberal training; in other words, just the right kind for a young gentleman from a privileged family. Naturally, when the humanists of the Renaissance replaced the primarily religious education of the Middle Ages with a more secular type, they welcomed the guidance of an ancient writer such as Plutarch. For he proved to them that a cultured mind could combine philosophical and genteel interests with interest in such virtues as heroic self-assertion, glory, and statesmanship. And that was the combination fitted for the aspirations of the Renaissance.

The following selections are from *The Education of Children*, Volume I of Plutarch's *Moralia*, in F. C. Babbitt's translation, published by the Harvard University Press in 1927, in the Loeb Classical Library.

THE EDUCATION OF CHILDREN

1. Let us consider what may be said of the education of free-born children, and what advantages they should enjoy to give them a sound character when they grow up.

2. It is perhaps better to begin with their parentage first; and I should advise those desirous of becoming fathers of notable offspring to abstain from random cohabitation with women; I mean with such women as courtesans and concubines. For those who are not well-born, whether on the father's or the mother's side, have an indelible disgrace in their low birth, which accompanies them throughout their lives, and offers to anyone desiring to use it a

90

ready subject of reproach and insult. Wise was the poet who declares:

> The home's foundation being wrongly laid,
> The offspring needs must be unfortunate.[1]

．　　．　　．　　．　　．

3. In this connexion we should speak of a matter which has not been overlooked by our predecessors. What is this? It is that husbands who approach their wives for the sake of issue should do so only when they have either not taken any wine at all, or at any rate, a very moderate portion. For children whose fathers have chanced to beget them in drunkenness are wont to be fond of wine, and to be given to excessive drinking. Wherefore Diogenes, observing an emotional and crack-brained youth, said, "Young man, your father must have been drunk when he begot you!" So much for my views on the subject of birth. We must now speak of education.

4. As a general statement, the same assertion may be made in regard to moral excellence that we are in the habit of making in regard to the arts and sciences, namely, that there must be a concurrence of three things in order to produce perfectly right action, and these are: nature, reason, and habit. By reason I mean the act of learning, and by habit constant practice. The first beginnings come from nature, advancement from learning, the practical use from continued repetition, and the culmination from all combined; but so far as any one of these is wanting, the moral excellence must, to this extent, be crippled. For nature without learning is a blind thing, and learning without nature is an imperfect thing, and practice without both is an ineffective thing. Just as in farming, first of all the soil must be good, secondly, the husbandman skilful, and thirdly, the seed sound, so, after the same manner, nature is like to the soil, the teacher to the farmer, and the verbal counsels and precepts like to the seed. I should strenuously insist that all three qualities met together and formed a perfect union in the souls of those men who are celebrated among all mankind,—Pythagoras, Socrates, Plato, and all who have attained an ever-living fame.

Now it is a fortunate thing and a token of divine love if ever a heavenly power has bestowed all these qualities on any one man; but if anybody imagines that those not endowed with natural gifts, who yet have the chance to learn and to apply themselves in the right way to the attaining of virtue, cannot repair the want of their nature and advance so far as in them lies, let him know that he is

---

[1] Euripides, Hercules Furens 1261.

in great, or rather total, error. For indifference ruins a good natural endowment, but instruction amends a poor one; easy things escape the careless, but difficult things are conquered by careful application. . . . But why discuss the matter at length? For character is habit long continued, and if one were to call the virtues of character the virtues of habit, he would not seem to go far astray. I will cite but one more example on this point and then I shall desist from discussing it further. Lycurgus, the lawgiver of the Spartans, took two puppies of the same litter, and reared them in quite different ways, so that from the one he produced a mischievous and greedy cur, and from the other a dog able to follow a scent and to hunt. And then at a time when the Spartans were gathered together, he said, "Men of Sparta, of a truth habit and training and teaching and guidance in living are a great influence toward engendering excellence, and I will make this evident to you at once." Thereupon producing the two dogs, he let them loose, putting down directly in front of them a dish of food and a hare. The one dog rushed after the hare, and the other made for the dish. While the Spartans were as yet unable to make out what import he gave to this, and with what intent he was exhibiting the dogs, he said, "These dogs are both of the same litter, but they have received a different bringing-up, with the result that the one has turned out a glutton and the other a hunter." In regard to habits and manner of life let this suffice.

5. Next in order comes the subject of feeding. Mothers ought, I should say, themselves to feed their infants and nurse them themselves. For they will feed them with a livelier affection and greater care, as loving them inwardly, and, according to the proverb, to their finger-tips. But the goodwill of foster-mothers and nursemaids is insincere and forced, since they love for pay. . . . So, as I have said, mothers must endeavour, if possible, to nurse their children themselves; but if they are unable to do this, either because of bodily weakness (for such a thing can happen) or because they are in haste to bear more children, yet foster-mothers and nursemaids are not to be selected at random, but as good ones as possible must be chosen; and, first of all, in character they must be Greek. For just as it is necessary, immediately after birth, to begin to mould the limbs of the children's bodies in order that these may grow straight and without deformity, so, in the same fashion, it is fitting from the beginning to regulate the characters of children. For youth is impressionable and plastic, and while such minds are still tender lessons are infused deeply into them; but anything which has be-

92

come hard is with difficulty softened. For just as seals leave their impression in soft wax, so are lessons impressed upon the minds of children while they are young. . . .

6. Now there is another point which should not be omitted, that in choosing the younger slaves, who are to be the servants and companions of young masters, those should be sought out who are, first and foremost, sound in character, who are Greeks as well, and distinct of speech, so that the children may not be contaminated by barbarians and persons of low character, and so take on some of their commonness. The proverb-makers say, and quite to the point, "If you dwell with a lame man, you will learn to limp."

7. When now they attain to an age to be put under the charge of attendants, then especially great care must be taken in the appointment of these, so as not to entrust one's children inadvertently to slaves taken in war or to barbarians or to those who are unstable. Nowadays, the common practice of many persons is more than ridiculous; for some of their trustworthy slaves they appoint to manage their farms, others they make masters of their ships, others their factors, others they make house-stewards, and some even money-lenders; but any slave whom they find to be a wine-bibber and a glutton, and useless for any kind of business, to him they bring their sons and put them in his charge. But the good attendant ought to be a man of such nature as was Phoenix, the attendant of Achilles.

I come now to a point which is more important and weighty than anything I have said so far. Teachers must be sought for the children who are free from scandal in their lives, who are unimpeachable in their manners, and in experience the very best that may be found. For to receive a proper education is the source and root of all goodness. . . .

8. Briefly, then, I say (an oracle one might properly call it, rather than advice) that, to sum up, the beginning, the middle, and end in all these matters is good education and proper training; and it is this, I say, which leads on and helps towards moral excellence and towards happiness . . . Two elements in man's nature are supreme over all—mind and reason. The mind exercises control over reason, and reason is the servant of the mind, unassailable by fortune, impregnable to calumny, uncorrupted by disease, unimpaired by old age. For the mind alone grows young with increase of years, and time, which takes away all things else, but adds wisdom to avoid triviality and vulgarity in style . . .

10. Now the free-born child should not be allowed to go without

some knowledge, both through hearing and observation, of every branch also of what is called general education; yet these he should learn only incidentally, just to get a taste of them, as it were (for perfection in everything is impossible), but philosophy he should honour above all else. I can perhaps make my opinion clear by means of a figure: for example, it is a fine thing to voyage about and view many cities, but profitable to dwell only in the best one. And it was a clever saying of Bion, the philosopher, that, just as the suitors, not being able to approach Penelope, consorted with her maid-servants, so also do those who are not able to attain to philosophy wear themselves to a shadow over the other kinds of education which have no value. Wherefore it is necessary to make philosophy as it were the head and front of all education. For as regards the care of the body men have discovered two sciences, the medical and the gymnastic, of which the one implants health, the other sturdiness, in the body; but for the illnesses and affections of the mind philosophy alone is the remedy. For through philosophy and in company with philosophy it is possible to attain knowledge of what is honourable and what is shameful, what is just and what is unjust, what, in brief, is to be chosen and what to be avoided, how a man must bear himself in his relations with the gods, with his parents, with his elders, with the laws, with strangers, with those in authority, with friends, with women, with children, with servants; that one ought to reverence the gods, to honour one's parents, to respect one's elders, to be obedient to the laws, to yield to those in authority, to love one's friends, to be chaste with women, to be affectionate with children, and not to be overbearing with slaves; and, most important of all, not to be overjoyful at success or overmuch distressed at misfortune, nor to be dissolute in pleasures, nor impulsive and brutish in temper. These things I regard as pre-eminent among all the advantages which accrue from philosophy. For to have a generous heart in prosperity shows a man, to excite no envy withal shows a disciplined nature; to rule pleasure by reason marks the wise man, and not every man can master his passion. But I regard as perfect, so far as men can be, those who are able to combine and mingle political capacity with philosophy; and I am inclined to think that these are secure in the possession of two things which are of the greatest good: a life useful to the world in their public position, and the calm and untroubled life in their pursuit of philosophy. For there are three forms of life, of which the first is the practical life, the second the contemplative life, and the third the life of enjoyment. The last, which is dissolute and enslaved to pleasure, is bestial and mean, but the contemplative life, which falls short in practice, is not useful, while the practical life which has no portion in philosophy, is without culture or taste. One must try, then, as well as one can, both to take part in public life, and to lay hold of philosophy so far as the opportunity is granted. Such was the life of Pericles as a public man, such was Archytas of Tarentum, such was Dion of Syracuse, such was Epaminondas of Thebes, of whom the next to the last was the associate of Plato.

In regard to education I do not know why it is necessary to take the time to say more; but in addition to the foregoing, it is useful, or rather it is necessary, not to be indifferent about acquiring the works of earlier writers, but to make a collection of these, like a set of tools in farming. For the corresponding tool of education is the use of books, and by their means it has come to pass that we are able to study knowledge at its source.

11. It is not proper, either, to overlook the exercise of the body, but we should send the children to the trainer's and cultivate adequately this side of education with all diligence, not merely for the sake of gracefulness of body but also with an eye to strength; for sturdiness of body in childhood is the foundation of a hale old age. Just as in fair weather, then, one ought to prepare for storm, so also in youth one should store up discipline and self-restraint as a provision for old age. But the amount of bodily exercise should be so limited as not to be a drain on the children and make them too tired to study; for, according to Plato, sleep and weariness are the enemies of learning. But why do I introduce this subject here? Just because I am anxious to say that which is of greater importance than all the rest: it is for the contests of war that boys must be practised, by exercising themselves in throwing the javelin, shooting with the bow, and in hunting. "For the goods of the vanquished" in battle "are prizes offered to the victors." War has no place for a bodily condition produced by an indoor life, and a slenderly built soldier accustomed to military exercises forces his way through the masses of fleshy athletes.

But perchance someone may say, "What is this? You, who have promised to give directions in regard to the education of free-born children, are now evidently disregarding the education of the poor children of the common people, and you acknowledge that you are offering your suggestions for the rich only." To these it is not difficult to make reply. My dearest wish would be that my scheme of education should be generally useful; but if some, being needy in their private circumstances, shall be unable to avail themselves of

95

my directions, let them lay the blame therefor upon fortune and not upon him who gives this counsel. Even the poor must endeavour, as well as they can, to provide the best education for their children, but, if that be impossible, then they must avail themselves of that which is within their means. I have burdened the discussion with this minor matter so as to connect therewith in due order the other topics which tend toward the right education of the young.

12. This also I assert, that children ought to be led to honourable practices by means of encouragement and reasoning, and most certainly not by blows or ill-treatment, for it surely is agreed that these are fitting rather for slaves than for the free-born; for so they grow numb and shudder at their tasks, partly from the pain of the blows, partly from the degradation. Praise and reproof are more helpful for the free-born than any sort of ill-usage, since the praise incites them toward what is honourable, and reproof keeps them from what is disgraceful.

But rebukes and praise should be used alternately and in a variety of ways; it is well to choose some time when the children are full of confidence to put them to shame by rebuke, and then in turn to cheer them up by praises, and to imitate the nurses, who, when they have made their babies cry, in turn offer them the breast for comfort. Moreover in praising them it is essential not to excite and puff them up, for they are made conceited and spoiled by excess of praise.

13. In my time I have seen fathers in whom excessive affection had become the cause of no affection. What is it that I mean to say, in order that by the example I give I may make my argument more luminous? It is this: in their eagerness that their children may the sooner rank first in everything, they lay upon them unreasonable tasks, which the children find themselves unable to perform, and so come to grief; besides, being depressed by their unfortunate experiences, they do not respond to the instruction which they receive. . . .

It is right to rebuke some fathers who, after entrusting their sons to attendants and masters, do not themselves take cognizance at all of their instruction by means of their own eyes or their own ears. Herein they most fail in their duty; for they ought themselves every few days to test their children, and not rest their hopes upon the disposition of a hired person; for even those persons will devote more attention to the children if they know they must from time to time render an account. And in this connexion there is point as well as wit in the remark of the groom who said that nothing makes the horse so fat as the king's eye.

Above all, the memory of children should be trained and exercised; for this is, as it were, a storehouse of learning; and it is for this reason that the mythologists have made Memory the mother of the Muses, thereby intimating by an allegory that there is nothing in the world like memory for creating and fostering. This, then, is to be trained in either case, whether one's children be naturally gifted with a good memory, or, on the contrary, forgetful. For we shall thus strengthen nature's generous endowment, and thus fill out her deficiency; and while the first class of children will excel others, the second class will excel their former selves. The saying of Hesiod is admirably put:

> If even small upon the small you place
> And do this oft, the whole will soon be great.

Nor should parents forget that those branches of instruction which involve memory make no small contribution, not merely to education, but also to the practical activities of life; for the memory of past activities serves as a pattern of good counsel for the future.

14. Moreover, one's sons are to be kept from foul language; for, according to Democritus, "A word is a deed's shadow." Then, too, proper measures must be taken to ensure that they shall be tactful and courteous in their address; for nothing is so deservedly disliked as tactless characters. Besides, children may avoid getting themselves disliked by their associates if they do not prove totally unyielding in discussions. For it is a fine thing to understand, not only how to gain the victory, but also how to submit to defeat, in cases where victory is injurious; for there is really such a thing as a "Cadmean victory." As a witness of this I may quote Euripides the wise, who says:

> When of two speakers one is growing wroth,
> Wiser is he that yields in argument.

We must now lay down some rules of conduct which the young should follow no less but even more than those previously given. These are: To practise the simple life, to hold the tongue in check, to conquer anger, to control the hands. We must consider the importance of each of these; and they will be more intelligible if based on examples.

But besides all this, we should, as a most sacred duty, accustom children to speak the truth. For lying is fit for slaves only, and deserves to be hated of all men, and even in decent slaves it is not to be condoned.

15. So far I have felt no doubt or even hesitation in saying what I have said about the decorous conduct and modest behaviour of the young; but in regard to the topic now to be introduced I am of two opinions and two minds, and I incline now this way, now that, as though on a balance, being unable to settle down on either side; and a feeling of great reluctance possesses me, whether to introduce or to avoid the subject. Still I must venture to speak of it. What is it then? It is the question whether boys' admirers are to be permitted to associate with them and pass their time with them, or whether, on the contrary, they should be kept away and driven off from association with the youth. For when I have regard to those uncompromising fathers, harsh and surly in their manner, who think the society of admirers an intolerable outrage to their sons, I feel cautious about standing as its sponsor and advocate. But again, when I think of Socrates, Plato, Xenophon, Aeschines, Cebes, and that whole band of men who sanctioned affection between men, and thus guided the youth onward to learning, leadership, and virtuous conduct, I am of a different mind again, and am inclined to emulate their example. Euripides gives testimony in their favour when he says:

> Among mankind another love exists,
> That of an upright, chaste, and noble soul.

Nor may we omit the remark of Plato wherein jest and seriousness are combined. For he says that those who have acquitted themselves nobly ought to have the right to kiss any fair one they please. Now we ought indeed to drive away those whose desire is for mere outward beauty, but to admit without reserve those who are lovers of the soul. And while the sort of love prevailing at Thebes and in Elis is to be avoided, as well as the so-called kidnapping in Crete, that which is found at Athens and in Lacedaemon is to be emulated.

16. In this matter each man may be allowed such opinion as accords with his own convictions. But now that I have spoken of the orderly and decorous behaviour of children, I shall next pass to the period of adolescence, and say a very few words about it. I have often expressed my utter disapprobation of men who have been responsible for the introduction of depraved habits. For, while it is true that they have put attendants and teachers in charge of their

98

children, they nevertheless have allowed the impetuosity of youth to range unrestrained, when they ought, on the contrary, to have exercised greater caution and watchfulness over them when they were young men than when they were children. For who is not aware that the faults of children are trivial and altogether corrigible —heedlessness, perhaps, towards their attendants, or deceiving and refusing to mind their teachers? But the iniquities of early manhood are often monstrous and wicked—unlimited gluttony, theft of parents' money, gambling, revels, drinking-bouts, love affairs with young girls, and corruption of married women. The impulses of young men should therefore be kept fettered and restrained by careful supervision. For life's prime is prodigal in its pleasures, restive, and in need of a curb, so that parents who do not take hold of the reins with firm hand at this period of life, are manifestly, by their folly, giving to their sons licence for wrongdoing. Wise fathers ought, therefore, especially during this time, to be vigilant and alert, and to bring the young men to reason by instruction, by threats, by entreaties, by pointing out examples of men who through love of pleasure have become involved in misfortunes, and of those who, through their steadfastness, have gained for themselves approval and good repute. For these two things—hope of reward and fear of punishment—are, as it were, the elements of virtue. For the one renders men more eager for honourable pursuits while the other makes them averse to base actions. . . .

18. Now all these rules concern honour and good profit, but what follows concerns human nature. Take the fathers again: I do not think they should be utterly harsh and austere in their nature, but they should in many cases concede some shortcomings to the younger person, and remind themselves that they once were young. As physicians, by mixing bitter drugs with sweet syrups, have found that the agreeable taste gains access for what is beneficial, so fathers should combine the abruptness of their rebukes with mildness, and at one time grant some licence to the desires of their children, and slacken the reins a little, and then at another time draw them tight again. Most desirable is it that they should bear misdeeds with serenity, but if that be impossible, yet, if they be on occasion angered, they should quickly cool down. For it is better that a father should be quick-tempered than sullen, since a hostile and irreconcilable spirit is no small proof of animosity towards one's children. It is a good thing also to pretend not to know of some shortcomings, and to turn the old man's dull eye and dull ear to what they do, and

seeing, not to see, and, hearing, not to hear, sometimes, what goes on. Our friends' shortcomings we bear with: why should it be surprising that we bear with our children's? Though our slaves often suffer from a headache in the morning, we do not force them to confess a debauch. "You were niggardly once; well, now be liberal. You were indignant once; well, pardon now. He tricked you once with the help of a slave; restrain your anger. He once took away a yoke of cattle from the field, he once came home with breath reeking from yesterday's debauch; ignore it. Or smelling of perfume; do not say a word." In this fashion is restive youth gradually broken to harness.

19. An effort should be made to yoke in marriage those who cannot resist their desires, and who are deaf to admonitions. For marriage is the most secure bond for youth. One should, however, betroth to his sons women who are not greatly above them either in birth or wealth. The maxim "Keep to your own place" is wise, since those who take to wife women far above themselves unwittingly become not the husbands of their wives, but the slaves of their wives' dowries.

20. I will add but little more and then conclude my suggestions. Fathers ought above all, by not misbehaving and by doing as they ought to do, to make themselves a manifest example to their children, so that the latter, by looking at their fathers' lives as at a mirror, may be deterred from disgraceful deeds and words. For those who are themselves involved in the same errors as those for which they rebuke their erring sons, unwittingly accuse themselves in their sons' name. If the life they lead is wholly bad, they are not free to admonish even their slaves, let alone their sons. Besides, they are likely to become counsellors and instructors to their sons in their wrongdoing. For, wherever old men are lacking in decency, young men too are sure to be most shameless.

We must endeavour, therefore, to employ every proper device for the discipline of our children, emulating the example of Eurydice, who, although she was an Illyrian and an utter barbarian, yet late in life took up education in the interest of her children's studies. The inscription which she dedicated to the Muses sufficiently attests her love for her children:

> Eurydice of Hierapolis
> Made to the Muses this her offering
> When she had gained her soul's desire to learn.
> Mother of young and lusty sons was she,
> And by her diligence attained to learn
> Letters, wherein lies buried all our lore.

PLUTARCH

Now to put into effect all the suggestions which I have given is the province of prayer, perhaps, or exhortation. And even to follow zealously the majority of them demands good fortune and much careful attention, but to accomplish this lies within the capability of man.

QUINTILIAN c. 35–95 A.D.

ONE sometimes feels like asking heretically if it really was to the advantage of education that the Italian humanist Andrea Poggio, in 1410, discovered the lost manuscript of Quintilian's *Institutes of Oratory* among the dusty book shelves of the Monastery of St. Gallen.

For Quintilian has a narrow mind, not to be compared with great philosophers, nor even Plutarch. He is, so to speak, a "professional." The fundamental premises underlying Quintilian's pedagogy are either wrong or doubtful. He rightly attacks the degenerated philosophical schools of his time for their futility and the lack of usefulness in practical life. But this does not warrant his conclusion that we ought to put "oratory" (with a good portion of showmanship) on a par with philosophy in its broad and pure tradition. For the moment when in education, or civilization generally, the art of expression is set above the deeper experiences from which we draw our convictions, both education and civilization are bound to decay.

As a matter of history it turned out that those schools which put the main emphasis on style and language, such as the classical schools of the humanist period, tended to become formalistic, and drifted apart from the essential interests of man. This is the reason why today so many teachers are unable to see the good sides in the classical tradition and fail to imagine the loss civilization would incur if we demolish rather than try to revitalize this tradition for those fitted.

Why then, after all these negative statements, does Quintilian deserve a place in the history of educational thought? Because he penetrated more deeply than people before him into the problems of teaching; he had a sense for the importance of method; he had respect for the specific qualities of childhood and therefore taught his readers that education is more a process of understanding than of hardship and punishment. In all these respects he helped the schoolmen of the Renaissance and later periods to gradually change teaching from a process of imposition into a process of self-development.

The following selections are taken from Quintilian's *Institutes of Oratory* (*Institutio Oratoria*) in H. E. Butler's translation, published by the Harvard University Press in 1936, in the Loeb Classical Library.

INSTITUTES OF ORATORY, BOOK I

Preface: . . . My first book will be concerned with the education preliminary to the duties of the teacher of rhetoric. My second will

102

deal with the rudiments of the schools of rhetoric and with problems connected with the essence of rhetoric itself. The next five will be concerned with Invention, in which I include Arrangement. The four following will be assigned to Eloquence, under which head I include Memory and Delivery. Finally there will be one book in which our complete orator will be delineated; as far as my feeble powers permit, I shall discuss his character, the rules which should guide him in undertaking, studying and pleading cases, the style of his eloquence, the time at which he should cease to plead cases and the studies to which he should devote himself after such cessation. In the course of these discussions I shall deal in its proper place with the method of teaching by which students will acquire not merely a knowledge of those things to which the name of art is restricted by certain theorists, and will not only come to understand the laws of rhetoric, but will acquire that which will increase their powers of speech and nourish their eloquence. For as a rule the result of the dry textbooks on the art of rhetoric is that by straining after excessive subtlety they impair and cripple all the nobler elements of style, exhaust the lifeblood of the imagination and leave but the bare bones, which, while it is right and necessary that they should exist and be bound each to each by their respective ligaments, require a covering of flesh as well. . . .

There is however one point which I must emphasise before I begin, which is this. Without natural gifts technical rules are useless. Consequently the student who is devoid of talent will derive no more profit from this work than barren soil from a treatise on agriculture. There are, it is true, other natural aids, such as the possession of a good voice and robust lungs, sound health, powers of endurance and grace, and if these are possessed only to a moderate extent, they may be improved by methodical training. In some cases, however, these gifts are lacking to such an extent that their absence is fatal to all such advantages as talent and study can confer, while, similarly, they are of no profit in themselves unless cultivated by skilful teaching, persistent study and continuous and extensive practice in writing, reading and speaking.

I. I would, therefore, have a father conceive the highest hopes of his son from the moment of his birth. If he does so, he will be more careful about the groundwork of his education. For there is absolutely no foundation for the complaint that but few men have the power to take in the knowledge that is imparted to them, and that the majority are so slow of understanding that education is a waste of time and labour. On the contrary you will find that most are

103

quick to reason and ready to learn. Reasoning comes as naturally to man as flying to birds, speed to horses and ferocity to beasts of prey: our minds are endowed by nature with such activity and sagacity that the soul is believed to proceed from heaven. Those who are dull and unteachable are as abnormal as prodigious births and monstrosities, and are but few in number. A proof of what I say is to be found in the fact that boys commonly show promise of many accomplishments, and when such promise dies away as they grow up, this is plainly due not to the failure of natural gifts, but to lack of the requisite care. But, it will be urged, there are degrees of talent. Undoubtedly, I reply, and there will be a corresponding variation in actual accomplishment: but that there are any who gain nothing from education, I absolutely deny. The man who shares this conviction, must, as soon as he becomes a father, devote the utmost care to fostering the promise shown by the son whom he destines to become an orator.

Above all see that the child's nurse speaks correctly. The ideal, according to Chrysippus, would be that she should be a philosopher: failing that he desired that the best should be chosen, as far as possible. No doubt the most important point is that they should be of good character: but they should speak correctly as well. It is the nurse that the child first hears, and her words that he will first attempt to imitate. And we are by nature most tenacious of childish impressions, just as the flavour first absorbed by vessels when new persists, and the colour imparted by dyes to the primitive whiteness of wool is indelible. Further it is the worst impressions that are most durable. . . .

I prefer that a boy should begin with Greek, because Latin, being in general use, will be picked up by him whether we will or no; while the fact that Latin learning is derived from Greek is a further reason for his being first instructed in the latter. I do not however desire that this principle should be so superstitiously observed that he should for long speak and learn only Greek, as is done in the majority of cases. Such a course gives rise to many faults of language and accent; the latter tends to acquire a foreign intonation, while the former through force of habit becomes impregnated with Greek idioms, which persist with extreme obstinacy even when we are speaking another tongue. The study of Latin ought therefore to follow at no great distance and in a short time proceed side by side with Greek. The result will be that, as soon as we begin to give equal attention to both languages, neither will prove a hindrance to the other.

QUINTILIAN

Some hold that boys should not be taught to read till they are seven years old, that being the earliest age at which they can derive profit from instruction and endure the strain of learning. . . . Let us not therefore waste the earliest years: there is all the less excuse for this, since the elements of literary training are solely a question of memory, which not only exists even in small children, but is specially retentive at that age.

I am not however so blind to differences of age as to think that the very young should be forced on prematurely or given real work to do. Above all things we must take care that the child, who is not yet old enough to love his studies, does not come to hate them and dread the bitterness which he has once tasted, even when the years of infancy are left behind. His studies must be made an amusement: he must be questioned and praised and taught to rejoice when he has done well; sometimes too, when he refuses instruction, it should be given to some other to excite his envy, at times also he must be engaged in competition and should be allowed to believe himself successful more often than not, while he should be encouraged to do his best by such rewards as may appeal to his tender years. . . .

At any rate I am not satisfied with the course (which I note is usually adopted) of teaching small children the names and order of the letters before their shapes. Such a practice makes them slow to recognise the letters, since they do not pay attention to their actual shape, preferring to be guided by what they have already learned by rote. It is for this reason that teachers, when they think they have sufficiently familiarised their young pupils with the letters written in their usual order, reverse that order or rearrange it in every kind of combination, until they learn to know the letters from their appearance and not from the order in which they occur. It will be best therefore for children to begin by learning their appearance and names just as they do with men. The method, however, to which we have objected in teaching the alphabet, is unobjectionable when applied to syllables. I quite approve on the other hand of a practice which has been devised to stimulate children to learn by giving them ivory letters to play with, as I do of anything else that may be discovered to delight the very young, the sight, handling and naming of which is a pleasure.

As soon as the child has begun to know the shapes of the various letters, it will be no bad thing to have them cut as accurately as possible upon a board, so that the pen may be guided along the grooves. Thus mistakes such as occur with wax tablets will be rendered impossible; for the pen will be confined between the edges of the letters and will be prevented from going astray. Further by increasing the frequency and speed with which they follow these fixed outlines we shall give steadiness to the fingers, and there will be no need to guide the child's hand with our own. The art of writing well and quickly is not unimportant for our purpose, though it is generally disregarded by persons of quality. Writing is of the utmost importance in the study which we have under consideration and by its means alone can true and deeply rooted proficiency be obtained. But a sluggish pen delays our thoughts, while an unformed and illiterate hand cannot be deciphered, a circumstance which necessitates another wearisome task, namely the dictation of what we have written to a copyist. We shall therefore at all times and in all places, and above all when we are writing private letters to our friends, find a gratification in the thought that we have not neglected even this accomplishment.

As regards syllables, no short cut is possible: they must all be learnt, and there is no good in putting off learning the most difficult; this is the general practice, but the sole result is bad spelling. Further we must beware of placing a blind confidence in a child's memory. It is better to repeat syllables and impress them on the memory and, when he is reading, not to press him to read continuously or with greater speed, unless indeed the clear and obvious sequence of letters can suggest itself without its being necessary for the child to stop to think. The syllables once learnt, let him begin to construct words with them and sentences with the words. You will hardly believe how much reading is delayed by undue haste. If the child attempts more than his powers allow, the inevitable result is hesitation, interruption and repetition, and the mistakes which he makes merely lead him to lose confidence in what he already knows. Reading must therefore first be sure, then connected, while it must be kept slow for a considerable time, until practice brings speed unaccompanied by error. . . . And as we are still discussing minor details, I would urge that the lines, which he is set to copy, should not express thoughts of no significance, but convey some sound moral lesson. He will remember such aphorisms even when he is an old man, and the impression made upon his unformed mind will contribute to the formation of his character. He may also be entertained by learning the sayings of famous men and above all selections from the poets, poetry being more attractive to children. For memory is most necessary to an orator, as I shall point out in its proper place, and there is nothing like practice for strengthening and developing it. And at the tender age of which we are now speaking, when originality is impossible, memory is almost the only faculty which can be developed by the teacher. It will be worth while, by way of improving the child's pronunciation and distinctness of utterance, to make him rattle off a selection of names and lines of studied difficulty: they should be formed of a number of syllables which go ill together and should be harsh and rugged in sound: the Greeks call them "gags." This sounds a trifling matter, but its omission will result in numerous faults of pronunciation, which, unless removed in early years, will become a perverse and incurable habit and persist through life.

II. But the time has come for the boy to grow up little by little, to leave the nursery and tackle his studies in good earnest. This therefore is the place to discuss the question as to whether it is better to have him educated privately at home or hand him over to some large school and those whom I may call public instructors. The latter course has, I know, won the approval of most eminent authorities and of those who have formed the national character of the most famous states. It would, however, be folly to shut our eyes to the fact that there are some who disagree with this preference for public education owing to a certain prejudice in favour of private tuition. These persons seem to be guided in the main by two principles. In the interests of morality they would avoid the society of a number of human beings at an age that is specially liable to acquire serious faults: I only wish I could deny the truth of the view that such education has often been the cause of the most discreditable actions. Secondly they hold that whoever is to be the boy's teacher, he will devote his time more generously to one pupil than if he has to divide it among several. The first reason certainly deserves serious consideration. If it were proved that schools, while advantageous to study, are prejudicial to morality, I should give my vote for virtuous living in preference to even supreme excellence of speaking. But in my opinion the two are inseparable. I hold that no one can be a true orator unless he is also a good man and, even if he could be, I would not have it so. I will therefore deal with this point first.

It is held that schools corrupt the morals. It is true that this is sometimes the case. But morals may be corrupted at home as well. . . .

In the first place there is nothing to prevent the principle of "one teacher, one boy" being combined with school education. And even if such a combination should prove impossible, I should still prefer

107

the broad daylight of a respectable school to the solitude and obscurity of a private education. For all the best teachers pride themselves on having a large number of pupils and think themselves worthy of a bigger audience. On the other hand in the case of inferior teachers a consciousness of their own defects not seldom reconciles them to being attached to a single pupil and playing the part—for it amounts to little more—of a mere *paedagogus*. . . .

. . . Let me now explain my own views. It is above all things necessary that our future orator, who will have to live in the utmost publicity and in the broad daylight of public life, should become accustomed from his childhood to move in society without fear and habituated to a life far removed from that of the pale student, the solitary and recluse. His mind requires constant stimulus and excitement, whereas retirement such as has just been mentioned induces languor and the mind becomes mildewed like things that are left in the dark, or else flies to the opposite extreme and becomes puffed up with empty conceit; for he who has no standard of comparison by which to judge his own powers will necessarily rate them too high. . . . I say nothing of friendships which endure unbroken to old age having acquired the binding force of a sacred duty: for initiation in the same studies has all the sanctity of initiation in the same mysteries of religion. And where shall he acquire that instinct which we call common feeling, if he secludes himself from that intercourse which is natural not merely to mankind but even to dumb animals? Further, at home he can only learn what is taught to himself, while at school he will learn what is taught others as well. He will hear many merits praised and many faults corrected every day: he will derive equal profit from hearing the indolence of a comrade rebuked or his industry commended. Such praise will incite him to emulation, he will think it a disgrace to be outdone by his contemporaries and a distinction to surpass his seniors. All such incentives provide a valuable stimulus, and though ambition may be a fault in itself, it is often the mother of virtues . . . It is a good thing therefore that a boy should have companions whom he will desire first to imitate and then to surpass: thus he will be led to aspire to higher achievement. I would add that the instructors themselves cannot develop the same intelligence and energy before a single listener as they can when inspired by the presence of a numerous audience.

For eloquence depends in the main on the state of the mind, which must be moved, conceive images and adapt itself to suit the nature of the subject which is the theme of speech. Further the

108

loftier and the more elevated the mind, the more powerful will be the forces which move it: consequently praise gives it growth and effort increase, and the thought that it is doing something great fills it with joy. The duty of stooping to expend that power of speaking which has been acquired at the cost of such effort upon an audience of one gives rise to a silent feeling of disdain, and the teacher is ashamed to raise his voice above the ordinary conversational level. Imagine the air of a declaimer, or the voice of an orator, his gait, his delivery, the movements of his body, the emotions of his mind, and, to go no further, the fatigue of his exertions, all for the sake of one listener! Would he not seem little less than a lunatic? No, there would be no such thing as eloquence, if we spoke only with one person at a time.

III. The skilful teacher will make it his first care, as soon as a boy is entrusted to him, to ascertain his ability and character. The surest indication in a child is his power of memory. The characteristics of a good memory are twofold: it must be quick to take in and faithful to retain impressions of what it receives. The indication of next importance is the power of imitation: for this is a sign that the child is teachable: but he must imitate merely what he is taught, and must not, for example, mimic someone's gait or bearing or defects. For I have no hope that a child will turn out well who loves imitation merely for the purpose of raising a laugh. He who is really gifted will also above all else be good. For the rest, I regard slowness of intellect as preferable to actual badness. But a good boy will be quite unlike the dullard and the sloth. My ideal pupil will absorb instruction with ease and will even ask some questions; but he will follow rather than anticipate his teacher. Precocious intellects rarely produce sound fruit. By the precocious I mean those who perform small tasks with ease and, thus emboldened, proceed to display all their little accomplishments without being asked: but their accomplishments are only of the most obvious kind: they string words together and trot them out boldly and undeterred by the slightest sense of modesty. Their actual achievement is small, but what they can do they perform with ease. They have no real power and what they have is but of shallow growth: it is as when we cast seed on the surface of the soil: it springs up too rapidly, the blade apes the loaded ear, and yellows ere harvest time, but bears no grain. Such tricks please us when we contrast them with the performer's age, but progress soon stops and our admiration withers away.

Such indications once noted, the teacher must next consider what

109

treatment is to be applied to the mind of his pupil. There are some boys who are slack, unless pressed on; others again are impatient of control: some are amenable to fear, while others are paralysed by it: in some cases the mind requires continued application to form it, in others this result is best obtained by rapid concentration. Give me the boy who is spurred on by praise, delighted by success and ready to weep over failure. Such an one must be encouraged by appeals to his ambition; rebuke will bite him to the quick; honour will be a spur, and there is no fear of his proving indolent.

Still, all our pupils will require some relaxation, not merely because there is nothing in this world that can stand continued strain and even unthinking and inanimate objects are unable to maintain their strength, unless given intervals of rest, but because study depends on the good will of the student, a quality that cannot be secured by compulsion. Consequently if restored and refreshed by a holiday they will bring greater energy to their learning and approach their work with greater spirit of a kind that will not submit to be driven. I approve of play in the young; it is a sign of a lively disposition; nor will you ever lead me to believe that a boy who is gloomy and in a continual state of depression is ever likely to show alertness of mind in his work, lacking as he does the impulse most natural to boys of his age. Such relaxation must not however be unlimited: otherwise the refusal to give a holiday will make boys hate their work, while excessive indulgence will accustom them to idleness. There are moreover certain games which have an educational value for boys, as for instance when they compete in posing each other with all kinds of questions which they ask turn and turn about. Games too reveal character in the most natural way, at least that is so if the teacher will bear in mind that there is no child so young as to be unable to learn to distinguish between right and wrong, and that the character is best moulded, when it is still guiltless of deceit and most susceptible to instruction: for once a bad habit has become engrained, it is easier to break than bend. There must be no delay, then, in warning a boy that his actions must be unselfish, honest, self-controlled, and we must never forget the words of Virgil,

"So strong is custom formed in early years."

I disapprove of flogging, although it is the regular custom and meets with the acquiescence of Chrysippus, because in the first place it is a disgraceful form of punishment and fit only for slaves, and is in any case an insult, as you will realise if you imagine its

110

infliction at a later age. Secondly if a boy is so insensible to instruction that reproof is useless, he will, like the worst type of slave, merely become hardened to blows. Finally there will be absolutely no need of such punishment if the master is a thorough disciplinarian. As it is, we try to make amends for the negligence of the boy's *paedagogus,* not by forcing him to do what is right, but by punishing him for not doing what is right. And though you may compel a child with blows, what are you to do with him when he is a young man no longer amenable to such threats and confronted with tasks of far greater difficulty? Moreover when children are beaten, pain or fear frequently have results of which it is not pleasant to speak and which are likely subsequently to be a source of shame, a shame which unnerves and depresses the mind and leads the child to shun and loathe the light. Further if inadequate care is taken in the choices of respectable governors and instructors, I blush to mention the shameful abuse which scoundrels sometimes make of their right to administer corporal punishment or the opportunity not infrequently offered to others by the fear thus caused in the victims. I will not linger on this subject; it is more than enough if I have made my meaning clear. I will content myself with saying that children are helpless and easily victimised, and that therefore no one should be given unlimited power over them. I will now proceed to describe the subjects in which the boy must be trained, if he is to become an orator, and to indicate the age at which each should be commenced.

IV. As soon as the boy has learned to read and write without difficulty, it is the turn for the teacher of literature. My words apply equally to Greek and Latin masters, though I prefer that a start should be made with a Greek: in either case the method is the same. This profession may be most briefly considered under two heads, the art of speaking correctly and the interpretation of the poets; but there is more beneath the surface than meets the eye. For the art of writing is combined with that of speaking, and correct reading precedes interpretation, while in each of these cases criticism has its work to perform. The old school of teachers indeed carried their criticism so far that they were not content with obelising lines or rejecting books whose titles they regarded as spurious, as though they were expelling a supposititious child from the family circle, but also drew up a canon of authors, from which some were omitted altogether. Nor is it sufficient to have read the poets only; every kind of writer must be carefully studied, not merely for the subject matter, but for the vocabulary; for words often acquire

111

authority from their use by a particular author. Nor can such training be regarded as complete if it stop short of music, for the teacher
of literature has to speak of metre and rhythm: nor again if he be
ignorant of astronomy, can he understand the poets; for they, to
mention no further points, frequently give their indications of time
by reference to the rising and setting of the stars. Ignorance of
philosophy is an equal drawback, since there are numerous passages
in almost every poem based on the most intricate questions of natural philosophy, while among the Greeks we have Empedocles and
among our own poets Varro and Lucretius, all of whom have expounded their philosophies in verse. No small powers of eloquence
also are required to enable the teacher to speak appropriately and
fluently on the various points which have just been mentioned. For
this reason those who criticise the art of teaching literature as trivial
and lacking in substance put themselves out of court. Unless the
foundations of oratory are well and truly laid by the teaching of
literature, the superstructure will collapse. The study of literature
is a necessity for boys and the delight of old age, the sweet companion of our privacy and the sole branch of study which has more
solid substance than display. . . .

IX. I have now finished with two of the departments, with which
teachers of literature profess to deal, namely the art of speaking
correctly and the interpretation of authors; the former they call
methodicē, the latter *historicē*. We must however add to their
activities instruction in certain rudiments of oratory for the benefit
of those who are not yet ripe for the schools of rhetoric. Their
pupils should learn to paraphrase Aesop's fables, the natural successors of the fairy stories of the nursery, in simple and restrained
language and subsequently to set down this paraphrase in writing
with the same simplicity of style: they should begin by analysing
each verse, then give its meaning in different language, and finally
proceed to a freer paraphrase in which they will be permitted now
to abridge and now to embellish the original, so far as this may be
done without losing the poet's meaning. This is no easy task even
for the expert instructor, and the pupil who handles it successfully
will be capable of learning everything. He should also be set to
write *aphorisms, moral essays (chriae)* and *delineations of character (ethologiae)*, of which the teacher will first give the general
scheme, since such themes will be drawn from their reading. . . .

[*On the following pages Quintilian discusses "the remaining arts"
in which he thinks "boys ought to be instructed before being
handed over to the teacher of rhetoric." These arts are: music,*

geometry, the art of delivery (to be taught by the "comic actor") and gymnastics.]

XII. . . . We need have no fear at any rate that boys will find their work too exhausting: there is no age more capable of enduring fatigue. The fact may be surprising, but it can be proved by experiment. For the mind is all the easier to teach before it is set. This may be clearly proved by the fact that within two years after a child has begun to form words correctly, he can speak practically all without any pressure from outside. On the other hand how many years it takes for our newly imported slaves to become familiar with the Latin language. Try to teach an adult to read and you will soon appreciate the force of the saying applied to those who do everything connected with their art with the utmost skill "he started young!" Moreover boys stand the strain of work better than young men. Just as small children suffer less damage from their frequent falls, from their crawling on hands and knees and, a little later, from their incessant play and their running about from morn till eve, because they are so light in weight and have so little to carry, even so their minds are less susceptible of fatigue, because their activity calls for less effort and application to study demands no exertion of their own, since they are merely so much plastic material to be moulded by the teacher. And further owing to the general pliability of childhood, they follow their instructors with greater simplicity and without attempting to measure their own progress: for as yet they do not even appreciate the nature of their work. Finally, as I have often noticed, the senses are less affected by mere hard work than they are by hard thinking.

Moreover there will never be more time for such studies, since at this age all progress is made through listening to the teacher. Later when the boy has to write by himself, or to produce and compose something out of his own head, he will neither have the time nor the inclination for the exercises which we have been discussing. Since, then, the teacher of literature neither can nor ought to occupy the whole day, for fear of giving his pupil a distaste for work, what are the studies to which the spare time should preferably be devoted? For I do not wish the student to wear himself out in such pursuits: I would not have him sing or learn to read music or dive deep into the minuter details of geometry, nor need he be a finished actor in his delivery or a dancer in his gesture: if I did demand all these accomplishments, there would yet be time for them; the period allotted to education is long, and I am not speaking of duller wits. Why did Plato bear away the palm in all these branches of knowl-

113

edge which in my opinion the future orator should learn? I answer, because he was not merely content with the teaching which Athens was able to provide or even with that of the Pythagoreans whom he visited in Italy, but even approached the priests of Egypt and made himself thoroughly acquainted with all their secret lore. . . .

BOOK II

II. As soon therefore as a boy has made sufficient progress in his studies to be able to follow what I have styled the first stage of instruction in rhetoric, he should be placed under a rhetorician. Our first task must be to enquire whether the teacher is of good character. The reason which leads me to deal with this subject in this portion of my work is not that I regard character as a matter of indifference where other teachers are concerned, (I have already shown how important I think it in the preceding book), but that the age to which the pupil has now attained makes the mention of this point especially necessary. For as a rule boys are on the verge of manhood when transferred to the teacher of rhetoric and continue with him even when they are young men: consequently we must spare no effort to secure that the purity of the teacher's character should preserve those of tenderer years from corruption, while its authority should keep the bolder spirits from breaking out into licence. Nor is it sufficient that he should merely set an example of the highest personal self-control; he must also be able to govern the behaviour of his pupils by the strictness of his discipline.

Let him therefore adopt a parental attitude to his pupils, and regard himself as the representative of those who have committed their children to his charge. Let him be free from vice himself and refuse to tolerate it in others. Let him be strict but not austere, genial but not too familiar: for austerity will make him unpopular, while familiarity breeds contempt. Let his discourse continually turn on what is good and honourable; the more he admonishes, the less he will have to punish. He must control his temper without however shutting his eyes to faults requiring correction: his instruction must be free from affectation, his industry great, his demands on his class continuous, but not extravagant. He must be ready to answer questions and to put them unasked to those who sit silent. In praising the recitations of his pupils he must be neither grudging nor over-generous: the former quality will give them a distaste for work, while the latter will produce a complacent self-satisfaction. In correcting faults he must avoid sarcasm and above all

114

abuse: for teachers whose rebukes seem to imply positive dislike discourage industry. He should declaim daily himself and, what is more, without stint, that his class may take his utterances home with them. For however many models for imitation he may give them from the authors they are reading, it will still be found that fuller nourishment is provided by the living voice, as we call it, more especially when it proceeds from the teacher himself, who, if his pupils are rightly instructed, should be the object of their affection and respect. And it is scarcely possible to say how much more readily we imitate those whom we like.

IV. . . . It is worth while too to warn the teacher that undue severity in correcting faults is liable at times to discourage a boy's mind from effort. He loses hope and gives way to vexation, then last of all comes to hate his work and fearing everything attempts nothing. This phenomenon is familiar to farmers, who hold that the pruning-hook should not be applied while the leaves are yet young, for they seem to "shrink from the steel" and to be unable as yet to endure a scar. The instructor therefore should be as kindly as possible at this stage; remedies, which are harsh by nature, must be applied with a gentle hand: some portions of the work must be praised, others tolerated and others altered: the reason for the alterations should however be given, and in some cases the master will illumine an obscure passage by inserting something of his own. Occasionally again the teacher will find it useful to dictate whole themes himself that the boy may imitate them and for the time being love them as if they were his own. But if a boy's composition is so careless as not to admit of correction, I have found it useful to give a fresh exposition of the theme and to tell him to write it again, pointing out that he was capable of doing better: for there is nothing like hope for making study a pleasure. Different ages however demand different methods: the task set and the standard of correction must be proportioned to the pupil's strength. When boys ventured on something that was too daring or exuberant, I used to say to them that I approved of it for the moment, but that the time would come when I should no longer tolerate such a style. The result was that the consciousness of ability filled them with pleasure, without blinding their judgment. . . .

VIII. It is generally and not unreasonably regarded as the sign of a good teacher that he should be able to differentiate between the abilities of his respective pupils and to know their natural bent. The gifts of nature are infinite in their variety, and mind differs from mind almost as much as body from body. . . . One boy will be better adapted for the study of history, another for poetry, another for law, while some perhaps had better be packed off to the country. The teacher of rhetoric will distinguish such special aptitudes, just as our gymnast will turn one pupil into a runner, another into a boxer or wrestler or an expert at some other of the athletic accomplishments for which prizes are awarded at the sacred games. But on the other hand, he who is destined for the bar must study not one department merely, but must perfect himself in all the accomplishments which his profession demands, even though some of them may seem too hard for him when he approaches them as a learner. For if natural talent alone were sufficient, education might be dispensed with. . . .

IX. Though I have spoken in some detail of the duties of the teacher, I shall for the moment confine my advice to the learners to one solitary admonition, that they should love their masters not less than their studies, and should regard them as the parents not indeed of their bodies but of their minds. Such attachments are of invaluable assistance to study. For under their influence they find it a pleasure to listen to their teachers, believe what they say and long to be like them, come cheerfully and gladly to school, are not angry when corrected, rejoice when praised, and seek to win their master's affection by the devotion with which they pursue their studies. For as it is the duty of the master to teach, so it is the duty of the pupil to show himself teachable. The two obligations are mutually indispensable. And just as it takes two parents to produce a human being, and as the seed is scattered in vain, if the ground is hard and there is no furrow to receive it and bring it to growth, even so eloquence can never come to maturity, unless teacher and taught are in perfect sympathy.

XII. I must, however, admit that the general opinion is that the untrained speaker is usually the more vigorous. This opinion is due primarily to the erroneous judgment of faulty critics, who think that true vigour is all the greater for its lack of art, regarding it as a special proof of strength to force what might be opened, to break what might be untied and to drag what might be led. Even a gladiator who plunges into the fight with no skill at arms to help him, and a wrestler who puts forth the whole strength of his body the moment he has got a hold, is acclaimed by them for his outstanding vigour, although it is of frequent occurrence in such cases for the latter to be overthrown by his own strength and for the former to find the fury of his onslaught parried by his adversary with a supple turn of the wrist. But there are many details in this department of

116

our art which the unskilled critic will never notice. For instance, careful division under heads, although of the utmost importance in actual cases, makes the outward show of strength seem less than the reality; the unhewn block is larger than the polished marble, and things when scattered seem more numerous than when placed together. There is moreover a sort of resemblance between certain merits and certain defects: abuse passes for freedom of speech, rashness for courage, prodigality for abundance. But the untrained advocate will abuse too openly and too often, even though by so doing he imperils the success of the case which he has undertaken and not seldom his own personal safety as well. But even such violence will win men's good opinion, since they are only too pleased to hear another say things which nothing would have induced them to utter themselves. Such speakers are also less careful to avoid that other peril, the pitfall of style, and are so reckless in their efforts that sometimes in their passion for extravagance they light upon some really striking expression. But such success is rare and does not compensate for their other defects.

For the same reason the uninstructed sometimes appear to have a richer flow of language, because they say everything that can be said, while the learned exercise discrimination and self-restraint. To this must be added the fact that such persons take no trouble to prove their contentions, and consequently steer clear of the chilly reception given in our decadent law-courts to arguments and questions and seek only for such themes as may beguile the ears of the public even at the cost of appealing to the most perverted tastes. . . .

But these creatures have another weapon in their armoury: they seek to obtain the reputation of speaking with greater vigour than the trained orator by means of their delivery. For they shout on all and every occasion and bellow their every utterance "with uplifted hand," to use their own phrase, dashing this way and that, panting, gesticulating wildly and wagging their heads with all the frenzy of a lunatic. Smite your hands together, stamp the ground, slap your thigh, your breast, your forehead, and you will go straight to the heart of the dingier members of your audience. But the educated speaker, just as he knows how to moderate his style, and to impart variety and artistic form to his speech, is an equal adept in the matter of delivery and will suit his action to the tone of each portion of his utterances, while, if he has any one canon for universal observance, it is that he should both possess the reality and present the appearance of self-control. . . .

117

BOOK X

II. . . . The first point, then, that we must realise is that imitation alone is not sufficient, if only for the reason that a sluggish nature is only too ready to rest content with the inventions of others. For what would have happened in the days when models were not, if men had decided to do and think of nothing that they did not know already? The answer is obvious: nothing would ever have been discovered. Why, then, is it a crime for us to discover something new? Were primitive men led to make so many discoveries simply by the natural force of their imagination, and shall we not then be spurred on to search for novelty by the very knowledge that those who sought of old were rewarded by success? And seeing that they, who had none to teach them anything, have handed down such store of knowledge to posterity, shall we refuse to employ the experience which we possess of some things, to discover yet other things, and possess nought that is not owed to the beneficent activity of others? . . . Again, the greatest qualities of the orator are beyond all imitation, by which I mean, talent, invention, force, facility and all the qualities which are independent of art. Consequently, there are many who, after excerpting certain words from published speeches or borrowing certain particular rhythms, think that they have produced a perfect copy of the works which they have read, despite the fact that words become obsolete or current with the lapse of years, the one sure standard being contemporary usage; and they are not good or bad in virtue of their inherent nature (for in themselves they are no more than mere sounds), but solely in virtue of the aptitude and propriety (or the reverse) with which they are arranged, while rhythmical composition must be adapted to the theme in hand and will derive its main charm from its variety. . . .

III. Such are the aids which we may derive from external sources; as regards those which we must supply for ourselves, it is the pen which brings at once the most labour and the most profit. Cicero is fully justified in describing it as the best producer and teacher of eloquence, and it may be noted that in the *de Oratore* he supports his own judgment by the authority of Lucius Crassus, in whose mouth he places this remark. We must therefore write as much as possible and with the utmost care. For as deep ploughing makes the soil more fertile for the production and support of crops, so, if we improve our minds by something more than mere superficial study, we shall produce a richer growth of knowledge and

118

shall retain it with greater accuracy. For without the consciousness of such preliminary study our powers of speaking extempore will give us nothing but an empty flow of words, springing from the lips and not from the brain. It is in writing that eloquence has its roots and foundations, it is writing that provides that holy of holies where the wealth of oratory is stored, and whence it is produced to meet the demands of sudden emergencies. It is of the first importance that we should develop such strength as will not faint under the toil of forensic strife nor be exhausted by continual use. For it is an ordinance of nature that nothing great can be achieved in a moment, and that all the fairest tasks are attended with difficulty, while on births as well she has imposed this law, that the larger the animal, the longer should be the period of gestation. . . .

And it is not merely practice that will enable us to write at greater length and with increased fluency, although doubtless practice is most important. We need judgement as well. So long as we do not lie back with eyes turned up to the ceiling, trying to fire our imagination by muttering to ourselves, in the hope that something will present itself, but turn our thoughts to consider what the circumstances of the case demand, what suits the characters involved, what is the nature of the occasion and the temper of the judge, we shall acquire the power of writing by rational means. It is thus that nature herself bids us begin and pursue our studies once well begun. For most points are of a definite character and, if we keep our eyes open, will spontaneously present themselves. . . . We must not, therefore, persist in thinking that what is hard to find is necessarily best; for, if it seems to us that there is nothing to be said except that which we are unable to find, we must say nothing at all. On the other hand, there is a fault which is precisely the opposite of this, into which those fall who insist on first making a rapid draft of their subject with the utmost speed of which their pen is capable, and write in the heat and impulse of the moment. They call this their rough copy. They then revise what they have written, and arrange their hasty outpourings. But while the words and the rhythm may be corrected, the matter is still marked by the superficiality resulting from the speed with which it was thrown together. The more correct method is, therefore, to exercise care from the very beginning, and to form the work from the outset in such a manner that it merely requires to be chiselled into shape, not fashioned anew. Sometimes, however, we must follow the stream of our emotions, since their warmth will give us more than any diligence can secure.

119

The condemnation which I have passed on such carelessness in writing will make it pretty clear what my views are on the luxury of dictation which is now so fashionable. For, when we write, however great our speed, the fact that the hand cannot follow the rapidity of our thoughts gives us time to think, whereas the presence of our amanuensis hurries us on, and at times we feel ashamed to hesitate or pause, or make some alteration, as though we were afraid to display such weakness before a witness. As a result our language tends not merely to be haphazard and formless, but in our desire to produce a continuous flow we let slip positive improprieties of diction, which show neither the precision of the writer nor the impetuosity of the speaker. Again, if the amanuensis is a slow writer, or lacking in intelligence, he becomes a stumbling-block, our speed is checked, and the thread of our ideas is interrupted by the delay or even perhaps by the loss of temper to which it gives rise. . . .

BOOK XII

I. The orator then, whom I am concerned to form, shall be the orator as defined by Marcus Cato, "a good man, skilled in speaking." But above all he must possess the quality which Cato places first and which is in the very nature of things the greatest and most important, that is, he must be a good man. This is essential not merely on account of the fact that, if the powers of eloquence serve only to lend arms to crime, there can be nothing more pernicious than eloquence to public and private welfare alike, while I myself, who have laboured to the best of my ability to contribute something of value to oratory, shall have rendered the worst of services to mankind, if I forge these weapons not for a soldier, but for a robber. But why speak of myself? Nature herself will have proved not a mother, but a stepmother with regard to what we deem her greatest gift to man, the gift that distinguishes us from other living things, if she devised the power of speech to be the accomplice of crime, the foe to innocency and the enemy of truth. For it had been better for men to be born dumb and devoid of reason than to turn the gifts of providence to their mutual destruction. But this conviction of mine goes further. For I do not merely assert that the ideal orator should be a good man, but I affirm that no man can be an orator unless he is a good man. . . . There is one point at any rate which no one will question, namely, that the aim of every speech is to convince the judge that the case which it puts forward is true and honourable. Well then, which will do this best, the good man

120

or the bad? The good man will without doubt more often say what is true and honourable. But even supposing that his duty should, as I shall show may sometimes happen, lead him to make statements which are false, his words are still certain to carry greater weight with his audience. On the other hand bad men, in their contempt for public opinion and their ignorance of what is right, sometimes drop their mask unawares, and are impudent in the statement of their case and shameless in their assertions. Further, in their attempt to achieve the impossible they display an unseemly persistency and unavailing energy. For in lawsuits no less than in the ordinary paths of life, they cherish depraved expectations. But it often happens that even when they tell the truth they fail to win belief, and the mere fact that such a man is its advocate is regarded as an indication of the badness of the case.

.   .   .   .   .

II. Since then the orator is a good man, and such Goodness cannot be conceived as existing apart from virtue, virtue, despite the fact that it is in part derived from certain natural impulses, will require to be perfected by instruction. The orator must above all things devote his attention to the formation of moral character and must acquire a complete knowledge of all that is just and honourable. For without this knowledge no one can be either a good man or skilled in speaking, unless indeed we agree with those who regard morality as intuitive and as owing nothing to instruction: indeed they go so far as to acknowledge that handicrafts, not excluding even those which are most despised among them, can only be acquired by the result of teaching, whereas virtue, which of all gifts to man is that which makes him most near akin to the immortal gods, comes to him without search or effort, as a natural concomitant of birth. But can the man who does not know what abstinence is, claim to be truly abstinent? or brave, if he has never purged his soul of the fears of pain, death and superstition? or just, if he has never, in language approaching that of philosophy, discussed the nature of virtue and justice, or of the laws that have been given to mankind by nature or established among individual peoples and nations? What a contempt it argues for such themes to regard them as being so easy of comprehension! However, I pass this by; for I am sure that no one with the least smattering of literary culture will have the slightest hesitation in agreeing with me. I will proceed to my next point, that no one will achieve sufficient skill even in speaking, unless he makes a thorough study of all the workings of nature and forms his character on the precepts of philosophy and

121

the dictates of reason. For it is with good cause that Lucius Crassus, in the third book of the *de Oratore*, affirms that all that is said concerning equity, justice, truth and the good, and their opposites, forms part of the studies of an orator, and that the philosophers, when they exert their powers of speaking to defend these virtues, are using the weapons of rhetoric, not their own. But he also confesses that the knowledge of these subjects must be sought from the philosophers for the reason that, in his opinion, philosophy has more effective possession of them. And it is for the same reason that Cicero in several of his books and letters proclaims that eloquence has its fountain-head in the most secret springs of wisdom, and that consequently for a considerable time the instructors of morals and of eloquence were identical. Accordingly this exhortation of mine must not be taken to mean that I wish the orator to be a philosopher, since there is no other way of life that is further removed from the duties of a statesman and the tasks of an orator. For what philosopher has ever been a frequent speaker in the courts or won renown in public assemblies? Nay, what philosopher has ever taken a prominent part in the government of the state, which forms the most frequent theme of their instructions? None the less I desire that he, whose character I am seeking to mould, should be a "wise man" in the Roman sense, that is, one who reveals himself as a true statesman, not in the discussions of the study, but in the actual practice and experience of life. But inasmuch as the study of philosophy has been deserted by those who have turned to the pursuit of eloquence, and since philosophy no longer moves in its true sphere of action and in the broad daylight of the forum, but has retired first to porches and gymnasia and finally to the gatherings of the schools, all that is essential for an orator, and yet is not taught by the professors of eloquence, must undoubtedly be sought from those persons in whose possession it has remained. The authors who have discoursed on the nature of virtue must be read through and through, that the life of the orator may be wedded to the knowledge of things human and divine. But how much greater and fairer would such subjects appear if those who taught them were also those who could give them most eloquent expression! O that the day may dawn when the perfect orator of our heart's desire shall claim for his own possession that science that has lost the affection of mankind through the arrogance of its claims and the vices of some that have brought disgrace upon its virtues, and shall restore it to its place in the domain of eloquence, as though he had been victorious in a trial for the restoration of stolen goods!

122

QUINTILIAN

III. Our orator will also require a knowledge of civil law and of the custom and religion of the state in whose life he is to bear his part. For how will he be able to advise either in public or in private, if he is ignorant of all the main elements that go to make the state? How can he truthfully call himself an advocate if he has to go to others to acquire that knowledge which is all-important in the courts? He will be little better than if he were a reciter of the poets. For he will be a mere transmitter of the instructions that others have given him, it will be on the authority of others that he propounds what he asks the judge to believe, and he whose duty it is to succour the litigant will himself be in need of succour. It is true that at times this may be effected with but little inconvenience, if what he advances for the edification of the judge has been taught him and composed in the seclusion of his study and learnt by heart there like other elements of the case. But what will he do, when he is confronted by unexpected problems such as frequently arise in the actual course of pleading? Will he not disgrace himself by looking round and asking the junior counsel who sit on the benches behind him for advice? Can he hope to get a thorough grasp of such information at the very moment when he is required to produce it in his speech? Can he make his assertions with confidence or speak with native simplicity as though his arguments were his own? . . .

Let no one, however, regard the advice I have given as to the attention due to the development of character and the study of the law as being impugned by the fact that we are familiar with many who, because they were weary of the toil entailed on those who seek to scale the heights of eloquence, have betaken themselves to the study of law as a refuge for their indolence. Some of these transfer their attention to the praetor's edicts or the civil law, and have preferred to become specialists in *formulae*, or legalists, as Cicero calls them, on the pretext of choosing a more useful branch of study, whereas their real motive was its comparative easiness. Others are the victims of a more arrogant form of sloth; they assume a stern air and let their beards grow, and, as though despising the precepts of oratory, sit for a while in the schools of the philosophers, that, by an assumption of a severe mien before the public gaze and by an affected contempt of others they may assert their moral superiority, while leading a life of debauchery at home. For philosophy may be counterfeited, but eloquence never. . . .

See p. 641 for The Judaic Tradition.

ANCIENT AND MEDIEVAL CHRISTIANITY

THE BIBLE

The following selections are from the King James Version.

MATTHEW CHAPTER V

And seeing the multitudes, he went up into a mountain: and when he was set, his disciples came unto him:

2 And he opened his mouth, and taught them, saying,

3 Blessed *are* the poor in spirit: for their's is the kingdom of heaven.

4 Blessed *are* they that mourn: for they shall be comforted.

5 Blessed *are* the meek: for they shall inherit the earth.

6 Blessed *are* they which do hunger and thirst after righteousness: for they shall be filled.

7 Blessed *are* the merciful: for they shall obtain mercy.

8 Blessed *are* the pure in heart: for they shall see God.

9 Blessed *are* the peacemakers: for they shall be called the children of God.

10 Blessed *are* they which are persecuted for righteousness' sake: for their's is the kingdom of heaven.

11 Blessed are ye, when *men* shall revile you, and persecute *you,* and shall say all manner of evil against you falsely, for my sake.

12 Rejoice, and be exceeding glad for great *is* your reward in heaven: for so persecuted they the prophets which were before you.

13 ¶ Ye are the salt of the earth: but if the salt have lost his savour, wherewith shall it be salted? it is thenceforth good for nothing, but to be cast out, and to be trodden under foot of men.

14 Ye are the light of the world. A city that is set on an hill cannot be hid.

15 Neither do men light a candle, and put it under a bushel, but on a candlestick; and it giveth light unto all that are in the house.

16 Let your light so shine before men, that they may see your good works, and glorify your Father which is in heaven.

17 ¶ Think not that I am come to destroy the law, or the prophets: I am not come to destroy, but to fulfil.

18 For verily I say unto you, Till heaven and earth pass, one jot or one tittle shall in no wise pass from the law, till all be fulfilled.

19 Whosoever therefore shall break one of these least commandments, and shall teach men so, he shall be called the least in the kingdom of heaven: but whosoever shall do and teach *them,* the same shall be called great in the kingdom of heaven.

20 For I say unto you, That except your righteousness shall exceed *the righteousness* of the scribes and Pharisees, ye shall in no case enter into the kingdom of heaven.

21 ¶ Ye have heard that it was said by them of old time, Thou shalt not kill; and whosoever shall kill shall be in danger of the judgment:

22 But I say unto you, That whosoever is angry with his brother without a cause shall be in danger of the judgment: and whosoever shall say to his brother, Raca, shall be in danger of the council: but whosoever shall say, Thou fool, shall be in danger of hell fire.

23 Therefore if thou bring thy gift to the altar, and there rememberest that thy brother hath ought against thee;

24 Leave there thy gift before the altar, and go thy way; first be reconciled to thy brother, and then come and offer thy gift.

25 Agree with thine adversary quickly, whiles thou art in the way with him; lest at any time the adversary deliver thee to the judge, and the judge deliver thee to the officer, and thou be cast into prison.

26 Verily I say unto thee, Thou shalt by no means come out thence, till thou hast paid the uttermost farthing.

27 ¶ Ye have heard that it was said by them of old time, Thou shalt not commit adultery:

28 But I say unto you, That whosoever looketh on a woman to lust after her hath committed adultery with her already in his heart.

29 And if thy right eye offend thee, pluck it out, and cast *it* from thee: for it is profitable for thee that one of thy members should perish, and not *that* thy whole body should be cast into hell.

30 And if thy right hand offend thee, cut it off, and cast *it* from thee: for it is profitable for thee that one of thy members should perish, and not *that* thy whole body should be cast into hell.

31 It hath been said, Whosoever shall put away his wife, let him give her a writing of divorcement:

32 But I say unto you, That whosoever shall put away his wife, saving for the cause of fornication, causeth her to commit adultery: and whosoever shall marry her that is divorced committeth adultery.

128

33 ¶ Again, ye have heard that it hath been said by them of old time, Thou shalt not forswear thyself, but shalt perform unto the Lord thine oaths:

34 But I say unto you, Swear not at all; neither by heaven; for it is God's throne:

35 Nor by the earth; for it is his footstool: neither by Jerusalem; for it is the city of the great King.

36 Neither shalt thou swear by thy head, because thou canst not make one hair white or black.

37 But let your communication be, Yea, yea; Nay, nay: for whatsoever is more than these cometh of evil.

38 ¶ Ye have heard that it hath been said, An eye for an eye, and a tooth for a tooth:

39 But I say unto you, That ye resist not evil: but whosoever shall smite thee on thy right cheek, turn to him the other also.

40 And if any man will sue thee at the law, and take away thy coat, let him have *thy* cloke also.

41 And whosoever shall compel thee to go a mile, go with him twain.

42 Give to him that asketh thee, and from him that would borrow of thee turn not thou away.

43 ¶ Ye have heard that it hath been said, Thou shalt love thy neighbour, and hate thine enemy.

44 But I say unto you, Love your enemies, bless them that curse you, do good to them that hate you, and pray for them which despitefully use you, and persecute you;

45 That ye may be the children of your Father which is in heaven: for he maketh his sun to rise on the evil and on the good, and sendeth rain on the just and on the unjust.

46 For if ye love them which love you, what reward have ye? do not even the publicans the same?

47 And if ye salute your brethren only, what do ye more *than others?* do not even the publicans so?

48 Be ye therefore perfect, even as your Father which is in heaven is perfect.

CHAPTER VI

Take heed that ye do not your alms before men, to be seen of them: otherwise ye have no reward of your Father which is in heaven.

2 Therefore when thou doest *thine* alms, do not sound a trumpet before thee, as the hypocrites do in the synagogues and in the

streets, that they may have glory of men. Verily I say unto you, They have their reward.

3 But when thou doest alms, let not thy left hand know what thy right hand doeth:

4 That thine alms may be in secret: and thy Father which seeth in secret himself shall reward thee openly.

5 ¶ And when thou prayest, thou shalt not be as the hypocrites *are:* for they love to pray standing in the synagogues and in the corners of the streets, that they may be seen of men. Verily I say unto you, They have their reward.

6 But thou, when thou prayest, enter into thy closet, and when thou hast shut thy door, pray to thy Father which is in secret; and thy Father which seeth in secret shall reward thee openly.

7 But when ye pray, use not vain repetitions, as the heathen *do:* for they think that they shall be heard for their much speaking.

8 Be not ye therefore like unto them: for your Father knoweth what things ye have need of, before ye ask him.

9 After this manner therefore pray ye: Our Father which art in heaven, Hallowed be thy name.

10 Thy kingdom come. Thy will be done in earth, as *it is* in heaven.

11 Give us this day our daily bread.

12 And forgive us our debts, as we forgive our debtors.

13 And lead us not into temptation, but deliver us from evil: For thine is the kingdom, and the power, and the glory, for ever. Amen.

14 For if ye forgive men their trespasses, your heavenly Father will also forgive you:

15 But if ye forgive not men their trespasses, neither will your Father forgive your trespasses.

16 ¶ Moreover when ye fast, be not, as the hypocrites, of a sad countenance: for they disfigure their faces, that they may appear unto men to fast. Verily I say unto you, They have their reward.

17 But thou, when thou fastest, anoint thine head, and wash thy face;

18 That thou appear not unto men to fast, but unto thy Father which is in secret: and thy Father, which seeth in secret, shall reward thee openly.

19 ¶ Lay not up for yourselves treasures upon earth, where moth and rust doth corrupt, and where thieves break through and steal:

20 But lay up for yourselves treasures in heaven, where neither moth nor rust doth corrupt, and where thieves do not break through nor steal:

21 For where your treasure is, there will your heart be also.

22 The light of the body is the eye: if therefore thine eye be single, thy whole body shall be full of light.

23 But if thine eye be evil, thy whole body shall be full of darkness. If therefore the light that is in thee be darkness, how great *is* that darkness!

24 ¶ No man can serve two masters: for either he will hate the one, and love the other; or else he will hold to the one, and despise the other. Ye cannot serve God and mammon.

25 Therefore I say unto you, Take no thought for your life, what ye shall eat, or what ye shall drink; nor yet for your body, what ye shall put on. Is not the life more than meat, and the body than raiment?

26 Behold the fowls of the air: for they sow not, neither do they reap, nor gather into barns; yet your heavenly Father feedeth them. Are ye not much better than they?

27 Which of you by taking thought can add one cubit unto his stature?

28 And why take ye thought for raiment? Consider the lilies of the field, how they grow; they toil not, neither do they spin:

29 And yet I say unto you, That even Solomon in all his glory was not arrayed like one of these.

30 Wherefore, if God so clothe the grass of the field, which to day is, and to morrow is cast into the oven, *shall he* not much more *clothe* you, O ye of little faith?

31 Therefore take no thought, saying, What shall we eat? or, What shall we drink? or, Wherewithal shall we be clothed?

32 (For after all these things do the Gentiles seek:) for your heavenly Father knoweth that ye have need of all these things.

33 But seek ye first the kingdom of God, and his righteousness; and all these things shall be added unto you.

34 Take therefore no thought for the morrow: for the morrow shall take thought for the things of itself. Sufficient unto the day *is* the evil thereof.

CHAPTER VII

Judge not, that ye be not judged.

2 For with what judgment ye judge, ye shall be judged: and with what measure ye mete, it shall be measured to you again.

3 And why beholdest thou the mote that is in thy brother's eye, but considerest not the beam that is in thine own eye?

4 Or how wilt thou say to thy brother, Let me pull out the mote out of thine eye; and, behold, a beam *is* in thine own eye?

5 Thou hypocrite, first cast out the beam out of thine own eye; and then shalt thou see clearly to cast out the mote out of thy brother's eye.

6 ¶ Give not that which is holy unto the dogs, neither cast ye your pearls before swine, lest they trample them under their feet, and turn again and rend you.

7 ¶ Ask, and it shall be given you; seek, and ye shall find; knock, and it shall be opened unto you:

8 For every one that asketh receiveth; and he that seeketh findeth; and to him that knocketh it shall be opened.

9 Or what man is there of you, whom if his son ask bread, will he give him a stone?

10 Or if he ask a fish, will he give him a serpent?

11 If ye then, being evil, know how to give good gifts unto your children, how much more shall your Father which is in heaven give good things to them that ask him?

12 Therefore all things whatsoever ye would that men should do to you, do ye even so to them: for this is the law and the prophets.

13 ¶ Enter ye in at the strait gate: for wide *is* the gate, and broad *is* the way, that leadeth to destruction, and many there be which go in thereat:

14 Because strait *is* the gate, and narrow *is* the way, which leadeth unto life, and few there be that find it.

15 ¶ Beware of false prophets, which come to you in sheep's clothing, but inwardly they are ravening wolves.

16 Ye shall know them by their fruits. Do men gather grapes of thorns, or figs of thistles?

17 Even so every good tree bringeth forth good fruit; but a corrupt tree bringeth forth evil fruit.

18 A good tree cannot bring forth evil fruit, neither *can* a corrupt tree bring forth good fruit.

19 Every tree that bringeth not forth good fruit is hewn down, and cast into the fire.

20 Wherefore by their fruits ye shall know them.

21 ¶ Not every one that saith unto me, Lord, Lord, shall enter into the kingdom of heaven; but he that doeth the will of my Father which is in heaven.

22 Many will say to me in that day, Lord, Lord, have we not prophesied in thy name? and in thy name have cast out devils? and in thy name done many wonderful works?

23 And then will I profess unto them, I never knew you: depart from me, ye that work iniquity.

24 ¶ Therefore whosoever heareth these sayings of mine, and doeth them, I will liken him unto a wise man, which built his house upon a rock:

25 And the rain descended, and the floods came, and the winds blew, and beat upon that house; and it fell not: for it was founded upon a rock.

26 And every one that heareth these sayings of mine, and doeth them not, shall be likened unto a foolish man, which built his house upon the sand:

27 And the rain descended, and the floods came, and the winds blew, and beat upon that house; and it fell: and great was the fall of it.

28 And it came to pass, when Jesus had ended these sayings, the people were astonished at his doctrine:

29 For he taught them as *one* having authority, and not as the scribes.

.   .   .   .   .

I CORINTHIANS, CHAPTER XIII

Though I speak with the tongues of men and of angels, and have not charity, I am become *as* sounding brass, or a tinkling cymbal.

2 And though I have *the gift of* prophecy, and understand all mysteries, and all knowledge; and though I have all faith, so that I could remove mountains, and have not charity, I am nothing.

3 And though I bestow all my goods to feed *the poor,* and though I give my body to be burned, and have not charity, it profiteth me nothing.

4 Charity suffereth long, *and* is kind; charity envieth not; charity vaunteth not itself, is not puffed up,

5 Doth not behave itself unseemly, seeketh not her own, is not easily provoked, *thinketh no evil;*

6 Rejoiceth not in iniquity, but rejoiceth in the truth;

7 Beareth all things, believeth all things, hopeth all things, endureth all things.

8 Charity never faileth: but whether *there be* prophecies, they shall fail; whether *there be* tongues, they shall cease; whether *there be* knowledge, it shall vanish away.

9 For we know in part, and we prophesy in part.

10 But when that which is perfect is come, then that which is in part shall be done away.

11 When I was a child, I spake as a child, I understood as a child, I thought as a child: but when I became a man, I put away childish things.

12 For now we see through a glass, darkly; but then face to face: now I know in part; but then shall I know even as also I am known.

13 And now abideth faith, hope, charity, these three; but the greatest of these *is* charity.

THE ANCIENT CHURCH

TATIAN, ST. AUGUSTINE, ST. BASIL, ST. JEROME

IF THE center of a person's philosophy changes, his whole personality becomes modified. St. Basil says in his *Address to Young Men on the Right Use of Greek Literature:*

"We Christians, young men, hold that this human life is not a supremely precious thing . . . Neither pride of ancestry, nor bodily strength, nor beauty, nor greatness, nor the esteem of all men, nor kingly authority, nor indeed, whatever of human affairs may be called great, do we consider worthy of desire, or the possessors of them as objects of envy; but we place our hopes upon the things which are beyond, and in preparation for the life eternal do we all things that we do."

In the light of such transcendentalism many of the early Christians looked with suspicion at the philosophy and literature of the Greeks and Romans, their government, and their social life. Some were uncompromising, like Tatian, some wavering, like St. Augustine, some tried to find a reconciliation between the pagan tradition and the new faith, like St. Basil.

But whatever the standpoint, the heathen attitude of courageous self-assertion changed into an attitude of humility; the "fear of God" and the heroism of love, asceticism and martyrdom were esteemed more highly than the heroism of the warrior; no revelation or ultimate wisdom was supposed to spring from independent intellectual effort. Only the man who in full awareness of his own utter weakness opened his soul to the grace of God could expect to participate in the final mystery of Salvation.

The following selections taken from the *Address of Tatian to the Greeks* are from *The Ante-Nicene Fathers,* . . . Volume II, published in New York by Charles Scribner's Sons in 1885.

The selections from *The Confessions of Saint Augustine,* are from William Watts's translation, 1912, published in the Loeb Classical Library, by the Harvard University Press.

Selections from St. Basil's *Address to Young Men on the Right Use of Greek Literature* are taken from Yale Studies in English, Albert S. Cook, editor, volume XV, *Essays on the Study and Use of Poetry by Plutarch and Basil the Great,* translated from the Greek with an introduction by Frederick Morgan Padelford. This was published by Henry Holt and Company, New York, in 1902, and the passages are here reproduced by permission of the Yale University Press. The selections from Saint Basil's *The Longer Rules* are taken from *The Ascetic Works* of Saint Basil, translated into English with introduction and notes by W. K. L. Clarke and published in London and New York in Translations of Christian Literature, Series I, Greek Texts, by The Macmillan Company in 1925.

The selections from Saint Jerome's *Letter to Laeta* are taken from *Letter CVII* in *The Principal Works of St. Jerome,* translated by W. H. Fremantle, with the assistance of G. Lewis. This is included in A Select Library of Nicene and Post-Nicene Fathers of the Christian Church, Second Series, Volume VI, published in New York in 1893 by Charles Scribner's Sons. Selections from Saint Jerome's *Letter to Gaudentius* are in *Letter CXXVIII* of the same work.

TATIAN 2nd cent.

ADDRESS TO THE GREEKS

CHAPTER I.—THE GREEKS CLAIM, WITHOUT REASON, THE INVENTION OF THE ARTS. Be not, O Greeks, so very hostilely disposed towards the Barbarians, nor look with ill will on their opinions. For which of your institutions has not been derived from the Barbarians? . . . To the Babylonians you owe astronomy; to the Persians magic; to the Egyptians, geometry; to the Phoenicians, instruction by alphabetic writing. Cease, then to miscall these imitations inventions of your own. Orpheus, again taught you poetry and song; from him too, you learned the mysteries. The Tuscans taught you the plastic art; from the annals of the Egyptians you learned to write history; you acquired the art of playing the flute from Marsyas and Olympus,—these two rustic Phrygians constructed the harmony of the shepherd's pipe. The Tyrrhenians invented the trumpet; the Cycloped the smith's art; and a woman who was formerly a queen of the Persians, as Hellanicus tells us, the method of joining together epistolary tablets: her name was Atossa. Wherefore lay aside this conceit, and be not ever boasting of your elegance of diction; for, while you applaud yourselves, your own people will of course side with you. But it becomes a man of sense to wait for the testimony of others, and it becomes men to be of one accord also in the pronunciation of their language. But, as matters stand, to you alone it has happened not to speak alike even in common intercourse; for the way of speaking among the Dorians is not the same as that of the inhabitants of Attica, nor do the Aeolians speak like the Ionians. And, since such a discrepancy exists where it ought not to be, I am at a loss whom to call a Greek. And, what is strangest of all, you hold in honour expressions not of native growth, and by the intermixture of barbaric words have made your language a medley. On this account we have renounced your wisdom, though I was once a great proficient in it; for, as the comic poet says,—"These are gleaners' grapes and small talk,—Twittering places of swallows, corrupters of art." [Aristoph, *Ranae*, 92, 93] Yet those who eagerly pursue it shout lustily, and croak like so many ravens. You have, too, contrived the art of rhetoric to serve injustice and slander, selling the free power of your speech for hire, and often representing the same thing at one time as right, at another time as not good. The poetic art, again, you employ to describe battles, and the amours of the gods, and the corruption of the soul.

CHAPTER II.—THE VICES AND ERRORS OF THE PHILOS-OPHERS. What noble thing have you produced by your pursuit of philosophy? Who of your most eminent men has been free from vain boasting? Diogenes, who made such a parade of his independence with his tub, was seized with a bowel complaint through eating a raw polypus, and so lost his life by gluttony. Aristippus walking about in a purple robe, led a profligate life, in accordance with his professed opinions. Plato, a philosopher, was sold by Dionysius for his gormandizing propensities. And Aristotle, who absurdly placed a limit to Providence and made happiness to consist in the things which give pleasure, quite contrary to his duty as a preceptor flattered Alexander, Forgetful that he was but a youth; and he, showing how well he had learned the lessons of his master, because his friend would not worship him shut him up and carried him about like a bear or a leopard. He in fact obeyed strictly the precepts of his teacher in displaying manliness and courage by feasting, and transfixing with his spear his intimate and most beloved friend, and then, under a semblance of grief, weeping and starving himself, that he might not incur the hatred of his friends. I could laugh at those also who in the present day adhere to his tenets,—people who say that sublunary things are not under the care of Providence; and so, being nearer the earth than the moon, and below its orbit, they themselves look after what is thus left uncared for; and for those who have neither beauty, nor wealth, nor bodily strength, nor high birth, they have no happiness, according to Aristotle. Let such men philosophize for me!

.   .   .   .   .

CHAPTER XXV.—BOASTING AND QUARRELS OF THE PHI-LOSOPHERS. What great and wonderful things have your philosophers effected? They leave uncovered one of their shoulders; they let their hair grow long; they cultivate their beards; their nails are like the claws of wild beasts. Though they say that they want nothing, yet, like Proteus [the Cynic Peregrinus is meant], they need a currier for their wallet, and a weaver for their mantle, and a wood-cutter for their staff, and the rich [they need the rich to invite them to banquets], and a cook also for their gluttony. O man competing with the dog [the Cynic], you know not God, and so have turned to the imitation of an irrational animal. You cry out

138

in public with an assumption of authority, and take upon you to avenge your own self; and if you receive nothing, you indulge in abuse, and philosophy is with you the art of getting money. You follow the doctrines of Plato, and a disciple of Epicurus lifts up his voice to oppose you. Again, you wish to be a disciple of Aristotle, and a follower of Democritus rails at you. Pythagoras says that he was Euphorbus, and he is the heir of the doctrine of Pherecydes; but Aristotle impugns the immortality of the soul. You who receive from predecessors doctrines which clash with one another, you the inharmonious, are fighting against the harmonious. One of you asserts that God is body, but I assert that He is without body; that the world is indestructible, but I say that it is to be destroyed; that a conflagration will take place at various times, but I say that it will come to pass once for all; that Minos and Rhadamanthus are judges, but I say that God Himself is Judge; that the soul alone is endowed with it. What injury do we inflict upon you, O Greeks? Why do you hate those who follow the word of God, as if they were the vilest of mankind? It is not we who eat human flesh—they among you who assert such a thing have been suborned as false witnesses; it is among you that Pelops is made a supper for the gods, although beloved by Poseidon, and Kronos devours his children, and Zeus swallows Metis.

CHAPTER XXVI.—RIDICULE OF THE STUDIES OF THE GREEKS. Cease to make a parade of sayings which you have derived from others, and to deck yourselves like the daw in borrowed plumes. If each state were to take away its contribution to your speech, your fallacies would lose their power. While inquiring what God is, you are ignorant of what is in yourselves; and, while staring all agape at the sky, you stumble into pitfalls. The reading of your books is like walking through a labyrinth, and their readers resemble the cask of the Danaïds. Why do you divide time, saying that one part is past, and another present, and another future? For how can the future be passing when the present exist? As those who are sailing imagine in their ignorance, as the ship is borne along, that the hills are in motion, so you do not know that it is you who are passing along, but that time . . . remains present as long as the Creator wills it to exist. Why am I called to account for uttering my opinions, and why are you in such haste to put them all down? Were not you born in the same manner as ourselves, and placed under the same government of the world? Why say that wisdom is with you alone, who have not another sun, nor other risings of the stars, nor a more distinguished origin, nor a death

139

preferable to that of other men? The grammarians have been the beginning of this idle talk; and you who parcel out wisdom are cut off from the wisdom that is according to truth, and assign the names of the several parts to particular men; and you know not God, but in your fierce contentions destroy one another. And on this account you are all nothing worth. While you arrogate to yourselves the sole right of discussion, you discourse like the blind man with the deaf. Why do you handle the builder's tools without knowing how to build? Why do you busy yourselves with words, while you keep aloof from deeds, puffed up with praise, but cast down by misfortunes? Your modes of acting are contrary to reason, for you make a pompous appearance in public, but hide your teaching in corners. Finding you to be such men as these, we have abandoned you, and no longer concern ourselves with your tenets, but follow the word of God. Why, O man, do you set the letters of the alphabet at war with one another? Why do you, as in a boxing match, make their sounds clash together with your mincing Attic way of speaking, whereas you ought to speak more according to nature? For if you adopt the Attic dialect though not an Athenian, pray why do you not speak like the Dorians? How is it that one appears to you more rugged, the other more pleasant for intercourse?

CHAPTER XXVII.—THE CHRISTIANS ARE HATED UNJUSTLY. And if you adhere to *their* teaching, why do you fight against me for choosing such views of doctrine as I approve? Is it not unreasonable that, while the robber is not to be punished for the name he bears [Athenagoras, *Embassy*, ii. *infra*], but only when the truth about him has been clearly ascertained, yet we are to be assailed with abuse on a judgment formed without examination? Diagoras was an Athenian, but you punished him for divulging the Athenian mysteries; yet you who read his Phrygian discourses hate us. You possess the commentaries of Leo, and are displeased with our refutations of them; and having in your hands the opinions of Apion concerning the Egyptian gods, you denounce us as most impious. . . . Why do you advise me to be false to my principles? Why do you who say that you despise death exhort us to use art in order to escape it? I have not the heart of a deer; but your zeal for dialectics resembles the loquacity of Thersites. How can I believe one who tells me that the sun is a red-hot mass and the moon an earth? Such assertions are mere logomachies, and not a sober exposition of truth. How can it be otherwise than foolish to credit the books of Herodotus relating to the history of Hercules, which tell of an upper earth from which the lion came down that was

140

killed by Hercules? And what avails the Attic style, the sorites of philosophers, the plausibilities of syllogisms, the measurements of the earth, the positions of the stars, and the course of the sun? To be occupied in such inquiries is the work of one who imposes opinions on himself as if they were laws.

. . . . .

CHAPTER XLII.—CONCLUDING STATEMENT AS TO THE AUTHOR. These things, O Greeks, I Tatian, a disciple of the barbarian philosophy, have composed for you. I was born in the land of the Assyrians, having been first instructed in your doctrines, and afterwards in those which I now undertake to proclaim. Henceforward, knowing who God is and what is His work, I present myself to you prepared for an examination concerning my doctrines, while I adhere immovably to that mode of life which is according to God.

ST. AUGUSTINE 354–430

THE CONFESSIONS

BOOK I

CHAPTER VIII.—A DESCRIPTION OF HIS CHILDHOOD.
Growing on from the state of infancy, came I not into my childhood? Or rather came not that into me, and succeeded unto my
infancy? nor yet did my infancy depart; for whither went it? yet
now it was no more. For an infant I was no longer, that could not
speak; seeing now I began to prove a pretty prating boy. And this
I well remember, and I afterwards observed how I first learned to
speak. For my elders did not teach me this ability, by giving me
words in any certain order of teaching, (as they did letters afterwards), but by that mind which thou, my God, gavest me, I myself
with gruntings, varieties of voices, and various motions of my body,
strove to express the conceits of mine own heart, that my desire
might be obeyed; but could not bring it out, either all I would have,
or with all the signs I would. Then, I pondered in my memory:
when they named anything, and when at that name they moved
their bodies toward that thing, I observed it, and gathered thereby,
that that word which they then pronounced, was the very name of
the thing which they showed me. And that they meant this or that
thing, was discovered to me by the motion of their bodies, even by
that natural language, as it were, of all nations; which expressed
by the countenance and cast of the eye, by the action of other parts,
and the sound of the voice, discovers the affections of the mind,
either to desire, enjoy, refuse, or to avoid anything. And thus words
in divers sentences, set in their due places, and heard often over, I
by little and little collected, of what things they were the signs, and
having broken my mouth to the pronunciation of them, I by them
expressed mine own purposes. Thus, with those whom I conversed
withal, did I communicate the expressions of mine own desires; and
ventured thereby upon the troublesome society of human busi-

nesses, depending all this while upon the authority of my parents, and being at the beck of my elders.

CHAPTER IX.—THE HATRED THAT CHILDREN BEAR TO LEARNING, AND THEIR LOVE TO PLAYING. O God, my God! what miseries and what mockeries did I find in that age; whenas being yet a boy, obedience was propounded unto me, to those who advised me to get on in the world; and prove excellent in tongue-sciences, which should get me reputation amongst men, and deceitful riches? Thereupon was I sent to school, to get learning; whereby little knew I (wretch that I was) what profit might be obtained; and yet if I proved truantly at my book, I was presently beaten. For this discipline was commended by our ancestors; and divers passing the same course before our times, had chalked these troublesome ways out unto us, by which we were constrained to follow them; multiplying by this means both labour and sorrow to the sons of Adam.

Yet we observed, O Lord, how certain men would pray unto thee; and we learned of them; thinking thee (as far as we could apprehend) to be some great one; who wert able, (and yet not appearing to our senses) both to hear and help us. For being yet a boy, I began to pray unto thee, my Aid and Refuge, and even then brake the string of my tongue in praying to thee; and being yet a little one, I prayed to thee with no small devotion, that I might not be beaten at school. And when thou heardest not (which yet was not to be accounted folly in me), my corrections, which I then esteemed my greatest and most grievous affliction, were made sport at by my elders, yea and by mine own parents, who wished no hurt at all unto me. Is there any man, O Lord, of so great a spirit, cleaving to thee with so strong an affection; is there any man, I say, (for even a callousness may other-whiles do as much), who by devoutly applying himself unto thee, is so resolutely affected, that he can think so lightly of those racks and strappadoes, and such varieties of torments, (for the avoiding whereof men pray unto thee with so much fear all the world over), that he can make sport at those who most bitterly fear them; as our parents laughed at these torments, which we schoolboys suffered from our masters? For we were no less afraid of the rod, nor did we less earnestly pray to thee for the scaping of it, than others did of their tortures. And yet for all our fears, we too often played the truants; either in writing, or reading, or thinking upon our lessons, less than was required of us. For we wanted not, O Lord, either memory or capacity, (of which, considering our age, thou pleasedst to bestow enough upon us) but

143

our mind was all upon playing; for which we were beaten, even by those masters, who were doing as much themselves. But elder folks' idlenesses, must, forsooth, be called business, and when children do the like, the same men must punish them; and yet no man pities either children or men or both. But perhaps some indifferent judge might account me to be justly beaten for playing at ball, being yet a boy, because by that sport I was hindered in my learning, by which, when I came to be a man, I was to play the fool more unbeseemingly: or did my master, who now beat me, anything else? who, if in any trifling question he were foiled by another schoolmaster, he was presently more racked with choler and envy at him, than I was, when at a match at tennis-ball, I lost the game to my playfellow.

CHAPTER X.—HOW FOR HIS PLAY HE NEGLECTED HIS PARENTS' COMMANDMENTS. And yet I offended, O Lord God, thou Ruler and Creator of all natural things, of sins only the Ruler! I sinned, O Lord my God! in doing contrary to the commandments of my parents, and of those masters: for I might afterwards have made good use of my learning, which they were desirous I should obtain, whatsoever purpose they had in it. For I disobeyed them not out of desire of choosing better courses; but all out of a desire to play: aspiring to be captain in all sports, and to have mine ears tickled with feigned fables, to make them itch the more glowingly: the like desperate curiosity also sparkling through mine eyes, after the shows and plays of my elders: the authors whereof are esteemed to gain so much honour by it, that almost all the spectators wish the like to be their own children; whom for all that they gladly suffer to be beaten, if by such stage-plays they be hindered from their studies, by which they desire them to arrive one day to the ability of making the like. Look down upon these things mercifully, O Lord, and deliver us that now call upon thee: deliver also those that do not yet call upon thee; that they may call upon thee, and thou mayest deliver them.

.   .   .   .   .

CHAPTER XII.—HE IS FORCED TO HIS BOOK: WHICH GOD TURNED TO GOOD PURPOSE. But in this my childhood (wherein was less fear of me than in my youth) I loved not my book, and I hated to be forced to it: yet was I held to it notwithstanding: wherein it was very well for me, but I did not well for myself: for I would never have taken my learning, had I not been constrained to it. For no man does well against his will, though that which he does be good. Nor did they that forced me to it, very

144

well; but it was thou, my God, that didst the good to me. For they that held me to my learning, did not understand to what I would apply it, unless to satiate the insatiable desires of a rich beggary, and a dishonourable glory. But thou before whom the very hairs of our heads are numbered, didst convert the common error of them all who pressed me to learning, to mine own benefit; and my error, who would not learn, didst thou make use of for my punishment; of which I being then so little a boy, and so great a sinner, was not unworthy. Thus by their means who did not well by me, didst thou well for me: and upon me who was a sinner, thou inflictedst a deserved punishment. For thou hast appointed it, and so it proves, every man's inordinate affection shall be his own affliction.

CHAPTER XIII.—WITH WHAT STUDIES HE WAS CHIEFLY DELIGHTED. But what was the reason why of a child I should so naturally hate the Greek tongue when it was taught me, I cannot yet understand. Latin I loved very well: not that part which the elementary teachers enter us in, but that which the men of letters teach us.[1] For those first rudiments, to read, to write, and cipher, I accounted no less painful and troublesome than the Greek. But whence should this proceed, but from the sinfulness and vanity of this life? For I was but flesh, a wind that passeth away and cometh not again. For those first rudiments were better, because more certain, (seeing that by them, that skill was and is wrought in me, that I am able to read what I find written, and of myself to write what I will) than these latter; by which I was enforced to commit to memory the wanderings of I know not what Aeneas, while I forgot mine own: and to bewail dead Dido, because she killed herself for love; when in the mean time (wretch that I was) I with dry eyes endured myself dying towards thee, O God my Life!

For what can be more miserable than a wretch that pities not himself; one bemoaning Dido's death caused by loving of Aeneas, and yet not lamenting his own death, caused by not loving of thee, O God, thou Light of my soul, thou Bread of the internal mouth of my soul, and thou firmest Knot, marrying my soul and the bosom of my thoughts together? I did not love thee, and I committed fornication against thee, while in the mean time every one applauded me with Well done, well done! But the love of this world is fornication against God: which so applauds and encourages a spiritual fornicator, that it is even a shame for a man to be otherwise. But I bemoaned not all this; but dead Dido I bewailed, that killed herself by falling upon the sword: I myself following these

[1] I.e. the literature, not the grammar.

145

lower creatures of thine, forsaking thee; and myself being earth, hastening to the earth. But if I were forbidden to read these toys, how sorry would I be, for that I might not read that which would make me sorry. Such madnesses were esteemed to be more commendable and fluent learning, than the learning to write and read.

But let my God now cry unto my soul, and let thy truth say unto me, It is not so, it is not so; that first kind of learning was far better. For behold I am readier to forget the wanderings of Aeneas, and all such toys, than I am to write and read. True it is, that there are curtains at the entrance of Grammar Schools; but they signify not so much the cloth of state to privacy, as serve for a blind to the follies committed behind them. Let not these masters now cry out upon me, whom now I am out of fear of; whilst I confess to thee, my God, what my soul delights in; and rest contented with the reprehension of mine own evil ways, that I may love thy good ones. Let not those buyers or sellers of grammar exclaim upon me, for that if I ask them, whether that of the poet be true, that Aeneas ever came to Carthage: the unlearned will answer, they know not; and the learned will deny it to be true. But if I ask them with what letters Aeneas' name is written, every one that hath but learned so far, will pitch upon one truth, according to the agreement and will whereby men at first made rules for those characters. If I should ask again, which of the two would be most incommodious to the life of man to forget; to write and read, or, these poetical fictions; who sees not what any man would answer, that had not quite forgotten himself? I offended therefore being but a boy, when in my affection I preferred those vain studies to these more profitable: or rather, indeed, I utterly hated these, and was in love with those. But then, One and one makes two, and two and two makes four, was a harsh song to me; but The Wooden Horse full of Armed Men, and The Burning of Troy, and the Ghost of Creusa, was a most delightful spectacle of vanity.

CHAPTER XIV.—OF THE GREEK AND LATIN TONGUES. But why then did I hate the Greek literature that chants of such things? For Homer himself was skilful in contriving such fictions, and is most delightfully wanton; but yet very harsh to me being a schoolboy. I believe that Virgil is no less to Grecian children when they be compelled to learn him, as I was to learn Homer: for to say truth, the difficulty of learning a strange language, did sprinkle as it were with gall all the pleasures of those fabulous narrations. For I understood not a word of it, yet they vehemently pressed me and with most cruel threatenings and punishments, to make me

146

understand it. The time was also (when I was an infant) that I knew not a word of Latin; yet by marking I got that without any fear or tormenting, even by my nurses' prattlings to me, and the pretty tales of those that laughed upon me, and the sports of those that played with me.

So much verily I learnt without any painful burden to me of those that urged me, for that mine own heart put me to it to bring out mine own conceptions. Which I could never have done, had I not learned divers words, not of those that taught me, but of them that talked familiarly to me, in whose hearing I also brought forth whatsoever I had conceived. Hereby it clearly appears that a free curiosity hath more force in children's learning of languages, than a frightful enforcement can have. But the unsettledness of that freedom, this enforcement restrains: thy laws, O God, yea, thy laws, even from the schoolmaster's ferule, to the martyr's trials, being able to temper wholesome and bitter together; calling us back by that means unto thyself, even from that infectious sweetness, which at first allured us to fall away from thee.

CHAPTER XV.—HIS PRAYER TO GOD. Hear my prayer, O Lord, let not my soul faint under thy correction: nor let me faint in confessing unto thee thine own mercies, by which thou hast drawn me out of all mine own most wicked courses: that thyself mightest from hence forward grow sweet unto me, beyond all those allurements which heretofore I followed; and that I might most entirely love thee, and lay hold upon thy hand with all the powers of my heart, that thou mightest finally draw me out of all danger of temptation.

For behold, O Lord my King; whatsoever good I have learned, being a boy, unto thy service let it be directed, yea, whatsoever I speak or write, or read, or number, let all serve thee. For when I learned vain things, thou didst discipline me: and in those vanities, thou forgavest the sinfulness of my delight in them. In those studies I learned many useful words, but those might have been also learned in studies not so vain: which is, I confess, the safest way for children to be trained up in.

CHAPTER XVI.—AGAINST LASCIVIOUS FABLES. But woe unto thee, O thou torrent of human custom, who shall stop the course of thee? When wilt thou be dry? How long will thou continue tumbling the sons of Eve into that huge and hideous ocean, which they very hardly pass, who are shipped upon the Tree? Do I not read in thee of Jupiter sometimes thundering, and sometimes adultering? But verily both these could not one person do: but this

147

is feigned, that there might be authority to imitate true-acted adultery; false thunder the mean while playing the bawd to him. Yet which of our longrobed masters can with any patience hear a man that should in his school cry out saying: Homer feigned these, and ascribed men's faults unto the gods; but I had rather he had derived divine excellencies upon us. But more truly it is said, that Homer feigned these things indeed; and that by this attributing divine excellencies to most wicked mortals, crimes might not be accounted crimes: so that whosoever shall commit the like, seems not therein to imitate desperate people, but some heavenly deities.

This notwithstanding, O thou hellish torrent, are the sons of men cast into thee, with payments made, to learn these fables; and a great solemnity is made of it, when 'tis pleaded for openly in the assemblies, and in the sight of the laws, which allow stipends to the teachers over and above the payments of the scholars: yet, O torrent, thou art still beating upon thy rocks, roaring out, and crying: Here are fine words to be learned; here eloquence is attained: eloquence to necessary to persuade to business, and with advantage to express thoughts. But for all this, should we never so well have understood these words: The Golden Shower, The Lap, the Deceit, the Temple of Heaven, and such others written in the same place, had not Terence withal brought a lewd young man upon the stage, propounding Jupiter to himself for an example of his adultery; whilst he beholds a certain picture on the wall, wherein are set out to the life, the story of Jupiter raining a golden shower into Danae's lap, deceiving the simple maiden by that means? See how that young man provoked himself to lust, as if he had had a celestial authority for it:

'But what god do I imitate, saith he? Even that god who with a mighty thunder shakes the very arches of heaven: may I not then, frail flesh and blood, do as much? But I for my part did as much, yea, and gladly too.'

Plainly, these words are not so much the more easily learned by this filthy matter, but by these words the sin is more confidently committed. I blame not the words, which of themselves are like vessels choice and precious; but that wine of error which is in them, drunk to us by our intoxicated teachers. If we refused to pledge them, we were beaten: nor had we liberty to appeal unto any sober judge. All this notwithstanding, O my God, (in whose presence I now with security remember this) I did willingly learn these things; and unhappy I, was for this accounted a youth of much towardness.

CHAPTER XVII.—THE WAY OF EXERCISING YOUTH IN

REPEATING AND VARYING OF VERSES. Give me leave, O my God, to tell thee something of mine own wit, which was thy gift, and what dotages I spent it upon. My master put a task upon me, troublesome enough to my soul, and that upon terms of reward of commendations, or fear of shame and whipping: namely, that I should declaim upon those words of Juno, expressing both her anger and sorrow, that she could not keep off the Trojan King from going into Italy: which words I had heard that Juno never uttered; yet were we enforced to imitate the passages of these poetical fictions; and to vary that into prose which the poet had expressed in verse. And he declaimed with more applause, in whose action, according to the dignity of the person represented, there appeared an affection nearer to anger or grief, set out with words agreeable to the matter.

But to what end was this, O my true Life, my God? Why was my declamation more applauded than so many others of mine own age and form? Was not all this mere smoke and wind? And could no other subject be found to exercise my wit and tongue in? Thy praises, O Lord, thy praises, might have stayed the tender sprig of my heart upon the prop of thy Scriptures, that it might not have been cropped off by these empty vanities, to be caught up as a prey by those flying spirits. For by more ways than one is there sacrifice offered to the collapsed angels.

CHAPTER XVIII.—THAT MEN CARE MORE TO OBSERVE THE RULES OF GRAMMAR THAN THE LAWS OF GOD. But what wonder was it, if I were thus carried towards vanity, and estranged from thee, O my God; whenas such men were propounded to me to imitate, who should they deliver any of their own acts, though not evil, with any barbarism or solecism, they were utterly dashed out of countenance: but should they make a copious and neat oration of their own lusts, in a round and well followed style, would take a pride to be applauded for it. These things thou seest, O Lord, long suffering, and of much mercy and truth, and thou keepest silence; but wilt thou be silent for ever? Even now thou wilt draw out of this horrible pit, that soul that seeks after thee, and that thirsts after thy pleasures: whose heart saith unto thee, I have sought thy face, and thy face, Lord, will I seek. For I had straggled far away from thy countenance in the mistiness of my affections. For we neither go nor return, from, or to thee, upon our feet, or by distance of spaces: nor did that younger brother seek posthorses, or waggons, or ships, or fly away with visible wings, or take his journey by the motion of his hams, that living in a far country

149

he might prodigally waste that portion, which thou hadst given him at his departure. A sweet father, because thou gavest him his portion: yet far sweeter to the poor wretch returning: for that he went from thee out of a voluptuous affection; that is to say, a darkened one; and such that is, which is far from the countenance. Behold, O Lord God, and patiently behold, as thou still dost, how diligently the sons of men observe the rules of letters and syllables received from former speakers; and yet regard not the eternal covenants of everlasting salvation, received from thyself. Insomuch, that he who either holds or teaches the ancient rules of pronunciation, if contrary to grammar he shall pronounce *ominem,* (that is, a man) without H in the first syllable; he shall displease men more, than if against thy rules he should hate a man, although he be a man. As if any man should think his enemy to be more pernicious to him, than that hatred of his own is, whereby he is set against him: or imagine that he does worse scath to another man by persecuting him, than he does to his own heart, by contriving enmity against him. Certainly there is no more inward knowledge of Letters than this law of conscience, that one is doing to another what himself would not suffer. How secret art thou, O thou only great God, which dwellest in the Highest, and in silence, with an untiring destiny, dispersing blindness for punishments upon unlawful desires: when a man affects the credit of eloquence, standing before a mortal judge, a multitude of mortals standing about him, inveighing against his adversary with his fiercest hatred, he takes heed most watchfully, that his tongue trips not before men, and he call them *omines;* but takes not heed at all, lest through the fury of his spirit he should destroy a man out of the society of men.

CHAPTER XIX.—HOW HE WAS MORE CAREFUL TO AVOID BARBARISMS OF SPEECH, THAN CORRUPTION OF MANNERS. In the threshold of these customs lay I, wretched boy, and upon that stage I played my prizes; where I more feared to commit a barbarism in speaking, than I took care when I committed any, not to envy those that committed none. All this I declare and confess to thee, my God; but in these things I was by them applauded, to please whom, I then accounted equal to living honestly. For then I discerned not that whirlpool of filthiness whereinto I was cast from thine eyes. For in thine eyes, what was more filthy than I? Where also I displeased such as myself; with innumerable lies deceiving both my tutor, and masters, and parents: all for love of play, out of a desire to see toys, and a restless desire to imitate the stage.

Thievery also I committed out of my father's buttery and table;

either gluttony oft commanding me, or that I might have some-thing to give my playfellows, selling me their baubles, although they were as much delighted with them as myself. In these play-games I being often over-matched, did with a vain desire to be counted excellent, aspire to win though by foul play. And what was I so unwilling to endure, and what if I found out the deceit would I so fiercely wrangle at, as even those very tricks which I would put upon others? And being myself taken with the manner, I would rather fall flat out, than yield to it.

Is this that childish innocency? It is not, Lord, it is not. I cry thee mercy, O my God: for these are the same things, the very same, which as our years go on, leaving tutors and masters, leaving nuts, and balls, and birds, are done with regard to kings and gov-ernors, to the getting of gold, and manor houses, and slaves. But this boy's play passes over as more years come on, just as greater punishments follow after the ferule. Thou therefore, O our King, hast approved of the character of humility in the stature of child-hood, when thou sayest: To such belongeth the Kingdom of God.

. . . . . .

BOOK III

CHAPTER IV.—HOW TULLY'S HORTENSIUS' PROVOKED HIM TO STUDY PHILOSOPHY. Amongst these mad companions in that tender age of mine learned I the books of eloquence, wherein my ambition was to be eminent, all out of a damnable and vain-glorious end, puffed up with a delight of human glory. By the ordinary course of study I fell upon a certain book of one Cicero, whose tongue almost every man admires, though not so his heart. This book of his contains an exhortation to Philosophy, and 'tis called Hortensius. Now this book quite altered my affection, turned my prayers to thyself, O Lord, and made me have clean other pur-poses and desires. All my vain hopes I thenceforth slighted; and with an incredible heat of spirit I thirsted after the immortality of wisdom, and began now to rouse up myself, that I might turn again to theeward. For I made not use of that book to file my tongue with, which I seemed to buy with that exhibition which my mother allowed me, in that nineteenth year of my age, my father being dead two years before. I made not use of that book, I say, to sharpen my tongue withal, nor had it persuaded me to affect the fine language in it, but the matter of it.

How did I burn then, my God, how did I burn to fly from earthly

151

delights towards thee, and yet I knew not what thou meanedst to do with me! For with thee is wisdom. That love of wisdom is in Greek called Philosophy, with which that book inflamed me. Some there be that seduce others through Philosophy, under a great, a fair promising, and an honest name, colouring over and palliating their own errors: and almost all those who in the same and former ages had been of that stamp, are in that book censured and set forth: there also is that most wholesome advice of thy Spirit, given by thy good and devout servant, made plain: Beware lest any man spoil you through Philosophy and vain deceit after the tradition of men, after the rudiments of the world, and not after Christ. For in him dwelleth all the Fulness of the Godhead bodily. For my part, thou Light of my heart knowest, that the Apostolical Scriptures were scarce known to me at that time: but this was it that so delighted me in that exhortation, that it did not engage me to this or that sect, but left me free to love, and seek, and obtain, and hold, and embrace Wisdom itself, whatever it was. Perchance it was that book I was stirred up, and enkindled, and inflamed by: This thing only in such a heat of zeal took me off, that the name of Christ was not in it. For this Name, according to thy mercy, O Lord, this Name of my Saviour thy Son, had my tender heart even together with my mother's milk devoutly drunken in, and charily treasured up: so that what book soever was without that Name, though never so learned, politely and truly penned, did not altogether take my approbation.

CHAPTER V.—HE SETS LIGHTLY BY THE HOLY SCRIPTURES BECAUSE OF THE SIMPLICITY OF THE STYLE. I resolved thereupon to bend my studies towards the Holy Scriptures, that I might see what they were. But behold, I espy something in them not revealed to the proud, not discovered unto children, humble in style, sublime in operation, and wholly veiled over in mysteries; and I was not so fitted at that time, as to pierce into the sense, or stoop my neck to its coming. For when I attentively read these Scriptures, I thought not then so of them, as I now speak; but they seemed to me far unworthy to be compared to the stateliness of the Ciceronian eloquence. For my swelling pride soared above the temper of their style, nor was my sharp wit able to pierce into their sense. And yet such are thy Scriptures as grew up together with thy little ones. But I much disdained to be held a little one; and big swollen with pride, I took myself to be some great man.

.   .   .   .   .

ST. BASIL c. 330–379

ADDRESS TO YOUNG MEN

I. Many considerations, young men, prompt me to recommend to you the principles which I deem most desirable, and which I believe will be of use to you if you will adopt them. For my time of life, my many-sided training, yea, my adequate experience in those vicissitudes of life which teach their lessons at every turn, I have so familiarized me with human affairs, that I am able to map out the safest course for those just starting upon their careers. By nature's common bond I stand in the same relationship to you as your parents, so that I am no whit behind them in my concern for you. Indeed, if I do not misinterpret your feelings, you no longer crave your parents when you come to me. . . .

Do not be surprised if to you, who go to school every day, and who, through their writings, associate with the learned men of old, I say that out of my own experience I have evolved something more useful. Now this my counsel, that you should not unqualifiedly give over your minds to these men, as a ship is surrendered to the rudder, to follow whither they list, but that, while receiving whatever of value they have to offer, you yet recognize what it is wise to ignore. Accordingly, from this point on I shall take up and discuss the pagan writings, and how we are to discriminate among them.

II. We Christians, young men, hold that this human life is not a supremely precious thing, nor do we recognize anything as unconditionally a blessing which benefits us in this life only. Neither pride of ancestry, nor bodily strength, nor beauty, nor greatness, nor the esteem of all men, nor kingly authority, nor indeed, whatever of human affairs may be called great, do we consider worthy of desire, or the possessors of them as objects of envy; but we place our hopes upon the things which are beyond, and in preparation for the life eternal do we all things that we do. . . .

Into the life eternal the Holy Scriptures lead us, which teach us through divine words. But as long as our immaturity forbids our understanding their deep thought, we exercise our spiritual perceptions upon profane writings, which are not altogether different, and in which we perceive the truth as it were in shadows and in mirrors. Thus we imitate those who perform the exercises of military practice, for they acquire skill in gymnastics and in dancing, and then in battle reap the reward of their training. We must needs believe that the greatest of all battles lies before us, in preparation for which we must do and suffer all things to gain power. Consequently we must be conversant with poets, with historians, with orators, indeed with all men who may further our soul's salvation. Just as dyers prepare the cloth before they apply the dye, be it purple or any other color, so indeed must we also, if we would preserve indelible the idea of the true virtue, become first initiated in the pagan lore, then at length give special heed to the sacred and divine teachings, even as we first accustom ourselves to the sun's reflection in the water, and then become able to turn our eyes upon the very sun itself.

III. If, then, there is any affinity between the two literatures, a knowledge of them should be useful to us in our search for truth; if not, the comparison by emphasizing the contrast, will be of no small service in strengthening our regard for the better one. With what now may we compare these two kinds of education to obtain a simile? Just as it is the chief mission of the tree to bear its fruit in its season, though at the same time it puts forth for ornament the leaves which quiver on its boughs, even so the real fruit of the soul is truth, yet it is not without advantage for it to embrace the pagan wisdom, as also leaves offer shelter to the fruit, and an appearance not untimely. . . .

IV. Perhaps it is sufficiently demonstrated that such heathen learning is not unprofitable for the soul; I shall then discuss next the extent to which one may pursue it. To begin with the poets, since their writings are of all degrees of excellence, you should not study all of their poems without omitting a single word. When they recount the words and deeds of good men, you should both love and imitate them, earnestly emulating such conduct. But when they portray base conduct, you must flee from them and stop up your ears, as Odysseus is said to have fled past the song of the sirens, for familiarity with evil writings paves the way for evil deeds. Therefore the soul must be guarded with great care, lest through our love for letters it receive some contamination unaware, as men drink in poison with honey. We shall not praise the poets when they scoff and rail, when they represent fornicators and winebibbers, when they define blissfulness by groaning tables and wanton songs. Least

154

of all shall we listen to them when they tell us of their gods, and especially when they represent them as being many, and not at one among themselves. For, among these gods, at one time brother is at variance with brother, or the father with his children; at another, the children engage in truceless war against their parents. The adulteries of the gods and their amours, and especially those of the one whom they call Zeus, chief of all and most high, things of which one cannot speak, even in connection with brutes, without blushing, we shall leave to the stage.

I have the same words for the historians, and especially when they make up stories for the amusement of their hearers. And certainly we shall not follow the example of the rhetoricians in the art of lying. For neither in the courts of justice nor in other business affairs will falsehood be of any help to us Christians, who, having chosen the straight and true path of life, are forbidden by the gospel to go to law. But on the other hand we shall receive gladly those passages in which they praise virtue or condemn vice. For just as bees know how to extract honey from flowers, which to men are agreeable only for their fragrance and color, even so here also those who look for something more than pleasure and enjoyment in such writers may derive profit for their souls. Now, then, altogether after the manner of bees must we use these writings, for the bees do not visit all the flowers without discrimination, nor indeed do they seek to carry away entire those upon which they light, but rather, having taken so much as is adapted to their needs, they let the rest go. So we, if wise, shall take from heathen books whatever befits us and is allied to the truth, and shall pass over the rest. And just as in culling roses we avoid the thorns, from such writings as these we will gather everything useful, and guard against the noxious. So, from the very beginning, we must examine each of their teachings, to harmonize it with our ultimate purpose, according to the Doric proverb, 'testing each stone by the measuring-line.'

V. Since we must needs attain to the life to come through virtue, our attention is to be chiefly fastened upon those many passages from the poets, from the historians, and especially from the philosophers, in which virtue itself is praised. For it is of no small advantage that virtue become a habit with a youth, for the lessons of youth make a deep impression, because the soul is then plastic, and therefore they are likely to be indelible. . . .

Now as I have heard from one [Libanius, born at Antioch in 314] skilful in interpreting the mind of a poet, all the poetry of Homer is a praise of virtue, and with him all that is not merely accessory tends to this end. There is a notable instance of this where Homer first made the princess reverence the leader of the Cephallenians, though he appeared naked, shipwrecked, and alone, and then made Odysseus as completely lack embarrassment, though seen naked and alone, since virtue served him as a garment. And next he made Odysseus so much esteemed by the other Phaeacians that, abandoning the luxury in which they lived, all admired and emulated him, and there was not one of them who longed for anything else except to be Odysseus, even to the enduring of shipwreck. . . .

And, indeed, this is the truth, for other possessions belong to the owner no more than to another, and, as when men are dicing, fall now to this one, now to that. But virtue is the only possession that is sure, and that remains with us whether living or dead. . . .

VI. Almost all who have written upon the subject of wisdom have more or less, in proportion to their several abilities, extolled virtue in their writings. Such men must one obey, and must try to realize their words in his life. For he, who by his works exemplifies the wisdom which with others is a matter of theory alone, 'breathes; all others flutter about like shadows.' [Odys. X. 495] I think it is as if a painter should represent some marvel of manly beauty, and the subject should actually be such a man as the artist pictures on the canvas. To praise virtue in public with brilliant words and with long drawn out speeches, while in private preferring pleasures to temperance, and self-interest to justice, finds an analogy on the stage, for the players frequently appear as kings and rulers, though they are neither, nor perhaps even genuinely free men. . . . But every man is divided against himself who does not make his life conform to his words, but who says with Euripides, 'The mouth indeed hath sworn, but the heart knows no oath.' [Hippolytus 612] Such a man will seek the appearance of virtue rather than the reality. But to seem to be good when one is not so, is, if we are to respect the opinion of Plato [Rep. ii, 361] at all, the very height of injustice.

VII. After this wise, then, are we to receive those words from the pagan authors which contain suggestions of the virtues. But since also the renowned deeds of the men of old either are preserved for us by tradition, or are cherished in the pages of poet or historian, we must not fail to profit by them. . . .

But let us bring our discussion back again to the examples of noble deeds. A certain man once kept striking Socrates, the son of Sophroniscus, in the face, yet he did not resent it, but allowed full play to the ruffian's anger, so that his face was swollen and

156

bruised from the blows. Then when he stopped striking him, Socrates did nothing more than write on his forehead, as an artisan on a statue, who did it, and thus took out his revenge. Since these examples almost coincide with our teachings, I hold that such men are worthy of emulation. For this conduct of Socrates is akin to the precept that to him who smites you upon the one cheek, you shall turn the other also [Matt. v. 39]—thus much may you be avenged; . . . One who has been instructed in the pagan examples will no longer hold the Christian precepts impracticable. . . .

VIII. But let us return to the same thought with which we started, namely, that we should not accept everything without discrimination, but only what is useful. For it would be shameful should we reject injurious foods, yet should take no thought about the studies which nourish our souls, but as a torrent should sweep along all that came near our path and appropriate it. . . .

An analogy may be found in the athletic contests, or, if you will, in the musical contests; for the contestants prepare themselves by a preliminary training for those events in which wreaths of victory are offered, and no one by training for wrestling or for the pancratium would get ready to play the lyre or the flute. . . . Such power to compass one's end, either in music or in athletic contests, is developed by practice.

I have called to mind the wreaths and the fighters. These men endure hardships beyond number, they use every means to increase their strength, they sweat ceaselessly at their training, they accept many blows from the master, they adopt the mode of life which he prescribes, though it is most unpleasant, and, in a word, they so rule all their conduct that their whole life before the contest is preparatory to it. Then they strip themselves for the arena, and endure all and risk all, to receive the crown of olive, or of parsley, or some other branch, and to be announced by the herald as victor. [I Cor. ix. 24-27]

Will it then be possible for us, to whom are held out rewards so wondrous in number and in splendor that tongue can not recount them, while we are fast asleep and leading care-free lives, to make these our own by half-hearted efforts? . . . For after we have actually endured many hardships, we shall scarcely gain those blessings to which, as said above, nothing in human experience is comparable. Therefore we must not be lightminded, nor exchange our immortal hopes for momentary idleness, lest reproaches come upon us, and judgment befall us, not forsooth here among men, although judgment here is no easy thing for the man of sense to

157

bear, but at the bar of justice, be that under the earth, or wherever else it may happen to be. While he who unintentionally violates his obligations perchance receives some pardon from God, he who designedly chooses a life of wickedness doubtless has a far greater punishment to endure.

IX. 'What then are we to do?' perchance some one may ask. What else than to care for the soul, never leaving an idle moment for other things? Accordingly, we ought not to serve the body any more than is absolutely necessary, but we ought to do our best for the soul, releasing it from the bondage of fellowship with the bodily appetites; at the same time we ought to make the body superior to passion. We must provide it with the necessary food, to be sure, but not with delicacies, as those do who seek everywhere for waiters and cooks, and scour both earth and sea, like those bringing tribute to some stern tyrant. This is a despicable business, in which are endured things as unbearable as the torments of hell, where wool is combed into the fire, or water is drawn in a sieve and poured into a perforated jar, and where work is never done. Then to spend more time than is necessary on one's hair and clothes is, in the words of Diogenes, the part of the unfortunate or of the sinful. For what difference does it make to a sensible man whether he is clad in a robe of state or in an inexpensive garment, so long as he is protected from heat and cold? Likewise in other matters we must be governed by necessity, and only give so much care to the body as is beneficial to the soul. For to one who is really a man it is no less a disgrace to be a fop or a pamperer of the body than to be the victim of any other base passion. Indeed, to be very zealous in making the body appear very beautiful is not the mark of a man who knows himself, or who feels the force of the wise maxim: 'Not that which is seen is the man,' for it requires a higher faculty for any one of us, whoever he may be, to know himself. Now it is harder for the man who is not pure in heart to gain this knowledge than for a bleareyed person to look upon the sun.

To speak generally and so far as your needs demand, purity of soul embraces these things: to scorn sensual pleasures, to refuse to feast the eyes on the senseless antics of buffoons, or on bodies which goad one to passion, and to close one's ears to songs which corrupt the mind. . . .

In a word, he who would not bury himself in the mire of sensuality must deem the whole body of little worth, or must, as Plato puts it, pay only so much heed to the body as is an aid to wisdom, [Rep. iii. 403-412] or as Paul admonishes somewhere in a similar passage:

'Let no one make provision for the flesh, to fulfill the lusts thereof.' [Rom. xiii. 14.] Wherein is there any difference between those who take pains that the body shall be perfect, but ignore the soul, for the use of which it is designed, and those who are scrupulous about their tools, but neglectful of their trade? On the contrary, one ought to discipline the flesh and hold it under, as a fierce animal is controlled, and to quiet, by the lash of reason, the unrest which it engenders in the soul, and not, by giving full rein to pleasure, to disregard the mind, as a charioteer is run away with by unmanageable and frenzied horses. So let us bear in mind the remark of Pythagoras, who, upon learning that one of his followers was growing very fleshy from gymnastics and hearty eating, said to him, 'Will you not stop making your imprisonment harder for yourself?' Then it is said that since Plato foresaw the dangerous influence of the body, he chose an unhealthy part of Athens for his Academy, in order to remove excessive bodily comfort, as one prunes the rank shoots of the vines. Indeed I have even heard physicians say that over-healthiness is dangerous. Since, then, this exaggerated care of the body is harmful to the body itself, and a hindrance to the soul, it is sheer madness to be a slave to the body, and serve it.

If we were minded to disregard attention to the body, we should be in little danger of prizing anything else unduly. For of what use, now, are riches, if one scorns the pleasures of the flesh? I certainly see none, unless, as in the case of the mythological dragons, there is some satisfaction in guarding hidden treasure. . . .

Again, shall we, while manifestly ignoring riches and scorning sensual pleasures, court adulation and fulsome praise, vying with the fox of Archilochus [Poet, ranked by ancients as second only to Homer, flourished 650 B.C.] in cunning and craft? Of a truth there is nothing which the wise man must more guard against than the temptation to live for praise, and to study what pleases the crowd. Rather truth should be made the guide of one's life, so that if one must needs speak against all men, and be in ill-favor and in danger for virtue's sake, he shall not swerve at all from that which he considers right; . . .

Such a man now praises justice to those who esteem it, and now expresses opposite sentiments when he sees that wrong is in good repute; this is the fawner's trick. Just as the polypus is said to take the color of the ground upon which it lies, so he conforms his opinions to those of his associates.

X. To be sure, we shall become more intimately acquainted with these precepts in the sacred writings, but it is incumbent upon us, for the present, to trace, as it were, the silhouette of virtue in the pagan authors. For those who carefully gather the useful from each book are wont, like mighty rivers, to gain accessions on every hand. For the precept of the poet which bids us add little to little must be taken as applying not so much to the accumulation of riches, as of the various branches of learning. In line with this Bias [See Diogenes Laërtius i. 82-88] said to his son, who, as he was about to set out for Egypt, was inquiring what course he could pursue to give his father the greatest satisfaction: 'Store up means for the journey of old age.' By *means* he meant virtue, but he placed too great restrictions upon it, since he limited its usefulness to the earthly life. For if any one mentions the old age of Tithonus or of Arganthonius, or of that Methuselah who is said to have lacked but thirty years of being a millenarian, or even if he reckons the entire period since the creation, I will laugh as at the fancies of a child, since I look forward to that long, undying age, of the extent of which there is no limit for the mind of man to grasp, any more than there is of the life immortal. For the journey of this life eternal I would advise you to husband resources, leaving no stone unturned, as the proverb has it, whence you might derive any aid. From this task we shall not shrink because it is hard and laborious, but, remembering the precept that every man ought to choose the better life, and expecting that association will render it pleasant, we shall busy ourselves with those things that are best. For it is shameful to squander the present, and later to call back the past in anguish, when no more time is given.

In the above treatise I have explained to you some of the things which I deem the most to be desired; of others I shall continue to counsel you so long as life is allowed me. Now as the sick are of three classes, according to the degrees of their sickness, may you not seem to belong to the third, or incurable, class, nor show a spiritual malady like that of their bodies! For those who are slightly indisposed visit physicians in person, and those who are seized by violent sickness call physicians, but those who are suffering from a hopelessly incurable melancholy do not even admit the physicians if they come. May this now not be your plight, as would seem to be the case were you to shun these right counsels!

THE LONGER RULES

CHAPTER XV.—AT WHAT AGE SHOULD WE ALLOW PROFESSIONS TO BE MADE, AND WHEN MAY WE CONSIDER

THE PROFESSION OF VIRGINITY TO BE VALID? Since the Lord says: 'Suffer the children to come unto me' [Mark x. 14], and the Apostle praises him who from a babe has learned sacred letters [2 Tim. iii. 15], and elsewhere enjoins the bringing up of children in the nurture and admonition of the Lord [Eph. vi. 4], we judge every time, even that of early youth, to be fitting for the reception of novices. Those who are bereft of parents we accept without more ado, and become fathers of orphans after the example of Job's zeal [Job xxix. 12]; but such as are under their parents' control, when they are brought by them in person we receive in the presence of a number of witnesses, so as not to give a handle of accusation to those who seek one but rather to stop every unjust mouth that utters blasphemy against us. Accordingly we must receive them in accordance with the above principle, but it is expedient that they be not numbered and enrolled with the body of the brethren immediately—so that in case of failure on their part no reproaches fall on the life of godliness. They should be trained in all godliness as common children of the brotherhood, but both houses and meals, of boys and girls alike, should be kept separate, so that neither boldness nor excessive freedom towards their elders be engendered, but owing to rarity of meeting reverence for seniors be preserved. (Two other dangers will thus be obviated:) the encouragement to sin that arises from seeing the punishments inflicted on their elders for neglect of duty, should they ever happen to be careless, and the elation which often arises imperceptibly, when they see their seniors stumbling in matters where their own conduct is correct. For he that is childish in mind is no better than the child in years. So that it is not surprising if the same faults are often found in both. Furthermore it is inexpedient for the young through intercourse with their elders to show premature and rash zeal as regards those things in which their elders owing to their age are naturally decorous.

Therefore both for the above reasons and because it is seemly in other respects, it is right to keep the apartments of the boys and the elders separate. Besides, the house of the monks will not be disturbed by the repetition of lessons necessary for the young. But let the prayers ordered for daily use be common both to boys and elders. For both boys are commonly stirred up by the zeal of their elders and the seniors get no small help in prayer from the presence of children. But as regards sleep and rising, the hours of meals and their quantity and quality, let a separate regime and manner of life be prescribed suitable for boys. Let a monk of some age be put in

161

charge of them, surpassing the rest in experience and with a reputation for patience; able to correct the sins of youth with fatherly
compassion and skilled words, while he applies to each offence the
appropriate remedies, so that at the same time he both punishes the
sin and trains the soul in impassivity. For example: has a boy been
angry with his comrade? Then let him be compelled to appease
him and serve him in a manner befitting the offence. For the habit
of humbling oneself cuts out, so to speak, anger from the soul, just
as pride as a rule engenders it in us. Has a boy touched food between meals? Let him go without food for the best part of the day.
Has he been caught eating in a greedy or rude fashion? Let him be
debarred from food at meal time and be compelled to see the rest
eating as usual, so that he is punished by abstinence and taught to
behave himself. Has he uttered idle words, insulted his neighbour,
told lies, or said any other forbidden thing? Let him be disciplined
in the stomach and by enforced silence.

Moreover, their literary studies must be appropriate to their
ideal [. . . A completely different ideal of education for Christians
in the world is sketched in *Hom.* 22.]. Thus their teachers will use
the language of the Scriptures, and in place of myths will tell them
stories of wonderful deeds and educate them by maxims drawn
from the Proverbs and offer rewards for remembering both words
and things, so that they accomplish their purpose with delight and
mental relaxation finding neither tedium nor offence in their studies.
And such pupils being rightly trained will easily attain attention
and learn to avoid mental dissipation, if they are regularly examined
by their tutors as to their thoughts and wanderings of imagination.
For youth, being simple and guileless and unaccustomed to falsehood, confesses readily the secrets of the soul and, to avoid being
caught frequently dwelling on forbidden subjects, a boy will avoid
wrong thoughts and keep recalling his mind from them, fearing the
shame entailed by the scoldings he will receive.

So the soul must be led to practise good immediately and from
the outset, while it is still plastic and soft, pliable as wax, and easily
moulded by the shapes pressed upon it. So that when reason is
added and the power of discrimination it may run its course, starting from the elementary lessons it has already learned and the
examples of religion delivered to it; reason will suggest utilitarian
motives, habit will make success easy. . . .

One thing I omitted to say, and I had better add now. Since
some crafts must be practised from childhood, when any of the boys
seem fitted to learn, we do not forbid them to spend their days with

the teachers of the craft. But at night we restore them to their comrades, with whom also they must take their meals.

CHAPTER LIII.—HOW INSTRUCTORS IN ARTS ARE TO CORRECT DELINQUENT BOYS. Those who teach crafts, when their pupils' sin concerns the craft itself, must rebuke the fault themselves and correct the errors. But whatever sins argue moral perversion, such as disobedience and answering back, slothfulness at work, idle talk, falsehood, or whatever else of this sort is forbidden to the religious, such they must correct by taking the offenders to the superintendent of the common discipline, so that the amount and manner of the healing of their sins may be devised by him. For if rebuke is a doctoring of the soul, it is not every man's duty to rebuke, any more than to be a doctor, but only the duty of him to whom the Superior himself has entrusted it after full examination.

ST. JEROME c. 340–420

LETTER TO LAETA

[Laeta, the daughter-in-law of Paula, having written from Rome to ask Jerome how she ought to bring up her infant daughter (also called Paula) as a virgin consecrated to Christ, Jerome now instructs her in detail as to the child's training and education. Feeling some doubt, however, as to whether the scheme proposed by him will be practicable at Rome, he advises Laeta in case of difficulty to send Paula to Bethlehem where she will be under the care of her grandmother and aunt, the elder Paula and Eustochium. Laeta subsequently accepted Jerome's advice and sent the child to Bethlehem where she eventually succeeded Eustochium as head of the nunnery founded by her grandmother. The date of the letter is 403 A.D.]

3. . . . For, in answer to your prayers and those of the saintly Marcella, I wish to address you as a mother and to instruct you how to bring up our dear Paula, who has been consecrated to Christ before her birth and vowed to His service before her conception. . . . As then Paula has been born in answer to a promise, her parents should give her a training suitable to her birth. Samuel, as you know, was nurtured in the Temple, and John was trained in the wilderness. The first as a Nazarite wore his hair long, drank neither wine nor strong drink, and even in his childhood talked with God. The second shunned cities, wore a leathern girdle, and had for his meat locusts and wild honey [Matt. iii. 4.] . . .

4. Thus must a soul be educated which is to be a temple of God. It must learn to hear nothing and to say nothing but what belongs to the fear of God. It must have no understanding of unclean words, and no knowledge of the world's songs. Its tongue must be steeped while still tender in the sweetness of the psalms. Boys with their wanton thoughts must be kept from Paula: even her maids and female attendants must be separated from worldly associates. For if they have learned some mischief they may teach more. Get for her a set of letters made of boxwood or of ivory and called each by its proper name. Let her play with these, so that even her play

164

may teach her something. And not only make her grasp the right order of the letters and see that she forms their names into a rhyme, but constantly disarrange their order and put the last letters in the middle and the middle ones at the beginning that she may know them all by sight as well as by sound. Moreover, so soon as she begins to use the style upon the wax, and her hand is still faltering, either guide her soft fingers by laying your hand upon hers, or else have simple copies cut upon a tablet; so that her efforts confined within these limits may keep to the lines traced out for her and not stray outside of these. Offer prizes for good spelling and draw her onwards with little gifts such as children of her age delight in. And let her have companions in her lessons to excite emulation in her, that she may be stimulated when she sees them praised. You must not scold her if she is slow to learn but must employ praise to excite her mind, so that she be glad when she excels others and sorry when she is excelled by them. Above all you must take care not to make her lessons distasteful to her lest a dislike for them conceived in childhood may continue into her maturer years. The very words which she tries bit by bit to put together and to pronounce ought not to be chance ones, but names specially fixed upon and heaped together for the purpose, those for example of the prophets or the apostles or the list of patriarchs from Adam downwards as it is given by Matthew and Luke. In this way while her tongue will be well-trained, her memory will be likewise developed. Again, you must choose for her a master of approved years, life, and learning. A man of culture will not, I think, blush to do for a kinswoman or a highborn virgin what Aristotle did for Philip's son when, descending to the level of an usher, he consented to teach him his letters [Quintilian, Inst. I. i.]. Things must not be despised as of small account in absence of which great results cannot be achieved. The very rudiments and first beginnings of knowledge sound differently in the mouth of an educated man and of an uneducated. Accordingly you must see that the child is not led away by the silly coaxing of women to form a habit of shortening long words or of decking herself with gold and purple. Of these habits one will spoil her conversation and the other her character. She must not therefore learn as a child what afterwards she will have to unlearn. The eloquence of the Gracchi is said to have been largely due to the way in which from their earliest years their mother spoke to them [Quint. I. i.] Hortensius [the contemporary and rival of Cicero] became an orator while still on his father's lap. Early impressions are hard to eradicate from the mind. When once wool has been

165

dyed purple who can restore it to its previous whiteness? An un-used jar long retains the taste and smell of that with which it is first filled [Horace, Epist. I. ii. 69.]. Grecian history tells us that the imperious Alexander who was lord of the whole world could not rid himself of the tricks of manner and gait which in his child-hood he had caught from his governor Leonides [Quint. Inst. I. i.]. We are always ready to imitate what is evil; and faults are quickly copied where virtues appear unattainable. Paula's nurse must not be intemperate, or loose, or given to gossip. Her bearer must be respectable, and her foster-father of grave demeanour. When she sees her grandfather, she must leap upon his breast, put her arms round his neck, and, whether he likes it or not, sing Alleluia in his ears. She may be fondled by her grandmother, may smile at her father to shew that she recognizes him, and may so endear herself to everyone, as to make the whole family rejoice in the possession of such a rosebud. She should be told at once whom she has for her other grandmother and whom for her aunt; and she ought also to learn in what army it is that she is enrolled as a recruit, and what Captain it is under whose banner she is called to serve. Let her long to be with the absent ones and encourage her to make playful threats of leaving you for them.

5. Let her very dress and garb remind her to Whom she is promised. Do not pierce her ears or paint her face consecrated to Christ with white lead or rouge. Do not hang gold or pearls about her neck or load her head with jewels, or by reddening her hair make it suggest the fires of gehenna. Let her pearls be of another kind and such that she may sell them hereafter and buy in their place the pearl that is "of great price" [Matt. xiii. 46.]. . . .

7. When Paula comes to be a little older and to increase like her Spouse in wisdom and stature and in favour with God and man [Luke ii. 52.], let her go with her parents to the temple of her true Father but let her not come out of the temple with them. Let them seek her upon the world's highway amid the crowds and the throng of their kinsfolk, and let them find her nowhere but in the shrine of the scriptures [Luke ii. 43-46.], questioning the prophets and the apostles on the meaning of that spiritual marriage to which she is vowed. . . .

8. Let her not take food with others, that is, at her parents' table; lest she see dishes she may long for. Some, I know, hold it a greater virtue to disdain a pleasure which is actually before them, but I think it a safer self-restraint to shun what must needs attract you. Once as a boy at school I met the words: 'It is ill blaming what you

166

allow to become a habit.' Let her learn even now not to drink wine "wherein is excess" [Eph. v. 18.]. But as, before children come to a robust age, abstinence is dangerous and trying to their tender frames, let her have baths if she require them, and let her take a little wine for her stomach's sake [I Tim. v. 23]. Let her also be supported on a flesh diet, lest her feet fail her before they commence to run their course. But I say this by way of concession not by way of command; because I fear to weaken her, not because I wish to teach her self-indulgence. . . .

9. And let it be her task daily to bring to you the flowers which she has culled from scripture. Let her learn by heart so many verses in the Greek, but let her be instructed in the Latin also. For, if the tender lips are not from the first shaped to this, the tongue is spoiled by a foreign accent and its native speech debased by alien elements. You must yourself be her mistress, a model on which she may form her childish conduct. Never either in you nor in her father let her see what she cannot imitate without sin. Remember both of you that you are the parents of a consecrated virgin, and that your example will teach her more than your precepts. Flowers are quick to fade and a baleful wind soon withers the violet, the lily, and the crocus. Let her never appear in public unless accompanied by you. Let her never visit a church or a martyr's shrine unless with her mother. Let no young man greet her with smiles; no dandy with curled hair pay compliments to her. If our little virgin goes to keep solemn eves and all-night vigils, let her not stir a hair's breadth from her mother's side. She must not single out one of her maids to make her a special favourite or a confidante. What she says to one all ought to know. Let her choose for a companion not a handsome well-dressed girl, able to warble a song with liquid notes but one pale and serious, sombrely attired and with the hue of melancholy. Let her take as her model some aged virgin of approved faith, character, and chastity, apt to instruct her by word and by example. She ought to rise at night to recite prayers and psalms; to sing hymns in the morning; at the third, sixth and ninth hours to take her place in the line to do battle for Christ; and, lastly, to kindle her lamp and to offer her evening sacrifice. In these occupations let her pass the day, and when night comes let it find her still engaged in them. Let reading follow prayer with her, and prayer again succeed to reading. Time will seem short when employed on tasks so many and so varied.

10. Let her learn too how to spin wool, to hold the distaff, to put the basket in her lap, to turn the spinning wheel and to shape the

167

yarn with her thumb. Let her put away with disdain silken fabrics, Chinese fleeces, and gold brocades: the clothing which she makes for herself should keep out the cold and not expose the body which it professes to cover. Let her food be herbs and wheaten bread with now and then one or two small fishes. . . . Let her meals always leave her hungry and able on the moment to begin reading or chanting. I strongly disapprove—especially for those of tender years—of long and immoderate fasts in which week is added to week and even oil and apples are forbidden as food. I have learned by experience that the ass toiling along the high way makes for an inn when it is weary. . . .

11. When you go a short way into the country, do not leave your daughter behind you. Leave her no power or capacity of living without you, and let her feel frightened when she is left to herself. Let her not converse with people of the world or associate with virgins indifferent to their vows. Let her not be present at the wedding of your slaves and let her take no part in the noisy games of the household. . . .

12. Let her treasures be not silks or gems but manuscripts of the holy scriptures; and in these let her think less of gilding, and Babylonian parchment, and arabesque patterns, than of correctness and accurate punctuation. Let her begin by learning the psalter, and then let her gather rules of life out of the proverbs of Solomon. From the Preacher let her gain the habit of despising the world and its vanities. Let her follow the example set in Job of virtue and of patience. Then let her pass on to the gospels never to be laid aside when once they have been taken in hand. Let her also drink in with a willing heart the Acts of the Apostles and the Epistles. As soon as she has enriched the storehouse of her mind with these treasures, let her commit to memory the prophets, the heptateuch [i.e. Genesis, Exodus, Leviticus, Numbers, Deuteronomy, Joshua, Judges.], the books of Kings and of Chronicles, the rolls also of Ezra and Esther. When she has done all these she may safely read the Song of Songs but not before: for, were she to read it at the beginning, she would fail to perceive that, though it is written in fleshly words, it is a marriage song of a spiritual bridal. And not understanding this she would suffer hurt from it. Let her avoid all apocryphal writings, and if she is led to read such not by the truth of the doctrines which they contain but out of respect for the miracles contained in them; let her understand that they are not really written by those to whom they are ascribed, that many faulty elements have been introduced into them, and that it requires infinite

168

discretion to look for gold in the midst of dirt. Cyprian's writings let her have always in her hands. The letters of Athanasius [of these a large number are still extant. Over twenty of them are 'festal epistles' announcing to the churches the correct day on which to celebrate Easter] and the treatises of Hilary [these include commentaries on many parts of Scripture and a work on the Trinity] she may go through without fear of stumbling. Let her take pleasure in the works and wits of all in whose books a due regard for the faith is not neglected. But if she reads the works of others let it be rather to judge them than to follow them.

13. You will answer, 'How shall I, a woman of the world, living at Rome, surrounded by a crowd, be able to observe all these injunctions?' In that case do not undertake a burthen to which you are not equal. When you have weaned Paula as Isaac was weaned and when you have clothed her as Samuel was clothed, send her to her grandmother and aunt; give up this most precious of gems, to be placed in Mary's chamber and to rest in the cradle where the infant Jesus cried. Let her be brought up in a monastery, let her be one amid companies of virgins, let her learn to avoid swearing, let her regard lying as sacrilege, let her be ignorant of the world, let her live the angelic life, while in the flesh let her be without the flesh, and let her suppose that all human beings are like herself. . . .

LETTER TO GAUDENTIUS

[Gaudentius had written from Rome to ask Jerome's advice as to the bringing up of his infant daughter; whom after the religious fashion of the day he had dedicated to a life of virginity. Jerome's reply may be compared with his advice to Laeta (Letter CVII.) which it closely resembles. It is noticeable also for the vivid account which it gives of the sack of Rome by Alaric in A.D. 410. The date of the letter is A.D. 413.]

1. It is hard to write to a little girl who cannot understand what you say, of whose mind you know nothing, and of whose inclination it would be rash to prophesy. In the words of a famous orator "she is to be praised more for what she will be than for what she is" [Spes in ea magis laudanda est quam res. Cic. de Rep.]. For how can you speak of self-control to a child who is eager for cakes, who babbles on her mother's knee, and to whom honey is sweeter than any words? Will she hear the deep things of the apostle when all her delight is in nursery tales? Will she heed the dark sayings of the prophets when her nurse can frighten her by a frowning

169

face? Or will she comprehend the majesty of the gospel, when its splendour dazzles the keenest intellect? Shall I urge her to obey her parents when with her chubby hand she beats her smiling mother? For such reasons as these my dear Pacatula must read some other time the letter that I send her now. Meanwhile let her learn the alphabet, spelling, grammar, and syntax. To induce her to repeat her lessons with her little shrill voice, hold out to her as rewards cakes and mead and sweetmeats. She will make haste to perform her task if she hopes afterwards to get some bright bunch of flowers, some glittering bauble, some enchanting doll. She must also learn to spin, shaping the yarn with her tender thumb; for, even if she constantly breaks the threads, a day will come when she will no longer break them. Then when she has finished her lessons she ought to have some recreation. At such times she may hang round her mother's neck, or snatch kisses from her relations. Reward her for singing psalms that she may love what she has to learn. Her task will then become a pleasure to her and no compulsion will be necessary.

3a. . . . A girl should associate only with girls, she should know nothing of boys and should dread even playing with them. She should never hear an unclean word, and if amid the bustle of the household she should chance to hear one, she should not understand it. Her mother's nod should be to her as much a command as a spoken injunction. She should love her as her parent, obey her as her mistress, and reverence her as her teacher. She is now a child without teeth and without ideas, but, as soon as she is seven years old, a blushing girl knowing what she ought not to say and hesitating as to what she ought, she should until she is grown up commit to memory the psalter and the books of Solomon; the gospels, the apostles and the prophets should be the treasure of her heart. She should not appear in public too freely or too frequently attend crowded churches. All her pleasure should be in her chamber. She must never look at young men or turn her eyes upon curled fops; and the wanton songs of sweet voiced girls which wound the soul through the ears must be kept from her. The more freedom of access such persons possess, the harder is it to avoid them when they come; and what they have once learned themselves they will secretly teach her and will thus contaminate our secluded Danaë by the talk of the crowd. Give her for guardian and companion a mistress and a governess, one not given to much wine or in the apostle's words idle and a tattler, but sober, grave, industrious in spinning wool and one whose words will form her childish

170

mind to the practice of virtue. For, as water follows a finger drawn through the sand, so one of soft and tender years is pliable for good or evil; she can be drawn in whatever direction you choose to guide her. Moreover spruce and gay young men often seek access for themselves by paying court to nurses or dependants or even by bribing them, and when they have thus gently affected their approach they blow up the first spark of passion until it bursts into flame and little by little advance to the most shameless requests. And it is quite impossible to check them then, for the verse is proved true in their case: "It is ill rebuking what you have once allowed to become ingrained.". . .

4. The world sinks into ruin: yes! but shameful to say our sins still live and flourish. The renowned city, the capital of the Roman Empire, is swallowed up in one tremendous fire; and there is no part of the earth where Romans are not in exile. Churches once held sacred are now but heaps of dust and ashes; and yet we have our minds set on the desire of gain. We live as though we are going to die tomorrow; yet we build as though we are going to live always in this world. Our walls shine with gold, our ceilings also and the capitals of our pillars; yet Christ dies before our doors naked and hungry in the person of His poor. . . .

Such are the times in which our little Pacatula is born. Such are the swaddling clothes in which she draws her first breath; she is destined to know of tears before laughter and to feel sorrow sooner than joy. And hardly does she come upon the stage when she is called on to make her exit. Let her then suppose that the world has always been what it is now. Let her know nothing of the past, let her shun the present, and let her long for the future.

These thoughts of mine are but hastily mustered. For my grief for lost friends has known no intermission and only recently have I recovered sufficient composure to write an old man's letter to a little child. My affection for you, brother Gaudentius, has induced me to make the attempt and I have thought it better to say a few words than to say nothing at all. The grief that paralyses my will will excuse my brevity; whereas, were I to say nothing, the sincerity of my friendship might well be doubted.

THE MEDIEVAL
CHURCH

HRABANUS MAURUS, JOHN GERSON

THERE are several reasons why the medieval Church is not a gold mine for those who search for great documents on education proper. For centuries after the breakdown of the Roman Empire and the Migration of Nations human energy was absorbed in the sheer struggle for survival. What was left of intellectual activity mostly revolved around learning the rudiments of the "seven liberal arts" from second-hand sources, in the making of compilations, and in the writing of chronicles.

There are other reasons too for the relative silence of the medieval Church on educational matters. This Church was still much more an institution for the education of adults than for the education of the young. And this adult education was education in worship and ritual rather than formal training in literacy and secular knowledge. Probably not even a considerable portion of one per cent was schooled in the modern sense of the word. In addition, this schooling was transmission, for even in the ripe Middle Ages man lived in the shadow of the tradition, coming secularly from Aristotle, and religiously from Christ. His task was to interpret, not to change and add.

In the 12th century the external and cultural conditions of life improved, and one of the greatest and most rapidly ascending movements of thought began, the era of Christian Scholasticism. But even then the writings on education are negligible in comparison with the wealth and profoundness of theological thought. For example, Thomas Aquinas' *Concerning the Teacher* conceals more than it reveals the wisdom of the great religious philosopher, at least to the inexpert mind.

The following two selections come from the writings of Hrabanus Maurus, a priest born about 776 in Mainz, and John Gerson, who was the famous chancellor of the University of Paris around 1400. There is a charming simplicity in the mind of Hrabanus Maurus, who in all his books depends naively on older authorities. The simplicity in Gerson's tract *On Leading Children to Christ* is of a much higher nature. It is the simplicity of a man who despite all his scholastic learning and his fame as an ecclesiastical statesman knows that the best he still can do to merit the grace of the Lord is to teach and guide children.

"Let the little children come unto me . . ."

172

THE MEDIEVAL CHURCH

The selections from Maurus' *Education of the Clergy* are taken from *Great Pedagogical Essays, Plato to Spencer*, by F. V. N. Painter, published in New York by the American Book Company in 1905. The selections from Gerson's *Treatise on Leading Children to Christ* are taken from a translation of the Fourth Argument of Gerson's *Tractatus de Parvulis trahendis ad Christum*, made by the editor, based on *Joannis Gersonii . . . Opera Omnia*, Tomus Tertius, col. 285-291. This was published in Antwerp in 1706.

MAURUS c. 776–856

EDUCATION OF THE CLERGY

BOOK III.—I. An ecclesiastical education should qualify the sacred office of the ministry for divine service. It is fitting that those who from an exalted station undertake the direction of the life of the Church, should acquire fulness of knowledge, and that they further should strive after rectitude of life and perfection of development. They should not be allowed to remain in ignorance about anything that appears beneficial for their own information or for the instruction of those entrusted to their care. Therefore they should endeavor to grasp and include in their knowledge the following things: An acquaintance with Holy Scripture, the unadulterated truth of history, the derivative modes of speech, the mystical sense of words, the advantages growing out of the separate branches of knowledge, the integrity of life, that manifests itself in good morals, delicacy and good taste in oral discourse, penetration in the explanation of doctrine, the different kinds of medicine, and the various forms of disease. Any one to whom all this remains unknown, is not able to care for his own welfare, let alone that of others. . . .

II. The foundation, the content, and the perfection of all wisdom is Holy Scripture, which has taken its origin from that unchangeable and eternal Wisdom, which streams from the mouth of the Most High, which was begotten before every other creature through the Holy Spirit, which is a light incessantly beaming from the words of Holy Scripture. And when anything else deserves the name of wisdom it goes back in its origin to this one source of the wisdom of the Church. Every truth, which is discovered by any one, is recognized as true by the truth itself through the mediation of the truth; every good thing, which is in any way traced out, is recognized and determined as good by the good itself; all wisdom, which is brought to light by any one, is found to be wisdom by wisdom itself. And all that is found of truth and wisdom in the books of the philosophers of this world, dare be ascribed to nothing

174

else than just to truth and wisdom; for it was not originally invented by those among whose utterances it is found; it has much rather been recognized as something present from eternity, so far as wisdom and truth, which bring illumination to all with their instruction, have granted the possibility of such recognition. . . .

III. Now the Holy Scriptures, which come to the aid of the weakness of the human will, have, in dependence upon the one perfect language in which under favorable circumstances they might have spread over the whole globe, been widely circulated in the different languages of the translators, in order that they might be known to the nations unto salvation. Those who read them strive for nothing else than to grasp the thought and meaning of those who wrote them, in order thereby to fathom the will of God, at whose bidding and under whose direction, as we believe, they were written. But those who read superficially allow themselves to be deceived through manifold recurring passages, the sense of which is obscure, and the meaning of which is doubtful; they assign to what is read a meaning that does not belong to it; they seek errors where no errors are to be found; they surround themselves with an obscurity, in which they can not find the right path. I have no doubt that this has been so ordered by God's providence that the pride of man may be restrained through spiritual labor; in order that the knowledge of man may be divorced from pride, to which it easily falls a prey, and then loses its value entirely. . . .

IV. Above all it is necessary that he, who aims to attain the summit of wisdom, should be converted to the fear of the Lord, in order to know what the divine will bids us strive for and shun. The fear of the Lord fills us with the thought of our mortality and future death. With mortification of the flesh it nails, as it were, the movements of pride to the martyr cross of Christ. Then it is enjoined to be lowly in piety. Therefore we are not to raise any objection to the Holy Scriptures, either when we understand them and feel ourselves smitten by their words, or when we do not understand them, and give ourselves up to the thought that we can understand and grasp something better out of our own minds. We should remember that it is better and more conformable to truth, to believe what is written, even if the sense remains concealed from us, than to hold that for true which we are able to recognize by our own strength. . . .

XVIII. The first of the liberal arts is grammar, the second rhetoric, the third dialectic, the fourth arithmetic, the fifth geometry, the sixth music, the seventh astronomy.

Grammar takes its name from the written character, as the derivation of the word indicates [gramma i.e. written character, letter]. The definition of grammar is this: Grammar is the science which teaches us to explain the poets and historians; it is the art which qualifies us to write and speak correctly. Grammar is the source and foundation of the liberal arts. It should be taught in every Christian school, since the art of writing and speaking correctly is attained through it. How could one understand the sense of the spoken word or the meaning of letters and syllables, if one had not learned this before from grammar? How could one know about metrical feet, accent, and verses, if grammar had not given one knowledge of them? How should one learn to know the articulation of discourse, the advantages of figurative language, the laws of word formation, and the correct forms of words, if one had not familiarized himself with the art of grammar?

All the forms of speech, of which secular science makes use in its writings, are found repeatedly employed in the Holy Scriptures. Every one, who reads the sacred Scriptures with care, will discover that our [biblical] authors have used derivative forms of speech in greater and more manifold abundance than would have been supposed and believed. There are in the Scripture not only examples of all kinds of figurative expressions, but the designations of some of them by name; as, allegory, riddle, parable. A knowledge of these things is proved to be necessary in relation to the interpretation of those passages of Holy Scripture which admit of a twofold sense; an interpretation strictly literal would lead to absurdities. Everywhere we are to consider whether that, which we do not at once understand, is to be apprehended as a figurative expression in some sense. A knowledge of prosody, which is offered in grammar, is not dishonorable, since among the Jews, as St. Jerome testifies, the Psalter resounds sometimes with iambics, sometimes with Alcaics, sometimes chooses sonorous Sapphics, and sometimes even does not disdain catalectic feet. But in Deuteronomy and Isaiah, as in Solomon and Job, as Josephus and Origen have pointed out, there are hexameters and pentameters. Hence this art, though it may be secular, has nothing unworthy in itself; it should rather be learned as thoroughly as possible.

XIX. According to the statement of teachers, rhetoric is the art of using secular discourse effectively in the circumstances of daily life. From this definition rhetoric seems indeed to have reference merely to secular wisdom. Yet it is not foreign to ecclesiastical instruction. Whatever the preacher and herald of the divine law,

176

in his instruction, brings forward in an eloquent and becoming manner; whatever in his written exposition he knows how to clothe in adequate and impressive language, he owes to his acquaintance with this art. Whoever at the proper time makes himself familiar with this art, and faithfully follows its rules in speaking and writing, needs not count it as something blameworthy. On the contrary, whoever thoroughly learns it so that he acquires the ability to proclaim God's word, performs a good work. Through rhetoric anything is proved true or false. Who would have the courage to maintain that the defenders of truth should stand weaponless in the presence of falsehood, so that those, who dare to represent the false, should know how by their discourse to win the favor and sympathy of the hearers, and that, on the other hand the friends of truth should not be able to do this; that those should know how to present falsehood briefly, clearly, and with the semblance of truth, and that the latter, on the contrary, should clothe the truth in such an exposition that listening would become a burden, apprehension of the truth a weariness, and faith in the truth an impossibility?

XX. Dialectic is the science of the understanding, which fits us for investigations and definitions, for explanations, and for distinguishing the true from the false. It is the science of sciences. It teaches how to teach others; it teaches learning itself; in it the reason marks and manifests itself according to its nature, efforts, and activities; it alone is capable of knowing; it not only will, but can lead others to knowledge; its conclusions lead us to an apprehension of our being and of our origin; through it we apprehend the origin and activity of the good, of Creator and creature; it teaches us to discover the truth and to unmask falsehood; it teaches us to draw conclusions; it shows us what is valid in argument and what is not; it teaches us to recognize what is contrary to the nature of things; it teaches us to distinguish in controversy the true, the probable, and the wholly false; by means of this science we are able to investigate everything with penetration, to determine its nature with certainty, and to discuss it with circumspection.

Therefore the clergy must understand this excellent art and constantly reflect upon its laws, in order that they may be able keenly to pierce the craftiness of errorists, and to refute their fatal fallacies.

XXII. Arithmetic is the science of pure extension determinable by number; it is the science of numbers. Writers on secular science assign it, under the head of mathematics, to the first place, because it does not presuppose any of the other departments. Music, geometry, and astronomy, on the contrary, need the help of arithmetic;

without it they cannot arise or exist. We should know, however, that the learned Hebrew Josephus, in his work on Antiquities, Chapter VIII. of Book I., makes the statement that Abraham brought arithmetic and astronomy to the Egyptians; but that they as a people of penetrating mind, extensively developed from these germs the other sciences. The holy Fathers were right in advising those eager for knowledge to cultivate arithmetic, because in large measure it turns the mind from fleshly desires, and furthermore awakens the wish to comprehend what with God's help we can merely receive with the heart. Therefore the significance of number is not to be underestimated. Its very great value for an interpretation of many passages of Holy Scriptures is manifest to all who exhibit zeal in their investigations. Not without good reason is it said in praise of God, "Thou hast ordained all things by measure, number, and weight." [Book of Wisdom XI. 21.]

But every number, through its peculiar qualities, is so definite that none of the others can be like it. They are all unequal and different. The single numbers are different; the single numbers are limited; but all are infinite.

Those with whom Plato stands in especial honor will not make bold to esteem numbers lightly, as if they were of no consequence for the knowledge of God. He teaches that God made the world out of numbers. And among us the prophet says of God, "He forms the world by number." And in the Gospel the Saviour says, "The very hairs of your head are all numbered" [Matth. x. 30.]. . . . Ignorance of numbers leaves many things unintelligible that are expressed in the Holy Scripture in a derivative sense or with a mystical meaning.

XXIII. We now come to the discussion of geometry. It is an exposition of form proceeding from observation; it is also a very common means of demonstration among philosophers, who, to adduce at once the most full-toned evidence, declare that their Jupiter made use of geometry in his works. I do not know indeed whether I should find praise or censure in this declaration of the philosophers, that Jupiter engraved upon the vault of the skies precisely what they themselves draw in the sand of the earth.

When this in a proper manner is transferred to God, the Almighty Creator, this assumption may perhaps come near the truth. If this statement seems admissible, the Holy Trinity makes use of geometry in so far as it bestows manifold forms and images upon the creatures which up to the present day it has called into being, as in its adorable omnipotence it further determines the course of the stars, as it prescribes their course to the planets, and as it assigns to the fixed stars their unalterable position. For every excellent and well-ordered arrangement can be reduced to the special requirements of this science. . . .

This science found realization also at the building of the tabernacle and temple; the same measuring rod, circles, spheres, hemispheres, quadrangles, and other figures were employed. The knowledge of all this brings to him, who is occupied with it, no small gain for his spiritual culture.

XXIV. Music is the science of time intervals as they are perceived in tones. This science is as eminent as it is useful. He who is a stranger to it is not able to fulfil the duties of an ecclesiastical office in a suitable manner. A proper delivery in reading and a lovely rendering of the Psalms in the church are regulated by a knowledge of this science. Yet it is not only good reading and beautiful psalmody that we owe to music; through it alone do we become capable of celebrating in the most solemn manner every divine service. Music penetrates all the activities of our life, in this sense namely, that we above all carry out the commands of the Creator and bow with a pure heart to his commands; all that we speak, all that makes our hearts beat faster, is shown through the rhythm of music united with the excellence of harmony; for music is the science which teaches us agreeably to change tones in duration and pitch. When we employ ourselves with good pursuits in life, we show ourselves thereby disciples of this art; so long as we do what is wrong, we do not feel ourselves drawn to music. Even heaven and earth, as everything that happens here through the arrangement of the Most High, is nothing but music, as Pythagoras testifies that this world was created by music and can be ruled by it. Even with the Christian religion music is most intimately united; thus it is possible that to him, who does not know even a little music, many things remain closed and hidden. . . .

XXV. There remains yet astronomy which, as some one has said, is a weighty means of demonstration to the pious, and to the curious a grievous torment. If we seek to investigate it with a pure heart and an ample mind, then it fills us, as the ancients said, with great love for it. For what will it not signify, that we soar in spirit to the sky, that with penetration of mind we analyze that sublime structure, that we, in part at least, fathom with the keenness of our logical faculties what mighty space has enveloped in mystery! The world itself, according to the assumption of some, is said to have the shape of a sphere, in order that in its circumference it may be able

179

to contain the different forms of things. Thus Seneca, in agreement with the philosophers of ancient times, composed a work under the title, "The Shape of the World."

Astronomy, of which we now speak, teaches the laws of the stellar world. The stars can take their place or carry out their motion only in the manner established by the Creator, unless by the will of the Creator a miraculous change takes place. Thus we read that Joshua commanded the sun to stand still in Gibeon, that in the days of King Josiah the sun went backward ten degrees, and that at the death of the Lord the sun was darkened for three hours. We call such occurrences miracles, because they contradict the usual course of things, and therefore excite wonder. . . .

That part of astronomy, which is built up on the investigation of natural phenomena, in order to determine the course of the sun, of the moon, and stars, and to effect a proper reckoning of time, the Christian clergy should seek to learn with the utmost diligence, in order through the knowledge of laws brought to light and through the valid and convincing proof of the given means of evidence, to place themselves in a position, not only to determine the course of past years according to truth and reality, but also for further times to draw confident conclusions, and to fix the time of Easter and all other festivals and holy days, and to announce to the congregation the proper celebration of them.

XXVI. The seven liberal arts of the philosophers, which Christians should learn for their utility and advantage, we have, as I think, sufficiently discussed. We have this yet to add. When those, who are called philosophers, have in their expositions or in their writings, uttered perchance some truth, which agrees with our faith, we should not handle it timidly, but rather take it as from its unlawful possessors and apply it to our own use. . . .

GERSON 1363–1429

ON LEADING CHILDREN TO CHRIST.
FOURTH ARGUMENT.

In my defense. Also an admonition to allow me, the unworthy, to lead the children to Christ. ". . . *if a man be overtaken in a fault, ye which are spiritual, restore such an one in the spirit of meekness; considering thyself, lest thou also be tempted.*" (*Galatians*, vi, 1.)

A certain man who was a good judge of human customs once said: "The skill of skills is the guiding of souls." Yet there is nothing that the men of our time, even the clergy, approach with less skill than just this. The blind lead the blind. Nobody will be surprised to see this bring forth all kind of misery! Many persons consider it even below the dignity of a clergyman if, enjoying a good reputation or vested with high ecclesiastical honors, he devotes himself to this task, especially where children are concerned. This attitude has caused me also to become an object of public controversy and disdain, as in the public's eye I am of some importance in this question. Indeed, the Lord's disciples, at the time they had yet little understanding of things celestial, seem to have harbored the same absurd notion, in so far as they prevented children's being brought to the Lord. They thought it unworthy of Christ, their great master and doctor, to concern himself with such an insignificant matter. This very opinion shows their mistake, as does also the Lord's example and the above-quoted word of the Apostle, in which he admonishes the clergymen, to be the teachers of others, and to be endowed with the spirit of gentleness, and to look to themselves lest they be tempted. It is astonishing to think how rare such men are. Show me one, and I will tell you that he is spiritually inclined who judges everything according to spiritual principles; who has learned to suffer from the sufferings he had to undergo; who is not interested in himself, but in Jesus Christ; who is filled with love, humility, and piety to such an extent that vanity and greed find no room within him; who directs his thoughts towards Heaven; who though he were one of the angels of the Lord and conformed to their example, could be moved neither by praise nor by remonstrances; and who, for the sake of baser occupations neither turns from the high aim nor allows himself to be drawn into

181

ruinous impurity. For the rest: ". . . what is a man advantaged, if he gain the whole world, and lose himself, or be cast away?" (*Luke* ix, 25) What would be the benefit if he were not to listen to the command: "Take pity in thy soul, in order to please God." (*Jesus Sirach* xxx, 24) He, finally, is spiritually inclined, who is not attracted or tempted by any physical beauty, but who, entirely removed from all worldliness, dwells on the highest summit of reason, absorbed in keen conception of the character of the soul.

As long as you lack this, as long as either suspicions bring you suddenly unrest, or threats frighten you, as long as fame makes you proud or slander makes you despair: you are secularly and not spiritually inclined, you are not fitted to teach others in the spirit of gentleness. Thus it happens that I should have been reprimanded for my audacity rather than for my overgreat humility, in so far as I invade the domain of spiritually inclined men with the intention of teaching children who are ensnared in sin, just as though a turtle were to join the company of birds. Yet what shall I do? Some benevolent people think quite differently. They threaten me or the children lest they associate with me, they try this in many different ways; above all they think to demonstrate the justness of their procedure by a fourfold indication. They point out the difference in customs between me and the children; they mention that the dignity of my office reserves me for higher tasks; then they pretend that neither place nor time are suitable; and finally, they fear that the unusualness of the procedure would be condemned by envious people.

We shall discuss in a few words these various charges.

They maintain, and this is correct, that there is a great difference between my customs and those of my pupils. If nevertheless I want to be useful to them, then it is necessary that I adapt my habits to theirs, and that I step down in order to lift them up to my level.

"Love and majesty do not go together, nor have they common
             abode." (Ovid, *Metamorphoses* ii, 846-847).

But where there is no love, what good is instruction, as one neither likes to listen to it nor properly believes in the words heard, nor follows the commandments! Therefore it is best to forego all false dignity and to become a child among children. Yet, all sins have to be avoided, and all signs of impure love have to be held at bay. Also, it must be added, that our nature is inclined to resist, as Seneca proves. Our nature prefers guidance to force. Especially gifted people have the further characteristic—as the dumb creatures, the wild animals, and the birds teach us—that they are won and influ-

182

enced by flattery rather than by words of threat. Why after all, should extremely shy children hide their sins from one whom they neither hate nor fear? One who, in addition, has convinced them that he is benevolent, loyal, and friendly? But he will not be able to convince them unless he smiles kindly at the laughing ones, encourages those who play, praises their progress in learning, and when remonstrating, avoids all that is bitter or insulting. Then the children will feel he does not hate, but loves them like a brother.

Therefore, if one abolished the affable and encouraging inclination of a man towards children, he would weaken the effect of confession and the emotion it produces. I am convinced that the Apostle had this gentle spirit in his time. How else would he have become "all things to all men," in order to win Christ? If we were to except children, why should we become "a little child"? By what right, then, would he have commanded the fathers to treat their children humanely, not to arouse their wrath, and not to discourage them, if he had considered dealing with children something unworthy? But why should we lean upon arguments since the Apostle himself has expressed this: "We were," he says, "gentle among you, even as a nurse cherisheth her children?" (I *Thessalonians* ii, 7) Again, let us consider in what spirit the Apostle (*Galatians* vi, 1) commands us to educate sinners in the spirit of gentleness. And let us consider if even Christ, our law-giver, has not taught and acted before us in the same way. When loudly he had called: "Come unto me, all ye that labour and are heavy laden, and I will give you rest"; he added, as the case demanded: ". . . learn of me; for I am meek and lowly in heart." (*Matthew* xi, 28, 29.) We could take additional testimonies from the old stories of the fathers, where no means can be found that is more effective for the improvement and the purification of many than gentleness. "For there is nothing better among men than affability and gentleness," says the author of a comedy.[1] Did not John, who knew and announced divine secrets, kiss the hand of a cursed murderer and robber, so that he might win him? Who won the great teacher Augustinus as a beneficent star for the Church? Ambrosius. And by what means? By kindness and gentleness. Augustinus says of him: "I began to love him as a man, not as a teacher of truth, but as a man who manifested benevolence towards me." [2] O sage Ambrosius, true follower of the Lord!

[1] Terence, *The Brothers* V, iv 10-12: "From life itself I found that there be nothing better for man than gentleness and kindness."

[2] Augustinus, *Confessions* v, ch. 13: "And I began to love him, at the beginning, though, not as a teacher of truth, which I frankly despaired of in your church, but as a man who manifested benevolence towards me."

He did not say to Augustinus, who at that time was dominated by erroneous opinions: "Get thee hence, you are a sinner, a heretic, a blasphemer!" How much less would he have said similar things, in rising anger to the children who sought refuge with him!

If we further remember that Christ did nothing that was not full of meaning and dignity, we shall come to the opinion that his intention was not trifling when he called the children unto himself, while reproaching his beloved disciples for trying to keep them off. But then when the children came to him, he took them into his arms, laid his hands upon them and blessed them. (*Mark* x, 16) O gentle-hearted Jesus! Who, thereafter, would hesitate to be humble with children? Who would dare, in haughty pride, to boast of his greatness or his knowledge, and to despise the youth, ignorance, and weakness of children, if ". . . Christ came, who is over all, God blessed for ever." (*Romans* ix, 5) "In whom are hid all the treasures of wisdom and knowledge," (*Colossians* ii, 3) if in friendly gentleness you fold your holy arms about the children! Far, far be all pride from us. Also far be it from us to chase away indignantly the little ones! This sublime example of our Lord Jesus Christ overshadows even the humbleness for which the philosophers praise Socrates. For, after the business of the day, he was not ashamed to seek recreation by playing with the children in riding on a hobby-horse. O if the critical "Catoes" of our time had seen him! How would they have laughed at him! Yet, in the freedom of play we never let ourselves go so far as not to call detestable any impudence or shamelessness in bearing, word, or touch.

It is another kind of humbleness in the service of the Lord that David danced, naked, before the Ark of the Covenant and considered himself base in his own eyes; it is a different kind of self-humiliation, if one aims solely at the relaxation of the mind.

The first kind of humbleness is always the best; it allows no excess, and I can find no place where the word of *Jesus Sirach* iii, 18, also confirmed by Cicero in his work *On Offices*,[3] could be more suitably applied. The proverb reads: "The greater thou art, the more humble thyself." Therefore, Christ, who wanted to teach his disciples this kind of humbleness by word and example, gives them the following command: ". . . whosoever will be great among you, let him be your minister." (Matthew xx, 26) And further we see it from the quotation with which we started: "Whosoever shall not receive the kingdom of God as a little child, he shall not enter

---

[3] Cf. Cicero, *De Officiis* i, 26: "Those who ask that the higher we stand, the more affable we shall become, demand the right thing."

therein." (*Mark* x, 15) I say it before God and I do not lie thereby: for the past three years I have listened to the confessions of many little boys, and among those who confessed, were several already somewhat mature; they would never have confessed their sins to anybody who did not humble himself towards them and question them thoroughly, even if it were in the moment of death and if they deserved damnation. Therefore, let us admit the effect of gentleness and the results of careful examination and artful zeal in questions and admonitions, but how much more effective they are with the aid of God to whom we appeal, for whose help and mercy we hope.

I have also known some experienced men who have been father-confessors for many years. They have assured me that they have never or hardly ever found a man addicted to vices, who had ever before confessed them to anybody, and such people would not have confessed now, if the father confessors had not treated them with great caution and gentleness, if they had not, so to speak, cheated them with "pious delusion." About this topic I have, as I remember, written another essay; lately I have published in French a treatise about the recognition of such mistakes.[4]

I will deal more shortly with the three other objections. For I believe that I have sufficiently pointed out the dignity of my office or the rank which I hold as a teacher.

But as regards the opinion held by some that it is my duty to devote my energy to greater things, I do not know if there be anything greater to which to devote my modesty more profitably than, with the help of God, to snatch souls from the very doors of Hell and to implant such souls, as it were, once more in the children, or to water a not inconsiderable part of the garden of the Church. It is the children of whom I am thinking, bearing in mind that Christ gives them growth. But I am assured that by preaching publicly I should reach this aim in a more splendid manner. It may be that this will cause a greater stir, but in my opinion it will not have more effect and will not bear better fruit. As to the first point, it is Christ who puts us to shame in our pride, if we do not open the lips of wisdom except in the presence of many listeners. He taught by speaking at length to the Samaritan woman, and to her alone. But I will not deny that I should neglect the duty imposed by the dignity of the pulpit, if, in order to serve the profit of others, I should prove unworthy in the fulfillment of this duty. But in the absence of such a duty, as is usually the case, who will blame my

[4] *Opera*, Tomus ii, 446 f.: *Tractatus de arte audiendi confessiones.* (Preserved only in Latin.)

wholesome activity, since nobody would dare to raise an accusation against me, if I were to enjoy play or rest under these circumstances?

In a previous argument I have dealt in detail with the third accusation namely, that of the unsuitability of time and place. There can be no place more suitable, and more nearly above all suspicion, than the Church, open to everybody. Thereby, one avoids the proverb: "For every one that doeth evil hateth the light." (*St. John*, iii, 20).

Christ's command, too, reads to the effect: "Let your light so shine before men, that they may see your good works," (*Matthew* v, 16) and that one puts his candle in a candlestick. If others find this annoying by considering such action ostentatious, vain boasting, passion for glory, play-acting, hypocrisy, or anything similar, let them take care what they are saying. True, this is an offence which is being taken, but not offered. It is an offence which Pharisees take but not the children. Therefore, it has to be rejected, because neither the action proper, nor the circumstances under which the action is carried out, harbor anything that could cause spiritual damage. Besides, it must not surprise us that the beam of light, issuing from a good work, benefits healthy eyes, but is a nuisance and hateful to watering, squinting and inflamed eyes. "We are unto Good a sweet savour of Christ!" exclaims the Apostle. And what does he add? "To the one we are the savour of death unto death; and to the other the savour of life unto life." (II *Corinthians* ii, 15, 16) Whosoever observes how great the harvest of the Lord is and how few are the laborers—(I am speaking of capable laborers, for there are plenty of the other kind, and they are here, as Horace says, "to consume the fruits of the earth"—he will see that at no day, at no hour, at no place must such work be left undone.

As to the fourth charge, I will not deny that my activity has not been exercised by my predecessors in my office. I console myself with the words of the comedy: "As many people, so many opinions!"[5] If one were not free to start something new and excellent, the state would be in a bad way,—nay, if the state did not permit that way, it would perish. And yet, this enterprise is neither outstanding, nor exceptional, if with the permission or at the order of the bishop of the diocese, (who is the master of his harvest,) one has been commanded to this harvest, which may be reaped now in one, now in another manner. Now, after having obtained this permission, I am protected by the word of Christ: "Pray ye therefore

[5] Terence, *Phormio* II. Cf. Horace, *Satir.* II, i: "As of the heads, there are also thousands of opinions."

the Lord of the harvest, that he will send forth labourers into his harvest." (*Matthew* ix, 38) The same is found in the words of Isaiah (vi, 8) when to the question: "Whom shall I send and who will go for us?" he answers: "Here am I; send me."

There is nothing irregular or illegal in my action, because I have obtained permission from my superior, and because I do not undertake or suggest to listen to the confession of boys without informing their teachers of it. Finally, the Chancellor of the Church of Paris, be it by virtue of his official position, or at the command of the Apostolic Chair, has a not inconsiderable duty of supervision over the schools of Paris or many of them and their pupils. But what could be more suitable for such care than the pious decency of good manners?

However, to repeat what has already been said, friends raise the objection that my enemies will blame the novelty of the matter by pointing out either the curiosity, or the conceit, or the uselessness, or a too great superficiality, of this or that. This now, dear friends, is nothing new to me. I have reflected a good deal about all this and turned it over in my mind. For what kind of activity would be that of a well-known man who has remained free from blame or from false or absurd criticism? Yet, I swear by the salvation for which all of us hope, and I testify to it before the terrible chair of judgment of the just Lord—since nobody knows what is in man, except the spirit of man, which is in him,—that, according to the word of Christ, my work may be known by my fruits. And if perhaps they have found something false, shameless, ignoble in my teaching or my actions, yet I do not yield, I would rather be considered a wolf in sheep-clothing. But if the fruits of good work are apparent from without, I ask you not to condemn the inside of the tree with malevolence, else one would fall into the sin of thoughtless condemnation of his neighbor and one harms the children thereby, not rarely preventing their being led to Christ. Everyone, whoever he be, has to carry his load; I shall go free. And those who observe me I would beg to consider how much confidence I have in this work, because I have a good conscience. And I have and I invoke the testimony of the children who by their very nature are not apt to conceal anything.

This about my critics. But now I turn to the children, confident in the word of wisdom that "who is simple, let him turn in hither" (*Proverbs* ix, 4) without fear and trembling. Let everyone, no matter who he be, at least listen to the good admonitions from my lips. If I claim this virtue for myself, I do so not for myself, but for the

187

Lord. I shall lead him to the good, if I can; especially if I can make him examine, with a sorrowful soul, all the years of his life, and make him sweep out his mind with the broom of his own tongue. To do this, or anything else, I shall not force anyone against his will. Furthermore, I shall not try to ask for things that shall not be revealed; also, I shall not persuade him to reveal the secrets of his companions,—on the contrary, I shall prevent it! Further, nobody shall doubt that in every respect I shall preserve unbroken the seal of confession. I know how much confession is protected. I hope that those who confess will remain silent about themselves and me, and that they will not let themselves be persuaded by the silly and wrong curiosity of others, to do otherwise.

But perhaps there is one who is afraid of the severity of the penalty. There is no cause for this fear because I do not impose a penalty on the unwilling. I prefer the example of William of Paris,[6] and will rather send men to purgatory with a small penalty, voluntarily fulfilled, than cast them into hell with an unfulfilled penalty imposed against their will. Whosoever comes to me conscious of his sins, no matter how grave they are, he may say with David in deep contrition: "I have sinned." I will add immediately: "The Lord hath put away thy sin." (II *Samuel* xii, 13)

Finally I am convinced that penitence is perfected if the sin is wholeheartedly detested and cast off in the act of confession. Some one else may perhaps think that I hate and despise those whose confessions I have heard. Nothing is more erroneous! Rather, I will love him as a faithful son in Christ, further as a man who, as I know, fears God and has become good and pure, and further as a man who has entrusted himself completely to my loyalty, so that he revealed to me the ugly wounds of his soul, which perhaps he would never have shown to his loving parents. And thus I feel in my heart —truth knows it—how I am inclined to be more friendly and loving towards those whom I see liberated from great and serious peril of sin than towards those who suffer from less serious wounds. There has never, with my will, remained in my heart a trace of revenge or hatred during somebody's confession of sin, were it even the murder of his own parents. I know well that those who confess cannot at once overcome all reluctance and shame; but this is neither necessary nor useful. Reason, at last, will conquer shame, and thereafter this embarrassment will contribute not a little toward diminishing the penalty. Someone will perhaps complain to me:

[6] The author refers probably to William of Occam, who taught theology and philosophy at Paris.

"My mind is cold and unbelieving; what, then, do I profit from confession?" And if this is true, then he should hurry all the more ardently to the warming talk with God. Come to his fire; you will be warmed more than enough. Sometimes I see many who at the beginning are cold or even avoid or mock such a talk about their sins; but they go away warmed, comforted, and shedding tears. I frequently see such change. Once I felt such a worldly inclination when I wanted to persuade my own sisters to permanent celibacy. Yet, often I felt a deep conflict between my plans and ideas and the power of custom; the goal, which in my piety I had tried to reach, presented itself to me as something contradictory to tradition; I hesitated and changed my opinion and I almost tried to give up my sacred intention by turning my feet backwards, till finally, with God's kindly help, my eyes turned from the earth to heaven, from this death to life, from the flesh to eternity, till taught by reason and enlightened by the light of faith, I remembered the proverb: "Vanity of vanities; and all is vanity." (*Ecclesiastes* i, 2) Then I breathed, and was comforted and strengthened. All the more I want to admonish every one to recognize clearly what is right and pious and to obey pure truth instead of the talks of the crowd and the error of tradition. Let them not aim at what their hearts feel at the moment, but at what they ought to feel.

For the rest, I have the habit, and will not deny it, of advising those who confess to me to observe four things. With regard to their transgressions, I hate it above all if they are given to lies, to perjury, to slander, and further, if their hands are made to apply force and robbery, also lustful and unnatural touch, which is punished by worldly laws. First, they should guard as far as possible against giving others occasions to perdition or to sin; for such actions are of the devil. There is a good command: "*Si non caste, tamen caute*" (if not chaste, yet discreet), that means secret and alone, without offense or harm to anyone else. The second is that they endeavor to lead to betterment those whom they formerly tempted, or their companions in sin, or, in their stead, others, as far as they can do so unobtrusively, so that they themselves, who formerly did the devil's work now do the works of the angels. The third is that if they have sinned again—as weak human beings do— they should always, considering time and place, use confession as a remedy; confession is of no use—as I prove again and again—if it has not been a complete one, and if the confessor has not enumerated and explained all the sins he remembers, stressing accompanying details, and above all those that change the kind of sin. The

189

fourth point is—although I do not impose this as an obligation, but rather as an admonition—that they take up as their duty a regular but not too strenuous exercise for all the rest of their lives, not only in order to remind them of their sins, but also as a satisfaction for the properly confessed sins, and also as a safeguard against future sins. Hereby, I make it a habit to make them pray daily two "Lord's Prayers" and two "Ave Marias," the one in the morning, the other in the evening, and that, if possible, on their knees. But I seldom make a change in the arrangements of these exercises, according to the seriousness and the difference of the trespasses, as this is seldom carried out, and as such a change can also be made with other secret exercises of penalty. If, by doing so, I treat those free from sin and those laden with sin in an equal manner, I wish that the innocents would not complain about this. Their obligations are not smaller, since God has taken them under his protection and has prevented them from becoming equal to the sinners.

In order to help children to remember more easily this fourfold observation I have indulged in the art of poetry:

> Neither by deed nor by word shalt ever thou tempt the others:
> You are guilty enough, if corrupted yourself.
> Have you others corrupted by wicked doings and words,
> Secretly strive to guide them back to the path of right.
> Let not shame prevent your confessing all of your sins,
> Naming distinctly them all; confession, nothing else avails.
> If of confession you think, 'gainst relapse it will easily guard you;
> Therefore a marker think up, which of confession reminds.

And finally: "How long ye simple one, will ye love simplicity?" (*Proverbs* i, 22) "How long will you love vanity, and seek after leasing?" (*Psalm* iv, 2) Come confidingly! There is no snare laid on the path; no snake lurks in the grass. We shall profit from a mutual exchange of spiritual goods, because I have no desire for your worldly goods. I offer you instruction, you pay me with prayers; rather, we will pray mutually for each other's salvation. Thus we all shall bring joy to our guardian-angels, on whose day I am writing this. In this manner perhaps—but I do not want to say perhaps, but in certain hope—we will find mercy by our heavenly father, if on the way to him we obey his voice: I, by admonitions, you, by following them. There will not be lack of embracing, thanks, and devotion, giving us comfort in our present misery, and this will be followed by everlasting unison in complete glory. To this unity Jesus invites all of us who shall be children in the spirit; he wants us to answer his call in everlasting enthusiasm: "Suffer the little children to come unto me!" (*Mark* x, 14)

190

ISLAM

ISLAM

ALTHOUGH there were many good sides to the life of medieval man, he had to endure endless feudal fights, the continual struggle between the emperors and the popes, and the persecutions of heretics; but probably his greatest concern was the menace he felt from the Islamic world. In the West he was threatened by the Moors who for centuries occupied large parts of Spain, and in the East by the Turks who pushed from Asia Minor toward the Byzantine Empire. But much though medieval man hated the followers of Mohammed as heretics and political enemies, he could not help but admire parts of their culture, which in many respects was superior to his own. Cities such as Granada and Toledo in Spain, Baghdad in Mesopotamia, and Cairo in Egypt, were in medieval times centers of wealth, luxury, and higher learning. Without the Arabs much of the Greek philosophical tradition would have been lost to the world; in all likelihood, the medieval Christians found a model for their universities in the colleges of the Moors; in addition they served as middlemen between the Western world and India, where they had founded a powerful and highly cultured empire.

According to all we know, the defect of Arabic or Moslem education was that it concentrated almost exclusively on higher learning, and that it was, with few exceptions, theological, or, at best, historical, mathematical, and philosophical. Little attention was given to empirical research, except in certain fields of medicine. In all these respects Moslem learning was not different from Christian medieval scholasticism, but it was bound to fall behind when, with the coming of the Renaissance and of empirical science, Western scholarship opened up new avenues of mental development. With the fall of Baghdad to the Mongols in 1258 and the defeat of the Moorish principalities in Spain, ending with the capitulation of Granada to the Christians in 1492, also the cultural superiority of Islam was finished. The Turks, who continued their conquests up to the seventeenth century, were neither able nor willing to carry on the great tradition of Moslem learning.

The following quotation is taken from the essay *My Child* by the Arabian philosopher and theologian Ghazali, or Algazel (1058-1111), who taught Moslem theology at Baghdad, realized the incapacity of human reason if confronted with the great mysteries of God, immortality, and eternity, and tried to overcome the menace of scepticism by mysticism and an ascetic life. I have translated from Hammer-Purgstall, *O Kind! die berühmte ethische Abhandlung Ghasali's*, Arabisch und deutsch, Wien, Gedruckt bei U. Strauss' sel. Witwe, 1838.

The second quotation is chosen from the *Universal History* by Ibn Khaldoun (1332-1406), who is considered by some historians "the greatest intellect of his century." In his monumental work, which is mainly a history of the Berbers, Ibn Khaldoun attempted to explain the development of civilization with reference to intellectual, social, and climatic conditions. Thus he anticipated by four and five centuries the later works of Vico, Montesquieu, Herder, and Taine.

Historical Prolegomena was translated by the editor from *Prolégomènes Historiques d' Ibn Khaldoun*. Notices et extraits des Manuscrits de la Bibliothèque Impériale et autres Bibliothèques. Publiés par l' Institut Impérial de France, Tome XX, Paris, Imprimerie Impériale, 1865. The selection appears on page 425 and following pages, page 439, and page 446 and following pages.

AL-GHAZALI

O CHILD

In the name of God, the ever kind and ever pitying,

1. Know, my child and admired friend (may God prolong your life in His obedience and may He lead you on the path of His friends!) In the message of the Prophet (Whom God may bless with His Grace) you will find many pearls of wisdom . . . ; if you have His counsel you do not need mine, and if you have not been blessed with His wisdom what have you acquired during the past years?

2. O child, above all that which the messenger of God . . . has told his people, cherish this word: It is a sign of God's alienation from his servant if his servant begins to be occupied with things which are not his; a man who has lost an hour of his life in something other than that for which he has been created will feel the biting of his conscience on the day of his resurrection; he who is more than forty and has not more good than evil on his side will have his place prepared in eternal fire. This counsel is enough for those who profess the true knowledge.

3. O child, the counsel is easy but it is difficult to follow, for it is contrary to the taste of the man who follows his lusts; the things forbidden are dear to the heart especially of the one who seeks only the external side of knowledge, who is occupied with his own self, or who thinks of a great career as a judge and of the praise of the world. For such a man believes that mere erudition (without corresponding action) will be sufficient cause for his salvation and liberation; this is the belief of the philosophers. . . . But, thus says the messenger of God (Whom God may bless with His Grace), more than all other men will be punished at the day of resurrection the learned man whose knowledge has not helped him in the eyes of the Almighty.

8. O child, you may live as long as you wish yet your death will come; love what you wish, you will be separated from it; do what you wish, and you will have your reward for it. . . .

10. O child, knowledge without action is insanity, but action without knowledge is not action. Know that all knowledge can not

195

save you from sin and will not make you obedient, and will not free you from the fire of hell, unless you really act according to your knowledge.

.　.　.　.　.

17. We say that those who walk the path of truth need four things: the first, true faith in which there is no change, second, sincere repentance after which there is no return to sinfulness, third, the satisfaction of one's enemies so that none of them can ask anything from you, fourth, the acquisition of the knowledge of the law in so far as it is necessary for the fulfillment of God's commandments. You ought also to know of the future world, for you need it for your salvation. More than this is not necessary.

.　.　.　.　.

18. O child, if you act according to this tradition you do not need much knowledge, but contemplate [another story which is the following.] Hatim the deaf was one of the companions of Shakik of Balch (may God have pity on each). Shakik asked him one day, "You have now been my friend for thirty years, what have you acquired during this time?" Hatim answered, "I have acquired eight useful insights which are sufficient for me because from them I expect my liberation and salvation." Shakik said, "What are they?" And Hatim replied, "The first useful insight is: I have observed the people and have seen that each of them has one with whom he is friendly and loving; some accompany their friend through his last sickness and some to the edge of the grave. Then they all return and leave him single and alone, and none of them goes with him into the grave. I thought about it and said to myself: The best friend of man is one who follows him into the grave and stays there with him. I have found nothing but good deeds which I have chosen for my friends that they may be the light and friends in my grave and not desert me.

"The second useful insight is: I have seen men who follow their lusts and are anxious to satisfy their desires, and I thought about the word of God: But who fears the majesty of his Lord, and refrains his soul from lust, verily, he shall have the Paradise as his dwelling-place. I understood that the Koran has the real truth, thus I prepared myself to oppose my emotions. I girded myself for the battle with them until they voluntarily submitted to the commands of God.

"The third useful insight is: I have seen how everybody struggles to collect the goods of the world in order to preserve and keep them

196

in his hand; then I thought about the words of the Lord: that which is with you will pass away, that which is God's will remain. Then I turned my appetites away from the world toward the face of God the Highest and distributed my goods among the poor that they might serve me before God the Highest.

"The fourth useful insight is: I have seen some who believe that nobility and honor are judged by the size of their people and tribe, and they are proud of it; others believe that nobility and honor depend on the wealth of goods and positions, and the number of children of whom they can boast; others believe that nobility and honor come from the exploitation of men, their suppression, and from shedding their blood; and others believe that nobility and honor may be acquired by spending and wasting one's goods. Then I thought about the word of the Highest: The most worthy in the eyes of God is he who fears Him most. So I chose the fear of God; I believed that the Koran has a truth and that the opinions and illusions of men are vain and perishable.

"The fifth useful insight is: I have seen that some criticized the others; one blackmails the other, and I have found that this springs from the envy of others' good offices and knowledge. Then I thought of the word of God the Highest: We have distributed their subsistence among them in this world's life. Then I understood that the distribution from God the Highest comes from eternity and I envied nobody and was content with what God the Highest had given me.

"The sixth useful insight is: I have seen that people make enemies for many causes and intentions. Then I thought of the word of God the Highest: Satan is your enemy and hold him for such. And I knew that I was not permitted to make enemies except Satan.

"The seventh useful insight is: I have seen how each of us labors and struggles for food and sustenance so that he falls into temptation and does deeds forbidden, humiliates himself, and degrades himself. Then I thought of the words of the Highest: There is no animal on earth whose food does not depend on God. Then I knew that my food was with God and that He guarantees it, and I devoted myself to His service and cut off my greed for all which did not come from him.

"The eighth useful insight is: I have seen that each of us leans on one thing created, some on the world and money, some on gold and property, some on craft and art, and some on creatures of their own kind. Then I thought of the word of God the Highest: For him who puts his faith in God He will be all-sufficient, for God will attain his purpose, and God has assigned its destiny to everything. Trust in God, He will not mislead thee, He will reward you."

Then Shakik said, "God has led you with His wisdom, O Hatim; I have read the Pentateuch, the Psalms, the Gospel, and the Koran, and have found that these four books all turn around the same eight useful insights, and he who acts accordingly acts according to these four books."

IBN KHALDOUN

HISTORICAL PROLEGOMENA[1]

SECTION 60.—ABOUT THE SCIENCES AND THEIR DIFFERENT BRANCHES; ABOUT INSTRUCTION, ITS METHODS AND PROCEDURES, AND EVERYTHING CONNECTED WITH IT. . . . The introduction deals with reflection, the faculty which distinguishes man from other animals, which leads him to work for his subsistence in competition with his kind; which directs his attention toward the Being which he must adore and toward the revelations which the prophets have brought to us. It is by virtue of reflection that God has placed man in the position of subjecting all lower animals to himself and to subject them to his power; it is also reflection which has secured man's superiority over most of creation.

ABOUT REFLECTION

In order to understand the nature of reflection one must first know that it makes use of perception, which is the act by which the perceptive creature becomes conscious of that which is outside of him. Of all creatures the animals are the only ones which enjoy this faculty: they perceive external objects by means of the senses with which God has endowed them. There are five: hearing, seeing, smelling, tasting, and touching. The faculty of reflection . . . uses . . . certain powers which, situated in the ventricles of the brain, seize the forms of things, turn them into comprehension, and give them new forms by means of abstraction. Reflection . . . together with the faculty of comprehension, sorts and combines the sense impressions . . .

The faculty of reflection has different degrees of intensity: in the first place it gives us an understanding of the order of things as we find them in nature and human society so that, by the use of his own power, man can achieve the results he wants. This sort of reflection is composed, to a large degree, of concepts or simple ideas and is called *discerning intelligence*. With the help of this, man

---

[1] In translating parts of Ibn Khaldoun's treatise on reflection from a French translation, the editor feels somewhat like a medieval scholastic who—as well as he could—translated Aristotle into Latin from unreliable Arabic translations; especially since Ibn Khaldoun, in all likelihood, was influenced by the Arabic tradition of Aristotle. Yet, with all its drawbacks, this rather free translation may serve as a source of information until the English speaking world possesses a scholarly edition of Ibn Khaldoun.

procures the things which are useful, for instance, his sustenance, and avoids that which may do him harm. Reflection of the second degree of intensity teaches man to receive opinions and rules of conduct which he must observe in his transactions and in the government of his fellowmen. To a large extent, they are composed of affirmations or propositions, the validity of which gradually becomes verified by experience. One designates this kind of reflection as *experiential intelligence*. In the third degree of intensity reflection arrives at the real or hypothetical knowledge of things. For this it searches behind the senses and no act attaches itself to the things discovered. This is called *speculative intelligence*. It consists of concepts and affirmation combined according to a very particular manner and according to certain special conditions; thus it furnishes other insights of the class of concepts or the class of affirmations. Combining these insights with others, speculative intelligence produces more new insights. In the last result it forms a general idea of things existing according to their species, their classes, and their primary and secondary causes. In this way reflection finally completes itself and becomes pure intelligence and perceptive mind. That is that which one calls the *veritable nature of man*.

SECTION 60.—INSTRUCTION IS A PART OF THE ARTS. In order to acquire trained knowledge, in order to possess certain information, and to make oneself the master of it, one must have acquired the faculty of understanding the basic principles on which a particular branch of knowledge is founded. One must have studied the problems which belong to it and have acquainted oneself with its foundations and the character of all its ramifications. One does not become master of a branch of knowledge as long as one does not possess the faculty of which we are speaking here and which one must not confuse with that of listening and retention. We see sometimes that a problem of knowledge is comprehended similarly well both by a man versed in that matter and by a simple beginner, by the most erudite savant, and by a man of the people who has not received any instruction. But the faculty in question (understanding the basic principles) can be found only with the savant and instructed man; nobody else possesses it, and that shows that we must regard it as completely different for mere comprehension . . .

Because all corporal objects must be perceived by the senses their acquisition can only be achieved by instruction. Here is the reason why among the people of all countries and all generations one believes that in each science and each art the system of instruction is based on the authority and example of a very famous doctor. The differences which exist among the various systems of instruction with respect to technical terms prove that instruction itself has become a part of the arts. In effect, each of the most illustrious teachers in every field of scholarship had a particular terminology just as that which can still be observed with the professors of all arts. Consequently the technical terms are not a real part of true knowledge, for if this were so all the teachers would have only one and the same system of terminology. But look what differences exist between the terms employed by the ancients and those adopted by the moderns in all kinds of instruction, be it scholastic theology, or the fundamental principles of jurisprudence, or Arabic grammar, or law. And it is the same with any branch of knowledge one may begin to study; every teacher avails himself of a different terminology. This shows that the various terminologies employed in instruction represent as many arts though knowledge in itself is one. . . .

The talent of teaching, of practicing any art, and that of acting with ease in different circumstances, depending upon customs, augment the vigor of intelligence. They also give a high degree of clarity to the human mind because they are to the same degree faculties which influence the soul. We have already said that the soul is formed by means of perceptions and the faculties which cooperate with them. The sagacity of the Oriental peoples has been augmented by the impressions of their various cultural achievements on their soul. To believe that this sagacity is the result of a real difference in the nature of men is an error which only a vulgar man is able to commit. To be sure, if one compares a city dweller with an inhabitant of a desert one will discover in the first a mind endowed with penetration and sagacity. Therefore the peasant feels inferior in nature and intelligence to the city dweller. However, he deceives himself. The superiority of the latter comes from the perfect acquisition of the faculties which facilitate the exercise of the various arts and from the observation of the customs imposed upon him by the usage of habits of a sedentary life; all these are things of which the man of the desert has no idea. When people understand the practice of arts . . . all the individuals who miss them imagine that the other owes them to the superior nature of his intelligence and that the mentality of the inhabitants of the desert is inferior in organization and nature to the city dweller. But this is not the case.

201

THE HUMANIST EVOLUTION

AENEA SILVIO 1405–1464

WHEN we speak of the Renaissance we think of Bramante, Michelangelo, the Medici, of the great condottieri, and lives full of adventure. Not much of this greatness is reflected in the pedagogy of the Renaissance. It may be totally incorrect to characterize the Renaissance, which is the result of erupting individualism in all fields of life, simply as a "revival of Antiquity", yet such a phrase contains much truth with respect to the humanist educators of the time, even in the case of the great humanist Aenea Silvio, who became Pope Pius II. They almost exhaust themselves in quoting ancient authors and in recommending classical examples of style; one of these educators, Leonardo Bruno, goes so far as to dissuade his students from using any phrase in their Latin prose which they cannot find in Cicero, Livy, and Sallust. If people had followed this example it would have been the death rather than the beginning of originality.

Yet, to a degree, the spirit of the Renaissance makes itself felt even in pedagogy. Values are emphasized which did not play a role in medieval religious education, such as glory, excellence in the service for the prince, beauty, social distinction, and social success. Education is no longer for the life beyond, but a means for self-development and for mastering the various tasks of earthly life. And the goal of education is a kind of gentleman who impresses his friends not so much by his piety, but by his all-round education, his character, his appearance, his manners, and the way in which he takes his destiny into his own hands.

The following selections from *Aeneae Silvii de Liberorum Educatione* in the translation of Brother Joel Stanislaus Nelson are from Studies in Medieval Renaissance Latin Language and Literature, Volume XII. This was published in 1940 by the Catholic University of America Press.

AENEAE SILVII DE LIBERORUM EDUCATIONE

THE EDUCATION OF BOYS.[1] To the most serene prince, Ladislaus, king of Hungary and Bohemia and duke of mighty Austria, his lord, Aeneas, bishop of Trieste, sends hearty greetings.

If anyone ought to devote himself to virtue and to dedicate himself entirely to good deeds, no one who has any sense will deny that it is you, Ladislaus, illustrious king. For after you have completed

---

[1] The major part of all quotations in this treatise are taken from Plutarch's *De educatione puerorum* and from Quintilian's *Institutio oratoria*.

the years of your tutelage, you will be expected to rule great kingdoms and extensive realms, which you will be unable to govern
long unless you will be a man of consummate prudence. Kingdoms
are obedient to virtue, they resist vice. As formerly Rome did not
tolerate the cowardice of an emperor, so now Hungary despises the
sloth of a king. No one needs wisdom more than a sovereign; in
what manner will he govern "others rightly whom his own error has
perverted? A foolish king destroys both himself and his people;"
all things become better for a wise king. "By me," says Wisdom,
"Kings reign, and lawgivers decree justice." Do you, therefore,
while you are a boy and especially when you have grown, allow
yourself to be imbued with the best precepts. And to these ideals
you ought to be incited also by the example of your forbears, your
grandparents, paternal and maternal, who ruled the Roman empire
with the greatest glory, and especially of him who begot you, your
father, Albert, of honored and imperishable memory. It would be
most shameful for you to be a degenerate descendent of such as
these. It is fitting that he who assumes the realms of his forbears
should also inherit their virtues. You are succeeding to nobility:
take care that you be likewise an heir in morals. Nobility clothed
in holy morals is deserving of praise. Nothing vicious is noble.
"For who would call him noble-born who is unworthy of his family
and distinguished only by a famous name?" Indeed, as no one considers "mute animals superior stock" even though sprung of excellent sires "unless they are brave," so men cannot rightfully be called
noble unless they are commended by their own virtue. "It is a poor
thing," as Juvenal says, "to lean upon the fame of others, lest the
pillars having given way, the house fall in ruins." The pursuit of
learning offers the greatest assistance in acquiring virtue, and this
learning becomes none more than a king. Knowing this, the Roman
emperor in a letter, greatly exhorted the "king of the Franks" with
whom he was then allied in friendship, to be solicitous that his children be instructed in learning, "and he said that an illiterate king
was like a crowned ass." And I have learned that the Roman emperors, so long as the commonwealth flourished, were not illiterate,
but at home and abroad, in the senate and in the army learning prevailed; but it is evident to everybody that all virtues grew weak
after letters were neglected. For the "strength of the military arms
and of the imperial power itself was, as it were, cut off at the root."
"Indeed, Socrates," as is related by Boethius, thought "that commonwealths were happy" if their rulers "were lovers of wisdom." For
those men only are perfect who endeavor to mingle political capac-

ity with philosophy, and who procure for themselves a double good: for their life is devoted to the general benefit, and exposed to no disturbances, it is spent in the pursuit of philosophy with greatest tranquility." Princes and all who are destined to rule must endeavor with all their strength, "to take part in public life and to lay hold of philosophy in so far as it will seem appropriate for the times. . . .

In boys there are two subjects which must be informed: the body and the mind. We shall speak first of the care of the body, for we shall say that first the small body was formed in the womb of its mother and then the soul was infused. Next we shall embrace the instruction of the mind. Sometimes we shall treat them together. Some affirm that both should be done together, that the education of a boy should begin "from infancy," from the first "little finger-nail," as they say. But this period has passed for you, I hope not unfruitfully; we must hasten to your age. As yet you are still a boy: listen to the precepts which we give for the boy. While I am addressing you, I am also addressing and advising all your teachers who have care of you. They ought to remember what Plutarch wrote to the emperor Trajan, stating publicly that faults of pupils fall back upon their teachers, for indeed there were not lacking those who ascribed to Seneca the depraved character of Nero. "Whenever Socrates beheld a boy of good natural disposition ignorant, he is said to have struck his teacher. . . . Certainly the choice has been splendidly made for you, who have obtained such excellent teachers; if you observe their precepts you can acquire the reputation of an illustrious man and a famous king. "Just as farmers place stakes beside the small plants, so it is the duty of your instructors 'to encircle' you with teachings in keeping with a praise-worthy life and with admonitions whence will shoot forth the germs of very holy morals, for to receive a proper education is the source and root of virtue." Yet, let them "conduct you by advice, not by blows." For although it is customary for pupils to be flogged, and Chrisippus does not disapprove, and the words of Juvenal are applicable: "fearing the rod Achilles already grown to manhood would sing in his native mountains," yet, Quintilian and Plutarch have more weight with me "when they say that boys must be led to practice virtue, not by wounds or blows, but by admonitions and reason. Blows are becoming slaves, not freemen. For noble and especially for royal boys the praise and blame more than the blows of their elders bring due proportion. The former arouses to virtuous deeds, the latter restrains from disgrace;" yet in each case, meas-

207

ure must be applied "lest there be excess. For boys honored with unmeasured praise become proud, but visited with too much raillery they are broken and become lacking in spirit." Indeed, from blows hatred arises which endures even to manhood. But nothing is more disadvantageous for the pupil than to hate teachers whom, if one wishes to act rightly, "he will love not less than studies themselves and he will consider them as the parents, not indeed of his body but of his mind. This affection adds much to study." . . .

. . . . Shall we suffer the minds of boys to become intoxicated or shall we throttle with unmixed wine the growing intellect? Although by Germanic custom it is abominable to mix water with wine, yet in no way shall I be persuaded that strong wine should be placed on the tables of boys, unless it be weakened with water. . . . This is a foolish and vain precaution, that lest you might ever be drunk always to be drunk. Those who are nourished thus, when they drink greatly, do not lose their reason, but they have a foolish mind and are in continuous drunkenness. In this condition there is no memory, no liveliness of disposition, no aspiration for fine arts, no eagerness for glory or noble deeds. But that we may not seem to be contending with these beasts, whom we consider it a crime to reckon amongst men, let us turn to Plato and hear what that heavenly man has proclaimed about the drinking of wine. "For he wisely judged that to fulfill the obligation of sobriety," wine must not be drunk haphazardly, "but on the contrary the spirit is refreshed and renewed by a moderate and respectable relaxation while drinking. Now the drinking of wine must not be avoided entirely, because no one can seem really continent or very truly temperate whose life is not tested betwixt the very dangers of error and in the midst of the allurement of pleasure. He to whom all the pleasures and delights of feasts are unknown and who is entirely ignorant of them, if perchance his will should bring him, accident lead him, or necessity compel him to experience pleasures of this kind, will soon have to restrain his mind and spirit from being enticed and captivated." Therefore the boy must be fortified against the evil of wine that he may become temperate and continent "not by flight" as the Egyptians do nor by swilling as is pleasing to the Bohemian, "but that by moderation in use he may with strength of soul and continued resolution of mind become temperate and continent." We use wine not that it may master us "but that, our mind having been warmed and refreshed, we may destroy whatever chilling sadness or languishing timidity be there." This we do when we take wine in moderate and supportable quantities. . . .

208

As in the winter it is fitting to endure hardships with tranquility, "so in boyhood good morals ought to be assumed as the best provision for an old age of virtue." Who knows the changeable fortunes of life? There is nothing fixed under the sun; now men are rich, now they are poor, now they rule, again they serve; now they rejoice in health, again they are sick. "No one knows in the morning how evening will turn out." No one has so many protecting deities that he can promise himself the morrow. Wherefore Theseus," as Cicero says is related in Euripides, "was accustomed to say, 'For since I remembered what I had heard from a seer, I was contemplating my future miseries. I was always planning either bitter death or sad flight of exile or some other weight of evil, that if any misfortune should chance to happen no sudden care might tear me unprepared.'" But nothing offers a surer refuge against the attacks of unpropitious fortune than philosophy. "Hence when Dionysius the Younger, expelled from power and driven into exile, was asked what profit to him were Plato and philosophy, he replied: 'That I might bear with tranquil and calm spirit just such a change of fortune.'" Therefore whether circumstances be unpropitious or propitious to us we ought to have recourse to philosophy, which is the study of virtue, and of which kings especially should be lovers. . . .

Every age without learning is dark; and an illiterate ruler cannot do without another's guidance. And since the courts of kings are filled with flatterers, who will speak the truth to the ruler? . . .

Therefore greatest attention and zeal must be given to letters. It was once asked at what age boys ought to be assigned to learning. Hesiod thought not before the age of seven, since "that seemed the earliest age" capable of instruction and susceptible of labor; Eratosthenes likewise enjoined the same. But "Aristophanes and Chrysippus," with whom Quintilian agrees, held that "no time should be free from care." Therefore, training should have begun from the very cradle so that nurses might have contributed something to you. "These nurses Chrysippus would have wise, if possible," that no contagion might be contracted from them, for the worse things cling more tenaciously and "good things are easily changed into worse." "The words of a mother" seasoned with patience and elegance has often been profitable to sons, as many write concerning "Cornelia the mother of the Gracchi," whose eloquence redounded upon her sons. It makes a great deal of difference whether mothers or anyone else who rear boys be polished or coarse, prudent or foolish. But you have now escaped from the

209

yoke of a nurse; you lost your mother, very brilliant and eloquent beyond measure, before you could know her. But let us dismiss the past, more to be lamented than reformed. Let us turn to your present age.

We believe that you were instructed as is befitting a Christian, that you know the Lord's Prayer, the Salutation of the Blessed Virgin, the Gospel of John, the Creed, some prayers, what sins are mortal, the Gifts of the Holy Ghost, the Commandments of Almighty God, the Works of Mercy, and finally the way of saving the soul and leading it to heaven. . . .

. . . But let truthful boys be in your company, upright, chaste, and supporters of modesty and holiness; nor false nor deceivers, nor obstinate, nor drunkards, nor inclined to drunkenness, nor harmful. Let some of them know Hungarian, some Bohemian, some your native tongue, but all the Latin language; and let them speak in turn. And thus you will learn all these individual languages without labor as if in play, and you yourself will be able to address your subjects. Nothing will win the favor of a people towards their ruler more than the grace of speech. And in a certain manner, he seems unworthy of a kingdom who does not understand his people when they are complaining or demanding something. To have known many languages was of so much advantage to your maternal grandfather, a king of great heart, as not to have known them was disadvantageous for your father. Who does not commend "Mithridates, the ruler of Pontus, who spoke without any interpreter with the twenty-two nations over whom he held sway?" And I would not have you more attached to the Austrian people than to the Bohemian and Hungarian. All must be governed with equal zeal. As Plato says: "He does an unjust act who cares for one part of the state to such an extent that he neglects the other." This action has very frequently been the cause of disasters for rulers. And this is the chief factor that withdrew the most noble province of Italy from the empire; for the Teutonic kings, content with their native land alone, and attached too much to their firesides, neglected the government of Italy. Love, not less than the sword, guards kingdoms, but it will be impossible for him who does not love to be loved. Intercourse of language is a promoter of love. Therefore while your age permits, you must strive to be able by yourself to hear your subjects, to understand them, and to speak with them. Frequently some things occur which your subjects may wish to refer to you alone and which they would not entrust to an interpreter. A ruler, moreover, who always speaks through another deserves more the name of judge than king. Silence, as Homer says, brings honor to a woman but not to a man.

. . . But that you may be able to form your speech rightly, something must be said about what pertains to a boy. In the first place your voice must be formed; let it not be broken "with feminine shrillness," nor repeat the "tremulous tone of the aged," nor shout too much. "Let the words be expressed and let individual letters be enunciated with their proper sound; let not the final syllables be lost;" let not the voice be heard "in the throat" and let your tongue be unimpeded, "your mouth more unrestricted, and your speech more expressive." Your teachers will offer you "certain words and verses of selected difficulty, roughly united as it were, from many syllables harshly connected," that you may turn them about and pronounce "them as swiftly as possible." . . .

But since power of speaking, in which both words and thoughts are praised, cannot exist without the help of memory, there is need that "the boy exercise his memory. The mark of this ability is in children and has a threefold quality: it perceives without labor, it retains faithfully" and imitates easily. Something must be committed to memory daily, whether this be verses or important maxims from illustrious authors. "For memory is called the storehouse of learning and instruction, and in the fables is called the mother of the muses because it begets and nourishes. You will aid this in each quality whether you are mindful or forgetful by nature. For either you will strengthen the abundance or supply the defect and you will obey the verses of Hesiod. For thus he says: 'If you strive to add small bits to little things and you do that frequently, a huge pile is accumulated.'"

But because grammar is known to be the door of every discipline and holds more within than it displays outwardly, and seems hopeless if it learned from adolescence and youth, we wish to advise you in a few words not to despise this art as unworthy of the royal mind. "Nothing in grammar does any harm except what is superfluous." . . .

"Grammatica," as Quintilian says, "translated into Latin, signifies literature and has "three parts": "the science of speaking correctly, the explanation of poets" and other authors, and the "art of writing." We shall touch on certain points in all of these, matters such as are useful for you to hear, and not unpleasant for us to discuss. "The first part is the science of correct speaking." By correct speaking, we understand here that speech which is expressed with words suitably and duly joined, although it might otherwise be injurious, impudent, or less just. If, therefore, we wish to speak grammatically and correctly, we must learn the use of words, of which "some are native to us, some foreign, some simple, some proper, some transferred, some common, some coined," and the whole force of correct speaking consists in this, that we use these suitably and skillfully. . . . Many transferred meanings are usually introduced for the sake of elegance as "the light of speech, the distinction of race, the storms of the assembly, the thunder of eloquence." Still, let a "moderate and seasonable use of transferred meanings adorn your speech; frequent and excessive employment obscures and fills it with tediousness, and it becomes allegorical and enigmatic." And no small amount of judgment is necessary to recognize what is a proper and what is an inelegant transfer, . . . Coined words are those which each one newly forms for himself. . . . Everyone is not permitted to form new words. For Flaccus says this: "It has been and always will be allowable to produce a word marked with recent coinage; as the forests with their leaves are changed in the declining year and the first leaves fall, so the archaic meaning of words perishes and others duly born afresh flourish and become vigorous." But this prerogative should belong to those who in speaking and writing distinguished themselves. . . . Those who are of mediocre ability should not invent words but should use those that are current. But in all words, whether new or ancient, native or foreign, proper or transferred, there will be no honor or praise, unless they be well adapted to circumstances. And when there is a choice of two expressions, it is preferable to use that which is more euphonic and more easily understood. . . .

. . . If any one wishes to avoid faults in all these, it will be necessary for him to know four things which grammatical speech approves: reason, antiquity, authority, custom. . . .

The disciplines are interconnected and a person cannot gain one unless he acquires the light of another. For who has the art of correct speaking unless he has seen the poets, and read the historians and orators? Whence, except from these, is whatever there is of reason, of antiquity, of authority, and of custom in grammar? Wherefore, the second part of grammar requires not only that the aforementioned authors be read and understood, "but that every class of writers" who have been tried, approved, and discussed, should be read and understood, "not only because of their contents but also because of their words which frequently receive their authority from writers." Therefore it is advantageous and necessary that your teachers be very industrious in collecting, investigating,

212

and explaining them to you. The ancients decreed "that reading should commence with Homer and Vergil, although there is need of mature judgment to comprehend their virtues. But for the acquisition of this judgement, there is abundance of time nor will they be read but once. In the meantime, the mind of the boy will be exalted by the sublimity of the heroic verse, and will conceive ardor from the magnitude of affairs and be endowed with the noblest sentiments," as Augustine also approves in his first book of the *City of God.* But I do not see how Greek can be given to you, as a teacher of this subject is lacking. But I would say that you should acquire it, if you have the opportunity; for a knowledge of Greek, which not a few of the Latin emperors learned, would help not a little to direct the kingdom of Hungary, in which there are many Greeks, and would contribute much light to your Latin speech. For with me the authority of great Cato, who as an old man gave his attention to Greek letters, prevails more than that of Gaius Marius, who thought it disgraceful to learn this language whose teachers were slaves. We have the desire to learn this language but the opportunity is lacking; hence let us speak of Latin authors, of whom there is not such a great lack that with them we cannot acquire a fuller and more elegant Latin speech.

. . . . .

Receive this further instruction and learn what authors you should read while you are a boy. They are poets, historians, philosophers, and orators. For we shall reserve the theologians for another time, although some of those included under the name of philosophers might be given to a boy without danger as we shall afterwards indicate. For there is nothing which philosophy may ignore. Let the discernment of your teacher assist you in choosing the poets who may be entrusted to you. Among the epic poets let him prefer before all Vergil, whose eloquence, whose reputation, is so great that it can be augmented by no praise, diminished by no censure. In him the careful reader will discover the different kinds of style, which are thought to "be four: brevity, fullness, simplicity, and elegance." Lucan, a distinguished author of history, and Statius, who is quite polished, should not be neglected. Ovid is everywhere concise, everywhere delightful, but in many places too wanton; yet his most famous work, to which he gave the name *Metamorphoses,* ought in no wise to be cast aside, as the knowledge of this on account of the skill displayed in the stories is of no small profit. Others who write in heroic verse are far inferior to these and ought to be called versifiers rather than poets; I would consider

213

that Claudian and the author of the *Argonauts* least contemptible. Only three satirists are found among us today: Horace, Juvenal, and Persius. Martial also perhaps may seem a satirist, but his verse has not observed the laws of satire. Horace, a little younger than Vergil, was a man of much learning; he is useful everywhere whether you read his *odes,* his *epodes,* his *satires,* or his *Epistles.* Still, there are certain things in him which I would not wish to read nor explain to you while you are still a boy. Juvenal, a poet of great genius, has said many things too indiscreetly, yet in some satires he has shown himself so religious that he seems to yield to no teacher of our faith. Persius is too obscure but is useful. Martial is harmful; although flowery and elegant, he is packed with thorns, so that he does not permit the roses to be plucked without pricking. All those who write elegies should be withheld from a boy. For such as Tibullus, Propertius, Catullus, and whatever of Sappho has been translated among us, are very effeminate. For they continuously describe erotic things and lovers complain that they are deserted. Therefore, let them be put aside or let them be reserved for a more mature age. The writers of comedy can contribute much to eloquence, since they extend to all persons and affections. Of these we have only two, Plautus and Terence. The writers of tragedy are also very useful for boys, but besides Seneca, the nephew of the great Seneca, we have no Latin tragedian except Gregory Corario Venetu, who, when I was a youth, turned into tragedy the story of Tereus as found in Ovid. And since gravity and elegance are desired in speech, you will find the former in tragedy and the latter in comedy. But your teacher ought to take care that he may not seem to urge anything vicious while he selects comedies and tragedies. But let him order that the characters who speak and the emotions which follow be considered and meditated upon.

Indeed there is a galaxy of orators who can be read, but Cicero is the most brilliant of all and sufficiently pleasant and clear to beginners. He can not only be profitable but also loved, and I think that his book *de officiis* is not only useful but even necessary for you. Ambrose also wrote, an imitation of Cicero, a *de officiis,* a work not to be despised which I should think ought to be read most suitably with his, so that what of Cicero is not in harmony with our faith may be corrected from Ambrose. The works of Lactantius are elegant; there is nothing crude in Jerome; the books of Augustine are faultless; you can make use of Gregory with no small advantage. In our day the volumes of Leonardo Bruni, Guarino of Verona, Poggio of Florence, Ambrose the monk of Camaldoli, are concise

214

and fruitful for readers. Boys ought to read historians also, such as Livy and Sallust, although to understand them, there is need of maturity. Then we have Justin and Quintus Curtius and Arrian, whom Petrus Paulus translated, in all of whom we find truth and not fables. The History of Alexander ought to be run through. And to these men Valerius, the historian and philosopher, is not unworthy to be added. Suetonius should not be entrusted to a boy. Also stories from Genesis, the Books of Kings, the Book of Maccabees, the Books of Judith, Esdras, Esther, the Gospels, the Acts of the Apostles will be taken up with great profit. "For," as Cicero says, "history is the witness of time, the light of truth, the teacher of life, the messenger of antiquity." Therefore it is advantageous to know as many histories as possible and to train yourself in them, so that, by the example of others, you may know how to follow what is useful and to avoid what is harmful. Still we do not wish you to be engaged in superfluous work, and it is sufficient to have learned what is taken from or related by noted authors. But I would not permit in any manner the histories of the Bohemians or of the Hungarians to be given to a boy, if I had any authority. For they are written by the ignorant, containing many foolish things, many lies, no maxims, no ornaments of style. As Pliny says, no book is so bad that nothing useful can be taken from it, and therefore it may seem proper to entrust every sort of writer to the reader; yet they ought not to be given to boys but to men already learned. For unless boys be steeped in the best things, their intellects are depraved and they can acquire no discernment. And now, concerning the second part of grammar, you shall consider sufficient has been said. But we should, however, make one last observation, that these authors ought not to be approached all at the same time, and that we do not think that you must study them all necessarily and with great zeal, lest the enormity of the task should render literature hateful to you.

. . . . .

Perhaps some one might ask how "these things [namely the seven liberal arts] are to be learned or whether they can be transmitted and learned. Some deny this because the mind is confused and wearied by so many studies of such diversity. But these do not understand sufficiently how great is the power of the human mind, which is so busy, so active and which directs attention in every corner, so to say, that it can not even do only one thing but it expends all its power on many things, not only on the same day but even at the same moment of time. Who would not become dulled if he were to endure for a whole day one teacher of one art? The

215

spirit will be refreshed by a change as the stomach is invigorated by a moderate variety of food. Farmers cultivate at the same time their fields, their vineyards, their olive trees, and their groves; they care for their meadows, their herds, their flocks, and their bees." Why may not boys, whose dispositions are much more docile than those of young men, pursue the various disciplines, I would not say at the same moment but at the same time? Therefore those who direct you as a boy will take care that throughout the day you listen to different teachers, that you devote yourself now to grammar, now to dialectic, and now to another study, and they will not refuse a proper time for play and a proper time for bodily training.

But although the intellect is especially enlightened by studies of this kind, it is not immediately shown what is honorable, what is disgraceful, what is just, what must be chosen and what avoided. The known marks of virtue are not too deeply hidden in the poets, orators, and historians; from these things you must rise higher with all your affection; you must pass over to philosophy itself concerning which we made mention in the beginning. But here perhaps one of your companions will say: "What are you doing Aeneas? While the boy is sweating over the arts, seven of which you mentioned before, shall he pursue philosophy? Why do we return to this subject?" But such a one does not know what the name of philosopher connotes, the inventor of which name, it is agreed, was Pythagoras. For formerly when good and learned men were called wise he fled pride and wished to be called a philosopher, that is a lover of wisdom, not a wise man. Wisdom embraces not only the seven arts mentioned above but professes the knowledge of all things and of the causes by which these things exist. Wherefore one will not be called a philosopher because he has pursued the seven arts, but because he has acquired a part of philosophy. Philosophers at the beginning regarded natural causes alone and followed Thales, the Milesian, who is said to have first disputed concerning them. Then came Socrates who called moral philosophy out of the heavens. Therefore it came about that philosophy was divided into two parts: one is called natural and the other, moral. But through the intervention of Plato's divine genius, it was decided to add a third member, which is called rational.

But up to this point we have said little about the morals which should be learned from philosophy. Wherefore at the conclusion of the book but not at the conclusion of study we again send the boy to moral philosophy. "For this will point out with certain reason, what worship must be paid to the Divine Majesty, how we should act toward parents, nobles, foreigners, officials, soldiers, friends, wives, citizens, peasants, and slaves." This will teach you, O illustrious king, to despise avarice, a too great love of money, which as Sallust says no wise man ever desires. "This will advise you to observe modesty towards women, to hold your children and your neighbors dear, not to serve with the servants, to respect your elders, to obey the laws, to repress your anger, to despise pleasures, to pity the oppressed, to assist with your wealth, to confer worthy rewards, to grant justice to each and every one," to punish the guilty and, what is most important, "it will not allow you to be puffed up with joy at the favorable turns of fortune nor to be cast down with sadness at adverse misfortune," and will offer you a way by which you can live rightly and usefully command your subjects. For all these things should not be withheld from a boy, provided that a choice of books be made. Pleasing, clear and open, elegant and polished books should be given to him, as we said above. To the books mentioned can be added Cicero's *Tusculan disputations, de senectute, de amicitia,* and whatever he has written concerning morals. Seneca is to be received as useful and also Pliny in his Letters, and Boethius in his *de consolatione.* And I would not deny that more books of learned men than these exist which can safely be given to boys. But I demand discernment on the part of the teacher, that he be acquainted with books which are elegant and concise and acknowledged as authorities. But since that part of philosophy which is called ethics leaves no part of the human life untouched, but governs youths, young men and old, we believe that for the present we have pointed out sufficiently how much should be given to the boy and from what sources they should be learned. We shall have to speak more in detail in other books as the periods of your life will require if God the Creator of the world, and the Author of your soul will prolong our life—unless after we have said that you ought to read so many distinguished authors we shall judge it more modest to be silent than to speak anything further. But do you meanwhile so endeavor to practice and learn what you have been taught is proper for a boy, that you may be most eager for the other parts of this work. Farewell.

LUTHER 1483–1546

Luther is for some the hero of a new era, and for others the symbol of the final disintegration of medieval catholicity. But, however far the battle of opinions may extend, we can agree that the Protestant Reformation does represent the religious part of the movement toward individualism. As such it was bound to help the single man in his attempt to find a personal relation to God and the universe without the institution of the Church as the indispensable mediator between the individual and the Divine.

Nevertheless, it would be erroneous to believe that Luther really intended to expose Christian man merely to his own personal religious feelings. Medieval as he still was in many respects, he also needed a mediator: the Bible. Consequently, the primary goal of Protestant education was to enable people to read the sacred Scripture. The degree of influence of the Reformation on the freedom of higher studies and thought in general is a matter of controversy. But we cannot doubt that Protestantism was an enormous stimulus in the promotion of universal education, and that it made the governments of states and communities aware of their responsibilities in this respect.

The following selections from Luther's *Letter to the Mayors and Aldermen of All the Cities of Germany in Behalf of Christian Schools* and from Luther's *Sermon on the Duty of Sending Children to School* are taken from F. V. N. Painter's *Luther on Education,* published in Philadelphia by the Concordia Publishing House in 1890.

LETTERS TO THE MAYORS AND ALDERMEN

Grace and peace from God our Father and the Lord Jesus Christ. Honored and dear Sirs: Having three years ago been put under the ban and outlawed, I should have kept silent, had I regarded the command of men more than that of God. Many persons in Germany both of high and low estate assail my discourses and writings on that account, and shed much blood over them. But God who has opened my mouth and bidden me speak, stands firmly by me, and without any counsel or effort of mine strengthens and extends my cause the more, the more they rage, and seems, as the second Psalm says, to "have them in derision." By this alone any one not blinded by prejudice may see that the work is of God; for it exhibits the

218

divine method, according to which God's cause spreads most rapidly when men exert themselves most to oppose and suppress it.

Therefore, as Isaiah says, I will not hold my peace until the righteousness of Christ go forth as brightness, and his salvation as a lamp that burneth.[1] And I beseech you all, in the name of God and of our neglected youth, kindly to receive my letter and admonition, and give it thoughtful consideration. For whatever I may be in myself, I can boast with a clear conscience before God that I am not seeking my own interest, (which would be best served by silence,) but the interest of all Germany, according to the mission, (doubt it who will,) with which God has honored me. And I wish to declare to you frankly and confidently that if you hear me, you hear not me but Christ; and whoever will not hear me, despises not me but Christ.[2] For I know the truth of what I declare and teach; and every one who rightly considers my doctrine will realize its truth for himself.

First of all we see how the schools are deteriorating throughout Germany. The universities are becoming weak, the monasteries are declining, and, as Isaiah says, "The grass withereth, the flower fadeth, because the spirit of the Lord bloweth upon it,"[3] through the Gospel. For through the word of God the unchristian and sensual character of these institutions is becoming known. And because selfish parents see that they can no longer place their children upon the bounty of monasteries and cathedrals, they refuse to educate them. "Why should we educate our children," they say, "if they are not to become priests, monks, and nuns, and thus earn a support?"

The hollow piety and selfish aims of such persons are sufficiently evident from their own confession. For if they sought anything more than the temporal welfare of their children in monasteries and the priesthood, if they were deeply in earnest to secure the salvation and blessedness of their children, they would not lose interest in education and say, "if the priestly office is abolished, we will not send our children to school." But they would speak after this manner: "if it is true, as the Gospel teaches, that such a calling is dangerous to our children, teach us another way in which they may be pleasing to God and become truly blessed; for we wish to provide not alone for the bodies of our children, but also for their souls." Such would be the language of faithful Christian parents.

[1] An adaptation of Isaiah lxii. 1.
[2] A reference to Luke x. 16.
[3] Isaiah xl. 7.

It is no wonder that the devil meddles in the matter, and influences groveling hearts to neglect the children and the youth of the country. Who can blame him for it? He is the prince and god of this world,[4] and with extreme displeasure sees the Gospel destroy his nurseries of vice, the monasteries and priesthood, in which he corrupts the young beyond measure, a work upon which his mind is especially bent. How could he consent to a proper training of the young? Truly he would be a fool if he permitted such a thing in his kingdom, and thus consented to its overthrow: which indeed would happen, if the young should escape him, and be brought up to the service of God.

Hence he acted wisely at the time when Christians were educating and bringing up their children in a Christian way. Inasmuch as the youth of the land would have thus escaped him, and inflicted an irreparable injury upon his kingdom, he went to work and spread his nets, established such monasteries, schools, and orders, that it was not possible for a boy to escape him without the miraculous intervention of God. But now that he sees his snares exposed through the Word of God, he takes an opposite course, and dissuades men from all education whatever. He thus pursues a wise course to maintain his kingdom and win the youth of Germany. And if he secures them, if they grow up under his influence and remain his adherents, who can gain any advantage over him? He retains an easy and peaceful mastery over the world. For any fatal wound to his cause must come through the young, who, brought up in the knowledge of God, spread abroad the truth and instruct others.

Yet no one thinks of this dreadful purpose of the devil, which is being worked out so quietly that it escapes observation; and soon the evil will be so far advanced that we can do nothing to prevent it. People fear the Turks, wars, and floods, for in such matters they can see what is injurious or beneficial; but what the devil has in mind no one sees or fears. Yet where we would give a florin to defend ourselves against the Turks, we should give a hundred florins to protect us against ignorance, even if only one boy could be taught to be a truly Christian man; for the good such a man can accomplish is beyond all computation.

Therefore I beg you all, in the name of God and of our neglected youth, not to think of this subject lightly, as many do who see not what the prince of this world intends. For the right instruction of youth is a matter in which Christ and all the world are concerned.

[4] A reference to John xiv. 30.

220

Thereby are we all aided. And consider that great Christian zeal is needed to overcome the silent, secret, and artful machinations of the devil. If we must annually expend large sums on muskets, roads, bridges, dams, and the like, in order that the city may have temporal peace and comfort, why should we not apply as much to our poor, neglected youth, in order that we may have a skillful school-master or two?

There is one consideration that should move every citizen, with devout gratitude to God, to contribute a part of his means to the support of schools—the consideration that if divine grace had not released him from exactions and robbery, he would still have to give large sums of money for indulgences, masses, vigils, endowments, anniversaries, mendicant friars, brotherhoods, and other similar impositions. And let him be sure that where turmoil and strife exist, there the devil is present, who did not writhe and struggle so long as men blindly contributed to convents and masses. For Satan feels that his cause is suffering injury. Let this, then, be the first consideration to move you,—that in this work we are fighting against the devil, the most artful and dangerous enemy of men.

Another consideration is found in the fact that we should not, as St. Paul says, receive the grace of God in vain,[5] and neglect the present favorable time. For Almighty God has truly granted us Germans a gracious visitation, and favored us with a golden opportunity. We now have excellent and learned young men, adorned with every science and art, who, if they were employed, could be of great service as teachers. Is it not well known that a boy can now be so instructed in three years, that at the age of fifteen or eighteen he knows more than all the universities and convents have known heretofore? Yea, what have men learned hitherto in the universities and monasteries, except to be asses and blockheads? Twenty, forty years, it has been necessary to study, and yet one has learned neither Latin nor German! I say nothing of the shameful and vicious life in those institutions, by which our worthy youth have been so lamentably corrupted.

I should prefer, it is true, that our youth be ignorant and dumb rather than that the universities and convents should remain as the only sources of instruction open to them. For it is my earnest intention, prayer and desire that these schools of Satan either be destroyed or changed into Christian schools. But since God has so richly favored us, and given us a great number of persons who are competent thoroughly to instruct and train our young people, it is

[5] 2 Cor. vi. 1.

truly needful that we should not disregard His grace and let Him knock in vain. He stands at the door; happy are we if we open to Him. He calls us; happy is the man who answers Him. If we disregard His call, so that He passes by, who will bring Him back?

Let us consider the wretchedness of our former condition and the darkness in which we were enveloped. I believe Germany has never heard so much of the Word of God as at the present time; history reveals no similar period. If we let the gracious season pass without gratitude and improvement, it is to be feared that we shall suffer still more terrible darkness and distress. My dear countrymen, buy while the market is at your door; gather the harvest while the sun shines and the weather is fair: use the grace and Word of God while they are near. For know this, that the Word and grace of God are like a passing shower, which does not return where it has once been. The Divine favor once rested upon the Jews, but it has departed. Paul brought the Gospel into Greece; but now they have the Turks. Rome and Italy once enjoyed its blessings; but now they have the Pope. And the German people should not think that they will always have it; for ingratitude and neglect will banish it. Therefore seize it and hold it fast, whoever can; idle hands will have an evil year.

The third consideration is the highest of all, namely, God's command, which through Moses so often urges and enjoins that parents instruct their children, that the seventy-eighth Psalm says: "He established a testimony in Jacob and appointed a law in Israel, which he commanded our fathers that they should make them known to their children." And the fourth commandment also shows this, where he has so strictly enjoined children to obey their parents, that disobedient children were to be put to death. And why do old people live, except to care for, teach, and bring up the young? It is not possible for inexperienced youth to instruct and care for themselves; and for that reason God has commended them to us who are older and know what is good for them, and He will require a strict account at our hands. Therefore Moses gives this injunction: "Ask thy father, and he will show thee; thy elders, and they will tell thee." [6]

It is indeed a sin and shame that we must be aroused and incited to the duty of educating our children and of considering their highest interests, whereas nature itself should move us thereto, and the example of the heathen affords us varied instruction. There is no irrational animal that does not care for and instruct its young in

[6] Deut. xxxii. 7.

what they should know, except the ostrich, of which God says; "She leaveth her eggs in the earth, and warmeth them in the dust; and is hardened against her young ones, as though they were not hers." [7] And what would it avail if we possessed and performed all else, and became perfect saints, if we neglect that for which we chiefly live, namely, to care for the young? In my judgment there is no other outward offense that in the sight of God so heavily burdens the world, and deserves such heavy chastisement, as the neglect to educate children.

In my youth this proverb was current in the schools: "It is no less a sin to neglect a pupil than to do violence to a woman." It was used to frighten teachers. But how much lighter is this wrong against a woman (which as a bodily sin may be atoned for), than to neglect and dishonor immortal souls, when such a sin is not recognized and can never be atoned for? O eternal woe to the world! Children are daily born and grow up among us, and there are none, alas! who feel an interest in them; and instead of being trained, they are left to themselves. The convents and cathedral schools are the proper agencies to do it; but to them we may apply the words of Christ: "Woe unto the world because of offenses! Whoso shall offend one of these little ones which believe in me, it were better for him that a mill-stone were hanged about his neck, and that he were drowned in the depth of the sea." [8] They are nothing but destroyers of children.

But all that, you say, is addressed to parents; what does it concern the members of the council and the mayors? That is true; but how, if parents neglect it? Who shall attend to it then? Shall we therefore let it alone, and suffer the children to be neglected? How will the mayors and council excuse themselves, and prove that such a duty does not belong to them?

Parents neglect this duty from various causes.

In the first place, there are some who are so lacking in piety and uprightness that they would not do it if they could, but like the ostrich, harden themselves against their own offspring, and do nothing for them. Nevertheless these children must live among us and with us. How then can reason and, above all, Christian charity, suffer them to grow up ill-bred, and to infect other children, till at last the whole city be destroyed, like Sodom, Gomorrah, and some other cities?

In the second place, the great majority of parents are unqualified

[7] Job xxxix. 14, 16.
[8] Matt. xviii. 6, 7.

for it, and do not understand how children should be brought up and taught. For they have learned nothing but to provide for their bodily wants; and in order to teach and train children thoroughly, a separate class is needed.

In the third place, even if parents were qualified and willing to do it themselves, yet on account of other employments and household duties they have no time for it, so that necessity requires us to have teachers for public schools, unless each parent employ a private instructor. But that would be too expensive for persons of ordinary means, and many a bright boy, on account of poverty, would be neglected. Besides, many parents die and leave orphans; and how they are usually cared for by guardians, we might learn, even if observation were not enough, from the sixty-eighth Psalm, where God calls himself the "Father of the fatherless," as of those who are neglected by all others. Also there are some who have no children, and therefore feel no interest in them.

Therefore it will be the duty of the mayors and council to exercise the greatest care over the young. For since the happiness, honor, and life of the city are committed to their hands, they would be held recreant before God and the world, if they did not, day and night, with all their power, seek its welfare and improvement. Now the welfare of a city does not consist alone in great treasures, firm walls, beautiful houses, and munitions of war; indeed, where all these are found, and reckless fools come into power, the city sustains the greater injury. But the highest welfare, safety, and power of a city consists in able, learned, wise, upright, cultivated citizens, who can secure, preserve, and utilize every treasure and advantage.

In ancient Rome the boys were so brought up that at the age of fifteen, eighteen, twenty, they were masters not only of the choicest Latin and Greek, but also of the liberal arts, as they are called; and immediately after this scholastic training, they entered the army or held a position under the government. Thus they became intelligent, wise, and excellent men, skilled in every art and rich in experience, so that all the bishops, priests, and monks in Germany put together would not equal a Roman soldier. Consequently their country prospered; persons were found capable and skilled in every pursuit. Thus, in all the world, even among the heathen, schoolmasters and teachers have been found necessary where a nation was to be elevated. Hence in the Epistle to the Galatians Paul employs a word in common use when he says, "The law was our school-master." [9]

[9] Gal. iii. 24.

224

LUTHER

Since, then, a city must have well-trained people, and since the greatest need, lack, and lament is that such are not to be found, we must not wait till they grow up of themselves; neither can they be hewed out of stones nor cut out of wood; nor will God work miracles, so long as men can attain their object through means within their reach. Therefore we must see to it, and spare no trouble or expense to educate and form them ourselves. For whose fault is it that in all the cities there are at present so few skillful people except the rulers, who have allowed the young to grow up like trees in the forest, and have not cared how they were reared and taught? The growth, consequently, has been so irregular that the forest furnishes no timber for building purposes, but like a useless hedge, is good only for fuel.

Yet there must be civil government. For us, then, to permit ignoramuses and blockheads to rule when we can prevent it, is irrational and barbarous. Let us rather make rulers out of swine and wolves, and set them over people who are indifferent to the manner in which they are governed. It is barbarous for men to think thus: "We will now rule; and what does it concern us how those fare who shall come after us?" Not over human beings, but over swine and dogs should such people rule, who think only of their own interests and honor in governing. Even if we exercise the greatest care to educate able, learned and skilled rulers, yet much care and effort are necessary in order to secure prosperity. How can a city prosper, when no effort is made?

But, you say again, if we shall and must have schools, what is the use to teach Latin, Greek, Hebrew, and the other liberal arts? Is it not enough to teach the Scriptures, which are necessary to salvation, in the mother tongue? To which I answer: I know, alas! that we Germans must always remain irrational brutes, as we are deservedly called by surrounding nations. But I wonder why we do not also say: of what use to us are silk, wine, spices, and other foreign articles, since we ourselves have an abundance of wine, corn, wool, flax, wood, and stone in the German states, not only for our necessities, but also for embellishment and ornament? The languages and other liberal arts, which are not only harmless, but even a greater ornament, benefit, and honor than these things, both for understanding the Holy Scriptures and carrying on the civil government, we are disposed to despise; and the foreign articles which are neither necessary nor useful, and which besides greatly impoverish us, we are unwilling to dispense with. Are we not rightly called German dunces and brutes?

Indeed, if the languages were of no practical benefit, we ought still to feel an interest in them as a wonderful gift of God, with which he has now blessed Germany almost beyond all other lands. We do not find many instances in which Satan has fostered them through the universities and cloisters; on the contrary, these institutions have fiercely inveighed and continue to inveigh against them. For the devil scented the danger that would threaten his kingdom, if the languages should be generally studied. But since he could not wholly prevent their cultivation, he aims at least to confine them within such narrow limits, that they will of themselves decline and fall into disuse. They are to him no welcome guest, and consequently he shows them scant courtesy in order that they may not remain long. This malicious trick of Satan is perceived by very few.

Therefore, my beloved countrymen, let us open our eyes, thank God for this precious treasure, and take pains to preserve it, and to frustrate the design of Satan. For we cannot deny that, although the Gospel has come and daily comes through the Holy Spirit, it has come by means of the languages, and through them must increase and be preserved. For when God wished through the apostles to spread the Gospel abroad in all the world, he gave the languages for that purpose; and by means of the Roman empire he made Latin and Greek the language of many lands, that his Gospel might speedily bear fruit far and wide. He has done the same now. For a time no one understood why God had revived the study of the languages; but now we see that it was for the sake of the Gospel, which he wished to bring to light and thereby expose and destroy the reign of Antichrist. For the same reason he gave Greece a prey to the Turks, in order that Greek scholars, driven from home and scattered abroad, might bear the Greek tongue to other countries, and thereby excite an interest in the study of languages.

In the same measure that the Gospel is dear to us, should we zealously cherish the languages. For God had a purpose in giving the Scriptures only in two languages, the Old Testament in the Hebrew, and the New Testament in the Greek. What God did not despise, but chose before all others for His Word, we should likewise esteem above all others. St. Paul, in the third chapter of Romans, points out, as a special honor and advantage of the Hebrew language, that God's Word was given in it: "What profit is there of circumcision? Much every way; chiefly because that unto them were committed the oracles of God." [10] Likewise King David boasts in the one hun-

[10] Rom. iii. 1, 2.

226

dred and forty-seventh Psalm: "He showeth his word unto Jacob, his statutes and his judgments unto Israel. He hath not dealt so with any nation: and as for his judgments, they have not known them." [11] Hence the Hebrew language is called sacred. And St. Paul, in Romans i. 2, speaks of the Hebrew Scriptures as holy, no doubt because of the Word of God which they contain. In like manner the Greek language might well be called holy, because it was chosen, in preference to others, as the language of the New Testament. And from this language, as from a fountain, the New Testament has flowed through translations into other languages, and sanctified them also.

And let this be kept in mind, that we will not preserve the Gospel without the languages. The languages are the scabbard in which the Word of God is sheathed. They are the casket in which this jewel is enshrined; the cask in which this wine is kept; the chamber in which this food is stored. And, to borrow a figure from the Gospel itself, they are the baskets in which this bread, and fish, and fragments are preserved. If through neglect we lose the languages (which may God forbid), we will not only lose the Gospel, but it will finally come to pass that we will lose also the ability to speak and write either Latin or German. Of this let us take as proof and warning the miserable and shocking example presented in the universities and cloisters, in which not only the Gospel has been perverted, but also the Latin and German languages have been corrupted, so that the wretched inmates have become like brutes, unable to speak and write German or Latin, and have almost lost their natural reason.

The apostles considered it necessary to embody the New Testament in the Greek language, in order, no doubt, that it might be securely preserved unto us as in a sacred shrine. For they foresaw what has since taken place, namely, that when the divine revelation is left to oral tradition, much disorder and confusion arise from conflicting opinions and doctrines. And there would be no way to prevent this evil and to protect the simple-minded, if the New Testament was not definitely recorded in writing. Therefore it is evident that where the languages are not preserved, there the Gospel will become corrupted.

Experience shows this to be true. For immediately after the age of the apostles, when the languages ceased to be cultivated, the Gospel, and the true faith, and Christianity itself, declined more and more, until they were entirely lost under the Pope. And since

[11] Psalm cxlvii. 19, 20.

the time that the languages disappeared, not much that is note-worthy and excellent has been seen in the Church; but through ignorance of the languages very many shocking abominations have arisen. On the other hand, since the revival of learning, such a light has been shed abroad, and such important changes have taken place, that the world is astonished, and must acknowledge that we have the Gospel almost as pure and unadulterated as it was in the times of the apostles, and much purer than it was in the days of St. Jerome and St. Augustine. In a word, since the Holy Ghost, who does nothing foolish or useless, has often bestowed the gift of tongues, it is our evident duty earnestly to cultivate the languages, now that God has restored them to the world through the revival of learning.

But many of the church fathers, you say, have become saints and have taught without a knowledge of the languages. That is true. But to what do you attribute their frequent misunderstanding of the Scriptures? How often is St. Augustine in error in the Psalms and in other expositions, as well as Hilary, and indeed all those who have undertaken to explain the Scriptures without an acquaintance with the original tongues? And if perchance they have taught correct doctrine, they have not been sure of the application to be made of particular passages. For example, it is truly said that Christ is the Son of God. But what mockery does it seem to adversaries when as proof of that doctrine Psalm cx. 3 is adduced: "*Tecum principium in die virtutis*," since in the Hebrew no reference is made in that verse to the Deity. When the faith is thus defended with uncertain reasons and proof-texts, does it not seem a disgrace and mockery in the eyes of such adversaries as are acquainted with the Greek and the Hebrew? And they are only rendered the more obstinate in their error, and with good ground hold our faith as a human delusion.

What is the reason that our faith is thus brought into disgrace? It is our ignorance of the languages; and the only remedy is a knowledge of them. Was not St. Jerome forced to make a new translation of the Psalms from the Hebrew, because the Jews, when quotations were made from the Latin version, derided the Christians, affirming that the passages adduced were not found in the original? The comments of all the ancient fathers who, without a knowledge of the languages, have treated of the Scriptures (although they may teach nothing heretical), are still of such a character that the writers often employ uncertain, doubtful, and inappropriate expressions, and grope like a blind man along a wall, so that they often miss the

228

sense of the text and mould it according to their pious fancy, as in the example mentioned in the last paragraph. St. Augustine himself was obliged to confess that the Christian teacher, in addition to Latin, should be acquainted with Hebrew and Greek. Without this knowledge, the expositor will inevitably fall into mistakes; and even when the languages are understood, he will meet with difficulties.

With a simple preacher of the faith it is different from what it is with the expositor of the Scriptures, or prophet, as St. Paul calls him. The former has so many clear passages and texts in translations, that he is able to understand and preach Christ, and lead a holy life. But to explain the Scriptures, to deal with them independently, and oppose heretical interpreters, such a one is too weak without a knowledge of the languages. But we need just such expositors, who will give themselves to the study and interpretation of the Scriptures, and who are able to controvert erroneous doctrines; for a pious life and orthodox teaching are not alone sufficient. Therefore the languages are absolutely necessary, as well as prophets or expositors; but it is not necessary that every Christian or preacher be such a prophet, according to the diversity of gifts of which St. Paul speaks in I Corinthians xii. 8, 9, and in Ephesians iv. 11.

This explains why, since the days of the apostles, the Scriptures have remained in obscurity, and no reliable and enduring expositions have anywhere been written. For even the holy fathers, as we have said, are often in error, and because they were not versed in the languages, they seldom agree. St. Bernard was a man of great ability, so that I am inclined to place him above all other distinguished teachers, whether ancient or modern; but how often he trifles with the Scriptures, in a spiritual manner to be sure, and wrests them from their true meaning! For the same reason the Papists have said that the Scriptures are of obscure and peculiar import. But they do not perceive that the trouble lies in ignorance of the languages; but for this, nothing simpler has ever been spoken than the Word of God. A Turk must indeed speak unintelligibly to me, although a Turkish child of seven years understands him, because I am unacquainted with the language.

Hence it is foolish to attempt to learn the Scriptures through the comments of the fathers and the study of many books and glosses. For that purpose we ought to give ourselves to the languages. For the beloved fathers, because they were not versed in the languages, have often failed, in spite of their verbose expositions, to give the meaning of the text. You peruse their writings with great toil; and yet with a knowledge of the languages you can get the meaning of Scripture better than they do. For in comparison with the glosses of the fathers, the languages are as sunlight to darkness.

Since, then, it behooves Christians at all times to use the Bible as their only book and to be thoroughly acquainted with it, especially is it a disgrace and sin at the present day not to learn the languages, when God provides every facility, incites us to study, and wishes to have His word known. O how glad the honored fathers would have been, if they could have learned the languages, and had such access to the Holy Scriptures! With what pain and toil they scarcely obtained crumbs, while almost without effort we are able to secure the whole loaf! O how their industry shames our idleness, yea, how severely will God punish our neglect and ingratitude!

St. Paul, in 1 Corinthians xiv. 29,[12] enjoins that there be judgment upon doctrine—a duty that requires a knowledge of the languages. For the preacher or teacher may publicly read the whole Bible as he chooses, right or wrong, if there be no one present to judge whether he does it correctly or not. But if one is to judge, there must be an acquaintance with the languages; otherwise, the judging will be in vain. Hence, although faith and the Gospel may be preached by ordinary ministers without the languages, still such preaching is sluggish and weak, and the people finally become weary, and fall away. But a knowledge of the languages renders it lively and strong, and faith finds itself constantly renewed through rich and varied instruction. In the first Psalm the Scriptures liken such study to "a tree planted by the rivers of water, that bringeth forth its fruit in its season; its leaf also shall not wither."

We should not allow ourselves to be deceived because there are some who, while setting little store by the Scriptures, boast of the Spirit. Some also, like the Waldenses, do not regard the languages useful. But, dear friend, whatever such persons may say, I have also been in the Spirit, and have seen more of His power (if it is allowable to boast of one's self), than they will see in a year, however much they may vaunt themselves. I have also been able to accomplish somewhat, while they have remained without influence, and done little more than boast. I know full well that the Spirit does almost everything. Still I should have failed in my work, if the languages had not come to my aid, and made me strong and immovable in the Scriptures. I might without them have been pious; and preached the Gospel in obscurity; but I could not have disturbed the Pope, his adherents, and all the reign of Antichrist. The devil

[12] Let the prophets speak two or three, and let the other judge.

230

cares less for the Spirit within me than for my pen and linguistic knowledge. For while the Spirit takes nothing but myself away from him, the Holy Scriptures and the languages drive him from the world and break up his kingdom.

I can not praise the Waldenses for depreciating the languages. For although they taught no heresies, yet they often necessarily failed in their proof-texts, and remained unqualified and unskilled to contend against error for the true faith. Besides, their teaching is so unenlightened, and presented in such peculiar forms, not following the language of Scripture, that I fear it will not continue pure. For it is dangerous to speak of divine things in a manner or in words different from those employed in the Scriptures. In brief, they may lead holy lives and teach among themselves; but because they are without the languages, they will lack what others have lacked, namely, an assured and thorough handling of the Scriptures, and the ability to be useful to other nations. And because they could have done this, and would not, they will have an account to render before God for their neglect.

So much for the utility and necessity of the languages, and of Christian schools for our spiritual interests and the salvation of the soul. Let us now consider the body and inquire: though there were no soul, nor heaven, nor hell, but only the civil government, would not this require good schools and learned men more than do our spiritual interests? Hitherto the Papists have taken no interest in civil government, and have conducted the schools so entirely in the interests of the priesthood, that it has become a matter of reproach for a learned man to marry, and he has been forced to hear remarks like this: "Behold, he has become a man of the world, and cares nothing for the clerical state," just as if the priestly order were alone acceptable to God, and the secular classes, as they are called, belonged to Satan, and were unchristian. But in the sight of God, the former rather belong to Satan, while the despised masses (as happened to the people of Israel in the Babylonian captivity) remain in the land and in right relations with God.

It is not necessary to say here that civil government is a divine institution; of that I have elsewhere said so much, that I hope no one has any doubts on the subject. The question is, how are we to get able and skillful rulers? And here we are put to shame by the heathen, who in ancient times, especially the Greeks and Romans, without knowing that civil government is a divine ordinance, yet instructed the boys and girls with such earnestness and industry that, when I think of it, I am ashamed of Christians, and especially of our Germans, who are such blockheads and brutes that they can say: "Pray, what is the use of schools, if one is not to become a priest?" Yet we know, or ought to know, how necessary and useful a thing it is, and how acceptable to God, when a prince, lord, counsellor, or other ruler, is well-trained and skillful in discharging, in a Christian way, the functions of his office.

Even if there were no soul, (as I have already said,) and men did not need schools and the languages for the sake of Christianity and the Scriptures, still, for the establishment of the best schools everywhere, both for boys and girls, this consideration is of itself sufficient, namely, that society, for the maintenance of civil order and the proper regulation of the household, needs accomplished and well-trained men and women. Now such men are to come from boys, and such women from girls; hence it is necessary that boys and girls be properly taught and brought up. As I have before said, the ordinary man is not qualified for this task, and can not, and will not do it. Princes and lords ought to do it; but they spend their time in pleasure-driving, drinking, and folly, and are burdened with the weighty duties of the cellar, kitchen and bedchamber. And though some would be glad to do it, they must stand in fear of the rest, lest they be taken for fools or heretics. Therefore, honored members of the city councils, this work must remain in your hands; you have more time and better opportunity for it than princes and lords.

But each one, you say, may educate and discipline his own sons and daughters. To which I reply: We see indeed how it goes with this teaching and training. And where it is carried to the highest point, and is attended with success, it results in nothing more than that the learners, in some measure, acquire a forced external propriety of manner; in other respects they remain dunces, knowing nothing, and incapable of giving aid or advice. But were they instructed in schools or elsewhere by thoroughly qualified male or female teachers, who taught the languages, other arts, and history, then the pupils would hear the history and maxims of the world, and see how things went with each city, kingdom, prince, man, and woman; and thus, in a short time, they would be able to comprehend, as in a mirror, the character, life, counsels, undertakings, successes, and failures, of the whole world from the beginning. From this knowledge they could regulate their views, and order their course of life in the fear of God, having become wise in judging what is to be sought and what avoided in this outward life, and capable of advising and directing others. But the training which is given at home is expected to make us wise through our own expe-

232

rience. Before that can take place, we shall die a hundred times, and all through life act injudiciously; for much time is needed to give experience.

Now since the young must leap and jump, or have something to do, because they have a natural desire for it which should not be restrained, (for it is not well to check them in everything,) why should we not provide for them such schools, and lay before them such studies? By the gracious arrangement of God, children take delight in acquiring knowledge, whether languages, mathematics, or history. And our schools are no longer a hell or purgatory, in which children are tortured over cases and tenses, and in which with much flogging, trembling, anguish and wretchedness they learn nothing. If we take so much time and pains to teach our children to play cards, sing, and dance, why should we not take as much time to teach them reading and other branches of knowledge, while they are young and at leisure, are quick at learning, and take delight in it? As for myself,[13] if I had children and were able, I would have them learn not only the languages and history, but also singing, instrumental music, and the whole course of mathematics. For what is all this but mere child's play, in which the Greeks in former ages trained their children, and by this means became wonderfully skillful people, capable for every undertaking? How I regret that I did not read more poetry and history, and that no one taught me in these branches. Instead of these I was obliged with great cost, labor, and injury, to read Satanic filth, the Aristotelian and Scholastic philosophy, so that I have enough to do to get rid of it.

But you say, who can do without his children and bring them up, in this manner, to be young gentlemen? I reply: it is not my idea that we should establish schools as they have been heretofore, where a boy has studied Donatus and Alexander[14] twenty or thirty years, and yet has learned nothing. The world has changed, and things go differently. My idea is that boys should spend an hour or two a day in school, and the rest of the time work at home, learn some trade and do whatever is desired, so that study and work may go on together, while the children are young and can attend to both. They now spend tenfold as much time in shooting with crossbows, playing ball, running, and tumbling about.

In like manner, a girl has time to go to school an hour a day, and

[13] Luther was not yet married.

[14] Donatus wrote a Latin grammar used as a text-book during the Middle Ages. Alexander was the author of a commentary on Aristotle.

yet attend to her work at home; for she sleeps, dances, and plays away more than that. The real difficulty is found alone in the absence of an earnest desire to educate the young, and to aid and benefit mankind with accomplished citizens. The devil much prefers blockheads and drones, that men may have more abundant trials and sorrows in the world.

But the brightest pupils, who give promise of becoming accomplished teachers, preachers, and workers, should be kept longer at school, or set apart wholly for study, as we read of the holy martyrs, who brought up St. Agnes, St. Agatha, St. Lucian, and others. For this purpose also the cloisters and cathedral schools were founded, but they have been perverted into another and accursed use. There is great need for such instruction; for the tonsured crowd is rapidly decreasing, and besides, for the most part, the monks are unskilled to teach and rule, since they know nothing but to care for their stomachs, the only thing they have been taught. Hence we must have persons qualified to dispense the Word of God and the Sacraments, and to be pastors of the people. But where will we obtain them, if schools are not established on a more Christian basis, since those hitherto maintained, even if they do not go down, can produce nothing but depraved and dangerous corrupters of youth?

There is consequently an urgent necessity, not only for the sake of the young, but also for the maintenance of Christianity and of civil government, that this matter be immediately and earnestly taken hold of, lest afterwards, although we would gladly attend to it, we shall find it impossible to do so, and be obliged to feel in vain the pangs of remorse forever. For God is now graciously present, and offers his aid. If we despise it, we already have our condemnation with the people of Israel, of whom Isaiah says: "I have spread out my hands all the day unto a rebellious people." [15] And Proverbs i. 24-26: "I have stretched out my hand, and no man regarded: but ye have set at naught all my counsel, and would none of my reproof: I also will laugh at your calamity; I will mock when your fear cometh." Let us then take heed. Consider for example what great zeal Solomon manifested; for he was so much interested in the young that he took time, in the midst of his imperial duties, to write a book for them called Proverbs. And think how Christ himself took the little children in His arms! How earnestly He commends them to us, and speaks of their guardian angels,[16] in order that He

[15] Isaiah lxv. 2.
[16] Matt. xviii. 10.

234

may show us how great a service it is, when we rightly bring them up: on the other hand, how His anger kindles, if we offend the little ones, and let them perish.

Therefore, dear Sirs, take to heart this work, which God so urgently requires at your hands, which pertains to your office, which is necessary for the young, and which neither the world nor the Spirit can do without. We have, alas! lived and degenerated long enough in darkness; we have remained German brutes too long. Let us use our reason, that God may observe in us gratitude for His mercies, and that other lands may see that we are human beings, capable both of learning and of teaching, in order that through us, also, the world may be made better. I have done my part; I have desired to benefit the German states, although some have despised me and set my counsel at naught as knowing better themselves,— to all which I must submit. I know indeed that others could have accomplished it better; but because they were silent, I have done the best I could. It is better to have spoken, even though imperfectly, than to have remained silent. And I have hope that God will rouse some of you to listen to my counsel, and that instead of considering the adviser, you will let yourselves be moved by the great interests at stake.

Finally, this must be taken into consideration by all who earnestly desire to see such schools established and the languages preserved in the German states: that no cost nor pains should be spared to procure good libraries in suitable buildings, especially in the large cities, which are able to afford it. For if a knowledge of the Gospel and of every kind of learning is to be preserved, it must be embodied in books, as the prophets and apostles did, as I have already shown. This should be done, not only that our spiritual and civil leaders may have something to read and study, but also that good books may not be lost, and that the arts and languages may be preserved, with which God has graciously favored us. St. Paul was diligent in this matter, since he lays the injunction upon Timothy: "Give attendance to reading;" [17] and directs him to bring the books, but especially the parchments left at Troas.[18]

All the kingdoms that have been distinguished in the world have bestowed care upon this matter, and particularly the Israelites, among whom Moses was the first to begin the work, who commanded them to preserve the book of the law in the ark of God, and put it under the care of the Levites, that any one might procure

[17] 1 Tim. iv. 13.
[18] 2 Tim. iv. 13.

copies from them. He even commanded the king to make a copy of this book in the hands of the Levites. Among other duties, God directed the Levitical priesthood to preserve and attend to the books. Afterwards Joshua increased and improved this library, as did subsequently Samuel, David, Solomon, Isaiah, and many kings and prophets. Hence have come to us the Holy Scriptures of the Old Testament, which would not otherwise have been collected and preserved, if God had not required such diligence in regard to it.

After this example the collegiate churches and convents formerly founded libraries, although with few good books. And the injury resulting from the neglect to procure books and good libraries, when there were men and books enough for that purpose, was afterwards perceived in the decline of every kind of knowledge; and instead of good books, the senseless, useless, and hurtful books of the monks, the Catholicon, Florista, Graecista, Labyrinthus, Dormi Secure,[19] and the like were introduced by Satan, so that the Latin language was corrupted, and neither good schools, good instruction, nor good methods of study remained. And as we see, the languages and arts are, in an imperfect manner, recovered from fragments of old books rescued from the worms and dust; and every day men are seeking these literary remains, as people dig in the ashes of a ruined city after treasures and jewels.

Therein we have received our just due, and God has well recompensed our ingratitude, in that we did not consider His benefits, and lay up a supply of good literature when we had time and opportunity, but neglected it, as if we were not concerned. He in turn, instead of the Holy Scriptures and good books, suffered Aristotle and numberless pernicious books to come into use, which only led us further from the Bible. To these were added the progeny of Satan, the monks and the phantoms of the universities, which we founded at incredible cost, and many doctors, preachers, teachers, priests and monks, that is to say, great, coarse, fat asses, adorned with red and brown caps, like swine led with a golden chain and decorated with pearls; and we have burdened ourselves with them, who have taught us nothing useful, but have made us more and more blind and stupid, and as a reward have consumed all our property, and filled all the cloisters, and indeed every corner, with the dregs and filth of their unclean and noxious books, of which we can not think without horror.

Has it not been a grievous misfortune that a boy has hitherto been obliged to study twenty years or longer, in order to learn

[19] Names of Latin grammars and collections of sermons.

enough miserable Latin to become a priest and to read the mass? And whoever has succeeded in this, has been called blessed, and blessed the mother that has borne such a child! And yet he has remained a poor ignorant man all through life, and has been of no real service whatever. Everywhere we have had such teachers and masters, who have known nothing themselves, who have been able to teach nothing useful, and who have been ignorant even of the right methods of learning and teaching. How has it come about? No books have been accessible but the senseless trash of the monks and sophists. How could the pupils and teachers differ from the books they studied? A jackdaw does not hatch a dove, nor a fool make a man wise. That is the recompense of our ingratitude, in that we did not use diligence in the formation of libraries, but allowed good books to perish, and bad ones to survive.

But my advice is, not to collect all sorts of books indiscriminately, thinking only of getting a vast number together. I would have discrimination used, because it is not necessary to collect the commentaries of all the jurists, the productions of all the theologians, the discussions of all the philosophers, and the sermons of all the monks. Such trash I would reject altogether, and provide my library only with useful books; and in making the selection, I would advise with learned men.

In the first place, a library should contain the Holy Scriptures in Latin, Greek, Hebrew, German, and other languages. Then the best and most ancient commentators in Greek, Hebrew, and Latin.

Secondly, such books as are useful in acquiring the languages, as the poets and orators, without considering whether they are heathen or Christian, Greek or Latin. For it is from such works that grammar must be learned.

Thirdly, books treating of all the arts and sciences.

Lastly, books on jurisprudence and medicine, though here discrimination is necessary.

A prominent place should be given to chronicles and histories, in whatever languages they may be obtained; for they are wonderfully useful in understanding and regulating the course of the world, and in disclosing the marvelous works of God. O how many noble deeds and wise maxims produced on German soil have been forgotten and lost, because no one at the time wrote them down; or if they were written, no one preserved the books: hence we Germans are unknown in other lands, and are called brutes that know only how to fight, eat, and drink. But the Greeks and Romans, and even the Hebrews, have recorded their history with such particularity,

237

that even if a woman or child did any thing noteworthy, all the world was obliged to read and know it; but we Germans are always Germans, and will remain Germans.

Since God has so graciously and abundantly provided us with art, scholars, and books, it is time for us to reap the harvest and gather for future use the treasures of these golden years. For it is to be feared, (and even now it is beginning to take place,) that new and different books will be produced, until at last, through the agency of the devil, the good books which are being printed will be crowded out by the multitude of ill-considered, senseless, and noxious works. For Satan certainly designs that we should torture ourselves again with Catholicons, Floristas, Modernists, and other trash of the accursed monks and sophists, always learning, yet never acquiring knowledge.

Therefore, my dear Sirs, I beg you to let my labor bear fruit with you. And though there be some who think me too insignificant to follow my advice, or who look down upon me as one condemned by tyrants: still let them consider that I am not seeking my own interest, but that of all Germany. And even if I were a fool, and should yet hit upon something good, no wise man should think it a disgrace to follow me. And even if I were a Turk and heathen, and it should yet appear that my advice was advantageous, not for myself, but for Christianity, no reasonable person would despise my counsel. Sometimes a fool has given better advice than a whole company of wise men. Moses received instruction from Jethro.

Herewith I commend you all to the grace of God. May He soften your hearts, and kindle therein a deep interest in behalf of the poor, wretched, and neglected youth; and through the blessing of God may you so counsel and aid them as to attain to a happy Christian social order in respect to both body and soul, with all fullness and abounding plenty, to the praise and honor of God the Father, through Jesus Christ our Saviour. Amen.

Wittenberg, 1524.

DUTY OF SENDING CHILDREN TO SCHOOL

PART SECOND.—THE TEMPORAL BENEFIT OR INJURY ARISING FROM THE SUPPORT OR THE NEGLECT OF SCHOOLS. The second part of this discourse will be devoted to the temporal or secular benefit and injury resulting from a support or neglect of schools. In the first place, it is true that secular authority or station is in no way comparable to the spiritual office of

238

the ministry, as St. Paul calls it; for it is not so dearly purchased through the blood and death of the Son of God. It can not perform such great works and miracles as the ministerial office; for all the works of secular authority belong only to this temporal and transitory existence, such as caring for body, wife, child, house, goods, and honor, and whatever else pertains to the needs of the present life. As far then as eternal life surpasses temporal life, so far does the ministerial office surpass secular office; the one is the substance, the other is the shadow. For secular authority is an image, shadow, or figure of the authority of Christ; for the ministerial office, (where it exists as God ordained it,) brings and imparts eternal righteousness, eternal peace, and eternal life, as St. Paul declares in the fourth chapter of 2 Corinthians. But secular government maintains temporal and transitory peace, law, and life.

But it is still a beautiful and divine ordinance, an excellent gift of God, who ordained it, and who wishes to have it maintained as indispensable to human welfare; without it men could not live together in society, but would devour one another like the irrational animals.

. . . . . .

Accordingly, since our government in the German states is based on the imperial law of Rome, which embodies the wisdom and reason of our government, it follows that such a government can not be maintained, unless these laws are upheld. Now who will uphold them? Club-law and force will not do it; it must be done by means of knowledge and books; men must learn and understand the law and wisdom of our empire. Although it is an excellent thing when an emperor, prince or lord is wise and judicious by nature, so that he can administer justice without external aids, as could Frederick, Duke of Saxony, and Fabian von Feilitz (not to speak of the living); yet such rulers are rare, and their example is dangerous, so that it is always better to adhere to the written law, which carries with it authority, and serves as a safeguard against arbitrary action.

Now in civil government it is the jurists and scholars who uphold this law, and thereby maintain secular authority; and just as a pious theologian or sincere preacher in the kingdom of Christ is called a messenger of God, a saviour, prophet, priest, steward and teacher (as was said above), in like manner a pious jurist or a faithful scholar in the government of the emperor might be called a prophet, priest, messenger, and saviour. On the other hand, just as a heretic or hypocritical minister in the kingdom of Christ is a devil, thief,

239

murderer, blasphemer; in the same way a corrupt and unfaithful jurist in the government of the emperor is a thief, rogue, traitor, devil.

When I speak of jurists, I do not mean the doctors alone, but the whole body of civil officers—chancellors, secretaries, judges, advocates, notaries, and whatever else belongs to the civil administration, even the great crowd of advisers, as they are called, at court; for they exercise the functions of law and of jurists. And since an adviser through evil advice can easily become a traitor, it sometimes happens that under the form of friendly counsel sovereigns are basely betrayed.

You now see of what use an upright jurist can be; yea, who can fully set it forth? For whatever is God's ordinance and work, bears so much fruit that it can not be told or comprehended. First of all, such a jurist maintains and furthers with his legal knowledge (through divine institution) the whole structure of civil government—emperors, princes, lords, cities, states, people (as before stated), for all must be upheld through wisdom and justice. But who can sufficiently praise this work alone? It gives you protection of body and life against neighbors, enemies, murderers; protection also of wife, daughters, sons, house, servants, money, property, lands, and whatever you possess; for it is all comprehended, secured, and hedged about by law. How great a blessing that is, can not be told. Who can express the immeasurable benefits of peace? How much it gives and saves every year!

Such great works can your son do, and such a useful person can he become, if you direct him to the civil service and send him to school; and if you can become a sharer in this honor, and make such good use of your money, ought it not to be a great pleasure and glory to you? Think of your son as a messenger in the empire, an apostle of the emperor, a corner-stone and foundation of temporal peace on earth! Knowing, too, that God looks upon the service in this light, as indeed it deserves to be! For though we can not be justified and secure salvation by such works, it is still a joyful comfort that these works are well-pleasing to God, especially when such a man is a believer and a member of Christ's kingdom; for in that way we thank him for his benefits, and bring him the best thank-offering and the highest service.

You must indeed be an insensible and ungrateful creature, fit to be ranked among the brutes, if you see that your son may become a man to help the emperor maintain his dominions, sword, and crown—to help the prince govern his land, to counsel cities and

240

states, to help protect for every man his body, wife, child, property, and honor—and yet will not do so much as to send him to school and prepare him for this work! Tell me, what are all the chapters and cloisters doing in comparison with this? I would not give the work of a faithful, upright jurist and secretary for the righteousness of all the monks, priests, and nuns at their best. And if such great good works do not move you, the honor and desire of God alone should move you, since you know that you thereby express your gratitude to God, and render Him a service of surpassing excellence, as has been said. It is a shameful contempt of God that you do not bring up your children to such an excellent and divinely appointed calling, and that you strengthen them only in the service of appetite and avarice, teaching them nothing but to provide for the stomach, like a hog with its nose always in filth, and do not bring them up to this worthy station and office. You must either be insensible creatures, or else you do not love your children.

But hearken further: how if God demands your child for such office? For you are under obligation to help maintain civil order if you can. Now, beyond all doubt, it can not be maintained if people do not have their children instructed; and since more wisdom is required in civil office than in the ministry, it will be necessary to set apart for it the brightest boys. For in the ministry Christ works by His Spirit; but in civil government men must be guided by reason (which is the source of human laws): for God has placed secular government and our physical state under the control of reason (Gen. ii. 19), and has not sent the Holy Spirit for that purpose. Hence the functions of civil office are more difficult than those of the ministry, since the conscience can not rule, but must act, so to speak, in the dark.

If now you have a son capable of learning; if you can send him to school, but do not do it and go your way asking nothing about temporal government, law, peace, and so on; you are, to the extent of your ability, opposing civil authority like the Turk, yea, like the devil himself. For you withhold from the empire, principality, state, city, a saviour, comforter, corner-stone, helper; and so far as you are concerned, the emperor loses both his sword and crown, the state loses protection and peace, and it is through your fault (as much as lies in you) that no man can hold in security his body, wife, child, house, property. On the contrary, you freely offer them all upon a butcher's block, and give occasion for men to degenerate into brutes, and at last to devour one another. All this you certainly do, especially if you on purpose withdraw your child from such a

241

salutary station out of regard for his physical wants. Are you not a pretty and useful man in society! You daily enjoy the benefits of the government, and then as a return rob it of your son, dedicating him to avarice, and thus strive with all your might not to maintain government, law, and peace, but to destroy social order, though you possess and hold your body, life, property, and honor, through secular authority.

What do you think you deserve? Are you even worthy to dwell among men? What will God say, who has given you child and property that you might honor Him therewith, and consecrate your child to His service? Is it not serving God, if we help to maintain His ordinance of civil government? Now you neglect such service, as if it did not concern you, or as if you above all men were free and not bound to serve God; and you presume to do with your child what you please, even though the temporal and the spiritual kingdom of God perish; and at the same time you enjoy the protection, peace, and. law of the empire, and allow the ministry and Word of God to serve you, so that God becomes your servant: and yet you abuse all these benefits to turn your son from him, and to teach him the service of Mammon.

Do you not think God will pronounce such a judgment on your worldliness that you will perish with your children and property? Rather, is not your heart affrighted at the horror of your idolatry, at your contempt of God, your ingratitude, your destruction of the civil and religious ordinances of God, yea, at the injury you do all men? Well, I have declared unto you both the benefit and the injury you can do; and do which you will, God will surely repay you.

I will not here speak of the pleasure a scholar has, apart from any office, in that he can read at home all kinds of books, talk and associate with learned men, and travel and transact business in foreign lands. For this pleasure perhaps will move but few; but since you are seeking Mammon and worldly possessions, consider what great opportunities God has provided for schools and scholars; so that you need not despise learning from fear of poverty. Behold, emperors and kings must have chancellors, secretaries, counsellors, jurists and scholars; there is not a prince but must have chancellors, jurists, counsellors, scholars, and secretaries; likewise counts, lords, cities, states, castles, must have councils, secretaries, and other learned men; there is not a nobleman but must have a secretary. And to speak of ordinary scholars, where are the miners, merchants, and artisans? At the end of three years where are we to find educated men, when the want has already begun to be felt?

It looks as if kings would have to become jurists, princes chancellors, counts and lords secretaries, and mayors sextons.

If we do not soon begin to do something, we shall become Tartars and Turks, and ignoramuses will again be doctors and counsellors at court. Therefore I hold that there never was a better time for study than the present, not only because learning is so accessible and cheap, but also because great wealth and honor must follow; for those who study at this time will become such valuable people that two princes and three cities will contend for one scholar. If you look about you, you will find innumerable offices that will need learned men in less than ten years, and yet but few young people are being educated for them.

There is further a divine blessing attached to this sphere of activity; for God is pleased with the many excellent and useful works that belong to the secular condition, and that constitute a divine service. But avarice in seeking its end meets with contempt (even though its works be not sinful); evil deeds destroy all peace of mind, and such a life can not be called a service of God. Now I would rather earn ten florins with a work that might properly be called a service of God, than a thousand florins with a work that could not be called a service of God, but a service of self and Mammon.

In addition to this, there is worldly honor. For chancellors, scribes, jurists, and the people through them, occupy upper seats, help, advise and govern as said above, and in fact they here become lords on earth, though in person, birth, and station they are not so regarded. For Daniel says that he did the king's work. And it is true that a chancellor must perform imperial, kingly, princely functions and duties, a city scribe must do the work of the council and city, and that all with honor and the blessing of God, which gives happiness and salvation.

When they are not engaged in war but govern by law, what are emperors, kings, princes, (if we speak according to their work,) but mere scribes and jurists? For they concern themselves about the law, which is a legal and clerical work. And who governs the land and people in times of peace? Is it the knights and captains? I think it is the pen of the scribe. Meanwhile, what is avarice doing with its worship of Mammon? It can not come to such honor, and defiles its devotees with its rust-covered treasures.

Thus the emperor Justinian declares that "imperial majesty ought not only to be adorned with arms, but also to be armed with laws." Observe the peculiar phraseology this emperor uses, when he calls the laws his weapons, and weapons his adornment, and changes his scribes into cuirassiers and warriors. And he spoke well; for the laws are truly the right armor and weapons with which to protect the country and people, yea, the empire and government, (as has been sufficiently shown above,) so that wisdom is better than might. And pious jurists are the real warriors that preserve the emperor and princes. How many passages, if time permitted, might be given from the poets and the historians! Solomon himself in Ecclesiastes ix. 15 declares that a poor man by his wisdom saved a city from a powerful king.

Not that I would have soldiers, knights, and whatever else belongs to warfare, despised and repudiated; they also help (where they are obedient) to maintain peace and protect the land by force. Every thing has its honor before God, and its station and work.

I must also praise my craft, though I should be censured; just as St. Paul constantly praised his office, so that many thought he went too far and was proud. Whoever wishes to praise and honor soldiers, can find ground enough to do so, as I have elsewhere shown in strong terms. For I do not like those jurists and scribblers who have so high an opinion of themselves that they despise or mock other callings, as the extortionate priests and other adherents of the Papacy have hitherto done.

We should duly praise all the offices and works ordained of God, and not despise one for the sake of another; for it is written, "His work is honorable and glorious" (Ps. iii. 3). And again, Psalm civ. 24: "O Lord, how manifold are thy works! in wisdom hast thou made them all." And especially should preachers constantly inculcate such thoughts upon the people, school-teachers likewise upon their pupils, and parents upon their children, that these may learn what stations and offices are ordained of God. When they come to understand this, they should not despise, mock, or speak evil of them, but honor and esteem them. That is pleasing to God, and contributes to peace and unity; for God is a great Lord, and has many servants.

On the contrary, we find some conceited soldiers that fancy the name scribe is not worthy to be mentioned or heard by them. Well, pay no attention to it, but consider that these poor fellows must have some kind of pastime and pleasure. Let them make the most out of this; but you still remain a scribe in the eyes of God and the world. If they come together for any length of time, you see that they bestow the highest honor upon the quill, placing a feather on hat or helmet, as if they confessed by that act that the pen is the most excellent thing in the world, without which they would not be equipped for combat, nor for parade in times of peace, much less assemble in security; for they must also profit by the peace which the emperor's preachers and teachers (the jurists) maintain. Therefore, as you see, they give the place of honor to the instrument of our craft (and properly), since they gird the sword about the loins; there it hangs handsomely for their purpose: on the head it would not be becoming—there the feather must wave. If they have sinned against you, they have thus made atonement and should be forgiven.

. . . . . .

There are some who think that the office of scribe is an easy, insignificant office, but that to ride in armor and suffer heat, frost, dust, thirst, and other discomforts, is work. Verily that is an old story—no one knows where the shoe pinches another; every one feels only his own discomfort, and looks only at the comforts of another. It is true that it would be hard for me to ride in armor; but I should like to see the knight who could sit still the whole day and look in a book, though he were not required to read, think, or do any thing. Ask a chancery-clerk, preacher, orator, about the labor of writing and speaking; ask a school-master about the labor of teaching boys. The pen is a light instrument, it is true, and among all the trades there is no tool more easily procured than the pen; for it needs only a goose-quill, which can be found anywhere. But the best part of the body, as the head, and the noblest member, as the tongue, and the highest function, as speech, must here bear the brunt, and do most of the work, while in other occupations it is the hands, feet, back that labor, and the workman can at the same time sing and joke, which a writer must forego. Three fingers do it, (as is said of writers,) but the whole body and soul work at the same time.

When the ignoramuses about the illustrious emperor Maximilian complained that he employed so many scribes for embassies and other similar duties, he is said to have replied: "What shall I do? You can not be employed, so I must take scribes." And further: "I can make knights, but not doctors." I have heard also of a wise nobleman who said: "I shall let my son study; there is no great art in straddling a horse and becoming a knight,—a thing that is soon learned." And that is all well said.

I do not say this to depreciate the knightly order or any other, but to rebuke the ignorant fellows who despise all learning and culture, and praise nothing but wearing armor and straddling a horse, though they are seldom obliged to do it, and hence, the whole year through, have comfort, pleasure, honor, and money. It is indeed true that learning is light to carry, and that armor is heavy to carry; but on the other hand, to wear armor is easily learned, but an education is neither quickly acquired nor easily employed.

But to make an end of this matter, God is a wonderful sovereign, and it is his plan of work to make lords out of beggars, as he made the heaven and earth out of nothing; and in this no man will hinder Him, who is praised in all the world, as the 112th Psalm says: "Who is like unto the Lord our God, who dwelleth on high, who humbleth Himself to behold the things that are in heaven and in the earth? He raiseth up the poor out of the dust, and lifteth the needy out of the dunghill; that He may set him with princes, even with the princes of His people." Look at all the courts of kings and princes, and in cities and pastorates, and do you not see this Psalm fulfilled by many striking examples? You will there find jurists, doctors, counsellors, scribes, preachers, who struggled with poverty in acquiring an education, and who have risen by means of the pen to the position of lords, as this Psalm says, and like princes they help to govern the land and people. God does not wish that those who are born kings, princes, lords, and nobles should alone rule, but He desires also to have His beggars share in the government; otherwise, they would think that noble birth alone made lords and rulers, and that God had nothing to do with it.

It is true, as is sometimes said, that the Pope was once a student; therefore do not despise the boys who beg from door to door "a little bread for the love of God," [20] and when the groups of poor pupils sing before your house, remember that you hear, as this Psalm says, great princes and lords. I have myself been such a beggar pupil, and have eaten bread before houses, especially in the dear town of Eisenach, though afterwards my beloved father supported me at the University of Erfurt with all love and self-sacrifice, and by the sweat of his face helped me to the position I now occupy; but still I was for a time a poverty student, and according to this Psalm I have risen by the pen to a position which I would not exchange for that of the Turkish sultan, taking his wealth and giving up my learning. Yea, I would not exchange it for all the wealth of the world many times multiplied; and yet, beyond all

[20] Panem propter Deum.

246

doubt, I should not have attained my present station, if I had not gone to school and learned to write.

Without anxiety, then, let your son study, and if he should have to beg bread for a time, you give our God material out of which he can make a lord. It will remain true that your son and mine, that is to say, the children of the common people, will rule the world, both in spiritual and secular stations, as this Psalm testifies. For wealthy worldlings can not and will not do it; they are the priests and monks of Mammon, upon whom they are obliged to wait day and night; princes and lords by birth can not do it alone, and especially are they unable to fill the spiritual office of the ministry. Thus must both spiritual and secular government continue on earth in the hands of the common people and their children.

And pay no attention to the contempt which the ordinary devotee of Mammon manifests for culture, so that he says: "Well, if my son can read, write, and cipher, that is enough; for I am going to make a merchant out of him." Without scholars it would not be long till business men in their perplexity would be ready to dig a learned man out of the ground ten yards deep with their fingers; for the merchant will not long remain a merchant, if preaching and the administration of justice cease. I know full well that we theologians and jurists must remain, or else all other vocations will inevitably go to the ground with us; where theologians perish, there perishes also the Word of God, and nothing but heathen and devils are left; when jurists perish, there perish also law and peace, and nothing remains but robbery, murder, outrage, and force—the reign of wild beasts. But what the merchant will gain when peace vanishes, I shall let his ledger tell him; and the use of all his property when preaching ceases, let his conscience show him.

It is a ground of special vexation that such foolish and unchristian language is used by those who pretend to be evangelical, and who know how to beat down every opponent with Scripture; and yet, at the same time, they do not bestow honor enough upon God or their children to educate them for these divine and exalted offices, through which they could serve their Maker and the world, and in which their temporal wants would be provided for. On the contrary, they turn their children away from these callings, and urge them to the service of Mammon, in which their success is uncertain, their bodies and souls are endangered, and their lives can in no way be considered a service of God.

I should mention here how many learned men are needed in medicine and the other professions, in reference to which a book might be written, and six months spent in preaching. Where would our preachers, jurists, and physicians come from, if the liberal arts were not taught? It is from this source they all must come. But to speak of this in detail would carry me too far. To be brief, an industrious, pious school-master or teacher, who faithfully trains and educates boys, can never be sufficiently recompensed, and no money will pay him, as even the heathen Aristotle says. Yet this calling is shamefully despised among us, as if it were nothing— and at the same time we pretend to be Christians!

If I had to give up preaching and my other duties, there is no office I would rather have than that of school-teacher. For I know that next to the ministry it is the most useful, greatest, and best; and I am not sure which of the two is to be preferred. For it is hard to make old dogs docile and old rogues pious, yet that is what the ministry works at, and must work at, in great part, in vain; but young trees, though some may break in the process, are more easily bent and trained. Therefore let it be considered one of the highest virtues on earth faithfully to train the children of others, which duty but very few parents attend to themselves.

That physicians in a sense become lords, is everywhere apparent; and that they can not be dispensed with, is taught by experience; but that medicine is a useful, comforting, and salutary profession, and likewise an acceptable and divinely appointed service of God, appears not only from the work itself, but also from Scripture. The thirty-eighth chapter of Ecclesiasticus is devoted to the praise of physicians: "Honor a physician with the honor due unto him for the uses which you may have of him; for the Lord hath created him. For of the Most High cometh healing. The Lord hath created medicines out of the earth; and he that is wise will not abhor them. Was not the water made sweet with wood, that the virtue thereof might be known? With such doth He heal men, and taketh away their pains. Of such doth the apothecary make a confection; and of his works there is no end," etc. But I am going too far; other preachers may develop these points more fully, and show the people better than I can write it, what injury or benefit may here be done the world and posterity.

.   .   .   .   .

But I maintain that the civil authorities are under obligation to compel the people to send their children to school, especially such as are promising, as has elsewhere been said. For our rulers are certainly bound to maintain the spiritual and secular offices and callings, so that there may always be preachers, jurists, pastors, scribes, physicians, school-masters, and the like; for these can not be dispensed with. If the government can compel such citizens as are fit for military service to bear spear and rifle, to mount ramparts, and perform other martial duties in time of war; how much more has it a right to compel the people to send their children to school, because in this case we are warring with the devil, whose object it is secretly to exhaust our cities and principalities of their strong men, to destroy the kernel and leave a shell of ignorant and helpless people, whom he can sport and juggle with at pleasure. That is starving out a city or country, destroying it without a struggle, and without its knowledge. The Turk does differently, and takes every third child in his empire to educate for whatever he pleases. How much more should our rulers require children to be sent to school, who, however, are not taken from their parents, but are educated for their own and the general good, in an office where they have an adequate support.

Therefore, let him who can, watch; and wherever the government sees a promising boy, let him be sent to school. If the father is poor, let the child be aided with the property of the Church. The rich should make bequests to such objects, as some have done, who have founded scholarships; that is giving money to the Church in a proper way. You do not thus release the souls of the dead from purgatorial fire, but you help, through the maintenance of divinely appointed offices, to prevent the living from going to purgatory—yea, you secure their deliverance from hell and entrance into heaven, and bestow upon them temporal peace and happiness. That would be a praiseworthy, Christian bequest, in which God would take pleasure, and for which He would honor and bless you, that you might have joy and peace in Him. Now, my dear Germans, I have warned you enough; you have heard your prophet. God grant that we may follow His Word, to the praise and honor of our dear Lord, for His precious blood so graciously shed for us, and preserve us from the horrible sin of ingratitude and forgetfulness of His benefits. Amen.

ERASMUS 1466–1536

ERASMUS was probably the greatest scholar of the humanist period. He was also one of the first great liberals in Western culture.

As a scholar he quickly won the recognition of his contemporaries; nobody could deny the philological quality of his editions of the New Testament and of the Church Fathers. But, as every true liberal, he had to suffer for his liberalism. Since he attacked the corruption in Catholicism and the confusion of religion with ritualism and superstition, he was disliked by the clergy, though the Church bestowed honors on him. The Protestant reformers first expected him to be their friend. But he refused to join the new movement. It was for him too irrational; in addition, despite all his attacks against the mere show of tradition, he knew the value of the universality in the Greek-Roman-Christian heritage and was afraid of contributing to its disintegration. So the Protestants insulted him as a traitor.

He, like Plato, is the tragic symbol of the wise man who cannot support either of two opposing issues, not because he lacks strength and courage, but because his mind is too unimpeachable to conceal to itself the defects on either side. So he prefers to be alone.

Erasmus, especially in his *Praise of Folly,* could be extremely sarcastic, and thus he made for himself more enemies than was perhaps necessary. Yet, the essence of his character was kindness and a profound sympathy with humankind. And in all his fights against narrowness and fanaticism, and in all his personal tribulations, one figure always accompanied and comforted him—the figure of Christ.

The following selections from Erasmus' *The Education of a Christian Prince* are taken from the translation by Lester K. Born, published by Columbia University Press, New York, 1936, reprinted by permission of the publisher. The selections from *The Praise of Folly* are from a translation published in London by Adams and Co.; in Glasgow by Thomas D. Morison, in 1887.

THE EDUCATION OF A CHRISTIAN PRINCE

I.—. . . Nature created all men equal, and slavery was superimposed on nature, which fact the laws of even the pagans recognized. Now stop and think how out of proportion it is for a Christian to usurp full power over other Christians, whom the laws did not design to be slaves, and whom Christ redeemed from all slav-

250

ery. . . . And over them, who have the same Master as you, the Prince, Jesus Christ, will you impose the yoke of slavery?

You may treat them as you please, divide them off as you will, and even kill them. Surely he who has reduced his free subjects to slaves has put his power on a meaner level. The loftier the ideal to which you fashion your authority, the more magnificently and splendidly will you rule. Whoever protects the liberty and standing of your subjects is the one that helps your sovereign power. God gave the angels and men free will so that He would not be ruling over bondsmen, and so that He might glorify and add further grandeur to His kingdom. And who, now, would swell with pride because he rules over men cowed down by fear, like so many cattle?

. . . . .

III.—THE ARTS OF PEACE. Although the writers of antiquity divided the whole theory of state government into two sections, war and peace, the first and most important objective is the instruction of the prince in the matter of ruling wisely during times of peace, in which he should strive his utmost to preclude any future need for the science of war. In this matter it seems best that the prince should first know his own kingdom. This knowledge is best gained from [a study of] geography and history and from frequent visits through his provinces and cities. Let him first be eager to learn the location of his districts and cities, with their beginnings, their nature, institutions, customs, laws, annals, and privileges. No one can heal the body until he is thoroughly conversant with it. No one can properly till a field which he does not understand. To be sure, the tyrant takes great care in such matters, but it is the spirit, not the act, which singles out the good prince. The physician studies the functions of the body so as to be more adept in healing it; the poisoning assassin, to more surely end it! Next, the prince should love the land over which he rules just as the farmer loves the fields of his ancestors or as a good man feels affection toward his household. . . .

In the second place the prince will see to it that he is loved by his subjects in return, but in such way that his authority is no less strong among them. There are some who are so stupid as to strive to win good will for themselves by incantations and magic rings, when there is no charm more efficacious than good character itself; nothing can be more lovable than that, for, as this is a real and immortal good, so it brings a man true and undying good will. The best formula is this: let him love, who would be loved, so that he may attach his subjects to him as God has won the peoples of the world to Himself by His goodness.

They are also wrong who win the hearts of the masses by largesses, feasts, and gross indulgence. It is true that some popular favor, instead of affection, is gained by these means, but it is neither genuine nor permanent. In the meanwhile the greed of the populace is developed, which, as happens, after it has reached large proportions thinks nothing is enough. . . .

In the first place, then, he who would be loved by his people should show himself a prince worthy of love; after that it will do some good to consider how best he may win his way into their hearts. The prince should do this first so that the best men may have the highest regard for him and that he may be accepted by those who are lauded by all. They are the men he should have for his close friends; they are the ones for his counselors; they are the ones on whom he should bestow his honors and whom he should allow to have the greatest influence with him. . . .

For my part, I should like to see the prince born and raised among those people whom he is destined to rule, because friendship is created and confirmed most when the source of good will is in nature itself. The common people shun and hate even good qualities when they are unknown to them, while evils which are familiar are sometimes loved. This matter at hand has a twofold advantage to offer, for the prince will be more kindly disposed toward his subjects and certainly more ready to regard them as his own. The people on their part will feel more kindness in their hearts and be more willing to recognize his position as prince. For this reason I am especially opposed to the accepted [idea of] alliances of the princes with foreign, particularly with distant, nations.

. . . . .

. . . Good will is the opposite of hatred; respected authority, of contempt. Therefore it will be the duty of the prince to study the best way to win the former and avoid the latter. Hatred is kindled by an ugly temper, by violence, insulting language, sourness of character, meanness, and greediness; it is more easily aroused than allayed. A good prince must therefore use every caution to prevent any possibility of losing the affections of his subjects. You may take my word that whoever loses the favor of his people is thereby stripped of a great safeguard. On the other hand, the affections of the populace are won by those characteristics which, in general, are farthest removed from tyranny. They are clemency, affability, fair-

252

ness, courtesy, and kindliness. This last is to spur to duty, especially if they who have been of good service to the state, see that they will be rewarded at the hands of the prince. Clemency inspires to better efforts those who are aware of their faults, while forgiveness extends hope to those who are now eager to make recompense by virtuous conduct for the shortcomings of their earlier life and provides the steadfast with a happy reflection on human nature. Courtesy everywhere engenders love—or at least assuages hatred. This quality in a great prince is by far the most pleasing to the masses.

Contempt is most likely to spring from a penchant for the worldly pleasures of lust, for excessive drinking and eating, and for fools and clowns—in other words, for folly and idleness. Authority is gained by the following varied characteristics: in the first place wisdom, then integrity, self-restraint, seriousness, and alertness.

. . . . . .

A prince who is about to assume control of the state must be advised at once that the main hope of a state lies in the proper education of its youth. . . . Pliable youth is amenable to any system of training. Therefore the greatest care should be exercised over public and private schools and over the education of the girls, so that the children may be placed under the best and most trustworthy instructors and may learn the teachings of Christ and that good literature which is beneficial to the state. As a result of this scheme of things, there will be no need for many laws or punishments, for the people will of their own free will follow the course of right.

Education exerts such a powerful influence, as Plato says, that a man who has been trained in the right develops into a sort of divine creature, while on the other hand, a person who has received a perverted training degenerates into a monstrous sort of savage beast. Nothing is of more importance to a prince than to have the best possible subjects.

The first effort, then, is to get them accustomed to the best influences, because any music has a soothing effect to the accustomed ear, and there is nothing harder than to rid people through habit. None of those tasks will be too difficult if the prince himself adheres to the best manners. It is the essence of tyranny, or rather trickery, to treat the common citizen as animal trainers are accustomed to treat a savage beast: first they carefully study the way in which these creatures are quieted or aroused, and then they anger them or quiet them at their pleasure. This Plato has painstakingly pointed out. Such a course is an abuse of the emotions of the masses and is no help to them. However, if the people prove intractable and rebel against what is good for them, then you must bide your time and gradually lead them over to your end, either by some subterfuge or by some helpful pretence. This works just as wine does, for when that is first taken it has no effect, but when it has gradually flowed through every vein it captivates the whole man and holds him in its power.

If sometimes the whirling course of events and public opinion beat the prince from his course, and he is forced to obey the [exigencies of the] time, yet he must not cease his efforts as long as he is able to renew his fight, and what he has not accomplished by one method he should try to effect by another.

IV—ON TRIBUTES AND TAXES. A good prince will tax as lightly as possible those commodities which are used even by the poorest members of society; e.g., grain, bread, beer, wine, clothing, and all the other staples without which human life could not exist. But it so happens that these very things bear the heaviest tax in several ways; in the first place, by the oppressive extortion of the tax farmers, commonly called assisiae, then by import duties which call for their own set of extortionists, and finally by the monopolies by which the poor are sadly drained of their funds in order that the prince may gain a mere trifling interest.

. . . However, if some taxation is absolutely necessary and the affairs of the people render it essential, barbarous and foreign goods should be heavily taxed because they are not the essentials of livelihood but the extravagant luxuries and delicacies which only the wealthy enjoy; for example, linen, silks, dyes, pepper, spices, unguents, precious stones, and all the rest of that same category. But by this system only those who can well afford it feel the pinch. They will not be reduced to straightened circumstances as a result of this outlay but perchance may be made more moderate in their desires so that the loss of money may be replaced by a change for the better in their habits.

·   ·   ·   ·   ·

XI.—ON BEGINNING WAR. Although a prince ought nowhere to be precipitate in his plans, there is no place for him to be more deliberate and circumspect than in the matter of going to war. Some evils come from one source and others from another, but from war comes the shipwreck of all that is good and from it the sea of all calamities pours out. Then, too, no other misfortune clings so

254

steadfastly. War is sown from war; from the smallest comes the greatest; from one comes two; from jesting one comes a fierce and bloody one, and the plague arising in one place, spreads to the nearest peoples and is even carried into the most distant places.

A good prince should never go to war at all unless, after trying every other means, he cannot possibly avoid it. If we were of this mind, there would hardly be a war. Finally, if so ruinous an occurrence cannot be avoided, then the prince's main care should be to wage the war with as little calamity to his own people and as little shedding of Christian blood as may be, and to conclude the struggle as soon as possible. The really Christian prince will first weigh the great difference between man, who is an animal born for peace and good will, and beasts and monsters, who are born to predatory war; [he will weigh also] the difference between men and Christian men. Then let him think over how earnestly peace is to be sought and how honorable and wholesome it is; on the other hand [let him consider] how disastrous and criminal an affair war is and what a host of all evils it carries in its wake even if it is the most justifiable war—if there really is any war which can be called "just." Lastly, when the prince has put away all personal feelings, let him take a rational estimate long enough to reckon what the war will cost and whether the final end to be gained is worth that much— even if victory is certain, victory which does not always happen to favor the best causes. Weigh the worries, the expenditures, the trials, the long wearisome preparation. That barbaric flux of men in the last stages of depravity must be got together, and while you wish to appear more generous in favor than the other prince, in addition to paying out money you must coax and humor the mercenary soldiers, who are absolutely the most abject and execrable type of human being. Nothing is dearer to a good prince than to have the best possible subjects. But what greater or more ready ruin to moral character is there than war? There is nothing more to the wish of the prince than to see his people safe and prospering in every way. But while he is learning to campaign he is compelled to expose his young men to so many dangers, and often in a single hour to make many and many an orphan, widow, childless old man, beggar, and unhappy wretch.

The wisdom of princes will be too costly for the world if they persist in learning from experience how dreadful war is, so that when they are old men, they may say: "I did not believe that war was so utterly destructive!" But—and I call God to witness—with what countless afflictions on the whole world have you learned that idea! The prince will understand some day that it was useless to extend the territory of the kingdom and that what in the beginning seems a gain was [in reality] tremendous loss, but in the meantime a great many thousands of men have been killed or impoverished. These things should better be learned from books, from the stories of old men, from the tribulations of neighbors: "For many years this or that prince has been fighting on for such and such a kingdom. How much more is his loss than his gain!" Let the good prince establish matters of the sort that will be of lasting worth. Those things which are begun out of a fancy are to our liking while the fancy lasts, but the things which are based on judgment and which delight the young man, will also afford pleasure to the old man. Nowhere is this truth more to be observed than in the beginning of war.

Plato calls it sedition, not war, when Greeks war with Greeks; and if this should happen, he bids them fight with every restraint. What term should we apply, then, when Christians engage in battle with Christians, since they are united by so many bonds to each other? What shall we say when on account of a mere title, on account of a personal grievance, on account of a stupid and youthful ambition, a war is waged with every cruelty and carried on during many years?

Some princes deceive themselves that any war is certainly a just one and that they have a just cause for going to war. We will not attempt to discuss whether war is ever just; but who does not think his own cause just? Among such great and changing vicissitudes of human events, among so many treaties and agreements which are now entered into, now rescinded, who can lack a pretext—if there is any real excuse—for going to war? But the pontifical laws do not disapprove all war. Augustine approves of it in some instances, and St. Bernard praises some soldiers. But Christ himself and Peter and Paul everywhere teach the opposite. Why is their authority less with us than that of Augustine or Bernard? Augustine in one or two places does not disapprove of war, but the whole philosophy of Christ teaches against it. There is no place in which the apostles do not condemn it; and in how many places do those very holy fathers, by whom, to the satisfaction of some, war has been approved in one or two places, condemn and abhor it? Why do we slur over all these matters and fasten upon that which helps our sins? Finally, if any one will investigate the matter more carefully, he will find that no one has approved the kind of wars in which we are now commonly involved.

256

Certain arts are not countenanced by the laws on the ground that they are too closely allied to imposture and are too frequently practiced by deceit; for example, astrology and the so-called "alchemy," even if someone happens to be employing them for an honorable purpose. This restriction will be made with far more justice in the case of wars, for even if there are some which might be called "just," yet as human affairs are now, I know not whether there could be found any of this sort—that is, the motive for which was not ambition, wrath, ferocity, lust, or greed. It too often happens that nobles, who are more lavish than their private means allow, when the opportunity is presented stir up war in order to replenish their resources at home even by the plunder of their peoples. It happens sometimes that princes enter into mutual agreements and carry on a war on trumped-up grounds so as to reduce still more the power of the people, and secure their own positions through disaster to their subjects. Wherefore the good Christian prince should hold under suspicion every war, no matter how just.

People may lay down the doctrine that your rights must not be forsaken. In the first place those rights are connected to a large extent with the private affairs of the prince if he has acquired them through alliances. How unfair it would be to maintain them at the expense of such great suffering to the people; and while you are seeking some addition or other to your power, to plunder the whole kingdom and to plunge it into deadliest turmoil. If one prince offends another on some trivial matter (probably a personal one such as a marriage alliance or other like affair) what concern is this to the people as a whole? A good prince measures everything by the advantage of his people, otherwise he is not even a prince. He does not have the same right over men as over animals. A large part of the ruling authority is in the consent of the people, which is the factor that first created kings. If a disagreement arises between princes, why not go to arbiters? There are plenty of bishops, abbots, and learned men, or reliable magistrates, by whose judgment the matter could better be settled than by such slaughter, despoliation, and calamity to the world.

The Christian prince should first question his own right, and then if it is established without a doubt he should carefully consider whether it should be maintained by means of catastrophes to the whole world. Those who are wise sometimes prefer to lose a thing rather than to gain it, because they realize that it will be less costly . . . But what will be safe, they say, if no one maintains his rights? Let the prince insist by all means, if there is any ad-

257

vantage to the state, only do not let the right of the prince bear too hard on his subjects. But what is safe anywhere while everyone is maintaining his rights to the last ditch? We see wars arise from wars, wars following wars, and no end or limit to the upheaval! It is certainly obvious that nothing is accomplished by these means. Therefore other remedies should be given a trial. Not even between the best of friends will relations remain permanently harmonious unless sometimes one gives in to the other. A husband often makes some concession to his wife so as not to break their harmony. What does war cause but war? Courtesy, on the other hand, calls forth courtesy, and fairness, fairness. The fact that he can see, from the countless calamities which war always carries in its wake, that the greatest hardship falls on those to whom the war means nothing and who are in no way deserving of these catastrophes, will have an effect on the devoted and merciful prince.

After the prince has reckoned and added up the total of all the catastrophes [which would come] to the world (if that could ever be done), then he should think over in his own mind: "Shall I, one person, be the cause of so many calamities? Shall I alone be charged with such an outpouring of human blood; with causing so many widows; with filling so many homes with lamentation and mourning; with robbing so many old men of their sons; with impoverishing so many who do not deserve such a fate; and with such utter destruction of morals, laws, and practical religion? Must I account for all these things before Christ?" The prince cannot punish his enemy unless he first brings hostile activities upon his own subjects. He must fleece his people, and he must receive [into his realm] the soldier, who has been called ruthless (and not without justification) by Vergil. He must cut off his subjects from those districts which they formerly enjoyed for their own advantage; [or else the reverse], he must shut up his subjects in order to hem in the enemy. And it frequently happens that we inflict worse sufferings upon our own people than upon the enemy. It is more difficult, as well as more desirable, to build a fine city than to destroy it. But we see flourishing cities which are established by inexperienced and common people, demolished by the wrath of princes. Very often we destroy a town with greater labor and expense than that with which we could build a new one, and we carry on war at such great expense, such loss, such zeal, and pains, that peace could be maintained at one-tenth of these costs.

Let the good prince always lean toward that glory which is not steeped in blood nor linked with the misfortune of another. In war,

258

however fortunately it turns out, the good fortune of one is always the ruin of the other. Many a time, too, the victor weeps over a victory bought too dearly.

If you are not moved by devotion, nor by the calamity of the world, surely you will be stirred by the honor of the term "Christian." What do we think the Turks and Saracens are saying about us when they see that for century after century there has been no harmony between Christian princes; that no treaties have secured peace; that there has been no end to bloodshed; and that there has been less disorder among the heathen than among those who profess the most complete accord in following the teachings of Christ?

How fleeting, short, and delicate is the life of man, and how exposed to calamities, with so many diseases and accidents which are continually happening, such as the falling of buildings, shipwrecks, earthquakes, and lightning? There is no need, then, of wars to stir up misfortunes; and more calamities come from that source than from all else. It was the duty of the preachers to have uprooted completely the ideas of discord from the hearts of the common people. But now practically every Angle hates the Gaul, and every Gaul the Angle, for no other reason than that he is an Angle. The Irishman, just because he is an Irishman, hates the Briton; the Italian hates the German; the Swabian, the Swiss; and so on throughout the list. District hates district, and city (civitas) hates city. Why do these stupid names do more to divide us than the common name of Christ does to unite us?

Although we may grant some war to be just, yet, since we see that all men go mad over this scourge, it is the part of wise priests to deflect the minds of commoners and princes into different channels. Now we see them often as the very firebrands of war. The bishops are not ashamed to go about in the camp, and there is the cross, and there the body of Christ, and they mix His heavenly sacraments with things that are more than Tartarean and in such bloody discord produce the symbols of the greatest charity. What is more ridiculous, Christ in both camps, as if he were fighting against himself. It was not enough that war was tolerated among Christians, it must also be given the place of highest honor.

If the whole teaching of Christ do not everywhere inveigh against war; if a single instance of specific commendation of war can be brought forth in its favor, let us Christians fight. The Hebrews were allowed to engage in war, but only by consent of God. Our oracle, which we hear steadily in the Gospels, restrains us from war, and yet we wage war more madly than they. David was most

259

pleasing to God for various good qualities, and yet He forbade His temple to be built by Him on the one ground that he was tainted with blood; that is, he was a warrior. He chose the peaceful Solomon for this task. If these things were done among the Jews, what should be done among us Christians? They had a shadow of Solomon, we have the real Solomon, the Prince of Peace, Christ, who conciliates all things in heaven and earth.

Not even against the Turks do I believe we should rashly go to war, first reflecting in my own mind that the kingdom of Christ was created, spread out, and firmly established by far different means. Perchance then it is not right that it should be maintained by means differing from those by which it was created and extended. We see how many times under pretexts of wars of this kind the Christian people have been plundered and nothing else has been accomplished. Now, if the matter has to do with faith, that has been increased and made famous by the suffering of martyrs and not by forces of soldiery; but if it is for ruling power, wealth, and possessions, we must continuously be on guard lest the cause have too little of Christianity in it. But on the contrary, to judge from some who are conducting wars of this kind, it may more readily happen that we degenerate into Turks than that they become Christians through our efforts. First let us see that we ourselves are genuine Christians, and then, if it seems best, let us attack the Turks.

We have written elsewhere more extensively on the evils of war and should not repeat here. I will only urge princes of Christian faith to put aside all feigned excuses and all false pretexts and with wholehearted seriousness to work for the ending of that madness for war which has persisted so long and disgracefully among Christians, that among those whom so many ties unite there may arise a peace and concord. Let them develop their genius to this end, and for this let them show their strength, combine their plans, and strain every nerve. Whoever desires to appear great, let him prove himself great in this way. If any one accomplishes this, he will have done a deed far more magnificent than if he had subdued the whole of Africa by arms. It would not be so difficult to do, if everyone would cease to favor his own cause, if we could set aside all personal feelings and carry out the common aim, if Christ, not the world, was in our plans. Now, while everyone is looking out for his own interests, while popes and bishops are deeply concerned over power and wealth, while princes are driven headlong by ambition or anger, while all follow after them for the sake of their own gain, it is not surprising that we run straight into a whirlwind of affairs under the guidance of folly. But if, after common counsel, we should carry out our common task, even those things which are purely personal to each one would be more prosperous. Now even that for which we are fighting is lost.

I have no doubt, most illustrious of princes, but that you are of this mind; for you were born in that atmosphere and have been trained by the best and most honorable men along those lines. For the rest, I pray that Christ, who is all good and supreme, may continue to bless your worthy efforts. He gave you a kingdom untainted by blood; He would have it always so. He rejoices to be called the Prince of Peace; may you do the same, that by your goodness and your wisdom, at last there may be a respite from the maddest of mad wars. The memory of the misfortunes we have passed through will also commend peace to us, and the calamities of earlier times will render twofold the favor of your kindness.

THE PRAISE OF FOLLY

AN ORATION.—IT IS FOLLY WHO SPEAKS. How slightly soever I am esteemed in the common vogue of the world, for I well know how disingenuously Folly is decried, even by those who are themselves the greatest fools, yet it is from my influence alone that the whole universe receives her ferment of mirth and jollity. Of which this may be urged as a convincing argument, in that as soon as I appeared to speak before this numerous assembly all their countenances were gilded over with a lively sparkling pleasantness. You soon welcomed me with so encouraging a look, you spurred me on with so cheerful a hum, that truly in all appearance, you seemed now flushed with a good dose of reviving nectar, when as just before, you sate drowsy and melancholy, as if you were lately come out of some hermit's cell. But as it is usual, that as soon as the sun peeps from her eastern bed, and draws back the curtains of the darksome night; or as when, after a hard winter, the restorative spring breathes a more enlivening air, nature forthwith changes her apparel, and all things seem to renew their age; so at the first sight of me you all unmask, and appear in more lively colours.

That therefore with expert orators can scarce effect by all their little artifice of eloquence, to wit, a raising the attentions of their auditors to a composedness of thought, this a bare look from me has commanded. The reason why I appear in this odd kind of garb, you shall soon be informed of, if for so short a while you will have but the patience to lend me an ear. Yet not such a one as you are wont to hearken with to your reverend preachers, but as you listen withal to mountebanks, buffoons, and merry-andrews; in short, such as formerly were fastened to Midas, as a punishment for his affront to the god Pan. For I am now in a humour to act awhile the sophist, yet not of that sort who undertake the drudgery of tyrannizing over school boys, and teach a more than womanish knack of brawling. But in imitation of those ancient ones, who to avoid the scandalous epithet of wise, preferred this title of sophists; the task of these was to celebrate the worth of gods and heroes. Prepare therefore to be entertained with a panegyrick, yet not upon Hercules, Solon, or any other grandee, but on myself, that is, upon Folly.

. . . . .

I shall confine therefore my following discourse only to such as challenge the repute of wisdom, and seemingly pass for men of the soundest intellectuals. Among whom the Grammarians present themselves in the front, a sort of men who would be the most miserable, the most slavish, and the most hateful of all persons, if I did not in some way alleviate the pressures and miseries of their profession by blessing them with a bewitching sort of madness. For they are not only liable to those five curses, which they so oft recite from the first five verses of Homer, but to five hundred more of a worse nature; as always damned to thirst and hunger, to be choked with dust in their unswept schools. Schools, shall I term them, or rather elaboratories, nay, bridewells, and houses of correction.

To wear out themselves in fret and drudgery; to be deafened with the noise of gaping boys; and in short, to be stifled with heat and stench; and yet they cheerfully acquiesce in all these inconveniences, and, by the help of a fond conceit, think themselves as happy as any men living. Taking a great pride and delight in frowning and looking big upon the trembling Vurchins, in boxing, slashing, striking with the ferula, and in the exercise of all their other methods of tyranny. While thus lording it over a parcel of young, weak chits, they imitate the Cuman ass, and think themselves as stately as a lion, that domineers over all the inferior herd.

Elevated with this conceit, they can hold filth and nastiness to be an ornament; can reconcile their nose to the most intolerable smells; and finally, think their wretched slavery the most arbitrary kingdom, which they would not exchange for the jurisdiction of the most sovereign potentate. And they are yet more happy by a strong

262

persuasion of their own parts and abilities; for thus when their employment is only to rehearse silly stories, and poetical fictions, they will yet think themselves wiser than the best experienced philosopher; nay, they have an art of making ordinary people, such as their school boys' fond parents, to think them as considerable as their own pride has made them.

Add hereunto this other sort of ravishing pleasure. When any of them has found out who was the mother of Anchises, or has lighted upon some old unusual word, such as *bubsequa bovinator, manticulator,* or other like obsolete cramp terms; or can, after a great deal of poring, spell out the inscription of some battered monument; Lord! what joy, what triumph, what congratulating their success, as if they had conquered Africa, or taken Babylon the Great! When they recite some of their frothy, bombast verses, if any happen to admire them, they are presently flushed with the least hint of commendation, and more devoutly than Pythagoras for his grateful hypotheses, whereby they are now become actuated with a descent of Virgil's poetic soul.

Nor is any divertissement more pleasant, than when they meet to flatter and curry one another; yet they are so critical, that if any one hap to be guilty of the least slip, or seeming blunder, another shall presently correct him for it, and then to it they go in a tongue-combat with all the fervour, spleen, and eagerness imaginable. May Priscian himself be my enemy if what I am now going to say be not exactly true. I knew an old Sophister that was a Grecian, a latinist, a mathematician, a philosopher, a musician, and all to the utmost perfection, who, after threescore years' experience in the world, had spent the last twenty of them only in drudging to conquer the criticisms of grammar, and made it the chief part of his prayers, that his life might be so long spared till he had learned how rightly to distinguish betwixt the eight parts of speech, which no grammarian, whether Greek or Latin, had yet accurately done. If any chance to have placed that as a conjunction which ought to have been used as an adverb, it is a sufficient alarm to raise a war for doing justice to the injured word.

And since there have been as many several grammars, as particular grammarians, nay, more, for Aldus alone wrote five distinct grammars for his own share, the schoolmaster must be obliged to consult them all, sparing for no time nor trouble, though never so great, lest he should be otherwise posed in an unobserved criticism, and so by an irreparable disgrace lose the reward of all his toil. It is indifferent to me whether you call this folly or madness, since

263

you must needs confess that it is by my influence these school-tyrants, though in never so despicable a condition, are so happy in their own thoughts, that they would not change fortunes with the most illustrious Sophi of Persia.

The Poets, however somewhat less beholden to me, own a professed dependence on me, being a sort of lawless blades, that by prescription claim a license to a proverb, while the whole intent of their profession is only to smooth up and tickle the ears of fools. That by mere toys and fabulous shams, with which however ridiculous they are so bolstered up in an airy imagination, as to promise themselves an everlasting name, and promise, by their balderdash, at the same time to celebrate the never-dying memory of others. To these rapturous wits self-love and flattery are never-failing attendants; nor do any prove more zealous or constant devotees to folly.

The Rhetoricians likewise, though they are ambitious of being ranked among the Philosophers, yet are apparently of my faction, as appears among other arguments, by this more especially. In that among their several topics of completing the art of oratory, they all particularly insist upon the knack of jesting, which is one species of folly; as evident from the books of oratory ascribed to Herennius, put among Cicero's work, but done by some other unknown author. And in Quintilian, that great master of eloquence, there is one large chapter spent in prescribing the methods of raising laughter. In short, they may well attribute a great efficacy to folly, since on any argument they can many times by a slight laugh over what they could never seriously confute.

Of the same gang are those scribbling fops, who think to eternize their memory by setting up for authors. Among which, though they are all some way indebted to me, yet are those more especially so, who spoil paper in blotting it with mere trifles and impertinences. For as to those graver drudgers to the press, that write learnedly, beyond the reach of an ordinary reader, who durst submit their labours to the review of the most severe critic, these are not so liable to be envied for their honour, as to be pitied for their sweat and slavery. They make additions, blot out, write anew, amend, interline, turn it upside down, and yet can never please their fickle judgment, but that they shall dislike the next hour what they penned the former; and all this to purchase the airy commendations of a few understanding readers, which at most is but a poor reward for all their fastings, watchings, confinements, and brain-breaking tortures of invention. Add to this the impairing of their

264

health, the weakening of their constitution, their contracting sore eyes, or perhaps turning stark blind; their poverty, their envy, their debarment from all pleasures, their hastening on old age, their untimely death, and what other inconveniences of a like or worse nature can be thought upon: and yet the recompense for all this severe penance is at best no more than a mouthful or two of frothy praise.

These, as they are more laborious, so are they less happy than those, other hackney scribblers which I first mentioned, who never stand much to consider, but write what comes next at a venture, knowing that the more silly their composure, the more they will be bought up by the greater number of readers, who are fools and blockheads. And if they hap to be condemned by some few judicious persons, it is an easy matter by clamour to drown their censure, and to silence them by urging the more numerous commendations of others.

They are yet the wisest who transcribe whole discourses from others, and then reprint them as their own. By doing so they make a cheap and easy seizure to themselves of that reputation which cost the first author so much time and trouble to procure. If they are at any time pricked a little in conscience for fear of discovery, they feed themselves however with this hope, that if they be at last found plagiaries, yet at least for some time they have the credit of passing for the genuine authors.

It is pleasant to see how all these several writers are puffed up with the least blast of applause, especially if they walk along the streets, when their several pieces are laid open upon every bookseller's stall, when their names are embossed in a different character upon the title-page, sometime only with the two first letters, and sometime with fictious cramp terms, which few shall understand the meaning of. And of those that do, all shall not agree in their verdict of the performance. Some censuring, others approving it, men's judgments being as different as their palates, that being toothsome to one which is unsavoury and nauseous to another. Though it is a sneaking piece of cowardice for authors to put feigned names to their works, as if, like bastards of their brain, they were afraid to own them. Thus one styles himself Telemachus, another Stelenus, a third Polycrates, another Thrasymachus, and so on. By the same liberty we may ransack the whole alphabet, and jumble together any letters that come next to hand.

It is farther very pleasant when these coxcombs employ their pens in writing congratulatory epistles, poems, and panegyricks, upon each other, wherein one shall be charactered for the incomparable Callimachus; this shall be commended for a completer orator than Tully himself; a fourth shall be told by his fellow-fool that the divine Plato comes short of him for a philosophic soul.

Sometime again they take up the cudgels, and challenge out an antagonist, and so get a name by a combat at dispute and controversy, while the unwary readers draw sides according to their different judgments. The longer the quarrel holds the more irreconcilable it grows; and when both parties are weary, they each pretend themselves the conquerors, and both lay claim to the credit of coming off with victory. These fooleries make sport for wise men, as being highly absurd, ridiculous and extravagant. True, but yet these paper-combatants, by my assistance, are so flushed with a conceit of their own greatness, that they prefer the solving of a syllogism before the sacking of Carthage; and upon the defeat of a poor objection carry themselves more triumphant than the most victorious Scipio.

Nay, even the learned and more judicious, that have wit enough to laugh at the other's folly, are very much beholden to my goodness; which, except ingratitude have drowned their ingenuity, they must be ready upon all occasions to confess. Among these I suppose the lawyers will shuffle in for precedence, and they of all men have the greatest conceit of their own abilities. They will argue as confidentially as if they spoke gospel instead of law; they will cite you six hundred several precedents, though not one of them come near to the case in hand. They will muster up the authority of judgments, deeds, glosses, and reports, and tumble over so many musty records, that they make their employ, though in itself easy, the greatest slavery imaginable; always accounting that the best plea which they have took most pains for.

To these, as bearing great resemblance to them, may be added Logicians and Sophisters, fellows that talk as much by rote as a parrot; who shall run down a whole gossiping of old women, nay, silence the very noise of a belfry, with louder clappers than those of the steeple. And if their unappeasable clamorousness were their only fault it would admit of some excuse; but they are at the same time so fierce and quarrelsome, that they will wrangle bloodily for the least trifle, and be so over intent and eager, that they many times lose their game in the chase and fright away that truth they are hunting for. Yet self-conceit makes these nimble disputants such doughty champions, that armed with three or four close-linked syllogisms, they shall enter the lists with the greatest masters

266

of reason, and not question the foiling of them in an irresistible baffle. Nay, their obstinacy makes them so confident of their being in the right, that all the arguments in the world shall never convince them to the contrary.

Next to these come the Philosophers in their long beards and short cloaks, who esteem themselves the only favourites of wisdom, and look upon the rest of mankind as the dirt and rubbish of the creation. Yet these men's happiness is only a frantic craziness of brain; they build castles in the air, and infinite worlds in a *vacuum*. They will give you to a hair's breadth the dimensions of the sun, moon, and stars, as easily as they would do that of a flaggon or pipkin. They will give a punctual account of the rise of thunder, of the origin of winds, of the nature of eclipses, and of all the other obstrusest difficulties in physics, without the least demur or hesitation, as if they had been admitted into the cabinet council of nature, or had been eye-witnesses to all the accurate methods of creation; though alas nature does but laugh at all their puny conjectures. For they never yet made one considerable discovery, as appears in that they are unanimously agreed in no one point of the smallest moment; nothing so plain or evident but what by some or other is opposed and contradicted.

But though they are ignorant of the artificial contexture of the least insect, they vaunt however, and brag that they know all things, when indeed they are unable to construe the mechanism of their own body. Nay, when they are so purblind as not to be able to see a stone's cast before them, yet they shall be as sharp-sighted as possible in spying out ideas, universals, separate forms, first matters, quiddities, formalities, and a hundred such like niceties, so diminutively small, that were not their eyes extremely magnifying all the art of optics could never make them discernible.

But they then most despise the low grovelling vulgar when they bring out their parallels, triangles, circles, and other mathematical figures, drawn up in battalia, like to many spells and charms of conjuration in muster, with letters to refer to the explication of the several problems; hereby raising devils as it were, only to have the credit of laying them, and amusing the ordinary spectators into wonder, because they have not wit enough to understand the juggle. Of these some undertake to profess themselves judicial astrologers, pretending to keep correspondence with the stars, and so from their information can resolve any query. And though it is all but a presumptuous imposture, yet some to be sure will be so great fools as to believe them.

The divines present themselves next. But it may perhaps be most safe to pass them by, and not to touch upon so harsh a string as this subject would afford. Besides, the undertaking may be very hazardous; for they are a sort of men generally very hot and passionate; and should I provoke them, I doubt not would set upon me with a full cry, and force me with shame to recant, which if I stubbornly refuse to do, they will presently brand me for a heretic, and thunder out an excommunication, which is their spiritual weapon to wound such as lift up a hand against them.

It is true, no men own a less dependence on me yet have they reason to confess themselves indebted for no small obligations. For it is by one of my properties, self-love, that they fancy themselves, with their elder brother Paul, caught up into the third heaven, from whence, like shepherds indeed, they look down upon their flock, the laity, grazing as it were, in the vales of the world below. They fence themselves in with so many surrounders of magisterial definitions, conclusions, corollaries, propositions explicit and implicit, that there is no falling in with them. Or if they do chance to be urged to a seeming non-plus, yet they find out so many evasions, that all the art of man can never bind them so fast, but that an easy distinction shall give them a starting-hole to escape the scandal of being baffled.

They will cut asunder the toughest argument with as much ease as Alexander did the gordian knot; they will thunder out so many rattling terms as shall fright an adversary into conviction. They are exquisitely dexterous in unfolding the most intricate mysteries; they will tell you to a tittle all the successive proceedings of Omnipotence in the creation of the universe; they will explain the precise manner of original sin being derived from our first parents. They will satisfy you in what manner, by what degrees, and in how long a time, our Saviour was conceived in the Virgin's womb, and demonstrate in the consecrated wafer how accidents may subsist without a subject. Nay, these are accounted trivial, easy questions; they have yet far greater difficulties behind, which notwithstanding they solve with as much expedition as the former.

As namely, whether supernatural generation requires any instant of time for its acting? Whether Christ, as a son, bears a double specifically distinct relation to God the Father, and his virgin mother? Whether this proposition is possible to be true, the first person of the Trinity hated the second? Whether God, who took our nature upon him in the form of a man, could as well have become a woman, a devil, a beast, an herb, or a stone? And were it

268

so possible that the Godhead had appeared in any shape of an inanimate substance, how he should then have preached his gospel? Or how have been nailed to the cross? Whether if St. Peter had celebrated the eucharist at the same time our Saviour was hanging on the cross, the consecrated bread would have been transsubstantiated into the same body that remained on the tree? Whether in Christ's corporal presence in the sacramental wafer, his humanity be not abstracted from his Godhead? Whether after the resurrection we shall carnally eat and drink as we do in this life?

There are a thousand other more sublimated and refined niceties of notions, relations, quantities, formalities, quiddities, haeccities, and such like abstrusities, as one would think no one could pry into, except he had not only such cat's eyes as to see best in the dark, but even such a piercing faculty as to see through an inch-board, and spy out what really never had any being. And to these some of their tenets and opinions, which are so absurd and extravagant, that the wildest fancies of the Stoics, which they so much disdain and decry as paradoxes, seem in comparison just and rational. As their maintaining, that it is a less aggravating fault to kill a hundred men, than for a poor cobbler to set a stitch on the Sabbath-day; or, that it is more justifiable to do the greatest injury imaginable to others, than to tell the least lie ourselves.

And these subtleties are alchymized to a more refined sublimate by the abstracting brains of their several schoolmen; the Realists, the Nominalists, the Thomists, the Albertists, the Occamists, the Scotists. These are not all, but the rehearsal of a few only, as a specimen of their divided sects; in each of which there is much of deep learning, so much of unfathomable difficulty, that I believe the apostles themselves would stand in need of a new illuminating spirit, if they were to engage in any controversy with these new divines. St. Paul, no question, had a full measure of faith; yet when he lays down faith to be the substance of things not seen, these men carp at it for an imperfect definition, and would undertake to teach the apostles better logic. Thus the same holy author wanted for nothing of the grace of charity, yet, say they, he describes and defines it but very inaccurately, when he treats of it in the thirteenth chapter of his first epistle to the Corinthians.

The primitive disciples were very frequent in administering the holy sacrament, breaking bread from house to house; yet should they be asked of the *Terminus a quo* and the *Terminus ad quem,* the nature of transsubstantiation? The manner how one body can be in several places at the same time? The difference betwixt the

269

several attributes of Christ in heaven, on the cross, and in the consecrated bread? What time is required for the transsubstantiating
the bread into flesh? How it can be done by a short sentence pronounced by the priest, which sentence is a species of discreet quantity, that has no permanent *punctum*? Were they asked these, and
several other confused queries, I do not believe they could answer
so readily as our mincing school-men now-a-days take a pride to do.
They were well acquainted with the Virgin Mary, yet none of them
undertook to prove that she was preserved immaculate from original sin, as some of our divines very hotly contend for.

. . . . .

But alas, those notional divines, however condemned by the
soberer judgment of others, are yet mightily pleased with themselves, and are so laboriously intent upon prosecuting their crabbed
studies, that they cannot afford so much time as to read a single
chapter in any book of the whole bible. And while they thus trifle
away their mis-spent hours in trash and babble, they think that they
support the Catholic Church with the props and pillars of propositions and syllogisms, no less effectually than Atlas is feigned by the
poets to sustain on his shoulders the burden of a tottering world.

Their privileges, too, and authority are very considerable. They
can deal with any text of scripture as with a nose of wax, knead it
into what shape best suits their interest; and whatever conclusions
they have dogmatically resolved upon, they would have them as
irrepealably ratified as Solon's laws, and in as great force as the
very decrees of the papal chair. If any be so bold as to remonstrate
to their decisions, they will bring him on his knees to a recantation
of his impudence. They shall pronounce as irrevocably as an oracle,
this proposition is scandalous, that irreverent; this has a smack of
heresy, and that is bald and improper; so that it is not the being
baptised into the church, the believing of the scriptures, the giving
credit to St. Peter, St. Paul, St. Hierom, St. Augustin, nay, or St.
Thomas Aquinas himself, that shall make a man a Christian, except
he have the joint suffrage of these novices in learning, who have
blessed the world no doubt with a great many discoveries, which
had never come to light if they had not struck the fire of sublety out
of the flint of obscurity. These fooleries sure must be a happy
employ.

Farther, they make as many partitions and divisions in hell and
purgatory, and describe as many different sorts and degrees of
punishment as if they were very well acquainted with the soil and

270

situation of those infernal regions. And to prepare a seat for the blessed above, they invent new orbs, and a stately empyrean heaven, so wide and spacious as if they had purposely contrived it, that the glorified saints might have room enough to walk, to feast, or to take any recreation.

With these, and a thousand more such like toys, their heads are more stuffed and swelled than Jove, when he went big of Pallas in his brain, and was forced to use the midwifery of Vulcan's axe to ease him of his teeming burden. Do not wonder, therefore, that at public disputations they bind their heads with so many caps one over another; for this is to prevent the loss of their brains, which would otherwise break out from their uneasy confinement. It affords likewise a pleasant scene of laughter, to listen to these divines in their hotly managed disputations. To see how proud they are of talking such hard gibberish, and stammering out such blundering distinctions, as the auditors perhaps may sometimes gape at, but seldom apprehend.

And they take such a liberty in their speaking of Latin, that they scorn to stick at the exactness of syntax or concord; pretending it is below the majesty of a divine to talk like a pedagogue, and be tied to the slavish observance of the rules of grammar. Finally, they take a vast pride, among other citations, to allege the authority of their respective master, which word they bear as profound a respect to as the Jews did to their ineffable *tetragrammaton,* and therefore they will be sure never to write it any otherwise than in great letters, MAGISTER NOSTER. And if any happen to invert the order of the words, and say, *noster magister,* instead of *magister noster,* they will presently exclaim against him as a pestilent heretic and underminer of the catholic faith.

. . . . .

THE JESUIT ORDER

EVERY REVOLUTION creates its counter revolution, which either is quickly nipped in the bud, or becomes a source of increasing strength and discipline for the conservative forces.

The latter was the case with the Jesuit Order, founded by Ignatius of Loyola in 1539, which soon became one of the main agents of the Catholic reaction to the rising waves of Protestantism. Its energy reveals itself not only in its general role as the servant of the *Ecclesia Militans,* but also in its educational work. In the 17th and 18th centuries even ardent critics of the Jesuits acknowledged the effectiveness of their schools in which the Catholic tradition was taught together with carefully selected classics, and Christian obedience indoctrinated together with a strong sense for competition.

The *Ratio Studiorum,* issued in 1599, in which the educational program and method of the Order are laid down in the most minute detail, is one of the great masterpieces of committee work. It is the result of fifteen years of co-operation among the best educators of the Jesuit fathers, who carefully utilized all pedagogical experience available at their time. The *Ratio* is probably the most enduring of all educational regulations, for in spite of certain corrections it still serves as the directive for the Jesuit schools.

The following selections are taken from *St. Ignatius and the Ratio Studiorum,* edited by Edward A. Fitzpatrick, translation by A. R. Ball, published in 1933 by the McGraw-Hill Book Company.

THE *RATIO STUDIORUM* OF 1599

LETTER OF TRANSMISSION OF THE RATIO STUDIORUM OF 1599. The entire plan of our studies begun to be prepared fourteen years ago is now at length sent to the provinces finished and completely determined.

For although because of the great utility which it seemed it would afford to our studies, Very Reverend Father General had wished that it should be finished and put into use long ago, still up to the present time this could not well be done. For it was proper, in a matter so important and involved in so many difficulties, not to determine anything before the objections and the demands of the provinces should be carefully examined, so that as far as possible all might be satisfied and so that the work which hereafter ought to be put into practice by all should be more favorably received.

Wherefore whatever in the beginning had been discussed and determined with great labor and carefulness concerning our whole plan of study by the six fathers deputed (for this purpose) has been sent to the provinces with this design, that our doctors and those skilled in such matters should weigh all things carefully and exactly so that if they should notice anything in this plan which was less suitable or which could be framed more suitably they should set this forth and also what their opinion was of the whole plan, giving the reasons for their opinion.

And when almost all the provinces had done this laboriously and carefully, and when everything which had been suggested or proposed by them was diligently gone over at Rome a second time by the principal doctors of the Roman College, and by three Fathers who for this purpose had remained at Rome, Very Reverend Father General with the Father's assistant carefully studied it and again sent this plan so modified to the whole Society, and commanded that it should be exactly observed by all.

Nevertheless, he warns all the provincials that since new plans acquired more solidity from experiment they should take note of and afterwards send to Rome whatever the daily practice of teaching should reveal in each province so that finally the finishing touch might be put to the work and the plan of our studies after so much and so long-continued discussion should be firmly established.

But since the provincials who came to the fifth general congregation brought with them whatever had been remarked from the daily use in their provinces to be less suitable, and since the majority preferred above all else greater brevity in this plan, the whole plan of studies was again carefully examined with considerable labor and having considered the weight of the reasons which were brought forward by the provinces, it was decided what should be firmly established and all things as far as possible were reduced to a shorter and more convenient method; and this was so done that we may rightly hope that this final labor of ours will be approved by all.

Wherefore, this plan of studies which is now sent ought to be observed in the future by all of ours, setting aside all other plans which heretofore had been sent for the sake of experiment, and the careful effort of our doctors should be fixed on this that what is prescribed in this final *Ratio* should be put into execution readily

273

and cheerfully. And it will be so I readily persuade myself if all understand that our Reverend Father has this very much at heart.

Before the Superiors on whom especially this duty lies, Very Reverend Father General seriously and earnestly commands that they strive with as great zeal as possible that this matter which is so much commended in our *Constitutions,* and which it is believed will bring such rich advantages to all our students, be carried out by all readily and exactly.

Rome, January 8, 1599,

By Command of Very Reverend Father General,

JACOBUS DOMINICUS,

Secretary.

RATIO ATQUE INSTITUTIO STUDIORUM SOCIETATIS JESU.—RULES FOR THE PROVINCIAL. 1. *Purpose of the Studies of the Society.*—Since one of the principal functions of our Society is to transmit to those about us all of the schooling consistent with our Institute in such a way that they may be brought to a knowledge and love for our Creator and Redeemer, the Provincial shall realize that he must exert every effort to see to it that the manifold labor of our teaching achieves fully a result such as the grace of our vocation demands, a result such as fully corresponds to the manifold labor of our teaching.

.　　.　　.　　.　　.

16. *Requirements for Professors of Philosophy.*—Professors of philosophy (unless pressing need demands otherwise) should not only have finished the course of theology but also have reviewed it for two years, so that their doctrine may be the more firmly established and serve theology the better. If there are any too prone to innovations, or too liberal in their views, they shall certainly be removed from the responsibility of teaching.

.　　.　　.　　.　　.

28. *Time for the Teaching Period.*—He must try not to put in charge of classes any who have not yet studied philosophy, if they are to have philosophy, when there are some at hand who have already studied it.

29. *In What Class One Should Begin Teaching.*—He should take care that members of our Order begin their teaching with a class below them, so that they can advance yearly to a higher grade with the greater share of their pupils.

274

34. *Prohibition of Improper Books.*—§ 1. He shall take every precaution and consider it a matter of the greatest importance, that there be in our schools no books, of poets or others, which may harm uprightness and good morals, unless they have been expurgated of all improper words and statements; or if they cannot be completely expurgated, as in the case of Terence, they shall not be read, lest the nature of their statements offend purity of mind.

. . . . .

7. *Academies of Languages.*—The Rector shall see to it that academies of Hebrew and Greek are established for the members of the Order, in which they may practice twice or three times a week at some fixed time, at the time of recreation, for example, so that those who seek both publicly and privately for the knowledge and dignity of these languages may make some progress.

8. *Use of Latin.*—He shall see to it that the use of Latin is diligently preserved among the Scholastics; there shall be no exception from this rule of speaking Latin except on days of vacation and in hours of recreation, unless in some localities it seems good to the Provincial that the practice of speaking Latin be retained even at these times. He shall also see to it that when those of the Order who have not yet finished their studies write to other members of the Order, they shall write in Latin. Moreover, two or three times a year, when some celebration is held, such as at the recommencement of studies or the renewal of vows, both the philosophy and theology students shall prepare and post verses.

. . . . .

12. *Encouraging Externs to Rhetoric.*—Care should be taken that our boarding students attend rhetoric for a year (as far as each one can) before they enter philosophy; and the necessity of this must be made evident to their parents. Others who are externs should be urged to do the same, but should not be compelled if they are unwilling. But if any wish to enter upon philosophy while they are still boys, from whom some disturbance is to be feared, they may be treated as the *Constitutions* provide in the case of those who are not willing to be bound by any promise or to give their names for matriculation.

13. *Tragedies and Comedies.*—The subject of tragedies and comedies which must not be given except in Latin and on very rare occasions, ought to be sacred and pious, and nothing should be introduced between the acts which is not in Latin and is not

becoming; nor is a feminine rôle nor feminine attire to be introduced.

. . . . .

30. *What Books Are to Be Given to Students.*—He shall give to
the students of theology and philosophy not all books but certain
ones with the knowledge of the Rector and the advice of their masters, namely, besides the Summa of St. Thomas for the theologians,
and Aristotle for the students of philosophy, some select commentary which they can consult in private studies. All the theologians
shall have the Council of Trent and the volume of the Bible, the
reading of which ought to be familiar with them. Let him consider
along with the Rector whether they should have also some one
of the Fathers. And he shall give, moreover, to all the students of
theology and of philosophy some book pertaining to the study of
humanities and he shall advise them not to neglect to read this book
at certain times when it will be convenient.

COMMON RULES FOR ALL PROFESSORS OF HIGHER FAC-
ULTIES. 1. *Purpose.*—The special duty of a teacher shall be to
move his hearers, both within class and out, as opportunity offers,
to a reverence and love of God and of the virtues which are pleasing
in His sight, and to pursue all their studies to that end.

2. *Prayer before Class.*—To keep this in mind, someone shall
recite a short prayer adapted to this purpose at the beginning of
class, and the teacher and all the pupils shall listen attentively with
bared head; or at least the teacher shall sign himself with the sign
of the Cross and begin.

3. *Helping Students to Devotion.*—He shall also assist his pupils
by frequent prayers to God and by the example of his own religious
life. It will be appropriate for him not to neglect exhortations, at
least on the days before feast days, and at the beginning of the
longer vacations. He shall urge them strongly to pray to God, to
examine their consciences at evening, to receive frequently and
duly the sacraments of penance and the Eucharist, to attend Mass
daily and sermons on all feast days, to avoid bad habits, to detest
vice, and to cultivate the virtues worthy of a Christian.

4. *Obedience to the Prefect.*—He shall obey the Prefect of
Studies in all matters which pertain to studies and the discipline of
the classes; he shall give him for revision all theses before they are
presented; he shall not undertake to explain any book or writer not
in the usual course, or introduce any new method in teaching or
disputation.

5. *Moderation in Refuting.*—In those questions in which he is

276

free to hold either side, he shall defend his view in such a way as to allow moderate and kindly consideration for the opposite view, especially if the previous teacher has held that view. But if writers can be reconciled, he must be careful not to neglect to do so. Finally, he shall conduct himself with moderation in citing and refuting authorities.

6. *Avoiding New Opinions.*—Even in matters where there is no risk to faith and devotion, no one shall introduce new questions in matters of great moment, or any opinion which does not have suitable authority, without first consulting his superiors; he shall not teach anything opposed to the axioms of learned men or the general belief of scholars. Rather, all should follow closely the approved doctors and, as far as local custom permits, the views accepted in Catholic schools.

7. *Brevity in Refuting Others' Views and Proving his Own.*— He shall not bring forward any views which are useless, antiquated, absurd, or patently false; nor shall he use too much time in mentioning and refuting such views. He shall strive to prove his conclusions not by the number of his arguments but by their effectiveness. He shall not digress to extraneous matter, nor shall he treat any part of his subject-matter more extensively than circumstances require, nor in the wrong place. He shall not heap up possible objections, but shall bring forward briefly only the strongest of them, unless their refutation is quite clear from his explanation of the thesis.

8. *Authorities to Be Quoted Infrequently, but Accurately.*—He shall not cite the authorities of learned men too often; but if he has the evidence of outstanding writers to confirm his views, he shall faithfully quote the other's own words, if possible, but briefly, especially the sacred Scriptures, the Councils, and the holy Fathers. It does not befit the dignity of a teacher to cite any author which he has not himself read.

9. *Dictation.*—If anyone can teach without dictating, yet in such a way that the pupils can easily tell what ought to be written down, it is preferable for him not to dictate. Certainly teachers who dictate should not pause after every word, but speak for a single breath and then, if necessary, repeat the words; they should not dictate the entire thesis and then explain it, but dictate and explain in turn.

10. *Referring Students to Books.*—If the teacher brings forward material from books which are easily available, he shall explain rather than dictate; rather, he shall refer the students to those books which treat the matter in hand accurately and in detail.

11. *Repetitions in Class.*—After the lecture let him remain in the classroom or near the classroom for at least a quarter of an hour so that the students may approach him to ask questions, so that he may sometimes ask an account of the lectures, and so that the lectures may be repeated.

12. *Review at Home.*—Every day except Saturdays, vacations, and feast days, an hour is to be designated at which the members of the Order shall review the matter of their classes and hold disputations, so that in this way talents may be exercised and difficulties which have occurred may be removed. And so one or another should be told beforehand to recite from memory, but no longer than a quarter of an hour; then one or two should raise objections and a like number answer them; then if time remains, doubtful points should be raised; in order that such time may be left, the teacher shall insist strictly on the form of argumentation and, when no new points are raised, bring it to an end.

13. *General Repetitions.*—The repetition of all past lectures at the end of the year is to be so arranged that unless something interferes, a whole month should be left free not only from (regular) repetitions but also from lectures.

14. *Weekly Disputations.*—On Saturday, or some other day of the week, according to the custom of the school, there shall be a disputation in each class, lasting for two hours, or longer when there is a large attendance of externs. If there are two feast days in one week, or if the weekly vacation falls on a feast day, there shall be no disputation on Saturday, but a lecture; but if this shall happen for three successive weeks, one disputation shall be held.

15. *Monthly Disputations.*—Where the accepted custom of the school does not prevent, disputations should be held, in both the forenoon and the afternoon, on a fixed day every month except the last three summer months, or, if the number of pupils is small, every other month; as many pupils as there are teachers shall individually defend the questions of their respective teachers.

16. *Supporting the Objections.*—Some of our other learned men and teachers, although of other branches, shall be present at these disputations; to make the discussion more lively they shall press the objections which are raised; but shall not undertake the support of any argument in which the original objector is still arguing earnestly and with good effect. Visiting teachers shall also be permitted to do this and so may be invited to bring objections according to custom, unless the usage of the locality does not permit.

17. *Disputation Limited to the More Learned.*—Only the more

278

learned of the pupils shall engage in public disputation; others shall be instructed privately until they are so well trained as not to be considered unworthy of public appearance.

18. *Arrangement for the Disputation.*—The teacher shall consider the day of disputations no less fruitful and worthy of attention than a day of lecture, and remember that the benefit and spirit of the disputation depend upon him; he shall preside in such a way that he may himself seem to take part on both sides; he shall praise anything good which is said, and call it to the attention of all; if some unusually difficult objection is proposed, he shall make a brief suggestion to support the defender or direct the objector; he shall not keep silent too long, nor yet speak all the time, but let the pupils set forth what they know; he shall himself correct or amplify what is set forth; he shall order the objector to proceed as long as the objection has any force; in fact, he shall add to the difficulty and not pass over it if the one who is bringing objections proceeds too soon to a new objection; he shall not permit an objection which is practically answered to be pressed too far, nor an answer which is unsound to stand too long; after a discussion, he shall briefly define and explain the entire matter. If there is anything else which is customary to make disputations better attended or more spirited, it shall be carefully preserved.

19. *Conference with his Beadle.*—He shall occasionally consult with his helper, or Beadle, appointed by the Rector, and question him about the status of the entire class and the industry and progress of the externs; he shall see to it that the other performs his tasks faithfully and accurately.

20. *Progress of the Students.*—He shall, with the help of Divine grace, be earnest and diligent in all his duties and observant of the progress of his students, both in lectures and in other literary exercises; he shall not appear more friendly to one pupil than another; he shall despise no one; he shall attend to the studies of the poor the same as those of the rich; he shall especially seek the progress of each of his Scholastics.

RULES FOR THE PROFESSOR OF SACRED SCRIPTURE. 1. *Special Attention to Literal Meaning.*—He shall realize that his duties are to explain sacred literature piously, learnedly, and seriously, according to the true and literal meaning, in order to strengthen true faith in God and the establishment of sound morals.

2. *The Vulgate Edition.*—Among his other duties, it is especially important that he defend the version adopted by the Church.

3. *Observing and Comparing Phrases of Sacred Scripture.*—To

learn this true sense he shall carefully observe the expressions and phrases peculiar to sacred Scripture; he shall not only consider the context of the place which he is reading, but also carefully compare other places in which the same phrases have the same or different meanings.

4. *Hebrew and Greek Text.*—He shall present examples from the Hebrew and Greek, when it is advantageous, but briefly; but he shall do this only when some difference between these and the Vulgate edition needs to be reconciled, or when the idioms of the other languages afford greater insight or understanding.

. . . . .

12. *Brevity of Treatment.*—Let him not delay too long over each text of Scripture unless it be important and worth the delay and the effort lest the progress be too slow and he will gain his object best if he runs through the easier passages or even omits them. Let him not take up very much time in investigating the various kinds of reckonings of time or in locating the place in the whole land, or in other less useful matters of this kind (unless the passage itself necessarily demands this); it will be sufficient to indicate the authorities who have treated of such matters at length.

. . . . .

15. *Time for Allegories and Morals.*—He shall not omit the allegories and morals unless they are commonly known or are easily evident from the literal meaning or present something clever or striking; with regard to passages which are not of this nature, he shall merely indicate in which of the Fathers they are treated.

16. *No Controversies.*—If he happens on a passage over which there is controversy between us and heretics, or which is accustomed to be a matter for disputation among theology students, he shall explain the passage earnestly and carefully, especially if he speaks in opposition to the heretics, yet only in so far as it pertains to the question in hand—all other points he shall omit; so will he seem to be mindful of his position, to teach nothing but sacred Scripture.

. . . . .

RULES OF THE PROFESSOR OF SCHOLASTIC THEOLOGY.
1. *Duty.*—He shall realize that it is his duty to join a well-founded subtlety in disputation with an orthodox faith and devotion in such a way that the former shall especially serve the latter.

2. *Following St. Thomas.*—All members of our Order shall follow the teaching of St. Thomas in scholastic theology, and consider him as their special teacher; they shall center all their efforts in him so that their pupils may esteem him as highly as possible. However, they should realize that they are not confined to him so closely that they are never permitted to depart from him in any matter, since even those who especially profess to be Thomists occasionally depart from him, and it would not befit the members of our Order to be bound to St. Thomas more tightly than the Thomists themselves.

3. *With Some Exceptions.*—Therefore, in regard to the conception of Blessed Mary, and in regard to the solemnity of vows, let them follow the opinion which is more common at this time, and more generally received among theologians, and in questions merely philosophical and also in those which belong to Scripture and Canon Law, he will be allowed to follow other authorities also who have treated those subjects *ex professo*.

4. *Choice of Opinions on Doubtful Questions.*—On those questions in which the opinion of St. Thomas is not clear, or which he does not treat, if Catholic scholars do not agree, he may hold either side of the question, as provided in the Common Rules, Rule 5.

5. *Regard for Faith and Devotion.*—In teaching, he shall first have regard for strengthening faith and fostering devotion. Wherefore, in those questions which St. Thomas does not explicitly treat, no one shall teach anything which does not accord with the interpretation of the Church and with her traditions, or which tends to weaken the foundation of true devotion. Whence it comes that they are not to reject the accepted arguments, even though they are only probable, by which matters of faith are accustomed to be proved; nor shall any form new opinions hastily, unless from firmly established principles.

6. *Not to Assert Views Which Offend Catholics.*—If any opinions, regardless of authority, are known to be seriously offensive to the Catholics of any province or school, he shall not teach them or defend them there. When no doctrine of faith or uprightness of morals is involved, charitable prudence requires that the members of the Order accommodate their actions to those with whom they are dealing.

. . . . . .

RULES FOR THE PROFESSOR OF PHILOSOPHY. 1. *Purpose.* —Since the arts and the natural sciences prepare the mind for theology and help to a perfect knowledge and use of it and of them-

281

selves aid in reaching this end, the instructor, seeking in all things sincerely the honor and glory of God, shall so treat them as to prepare his hearers and especially ours for theology and stir them up greatly to the knowledge of their Creator.

2. *How Far Aristotle Is to Be Followed.*—In matters of any importance let him not depart from Aristotle unless something occurs which is foreign to the doctrine which academies everywhere approve of; much more if it is opposed to the orthodox faith, and if there are any arguments of this or any other philosopher against the faith, he will endeavor earnestly to refute them according to the Lateran Council.

3. *Authors Hostile to Christianity.*—He shall not read without careful selection or bring into class interpreters of Aristotle who are out of harmony with the Christian religion and he will take care that his students do not become influenced by them.

4. *Averroes.*—For this reason he shall not treat of the digressions of Averroes (and the same judgment holds for others of this kind) in any separate treatise, and if anything good is to be cited from him, let him bring it out without praise and, if possible, let him show that he has taken it from some other source.

5. *Philosophical Sects not to Be Followed.*—Let him not attach himself or his students to any philosophic sect as the Averroists, Alexandrians, and the like, and let him not cover over the errors of Averroes or Alexander or the others, but on account of these let him more sharply attack their authority.

6. *St. Thomas.*—Let him never speak except with respect of St. Thomas, following him readily as often as it is proper, or reverently and gravely differing from him if at any time he does not approve of him.

. . . . .

RULES FOR THE PROFESSOR OF MORAL PHILOSOPHY. 1. *His Position.*—Let him understand that it is no part of his position to digress to theological questions, but proceeding briefly in the text, to explain learnedly and seriously the principal heads of moral science which are had in the ten books of ethics of Aristotle.

. . . . .

9. *New Pupils.*—As far as is possible, let him add to the number of pupils no one who is not brought by his parents or by others who have him in charge; or anyone whom he does not know or about whom he cannot get information from others already known to

him. On the other hand, let him exclude no one on account of his lowly station in life or his poverty.

10. *Entrance Examinations.*—Let those who come for the first time be examined in this fashion: Let him ask them what studies they have cultivated, and to what extent; then order each of them to write something on an assigned topic; let him demand a few rules of the subjects which they have studied; let him set forth either a few short sentences to be translated into Latin, or, if there be need, something from some author to be explained.

11. *Admission.*—Let him admit any whom he knows to be well instructed and of good character and disposition. Let him explain to them the rules of our scholars so that they may learn what they should become. Let him write in a book the name of each, his surname, his nationality, his age, his parents or those who have the care of him, and whether any of his scholars know their homes; let him also note the day and year on which each was admitted. Finally let him place each one in that class and under that instructor to whom he is suited, so that he may be able to seem fit for a higher class rather than unfit for his own.

12. *Who Must not Be Admitted.*—In the highest class let him admit neither youths nor boys of too tender years, unless they are especially suited, even if they be sent for the sake of good education.

. . . . . .

37. *The Censor, or Praetor.*—According to the customs of each district, let him appoint his public Censor in each class, or, if the name censor is too little pleasing, a Chief Decurion or Praetor; and that he may be respected by his fellow pupils, let him be honored with some privilege, and let him have the right, with the approval of the master, of begging off some lighter penalties for his fellow pupils. Let him watch whether any one of the pupils walks out into the courtyard before the signal is given, or enters another class, or leaves his own class or place; let him report to the Prefect whoever were absent during the day, if anyone not a pupil has entered the class, and whether any fault has been committed in class, whether the master was present or not.

38. *The Corrector.*—Because of those who have erred either in industry or in those matters which pertain to good morals, and since mere good words and urgings will not affect them, let there be appointed a Corrector who is not of the Society; when such a one cannot be had, let another method be thought out by which they may be punished in some convenient way: let them not be punished in

283

class for offenses committed around the house, except rarely and for good cause.

39. *The Case of Those Who Refuse Corrections.*—Those who refuse punishment are either to be compelled, if it can safely be done, or if at any time that would seem improper, namely, with older students, they are to be forbidden to attend our school with the knowledge, however, of the Rector; and the same is for those who are frequently absent from class.

40. *Removing From School.*—When neither words nor the punishment by the Corrector prevail, and there is no hope of improvement, and if he seems to be a scandal to the others, it is better to remove him from classes than to retain him when he himself will profit but little and will injure others. However, this decision is to be left to the Rector, that all may proceed to the glory and service of God, as is fitting.

41. *Punishment.*—If an occasion arises when it is not a sufficient remedy for the scandal given to expel from classes, let him bring the matter before the Rector that he may decide what further is fitting to be done. Still as much as is possible the affair must be conducted in a spirit of gentleness, with peace and charity toward all.

42. *No One to Be Permitted to Return to Class.*—A return to our classes is allowed to no one who was once expelled or who left without sufficient cause, unless the Rector is previously consulted, who shall then decide what is best.

. . . . .

40. *Method of Punishment.*—Let there be no haste in punishing, nor too much in accusing; let him rather dissimulate, when he can without hurt to anyone; and let him not punish anyone himself (for that is the duty of the Corrector), but abstain entirely from injury in word or attack in deed; let him not call anyone by any name other than his own, or his surname; sometimes it is helpful, in place of punishment, to add some literary task beyond the daily assignment. Let him refer to the Prefect any unusual or severe penalty, especially for misdeeds committed outside the class, and those who refuse correction, especially if they are of higher rank.

. . . . .

47. *Familiarity and Conversation.*—Let him not seem to be more familiar with one than with another; and outside the time of class let him not speak with them except briefly and concerning serious matters and in an open place, that is, not within the classroom, but

284

before the doors of the classroom, or in the courtyard, or at the door of the college, and only for greater edification.

. . . . .

RULES FOR PROFESSORS OF RHETORIC. 1. *Grade.*—The grade of this class cannot be easily assigned to certain definite ends: for it instructs to perfect eloquence, which embraces the two highest faculties, oratory and poetry (of these two, however, the preference is always given to oratory); nor does it serve only for usefulness, but also nourishes culture.

Nevertheless it can be said in general that it is confined to three great fields, the precepts of oratory, style, and erudition.

As to the precepts, Quintilian and Aristotle may be added to Cicero. Although precepts may be looked for and noted in other sources, still in the daily prelections nothing is to be explained except the rhetorical books of Cicero and the rhetoric of Aristotle, and, if he likes, the poetics of Aristotle. Style is to be learned only from Cicero (although the most approved historians and poets may be tasted); all of his books are well adapted for the study of style; but let only the orations be given as prelections, so that the principles of the art may be seen as practiced in the speeches.

Let erudition be derived from history and the customs of tribes, from Scriptural authority, and from all doctrine, but in small quantity as benefits the capacity of the students. In Greek the following belong to rhetoric especially the quantity of syllables and the fuller knowledge of authors and of dialects.

. . . . .

12. *Concertatio.*—Yet there be established a concertatio, or exercise, first in correcting those points which one of the rivals finds in the oration of the other; then in those things with which they were occupied during the first hour, each making the other a proposition in turn; then in distinguishing and forming figures; then in reciting and applying the precepts of rhetoric, or letters, or poetry, or history; then in setting forth the more difficult parts in authors and in explaining the difficulties; then in investigating the customs of the ancients and matters of erudition. Also in hieroglyphics, Pythagorean symbols, apothegms, adages, emblems and enigmas, or both a poem and an oration suitable to the students of humanities should be recited from the pulpit every other Saturday by one or another student in the last half-hour of the afternoon.

13. *Greek Prelection.*—The prelection of Greek, whether of ora-

285

tors, historians, or poets, should be only from the ancient and classical writers, Demosthenes, Plato, Thucydides, Homer, Hesiod, Pindar, and others of this nature (provided they are expurgated), among whom should be preserved, by every right, SS. Nazianzen, Basil, and Chrysostom.

. . . . .

18. *Affixing Poems.*—Let choice poems written by the pupils be affixed to the walls of the classroom nearly every other month, to celebrate any rather famous day, or the announcement of a magistracy, or some other occasion. Moreover, according to the custom of the region, there may be short prose selections, such as inscriptions for coats of arms, churches, sepulchres, gardens, or statues; or descriptions, as of a city, a harbor, or an army; or narratives, as of some deed of one of the Saints, and there may be added, but not without the consent of the Rector, drawings which represent some motto or some proposed subject.

19. *Private Drama.*—Occasionally the master is allowed to propose to the scholars, for a subject, some short action as of an eclogue, drama, or dialogue; so that those which have been written the best of all may be presented within the class, parts being assigned to the student, but without any elaborate staging.

. . . . .

RULES FOR THE PROFESSOR OF HUMANITIES. 1. *Grade.*— In the first rule, for such knowledge of language as consists especially in propriety and copiousness, let there be explained in the daily prelections Cicero alone of the orators in those books of his which contain his philosophy or morals; of the historians, Caesar, Sallust, Livy, Curtius, and others of the same kind; of the poets, especially Virgil, excepting some of the eclogues and the fourth book of the Aeneid.

Let a brief summary of the precepts of rhetoric from Cyprian be given in the second semester; during which time omitting the philosophic writings of Cicero. Some of his easier orations as the *Pro lege Manilea, Pro Archia, Pro Marcello,* and others addressed to Caesar can be taken. Of the Greek language, that part belongs to this class which is properly called syntax, taking care in the meantime that they understand the Greek writers fairly well, and know how to write Greek somewhat.

. . . . .

MONTAIGNE 1533–1592

With Antiquity and the Renaissance, with Humanism and the Reformation, and with turbulent 16th century France in the background, such a complicated and rich personality as that of Montaigne was bound to appear: not a religious fighter like Luther or Ignatius of Loyola, not a liberal like Erasmus, but an individualist with such a degree of experience in the conflicts of human nature that scepticism offered itself as the most adequate position. "Que sais-je?"—"What do I know?"—so he wrote under his coat of arms. Yet, though he denies the possibility of ultimate knowledge, Montaigne's scepticism is not of the desperate, but of the disciplined sort. He appreciates kindness, understanding, and the standards of religious and moral convention. For him they are the means and the holds which prevent humanity from falling completely into pieces, and therefore the wise man ought to stick to them.

Naturally, the *Essays* in which Montaigne develops his philosophy of life have always been appreciated by men of the world who are too experienced to have illusions, but still enjoy excellence of intellect and character and are, consequently, unwilling to live a life of complete disenchantment. But even for people of ordinary experience Montaigne has much to say, for he knows men better than many of us may know ourselves. His psychological genius reveals itself especially in his ideas on education. Though outmoded with respect to their aristocratic emphasis, they nevertheless contain fundamental insights into the conditions of human development. Locke, in his *Some Thoughts on Education,* borrowed widely from Montaigne. And many of the modern theories and practices of education, such as the emphasis on spontaneity and on personal assimilation of knowledge instead of book-learning, are anticipated in Montaigne's essays.

The following selections are from Montaigne's *The Education of Children* translated by L. E. Rector and published by D. Appleton and Company, New York, 1899, in the International Education Series.

THE EDUCATION OF CHILDREN

TO MADAME DIANE DE FOIX, COUNTESS OF GARSON. . . .
A friend of mine . . . told me, the other day, in my own house, I should have enlarged a little more upon the education of children. Now, madam, were my abilities equal to the subject, I could not possibly employ them better than in presenting them to your little

287

son. Moreover, the old right you have ever had and still have over my service urges me with more than ordinary respect to wish all honour, welfare, and advantage to whatever may in any way concern you and yours. I mean to show by this that the greatest and most important difficulty of human effort is the training and education of children.

In matters of husbandry, all that precedes sowing, setting, and planting, even planting itself, is certain and easy. But when that which was sown, set, and planted takes life, there is a great deal more to be done, and it requires great care to bring it to perfection. So with men, continual cares, diligent attendance, doubts and fears, daily wait upon their parents and tutors before they can be nurtured and brought to any good. Their inclinations, while they are young, are so uncertain, their dispositions so variable, their promises so changing, their hopes so false, and their actions so doubtful, that it is very hard, even for the wisest, to place any certain judgment upon them or to feel assured of success. Look at Cymon and Themistocles, and a thousand others, whose manhood gave the lie to the ill-promise of their early youth. The young whelps of both dogs and bears show their natural disposition from the first; but men embracing this custom or fashion, following that humour or opinion, admitting this or that passion, conforming to certain laws, are changed and soon disguised. And yet, for want of a ready foresight of the natural propensity of the mind, much time is wasted in trying to teach children those things for which, by their natural constitution, they are totally unfit. Notwithstanding these difficulties my advice is, to bring them up in the best and most profitable studies without being too superstitious or taking too much notice of those light prognostics which they give of themselves in their infancy. Without offence to Plato, in his Republic, I think he allows them too much authority.

·　·　·　·　·

Upon the choice of a tutor you shall provide for your son depends the whole success of his education and bringing up. A gentleman born of noble parentage and heir of a house which aims at true learning should be disciplined not so much for the practical use he could make of it—so abject an end is unworthy the grace and favour of the Muses, and, besides, bids for the regard of others—not for external use and ornament, but to adorn and enrich his inward mind, desiring rather to form an able and efficient man than a learned man. My desire is, therefore, that the parents or guard-

288

ians of such a gentleman be very careful in choosing his tutor, whom I would commend for having a well-made rather than a well-filled head, yet both are desirable. And I would prefer wisdom, judgment, civil manners, and modest behaviour to bare and mere literal learning. And in his teaching I would advise a new course. Some never cease brawling in their pupils' ears, as if they were pouring into a funnel, to follow their book. I would have a tutor correct this, and on taking up a subject, according to the child's capacity, I would have him show it to his pupil, who may know thereby a little of all things, and how to choose and distinguish them without the help of others; sometimes opening for him the way, at other times leaving him to open it for himself. I would not have the tutor do all the talking, but allow the pupil to speak when his turn comes. . . . The tutor should make his pupil, like a young horse, trot before him in order that he may the better judge of his pace, determine how long he will hold out, and, accordingly, what may fit his strength. Lacking this knowledge we often spoil all. To make a good choice and to keep the right proportions is one of the hardest things I know. It is a sign of a noble and undaunted spirit, to know how far to condescend to childish proceedings, how to second, and how to guide them. As for myself, I can more easily walk up than down a hill.

Those who, according to our way of teaching, undertake in the same lessons and in the same manner of instruction to direct many pupils of different intellects and dispositions, seldom meet with more than two or three who reap any good by their discipline or who come to any perfection.

I would not only have the instructor demand an account of the words contained in a lesson, but of the sense and substance; and judge of the profit he has made of it, not by the testimony of his memory but by his own judgment. What he has lately learned cause him to set forth in a hundred various ways, and then to apply it to as many different subjects as possible, to determine whether he has apprehended the same and made it a part of himself, taking instruction of his progress from the Institutions of Plato. It is a sign of crudity and indigestion for a man to throw up his meat as he swallowed it. The stomach has not done its work unless it has changed the form and altered the condition of the food given to it. We see men gape after nothing but learning, and when they say such a one is a learned man, they think they have said enough. Our minds move at another's pleasure, bound and compelled to serve the fancies of others, brought under by authority and forced to accept their bare lesson. We have been so subjected to harp upon one string, that we have no power left to carry out our own wills. Our vigour and liberty are extinct. "Nunquam tutelæ suæ fiunt." (Seneca, *Epist*. 33.) ("They never become their own masters.")

. . . . .

I would have the tutor make the child examine and thoroughly sift all things, and harbour nothing in his head by mere authority or upon trust. Aristotle's principles should no more be axioms to him than those of the Stoics or Epicureans. Let different judgments be submitted to him; he may be able to distinguish truth from falsehood; if not, he may remain in doubt.

> "No less it pleases me
> To doubt, than wise to be."
> (Dante, *Inferno* xi, 93.)

If by his own thinking he embraces the opinions of Xenophon or of Plato, the opinions will be no longer theirs, but will become his own. He that merely follows another, seeks nothing, finds nothing. "Non sumus sub rege; sibi quisque se vindicet." (Seneca, *Epist*. 33.) ("We are not under a king; each one may dispose of himself.") Let him at least know that he does know. He must imbibe their knowledge, but not adopt their dogmas; when he knows how to apply, he may at once forget when or whence he had his learning.

Truth and reason are common to all, and belong no more to him who spoke them first than to him who shall speak them hereafter. . . .

Study should make us wiser. It is the understanding, says Epicharmus, that sees and hears, that moves, sways, and rules all. Everything else is blind, senseless, and without spirit, and by depriving a pupil of liberty to do things for himself we make him servile and cowardly. Who ever inquires of his pupil what he thinks of rhetoric, of grammar, of this or of that sentence of Cicero? Our teachers stick them full-feathered in our memories, and there establish them like oracles, of which the very words and letters are the substance of the thing. To know by heart only is not to know at all; it is simply to keep what one has committed to his memory. What a man knows directly, that will he dispose of without turning to his book or looking to his pattern. A mere bookish knowledge is useless. It may embellish actions, but it is not a foundation for them. According to Plato, constancy, faith, and sincerity are true

290

philosophy. As for other kinds of knowledge, they are garish paintings. Le Paluel and Pompey, those two noted dancers of our time, might as well teach a man to do their tricks and high capers by simply looking on and without stirring out of his place, as for some pedantical fellow to instruct our mind without moving or putting it to work. I should like to find one who would teach us to manage a horse, to toss a spear, to shoot, to play upon the lute, or to sing without any practice; yet these men would teach us to judge and how to speak well without any exercise in speaking or judging. Now, while we are in our apprenticeship to learning, actions or objects which present themselves to our eyes may serve us instead of a book. The knavish trick of a page, the foolishness of a servant, a jest at table, are so many new subjects for us to work upon.

And for this very reason the society of men, the visiting of foreign countries, observing people and strange customs, are very necessary; not to be able, after the manner of our young French gallants, to repeat how many paces the Santa Rotunda is in circuit, or of the richness of Signiora Livia's attire, or how much longer or broader the face of Nero is, which they have seen in some old ruin of Italy, than one seen on some medal. But they should be able to give an account of the ideas, manners, customs, and laws of the nations they have visited. That he may whet and sharpen his wits by rubbing them upon those of others, I would have a boy sent abroad very young; and in order to kill two birds with one stone, he should first see those neighbouring countries whose languages differ most from ours. For unless a man's tongue be formed to them in his youth, he can never acquire the true pronunciation.

. . . . .

It is not enough to fortify his soul; you must also make his muscles strong. The mind will be oppressed if not assisted by the body; it is too much for her alone to discharge two offices. . . .

A boy must be broken in by the hardship of severe exercises to endure the pain of colic, of cauteries, of falls, of dislocations, and even of imprisonment and the rack itself. By misfortune he may be reduced to the worst of these, which, as we have seen, sometimes befall the good as well as the bad. As for proofs, in our present civil war whoever draws his sword against the laws, threatens all honest men with the whip and halter.

Moreover, by living at home the authority of the tutor, which ought to be sovereign over the child, is often checked, interrupted, and hindered by the presence of the parents. Besides, the respect the whole household bear him as their master's son is, in my opinion, no small hindrance during these tender years.

In my intercourse with men of the world I have often observed this fault, that, instead of gathering information from others, we make it our whole business to give them our own, and are more concerned how to expose and set out our own commodities than how to acquire new. Silence and modesty are excellent qualities in conversation, and one should therefore train up the boy to be sparing and close-handed with what he knows when once acquired, and to refrain from reproving every idle saying or ridiculous story spoken or told in his presence. It is a great rudeness to controvert everything that is not agreeable to our palate. Let him be satisfied with correcting himself, and not seem to condemn in others what he would not do himself, nor dispute against common custom. "Licet sapere, sine pompa, sine invidia." ("Let him be wise without ostentation and without envy." Seneca, *Epistle* 103.) Let him avoid those ancient fashions and the childish ambition of trying to appear something better and greater than other people, proving himself in reality something less; and, as though finding fault were a proof of genius, seeking to found a special reputation thereon.

. . . . .

Let conscience and virtue shine in his speech, and let him have reason for his chief guide. Make him understand that to acknowledge the error he shall discover in his own argument, though only perceived by himself, is an effect of judgment and sincerity, which are the principal things he is to seek after; that obstinacy and contention are common qualities best becoming a mean soul; and that to recollect and to correct himself and to forsake a bad argument in the heat of dispute are noble and rare philosophic qualities.

In company he should have his eye and ear in every corner of the room, for I notice that the places of greatest honour are usually taken by the most unworthy and least capable, and that the greatest fortunes are not always possessed by the best men. I have been present when those at the upper end of the table have been only commending the hangings about the room or the flavour of the wine, while at the lower end many fine things have been lost or thrown away. Let him examine every one's talent—that of a herdsman, a mason, a stranger, or a traveller. A man may learn something from every one of these which he can use at some time or another. Even the folly and weakness of others will contribute to his instruc-

292

tion. By observing the graces and manners of others, he will acquire for himself the emulation of the good and a contempt for the bad. Let an honest curiosity be awakened in him to search out the nature and design of all things. Let him investigate whatever is singular and rare about him—a fine building, a fountain, an eminent man, the place where a battle was anciently fought, the passage of Caesar or of Charlemagne. . . .

In this acquaintance of men, my purpose is that he should give his chief attention to those who live in the records of history. He shall by the aid of books inform himself of the worthiest minds of the best ages. History is an idle study to those who choose to make it so, but of inestimable value to such as can make use of it; the only study Plato says, the Lacedaemonians reserved to themselves. Touching this point, what profit may he not reap by reading the Lives of Plutarch? But, above all, let the tutor remember to what end his instruction is directed, and not so much imprint in his pupil's memory the date of the ruin of Carthage as the character of Hannibal and of Scipio; nor so much where Marcellus died as why it was unworthy of his duty that he died there. Let him read history, not as an amusing narrative, but as a discipline of the judgment. It is this study to which, in my opinion, we apply ourselves with the most differing and uncertain measures. I have read a hundred things in Livy that another has not, or has not taken the least notice of; and Plutarch has read a hundred more than ever I could find, or than, peradventure, the author ever set down. To some it is a mere language study, but to others a perfect anatomy of philosophy, by which the most secret and abstruse parts of our human natures are penetrated. There are in Plutarch many discourses worthy of being carefully read and observed, for he is, in my opinion, the greatest master in that kind of writing; but there are a thousand other matters which he has only touched upon, where he only points with his finger to direct us which way we may go if we will. He contents himself sometimes with only giving one brief touch to the main point of the question, and leaves the rest for us to find out for ourselves. . . .

Human understanding is marvellously enlightened by daily conversation with men and by travelling abroad. In ourselves we are dull and stupid, and have our sight limited to the end of our nose. When Socrates was asked of what country he was, he did not answer, "Of Athens," but "Of the world." (Plutarch, *On Exile.*) His imagination was rich and expansive, and he embraced the whole world for his country, extending his society, his friendship, his

293

knowledge to all mankind, not as we do, who look no farther than our feet. When the vines of our village are nipped by frost, the parish priest immediately concludes that the wrath of God hangs over our head and threatens all mankind, and says that the cannibals have already got the pip. Who is it, seeing these civil wars of ours, does not cry out that the machine of the world is upsetting and that the day of judgment is at hand, never remembering that there have been many worse revolutions, and that in the meantime people are very happy in ten thousand other parts of the earth and never think of us.

. . . . .

He shall also learn what secret springs move us, and the reason of our various irresolutions; for, I think, the first doctrines with which one seasons his understanding ought to be those that rule his manners and direct his sense; that teach him to know himself, how to live and how to die well. Among the liberal studies let us begin with those which make us free; . . .

After having taught our pupil what will make him wise and good, you may then teach him the elements of logic, physics, geometry, and rhetoric. After training, he will quickly make his own that science which best pleases him. He should be instructed sometimes by a talk, sometimes by reading. At times the tutor should put the author himself into his hands, at other times give him only the pith and substance of it. And if the tutor does not know enough about books to refer the pupil to the choicest parts, a literary man might be employed to assist in this matter. . . . According to my method of teaching, the mind has something to feed upon and to digest. . . .

It is a thousand pities that matters should be at such a pass, in this age of ours, that philosophy, even with men of understanding, is looked upon as vane and fantastic, a thing of no use, no value, either in opinion or effect. And I think these sophists, by making the study difficult, are to blame for this state of affairs. People do wrong to represent it to children as an extremely difficult task, and set it forth with such a frowning, grim, and formidable aspect. Who has disguised her with this false, pale, and hideous countenance? There is nothing more airy, more gay, more frolicsome. She presents nothing to our eyes and preaches nothing to our ears but feasting and jollity. A sad and melancholy look shows she does not live there.

. . . . .

Now the tutor whom I would have, knowing it to be his duty to arouse affection as well as reverence for virtue, should teach his pupil that the poets have always accommodated themselves to public feeling, and will therefore impress upon his charge that the gods have planted far more toil in the avenues which lead to pleasure than in those which will take him to wisdom. . . .

Such a tutor will make his pupil feel that the height and value of true virtue consist in the facility, utility, and pleasure of its exercise; so far from difficult that children as well as men, the simple as well as the wise, may make it their own; and that by order and good conduct, not by force, is virtue to be acquired. . . .

If the pupil should happen to be of such a contrary disposition that he prefers an idle tale to the true story of some noble expedition; who at the beat of the drum that excites the youthful ardour of his companions leaves that to follow another that calls to a bear dance or to tumbling, juggling tricks, or who does not find it more delightful to return all weary and dusty from a victorious combat than from a tennis game; for such a one I see no remedy except to bind him as apprentice to make mince pies, even though he be the son of a duke. I believe with Plato, that children are to be placed in life not according to the condition of the father, but according to their own capacity. (Plato, *Republic* iv.)

．　．　．　．　．

Yet, for all that, I would not have this pupil of ours imprisoned and made a slave to his book, nor have him acquire the morose and melancholy disposition of a sour, ill-natured pedant. I would not have his spirit cowed and subdued by tormenting him fourteen or fifteen hours a day, as some do, making a pack horse of him. Neither should I think it good, if it be discovered that he is too much addicted to reading. Too much study diverts him from better employment, and renders him unfit for the society of men. Many a time have I seen men totally useless on account of an immoderate thirst for knowledge. . . . Neither would I have the noble manners of my pupil spoiled by the incivility and barbarity of other people. French wisdom was anciently turned into a proverb, "early, but does not continue." Nothing can be prettier than the children of France, but they ordinarily deceive the hopes and expectations of parents, and grow up to be men of very ordinary ability. I have heard men of good understanding insist that these colleges of ours make our children the animals they turn out to be. But to our young friend, a closet, a garden, the table, his bed, solitude, company, morning and evening—all hours and all places of study shall be the same.

.   .   .   .   .

By this method of instruction my young pupil will be much better employed than those who are at college. The steps we take in walking to and fro in a gallery, though they are three times as many, do not weary us so much as those we take in a formal journey; so our lessons, occurring as it were accidentally, without any set obligation of time and place, and falling in naturally with every action, will be learned as a pleasure, not as a task. Our very exercises and recreations, running, wrestling, dancing, hunting, riding, and fencing, will be a part of his study. I would have his manners, behaviour, and bearing cultivated at the same time with his mind. It is not the mind, it is not the body we are training: it is the man, and we must not divide him into two parts. . . .

As to the rest, this method ought to be carried on with a firm gentleness, quite contrary to the practice of our pedants, who, instead of tempting and alluring children to study, present nothing before them but rods and ferules, horror and cruelty. Away with this violence! away with this compulsion! nothing, I believe, more dulls and degenerates a well born nature. If you would have a child fear shame and punishment, do not harden him to them. Accustom him to heat and cold, to wind and sun, and to dangers that he ought to despise. Wean him from effeminacy in eating and drinking, clothes and lodging, that he may not be a gay fellow, a dude, but a hardy, sinewy, and vigorous young man. I have been of this opinion all my life, and still hold to it.

The strict government of our colleges has always displeased me; less harm would have been done had they erred on the indulgent side. They are mere jails, where youths are corrupted by being punished before they have done any wrong. Go into one of these institutions during lesson hours, and you hear nothing but the outcries of boys being punished and the thundering of pedagogues drunk with fury. A pretty way it is to tempt these tender and timorous souls to love their books—a furious countenance, rod in hand! O wicked and pernicious manner of teaching! Besides, Quintilian (*Inst. Orat. i, 3*) has well observed that this insolent authority is often attended by dangerous consequences, particularly in the matter of punishments. How much more respectable it would be to see our classrooms strewn with green boughs and flowers than with bloody birch rods. Were it left to my ordering, I should paint the school with pictures of joy and gladness, Flora and the Graces, as the philosopher Speusippus (Diogenes Laertius iv, 1) did his. Where their profit is there should also be their pleasure. Such viands as are proper and wholesome for children should be seasoned with sugar, and such as are dangerous with gall. . . .

All oddity of manner and self-consciousness should be avoided as obnoxious to society. . . .

Young bodies are supple, one should therefore bend them to fit all fashions and customs. Provided he can restrain the appetite and the will within limits, let a young man accustom himself to all nations and companies, even to debauchery and excess, if he do so simply out of regard to the customs of a place. Let him be able to do everything, but love to do nothing but what is good. . . . Let the young man laugh, carouse, and debauch with his prince; I would have him, even in his excesses, surpass his companions in ability and vigour, so that he may not refrain from such pleasures through lack of power or knowledge, but for lack of will.

. . . . .

A boy should not so much memorize his lesson as practice it. Let him repeat it in his actions. We shall discover if there be prudence in him by his undertakings; goodness and justice, by his deportment; grace and judgment, by his speaking; fortitude, by his sickness; temperance, by his pleasures; order, by the management of his affairs; and indifference, by his palate, whether what he eats and drinks be flesh or fish, wine or water. . . . The conduct of our lives is the true mirror of our doctrine. Zeuxidamus, to one who asked him why the Lacedaemonians did not write down their laws of chivalry and have their young men read them, replied, "Because we would rather accustom them to deeds than to writings." With such a one compare, after fifteen or sixteen years of study, one of our college Latinists, who has thrown away all his time in learning to speak. The world is nothing but babble, and I have never yet seen a man who did not say too much rather than too little. And yet half of our life goes this way. We are kept four or five years learning words and tacking them together into phrases, as many more to combine these into paragraphs, and another five is spent in learning how to weave them together into an intricate and rhetorical style. Let us leave such work to those who make it a trade.

. . . . .

Let our pupil be furnished with things—words will come only too fast; if they do not come readily, he will reach after them. I have

297

heard some make excuses because they can not express themselves, and pretend to have their heads full of a great many very fine things which for want of words they can not bring out. Do you know what I think of such people? I think they are nothing but shadows of imperfect images; they have no thoughts within, and consequently can not bring any out. They do not know themselves what they are trying to say, and if you notice how they haggle and stammer, you will soon conclude their pretensions to learning are downright false. For my part I hold, and Socrates is positive in it, that whoever has in his mind a clear and vivid idea, will express it well enough in one way or another; and if he be dumb, by signs.

"Verbaque provisam rem non invita sequentur."
("When matter they foreknow,
Words voluntarily flow.")—Horace, *Ars Poetica*, 311.

. . . . .

I have been ready enough to imitate the negligent garb which is observable among the young men of our time, to wear my cloak on one shoulder, my hat on one side, and one stocking somewhat more disorderly than the other, thereby expressing a sort of manly disdain for these exotic ornaments. But I find carelessness of even greater use in speaking. All affectation, particularly in the French gaiety and freedom, is ungraceful in a courtier; and in a monarchy every gentleman ought to be trained according to the court model, which requires an easy and natural negligence. . . . The eloquence which calls attention to itself, injures the subject it would advance. In our dress it is ridiculous effeminacy to distinguish ourselves by a peculiar fashion; so in language, to study new phrases and to affect words that are not in current use proceeds from a childish and scholastic ambition. As for me, may I never use any other language than what will be understood in the markets of Paris! Aristophanes was out of the way when he reproved Epicurus, for his simplicity and the design of his oratory, which was only a perspicuity of speech.

This imitation of words by its own facility immediately disperses itself through a whole people. But the imitation of judgment in applying these words is of slower growth. Most readers when they find a robe like their own imagine it contains a body like their own; but force and sinews are not to be borrowed, though the attire may be. Most of those I converse with speak the same language I here write, but whether they think the same thoughts I can not say. The Athenians, says Plato, study length and elegance of speaking; the

Lacedæmonians affect brevity; but the people of Crete aim more at richness of thought than at fertility of speech, and these are the best.

. . . . .

My late father having made most careful inquiry of the wisest men as to the best method of education, was cautioned by them against the systems then in use. They believed that the long time required to learn the languages of those people who were born to them was the sole reason we can never attain to the grandeur of soul and perfection of knowledge of the ancient Greeks and Romans. I do not think, however, that is the only cause. The expedient my father found out was this: In my infancy, and before I began to speak, he committed me to the care of a German (who has since died, a famous physician in France) totally ignorant of our language but very well versed in Latin. This man, whom my father had sent for and paid a large salary, had me continually with him. He was assisted by two Germans of inferior learning, but none of them conversed in any other language but Latin. As for the rest of the family, it was an inviolable rule that neither himself nor my mother, nor the servants, should speak anything in my company but such Latin words as everyone had learned to talk with me. You can hardly imagine what an advantage this proved to be to the whole family. My father and my mother learned Latin enough to understand it perfectly well, and to speak it to such a degree as was necessary for ordinary use; as well also did the servants who were most frequently with me. In short, we were all so Latinized that it overflowed to the neighbouring towns, where it yet remains in several Latin appellations of artisans and their tools. As for myself, I was more than six years of age before I understood either French or Perigordian any more than Arabic. I had learned to speak as pure Latin as my master himself without art, book, grammar or precept, whipping or a single tear. . . .

As to Greek, of which I have but a smattering, my father proposed to teach it by a new device, making of it a sort of sport and recreation. We tossed our declensions and conjugations to and fro, after the manner of those who by certain games at table and chess learn geometry and arithmetic. Among other things, he had been advised to make me enjoy study and duty; to accept them of my own free will, and to educate my soul in all liberty and delight, without any severity or constraint. He believed almost to superstition that it was wrong to arouse children suddenly from a sound sleep, in which they are more deeply lost than we are. I was always awakened by the sound of some musical instrument, a special musician being provided for that purpose.

By these examples alone you may judge of the prudence and affection of my good father, who is not to be blamed because he did not reap fruits commensurate with his exquisite toil and careful culture. For this result there are two reasons. First, a sterile and improper soil. Though of a stronger, healthy constitution, a gentle and tractable disposition, I was heavy, idle, and sluggish. They could not arouse me to any exercise or recreation, nor even get me out to play. What I saw, I saw clearly enough, and, despite this laziness, possessed a lively imagination and opinions far above my years. I had a slow mind that would go no faster than it was led, weak creative power, and, above all, a poor memory. With all these defects it is not strange my father could make but little of me. Secondly, like those who, impatient of a long and steady cure, submit to all sorts of nostrums and listen to every quack, so the good man, fearful of his plan, and having no longer the persons he had brought out of Italy, allowed himself to be overruled by the common opinion which always follows the lead of what goes before, like cranes, and sent me at six years of age to the College of Guienne, at that time the best and most flourishing in France. Even there he provided the most able tutor, and obtained many privileges for me contrary to college rules. And yet with all these precautions it was a college still. My Latin immediately grew corrupt, and by discontinuance I lost all use of it. This new plan of education, therefore, was of no benefit to me except to skip me over some of the lower classes and place me in the highest. I left college when I was thirteen, but without any improvement that I can boast of, though I finished the whole course, as they call it.

The first thing that gave me any taste for books was the pleasure I took in reading the fables of Ovid's Metamorphoses. When but seven or eight years old I would steal away from all other diversions to read them. They were written in my own natural language, the easiest tales I was acquainted with, and the subject was suited to my age and capacity. So carefully was I taught that I knew nothing of Lancelot du Lac, Amadis de Gaul, Huon of Bordeaux, and such idle, time-consuming, and pernicious books in which most children delight. To this day I do not know what those books contain. Of course, I thought little of my prescribed lessons, and right here it was greatly to my advantage to have a sensible tutor wise enough to connive at this and other irregularities of the same nature. In this

300

way I ran through Virgil's Aeneid, then Terence, then Plautus, and some Italian comedies, allured by the pleasure of the subject. On the other hand, had my tutor been so foolish as to deprive me of this amusement, I verily believe I would have brought nothing away from college but a hatred of books, as most of our young gentlemen do. He was very discreet about that business, apparently taking no notice, and whetting my appetite by allowing me only such time for this reading as I could steal from my regular studies.

. . . . .

I have always taxed persons with impertinence who condemn these entertainments, and with injustice those who refuse such comedies as are worth seeing, to come into our towns and begrudge the people that public amusement. A sensible plan of government takes care to assemble citizens not only to the solemn duties of devotion, but also to sports and spectacles. Society and friendship are augmented by it; and, besides, can there possibly be afforded a more orderly diversion than one which is performed in the sight of everyone, and often in the presence of the supreme magistrate himself? I, for my part, think it desirable that the prince should sometimes gratify his people at his own expense, out of paternal kindness, as it were. In large cities theatres should be erected for such entertainments, if for nothing more than to divert people from private and worse actions.

To return to my subject: There is nothing like alluring the appetite and affection, otherwise you make nothing but so many asses laden with books. By virtue of the lash, you give them a pocketful of learning to keep, whereas you should not only lodge it with them, but marry it to them, and make it a part of their very minds and souls.

. . . . .

THE NEW METHOD OF THINKING

BACON   DESCARTES   GALILEO

THE NEW METHOD

It was a slow and silent revolution—this gradual rise of the scientific and experimental attitude in western man. Though first couched in deductive theological inquiry, it actually began with the introduction of Aristotelian logic into the Scholastic universities of the 13th century. In the next two centuries men increasingly set human reason against the authority of tradition and revelation; in the course of time they began to doubt even Aristotle and to test his statements by dint of observation and experiment.

Some men were thrown into prison, like Galileo, others were burned, like Michael Servetus, but compared with any other great change in the history of mankind, casualties were small in numbers.

Yet, to a greater degree than the disputes of theologians, the new method of thinking changed our life, our economics, politics, production, and the programs and practices of our schools. Its spirit is expressed in the following statements.

Francis Bacon wrote in the *Great Instauration:* "Knowledge and human powers are synonymous, since the ignorance of the cause frustrates the effect. For nature is only subdued by submission, and that which in contemplative philosophy corresponds with the cause, in practical science becomes the rule."

Descartes wrote in his *Discourse on the Method of Rightly Conducting the Reason and Seeking for Truth in the Sciences:* "For it seemed to me that I might meet with much more truth in the reasonings that each man makes on the matters that specially concern him, and the issue of which would very soon punish him if he made a wrong judgment, than in the case of those made by a man of letters in his study touching speculations which lead to no result."

Finally, Galileo wrote in his Letter to the Grandduchess of Toscany: "This therefore being granted [that the Scripture has been written for the salvation of souls, and not for secular knowledge] methinks that in the discussion of natural problems, we ought not to begin at the authority of places of Scripture, but at sensible experiments and necessary demonstrations. . . ."

Selections from Bacon's *Novum Organum* are taken from *The Works.* . . . A New Edition in three volumes . . . by Basil Montagu (Philadelphia: Carey and Hart, 1842). Selections from Descartes' *Discourse* are taken from his *Philosophical Works,* translated by Elizabeth S. Haldane and G. R. T. Ross, published in England by the Cambridge University Press; in New York by The Macmillan Company, 1911-1912. Thomas Salusbury's *Mathematical Collections and Translations,* published in London in 1661, part I, is the source of selections from Galileo's *Letter to the Grandduchess of Toscany.*

BACON 1561–1626

NOVUM ORGANUM

THE GREAT INSTAURATION. SUMMARY OF THE SECOND
PART, DIGESTED IN APHORISMS.—APHORISMS ON THE
INTERPRETATION OF NATURE AND THE EMPIRE OF
MAN. 1. Man, as the minister and interpreter of nature, does and
understands as much as his observations on the order of nature,
either with regard to things or the mind, permit him, and neither
knows nor is capable of more.

2. The unassisted hand, and the understanding left to itself, possess but little power. Effects are produced by the means of instruments and helps, which the understanding requires no less than the
hand. And as instruments either promote or regulate the motion of
the hand, so those that are applied to the mind prompt or protect
the understanding.

3. Knowledge and human power are synonymous, since the ignorance of the cause frustrates the effect. For nature is only subdued by submission, and that which in contemplative philosophy
corresponds with the cause, in practical science becomes the *rule*.

4. Man, whilst operating, can only apply or withdraw natural
bodies; nature, internally, performs the rest.

5. Those who become practically versed in nature, are the mechanic, the mathematician, the physician, the alchymist, and the
magician; but all (as matters now stand) with faint efforts and
meagre success.

6. It would be madness, and inconsistency, to suppose that things
which have never yet been performed, can be performed without
employing some hitherto untried means.

7. The creations of the mind and hand appear very numerous, if
we judge by books and manufactures: but all that variety consists of
an excessive refinement, and of deductions from a few well known
matters; not of a number of axioms.

8. Even the effects already discovered are due to chance and experiment, rather than to the sciences. For our present sciences are

306

nothing more than peculiar arrangements of matters already discovered, and not methods for discovery, or plans for new operations.

9. The sole cause and root of almost every defect in the sciences is this; that whilst we falsely admire and extol the powers of the human mind, we do not search for its real helps.

10. The subtilty of nature is far beyond that of sense or of the understanding: so that the specious meditations, speculations, and theories of mankind, are but a kind of insanity, only there is no one to stand by and observe it.

11. As the present sciences are useless for the discovery of effects, so the present system of logic is useless for the discovery of the sciences.

12. The present system of logic rather assists in confirming and rendering inveterate the errors founded on vulgar notions, than in searching after truth; and is therefore more hurtful than useful.

13. The syllogism is not applied to the principles of the sciences, and is of no avail in intermediate axioms, as being very unequal to the subtilty of nature. It forces assent, therefore, and not things.

14. The syllogism consists of propositions, propositions of words, words are the signs of notions. If, therefore, the notions (which form the basis of the whole) be confused and carelessly abstracted from things, there is no solidity in the superstructure. Our only hope, then, is in genuine induction.

15. We have no sound notions either in logic or physics; substance, quality, action, passion, and existence are not clear notions; much less, weight, levity, density, tenuity, moisture, dryness, generation, corruption, attraction, repulsion, element, matter, form, and the like. They are all fantastical and ill defined.

16. The notions of less abstract natures, as man, dog, dove; and the immediate perceptions of sense, as heat, cold, white, black, do not deceive us materially, yet even these are sometimes confused by the mutability of matter and the intermixture of things. All the rest, which men have hitherto employed, are errors; and improperly abstracted and deduced from things.

17. There is the same degree of licentiousness and error in forming axioms, as in abstracting notions: and that in the first principles, which depend on common induction. Still more is this the case in axioms and inferior propositions derived from syllogisms.

18. The present discoveries in science are such as lie immediately beneath the surface of common notions. It is necessary, however, to penetrate the more secret and remote parts of nature, in order to

abstract both notions and axioms from things, by a more certain and guarded method.

19. There are and can exist but two ways of investigating and discovering truth. The one hurries on rapidly from the senses and particulars to the most general axioms; and from them as principles and their supposed indisputable truth derives and discovers the intermediate axioms. This is the way now in use. The other constructs its axioms from the senses and particulars, by ascending continually and gradually, till it finally arrives at the most general axioms, which is the true but unattempted way.

20. The understanding when left to itself proceeds by the same way as that which it would have adopted under the guidance of logic, namely, the first. For the mind is fond of starting off to generalities, that it may avoid labour, and after dwelling a little on a subject is fatigued by experiment. But these evils are augmented by logic, for the sake of the ostentation of dispute.

21. The understanding when left to itself in a man of a steady, patient, and reflecting disposition, (especially when unimpeded by received doctrines,) makes some attempt in the right way, but with little effect; since the understanding, undirected and unassisted, is unequal to and unfit for the task of vanquishing the obscurity of things.

22. Each of these two ways begins from the senses and particulars, and ends in the greatest generalities. But they are immeasurably different; for the one merely touches cursorily the limits of experiment, and particulars, whilst the other runs duly and regularly through them; the one from the very outset lays down some abstract and useless generalities, the other gradually rises to those principles which are really the most common in nature.

23. There is no small difference between the *idols* of the human mind, and the *ideas* of the divine mind; that is to say, between certain idle dogmas, and the real stamp and impression of created objects, as they are found in nature.

24. Axioms determined upon in argument can never assist in the discovery of new effects: for the subtilty of nature is vastly superior to that of argument. But axioms properly and regularly abstracted from particulars, easily point out and define new particulars, and therefore impart activity to the sciences.

25. The axioms now in use are derived from a scanty handful, as it were, of experience, and a few particulars of frequent occurrence, whence they are of much the same dimensions or extent as their origin. And if any neglected or unknown instance occurs, the

axiom is saved by some frivolous distinction, when it would be more consistent with truth to amend it.

26. We are wont, for the sake of distinction, to call that human reasoning which we apply to nature, the anticipation of nature, (as being rash and premature;) and that which is properly deduced from things, the interpretation of nature.

27. Anticipations are sufficiently powerful in producing unanimity, for if men were all to become even uniformly mad, they might agree tolerably well with each other.

28. Anticipations again will be assented to much more readily than interpretations; because, being deduced from a few instances, and these principally of familiar occurrence, they immediately hit the understanding, and satisfy the imagination; whilst, on the contrary, interpretations, being deduced from various subjects, and these widely dispersed, cannot suddenly strike the understanding; so that, in common estimation, they must appear difficult and discordant, and almost like the mysteries of faith.

29. In sciences founded on opinions and dogmas, it is right to make use of anticipations and logic, if you wish to force assent rather than things.

30. If all the capacities of all ages should unite and combine and transmit their labours, no great progress will be made in learning by anticipations; because the radical errors, and those which occur in the first process of the mind, are not cured by the excellence of subsequent means and remedies.

31. It is in vain to expect any great progress in the sciences by the superinducing or engrafting new matters upon old. An instauration must be made from the very foundations, if we do not wish to revolve forever in a circle, making only some slight and contemptible progress.

32. The ancient authors, and all others, are left in undisputed possession of their honours. For we enter into no comparison of capacity or talent, but of method; and assume the part of a guide, rather than of a critic.

33. To speak plainly, no correct judgment can be formed, either of our method, or its discoveries, by those anticipations which are now in common use; for it is not to be required of us to submit ourselves to the judgment of the very method we ourselves arraign.

34. Nor is it an easy matter to deliver and explain our sentiments: for those things which are in themselves new can yet be only understood from some analogy to what is old.

35. Alexander Borgia said of the expedition of the French into

Italy, that they came with chalk in their hands to mark up their lodgings, and not with weapons to force their passage. Even so do we wish our philosophy to make its way quietly into those minds that are fit for it, and of good capacity. For we have no need of contention where we differ in first principles, and our very notions, and even in our forms of demonstration.

36. We have but one simple method of delivering our sentiments: namely, we must bring men to particulars, and their regular series and order, and they must for a while renounce their notions and begin to form an acquaintance with things.

37. Our method and that of the skeptics agree in some respects at first setting out: but differ most widely and are completely opposed to each other in their conclusion. For they roundly assert that nothing can be known; we, that but a small part of nature can be known by the present method. Their next step, however, is to destroy the authority of the senses and understanding, whilst we invent and supply them with assistance.

38. The idols and false notions which have already preoccupied the human understanding, and are deeply rooted in it, not only to beset men's minds, that they become difficult of access, but, even when access is obtained, will again meet and trouble us in the instauration of the sciences, unless mankind, when forewarned, guard themselves with all possible care against them.

39. Four species of idols beset the human mind: to which (for distinction's sake) we have assigned names: calling the first idols of the tribe; the second idols of the den; the third idols of the market; the fourth idols of the theatre.

40. The formation of notions and axioms on the foundation of true induction, is the only fitting remedy, by which we can ward off and expel these idols. It is, however, of great service to point them out. For the doctrine of idols bears the same relation to the interpretation of nature, as that of confutation of sophisms does to common logic.

41. The idols of the tribe are inherent in human nature, and the very tribe or race of man. For man's sense is falsely asserted to be the standard of things. On the contrary, all the perceptions, both of the senses and the mind, bear reference to man, and not to the universe, and the human mind resembles those uneven mirrors, which impart their own properties to different objects, from which rays are emitted, and distort and disfigure them.

42. The idols of the den are those of each individual. For everybody (in addition to the errors common to the race of man) has his

own individual den or cavern, which intercepts and corrupts the light of nature; either from his own peculiar and singular disposition, or from his education and intercourse with others, or from his reading, and the authority acquired by those whom he reverences and admires, or from the different impressions produced on the mind, as it happens to be preoccupied and predisposed, or equable and tranquil, and the like: so that the spirit of man (according to its several dispositions) is variable, confused, and as it were actuated by chance; and Heraclitus said well that men search for knowledge in lesser worlds, and not in the greater or common world.

43. There are also idols formed by the reciprocal intercourse and society of man with man, which we call idols of the market, from the commerce and association of men with each other. For men converse by means of language; but words are formed at the will of the generality; and there arises from a bad and unapt formation of words a wonderful obstruction to the mind. Nor can the definitions and explanations, with which learned men are wont to guard and protect themselves in some instances, afford a complete remedy: words still manifestly force the understanding, throw every thing into confusion, and lead mankind into vain and innumerable controversies and fallacies.

44. Lastly, there are idols which have crept into men's minds from the various dogmas of peculiar systems of philosophy, and also from the perverted rules of demonstration, and these we denominate idols of the theatre. For we regard all the systems of philosophy hitherto received or imagined, as so many plays brought out and performed, creating fictitious and theatrical worlds. Nor do we speak only of the present systems, or of the philosophy and sects of the ancients, since numerous other plays of a similar nature can be still composed and made to agree with each other, the causes of the most opposite errors being generally the same. Nor, again, do we allude merely to general systems, but also to many elements and axioms of sciences, which have become inveterate by tradition, implicit credence, and neglect. We must, however, discuss each species of idols more fully and distinctly, in order to guard the human understanding against them.

DESCARTES 1596–1650

DISCOURSE ON THE METHOD OF RIGHTLY CONDUCTING THE REASON AND SEEKING FOR TRUTH IN THE SCIENCES

If this Discourse appears too long to be read all at once, it may be separated into six portions. And in the first there will be found various considerations respecting the sciences; in the second, the principal rules regarding the Method which the author has sought out; while in the third are some of the rules of morality which he has derived from this Method. In the fourth are the reasons by which he proves the existence of God and of the human soul, which form the foundation of his Metaphysic. In the fifth, the order of the questions regarding physics which he has investigated, and particularly the explanation of the movement of the heart, and of some other difficulties which pertain to medicine, as also the difference between the soul of man and that of the brutes. And in the last part the questions raised relate to those matters which the author believes to be requisite in order to advance further in the investigation of nature, in addition to the reasons that caused him to write.

PART I

Good sense is of all things in the world the most equally distributed, for everybody thinks himself so abundantly provided with it, that even those most difficult to please in all other matters do not commonly desire more of it than they already possess. It is unlikely that this is an error on their part; it seems rather to be evidence in support of the view that the power of forming a good judgment and of distinguishing the true from the false, which is properly speaking what is called Good sense or Reason, is by nature equal in all men. Hence too it will show that the diversity of our opinions does not proceed from some men being more rational than others, but solely from the fact that our thoughts pass through diverse channels and the same objects are not considered by all.

For to be possessed of good mental powers is not sufficient; the principal matter is to apply them well. The greatest minds are capable of the greatest vices as well as of the greatest virtues, and those who proceed very slowly may, provided they always follow the straight road, really advance much faster than those who, though they run, forsake it.

For myself I have never ventured to presume that my mind was in any way more perfect than that of the ordinary man; I have even longed to possess thought as quick, or an imagination as accurate and distinct, or a memory as comprehensive or ready, as some others. And besides these I do not know any other qualities that make for the perfection of the human mind. For as to reason or sense, inasmuch as it is the only thing that constitutes us men and distinguishes us from the brutes, I would fain believe that it is to be found complete in each individual, and in this I follow the common opinion of the philosophers, who say that the question of more or less occurs only in the sphere of the *accidents* and does not affect the *forms* or natures of the *individuals* in the same *species*.

But I shall not hesitate to say that I have had great good fortune from my youth up, in lighting upon and pursuing certain paths which have conducted me to considerations and maxims from which I have formed a Method, by whose assistance it appears to me I have the means of gradually increasing my knowledge and of little by little raising it to the highest possible point which the mediocrity of my talents and the brief duration of my life can permit me to reach. For I have already reaped from it fruits of such a nature that, even though I always try in the judgments I make on myself to lean to the side of self-depreciation rather than to that of arrogance, and though, looking with the eye of a philosopher on the diverse actions and enterprises of all mankind, I find scarcely any which do not seem to me vain and useless, I do not cease to receive extreme satisfaction in the progress which I seem to have already made in the search after truth, and to form such hopes for the future as to venture to believe that, if amongst the occupations of men, simply as men, there is some one in particular that is excellent and important, that is the one which I have selected.

It must always be recollected, however, that possibly I deceive myself, and that what I take to be gold and diamonds is perhaps no more than copper and glass. I know how subject we are to delusion in whatever touches ourselves, and also how much the judgments of our friends ought to be suspected when they are in our favour. But in this Discourse I shall be very happy to show the paths I have followed, and to set forth my life as in a picture, so that everyone may judge of it for himself; and thus in learning from the common talk what are the opinions which are held of it, a new means of obtaining self-instruction will be reached, which I shall add to those which I have been in the habit of using.

Thus my design is not here to teach the Method which everyone should follow in order to promote the good conduct of his Reason, but only to show in what manner I have endeavoured to conduct my own. Those who set about giving precepts must esteem themselves more skilful than those to whom they advance them, and if they fall short in the smallest matter they must of course take the blame for it. But regarding this Treatise simply as a history, or, if you prefer it, a fable in which, amongst certain things which may be imitated, there are possibly others also which it would not be right to follow, I hope that it will be of use to some without being hurtful to any, and that all will thank me for my frankness.

I have been nourished on letters since my childhood, and since I was given to believe that by their means a clear and certain knowledge could be obtained of all that is useful in life, I had an extreme desire to acquire instruction. But so soon as I had achieved the entire course of study at the close of which one is usually received into the ranks of the learned, I entirely changed my opinion. For I found myself embarrassed with so many doubts and errors that it seemed to me that the effort to instruct myself had no effect other than the increasing discovery of my own ignorance. And yet I was studying at one of the most celebrated Schools in Europe, where I thought that there must be men of learning if they were to be found anywhere in the world. I learned there all that others learned; and not being satisfied with the sciences that we were taught, I even read through all the books which fell into my hands, treating of what is considered most curious and rare. Along with this I knew the judgments that others had formed of me, and I did not feel that I was esteemed inferior to my fellow-students, although there were amongst them some destined to fill the places of our masters. And finally our century seemed to me as flourishing, and as fertile in great minds, as any which had preceded. And this made me take the liberty of judging all others by myself and of coming to the conclusion that there was no learning in the world such as I was formerly led to believe it to be.

I did not omit, however, always to hold in esteem those exercises which are the occupation of the Schools. I knew that the Languages which one learns there are essential for the understanding

314

of all ancient literature; that fables with their charm stimulate the mind and histories of memorable deeds exalt it; and that, when read with discretion, these books assist in forming a sound judgment. I was aware that the reading of all good books is indeed like a conversation with the noblest men of past centuries who were the authors of them, nay a carefully studied conversation, in which they reveal to us none but the best of their thoughts. I deemed Eloquence to have a power and beauty beyond compare; that Poesy has most ravishing delicacy and sweetness; that in Mathematics there are the subtlest discoveries and inventions which may accomplish much, both in satisfying the curious, and in furthering all the arts, and in diminishing man's labour; that those writings that deal with Morals contain much that is instructive, and many exhortations to virtue which are most useful; that Theology points out the way to Heaven; that Philosophy teaches us to speak with an appearance of truth on all things, and causes us to be admired by the less learned; that Jurisprudence, Medicine and all other sciences bring honour and riches to those who cultivate them; and finally that it is good to have examined all things, even those most full of superstition and falsehood, in order that we may know their just value, and avoid being deceived by them.

But I considered that I had already given sufficient time to languages and likewise even to the reading of the literature of the ancients, both their histories and their fables. For to converse with those of other centuries is almost the same thing as to travel. It is good to know something of the customs of different peoples in order to judge more sanely of our own, and not to think that everything of a fashion not ours is absurd and contrary to reason, as do those who have seen nothing. But when one employs too much time in travelling, one becomes a stranger in one's own country, and when one is too curious about things which were practised in past centuries, one is usually very ignorant about those which are practised in our own time. Besides, fables make one imagine many events possible which in reality are not so, and even the most accurate of histories, if they do not exactly misrepresent or exaggerate the value of things in order to render them more worthy of being read, at least omit in them all the circumstances which are basest and least notable; and from this fact it follows that what is retained is not portrayed as it really is, and that those who regulate their conduct by examples which they derive from such a source, are liable to fall into the extravagances of the knights-errant of Romance, and form projects beyond their power of performance.

I esteemed Eloquence most highly and I was enamoured of Poesy, but I thought that both were gifts of the mind rather than fruits of study. Those who have the strongest power of reasoning, and who most skilfully arrange their thoughts in order to render them clear and intelligible, have the best power of persuasion even if they can but speak the language of Lower Brittany and have never learned Rhetoric. And those who have the most delightful original ideas and who know how to express them with the maximum of style and suavity, would not fail to be the best poets even if the art of Poetry were unknown to them.

Most of all was I delighted with Mathematics because of the certainty of its demonstrations and the evidence of its reasoning; but I did not yet understand its true use, and, believing that it was of service only in the mechanical arts, I was astonished that, seeing how firm and solid was its basis, no loftier edifice had been reared thereupon. On the other hand I compared the works of the ancient pagans which deal with Morals to palaces most superb and magnificent, which are yet built on sand and mud alone. They praise the virtues most highly and show them to be more worthy of being prized than anything else in the world, but they do not sufficiently teach us to become acquainted with them, and often that which is called by a fine name is nothing but insensibility, or pride, or despair, or parricide.

I honoured our Theology and aspired as much as anyone to reach to heaven, but having learned to regard it as a most highly assured fact that the road is not less open to the most ignorant than to the most learned, and that the revealed truths which conduct thither are quite above our intelligence, I should not have dared to submit them to the feebleness of my reasonings; and I thought that, in order to undertake to examine them and succeed in so doing, it was necessary to have some extraordinary assistance from above and to be more than a mere man.

I shall not say anything about Philosophy, but that, seeing that it has been cultivated for many centuries by the best minds that have ever lived, and that nevertheless no single thing is to be found in it which is not subject of dispute, and in consequence which is not dubious, I had not enough presumption to hope to fare better there than other men had done. And also, considering how many conflicting opinions there may be regarding the self-same matter, all supported by learned people, while there can never be more than one which is true, I esteemed as well-nigh false all that only went as far as being probable.

316

Then as to the other sciences, inasmuch as they derive their principles from Philosophy, I judged that one could have built nothing solid on foundations so far from firm. And neither the honour nor the promised gain was sufficient to persuade me to cultivate them, for, thanks be to God, I did not find myself in a condition which obliged me to make a merchandise of science for the improvement of my fortune; and, although I did not pretend to scorn all glory like the Cynics, I yet had very small esteem for what I could not hope to acquire, excepting through fictitious titles. And, finally, as to false doctrines, I thought that I already knew well enough what they were worth to be subject to deception neither by the promises of an alchemist, the predictions of an astrologer, the impostures of a magician, the artifices or the empty boastings of any of those who make a profession of knowing that of which they are ignorant.

This is why, as soon as age permitted me to emerge from the control of my tutors, I entirely quitted the study of letters. And resolving to seek no other science than that which could be found in myself, or at least in the great book of the world, I employed the rest of my youth in travel, in seeing courts and armies, in intercourse with men of diverse temperaments and conditions, in collecting varied experiences, in proving myself in the various predicaments in which I was placed by fortune, and under all circumstances bringing my mind to bear on the things which came before it, so that I might derive some profit from my experience. For it seemed to me that I might meet with much more truth in the reasonings that each man makes on the matters that specially concern him, and the issue of which would very soon punish him if he made a wrong judgment, than in the case of those made by a man of letters in his study touching speculations which lead to no result, and which bring about no other consequences to himself excepting that he will be all the more vain the more they are removed from common sense, since in this case it proves him to have employed so much the more ingenuity and skill in trying to make them seem probable. And I always had an excessive desire to learn to distinguish the true from the false, in order to see clearly in my actions and to walk with confidence in this life.

It is true that while I only considered the manners of other men I found in them nothing to give me settled convictions; and I remarked in them almost as much diversity as I had formerly seen in the opinions of philosophers. So much was this the case that the greatest profit which I derived from their study was that, in seeing

317

many things which, although they seem to us very extravagant and ridiculous, were yet commonly received and approved by other great nations, I learned to believe nothing too certainly of which I had only been convinced by example and custom. Thus little by little I was delivered from many errors which might have obscured our natural vision and rendered us less capable of listening to Reason. But after I had employed several years in thus studying the book of the world and trying to acquire some experience, I one day formed the resolution of also making myself an object of study and of employing all the strength of my mind in choosing the road I should follow. This succeeded much better, it appeared to me, than if I had never departed either from my country or my books.

· · · · · ·

But like one who walks alone and in the twilight I resolved to go so slowly, and to use so much circumspection in all things, that if my advance was but very small, at least I guarded myself well from falling. I did not wish to set about the final rejection of any single opinion which might formerly have crept into my beliefs without having been introduced there by means of Reason, until I had first of all employed sufficient time in planning out the task which I had undertaken, and in seeking the true Method of arriving at a knowledge of all the things of which my mind was capable.

Among the different branches of Philosophy, I had in my younger days to a certain extent studied Logic; and in those of Mathematics, Geometrical Analysis and Algebra—three arts or sciences which seemed as though they ought to contribute something to the design I had in view. But in examining them I observed in respect to Logic that the syllogisms and the greater part of the other teaching served better in explaining to others those things that one knows (or like the art of Lully, in enabling one to speak without judgment of those things of which one is ignorant) than in learning what is new. And although in reality Logic contains many precepts which are very true and very good, there are at the same time mingled with them so many others which are hurtful or superfluous, that it is almost as difficult to separate the two as to draw a Diana or a Minerva out of a block of marble which is not yet roughly hewn. And as to the Analysis of the ancients and the Algebra of the moderns, besides the fact that they embrace only matters the most abstract, such as appear to have no actual use, the former is always so restricted to the consideration of symbols that it cannot exercise the Understanding without greatly fatiguing the

318

Imagination; and in the latter one is so subjected to certain rules and formulas that the result is the construction of an art which is confused and obscure, and which embarrasses the mind, instead of a science which contributes to its cultivation. This made me feel that some other Method must be found, which, comprising the advantages of the three, is yet exempt from their faults. And as a multiplicity of laws often furnishes excuses for evil-doing, and as a State is hence much better ruled when, having but very few laws, these are most strictly observed; so, instead of the great number of precepts of which Logic is composed, I believed that I should find the four which I shall state quite sufficient, provided that I adhered to a firm and constant resolve never on any single occasion to fail in their observance.

The first of these was to accept nothing as true which I did not clearly recognise to be so: that is to say, carefully to avoid precipitation and prejudice in judgments, and to accept in them nothing more than what was presented to my mind so clearly and distinctly that I could have no occasion to doubt it.

The second was to divide up each of the difficulties which I examined into as many parts as possible, and as seemed requisite in order that it might be resolved in the best manner possible.

The third was to carry on my reflections in due order, commencing with objects that were the most simple and easy to understand, in order to rise little by little, or by degrees, to knowledge of the most complex, assuming an order, even if a fictitious one, among those which do not follow a natural sequence relatively to one another.

The last was in all cases to make enumerations so complete and reviews so general that I should be certain of having omitted nothing.

Those long chains of reasoning, simple and easy as they are, of which geometricians make use in order to arrive at the most difficult demonstrations, had caused me to imagine that all those things which fall under the cognizance of man might very likely be mutually related in the same fashion; and that, provided only that we abstain from receiving anything as true which is not so, and always retain the order which is necessary in order to deduce the one conclusion from the other, there can be nothing so remote that we cannot reach to it, nor so recondite that we cannot discover it. And I had not much trouble in discovering which objects it was necessary to begin with, for I already knew that it was with the most simple and those most easy to apprehend. Considering also that of all

319

those who have hitherto sought for the truth in the Sciences, it has been the mathematicians alone who have been able to succeed in making any demonstrations, that is to say producing reasons which are evident and certain, I did not doubt that it had been by means of a similar kind that they carried on their investigations. I did not at the same time hope for any practical result in so doing, except that my mind would become accustomed to the nourishment of truth and would not content itself with false reasoning. But for all that I had no intention of trying to master all those particular sciences that receive in common the name of Mathematics; but observing that, although their objects are different, they do not fail to agree in this, that they take nothing under consideration but the various relationships or proportions which are present in these objects, I thought that it would be better if I only examined these proportions in their general aspect, and without viewing them otherwise than in the objects which would serve most to facilitate a knowledge of them. Not that I should in any way restrict them to these objects, for I might later on all the more easily apply them to all other objects to which they were applicable. Then, having carefully noted that in order to comprehend the proportions I should sometimes require to consider each one in particular, and sometimes merely keep them in mind, or take them in groups, I thought that, in order the better to consider them in detail, I should picture them in the form of lines, because I could find no method more simple nor more capable of being distinctly represented to my imagination and senses. I considered, however, that in order to keep them in my memory or to embrace several at once, it would be essential that I should explain them by means of certain formulas, the shorter the better. And for this purpose it was requisite that I should borrow all that is best in Geometrical Analysis and Algebra, and correct the errors of the one by the other.

. . . . .

But, having the intention of devoting all my life to the investigation of a knowledge which is so essential, and having discovered a path which appears to me to be of such a nature that we must by its means infallibly reach our end if we pursue it, unless, indeed, we are prevented by the shortness of life or by lack of experience, I judged that there was no better provision against these two impediments than faithfully to communicate to the public the little which I should myself have discovered, and to beg all well-inclined

320

persons to proceed further by contributing, each one according to his own inclination and ability, to the experiments which must be made, and then to communicate to the public all the things which they might discover, in order that the last should commence where the preceding had left off; and thus, by joining together the lives and labours of many, we should collectively proceed much further than any one in particular could succeed in doing.

I remarked also respecting experiments, that they become so much the more necessary the more one is advanced in knowledge, for to begin with it is better to make use simply of those which present themselves spontaneously to our senses, and of which we could not be ignorant provided that we reflected ever so little, rather than to seek out those which are more rare and recondite; the reason of this is that those which are more rare often mislead us so long as we do not know the causes of the more common, and the fact that the circumstances on which they depend are almost always so particular and so minute that it is very difficult to observe them. But in this the order which I have followed is as follows: I have first tried to discover generally the principles or first causes of everything that is or that can be in the world, without considering anything that might accomplish this end but God Himself who has created the world, or deriving them from any source excepting from certain germs of truths which are naturally existent in our souls. After that I considered which were the primary and most ordinary effects which might be deduced from these causes, and it seems to me that in this way I discovered the heavens, the stars, an earth, and even on the earth, water, air, fire, the minerals and some other such things, which are the most common and simple of any that exist, and consequently the easiest to know. Then, when I wished to descend to those which were more particular, so many objects of various kinds presented themselves to me, that I did not think it was possible for the human mind to distinguish the forms or species of bodies which are on the earth from an infinitude of others which might have been so if it had been the will of God to place them there, or consequently to apply them to our use, if it were not that we arrive at the causes by the effects, and avail ourselves of many particular experiments. In subsequently passing over in my mind all the objects which have ever been presented to my senses, I can truly venture to say that I have not there observed anything which I could not easily explain by the principles which I had discovered. But I must also confess that the power of nature is so ample and so vast, and these principles are so simple and general, that I observed hardly any particular effect as to which I could not at once recognise that it might be deduced from the principles in many different ways; and my greatest difficulty is usually to discover in which of these ways the effect does depend upon them.

GALILEO 1564–1642

LETTER TO THE GRANDDUCHESS OF TOSCANY

TO HER MOST SERENE HIGHNES THE GRAN DUCHESS
MOTHER. Some years since, as Your most Serene Highness well
knoweth, I did discover many particulars in Heaven that had been
unseen and unheard of untill this our Age; which, as well for their
novelty, as for certain consequences which depend upon them,
clashing with some Physical propositions commonly received by the
Schools, did stir up against me no small number of such as professed the vulgar Philosophy in the Universities; as if I had with my
own hand newly placed these things in Heaven to obscure and disturb Nature and the Sciences: who forgetting that the multitude of
Truths contribute, and concur to the investigation, augmentation,
and establishment of the Arts, and not to their diminution, and destruction; and at the same time shewing themselves more affectionate to their own Opinions, than to Truth, went about to deny, and
to disprove those Novelties; of which their very sense, had they but
pleased to have intentsly beheld them, would have rendered them
thorowly assured. And to this purpose they alledged sundry things,
and published certain Papers fraughted with vain discourses; and
which was a more gross errour, interwoven with the attestations of
the Sacred Scriptures, taken from places by them not rightly understood, and which did not any thing concern the point for which
they were produced Into which errour perhaps they would not
have run, if they had but been advertised of a most profitable
Document which S. *Augustine* giveth us, concerning our proceeding
warily, in making positive determinations in points that are obscure
and hard to be understood by the meer help of ratiocination; where
treating (as we) of a certain natural conclusion concerning Celestial Bodies, he thus writes: *But now having evermore a respect to
the moderation of pious Gravity, we ought to believe nothing un-
advisedly in a doubtful point; lest we conceive a prejudice against
that, in favour to our Errour, which Truth hereafter may discover
to be no wise contrary to the Sacred Books either of the Old, or
New Testament.*

It hath since come to pass, that Time hath by degrees discovered to every one the truths before by me indicated: and together with the truth of the fact, a discovery hath been made of the difference of humours between those who simply and without passion did refuse to admit such like *Phænomena* for true, and those who to their incredulity had added some discomposed affection: For as those who were better grounded in the Science of Astronomy, and Natural Philosophy, became satisfied upon my first intimation of the news; so all those who stood not in the Negative, or in doubt for any other reason, but because it was an unlookt-for-Novelty, and because they had not an occasion of seeing a sensible experiment thereof, did by degrees come to satisfie themselves: But those, who besides the love they bore to their first Errour, have I know not what imaginary interess to render them disaffected; not so much towards the things, as towards the Author of them, not being able any longer to deny them, conceal themselves under an obstinate silence; and being exasperated more than ever by that whereby those others were satisfied and convinced, they divert their thoughts to other projects, and seek to prejudice me some other wayes: of whom I profess that I would make no more account than I have done of those who heretofore have contradicted me (at whom I alwaies laugh, as being assured of the issue that the business is to have) but that I see that those new Calumnies and Persecutions do not determine in our greater or lesser Learning (in which I will scarce pretend to any thing) but extend so far as to attempt to asperse me with Crimes which ought to be, and are more abhorred by me than Death it self: Nor ought I to content my self that they are known to be unjust by those onely who know me and them, but by all men whatsoever. They persisting therefore in their first Resolution, Of ruining me and whatsoever is mine, by all imaginable waies; and knowing how that I in my Studies of Astronomy and Philosophy hold, as to the Worlds Systeme, That the Sun, without changing place, is situate in the Centre of the Conversion of the Celestial Orbes; and that the Earth, convertible about its own Axis, moveth it self about the Sun: And moreover understanding, that I proceed to maintain this Position, not onely by refuting the Reasons of *Ptolomy* and *Aristotle,* but by producing many on the contrary; and in particular, some Physical pertaining to Natural Effects, the causes of which perhaps can be by no other way assigned; and others Astronomical depending upon many circumstances and encounters of new Discoveries in Heaven, which manifestly confute the Ptolomaick Systeme, and admirably agree with

324

and confirm this other Hypothesis: and possibly being ashamed to see the known truth of other Positions by me asserted, different from those that have been commonly received; and therefore distrusting their defence so long as they should continue in the Field of Philosophy: for these respects, I say, they have resolved to try whether they could make a Shield for the fallacies of their Arguments of the Mantle of a feigned Religion, and of the Authority of the Sacred Scriptures, applyed by them with little judgment to the confutation of such Reasons of mine as they had neither understood, nor so much as heard.

And first, they have indeavoured, as much as in them lay, to divulge an opinion thorow the Universe, that those Propositions are contrary to the Holy Letters, and consequently Damnable and Heretical: And thereupon perceiving, that for the most part, the inclination of Mans Nature is more prone to imbrace those enterprizes, whereby his Neighbour may, although unjustly, be oppressed, than those from whence he may receive just incouragement; it was no hard matter to find those Complices, who for such (that is, for Damnable and Heretical) did from their Pulpits with unwonted confidence preach it, with but an unmerciful and less considerate injury, not only to this Doctrine, and to its followers, but to all Mathematicks and Mathematicians together. Hereupon assuming greater confidence, and vainly hoping that that Seed which first took root in their unfound mindes, might spread its branches, and ascend towards Heaven, they went scattering rumours up and down among the People, That it would, ere long be condemned by Supreme Authority: and knowing that such a *Censure* would supplant not onely these two Conclusions of the Worlds Systeme, but would make all other Astronomical and Physical Observations that have correspondence and necessary connection therewith to become damnable, to facilitate the business they seek all they can to make this opinion (at least among the vulgar) to seem new, and peculiar to my self, not owning to know that *Nicholas Copernicus* was its Authour, or rather Restorer and Confirmer: a person who was not only a Catholick, but a Priest, Canonick, and so esteemed, that there being a Dispute in the *Lateran Council,* under *Leo X.* touching the correction of the Ecclesiastick Calendar, he was sent for to *Rome* from the remotest parts of *Germany,* for to assist in this Reformation, which for that time was left imperfect, onely because as then the true measure of the Year and Lunar Moneth was not exactly known: whereupon it was given him in charge by the Bishop of *Sempronia,* at that time Super-intendent in that Affair, to search with reiterated studies and pains for greater light and certainty, touching those Cœlestial Motions. Upon which, with a labour truly *Atlantick* and with his admirable Wit, setting himself again to that Study, he made such a progress in these Sciences, and reduced the knowledge of the Cœlestial Motions to such exactnesse, that he gained the title of an Excellent *Astronomer*. And, according unto his Doctrine, not only the Calendar hath been since regulated, but the Tables of all the Motions of the Planets have also been calculated: and having reduced the said Doctrine into six Books, he published them to the World at the instance of the Cardinal of *Capua*, and of the Bishop of *Culma*. And in regard that he had re-assumed this so laborious an enterprize by the order of The Pope; he dedicated his Book *De Revolutionibus Cœlestibus* to His Successour, namely *Paul* III. which, being then also Printed, hath been received by The Holy Church, and read and studied by all the World, without any the least umbrage of scruple that hath ever been conceived at his Doctrine; The which, whilst it is now proved by manifest Experiments and necessary Demonstrations to have been well grounded, there want not persons that, though they never saw that same Book intercept the reward of those many Labours to its Authour, by causing him to be censured and pronounced an Heretick; and this, only to satisfie a particular displeasure conceived, without any cause, against another man, that hath no other interest in *Copernicus,* but only as he is an approver of his Doctrine.

Now in regard of these false aspersions, which they so unjustly seek to throw upon me, I have thought it necessary for my justification before the World (of whose judgment in matters of Religion and Reputation I ought to make great esteem) to discourse concerning those Particulars, which these men produce to scandalize and subvert this Opinion, and in a word, to condemn it, not only as false, but also as Heretical; continually making an Hipocritical Zeal for Religion their shield; going about moreover to interest the Sacred Scriptures in the Dispute, and to make them in a certain sense Ministers of their deceiptful purposes: and farthermore desiring, if I mistake not, contrary to the intention of them, and of the Holy Fathers to extend (that I may not say abuse) their Authority, so as that even in Conclusions meerly Natural, and not *de Fide,* they would have us altogether leave Sense and Demonstrative Reasons, for some place of Scripture which sometimes under the apparent words may contain a different sense. Now I hope to shew with how much greater Piety and Religious Zeal I proceed, than they do, in that I propose not, that the Book of *Copernicus* is not to be condemned, but that it is not to be condemned, as they would have it; without understanding it, hearing it, or so much as seeing it; and especially he being an Author that never treateth of matters of Religion or Faith; nor by Reasons any way depending on the Authority of Sacred Scriptures whereupon he may have erroniously interpreted them; but alwaies insists upon Natural Conclusions belonging to the Celestial Motions, handled with Astronomical and Geometrical Demonstrations. Not that he had not a respect to the places of the Sacred Leaves, but because he knew very well that his said Doctrine being demonstrated, it could not contradict the Scriptures, rightly, and according to their true meaning understood. And therefore in the end of his Epistle Dedicatory, speaking to The Pope, he saith thus: If *there should chance to be any Matæologists, who though ignorant in all the Mathematicks, yet pretending a skill in those Learnings, should dare, upon the authority of some place of Scripture wrested to their purpose, to condemn and censure this my Hypothesis, I value them not, but shall slight their inconsiderate Judgement. For it is not unknown, that* Lactantius *(otherwise a Famous Author, though mean Mathematician) writeth very childishly touching the Form of the Earth, when he scoffs at those who affirm the Earth to be in Form of a Globe. So that it ought not to seem strange to the Ingenious, if any such should likewise now deride us. The Mathematicks are written for Mathematitians, to whom (if I deceive not my self) these Labours of mine shall seem to add something, as also to the Common-weale of the Church, whose Government is now in the hands of Your Holiness.*

And of this kinde do these appear to be who indeavour to perswade that *Copernicus* may be condemned before his Book is read; and to make the World believe that it is not onely lawfull but commendable so to do, produce certain Authorities of the Scripture, of Divines, and of Councils; which as they are by me had in reverence, and held of Supream Authority, insomuch that I should esteem it high temerity for any one to contradict them whilst they are used according to the Institutes of Holy Church, so I believe that it is no errour to speak, so long as one hath reason to suspect that a person hath a desire, for some concern of his own, to produce and alledge them, to purposes different from those that are in the most Sacred intention of The Holy Church. Therefore I not onely protest (and my sincerity shall manifest it self) that I intend to submit my self freely to renounce those errors, into which, through ignorance, I may run in this Discourse of matters pertaining to

327

Religion; but I farther declare, that I desire not in these matters to engage dispute with any one, although it should be in points that are disputable: for my end tendeth onely to this, That if in these considerations, besides my own profession, amongst the errours that may be in them, there be any thing apt to give others an hint of some Notion beneficial to the Holy Church, touching the determining about the *Copernican* Systeme, it may be taken and improved as shall seem best to my Superiours: If not, let my Book be torn and burnt; for that I do neither intend, nor pretend to gain to my self any fruit from my writings, that is not Pious and Catholick. And moreover, although that many of the things that I observe have been spoken in my own hearing, yet I shall freely admit and grant to those that spake them, that they never said them, if so they please, but confess that I might have been mistaken: And therefore what I say, let it be supposed to be spoken not by them, but by those which were of this opinion.

The motive therefore that they produce to condemn the Opinion of the Mobility of the Earth, and Stability of the Sun, is, that reading in the Sacred Leaves, in many places, that the Sun moveth, that the Earth standeth still; and the Scripture not being capable of lying, or erring, it followeth upon necessary consequence, that the Position of those is Erronious and Heretical, who maintain that the Sun of itself is immoveable, and the Earth moveable.

Touching this Reason I think it fit in the first place, to consider, That it is both piously spoken, and prudently affirmed, That the Sacred Scripture can never lye, when ever its true meaning is understood: Which I believe none will deny to be many times very abstruce, and very different from that which the bare sound of the words signifieth. Whence it cometh to pass, that if ever any one should constantly confine himself to the naked Grammatical Sence, he might, erring himself, make not only Contradictions and Propositions remote from Truth to appear in the Scriptures, but also gross Heresies and Blasphemies: For that we should be forced to assign to God feet, and hands, and eyes, yea more corporal and humane affections, as of Anger, of Repentance, of Hatred, nay, and sometimes the Forgetting of things past, and Ignorance of those to come: Which Propositions, like as (so the Holy Ghost affirmeth) they were in that manner pronounced by the Sacred Scriptures, that they might be accommodated to the Capacity of the Vulgar, who are very rude and unlearned; so likewise, for the sakes of those that deserve to be distinguished from the Vulgar, it is necessary that grave and skilful Expositors produce the true senses of them, and

328

shew the particular Reasons why they are dictated under such and such words. And this is a Doctrine so true and common amongst Divines, that it would be superfluous to produce any attestation thereof.

Hence methinks I may with much more reason conclude, that the same holy Writ, when ever it hath had occasion to pronounce any natural Conclusion, and especially, any of those which are more abstruce, and difficult to be understood, hath not failed to observe this Rule, that so it might not cause confusion in the mindes of those very people, and render them the more contumacious against the Doctrines that were more sublimely mysterious: For (like as we have said, and as it plainly appeareth) out of the sole respect of condescending to Popular Capacity, the Scripture hath not scrupled to shadow over most principal and fundamental Truths, attributing, even to God himself, qualities extreamly remote from, and contrary unto his Essence. Who would positively affirm that the Scripture, laying aside that respect, in speaking but occasionally of the Earth, of the Water, of the Sun, or of any other Creature, hath chosen to confine it self, with all vigour, within the bare and narrow literal sense of the words? And especially, in mentioning of those Creatures, things not at all concerning the primary Institution of the same Sacred Volume, to wit, the Service of God, and the salvation of Souls, and in things infinitely beyond the apprehension of the Vulgar?

This therefore being granted, methinks that in the Discussion of Natural Problemes, we ought not to begin at the authority of places of Scripture; but at Sensible Experiments and Necessary Demonstrations: For, from the Divine Word, the Sacred Scripture and Nature did both alike proceed; the first, as the Holy Ghosts Inspiration; the second, as the most observant Executrix of Gods Commands: And moreover it being convenient in the Scriptures (by way of condescension to the understanding of all men) to speak many things different, in appearance; and so far as concernes the naked signification of the words, from absolute truth: But on the contrary, Nature being inexorable and immutable, and never passing the bounds of the Laws assigned her, as one that nothing careth whether her abstruse reasons and methods of operating be, or be not exposed to the Capacity of Men; I conceive that that, concerning Natural Effects, which either Sensible Experience sets before our eyes, or Necessary Demonstrations do prove unto us, ought not, upon any account, to be called into question, much less condemned upon the testimony of Texts of Scripture, which may, under their words, couch Senses seemingly contrary thereto; In regard that every Expression of Scripture is not tied to so strict conditions, as every Effect of Nature: Nor doth God less admirably discover himself unto us in Nature's Actions, than in the Scriptures Sacred Dictions. Which peradventure *Tertullian* intended to express in those words: *We conclude, God is known; first, by Nature, and then again more particularly known by Doctrine: by Nature, in his Works; by Doctrine, in his Word preached.*

But I will not hence affirm, but that we ought to have an extraordinary esteem for the Places of Sacred Scripture, nay, being come to a certainty in any Natural Conclusions, we ought to make use of them, as most apposite helps to the true Exposition of the same Scriptures, and to the investigation of those Senses which are necessarily conteined in them, as most true, and concordant with the Truths demonstrated.

This maketh me to suppose, that the Authority of the Sacred Volumes was intended principally to perswade men to the belief of those Articles and Propositions, which, by reason they surpass all humane discourse, could not by any other Science, or by any other means be made credible, than by the Mouth of the Holy Spirit it self. Besides that, even in those Propositions, which are not *de Fide*, the Authority of the same Sacred Leaves ought to be preferred to the Authority of all Humane Sciences that are not written in a Demonstrative Method, but either with bare Narrations, or else with probable Reasons; and this I hold to be so far convenient and necessary, by how far the said Divine Wisdome surpasseth all humane Judgment and Conjecture. But that that self same God who hath indued us with Senses, Discourse, and Understanding hath intended, laying aside the use of these, to give the knowledg of those things by other means, which we may attain by these, so as that even in those Natural Conclusions, which either by Sensible Experiments or Necessary Demonstrations are set before our eyes, or our Understanding, we ought to deny Sense and Reason, I do not conceive that I am bound to believe it; and especially in those Sciences, of which but a small part, and that divided into Conclusions is to be found in the Scripture: Such as, for instance, is that of *Astronomy*, of which there is so small a part in Holy Writ, that it doth not so much as name any of the Planets, except the Sun and the Moon, and once or twice onely *Venus* under the name of *Lucifer*. For if the Holy Writers had had any intention to perswade People to believe the Dispositions and Motions of the Coelestial Bodies; and that consequently we are still to derive that knowledge

330

from the Sacred Books they would not, in my opinion, have spoken so little thereof, that it is as much as nothing, in comparison of the infinite admirable Conclusions, which in that Science are comprized and demonstrated. Nay, that the Authours of the Holy Volumes did not only not pretend to teach us the Constitutions and Motions of the Heavens and Stars, their Figures, Magnitudes, and Distances, but that intentionally (albeit that all these things were very well known unto them) they forbore to speak of them, is the opinion of the Most Holy & Most Learned Fathers: and in S. *Augustine* we read the following words. *It is likewise commonly asked, of what Form and Figure we may believe Heaven to be, according to the Scriptures: For many contend much about those matters, which the greater prudence of our Authors hath forborn to speak of, as nothing furthering their Learners in relation to a blessed life; and, (which is the chiefest thing) taking up much of that time which should be spent in holy exercises. For what is it to me whether Heaven, as a Sphere, doth on all sides environ the Earth, a Mass ballanced in the middle of the World; or whether like a Dish it doth onely cover or overcast the same? But because belief of Scripture is urged for that cause, which we have oft mentioned, that is, That none through ignorance of Divine Phrases, when they shall find any thing of this nature in, or hear any thing cited out of our Bibles which may seem to oppose manifest Conclusions, should be induced to suspect their truth, when they admonish, relate, & deliver more profitable matters Briefly be it spoken, touching the Figure of Heaven, that our Authors knew the truth: But the H. Spirit would not, that men should learn what is profitable to none for salvation.*

And the same intentional silence of these sacred Penmen in determining what is to be believed of these accidents of the Celestial Bodies, is again hinted to us by the same Father in the ensuing 10. Chapter upon the Question, Whether we are to believe that Heaven moveth, or standeth still, in these words: *There are some of the Brethren that start a question concerning the motion of Heaven, Whether it be fixed, or moved: For if it be moved (say they) how is it a Firmament? If it stand still, how do these Stars which are held to be fixed go round from East to West, the more Northern performing shorter Circuits near the Pole; so that Heaven, if there be another Pole, to us unknown, may seem to revolve upon some other Axis; but if there be not another Pole, it may be thought to move as a Discus? To whom I reply, That these points require many subtil and profound Reasons, for the making out whether they*

331

be really so, or no; the undertakeing and discussing of which is neither consistent with my leasure, nor their duty, whom I desire to instruct in the necessary matters more directly conducing to their salvation, and to the benefit of The Holy Church.

From which (that we may come nearer to our particular case) it necessarily followeth, that the Holy Ghost not having intended to teach us, whether Heaven moveth or standeth still; nor whether its Figure be in Form of a Sphere, or of a Discus, or distended *in Planum:* Nor whether the Earth be contained in the Centre of it, or on one side; he hath much less had an intention to assure us of other Conclusions of the same kinde, and in such a manner, connected to these already named, that without the determination of them, one can neither affirm one or the other part; which are, The determining of the Motion and Rest of the said Earth, and of the Sun. And if the same Holy Spirit hath purposely pretermitted to teach us those Propositions, as nothing concerning his intention, that is, our salvation; how can it be affirmed, that the holding of one part rather than the other, should be so necessary, as that it is *de Fide,* and the other erronious? Can an Opinion be Heretical, and yet nothing concerning the salvation of souls? Or can it be said that the Holy Ghost purposed not to teach us a thing that concerned our salvation? I might here insert the Opinion of an Ecclesiastical Person, raised to the degree of *Eminentissimo,* to wit, *That the intention of the Holy Ghost, is to teach us how we shall go to Heaven, and not how Heaven goeth.*

But let us return to consider how much necessary Demonstrations, and sensible Experiments ought to be esteemed in Natural Conclusions; and of what Authority Holy and Learned Divines have accounted them, from whom amongst an hundred other attestations, we have these that follow: *We must also carefully heed and altogether avoid in handling the Doctrine of* Moses, *to avouch or speak any thing affirmatively and confidently which contradicteth the manifest Experiments and Reasons of Philosophy, or other Sciences. For since all Truth is agreeable to Truth, the Truth of Holy Writ cannot be contrary to the solid Reasons and Experiments of Humane Learning.*

. . . . .

Now as to these Determinations, I have had occasion to consider some particulars (which I will purpose) for that I was made cautious thereof, by those who understand more than I in these businesses, and to whose judgements I alwaies submit myself. And first

I could say, that there might possibly a certain kinde of equivocation interpose, in that they do not distinguish the preheminences whereby Sacred *Theologie* meriteth the Title of Queen.

Again, to command the very Professors of *Astronomy*, that they of themselves see to the confuting of their own Observations and Demonstrations, as those that can be no other but Falacies and Sophismes, is to enjoyn a thing beyond all possibility of doing: For it is not onely to command them that they do not see that which they see, and that they do not understand that which they understand; but that in seeking, they finde the contrary of that which they happen to meet with. Therefore before that this is to be done, it would be necessary that they were shewed the way how to make the Powers of the Soul to command one another, and the inferior the Superior; so that the imagination and will might, and should believe contrary to what the Intellect understands: I still mean in Propositions purely Natural, and which are not *de Fide,* and not in the Supernatural, which are *de Fide.*

I would entreat these Wise and Prudent Fathers, that they would withal diligence consider the difference that is between Opinable and Demonstrative Doctrines: To the end, that well weighing in their minds with what force Necessary Illations oblige, they might the better ascertain themselves, that it is not in the Power of the Professors of Demonstrative Sciences to change their Opinions at pleasure, and apply themselves one while to one fide, and another while to another; and that there is a great difference between commanding a Methametitian or a Philosopher, and the disposing of a Lawyer or a Merchant; and that the demonstrated Conclusions touching the things of Nature and of the Heavens cannot be changed with the same facility, as the Opinions are touching what is lawful or not in a Contract, Bargain, or Bill of Exchange. This difference was well understood by the Learned and Holy Fathers, as their having been at great pains to confute many Arguments, or to say better, many Philosophical Fallacies, doth prove unto us; and as may expresly be read in some of them, and particularly we have in S. *Augustine* the following words: *This is to be held for an undoubted Truth. That we may be confident, that whatever the Sages of this World have demonstrated touching Natural Points, is no waies contrary to our Bibles: And in case they teach any thing in their Books that is contrary to the Holy Scriptures, we may without any scruple conclude it to be most false; And according to our ability let us make the same appear: And let us so keep the Faith of our Lord, in whom are hidden all the Treasures of Wisdom; that we be*

333

neither seduced with the Loquacity of false Philosophy, nor feared by the superstition of a counterfeit Religion.

From which words, I conceive that I may collect this Doctrine, namely, That in the Books of the Wise of this World, there are contained some Natural truths that are solidly demonstrated, and others again that are barely taught; and that as to the first sort, it is the Office of wise Divines to shew that they are not contrary to the Sacred Scriptures; As to the rest, taught, but not necessarily demonstrated, if they shall contain any thing contrary to the Sacred Leaves, it ought to be held undoubtedly false, and such it ought by all possible waies to be demonstrated.

If therefore Natural Conclusions veritably demonstrated, are not to be postposed to the Places of Scripture, but that it ought to be shewn how those Places do not interfer with the said Conclusions; then its necessary before a Physical Proposition be condemned, to shew that it is not necessarily demonstrated; and this is to be done not by them who hold it to be true, but by those who judge it to be false. And this seemeth very reasonable, and agreeable to Nature; that is to say, that they may much more easily find the fallacies in a Discourse, who believe it to be false, than those who account it true and concludent. Nay, in this particular it will come to passe, that the followers of this opinion, the more that they shall turn over Books, examine the Arguments, repeat the Observations, and compare the Experiments, the more shall they be confirmed in this belief. And your Highness knoweth what happened to the late Mathematick Professor in the University of *Pisa*, Who betook himself in his old age to look into the Doctrine of *Copernicus*, with hope that he might be able solidly to confute it (for that he held it so far to be false, as that he had never studied it) but it was his fortune, that as soon as he had understood the grounds, proceedings, and demonstrations of *Copernicus*, he found himself to be perswaded, and of an opposer became his most confident Defender. I might also nominate other Mathematicians, who being moved by my last Discoveries, have confessed it necessary to change the formerly received Constitution of the World, it not being able by any means to subsist any longer.

If for the banishing this Opinion and Hypothesis out of the World, it were enough to stop the mouth of one alone, as it may be they perswade themselves who measuring others judgements by their own, think it impossible that this Doctrine should be able to subsist and finde any followers, this would be very easie to be done, but the business standeth otherwise: For to execute such a deter-

334

mination, it would be necessary to prohibite not onely the Book of *Copernicus*, and the Writings of the other Authors that follow the same opinion, but to interdict the whole Science of *Astronomy;* and which is more, to forbid men looking towards Heaven, that so they might not see *Mars* and *Venus* at one time neer to the Earth, and at another farther off, with such a difference that the latter is found to be fourty times, and the former sixty times bigger in surface at one time than at another; and to the end, that the same *Venus* might not be discovered to be one while round, and another while forked, with most subtil hornes: and many other sensible Observations which can never by any means be reconciled to the *Ptolomaick* Systeme, but are unanswerable Arguments for the *Copernican.*

But the prohibiting of *Copernicus* his Book, now that by many new Observations, and by the application of many of the Learned to the reading of him, his Hypothesis and Doctrine doth every day appear to be more true, having admitted and tolerated it for so many years, whilst he was lesse followed, studied, and confirmed, would seem, in my judgment, an affront to Truth, and a seeking the more to obscure and suppresse her, the more she sheweth her self clear and perspicuous.

The abolishing and censuring, not of the whole Book, but onely so much of it as concerns this particular opinion of the *Earths Mobility*, would, if I mistake not, be a greater detriment to souls, it being an occasion of great scandal, to see a Position proved, and to see it afterwards made an Heresie to believe it.

The prohibiting of the whole Science, what other would it be but an open contempt of an hundred Texts of the Holy Scriptures, which teach us, That the Glory, and the Greatnesse of Almighty God is admirably discerned in all his Works, and divinely read in the Open Book of Heaven? Nor let any one think that the Lecture of the lofty conceits that are written in those Leaves finish in only beholding the Splendour of the Sun, and of the Stars, and their rising and setting, (which is the term to which the eyes of bruits and of the vulgar reach) but there are couched in them mysteries so profound, and conceipts so sublime, that the vigils, labours, and studies of an hundred and an hundred acute Wits, have not yet been able thorowly to dive into them after the continual disquisition of some thousands of years. But let the Unlearned believe, that like as that which their eyes discern in beholding the aspect of a humane body, is very little in comparison of the stupendious Artifices, which an exquisite and curious Anatomist or Philosopher finds in the same when he is searching for the use of so many Muscles, Tendons,

Nerves, and Bones; and examining the Offices of the Heart, and of the other principal Members, seeking the seat of the vital Faculties, noting and observing the admirable structures of the Instruments of the Senses, and, without ever making an end of satisfying his curiosity and wonder, contemplating the Receptacles of the Imagination, of the Memory, and of the Understanding; So that which represents it self to the meer sight, is as nothing in comparison and proportion to the strange Wonders, that by help of long and accurate Observations the Wit of Learned Men discovereth in Heaven. And this is the substance of what I had to consider touching this particular.

THE DEVELOPMENT OF MODERN
EDUCATION

COMENIUS 1592–1670

THE LIFE and work of Comenius are characterized by a span of experience as only men of unusual comprehension and imagination are able to encompass. Because he fought for the religious and national liberty of his Moravian Brethren, whose Bishop he was at the period of the Thirty Years' War, he was a refugee for most of his life; yet all his writings breathe an atmosphere of peace and hope. He was continuously faced with the abysses of human cruelty, fanaticism, and the imperialistic struggle for power, yet he believed in the final victory of the "Way of Light," in the educability of men, and in their capacity to build up a league of nations and use an international language. He never wavered in his pietist faith; as most of his contemporaries he was not even free from superstition and magic beliefs; yet, he never was "orthodox." Rather he allowed elements of pantheism and theosophy to enter into his Weltanschauung. And despite his mystical transcendentalism he made a grand attempt to transfer the "inductive method," so ardently espoused by Francis Bacon, to the theory and practice of education.

The results of this attempt were an illustrated textbook, the *Orbis Pictus*, used in most western nations for more than a century and a half, and the *Great Didactic*. The main defect of the latter is that the author mistakenly uses analogies between animal and human life as examples of cause and effect. Yet, the *Great Didactic* is a great step toward a coherent discipline, and as such reveals in essence all those elements on which any modern system of education has to be built: a definition of goal, a psychology of human nature as a basis for interconnecting the methods of education with the laws of mental growth, and, finally, a consideration of the role of education within human society.

Selections from Comenius' *Didactica Magna* are translated by the editor from the German edition by Wilhelm Altemöller, Paderborn, Ferdinand Schöningh, 1905. The selection from *The Way of Light (Via Lucis)* is from the translation into English with an introduction by E. T. Campagnac, published by the University Press of Liverpool in 1939, page 18.

THE GREAT DIDACTIC

IN WHICH IS PRESENTED A GENERALLY VALID ART OF TEACHING EVERYTHING TO EVERYONE, OR, RELIABLE AND PERFECT DIRECTIONS FOR ERECTING SCHOOLS IN ALL COMMUNITIES, TOWNS, AND VILLAGES OF ANY

CHRISTIAN STATE. In these schools all youth of both sexes, without exception, can be instructed in the sciences, improved in their morals, filled with piety, and, in suchwise, be equipped in early years for all that belongs to the life here and beyond. This will be done by a concise, agreeable, and thorough form of instruction which:

> derives its reasons from the genuine nature of things,
>
> proves its truth by dint of adequate examples taken from the mechanical arts,
>
> arranges the sequence of instruction by years, months, days, and hours, and finally,
>
> shows an easy and safe way for the happy pursuit of all these suggestions.

The Beginning and End of our Didactic will be:
To seek and find a method by which the teachers teach less and the learners learn more, by which the schools have less noise, obstinacy, and frustrated endeavor, but more leisure, pleasantness, and definite progress, and by which the Christian State will suffer less under obscurity, confusion, and conflict, and will enjoy a greater amount of light, order, peace, and quiet.

. . . . .

Chapter 2. Man's Ultimate Goal Lies Outside this Life.
. . . All our doing and suffering tells us that we do not achieve our ultimate goal here on earth, but that all that is in us and we ourselves aim farther. For what we are, do, think, talk, contemplate, acquire, and possess is only a kind of ladder on which we always climb toward a higher rung, but never reach the top. After man has begun his life in the form of an amorphous mass he gradually takes on the contours of a body and later on begins to move. After birth the senses awake, then knowledge arises as a consequence of observation, and finally, will assumes the office of the pilot by addressing itself to certain things and going away from other things.

Also within the single levels of development we discover a definite improvement. Just as the rays of the rising sun emerge out of darkness so knowledge of things gradually increases, and as long as life lasts more and more light is added. Also our actions are insignificant, feeble, and awkward at the beginning; but gradually the faculties of the soul unfold together with the faculties of the body, and in a noble mind all this aspires higher and higher without

340

limits; for in this life there is no fulfillment for our wishes and desires. . . .

Chapter 4. There are Three Steps of Preparation for Eternity; Knowledge of Oneself (and at the same time of all things), Self-Control, and Direction toward God.

Apparently the highest destination of man is eternal blessedness. But there are also subordinate purposes which are expressed in God's decision at the creation

1 Moses 1:26.—And God said, Let us make man in our image, after our likeness; and let them have domination over the fish and the sea, and over the fowl of the air, and over the cattle, and over all the earth.

Therefore man is destined to be among the visible creatures:
1. the reasonable
2. the ruler over all creatures
3. the image and joy of his Creator

Therefore the natural demands upon man are that first he understand all things, second he can rule over all things and himself, and third that he and all things be related to God as the Source. Expressed in well-known terms these demands can be called, first, systematic education, second, virtue or morality, third, religion or piety.

Under systematic education has to be understood the comprehensive knowledge of things, arts, and languages; under virtue not only decorum but also the whole inner and outer order of action; under religion the reverence through which the human mind leans toward and connects itself with the Supreme Being. In the vision of these three demands lies the whole advantage of man, for they alone are the foundation of the present and future life; all other things (health, vigor, beauty, property, prestige, friendship, success, and long life) are only decorations of life if they are granted by God. But they can also be unnecessary luster, useless ballast, and dangerous obstacles if someone struggles for them too ardently, and devotes himself to them so onesidedly that he neglects the more eminent values.

.　　.　　.　　.　　.

Chapter 6. If Man is To Be Man He Must be Educated.

Nature gives the germinal capacities for knowledge, morality, and religion, but it does not give knowledge, morality and religion themselves. Rather these are acquired through learning, acting, and

praying. Therefore somebody rightly has defined man as an edu-
cable animal since he cannot become man unless he is educated.

. . . . .

Hence all who are born as human beings need education because
they are destined to be real men, not wild beasts, dull animals, and
clumps of wood. From this also follows: the better one is educated
the more he excels others.

Chapter 7. The Education of Man is Best Done in his Early
Youth, and Only Then will it Succeed.

It is a property of all things becoming that they can easily be bent
and formed as long as they are tender, but that they refuse to obey
when they have hardened. Soft wax can be modeled and re-
modeled, hard wax will crumble. The young tree can be planted,
replanted, trimmed, and bent to any shape; not so the grown. So
also the hands and limbs of man can be trained for art and craft
only during childhood, as long as the sinews are soft. If someone is
to become a good scribe, painter, tailor, smith, musician, etc., he
must devote himself to his vocation as long as his imagination is
still flexible and his fingers still elastic. In the same way piety must
be implanted into the hearts during infancy lest it not root. If we
want to educate a person in virtue we must polish him at a tender
age. And if someone is to advance toward wisdom he must be
opened up for it in the first years of his life when his industriousness
is still burning, his mind is malleable, and his memory still strong.
Says Seneca in his 36th letter, "An old man who occupies himself
with the elementary is despicable and ridiculous; youth should
learn, old men ought to apply."

. . . . .

Chapter 8. Youth Must be Educated in Common; for This We
Need Schools.

. . . It would be most natural that the parents who have given
their children physical life should lead them also toward a rational,
decent, and sacred life. . . . But in consequence of the growth of
the population and business only few parents have still the necessary skill and time to educate their children. Therefore many parents have followed wise counsel and entrusted their children to
selected, erudite, and moral persons for the purpose of education. . . .

It is in the interest of the whole Christian commonwealth that for

342

each well-ordered community a school be established as a common place for educating youth.

Chapter 9. All Youth of Both Sexes must be Entrusted to the Schools.

Not only the children of the rich and noble but all children ought to be educated in the same way whether they are nobles or commoners, rich or poor, boys or girls, or whether they come from cities, towns, or villages. That is evident for the following reasons:

First, all men are born for the same main purpose; they are to be human beings, i.e., rational creatures, masters over the other creatures, and images of the Creator. . . . God himself often testifies that before Him all things are equal. Therefore if we educate only a few and exclude the rest, we act unjustly not only against our fellow men but also against God who wishes to be known, loved, and praised by all. This will be the case all the more that the light of knowledge shines. For we love to the degree which we know.

Second, we do not know for which calling divine dispensation has destined one or the other of us. So much at least is known, that God has chosen the most perfect tools of his glory out of the poorest, humblest, and unknown people. Thus let us imitate the divine sun which gives light, warmth, and life to the whole earth so that all that is able to live, flower, and bear fruit may do so.

Third, it is no contradiction that some are by nature feeble and dull; this fact but commends, and calls for, the universal cultivation of the minds. . . . Also it is difficult to find a person so defective that he could not be helped in one or the other direction; and if dull people may achieve nothing in scholarship their morals can be improved. After all, experience shows that some less gifted people have acquired so much knowledge that they have surpassed the more gifted. . . . Only those therefore ought to be excluded from education whom God has deprived totally of sense and reason.

Fourth, nor can there be given sufficient reason why the female sex should be excluded from studying. For also girls are images of God; they participate in his Grace and in the future kingdom of God, and they are equipped with the same industriousness and capacity for wisdom.

· · · · ·

Chapter 12. Schools can be Improved.

I promise a kind of school in which:

1. The whole youth is being educated (except those whom God has denied reason).

2. There should be taught all that can make men wise, honest, and pious.

3. Education, which is preparation for life, should be finished before adulthood.

4. Education should be carried out not with beating, severity and any kind of coercion, but easily, pleasantly, and, so to speak, by its own momentum.

5. Not a semblance of education ought to be provided, but genuine education, not a superficial but thorough education; that means the rational animal man should be led by his own rather than a foreign reason. He should get accustomed to penetrating to the real roots of things and to take into himself their true meaning and usage, rather than read, perceive, memorize, and relate other people's opinions. The same ought to be the case with respect to morality and piety.

6. Education ought not to be painful but as easy as possible, everyday only four hours ought to be spent for public instruction, and this in such a way that one teacher should suffice for the simultaneous instruction of a hundred pupils. And he should do that ten times more easily than is now done with one pupil.

. . . . .

Chapter 14. The Exact Method of Teaching has to be Borrowed from Nature. . . .

. . . If the natural order of learning is completely discovered then there will not be any difference between the development of art and the growth of nature. For Cicero says very truly, "If we follow nature as our guide we will never go astray." . . . Therefore guided by nature we will explore the principles useful for, first, the prolongation of life in order to learn all that is necessary; second, the limitation of subject-matter in order to learn more quickly; third, grasping the right occasion in order to learn more effectively; fourth, the unfolding of the mind in order to learn more easily; fifth, the sharpening of the judgment in order to learn more thoroughly. Each of these points will be discussed in a special chapter, but with the limitation of subject-matter we will deal last.

. . . . .

Chapter 16. General Postulates of Teaching and Learning. . . .

First postulate: Nature follows a well-ordered time plan. . . . Hence all material of learning must be so divided according to age levels that only that is assigned to the child which is within the compass of his capacity.

344

Second postulate: Nature prepares the material before it begins to form it. . . . Schools fail in this principle very often. . . . Hence in order to improve teaching the following have to be done. 1. One has to have books and other adequate tools ready. 2. Perception must come before language. 3. Language must be learned not from grammar but from fitting authors. 4. Observation has to precede analysis. And 5. Examples have to precede the rules.

Third postulate: Nature chooses fitting materials for its activity. . . . Therefore in the future: First, each child entrusted to a school ought to stay in it. Second, the minds of the pupils should be made susceptible to the subject chosen for treatment. Third, all obstacles ought to be removed from the pupil.

Fourth postulate: Nature does not get confused, but proceeds by carefully distinguishing the single objects. . . . Therefore pupils in schools ought to be occupied with only one subject at any one time.

Fifth postulate: Nature begins its activities from within. . . . Therefore in the future:

1. First one ought to train the knowledge of things, second the memory, and third the language and the hand.

2. The teacher should explore and apply all means and ways for making the acquisition of knowledge possible.

Sixth postulate: Nature begins all its formation with the most general and finishes with the single. . . . Hence the individual sciences are badly taught unless a simple and general survey of the total knowledge is given before. And one ought never to instruct anybody in such a way that he becomes perfect in one branch of knowledge to the exclusion of others. Furthermore, the arts, sciences, and languages are badly taught unless one begins with the elements.

Seventh postulate: Nature does not skip but proceeds evenly. . . . Therefore in the future:

1. The totality of the studies ought to be classified so that each step prepares for the next one.

2. There ought to be a carefully planned schedule so that each year, month, day, and hour may have its special task.

3. This schedule ought to be followed rigidly so that nothing is skipped or confused.

Eighth postulate: If nature begins it does not stop before it has finished . . . Hence:

1. The pupil ought to stay in his institution until he becomes an educated, moral, and pious person.

345

2. The school ought to be situated in a quiet place.

3. Assignments ought to be finished without interruption.

4. Truancy and loafing ought not to be permitted.

Ninth postulate: Nature avoids contrasts and dangers. . . . Hence, care ought to be taken:

1. That the pupils have only such books which are fitting for their grade.

2. That these books be of such a kind that they can be called funnels of wisdom, virtue, and piety.

3. That disorderly behavior not be tolerated in schools and their surroundings.

If all this is carefully observed the schools can hardly miss their purpose.

Chapter 17. Requisites for easy teaching and learning.

After we have discussed the means by which the teacher can safely achieve his aim we are now going to see how these means have to be adjusted to the intellectual qualities of the student in order to make the process of learning and teaching easy and pleasant.

It will be evident that, here again, we will succeed if we follow in the steps of nature. This means that instruction:

1. Must begin early and before the mind is corrupted.

2. The minds must be made ready for it.

3. It must proceed from the general to the particular, and,

4. From the easier to the more difficult.

5. Progress must not be rushed.

6. The minds must not be forced to do anything but that to which they aspire according to their age and motivation.

7. Everything must be related through sense impression, if possible.

8. Everything must be applied immediately, and,

9. Everything must be taught consistently according to one and the same method.

THE WAY OF LIGHT (VIA LUCIS)

"For there is inborn in human nature a love of liberty—for liberty man's mind is convinced that it was made—and this love can by no means be driven out: so that, wherever and by whatever means it feels that it is being hemmed in and impeded, it cannot but seek a way out and declare its own liberty."

PETTY 1632–1687

EDUCATIONAL thought is a highly sensitive barometer of social change. When after the Revolution of 1648 England became, for some years, dominated by the middle classes, emphasis was laid more on a moral and industrial life than on aristocratic self-development. During this period a number of pamphlets were published which demanded a much more useful sort of school than those established by the Renaissance humanists.

Thus Sir William Petty, known to the historians of science for his pioneer work in social statistics, intended in his *Advice for Advancement of Some Particular Parts of Learning*, "onely to shew where our owne shoe pincheth us, or to point at some pieces of Knowledge, the improvement whereof . . . would make much to the generall good and comfort of all mankind."

Utilitarian though the educational ideals of Sir William and his friends are to a degree, they are nevertheless amazingly bold and progressive. Actually, they demand something we have not yet achieved today: institutions of learning which are at the same time places for a "Generall Randevouz" of all people engaged in professional or business work, or a kind of "Community Center." In this way scholarship and learning would be taken out of their isolation, and the schools would become part of a large national organization for the promotion of both systematic study and systematic application in all fields of human activity.

Unfortunately, the revolutionaries around Cromwell were too busy with other things to bother about the dreams of the educators, and when in 1660 Cromwell's regime gave place to the Restoration, advanced education in England became for almost two hundred years a privilege of a very small group of the population. If the "Advice" of Sir William Petty had been heeded, education would have contributed much more than it really has in the slow advance toward social democracy.

The following selections are from W.[illiam] P.[etty's] *Advice to Mr. Samuel Hartlib for the Advancement of some Particular Parts of Learning*, published in London in 1648.

THE ADVICE FOR ADVANCEMENT OF SOME PARTICULAR PARTS OF LEARNING

To give an exact Definition or nice Division of Learning, or of the Advancement thereof, we shall not undertake (it being already so accurately done by the great Lord *Verulam*) Intending only to

347

shew where our owne shoe pincheth us, or to point at some pieces of Knowledge, the improvement wherof (as we at least conceive) would make much to the generall good and comfort of all mankind, and withall to deliver our own opinion by what meanes they may be raised some one degree neerer to perfection.

But before we can meddle with this great Work, we must first think of getting Labourers, by appointing some Generall Randevouz, where all men either able or willing to take up armes against the many difficulties thereof, may finde entertainment. That is to say, We must recommend the Institution of an Office of common Addresse according to the projection of Master *Hartlib* (that painfull and great instrument of this Designe) whereby the wants and desires of all may bee made knowne unto all, where men may know what is already done in the buisinesse of Learning. What is at present in doing, and what is intended to be done: to the end, that by such a generall communication of designes, and mutuall assistance; The wits and endevours of the world may no longer be as so many scattered coales or firebrands, which for want of union, are soone quenched, whereas being but layed together they would have yeeled a comfortable light and heat. For me thinkes the present condition of men is like a field where a battle hath beene lately fought, where we may see many leggs, and armes, and eyes lying here and there, which for want of a union and a soule to quicken and enliven them, are good for nothing but to feed Ravens; and infect the aire. So we see many Wittes and Ingenuities lying scattered up and downe the world, whereof some are now labouring to doe what is already done, and pusling themselves to reinvent what is already invented, others we see quite stuck fast in difficulties, for want of a few Directions, which some other man (might he be met withall) both could and would most easily give him; againe one man wants a small summe of mony, to carry on some designe, that requires it, and there is perhaps another, who hath twice as much ready to bestow on the same designe, but these two having no Meanes ever to heare the one of the other, the good Work intended and desired, by both parties doth utterly perish and come to nothing: But this we passe over sleightly, though very fundamentall to our businesse, because the Master-builder thereof himself hath done it so solidly. Having by this means procured work-men and what else is necessary to the Worke, that which we would have them to labour in, is, How to finde out such Arts as are yet undiscovered, How to learne what is already known, by more compendious and

348

facile wayes, and to apply it to more, and those more noble uses, how to work in men an higher esteeme of Learning so as to give occasion, encouragement and opportunity to more Men to apply themselves to its Advancement.

The next thing then to be done, will be, First, to see what is well and sufficiently done already, exploding whatsoever is nice, contentious and meery phantasticall. All which must in some measure be suppressed and brought into disgrace and contempt with all men.

2. This survey may be made by perusing al Booksand taking notice of all Mechanicall Inventions.

3. In this perusall, all the Reall or Experimentall Learning may be sifted and collected out of the said Books.

4. There must be appointed able Readers of all such Books, with certaine and well limited Directions what to collect out of them.

5. Every Book must be so read by two severall Persons apart, to prevent mistakes and failings from the said Directions.

6. The Directions for Reading must be such, as the Readers observing them, may exactly agree in their Collections.

7. Out of all these Bookes one Booke or great Worke may be made, though consisting of many Volumes.

8. The most Artificiall Indices Tables or other Helps for the ready finding, remembring, and well understanding all things contained in these Bookes must be contrived and put in practice.

Having thus taken the height or pitch wherunto al Arts and Sciences whatsoever, are already come; and observed where they now stick, the ablest Men in every respective Faculty must be set apart, to drive them on further with sufficient maintenance, and encouragement for the same. Whereunto it is requisite that two or three, one under another, be employed about each Faculty, to the end that some of them dying, or any other wise failing, there may never want men acquainted with the whole Designe, and able to carry it on, with the help of others to be admitted under them; And that at least yearly Accompts be taken of those mens endeavours, and rewards be proportioned to them accordingly.

And now we shall think of whetting our tooles and preparing sharp Instruments for this hard work, by delivering our thoughts concerning Education, which are,

1. That there be instituted *Ergastula Literaria,* Literary-workhouses, where Children may be taught as well to doe something towards their living, as to Read and Write.

349

That the businesse of Education be not (as now) committed to the worst and unworthiest of men, but that it be seriously studied and practised by the best and abler persons.

That all Children of above seven yeares old may be presented to this kind of Education, none being to be excluded by reason of the poverty and unability of their Parents, for hereby it hath come to passe, that many are now holding the Plough, which might have beene made fit to steere the State. Wherefore let such poor children be imployed on works wherby they may earne their living, equall to their strength and understanding, and such as they may performe as well as elder and abler persons, *viz.* attending Engines, &c. And if they cannot get their whole living, and their Parents can contribute nothing at all to make it up, let them stay somewhat the longer in the Work-house.

That since few children have need of reading before they know, or can be acquainted with the Things they read of, or of writing, before their thoughts are worth the recording, or they are able to put them into any forme, (which we call inditing) much lesse of learning languages, when there bee Books enough for their present use in their owne mother Tongue; our opinion is, that those Things being withall somewhat above their capacity, (as being to be attained by Judgement, which is weakest in children) be deferred awhile, and others more needfull for them, such as are in the order of Nature before those afore mentioned, and are attainable by the help of Memory, which is either most strong or unpreoccupied in children, be studied before them. We wish therefore that the Educands be taught to observe and remember all sensible Objects and Actions, whether they be Naturall or Artificiall, which the Educators must upon all occasions expound unto them.

That they use such Exercises whether in work, or for recreation, as tend to the health, agility and strength of their bodies.

That they be taught to Read by much more compendious meanes then are in common use, which is a thing certainly very easie and feasible.

That they be not onely taught to Write according to our Common Way, but also to Write Swiftly and in Reall Characters, as likewise the dextrous use of the Instruments for Writing many Copies of the same thing at once.

That the Artificiall Memory be thought upon, and if the precepts thereof be not too farre above Childrens Capacities, We conceive it not improper for them to learn that also.

350

That in no case the Art of Drawing and designing be omitted, to what course of Life soever those children are to be applied, since the use thereof for expressing the conceptions of the mind, seemes (at least to us) to be little inferiour to that of Writing, and in many cases performeth what by words is impossible.

That the Elements of Arithmetick and Geometry be by all studied, being not onely of great and frequent use in all humane Affaires but also sure guides and helps to Reason, and especiall Remedies for a volatile and unstedy mind.

That effectuall Courses be taken to try the Abilities of the Bodies and Minds of Children, the strength of their Memory, inclination of their Affections either to Vice or Vertue, and to which of them in particular, and withall to alter what is bad in them, and increase and improve what is good, applying all, whether good or bad, to the least Inconveniencie and most Advantage.

That such as shall have need to learne Forraine Languages (the use whereof would be much lessened, were the Reall and Common Characters brought into practise) may be taught them by incomparably more easie wayes then are now usuall.

That no ignoble, unnecessary, or condemned Part of Learning be taught in those houses of Education, so that if any man shall vainely fall upon them, he himselfe onely may be blamed.

That such as have any naturall ability and fitnesse to Musick be Encouraged and Instructed therein.

That all Children, though of the highest ranke, be taught some gentile Manufacture in their minority, such as are

Turning of curious Figures.

Making Mathematicall Instruments, Dialls, and how to use them in Astronomicall Observations.

Making Watches and other Trochilick motions.

Limning and Painting on Glasse or in Oyle Colours.

Graving, Etching, Carving, Embossing and Molding in sundry matters.

The Lapidaries Art of knowing, cutting and setting Iewells.

Grinding of Glasses Dioptricall and Catoptricall.

Botanicks and Gardening.

Making Musicall Instruments.

Navarchy and making Modells for buildings and rigging of Ships.

Architecture and making Modells for houses.

The Confectioners, Perfumers or Diers Arts.

Chymistry, refining Metalls and Counterfeiting Iewells.

Anatomy making Sceletons and excarnating bowells.

Making Mariners Compasses, Globes, and other Magnetick Devices.

And all, for these Reasons.

1. They shall be lesse subject to be cousened by Artificers.

2. They will become more industrious in generall.

3. They will certainly bring to passe most excellent Works, being as Gentlemen, ambitious to excell ordinarie Work-men.

4. They being able to make Experiments themselves, may doe it with lesse charge, and more care then others will doe it for them.

5. The *Resp. Artium* will be much advanced, when such as are rich and able, are also willing to make Luciferous Experiments.

6. It may engage them to be Mecænates and Patrons of Arts.

7. It will keepe them from worse occasions of spending their time and estates.

8. As it will be a great Ornament in prosperity, so it wil be a great Refuge and stay in adversity and common calamity.

As for what remaines of Education, we cannot but hope that those, whom we have desired should make it their trade, will Supply it, and render the Idea therof much more perfect.

We have already recommended the studie of the Elements of Arithmetick and Geometry to all Men in generall, but they being the best grounded parts of Speculative knowledge, and of so Vast use in all Practicall Arts. We cannot but commend deeper enquiries into them. And although the way of advancing them in particular, may be drawne from what we have already delivered, concerning the Advancement of learning in generall, yet for the more explicite understanding of our meaning herein, we referre to Master *Pells* most excellent Idea thereof, written to Master *Hartlib*.

In the next place for the Advancement of all Mechanicall Arts and Manufactures, we wish that there were erected a Gymnasium Mechanicum or a Colledge of Trades-men (or for more expedition untill such a place could be built, that the most convenient houses for such a purpose may be either bought or hired) wherein we would that one at least of every Trade (but the Prime most Ingenious Work-man, the most desirous to improve his Art,) might be allowed therein, a handsom dwelling Rent free, which with the Credit of being admitted into this Society, and the quick sale which certainly they would have of their Commodities, when all men would repaire thither, as to a Market of rare and exquisite pieces of Workmanship, would be a sufficient Motive to attract the very

352

ablest Mechanicks, and such as we have described, to desire a fellowship in this Colledge.

From this Institution we may clearly hope when the excellent in all Arts are not onely Neighbours, but intimate Friends and Brethren, united in a Common desire and zeal to promote them, that all Trades will miraculously prosper, and new Inventions would be more frequent, then new fashions of Clothes and household-stuffe. Here would be the best and most effectuall opportunities and meanes, for writing a History of Trades in perfection and exactnesse, and what Experiments and stuffe would all those Shops and Operations afford to Active and Philosophicall heads, out of which, to extract that Interpretation of Nature, whereof there is so little, and that so bad as yet extant in the world?

Within the walls of this Gymnasium or College, should be a Nosecomium Academicum according to the most exact and perfect Idea thereof a compleate *Theatrum Botanicum,* stalls and Cages for all strange Beastes and Birds, with Ponds and Conservatories for all exotick Fishes, here all Animalls capable thereof should be made fit for some kind of labour and imployment, that they may as well be of use living as dead; here should be a Repositorie of all kind of Rarities Naturall and Artificiall pieces of Antiquity, Modells of all great and noble Engines, with Designes and Platformes of Gardens and Buildings. The most Artificiall Fountaines and Water-works, a Library of Select Bookes, an Astronomicall Observatory for celestiall Bodies and Meteor, large pieces of Ground for severall Experiments of Agriculture, Galleries of the rarest Paintings and Statues, with the fairest Globes, and Geographcall Maps of the best descriptions, and so farre as is possible, we would have this place to be the Epitome or Abstract of the whole world. So that a man conversant within those walls, would certainly prove a greater Schollar, then the Walking Libraries so called, although he could neither write nor read. But if a Child, before he learned to read or write, were made acquainted with all Things, and Actions (as he might be in this Colledge) how easily would he understand all good Bookes afterwards, and smell out the fopperies of bad ones. As for the Situation, Modell, Policy Oeconomy, with the Number of Officers and Retainers to this Colledge, and the Priviledges thereof, it is as yet time enough to delineate. Only we wish that a Society of Men might be instituted as carefull to advance Arts as the Iesuites are to Propagate their Religion for the government and mannaging of it.

But what relish will there be in all those dainties whereof we have

353

spoken, if we want a palate to tast them, which certainly is Health, the most desirable of all earthly blessings, and how can we in any reason expect Health, when there are so many great difficulties in the curing of diseases and no proportionable Course taken to re- move them? we shall therefore pursue the Meanes of acquiring the Publicke Good and comfort of Mankind a little further, and vent our conceits concerning a Nosocomium Academicum or an Hospitall to cure the Infirmities both of Physician and Patient.

We intended to have given the most perfect Idea of this Noso- comium Academicum, and consequently to have treated of the Situation and Fabrick of the House, Garden, Library, Chymicall Laboratorie, Anatomicall Theator, Apotheca, with all the Instru- ments and Furniture belonging to each of them, as also of the whole Policy and Oeconomy thereof. But since such a work could not be brought to passe without much charge (the very naming wherof doth deter men even from the most noble and necessary Attempts) we are contented to pourtray only such a Nosocomium, as may be made out of one of our old Hospitals, without any new donations or creeping to Benefactors, onely with a little paines taken by the Reforming hand of Authority. For we do not doubt, but that we have so contrived the businesse, that there is no Hospitall in its cor- rupt estate, can be more thriftily managed then Ours. For the Number of our Ministers are no greater then usuall, and absolutly necessary, their Pensions no larger then are allowed to those, who do not make the service of the Hospital, the sixth part of their Employment and meanes of subsistance, and yet we give encour- agement enough to able men to undertake it, without medling with any other businesse, which we strictly forbid. For as the Salaries are but small, so the Charge of the Ministers is not great (they being all to be unmarried Persons) their Accommodation handsome, their Employment (being a work of Publike and highest Charity) hon- ourable, and to Philosophicall Men, (who onely are to have a hand in this businesse) most pleasant and delightfull. Besides when their respective times are expired, their profit and esteeme in the world cannot but be very great. For their way of breeding will both procure them practice among such as are able to reward them, and give them a dexterity and ability, to manage and go thorough a great deale thereof. . . .

LOCKE 1632–1704

THOSE who know Quintilian, Comenius, and Montaigne will not find any surprisingly new ideas in Locke's *Some Thoughts Concerning Education*. At the end of the 17th century educational theory was sufficiently ahead of practice to know that encouragement is a better means of motivating than punishment, that character is of higher value than book-learning, and that educational programs will be effective only to the degree to which they are adequate to the individuality of the child.

The great influence of Locke's *Thoughts* springs from the fact that they expressed exactly that which the best members of the English ruling class wished their children to become: gentlemen with respect for moral standards, religion, and convention, with balanced judgment and good common sense, with knowledge helpful for a practical life and decent forms of leisure, and a strong sense for independence as far as their own class was concerned.

Only in two respects did the English upper class deviate from Locke. They preferred the aristocratic schools of Eton and Harrow to the private tutor recommended by the great philosopher, and, up to the end of the 19th century, they allowed the classical and humanistic subjects to dominate the program in these schools. Probably for both they saw good reason.

The following selections are from John Locke's *Some Thoughts on Education*. . . . Boston, 1830, in the Library of Education, Volume I.

SOME THOUGHTS ON EDUCATION

DEDICATION TO EDWARD CLARKE, OF CHIPLEY, ESQU.

. . . I myself have been consulted of late by so many who profess themselves at a loss how to breed their children, and the early corruption of youth is now become so a complaint, that he cannot be thought wholly impertinent who brings the consideration of this matter on the stage, and offers something, if it be but to excite others, or afford matter of correction. For errors in education should be less indulged than any: these, like faults in the first concoction, that are never mended in the second or third, carry their afterwards-incorrigible taint with them through all the parts and stations of life. . . .

But my business is not to recommend this treatise to you, whose opinion of it I know already; nor it to the world, either by your opinion or patronage. The well educating of their children is so much the duty and concern of parents, and the welfare and prosperity of the nation so much depends on it, that I would have every one lay it seriously to heart; and after having well examined and distinguished what fancy, custom, or reason advises in the case, set his helping hand to promote every where that way of training up youth, with regard to their several conditions, which is the easiest, shortest, and likeliest to produce virtous, useful, and able men in their distinct callings; though that most to be taken care of is the gentleman's calling. For if those of that rank are by their education once set right, they will quickly bring all the rest into order. . . .

(1) A sound mind in a sound body, is a short but full description of a happy state in this world: he that has these two, has little more to wish for; and he that wants either of them, will be but little the better for any thing else. Men's happiness or misery is most part of their own making. He whose mind directs not wisely, will never take the right way; and he whose body is crazy and feeble, will never be able to advance in it . . .

(2) I imagine the minds of children as easily turned, this or that way as water itself; and though this be the principal part, and our main care should be about the inside, yet the clay cottage is not to be neglected. I shall therefore begin with the case, and consider first the health of the body, as that which perhaps you may be rather expect, from that study I have been thought more peculiarly to have applied myself to; and that also which will be soonest despatched, as lying, if I guess not amiss, in a very little compass. . . .

(27) As the strength of the body lies chiefly in being able to endure hardship, so also does that of the mind. And the great principle and foundation of all virtue and worth is placed in this, that a man is able to deny himself his own desires, cross his own inclinations, and purely follow what reason directs as best, though the appetite lean the other way.

(28) The great mistake I have observed in people's breeding their children has been, that this has not been taken care enough of in its due season; that the mind has not been made obedient to discipline, and pliant to reason, when at first it was most tender, most easy to be bowed. Parents being wisely ordained by nature to love their children, are very apt, if reason watch not that natural affection very warily; are apt, I say, to let it run into fondness. They love their little ones, and it is their duty: but they often with them

356

cherish their faults too. They must not be crossed, forsooth; they must be permitted to have their wills in all things; and they being in their infancies not capable of great vices, their parents think they may safely enough indulge their little irregularities, and make themselves sport with that pretty perverseness, which they think well enough becomes that innocent age. But to a fond parent, that would not have his child corrected for a perverse trick, but excused it, saying it was a small matter; Solon very well replied, 'Ay, but custom is a great one'. . . .

(30) For if the child must have grapes, or sugar-plums, when he has a mind to them, rather than make the poor baby cry, or be out of humour; why, when he is grown up, must he not be satisfied too, if his desires carry him to wine or women? They are objects as suitable to the longing of twenty-one or more years, as what he cried for, when little, was to the inclinations of a child. The having desires accommodated to the apprehensions and relish of those several ages is not the fault; but the not having them subject to the rules and restraints of reason: the difference lies not in the having or not having appetites, but in the power to govern, and deny ourselves in them. He that is not used to submit his will to the reason of others, when he is young, will scarce hearken or submit to his own reason, when he is of an age to make use of it. And what kind of a man such a one is like to prove, is easy to foresee. . . .

(35) I imagine every one will judge it reasonable, that their children, when little, should look upon their parents as their lords, their absolute governors; and, as such, stand in awe of them: and that, when they come to riper years, they should look on them as their best, as their only sure friends: and, as such, love and reverence them. The way I have mentioned, if I mistake not, is the only one to obtain this. We must look upon our children, when grown up, to be like ourselves; with the same passions, the same desires. We would be thought rational creatures, and have our freedom; we love not to be uneasy under constant rebukes and brow-beatings; nor can we bear severe humours, and great distance, in those we converse with. Whoever has such treatment when he is a man, will look out other company, other friends, other conversation, with whom he can be at ease. If therefore a strict hand be kept over children from the beginning, they will in that age be tractable, and quietly submit to it, as never having known any other: and if, as they grow up to the use of reason, the rigour of government be, as they deserve it, gently relaxed, the father's brow more smoothed to them, and the distance by degrees abated: his former restraints

will increase their love, when they find it was only a kindness for them, and a care to make them capable to deserve the favour of their parents, and the esteem of every body else.

(40) . . . On the other side, if the mind be curbed, and humbled too much in children; if their spirit be abased and broken much, by too strict an hand over them; they lose all their vigour and industry, and are in a worse state than the former. For extravagant young fellows, that have liveliness and spirit, come sometimes to be set right, and so make able and great men: but dejected minds, timorous and tame, and low spirits, are hardly ever to be raised, and very seldom attain to any thing. To avoid the danger that is on either hand is the great art: and he that has found a way how to keep up a child's spirit, easy, active, and free; and yet, at the same time, to restrain him from many things that are uneasy to him; he, I say, that knows how to reconcile these seeming contradictions, has, in my opinion, got the true secret of education. . . .

(50) The rewards and punishments, then, whereby we should keep children in order are quite of another kind; and of that force, that when we can get them once to work, the business, I think, is done, and the difficulty is over. Esteem and disgrace are, of all others, the most powerful incentives to the mind, when once it is brought to relish them. If you can once get into children a love of credit, and an apprehension of shame and disgrace, you have put into them the true principle, which will constantly work, and incline them to the right. But, it will be asked, How shall this be done?

I confess, it does not, at first appearance, want some difficulty; but yet I think it worth our while to seek the ways, (and practise them when found,) to attain this, which I look on as the great secret of education. . . .

(57) But if a right course be taken with children, there will not be so much need of the application of the common rewards and punishments, as we imagined, and as the general practice has established. For all their innocent folly, playing, and childish actions, are to be left perfectly free and unrestrained, as far as they can consist with the respect due to those that are present; and that with the greatest allowance. If these faults of their age, rather than of the children themselves, were, as they should be, left only to time, and imitation, and riper years to cure, children would escape a great deal of misapplied and useless corrections; which either fails to overpower the natural disposition of their childhood, and so, by an ineffectual familiarity, makes correction in other necessary cases of less use; or else if it be of force to restrain the natural gaiety of that

358

age, it serves only to spoil the temper both of body and mind. If the noise and bustle of their play prove at any time inconvenience, or unsuitable to the place or company they are in, (which can only be where their parents are,) a look, or a word from the father or mother, if they have established the authority they should, will be enough either to remove, or quiet them for that time. But this gamesome humour, which is wisely adapted by nature to their age and temper, should rather be encouraged, to keep up their spirits and improve their strength and health, than curbed or restrained; and the chief art is to make all that they have to do, sport and play too.

(58) And here give me leave to take notice of one thing I think a fault in the ordinary method of education; and that is, the charging of children's memories, upon all occasions, with rules and precepts, which they often do not understand, and are constantly as soon forgot as given. If it be some action you would have done, or done otherwise; whenever they forget, or do it awkwardly, make them do it over and over again, till they are perfect; whereby you will get these two advantages: first, to see whether it be an action they can do, or is fit to be expected of them. For sometimes children are bid to do things, which upon trial, they are found not able to do; and had need be taught and exercised in, before, they are required to do them. But it is much easier for a tutor to command than to teach. Secondly, another thing got by it will be this, that by repeating the same action, till it be grown habitual in them, the performance will not depend on memory, or reflection, the concomitant of prudence and age, and not of childhood; but will be natural in them. Thus, bowing to a gentleman when he salutes him, and looking in his face when he speaks to him, is by constant use as natural to a well-bred man, as breathing; it requires no thought, no reflection. Having this way cured in your child any fault, it is cured for ever: and thus, one by one, you may weed them out all, and plant what habits you please. . . .

(60) But pray remember, children are not to be taught by rules, which will be always slipping out of their memories. What you think necessary for them to do, settle in them by an indispensable practice, as often as the occasion returns; and, if it be possible, make occasions. This will beget habits in them, which, being once established, operate of themselves easily and naturally, without the assistance of the memory. But here let me give two cautions: 1. The one is, that you keep them to the practice of what you would have grow into a habit in them, by kind words and gentle admoni-

tions, rather as minding them of what they forget, than by harsh rebukes and chiding, as if they were wilfully guilty. 2dly. Another thing you are to take care of, is, not to endeavour to settle too many habits at once, lest by a variety you confound them, and so perfect none. When constant custom has made any one thing easy and natural to them, and they practise it without reflection, you may then go on to another.

This method of teaching children by a repeated practice, and the same action done over and over again, under the eye and direction of the tutor, till they have got the habit of doing it well, and not by relying on rules trusted to their memories; has so many advantages, which way soever we consider it, that I cannot but wonder, (if ill customs could be wondered at in any thing,) how it could possibly be so much neglected. I shall name one more that comes now in my way. By this method we shall see, whether what is required of him be adapted to his capacity, and any way suited to the child's natural genius and constitution: for that too must be considered in a right education. We must not hope wholly to change their original tempers, nor make the gay pensive and grave, nor the melancholy sportive, without spoiling them. God has stamped certain characters upon men's minds, which, like their shapes, may perhaps be a little mended; but can hardly be totally altered and transformed into the contrary. . . .

(64) Having named company, I am almost ready to throw away my pen, and trouble you no farther on this subject. For since that does more than all precepts, rules and instructions, methinks it is almost wholly in vain to make a long discourse of other things, and to talk of that almost to no purpose. For you will be ready to say, 'What shall I do with my son? If I keep him always at home, he will be in danger to be my young master; and if I send him abroad, how is it possible to keep him from the contagion of rudeness and vice, which is every where so in fashion? In my house he will perhaps be more innocent, but more ignorant too of the world: wanting there change of company, and being used constantly to the same faces, he will, when he comes abroad, be a sheepish or conceited creature.'

I confess, both sides have their inconveniences. Being abroad, it is true, will make him bolder, and better able to bustle and shift amongst boys of his own age; and the emulation of school-fellows often puts life and industry into young lads. But till you can find a school, wherein it is possible for the master to look after the manners of his scholars, and can show as great effects of his care of

360

forming their minds to virtue and their carriage to good breeding, as of forming their tongues to the learned languages; you must confess, that you have a strange value for words, when, preferring the languages of the ancient Greeks and Romans to that which made them such brave men, you think it worth while to hazard your son's innocence and virtue for a little Greek and Latin. For, as for that boldness and spirit which lads get amongst their play-fellows at school, it has ordinarily such a mixture of rudeness and an ill-turned confidence, that those misbecoming and disingenious ways of shifting in the world must be unlearned, and all the tincture washed out again, to make way for better principles, and such manners as make a truly worthy man. He that considers how diametrically opposite the skill of living well, and managing, as a man should do, his affairs in the world, is to that malapertness, tricking, or violence, learnt among schoolboys, will think the faults of a privater education, infinitely to be preferred to such improvements; and will take care to preserve his child's innocence and modesty at home, as being nearer of kin, and more in the way of those qualities, which make an useful and able man. Nor does any one find, or so much as suspect, that that retirement and bashfulness, which their daughters are brought up in, makes them less knowing or less able women. Conversation, when they come into the world, soon gives them a becoming assurance; and whatsoever beyond that, there is of rough and boisterous, may in men be very well spared too; for courage and steadiness, as I take it, lie not in roughness and ill breeding.

Virtue is harder to be got than a knowledge of the world; and, if lost in a young man, is seldom recovered. . . . And therefore I cannot but prefer breeding of a young gentleman at home in his father's sight, under a good governor, as much as the best and safest way to this great and main end of education; when it can be had, and is ordered as it should be. Gentlemen's houses are seldom without variety of company: they should use their sons to all the strange faces that come there, and engage them in conversation with men of parts and breeding, as soon as they are capable of it. And why those, who live in the country, should not take them with them, when they make visits of civility to their neighbours, I know not: this I am sure, a father that breeds his son at home, has the opportunity to have him more in his own company, and there give him what encouragement he thinks fit; and can keep him better from the taint of servants, and the meaner sort of people, than is possible to be done abroad. But what shall be resolved in the case, must in

great measure be left to the parents to be determined by their circumstances and conveniences. Only I think it the worst sort of good
husbandry for a father not to strain himself a little for his son's
breeding; which, let his condition be what it will, is the best portion he can leave him. But if, after all, it shall be thought by some
that the breeding at home has too little company, and that ordinary
schools not such as it should be for a young gentleman, I think
there might be ways found out to avoid the inconveniences on the
one side and the other.

(65) Having under consideration how great the influence of
company is, and how prone we are all, especially children, to imitation; I must here take the liberty to mind parents of this one
thing, viz. that he that will have his son have a respect for him and
his orders, must himself have a great reverence for his son. 'Max-
ima debetur pueris reverentia.' You must do nothing before him,
which you would not have him imitate. If any thing escape you,
which you would have pass for a fault in him, he will be sure to
shelter himself under your example, and shelter himself so, as that
it will not be easy to come at him to correct it in him the right way.
If you punish him for what he sees you practise yourself, he will
not think that severity to proceed from kindness in you, or carefulness to amend a fault in him; but will be apt to interpret it the
peevishness and arbitrary imperiousness of a father, who, without
any ground for it, would deny his son the liberty and pleasure he
takes himself. Or if you assume to yourself the liberty you have
taken, as a privilege belonging to riper years, to which a child must
not aspire, you do but add new force to your example, and recommend the action the more powerfully to him. For you must always
remember, that children affect to be men earlier than is thought;
and they love breeches, not for their cut, or ease, but because the
having them is a mark or a step towards manhood. What I say of
the father's carriage before his children, must extend itself to all
those who have any authority over them, or for whom he would
have them have any respect. . . .

(67) . . . None of the things they are to learn should ever be
made a burden to them, or imposed on them as a task. Whatever
is so proposed presently becomes irksome: the mind takes an aversion to it, though before it were a thing of delight or indifference.
Let a child be but ordered to whip his top at a certain time every
day, whether he has or has not a mind to it; let this be required of
him as a duty, wherein he must spend so many hours morning and
afternoon, and see whether he will not soon be weary of any play

362

at this rate. Is it not so with grown men? What they do cheerfully of themselves, do they not presently grow sick of, and can no more endure, as soon as they find it is expected of them as a duty? Children have as much a mind to show that they are free, that their own good actions come from themselves, that they are absolute and independent, as any of the proudest of you grown men, think of them as you please.

(68) . . . As a consequence of this, they should seldom be put about doing even those things you have got an inclination in them to, but when they have a mind and disposition to it. He that loves reading, writing, music, &c. finds yet in himself certain seasons wherein those things have no relish to him: and, if at that time he forces himself to it, he only pothers and wearies himself to no purpose. So it is with children. This change of temper should be carefully observed in them, and the favourable seasons of aptitude and inclination be heedfully laid hold of: and if they are not often enough forward of themselves, a good disposition should be talked into them, before they be set upon any thing. This I think no hard matter for a discreet tutor to do, who has studied his pupil's temper, and will be at a little pains to fill his head with suitable ideas, such as may make him in love with the present business. By this means a great deal of time and tiring would be saved: for a child will learn three times as much when he is in tune, as he will with double the time and pains, when he goes awkwardly, or is dragged unwillingly to it. If this were minded as it should, children might be permitted to weary themselves with play, and yet have time enough to learn what is suited to the capacity of each age. But no such thing is considered in the ordinary way of education, nor can it well be. That rough discipline of the rod is built upon other principles, has no attraction in it, regards not what humour children are in, nor looks after favourable seasons of inclination. And indeed it would be ridiculous, when compulsion and blows have raised an aversion in the child to his task, to expect he should freely of his own accord leave his play, and with pleasure court the occasions of learning: whereas, were matters ordered right, learning any thing they should be taught might be made as much a recreation to their play, as their play is to their learning. . . .

(75) It will perhaps be wondered that I mention reasoning with children: and yet I cannot but think that the true way of dealing with them. They understand it as early as they do language; and if I misobserve not, they love to be treated as rational creatures sooner than is imagined. It is a pride should be cherished in them,

and, as much as can be, made the greatest instrument to turn them by.

But when I talk of reasoning, I do not intend any other but such as is suited to the child's capacity and apprehension. Nobody can think a boy of three or seven years old should be argued with as a grown man. Long discourses, and philosophical reasonings, at best amaze and confound, but do not instruct, children. When I say, therefore, that they must be treated as rational creatures, I mean, that they should make them sensible, by the mildness of your carriage, and the composure, even in your correction of them, that what you do is reasonable in you, and useful and necessary for them; and that it is not out of caprice, passion, or fancy, that you command or forbid them any thing. This they are capable of understanding; and there is no virtue they should be excited to, nor fault they should be kept from, which I do not think they may be convinced of: but it must be by such reasons as their age and understanding are capable of, and those proposed always in very few and plain words. The foundations on which several duties are built, and the fountains of right and wrong, from which they spring, are not, perhaps, easily to be let into the minds of grown men, not used to abstract their thoughts from common received opinions. Much less are children capable of reasonings from remote principles. They cannot conceive the force of long deductions: the reasons that move them must be obvious, and level to their thoughts, and such as may, (if I may so say,) be felt and touched. But yet, if their age, temper, and inclinations be considered, they will never want such motives as may be sufficient to convince them. If there be no other more particular, yet these will always be intelligible, and of force, to deter them from any fault fit to be taken notice of in them, viz. that it will be a discredit and disgrace to them, and displease you. . . .

(83) As the father's example must teach the child respect for his tutor; so the tutor's example must lead the child into those actions he would have him do. His practice must by no means cross his precepts, unless he intend to set him wrong. It will be to no purpose for the tutor to talk of the restraint of the passions, whilst any of his own are let loose; and he will in vain endeavour to reform any vice or indecency in his pupil which he allows in himself. Ill patterns are sure to be followed more than good rules: and therefore he must also carefully preserve him from the influence of ill precedents, especially the most dangerous of all, the examples of the servants; from whose company he is to be kept, not by prohibi-

364

tions for that will but give him an itch after it, but by other ways I have mentioned. . . .

(87) . . . The tutor therefore ought, in the first place to be well-bred: and a young gentleman, who gets this one qualification from his governor, sets out with great advantage; and will find, that this one accomplishment will more open his way to him, get him more friends, and carry him farther in the world, than all the hard words, or real knowledge, he has got from the liberal arts, or his tutor's learned encyclopedia; not that those should be neglected, but by no means preferred, or suffered to thrust out the other.

(88) Besides being well-bred, the tutor should know the world well; the ways, the humours, the follies, the cheats, the faults of the age he is fallen into, and particularly of the country he lives in. These he should be able to show to his pupil, as he finds him capable; teach him skill in men, and their manners; pull off the mask which their several callings and pretences cover them with; and make his pupil discern what lies at the bottom, under such appearances; that he may not, as unexperienced young men are apt to do, if they are unwarned, take one thing for another, judge by the outside, and give himself up to show, and the insinuation of a fair carriage, or an obliging application. A governor should teach his scholar to guess at, and beware of, the designs of men he hath to do with, neither with too much suspicion, nor too much confidence; but, as the young man is by nature most inclined to either side, rectify and bend him the other way. He should accustom him to make, as much as is possible a true judgment of men by those marks which serve best to show what they are, and give a prospect into their inside; which often shows itself in little things; especially when they are not in parade, and upon their guard. He should acquaint him with the true state of the world, and dispose him to think no man better or worse, wiser or foolisher, than he really is. Thus, by safe and in sensible degrees, he will pass from a boy to a man; which is the most hazardous step in all the whole course of life. This therefore should be carefully watched, and a young man with great diligence handed over it; and not, as now usually is done, be taken from a governor's conduct, and all at once thrown into the world under his own, not without manifest danger of immediate spoiling; there being nothing more frequent, than instances of the great looseness, extravagancy, and debauchery, which young men have run into, as soon as they have been let loose from a severe and strict education. . . .

The only fence against the world is a thorough knowledge of it:

into which a young gentleman should be entered by degrees, as he can bear it; and the earlier the better, so he be in safe and skilful hands to guide him. The scene should be gently opened, and his entrance made step by step, and the dangers pointed out that attend him, from the several degrees, tempers, designs, and clubs of men. He should be prepared to be shocked by some, and caressed by others; warned who are like to oppose, who to mislead, who to undermine him, and who to serve him. He should be instructed how to know and distinguish men; where he should let them see, and when dissemble the knowledge of them, and their aims and workings. And if he be too forward to venture upon his own strength and skill, the perplexity and trouble of a misadventure now and then, that reaches not his innocence, his health, or reputation, may not be an ill way to teach him more caution. . . .

A great part of the learning now in fashion in the schools of Europe, and that goes ordinarily into the round of education, a gentleman may, in a good measure, be unfurnished with, without any great disparagement to himself, or prejudice to his affairs. But prudence and good breeding are, in all the stations and occurrences of life, necessary; and most young men suffer in the want of them, and come rawer, and more awkward, into the world than they should, for this very reason because these qualities, which are, of all other, the most necessary to be taught, and stand most in need of the assistance and help of a teacher, are generally neglected, and thought but a slight, or no part of a tutor's business. Latin and learning make all the noise: and the main stress is laid upon his proficiency in things, a great part whereof belongs not to a gentleman's calling; which is to have the knowledge of a man of business, a carriage suitable to his rank, and to be eminent and useful in his country, according to his station. . . . But to initiate his pupil in any part of learning, as far as is necessary for a young man in the ordinary course of his studies, an ordinary skill in the governor is enough. Nor is it requisite that he should be a thorough scholar, or possess in perfection all those sciences, which it is convenient a young gentleman should have a taste of, in some general view, or short system. A gentleman that would penetrate deeper, must do it by his own genius and industry afterwards; for nobody ever went far in knowledge, or became eminent in any of the sciences, by the discipline and constraint of a master.

The great work of a governor is to fashion the carriage, and form the mind; to settle in his pupil good habits, and the principles of virtue and wisdom; to give him, by little and little, a view of man-

366

kind; and work him into a love and imitation of what is excellent and praiseworthy; and, in the prosecution of it, to give him vigour, activity, and industry. The studies which he sets him upon are but, as it were, the exercises of his faculties, and employment of his time, to keep him from sauntering and idleness, to teach him application, and accustom him to take pains, and to give him some little taste of what his own industry must perfect. For who expects, that under a tutor a young gentleman should be an accomplished critic, orator, or logician; go to the bottom of metaphysics, natural philosophy, or mathematics; or be a master in history or chronology? Though something of each of these is to be taught him: but it is only to open the door, that he may look in, and, as it were, begin an acquaintance, but not to dwell there: and a governor would be much blamed, that should keep his pupil too long, and lead him too far in most of them. But of good breeding, knowledge of the world, virtue, industry, and a love of reputation, he cannot have too much: and, if he have these, he will not long want what he needs or desires of the other.

. . . . . .

(92) Familiarity of discourse, if it can become a father to his son, may much more be condescended to by a tutor to his pupil. All their time together should not be spent in reading of lectures, and magisterially dictating to him what he is to observe and follow; hearing him in his turn, and using him to reason about what is proposed, will make the rules go down the easier, and sink the deeper, and will give him a liking to study and instruction: and he will then begin to value knowledge, when he sees that it enables him to discourse: and he finds the pleasure and credit of bearing a part in the conversation, and of having his reasons sometimes approved and hearkened to. . . .

(93) When, by making your son sensible that he depends on you, and is in your power, you have established your authority; and by being inflexibly severe in your carriage to him, when obstinately, persisting in any ill-natured trick which you have forbidden, especially lying, you have imprinted on his mind that awe which is necessary; and on the other side, when, (by permitting him the full liberty due to his age, and laying no restraint in your presence to those childish actions, and gaiety of carriage, which, whilst he is very young, are as necessary to him as eat or sleep,) you have reconciled him to your company, and made him sensible of your care and love of him by indulgence and tenderness, especially caressing

367

him on all occasions wherein he does any thing well, and being kind to him, after a thousand fashions, suitable to his age, which nature teaches parents better than I can: when, I say, by these ways of tenderness and affection, which parents never want for their children, you have also planted in him a particular affection for you; he is then in the state you could desire, and you have formed in his mind that true reverence, which is always afterwards carefully to be continued and maintained in both parts of it, love and fear, as the great principles whereby you will always have hold upon him to turn his mind to the ways of virtue and honour. . . .

(104) As to having and possessing of things, teach them to part with what they have, easily and freely to their friends; and let them find by experience, that the most liberal has always most plenty, with esteem and commendation to boot, and they will quickly learn to practise it. This, I imagine, will make brothers and sisters kinder and civiller to one another, and consequently to others, than twenty rules about good manners, with which children are ordinarily perplexed and cumbered. Covetousness, and the desire of having in our possession, and under our dominion, more than we have need of, being the root of all evil, should be early and carefully weeded out; and the contrary quality, or a readiness to impart to others, implanted. This should be encouraged by great commendation and credit, and constantly taking care, that he loses nothing by his liberality. Let all the instances he gives of such freeness be always repaid, and with interest; and let him sensibly perceive that the kindness he shows to others is no ill husbandry for himself; but that it brings a return of kindness, both from those that receive it, and those who look on. Make this a contest among children, who shall outdo one another this way. And by this means, by a constant practice, children having made it easy to themselves to part with what they have, goodnature may be settled in them into an habit, and they may take pleasure, and pique themselves in being kind, liberal, and civil to others.

If liberality ought to be encouraged, certainly great care is to be taken that children transgress not the rules of justice: and whenever they do, they should be set right; and, if there be occasion for it, severely rebuked.

Our first actions being guided more by self-love than reason or reflection, it is no wonder that in children they should be very apt to deviate from the just measure of right and wrong, which are in the mind the result of improved reason and serious meditation. This the more they are apt to mistake, the more careful guard ought

368

to be kept over them, and every least slip in this great social virtue taken notice of and rectified; and that in things of the least weight and moment, both to instruct their ignorance, and prevent ill habits, which, from small beginnings, in pins and cherry-stones, will, if let alone grow up to higher frauds, and be in danger to end at last in downright hardened dishonesty.

(109) . . . Fortitude is the guard and support of the other virtues; and without courage a man will scarce keep steady to his duty, and fill up the character of a truly worthy man.

Courage, that makes us bear up against dangers that we fear, and evils that we feel, is of great use in an estate, as ours is in this life, exposed to assaults on all hands: and therefore it is very advisable to get children into this armour as early as we can. Natural temper, I confess, does here a great deal; but even where that is defective, and the heart is in itself weak and timorous, it may, by a right management, be brought to a better resolution. What is to be done to prevent breaking children's spirits by frightful apprehensions instilled into them when young, or bemoaning themselves under every little suffering, I have already taken notice. How to harden their tempers, and raise their courage, if we find them too much subject to fear, is farther to be considered.

True fortitude I take to be the quiet possession of a man's self, and an undisturbed doing his duty, whatever evil besets, or danger lies in his way. This there are so few men attain to, that we are not to expect it from children. But yet something may be done; and a wise conduct, by insensible degrees, may carry them farther than one expects.

The neglect of this great care of them, whilst they are young, is the reason, perhaps, why there are so few that have this virtue, in its full latitude, when they are men. I should not say this in a nation so naturally brave as ours is, did I think that true fortitude required nothing but courage in the field, and a contempt of life in the face of an enemy. This, I confess, is not the least part of it, nor can be denied the laurels and honours always justly due to the valour of those who venture their lives for their country. But yet this is not all: dangers attack us in other places besides the field of battle; and though death be the king of terrors, yet pain, disgrace, and poverty, have frightful looks, able to discompose most men, whom they seem ready to seize on: and there are those who condemn some of these, and yet are heartily frighted with the other. True fortitude is prepared for dangers of all kinds, and unmoved, whatsoever evil it be that threatens: I do not mean unmoved with

369

any fear at all. Where danger shows itself, apprehension cannot, without stupidity, be wanting. Where danger is, sense of danger should be; and so much fear as should keep us awake, and excite our attention, industry, and vigour; but not disturb the calm use of our reason, nor hinder the execution of what that dictates.

The first step to get this noble and manly steadiness, is, what I have above mentioned, carefully to keep children from frights of all kinds, when they are young. Let not any fearful apprehensions be talked into them, nor terrible objects surprise them. . . .

But since the great foundation of fear in children is pain, the way to harden and fortify children against fear and danger, is to accustom them to suffer pain. This, it is possible, will be thought, by kind parents, a very unnatural thing towards their children; and by most, unreasonable, to endeavour to reconcile any one to the sense of pain, by bringing it upon him. It will be said, it may perhaps give the child an aversion for him that makes him suffer; but can never recommend to him suffering itself. This is a strange method. You will not have children whipped and punished for their faults; but you would have them tormented for doing well, or for tormenting's sake. I doubt not but such objections as these will be made, and I shall be thought inconsistent with my self, or fantastical, in proposing it. I confess, it is a thing to be managed with great discretion; and therefore it falls not out amiss, that it will not be received or relished, but by those who consider well, and look into the reason of things. I would not have children much beaten for their faults, because I would not have them think bodily pain, for the same reason, that they might be accustomed to bear it without looking on it as the greatest evil. How much education may reconcile young people to pain and sufferance, the examples of Sparta do sufficiently show: and they who have once brought themselves not to think bodily pain the greatest of evils, or that which they ought to stand most in fear of, have made no small advance towards virtue. But I am not so foolish to propose the Lacedaemonian discipline in our age or constitution: but yet I do say, that inuring children gently to suffer some degrees of pain without shrinking, is a way to gain firmness to their minds, and lay a foundation for courage and resolution in the future part of their lives. . . .

(110) One thing I have frequently observed in children, that when they have got possession of any poor creature, they are apt to use it ill; they often torment and treat very roughly young birds, butterflies, and such other poor animals, which fall into their hands,

370

and that with a seeming kind of pleasure. This, I think, should be watched in them; and if they incline to any such cruelty, they should be taught the contrary usage; for the custom of tormenting and killing of beasts will by degrees, harden their minds even towards men; and they who delight in the suffering and destruction of inferior creatures, will not be apt to be very compassionate or benign to those of their own kind. Our practice takes notice of this, in the exclusion of butchers from juries of life and death. Children should from the beginning be bred up in an abhorrence of killing or tormenting any living creature, and be taught not to spoil or destroy any thing, unless it be for the preservation or advantage of some other that is nobler. And truly, if the preservation of all mankind, as much as in him lies, were every one's persuasion, as indeed it is every one's duty, and the true principle to regulate our religion, politics, and morality by, the world would be much quieter, and better-natured, than it is. But to return to our present business; I cannot but commend both the kindness and prudence of a mother I knew, who was wont always to indulge her daughters, when any of them desired dogs, squirrels, birds, or any such things, as young girls used to be delighted with: but then, when they had them, they must be sure to keep them well, and look diligently after them, that they wanted nothing, or were not ill used; for, if they were negligent in their care of them, it was counted a great fault, which often forfeited their possession; or at least they failed not to be rebuked for it, whereby they were early taught diligence and good-nature. And indeed I think people should be accustomed, from their early cradles, to be tender to all sensible creatures, and to spoil or waste nothing at all. . . .

(111) Another way to instil sentiments of humanity, and to keep them lively in young folks, will be, to accustom them to civility, in their language and deportment towards their inferiors, and the meaner sort of people, particularly servants. It is not unusual to observe the children, in gentlemen's families, treat the servants of the house with domineering words, names of contempt, and an imperious carriage; as if they were of another race, and species beneath them. Whether ill example, the advantage of fortune, or their natural vanity, inspire this haughtiness, it should be prevented or weeded out; and a gentle, courteous, affable carriage towards the lower ranks of men, placed in the room of it. . . .

(112) Curiosity in children, . . . is but an appetite after knowledge, and therefore ought to be encouraged in them, not only as a good sign, but as the great instrument nature has provided, to re-

move that ignorance they were born with, and which without this busy inquisitiveness will make them dull and useless creatures. The ways to encourage it, and keep it active and busy, are, I suppose, these following:

1. Not to check or discountenance any inquiries he shall make, nor suffer them to be laughed at; but to answer all his questions, and explain the matters he desires to know, so as to make them as much intelligible to him, as suits the capacity of his age and knowledge. . . .

(124) Play-things, I think, children should have, and of divers sorts; but still to be in the custody of their tutors, or somebody else, whereof a child should have in his power but one at once, and should not be suffered to have another, but when he restored that: this teaches them, betimes to be careful of not losing or spoiling the things they have; whereas plenty and variety, in their own keeping, makes them wanton and careless, and teaches them from the beginning to be squanderers and wasters. . . .

(124) . . . How then shall they have the play-games you allow them, if none must be bought for them? I answer, they should make them themselves, or at least endeavour it, and set themselves about it; till then they should have none, and till then, they will want none of any great artifice. A smooth pebble, a piece of paper, the mother's bunch of keys, or any thing they cannot hurt themselves with, serves as much to divert little children, as those more chargeable and curious toys from the shops, which are presently put out of order and broken. Children are never dull or out of humour for want of such play-things, unless they have been used to them: when they are little, whatever occurs serves the turn; and as they grow bigger, if they are not stored by the expensive folly of others, they will make them themselves. Indeed, when they once begin to set themselves to work about any of their inventions, they should be taught and assisted; but should have nothing whilst they lazily sit still, expecting to be furnished from other hands without employing their own: and if you help them where they are at a stand, it will more endear you to them, than any chargeable toys you shall buy for them. Play-things which are above their skill to make, as tops, gigs, battledores, and the like, which are to be used with labour, should, indeed, be procured them: these, it is convenient, they should have, not for variety, but exercise; but these, too, should be given them as bare as might be. If they had a top, the scourge-stick and leather-strap should be left to their own making and fitting. If they sit gaping to have such things drop into

372

their mouths, they should go without them. This will accustom them to seek for what they want in themselves, and in their own endeavours; whereby they will be taught moderation in their desires, application, industry, thought, contrivance, and good husbandry; qualities that will be useful to them when they are men, and therefore cannot be learned too soon, nor fixed too deep. All the plays and diversions of children should be directed towards good and useful habits, or else they will introduce ill ones. Whatever they do, leaves some impressions on that tender age, and from thence they receive a tendency to good or evil: and whatever hath such an influence, ought not to be neglected. . . .

. . . . .

(141) You will wonder, perhaps, that I put learning last, especially if I tell you I think it the least part. This may seem strange in the mouth of a bookish man: and this making usually the chief, if not only bustle and stir about children, this being almost that alone which is thought on, when people talk of education, makes it the greater paradox. When I consider what ado is made about a little Latin and Greek, how many years are spent in it, and what a noise and business it makes to no purpose, I can hardly forbear thinking, that the parents of children still live in fear of the schoolmaster's rod, which they look on as the only instrument of education; as if a language or two were its whole business. How else is it possible, that a child should be chained to the oar seven, eight, or ten of the best years of his life, to get a language or two, which I think might be had at a great deal cheaper rate of pains and time, and belearned almost in playing?

Forgive me, therefore, if I say, I cannot with patience think, that a young gentleman should be put into the herd, and be driven with a whip and scourge, as if he were to run the gauntlet through the several classes, 'ad capiendum ingenii cultum.' 'What then, say you, would you not have him write and read? Shall he be more ignorant than the clerk of our parish, who takes Hopkins and Sternhold for the best poets in the world, whom yet he makes worse than they are, by his ill reading?' Not so, not so fast, I beseech you. Reading, and writing, and learning, I allow to be necessary, but yet not the chief business. I imagine you would think him a very foolish fellow, that should not value a virtuous, or a wise man, infinitely before a great scholar. Not but that I think learning a great help to both, in well disposed minds; but yet it must be confessed also, that in others not so disposed, it helps them only to be the more

373

foolish, or worse men. I say this, that, when you consider of the breeding of your son, and are looking out for a school-master, or a tutor, you would not have, (as is usual,) Latin and logic only in your thoughts. Learning must be had, but in the second place as subservient only to greater qualities. Seek out somebody, that may know how discreetly to frame his manners: place him in hands, where you may, as much as possible, secure his innocence, cherish and nurse up the good and gently correct and weed out any bad inclinations, and settle in him good habits. This is the main point; and this being provided for, learning may be had into the bargain; and that, as I think, at a very easy rate, by methods that may be thought on.

. . . . .

(144) I have therefore thought, that if play-things were fitted to this purpose, as they are usually to none, contrivances might be made to teach children to read, whilst they thought they were only playing. For example: What if an ivory-ball were made like that of the royal oak lottery, with thirty-two sides, or one rather of twenty-four or twenty-five sides; and upon several of those sides pasted on an A, upon several others B, on others C, and on others D? I would have you begin with but these four letters, or perhaps only two at first; and when he is perfect in them, then add another; and so on, till each side having one letter, there be on it the whole alphabet. This I would have others play with before him, it being as good a sort of play to lay a stake who shall first throw an A or B, as who upon dice shall throw six or seven. This being a play amongst you, tempt him not to it, lest you make it business; for I would not have him understand it is any thing but a play of older people, and I doubt not but he will take to it of himself. And that he may have the more reason to think it is a play, that he is sometimes in favour admitted to; when the play is done, the ball should be laid up safe out of his reach, that so it may not, by his having it in his keeping at any time, grow stale to him.

(145) To keep up his eagerness to it, let him think it a game belonging to those above him: and when by this means he knows the letters, by changing them into syllables, he may learn to read, without knowing how he did so, and never have any chiding or trouble about it, nor fall out with books, because of the hard usage and vexation they have caused him. Children, if you observe them, take abundance of pains to learn several games, which, if they should be enjoined them, they would abhor as a task, and business. I know

374

a person of great quality, (more yet to be honoured for his learning and virtue, than for his rank and high place,) who, by pasting
on the six vowels, (for in our language Y is one,) on the six sides
of a die, and the remaining eighteen consonants on the sides of
three other dice, has made this a play for his children, that he shall
win, who at one cast, throws most words on these four dice;
whereby his eldest son, yet in coats, has played himself into spelling, with great eagerness, and without once having been chid for
it, or forced to it.

· · · · ·

(150) When by these gentle ways he begins to be able to read,
some easy pleasant book, suited to his capacity, should be put into
his hands, wherein the entertainment that he finds, might draw him
on, and reward his pains in reading; and yet not such as should fill
his head with perfectly useless trumpery, or lay the principles of
vice and folly. To this purpose I think Aesop's Fables the best, which
being stories apt to delight and entertain a child, may yet afford useful reflections to a grown man; and if his memory retain them all
his life after, he will not repent to find them there, amongst his
manly thoughts, and serious business. If his Aesop has pictures in
it, it will entertain him much the better, and encourage him to read,
when it carries the increase of knowledge with it: for such visible
objects children hear talked of in vain, and without any satisfaction,
whilst they have no ideas of them; those ideas being not to be had
from sounds, but from the things themselves, or their pictures. And
therefore, I think, as soon as he begins to spell, as many pictures
of animals should be got him as can be found, with the printed
names to them, which at the same time will invite him to read, and
afford him matter of inquiry and knowledge. Reynard the Fox is
another book, I think, may be made use of to the same purpose.
And if those about him will talk to him often about the stories he
has read, and hear him tell them, it will, besides other advantages,
add encouragement and delight to his reading, when he finds there
is some use and pleasure in it. These baits seem wholly neglected
in the ordinary method; and it is usually long before learners find
any use or pleasure in reading, which may tempt them to it, and
so take books only for fashionable amusements, or impertinent
troubles, good for nothing.

(151) The Lord's prayer, the creed, and ten commandments, it
is necessary he should learn perfectly by heart; but, I think, not by
reading them himself in his primer, but by somebody's repeating

them to him, even before he can read. But learning by heart, and learning to read, should not, I think, be mixed, and so one made to clog the other. But his learning to read should be made as little trouble or business to him as might be.

.　.　.　.　.

(156) As soon as he can speak English, it is time for him to learn some other language: this nobody doubts of, when French is proposed. . . . But because French is a living language, and to be used more in speaking, that should be first learned [before Latin], that the yet pliant organs of speech might be accustomed to a due formation of those sounds, and he get the habit of pronouncing French well, which is the harder to be done the longer it is delayed.

(157) When he can speak and read French well, which in this method is usually in a year or two, he should proceed to Latin, which it is a wonder parents, when they have had the experiment in French, should not think ought to be learned the same way, by talking and reading. Only care is to be taken, whilst he is learning these foreign languages, by speaking and reading nothing else with his tutor, that he do not forget to read English, which may be preserved by his mother, or somebody else, hearing him read some chosen parts of the scripture or other English book, every day.

(158) Latin I look upon as absolutely necessary to a gentleman; and indeed custom, which prevails over every thing, has made it so much a part of education, that even those children are whipped to it, and made spend many hours of their precious time uneasily in Latin, who, after they are once gone from school, are never to have more to do with it, as long as they live. Can there be any thing more ridiculous, than that a father should waste his own money, and his son's time, in setting him to learn the Roman language, when, at the same time, he designs him for a trade, wherein he, having no use of Latin, fails not to forget that little which he brought from school, and which it is ten to one he abhors for the ill usage it procured him? Could it be believed, unless we had every where amongst us examples of it, that a child should be forced to learn the rudiments of a language, which he is never to use in the course of life that he is designed to, and neglect all the while the writing a good hand, and casting accounts, which are of great advantage in all conditions of life, and to most trades indispensably necessary? But though these qualifications, requisite to trade and commerce, and the business of the world, are seldom

or never to be had at grammar-schools; yet thither not only gentlemen send their younger sons intended for trades, but even tradesmen and farmers fail not to send their children, though they have neither intention nor ability to make them scholars. If you ask them, why they do this? they think it as strange a question, as if you should ask them why they go to church? Custom serves for reason, and has, to those that take it for reason, so consecrated this method, that it is almost religiously observed by them; and they stick to it, as if their children had scarce an orthodox education, unless they learned Lilly's grammar.

(159) But how necessary soever Latin be to some, and is thought to be to others, to whom it is of no manner of use or service, yet the ordinary way of learning it in a grammar-school, is that, which having had thoughts about, I cannot be forward to encourage. The reasons against it are so evident and cogent, that they have prevailed with some intelligent persons to quit the ordinary road, not without success, though the method made use of was not exactly that which I imagine the easiest, and in short is this: to trouble the child with no grammar at all, but to have Latin, as English has been, without the perplexity of rules, talked into him; for, if you will consider it, Latin is no more unknown to a child, when he comes into the world, than English: and yet he learns English without master, rule, or grammar: and so might he Latin too, as Tully did, if he had somebody always to talk to him in this language. And when we so often see a French-woman teach an English girl to speak and read French perfectly in a year or two, without any rule of grammar, or any thing else but prattling to her; I cannot but wonder, how gentlemen have been overseen this way for their sons, and thought them more dull or incapable than their daughters.

(160) If, therefore, a man could be got, who himself speaking good Latin, would always be about your son, talk constantly to him, and suffer him to speak or read nothing else, this will be the true and genuine way, and that which I would propose, not only as the easiest and best, wherein a child might, without pains or chiding, get a language, which others are wont to be whipped for at school, six or seven years together; but also as that, wherein at the same time he might have his mind and manners formed, and he be instructed to boot in several sciences, such as are a good part of geography, astronomy, chronology, anatomy, besides some parts of history, and all other parts of knowledge of things, that fall under the senses, and require little more than memory. For there, if we

would take the true way, our knowledge should begin, and in those things be laid the foundation; and not in the abstract notions of logic and metaphysics, which are fitter to amuse, than inform the understanding, in its first setting out towards knowledge. When young men have had their heads employed a while in those abstract speculations, without finding the success and improvement, or that use of them which they expected, they are apt to have mean thoughts either of learning or themselves; they are tempted to quit their studies, and throw away their books, as containing nothing but hard words, and empty sounds; or else to conclude, that if there be any real knowledge in them, they themselves have not understandings capable of it. That this is so, perhaps I could assure you upon my own experience. Amongst other things to be learned by a young gentleman in this method, whilst others of his age are wholly taken up with Latin and languages, I may also set down geometry for one, having known a young gentleman, bred something after this way, able to demonstrate several propositions in Euclid, before he was thirteen.

(161) . . . The great skill of a teacher is to get and keep the attention of his scholar: whilst he has that, he is sure to advance as fast as the learner's abilities will carry him; and without that, all his bustle and pother will be to little or no purpose. To attain this, he should make the child comprehend, (as much as may be,) the usefulness of what he teaches him; and let him see, by what he has learned, that he can do something which he could not do before; something which gives him some power and real advantage above others, who are ignorant of it. To this he should add sweetness in all his instructions; and by a certain tenderness in his whole carriage, make the child sensible that he loves him, and designs nothing but his good; the only way to beget love in the child, which will make him hearken to his lessons, and relish what he teaches him.

.   .   .   .   .

(170) I hear it is said, that children should be employed in getting things by heart, to exercise and improve their memories. I could wish this were said with as much authority of reason, as it is with forwardness of assurance; and that this practice were established upon good observation, more than old custom; for it is evident, that strength of memory is owing to a happy constitution, and not to any habitual improvement got by exercise. It is true what the mind is intent upon, and for fear of letting it slip, often imprints afresh on itself by frequent reflection, that it is apt to retain, but

378

still according to its own natural strength of retention. An impression made on beeswax or lead will not last so long as on brass or steel. Indeed, if it be renewed often, it may last the longer; but every new reflecting on it is a new impression, and it is from thence one is to reckon, if one would know how long the mind retains it. But the learning pages of Latin by heart, no more fits the memory for retention of any thing else, than the graving of one sentence in lead, makes it the more capable of retaining firmly any other character. . . .

[The curriculum Locke recommends includes besides English, French and Latin, also geography, arithmetic, astronomy, geometry, chronology, history, civil law, English law, rhetoric, logic and a versity in style and letters.]

* * * * *

(183) . . . To write and speak correctly gives a grace and gains a favourable attention to what one has to say: and, since it is English that an English gentleman will have constant use of, that is the language he should chiefly cultivate, and wherein most care should be taken to polish and perfect his style. . . .

. . . I am not here speaking against Greek and Latin; I think they ought to be studied, and the Latin at least, understood well, by every gentleman. But whatever foreign languages a young man meddles with, (and the more he knows, the better,) that which he should critically study and labour to get a facility, clearness, and elegancy to express himself in, should be his own, and to this purpose he should daily be exercised in it.

* * * * *

(187) . . . to the study of natural philosophy: though the world be full of systems of it, yet I cannot say, I know any one which can be taught a young man as a science, wherein he may be sure to find truth and certainty, which is what all sciences give an expectation of. I do not hence conclude, that none of them are to be read; it is necessary for a gentleman in this learned age to look into some of them, to fit himself for conversation; but whether that of Des Cartes be put into his hands, as that which is the most in fashion, or it be thought fit to give him a short view of that and several others also; I think the systems of natural philosophy that have obtained in this part of the world, are to be read more to know the hypotheses, and to understand the terms, and ways of talking, of the several sects,

than with hopes to gain thereby a comprehensive scientifical and satisfactory knowledge of the works of nature.

.   .   .   .   .

(191) Music is thought to have some affinity with dancing, and a good hand, upon some instruments, is by many people mightily valued. But it wastes so much of a young man's time, to gain but a moderate skill in it, and engages often in such odd company, that many think it much better spared: and I have, amongst men of parts and business, so seldom heard any one commended or esteemed for having an excellency in music, that amongst all those things, that ever came into the list of accomplishments, I think I may give it the last place.

.   .   .   .   .

(195) I have one thing more to add, which as soon as I mention, I shall run the danger of being suspected to have forgot what I am about, and what I have above written concerning education, all tending towards a gentleman's calling, with which a trade seems wholly to be inconsistent. And yet, I cannot forbear to say, I would have him learn a trade, a manual trade; nay, two or three, but one more particularly.

(196) The busy inclination of children being always to be directed to something that may be useful to them, the advantages proposed from what they are set about may be considered of two kinds; 1. Where the skill itself, that is got by exercise, is worth the having. Thus skill not only in languages, and learned sciences, but in painting, turning, gardening, tempering, and working in iron, and all other useful arts, is worth the having. 2. Where the exercise itself, without any consideration, is necessary or useful for health. Knowledge in some things is so necessary to be got by children, whilst they are young, that some part of their time is to be allotted to their improvement in them, though those employments contribute nothing at all to their health: such are reading, and writing, and all other sedentary studies, for the cultivating of the mind, which unavoidably take up a great part of gentlemen's time, quite from their cradles. Other manual arts which are both got and exercised by labour, do many of them by that exercise, not only increase our dexterity and skill, but contribute to our health too; especially such as employ us in the open air. In these, then, health and improvement may be joined together; and of these should some fit ones be chosen, to be made the recreations of one, whose chief business is

380

with books and study. In this choice the age and inclination of the person is to be considered, and constraint always to be avoided in bringing him to it. For command and force may often create, but can never cure an aversion; and whatever any one is brought to by compulsion, he will leave as soon as he can, and be little profited and less recreated by, whilst he is at it.

·　·　·　·　·

(203) To the arts above mentioned may be added perfuming, varnishing, graving, and several sorts of working in iron, brass, and silver: and if, as it happens to most young gentlemen, that a considerable part of his time be spent in a great town, he may learn to cut, polish, and set precious stones, or employ himself in grinding and polishing optical glasses. . . .

(204) But if his mistaken parents, frightened with the disgraceful names of mechanic and trade, shall have an aversion to any thing of this kind in their children; yet there is one thing relating to trade, which, when they consider, they will think absolutely necessary for their sons to learn.

Merchant's accounts, though a science not likely to help a gentleman to get an estate, yet possibly there is not any thing of more use and efficacy to make him preserve the estate he has. It is seldom observed, that he who keeps an account of his income and expenses, and thereby has constantly under view the course of his domestic affairs, lets them run to ruin; and I doubt not but many a man gets behind-hand, before he is aware, or runs further on, when he is once in, for want of this care, or the skill to do it. I would therefore advise all gentlemen to learn perfectly merchant's accounts, and not to think it is a skill that belongs not to them, because it has received its name from, and has been chiefly practised by, men of traffic.

·　·　·　·　·

(206) The last part, usually, in education is travel, which is commonly thought to finish the work, and complete the gentleman. I confess, travel into foreign countries has great advantages; but the time usually chosen to send young men abroad, is, I think, of all other, that which renders them least capable of reaping those advantages. Those which are proposed, as to the main of them, may be reduced to these two: first, language; secondly, an improvement in wisdom and prudence, by seeing men, and conversing with people of tempers, customs, and ways of living, different from one

381

another, and especially from those of his parish or neighbourhood. But from sixteen to one-and-twenty, which is the ordinary time of travel, men are, of all their lives, the least suited to these improvements. The first season to get foreign languages, and form the tongue to their true accents, I should think, should be from seven to fourteen or sixteen; and then, too, a tutor with them is useful and necessary, who may, with those languages teach them other things. . . .

．　．　．　．　．

(210) Though I am now come to a conclusion of what obvious remarks have suggested to me concerning education, I would not have it thought that I look on it as a just treatise on this subject. There are a thousand other things that may need consideration; especially if one should take in the various tempers, different inclinations, and particular defaults, that are to be found in children; and prescribe proper remedies. The variety is so great, that it would require a volume; nor would that reach it. Each man's mind has some peculiarity, as well as his face, that distinguishes him from all others; and there are possibly scarce two children, who can be conducted by exactly the same method. Besides that, I think a prince, a nobleman, and an ordinary gentleman's son, should have different ways of breeding. But having had here only some general views, in reference to the main end and aims in education, and those designed for a gentleman's son, whom, being then very little, I considered only as white paper, or wax, to be moulded and fashioned as one pleases; I have touched little more than those heads, which I judged necessary for the breeding of a young gentleman of his condition in general; and have now published these my occasional thoughts, with this hope, that, though this be far from being a complete treatise on this subject, or such as that every one may find what will just fit his child in it; yet it may give some small light to those, whose concern for their dear little ones makes them so irregularly bold, that they dare venture to consult their own reason in the education of their children, rather than wholly to rely upon old custom.

ROUSSEAU 1712–1778

IN THE SECOND half of the 18th century Jean Jacques Rousseau's gospel of Retournez à la Nature moved some enthusiastic mothers to harden their babies by ducking them into ice cold water which eventually brought on death. Others exposed their children to all kinds of psychological experiments and raised mental wrecks. There has rarely been a prophet whose symbolic language was not taken too literally by narrow-minded neophytes so that in many cases more harm than good was done.

For Rousseau himself education was nothing less than an essential part in his revolutionary plan to lead mankind from absolutism and authoritarianism toward freedom and independence. The *Émile* can be valued fully only if understood as the educational counterpart to the political *Social Contract.* In consequence of the work of Rousseau, and another great Swiss, Pestalozzi, even the admonitions of earlier educators came to be taken more seriously. Youngsters were no longer regarded as little grown-ups and punished accordingly if they did not live up to the expectation; some teachers, at least, became more interested in their pupils than in the mere conveyance of subject matter; and the children of the wealthy were no longer clad in the straitjackets of adult clothes but permitted to move their little bodies as they pleased. However, there are still a lot of pre-Rousseauist teachers and parents.

There has always been much discussion about Rousseau's own problematic personality. Yet, it was his very deviation from the norm that allowed him to see the lie in false conformity and conventionality. But whenever a man destroys old habits of thought and practice, he creates danger, for though he creates avenues for the bold, he takes safety away from the little minds.

The following article was taken from *Selections from Emilius; or, a Treatise of Education, translated from the French of J. J. Rousseau, Citizen of Geneva,* in three volumes, published in Edinburgh in 1773.

ÉMILE;[1] OR, A TREATISE OF EDUCATION

BOOK I

All things are good as they come out of the hands of their Creator, but every thing degenerates in the hands of man. He compels one

---

[1] The Latin form Emilius, which was chosen for the 1773 Edinburgh edition, has been replaced by the original form Émile.

soil to nourish the productions of another, and one tree to bear the fruits of another. He blends and confounds elements, climates, and seasons: he mutilates his dogs, his horses, and his slaves: he defaces, he confounds every thing: he delights in deformity and monsters. He is not content with any thing in its natural state, not even with his own species. His very offspring must be trained up for him, like a horse in the menage, and be taught to grow after his own fancy, like a tree in his garden.

Without this, matters would be still worse than they are, and our species would not be civilized but by halves. Should a man, in a state of society, be given up, from the cradle, to his own notions and conduct, he would certainly turn out the most preposterous of human beings. The influence of prejudice, authority, necessity, example, and all those social institutions in which we are immerged, would stifle in him the emotions of nature, and substitute nothing in their place. His humanity would resemble a shrub, growing by accident in the high way, which would soon be destroyed by the casual injuries it must receive from the frequent passenger.

$$. \quad . \quad . \quad . \quad .$$

We are born weak, we have need of help; we are born destitute of every thing, we stand in need of assistance; we are born stupid, we have need of understanding. All that we are not possessed of at our birth, and which we require when grown up, is bestowed on us by education.

This education we receive from nature, from men, or from circumstances. The constitutional exertion of our organs and faculties is the education of nature: the uses we are taught to make of that exertion, constitute the education given us by men; and in the acquisitions made by our own experience, on the objects that surround us, consists our education from circumstances.

We are formed, therefore, by three kinds of masters. The pupil, in whom the effects of their different lessons are contradictory, is badly educated and can never be consistent with himself. He in whom they are perfectly consonant, and always tend to the same point, hath only attained the end of a complete education. His life and actions demonstrate this, and that he alone is well brought up.

Of these three different kinds of education, that of nature depends not on ourselves; and but in a certain degree that of circumstances: the third, which belongs to men, is that only we have in our power: and even of this we are masters only in imagination; for

384

who can flatter himself, he will be able entirely to govern the discourse and actions of those who are about a child?

No sooner, then, doth education become an art, or profession, than it is almost impossible it should succeed, as the concurrent circumstances necessary to its success are not to be depended on. All that can be done with our utmost solicitude, is to approach as near as possible the end we aim at, attributing it to good fortune if it be attained.

If it be asked, what is this end? it may be answered, that of nature, which has been already proved. For, since the concurrence of three kinds of education is necessary to its perfection, it is by that one, which is entirely independent of us, we must regulate the two others. But perhaps this word, *Nature*, may appear vague and equivocal; let us therefore endeavour to give it a precise and determinate meaning.

Nature, it has been said, is only habit. But to what purpose is this said? Are there not habits, which are contracted only upon compulsion, and which can never suppress the tendency of nature? Such is, for example, the habitual growth of plants, restrained from pursuing their vertical direction. Take off the restraint, and it is true, they preserve the inclination they have been compelled to take: but, you will find, the rise of the sap has not on that account changed its primitive direction; if the plant continues to vegetate, its future growth becomes still upwards.

It is the same with the inclinations and dispositions of mankind. While we remain in exactly the same situation in which they were acquired, we may retain even the most unnatural habits; but as soon as circumstances change the force of habit ceases, and that of nature exerts itself. Education itself is certainly nothing but habit: but are there not persons in whom the impressions they received in education are effaced? Are there not others, again, that retain them? Whence arises this difference? if it be pretended that by nature is only meant habits conformable to nature, the position itself is unmeaning and absurd.

·　·　·　·　·

To be something, to be consistent with one's self, and always the same individual, our words and actions should agree; we should be always determined in that part we ought to take; we should take it with an high hand, and persevere. If such a prodigy could be found, we might then know whether he be a man or a citizen, or how he can so manage as to be at once both the one and the other.

From these objects, which are necessarily opposed to each other, arise two contrary forms of institution; the one public and general, the other domestic and particular.

. . . . .

It must be observed, I do not esteem, as public institutions, those ridiculous establishments that go by the name of Universities.[2] I regard just as little the education acquired by an intercourse with the world, because that experience, aiming at two contrary ends, falls short of both. It is only calculated to make men deceitful, appearing always to interest themselves in the good of others, and being never interested in any thing but what relates to their own. As these pretensions are also become general, there is no one deceived by them; so that it is only to much pains thrown away.

From these contradictions arises that which we constantly experience in ourselves. Impelled by nature and custom contrary ways, and forced to yield in a degree to both impulses, we take a route in the mean direction of both, that leads us neither to the end of one or the other. Thus held in suspense, and wavering, during the whole course of our lives, we end our days without being able to render ourselves consistent and without ever being good for any thing to ourselves or others.

There remains then only a private education, or that of nature. But of what use to others, it may be said, would a man be, educated only for himself? Perhaps, if the twofold object proposed could be reduced to a single one, in taking from man his contradictory motives of action, we should remove a great obstacle to his happiness. To judge of this, we should see him quite formed; should have observed his inclinations and propensities, have traced their progress, and attended them throughout; in a word, we should be made acquainted with the natural man. I flatter myself the reader will have made some advance in these researches, after having perused this treatise.

In order to form this extraordinary man, let us consider first what we have to do. Much, doubtless, depends on preventing any thing from being done. When the wind only is against us, we have noth-

[2] There are, indeed, professors, both in the academy of Geneva and in the university of Paris, for whom I have the greatest love and esteem, and think them very capable of instructing youth were they not tied down to establish customs. I would advise one of them to publish the project he has formed of a reformation therein. Perhaps an attempt may, some time or other, be made to remove the evil, when it is seen to be not without remedy.

ing to do but steer close and shape our course to windward: but in a strong current, if we would not lose ground, we must drop anchor. Take care, young pilot, that your cable does not veer, and your ship drive, before you are aware.

According to the order of society, in which the respective places of individuals are fixed, every one ought to be educated for that which he is to fill. A man formed for one place, if taken out of it, would be fit for no other, and consequently good for nothing. In this state, education is useful only as fortune seconds the intentions of parents; in every other case it would be hurtful to the pupil, were it only on account of the prejudices it might instil. In Egypt, where the son was obliged to follow the occupation or profession of his father, education had at least a determinate end; but among us, where rank and profession are only permanent, and persons continually changing; a father would not know whether, in bringing up his child to his own profession, he might be doing him good or ill.

According to the order of nature, all men being equal, their common vocation is the profession of humanity; and whoever is well educated to discharge the duties of a man, cannot be badly prepared to fill up any of those offices that have a relation to him. It matters little to me, whether my pupil be designed for the army, the bar, or the pulpit. Nature has destined us to the offices of human life, antecedent to the destination of our parents concerning the part we are to act in society. To live is the profession I would teach him. When I have done with him, it is true, he will be neither a lawyer, a soldier, nor a divine. Let him first be a man; he will on occasion as soon become any thing else, that a man ought to be, as any other person whatever. Fortune may remove him from one rank to another as she pleases, he will be always sound in his place. *Occupavite, fortuna, atque cepi: omnesque aditus tuos interclusi, ut ad me aspirare non posses.* (Tuscul. V.)

Our chief study is that of human life; the good and evil of which he that is best able to support, is, in my opinion, the best educated; and hence it follows that true education consists less in precept than action. . . .

In general, little more is thought of in the education of a child, than to preserve his being: this is not enough: he ought to learn how to preserve himself when he is grown up to manhood; to support the shocks of fortune, to bear riches or poverty; and to live, if occasion require, either amidst mountains of ice in Greenland, or on the burning rocks of Malta. You may take what precaution you will to preserve his life; he must inevitably die; and though his death may

387

not be justly charged to your solicitude, your pains will be in a great measure thrown away. It is less needful to preserve your child from death, than to teach him how to live. To live is not merely to breathe; it is to act, to make a proper use of our organs, our senses, our faculties, and of all those parts of the human frame which contribute to the consciousness of our existence. The man who has lived most, is not he who hath survived the greatest number of years, but he who has experienced most of life. A man may be buried at an hundred years of age, who died in his cradle. Such a one would have been a gainer by dying young, at least if he had lived, in our sense of the word, till the time of his decease.

All our wisdom consists in servile prejudice; all our customs are nothing but subjection, confinement, and restraint. Civilized man is born, lives, and dies in slavery: at his birth he is bound up in swaddling-cloaths, and at his death nailed down in his coffin. As long as he wears the appearance of the human form, he is confined by our institutions. . . .

But should mothers again condescend to nurse their children, manners would form themselves, the sentiments of nature would revive in our hearts, the state would be repeopled; this principal point, this alone would reunite every thing. A taste for the charms of a domestic life is the best antidote against corruption of manners. The noise and bustle of children, which is generally thought troublesome, becomes hence agreeable; it is these that render parents more necessary, more dear, to each other, and strengthen the ties of conjugal affection. When a family is all lively and animated, domestic concerns afford the most delightful occupation to a woman, and the most agreeable amusement to a man. Hence, from the correction of this one abuse, will presently result a general reformation; nature will soon re-assume all its rights. Let wives but once again become mothers, and the men will presently again become fathers and husbands.

. . . . .

Man is born to suffer in every stage of his existence. Even self-preservation is attended with some degree of pain. Happy are we that in our infancy we are susceptible only of physical evils! Evils much less cruel, much less terrible than others, and more seldom capable of reconciling us to death. Men never destroy themselves to get rid of the gout; the anguish of the mind only is productive of despair. We lament the state of infants, whereas it is our own that

388

is most to be lamented. Our greatest evils are derived from ourselves.

A child as soon as it is born begins to cry; great part of its earliest infancy being spent in tears. Sometimes we dance it about and soothe it; at others threaten and beat it, in order to make it silent. We always either do that which is pleasing to the child, or exact of it what pleases ourselves; either submitting to its humours, or obliging it to submit to ours. There is no medium, it must either command or obey. Hence the first ideas it acquires, are those of tyranny and servitude. Before it can speak it learns to command, and before it can act it is taught obedience; nay, sometimes it is punished before it be conscious of a fault, at least before it can commit one. Thus it is we early instil into their tender minds those passions which we afterwards impute to nature, and after having taken the pains to make them vitious, complain that we found them so.

In this manner a child passes six or seven years under the care of the women, the constant victim of their caprices and his own. After he has learned of them what they usually teach, that is, after they have burdened his memory with words without meaning, and things of no consequence; after they have corrupted his natural disposition by the passions they have implanted, this factitious being is turned over to the care of a preceptor, who proceeds in the development of those artificial buds already formed, teaching him every thing except the knowledge of himself, the business of human life, and the attainment of happiness. So that when this slavish and tyrannical infant, replete with science and deprived of sense, equally debilitated both in body and mind, comes at length to enter on the world, it is no wonder that the display he makes of his folly, vanity and vice, should cause us to lament the misery and perverseness of human nature. We are, however, mistaken: such is the man of our caprices; that of nature is differently constituted. Are you desirous of preserving his original form? begin with him as soon as he comes into the world: make yourself master of him as soon as he is born, nor quit him afterwards till he is grown up to manhood: without this you will never perfectly succeed. . . .

Much has been said and written on the qualifications of a good governor. The first that I should require of him, and which would include a great many others, is, that he should not be venal. There are some professions so noble that they cannot be practised for hire, without shewing the professor unworthy of them: such is the profession of arms, and such that of moral institutions. To whom, then, shall I intrust the education of my child?—I have already told you: to yourself. But I am incapable.—Are you indeed incapable? Make then a friend. I see no other resource.

What a sublime idea do I entertain of a complete tutor! In fact, to be able to form the man, one ought either to be his father or something more than man one's self. Yet such is the office you carelessly confer on the merest mercenaries.

The more I reflect on this subject, the more I perceive new difficulties arise. It is necessary the governor should have been educated for his pupil, that his domestics should have been educated for their master, that every one who comes near him should have received the same impressions which they are to communicate to him; and thus education on education becomes necessary nobody knows how far. How can a child be properly educated by one who has not been properly educated himself? But where is such an extraordinary mortal to be found? I confess I am ignorant. In these abject times, who knows what degree of virtue the human mind may attain? Yet suppose this prodigy found. It is in examining what he ought to do, that we shall see what he ought to be. I can venture to pronounce beforehand, however, that the father who is the most sensible of the value of a good governor, will be the first to do without one; as he will find it more difficult to procure one, than to become such himself. Or is he desirous, in such a case, to make a friend? let him educate his child to that end; he then will have no need to seek one elsewhere, and nature will have already done half his work. . . .

But, though I hold myself incapacitated to undertake the most useful part of this arduous task, I shall venture to attempt that which is the most easy. To follow the example of many others, I shall not set my hand to the work, but to the pen; and instead of doing it myself, endeavour to advise others what ought to be done.

In attempts of this kind, their authors, generally very easy about the consistency of a theory they are not concerned to put in practice, lay down, without scruple, a number of fine precepts impossible to be followed; and for want of being sufficiently circumstantial and exemplary in their application, render even those which are practicable useless.

I have, therefore, in this work, made choice of an imaginary pupil, and have taken the liberty to suppose myself of a proper age in health, and possessed of the requisite abilities to undertake his education, to conduct him from the time of his birth, till, grown up to maturity, he may stand in need of no other guide than himself.

. . . . .

I shall here observe only, in contradiction to the common opinion, that the governor of a child should be young, even as young as possible, consistent with his having attained necessary discretion and sagacity. I would have him be himself a child, that he might become the companion of his pupil, and gain his confidence by partaking of his amusements. There are not things in common enough between infancy and manhood, to form a solid attachment at so great a distance. Children sometimes caress old men, but they never love them.

. . . . .

The poor stand in no need of education; that of their station is confined, and they cannot attain any other. On the contrary, the education of those who are in a wealthy station, is that which is the least adapted to their own good, or to the good of society. Add to this, that an education adapted to the nature of things, ought to qualify a man for all conditions of life: now it is certainly less reasonable to educate the poor for a high station, than the rich for a low one; for, in proportion to the number of both, there are much fewer persons who become rich, than there are who become poor, as it is much easier to spend a fortune than to acquire one. Our pupil therefore shall be rich: thus we are sure at least of forming one man the more; a poor one may become a man of himself.

It is for the same reason, I shall not be sorry that Émile should be also of noble birth; as we are sure of snatching one victim from the absurdities of prejudice.

Émile is an orphan. It is to no purpose he should have a father or mother. As I charge myself with their obligations, I succeed to their rights and authority. He ought indeed to honour his parents, but complacence is all that is due to me. This is the first, or rather the only condition I make with him.

. . . . .

I say it again, the education of a man commences at his birth: before he can speak, before he can understand, he is already instructed. Experience is the forerunner of precept; the moment he knows the features of his nurse, he may be said to have acquired

391

considerable knowledge. Trace the progress of the most ignorant of mortals, from his birth to the present hour, and you will be astonished at the knowledge he has acquired. If we divide all human science into two parts, the one consisting of that which is common to all men, and the other of what is peculiar to the learned, the latter will appear insignificant and trifling in comparison with the other. But we think nothing of general acquisitions, because they are made insensibly, and even before we arrive at the age of reason; knowledge becomes conspicuous only in its difference on comparison; just as in working algebraic equations, common quantities are struck out and stand for nothing.

. . . . .

The only habit in which a child should be indulged, is that of contracting none; he should not be permitted to exercise one arm more than the other; we should not accustom him to present his right hand oftener than his left, or to make use of one more than the other; he should not be used to eat, sleep, or do any thing, at stated hours, or not to be left alone, whether in the day or night. Prepare early for his enjoyment of liberty, and the exercise of his natural abilities, by leaving him in full possession of them unrestrained by artificial habits, and by putting him in a situation to be always master of himself, and to do whatever his resolution prompts him, as soon as he is able to form one.

. . . . .

As it grows up, a child acquires strength, and becomes less active and restless; it contracts its powers more within itself. The body and soul, if I may so say, keep each other in aequilibrio; and nature requires no greater quantity of motion than is necessary to our preservation. But the desire of command doth not cease with the motives that gave rise to it; the notion of superiority is flattering to self-love, and is increased by habit: thus caprice succeeds to necessity, and the force of prejudice and opinion takes root in the mind.

The principle once known, we see clearly the track wherein we began to deviate from nature: let us inquire then, what must be done, in order to prevent our going astray. So far from being endued with superfluous abilities, children have at first hardly sufficient for the purposes nature requires; it is requisite therefore to leave them at full liberty to employ those she hath given them, and which they cannot abuse: this is my first maxim.

It is our duty to assist them, and supply their deficiencies, whether of body or mind, in every circumstance of physical necessity. Second maxim.

Every assistance afforded them should be confined to real utility, without administering any thing to the indulgence of their caprice or unreasonable humours; for they will never be capricious unless through neglect, or in some particular circumstance depending on their constitution. Third maxim.

The meaning of their language and signs ought to be carefully studied, in order to be able to distinguish, in an age when they know not how to dissemble, between those inclinations that arise immediately from nature, and what are only fantastical. Fourth maxim.

The design and tendency of these rules are, to give children more real liberty and less command; to leave them more to do of themselves than to require of others. Thus, by being early accustomed to confine their desires to their abilities, they will be little affected with the want of what is out of their power.

.   .   .   .   .

BOOK II

WE ARE come now to the second period of life, at which the state of infancy, properly speaking, ends, and that of puerility begins. . . .

Life is the most precarious at its commencement; the less time we have existed, the less hope have we of future existence. Of all the children that are born, the half only, at most, arrive at the age of fourteen, and it is very probable yours may not reach the age of manhood.

What can we think, then, of that barbarous method of education, by which the present is sacrificed to an uncertain future; by which a child is laid under every kind of restraint, and is made miserable, by way of preparing him for we know not what pretended happiness, which there is reason to believe he may never live to enjoy? Supposing it not unreasonable in its design, how can we see, without indignation, the unhappy innocents subjected to a yoke of insupportable rigour, and condemned like galley-slaves to continual labour, without being assured that such mortifications and restrictions will ever be of any service to them? The age of cheerfulness and gaiety is spent in the midst of tears, punishments, threats, and slavery. We torment the poor creatures, for their future good; and perceive not that death is at hand, and ready to seize them amidst all this sorrowful preparation for life. Who can tell how many children have fallen victims to the extravagant sagacity of their parents and guardians? Happy to escape such cruelty, the only advantage the poor sufferers reaped from the evils they endured, being to die without regretting a life of misery.

Man, be humane! It is the first, the chief of moral duties, to exercise humanity to every thing, of what age or condition soever, that is relative to man. What! is wisdom void of humanity? Have a tender regard for children; indulge them in their diversions, their pleasures, and in every thing dictated by their harmless natures.

Who is there among us that has not, at times, looked back with regret on that period of our lives, wherein the countenance was always smiling, and the heart as constantly at ease. Why will you deprive the little innocents of the enjoyment of a season so short and transient? of a blessing so precious, which they cannot abuse? Why will you clog, with bitterness and sorrow, those rapid moments which will return no more for them than for you? Ye fathers, do you know when the stroke of death shall fall on your offspring? Lay not up in store, then, for your own sorrow, by depriving them of the enjoyment of the few moments nature has allotted them: as soon as they become sensible of the pleasures of existence, let them enjoy it, so that whenever it may please God to call them home, they may not die without tasting of life.

. . . . .

To prevent our running into chimeras, let us never lose sight of what is befitting our situation. Humanity has its place in the order and constitution of things; the state of infancy in those of human life; men should be considered as men, and children as children. To assign both their separate places, and regulate the human passions, agreeable to the constitution of man, are all that can be done for his happiness. The rest depends on circumstances which are not in our power. . . .

In what then consists human wisdom, or the means of acquiring happiness? To diminish our desires is certainly not the method; for if these were less than our abilities, part of our faculties would remain useless and inactive, and we should enjoy but half of our being. Nor is it, on the other hand, to extend our natural capacity for enjoyment; for if our desires, at the same time, be extended in a greater proportion, we should only become thereby the more miserable.

It must consist, therefore, in lessening the disproportion between our abilities and our desires; and in reducing our inclinations and our powers to a perfect equilibrium. It is in such a situation, and that only, that all our faculties may be employed; and yet the mind preserve its tranquillity, and the body its due regularity and ease.

．　．　．　．　．

The material universe has its limits, the imaginary world is infinite: as we cannot enlarge the one, therefore, let us contract the other; for it is their difference only that gives birth to all those inconveniences that make us really unhappy. If we except the blessings or strength, health, and the testimony of a good conscience, all the other conveniences and pleasures of life depend on opinion: except pain of body and remorse of conscience, all our evils are imaginary. This principle, it may be said, is trite and common. I confess it: but the practical application of it is not common; and it is of the practice only I am now speaking.

．　．　．　．　．

That foresight, which carries us beyond ourselves, and often transports us in imagination to scenes we shall never arrive at, this it is which is the true source of all our miseries. What frenzy is it, in a being so transitory as man, to keep always looking forward to a futurity that seldom arrives, and to neglect the present of which he is so certain! A frenzy by so much the more fatal, as it increases with age, and as old men, always distrustful, provident, and covetous, had rather deny themselves necessaries to-day, than run the chance of wanting them an hundred years hence. Thus we lay hold and are tenacious of every thing; time, place, persons, and circumstances, all that is, or may be, becomes of consequence to our welfare: our own persons are thus the least part of ourselves. Every part of its extensive surface. Is it to be wondered at that our evils should multiply, and that we should feel in all those parts wherein we are capable of being wounded? How many sovereigns have been made unhappy by the loss of countries they have never seen? How many merchants are required to trade to the Indies, to furnish out the cries of Paris?

．　．　．　．　．

Confine, O man, thy existence within thyself, and thou wilt be no longer miserable. Remain in the place nature hath assigned you in the scale of beings: spurn not against the hard law of necessity, nor waste, by our opposition, that strength which heaven hath bestowed on you, not to extend and prolong your existence, but only to preserve it during its own time and in its own manner. Your liberty, your power, extend as far as your natural faculties, and no farther; all the rest is only slavery, illusion, and deceit. Authority itself is servile, when it is founded on opinion; for you depend on the prejudices of those whom you govern by the force of prejudice. To govern them according to your own pleasure, you must govern them agreeable to theirs. They have only to change their mode of thinking, and you will be obliged to change yours of acting.

.   .   .   .   .

He only performs the actions of his own will, who stands in no need of the assistance of others to put his designs in execution: and hence it follows, that the greatest of all blessings is not authority, but liberty. A man truly free, wills only what he is able to perform, and performs what he pleases. This is my fundamental maxim. It need only be applied to a state of infancy, and all the rules of education will naturally flow from it.

A wise man knows and will keep his place; but a child is ignorant of his, and therefore cannot confine himself to it. There are a thousand avenues through which he will be apt to escape: it belongs to those who have the care of his education, therefore, to prevent him; a task, by the way, which is not very easy. He should be neither treated as an irrational animal, nor as a man; but simply as a child: he should be made sensible of his weakness, but not abandoned to suffer by it; he should be taught dependence, and not merely obedience; he should be instructed to ask, and not to command. He is in a state of submission to others, only because of his wants, and because they know better than himself what is good or hurtful for him. No one hath a right, not even the father of a child, to command it to do any thing that is useless.

.   .   .   .   .

Excessive severity, as well as excessive indulgence, should be equally avoided. If you leave children to suffer, you expose their health, endanger their lives, and make them actually miserable; on the other hand, if you are too anxious to prevent their being sensible of any kind of pain and inconvenience, you only pave their way to feel much greater; you enervate their constitutions, make them tender and effeminate; in a word, you remove them out of their situation as men, into which they must hereafter return in spite of all your solicitude. In order not to expose them to the few evils nature would inflict on them, you provide for them many which they would otherwise never have suffered.

396

... the words *command* and *obey* should have no place in his dictionary, much less those of *duty* and *obligation;* but those of power, necessity, impotence, and restraint, ought to stand forth in capitals.

. . . . .

We may reduce almost all the lessons of morality that have, or can be, formed for the use of children, to the following formula.

MASTER. You must not do so.

CHILD. And why must I not do so?

MASTER. Because it is naughty.

CHILD. Naughty! what is that being naughty?

MASTER. Doing what you are forbid.

CHILD. And what harm is there in doing what one is forbid?

MASTER. The harm is, you will be whipped for disobedience.

CHILD. Then I will do it so that no body shall know any thing of the matter.

MASTER. O, but you will be watched.

CHILD. Ah! but then I will hide myself.

MASTER. Then you will be examined.

CHILD. Then I will tell a fib.

MASTER. But you must not tell fibs.

CHILD. Why must not I?

MASTER. Because it is naughty, etc.

Thus we go round the circle; and yet, if we go out of it, the child understands us no longer. Are not these very useful instructions, think you? I could be very curious to know what could be substituted in the place of this fine dialogue. Locke himself would certainly have been embarrassed had he been asked so puzzling a question. To distinguish between good and evil, to perceive the reasons on which our moral obligations are founded, is not the business, as it is not within the capacity, of a child.

Nature requires children to be children before they are men. By endeavouring to pervert this order, we produce forward fruits, that have neither maturity nor taste, and will not fail soon to wither or corrupt. Hence it is we have so many young professors and old children. Childhood hath its manner of seeing, perceiving, and thinking, peculiar to itself; nor is there any thing more absurd than our being anxious to substitute our own in its stead. I would as soon require an infant to be five feet high, as a boy to have judgment at ten years of age. In fact, of what use would reason be to

397

him at that age? Reason is given us as a check upon our power; a child has no need of such restraint.

. . . . .

Treat your pupil according to his years. Put him at first into his place, and keep him there so strictly, that he may never afterwards be tempted to go from it. Thus, before he may have learned what prudence is, he will have practised the most important of all its lessons. Never command him to do any thing in the world. Let him not even imagine you pretend to have any authority over him. Let him only be made sensible that he is weak, and you are strong; that, from your situation and his, he lies necessarily at your mercy: let him know, let him learn to perceive this circumstance; let him early feel on his aspiring crest the hard yoke nature hath imposed on man, the heavy yoke of necessity under which every finite being must bow; let him see that necessity in the nature and constitution of things, and not in the caprices[3] of mankind. The bridle of his restraint should be force, and not authority. As to doing those things from which he ought to abstain, forbid him not, but prevent him, without explanation or argument: whatever you indulge him in, grant it to his first request without solicitation or intreaty, and particularly without making any conditions. Grant with pleasure, and refuse with reluctance; but, I say again, let all your denials be irrevocable; let no importunity overcome your resolution; let the *no!* once pronounced, be as a brasen wall, against which when a child hath some few times exhausted his strength without making any impression, he will never attempt to overthrow it again.

. . . . .

. . . It is very strange, that, ever since mankind have taken it into their heads to trouble themselves so much about the education of children, they should never have thought of any other instruments to effect their purpose than those of emulation, jealousy, envy, pride, covetousness, and servile fear; all passions, the most dangerous, the most apt to ferment, and the most proper to corrupt the soul, even before the body is formed. With every premature instruction we instill into the head, we implant a vice in the bottom of the heart. Senseless preceptors, those, who think they work wonders, by making children actually vitious, in order to instruct

[3] We may be very certain that a child will think every injunction capricious that is contrary to its inclinations, and for which it sees not a reason. Now a child sees no manner of reason in any thing that contradicts its own humour.

398

them in the theory of virtue, and then gravely tell us, Such is man. Yes, such, indeed, is the man of your making.

Almost every method has been tried but one, and that the only one which can succeed, natural liberty duly regulated. No one ought to undertake the education of a child who cannot conduct him at pleasure, merely by the maxims of possibility and impossibility. The sphere of both being equally unknown to infancy, it may be extended or contracted as we please. A child may be equally excited or restrained, by the single plea of necessity, without murmuring: he may be rendered pliant and docile by the force of circumstance only, without ever giving occasion to sow the seeds of vice in his heart: for the passions will never be irritated so long as they must be exerted without effect. Give your pupil no kind of verbal instructions; he should receive none but from experience: inflict on him no kind of punishment, for he knows not what it is to be in fault: require him never to ask pardon, for he cannot offend you. As he is insensible of all moral obligation, he cannot do any thing morally evil, or that is deserving of punishment or reprimand.

. . . . .

Let us lay down as an incontestable maxim, That the first emotions of nature are always right: there is no original perversity in the human heart. I will venture to say, there is not a single vice to be found there, that one could not say how and which way it entered. The only passion natural to man is the love of himself, or self-love taken in an extensive sense. This passion considered in itself, or as relative to us, is good and useful; and, as it has no necessary relation to any one else, it is in that respect naturally indifferent: it becomes good or evil, therefore, from our application of it, and the several relations we give it. Till the guide of self-love, then, which is reason, appears, a child should do nothing merely because he is seen or heard, nothing from causes merely relative to others, but only those things which nature requires and infligates; and then he will never do wrong.

. . . . .

May I venture here to lay down the greatest, most important, and most useful rule of education? It is this, Not to gain time, but to lose it. The generality of readers will be so good as to excuse my paradoxes; there is an absolute necessity for them in making reflections: and, say what you will, I had rather be remarkable for hunt-

399

ing after a paradox, than for being misled by prejudice. The most critical interval of human life is that between the hour of our birth and twelve years of age. This is the time wherein vice and error take root, without our being possessed of any instrument to destroy them: and when the implement is found, they are so deeply grounded, that they are no longer to be eradicated. If children took a leap from their mother's breast, and at once arrived at the age of reason, the methods of education now usually taken with them would be very proper; but according to the progress of nature, they require those which are very different. We should not tamper with the mind, till it has acquired all its faculties: for it is impossible it should perceive the light we hold out to it while it is blind; or that it should pursue, over an immense plain of ideas, that route which reason hath so slightly traced as to be perceptible only to the sharpest sight.

The first part of education, therefore, ought to be purely negative. It consists, neither in teaching virtue nor truth; but in guarding the heart from vice, and the mind from error. If you could be content to do nothing yourself, and could prevent any thing being done by others; if you could bring up your pupil healthy and robust to the age of twelve years, without his being able to distinguish his right hand from his left, the eyes of his understanding would be open to reason at your first lesson; void both of habit and prejudice, his passions would not operate against your endeavours, and he would become, under proper instructions, the wisest of men. It is thus, by attempting nothing in the beginning, you might produce a prodigy of education.

Take the road directly opposite to that which is in use, and you will almost always do right. As we think it not enough children should be children, but it is expected they should be masters of arts; so fathers and preceptors think they can never have too many checks, corrections, reprimands, menaces, promises, instructions, fair speeches, and fine arguments. You will act wiser than all this, by being reasonable yourself, and never arguing with your child, particularly in striving to reconcile him to what he dislikes: for to use him to reason only upon disagreeable subjects, is the way to disgust him, and bring argument early into discredit with a mind incapable of understanding it. Exercise his corporeal organs, senses, and faculties, as much as you please; but keep his intellectual ones inactive as long as possible. Be cautious of all the sentiments he acquires previous to the judgment which should enable him to scrutinize them. Prevent or restrain all foreign impressions;

400

and, in order to hinder the rise of evil, be not in too great a hurry to instil good; for it is only such when the mind is enlightened by reason. Look upon every delay as an advantage; it is gaining a great deal, to advance without losing any thing: let the infancy of children therefore have time to ripen. In short, whatever instruction is necessary for them, take care not to give it them to-day, if it may be deferred without danger till to-morrow.

. . . . .

The first obligations we lie under, respect ourselves: our primary sentiments centre in our own existence; all our natural emotions, at first, relating to self-preservation. Hence, our first sense of justice arises not from what we owe to others, but from what is due from them to us: a circumstance which manifests another blunder in the common methods of education; wherein, by talking to children of their duties instead of their claims, we begin by telling them the reverse of what we ought to do, by endeavouring to inculcate what they cannot understand, and of course that in which they cannot be interested.

. . . . .

Forward, pratting children, usually make but ordinary men: I know no observation more certain and general than this. There is nothing more difficult than to distinguish, in children, between real stupidity and that apparent dullness which is the usual indication of strong intellects. It may appear strange, at first sight, that two such different extremes should be indicated by the same signs, and yet it is nevertheless what we ought to expect: for at an age when we have as yet acquired no true ideas, all difference between a child of genius and one that has none, is, that the latter admits only of false ideas of things; while the former, meeting with none but such, refuses to admit any: both therefore appear to be equally dull; the one because he has no capacity for the comprehension of things, and the other because the representations of things are not adapted to his capacity. The only means to distinguish between them depend on accident, which may offer to the latter some idea within his comprehension; whereas the former is always the same in all places and circumstances.

. . . . .

The apparent facility with which children seem to learn, operates greatly to their prejudice, and, though we do not observe it, is a

401

plain proof they learn nothing. The delicate texture of their brain reflects, like a mirrour, every object presented to them; but nothing penetrates the substance, or remains behind. A child retains the words, but the ideas accompanying them are reflected back again; those who hear him repeat, may understand what he means; but he himself knows nothing of the matter.

Although the memory and judgment are two faculties essentially different; yet the one cannot unfold itself without the other. Before a child arrives at years of understanding, he entertains not the ideas, but simply the images, of things; the difference between which consists in that such images are only the direct paintings of perceptible objects, and ideas are the notions of such objects determined by their respective relations to each other. A single image may subsist in the mind that is sensible of it; but every idea necessarily supposes the concomitance of others. To simple imagination, or the mere formation of images, nothing more is necessary than to have seen objects; but to conceive any thing about their existence, or to form ideas of them, it is required that we should be able to compare them. Our sensations are merely passive, whereas our perceptions, or the ideas formed in consequence of those sensations, rise from an active principle capable of judging of them. This will be hereafter demonstrated.

I say, therefore, that children, being incapable of forming a judgment of things, have no real memory. They retain, it is true, sounds, figures, and sensations; but seldom ideas, and still more seldom the connections between them. In objecting to what I advance, that children may be taught geometrical elements, this instance may be supposed to make against me; on the contrary, however, it makes for me. It may be shewn, that, so far are they from being capable of reasoning of themselves, they are incapable of retaining the arguments of others; for, trace these little geometricians in the solving any problem, and you will see they retain only the exact impression of the figure, and the terms of the demonstration. On the least unforeseen objection, they are quite at a loss; vary the figure, and they are totally disconcerted; all their knowledge lies clearly in their sensations, and has not penetrated into the understanding. Their memory itself, however retentive, is as little perfect as their other faculties; as they are almost always obliged to learn, when they are grown up, the meaning of the words they got by rote in their childhood.

I am far, however, from thinking that children are capable of no

402

kind of reasoning.[4] On the contrary, I observe that they reason very well as to things they are acquainted with, and which regard their present and obvious interest. But it is in the depth of their knowledge we deceive ourselves, in attributing to them what they have not, and setting them to reason about things they cannot comprehend. We are still farther deceived, in wanting to render them attentive to such considerations as cannot in any degree affect them, such as their future interest, their happiness when they come to be men, the esteem in which they will be held when grown up, and so forth; all which pleas, when made use of to beings void of all foresight, absolutely signify nothing, nor can serve to any good purpose. Now, all the studies imposed on these poor unfortunates, tend to such objects as are entirely foreign to their minds. Judge then of the attention they are like to bestow on them.

· · · · ·

That kind of memory which is possessed by children, may, without setting them to study books, be fully employed. Every thing they see, or hear, appears striking, and they commit it to memory. A child keeps in his mind a register of the actions and conversation of those who are about him; every scene he is engaged in, is a book, from which he insensibly enriches his memory, treasuring up his store till time shall ripen his judgement, and turn it to profit. It is in the choice of these scenes and objects, in the care of presenting those constantly to his view which he ought to be familiar with, and in hiding from him such as are improper, that consists the true art of cultivating this primary faculty of a child. By such means also it is that we should endeavour to form that magazine of knowledge

[4] I have an hundred times, while I have been writing, made this reflection, viz. That it is impossible, in a long work, to give always precisely the same meaning to the same words. There is no language rich and copious enough, to furnish as many terms, turns, and phrases, as our ideas may require modifications. The method of defining all our terms, and constantly substituting the definition in the place of what is defined, is very accurate; but it is impracticable; for how shall we avoid running round the circle? Definitions might be very useful, did we not make use of words in their construction. I am persuaded, however, a writer may be perspicuous and clear, notwithstanding the poverty of our language; not, indeed, by taking words always in the same acceptation; but in so managing the matter, that every time a word is made use of, the acceptation given it shall be determined by the sense of the period. In some places, I say, children are incapable of reasoning; in others again, I make them reason very acutely; and yet I do not think I am contradictory in my sentiments; tho' I cannot deny that I frequently contradict myself in my expressions.

which should serve for his education in youth, and to regulate his conduct afterwards. This method, it is true, is not productive of little prodigies of learning, nor doth it tend to enhance the characters of the governess or preceptor; but it is the way to form robust and judicious men, persons sound in body and mind, who, without being admired while children, know how to make themselves respected when grown up.

Emilius shall never be set to learn any thing by heart, not even fables, not even the fables of Fontaine, simple and beautiful as they are; for the words of a fable are no more the fable itself, than those of a history are the history. How is it possible men can be so blind as to call fables the moral lectures for children, without reflecting that the apologue, in amusing, only deceives them; and that, seduced by the charms of falsehood, the truth couched underneath it escapes their notice? Yet so it is; and the means which are thus taken to render instruction agreeable prevents their profiting by it. Fables may instruct grown persons, but the naked truth should ever be presented to children: for if we once spread over it a veil, they will not take the trouble to draw it aside in order to look at it.

Children universally read the fables of Fontaine, and yet there is not one who understands them. It would be still worse, however, if they did understand them; for the moral is so complicated and disproportionate to their capacities, that it would rather induce them to vice than virtue. Here, again, you will say, I am at my paradoxes: be it so; let us see whether what I affirm be not true.

I advance, that a child does not comprehend the fables which he gets by rote; because, whatever pains we take to render them simple, the instruction we would deduce from them is attended with other ideas above his capacity; and because that even the poetic turn given them, in order to make them the more easily remembered, makes them, at the same time, the less easily comprehended; so that they are rendered entertaining at the expense of perspicuity. Not to mention many of these fables that are totally unintelligible and useless to children, and which nevertheless are indiscreetly taught them because they are found mixed with the rest, we shall confine ourselves to those which the author appears to have written expressly for children.

It has been made a matter of great importance, to find out the best method of teaching children to read; to this end cards and other implements have been invented, so various and numerous, that they made the nursery resemble the workshop of a printer. Mr. Locke would have a child taught to read by means of letters carved on

404

dice. Is not this an excellent invention! A more certain method than any of these, and that which is nevertheless always neglected, is to excite in children a desire to learn. Give a child this desire, and do as you will with your cards and dice; any method will then be sufficient.

The grand motive, indeed the only one that is certain and effectual, is present interest. Émile sometimes receives written invitations from his father, mother, and other friends, to dinner, to go on a party of pleasure, or to see some public entertainment. These invitations are short, plain, precise, and well written. When received, it is necessary for him to find somebody to read them to him: such a person is not always at hand, or complaisant enough to comply with his request. Thus the opportunity is lost: the billet, indeed, is read to him afterwards, but then it is too late to obey the summons. How ardently must he wish on such an occasion to be able to read himself! He receives others, equally short and interesting: he sets immediately about deciphering them; sometimes receiving assistance, and at others denied it. By dint of study, he at length hammers out that he is invited to go to-morrow to eat cream; but where or with whom he cannot discover. How many efforts will he not make to find out the rest: Émile will learn to read by such means as these, without standing in need of horn-books, cards, or dice. I might here speak of teaching him to write; but I am ashamed of descending to such trifling objects in a treatise on education.

. . . . . .

I am teaching the young preceptor a very difficult art; that of instructing without precepts, and of doing every thing in the way of education by doing nothing. This art, I must confess, is not adapted to your age or views; it is not calculated to make an immediate display of your talents, nor to recommend you to the generality of fathers: it is the only one, however, in which you can succeed in the education of your pupil; you will never accomplish your design of forming sensible men, unless you begin by making playful children. This was the method of education among the Spartans: instead of tying down their sons to their books, they were taught to look out sharp for their dinner. Were they the greater blockheads for this when they grew up? The force and keenness of their repartees are, on the contrary, well known. Formed for universal conquest, they triumphed over their enemies in every kind of warfare; the talkative

405

Athenians being equally afraid both of their tongues and their swords.

. . . . .

To exercise any art, we must begin by procuring the necessary implements; and to employ those implements to any good purpose, they should be made sufficiently solid for their intended use. To learn to think, therefore, we should exercise our limbs, and our organs, which are the instruments of our intelligence; and in order to make the best use of those instruments, it is necessary that the body furnishing them should be robust and hearty. Thus, so far is a sound understanding from being independent on the body, that it is owing to a good constitution that the operations of the mind are effected with facility and certainty.

. . . . .

When a child plays at battle-door and shuttle-cock, he exercises his eye and arm; when he whips a top, he acquires fresh strength by exerting what he possesses: but in this exercise what does he learn? I have often asked, why children are not made to apply themselves to many of those games of skill and dexterity which are practised by men, such as tennis, fives, and billiards, or to play on musical instruments? To this question it hath been constantly replied, that some of these diversions are above their capacity, and that their limbs and organs are not sufficiently formed for the others. These reasons, however, appear to me very unsatisfactory; a child, it is true, has not the stature of a man, and yet he wears cloaths made in the same form and manner. I do not mean that he should play with the same mass, or at a billiard-table three feet high; that he should make one in a party at our tennis-courts, or that we should load his little arm with our heavy rackets: he might exercise himself, how-ever, in a saloon, where means should be previously taken to secure the windows; he might at first make use of soft balls, his rackets might be made of light wood, afterwards of parchment, and at length of cat-gut, as he increased in strength. You prefer the shut-tlecock, because it is less fatiguing and dangerous. For both these reasons, however, you are in the wrong. This is mere womens play: but you will find no woman who is not frightened at the motion of a tennis-ball. Their white and delicate skins are not adapted to bruises, nor are their complexions and features to be marred by contusions. But men, destined to be hardy and vigorous, must not expect to become such without peril; and what defence can we be

406

supposed capable of making, if we are never attacked? We always indulge ourselves in those amusements at which we may remain inexpert without danger; a shuttlecock, in falling, hurts nobody: but nothing renders the arms so active as the necessity of securing the head, nor the sight so quick as that of preserving the eyes. To spring from one side of a tennis-court to the other; to judge of the rebounding of a ball while it is in the air; and to return it with a sure and steady arm; these are diversions less adapted to the amusement of grown persons, than proper to form them in youth.

. . . . .

BOOK III

Although, till the age of puberty, the whole course of life be one continued series of imbecility, there is a certain period in this first age of life, in which the progress of his passions exceeding that of his necessities, the growing animal, though absolutely weak, becomes relatively strong. His wants not being wholly displayed, his actual abilities are more than sufficient to provide for those which he really feels. Considered as a man, he is very weak; but as a child, he is abundantly strong. Whence proceeds the weakness of man? From the disproportion he finds between his faculties and his desires. It is our passions that render us feeble; because, to gratify them, requires greater powers than nature has furnished us with. Diminish, then, the number, check the extravagance, of our desires, and you increase your powers of gratification. He who can compass more than he requires, hath ability to spare, and is certainly a powerful being. Here begins the third stage of infancy, of which I am now about to treat; it being that state of childhood which approaches nearly to puberty, without being quite arrived at the term.

At twelve or thirteen years of age, the faculties of a child display themselves more rapidly than his wants. The most impetuous, the most coercive of all physical necessities he hath not yet experienced. The very organs that provide for its gratification are as yet imperfect, and seem to wait the exertion of the will to capacitate them for action. Unaffected by the inclemency of the weather, or the change of seasons, his natural heat supplies the artificial warmth of apparel, and his keenness of appetite the provocatives of fauces. At his age, whatever is but nourishing, is good; if he be drowsy, he stretches himself on the ground, and falls asleep. Whatever he hath occasion for, is within his reach; he craves not after imaginary

407

dainties; he feels no disgust from prepossession. His desires confined within the sphere of his abilities, he is not only capable of providing for himself, but possess superfluous faculties for which he has no use. This, however, is the only time, during life, in which he will be in such a situation.

. . . . .

The earth is the island on which mankind are cast, and the most striking objects of their observation is the sun. As soon as our ideas begin to extend beyond ourselves, our attention will therefore naturally be ingrossed between two such interesting subjects. Hence the philosophy of almost every savage nation is confined solely to the imaginary divisions of the earth, and the divinity of the sun. 'What an excursion!' cries the reader. 'We were but just now employed about objects that immediately surround us, and we are now traversing the globe, and soaring to the distant extremities of the universe.' This excursion, however, is the simple effect of the progress of our faculties, and the bent of our understanding. During our infant state of weakness and incapacity, all our thoughts, influenced by self-preservation, are confined within ourselves. On the contrary, in a more advanced age, as our abilities increase, the desire of improving our existence carries us out of ourselves, and our ideas extend to their utmost limits. As the intellectual world, however, is as yet unknown to us, our thoughts cannot extend farther than we can see; but our comprehension dilates itself with the bounds of space.

Let us convert our sensations into ideas; but let us not fly at once from sensible to intellectual objects. It is by a due and rational attention to the former we can only attain the latter. In the first operations of the understanding, let our senses then always be our guide, the world our only book, and facts our sole preceptors. Children, when taught to read, learn that only; they never think; they gain no information; all their learning consists in words.

Direct the attention of your pupil to the phaenomena of nature, and you will soon awaken his curiosity; but to keep that curiosity alive, you must be in no haste to satisfy it. Put questions to him adapted to his capacity, and leave him to resolve them. Let him take nothing on trust from his preceptor, but on his own comprehension and conviction: he should not learn, but invent the sciences. If ever you substitute authority in the place of argument, he will reason no longer; he will be ever afterwards bandied like a shuttlecock between the opinions of others.

408

ROUSSEAU

. . . Talk not to children in a language they do not comprehend; make use of no pompous descriptions, no flowers of speech, no tropes and figures, no poetry; taste and sentiment are at present quite out of the question: simplicity, gravity, and precision are all that are yet required; the time will come but too soon when we must assume a different style.

A pupil educated agreeable to these maxims, and accustomed to receive no assistance till he has discovered his own inabilities, will examine every new object with a long and silent attention. He will be thoughtful without asking questions. Content yourself, therefore, with presenting proper objects opportunely to his notice, and when you see they have sufficiently excited his curiosity, drop from leading laconic questions, which may put him in the way of discovering the truth.

. . . . .

To accustom a child to give attention to objects, and to make sensible truths appear striking to his imagination, it is necessary to keep him some time in suspense before they are explained or discovered to him. If he should not sufficiently comprehend the nature of the present question by the means proposed, it may be rendered still more obvious by diversifying the terms of it. If he cannot comprehend in what manner the sun proceeds from its setting to its rising, he knows at least how it proceeds from its rising to its setting: he hath ocular information of this. Explain the first question, then, by the second; and if your pupil be not extremely dull indeed, the analogy is too obvious to escape him.

Such is our first lecture in cosmography.

As we proceed slowly from one sensible idea to another, making ourselves familiarly acquainted with each as we go on, and as our pupil's attention is never required upon compulsion, the distance will be very considerable, from the object of this first lesson, to the knowledge of the sun's course and the figure of the earth: but as the apparent motion of all the heavenly bodies depends on the same principle, and as the first observation naturally leads to all the rest, it requires less capacity, though more time, to proceed from the diurnal rotation of the earth to the calculation of an eclipse, than to acquire clear ideas of the phaenomenon of day and night.

. . . . .

When he asks a question, be your answer always calculated rather to keep alive than satisfy his curiosity; especially when you observe

409

he has a mind to trifle rather than be instructed. You ought to pay less regard to the terms of interrogation, than to his motives for enquiry. This conduct becomes of the greatest importance when a child begins to reason.

The sciences are connected together by a series of propositions, all dependent on some general and common principles, which are gradually displayed. The philosophers make use of these; with us they are as yet out of the question. There is another chain of reasoning, of a different construction, by which every particular object is connected to some other, and points out that which succeeds it. This order of succession, which, from our natural curiosity, keeps alive our attention, is generally made use of by grown persons, and is peculiarly adapted to children.

.   .   .   .   .

We acquire, without doubt, notions more clear and certain, of things we thus learn of ourselves, than of those we are taught by others. Another advantage also resulting from this method is, that we do not accustom ourselves to a servile submission to the authority of others; but, by exercising our reason, grow every day more ingenious in the discovery of the relations of things, in connecting our ideas, and in the contrivance of machines; whereas, by adopting those which are put into our hands, our invention grows dull and indifferent, as the man who never dresses himself, but is served in every thing by his servants, and drawn about every where by his horses, loses by degrees the activity and use of his limbs. Boileau boasted that he had taught Racine to rhyme with much difficulty: among the many admirable methods taken to abridge the study of the sciences, we are in great want of one to make us learn them with difficulty.

The most obvious advantage of these slow and laborious researches, is to preserve, in the cultivation of speculative studies, the activity of the body; to preserve the suppleness of the limbs, and to be always busied in some manual operation, or employment, of use to mankind. The diversity of instruments, invented to direct us in our experiments, and make up for the deficiency of our organs of sense, makes us neglect the exercise of the latter. A theodolite dispenses with our estimating the extent of angles; the eye, which is capable of measuring distances with great exactness, gives up the task to the chain; the steel-yard excuses me from judging of the weight of any thing by poising it in my hand. Thus the more ingenious and accurate our instruments, the more unsusceptible and

410

inexpert become our organs: by assembling a heap of machinery about us, we find afterwards none in ourselves.

But when we set about the construction of these machines ourselves, and employ therein that sagacity and address which are required to do without them, we lose nothing: on the contrary, we gain every thing; and, by adding the knowledge of art to nature, become more ingenious without being less dexterous. If, instead of keeping a boy poring over books, I employ him in a work-shop, his hands will be busied to the improvement of his understanding; he will become a philosopher while he thinks himself only an artisan. In short, this practice hath other uses which I shall speak of hereafter, and show in what manner these philosophical amusements lead to the exercise of the proper functions of a man.

I have already observed, that the mere speculative part of science is by no means adapted to children, even when they approach adolescency; it is proper, nevertheless, though you do not enter with them too profoundly into the depth of physical theory, to connect their experiments by some chain of deduction, that they may arrange them in some order in their minds, for the sake of remembering them: for it is very difficult to retain separate and independent facts and conclusions long in the memory, without some leading clue for occasional recollection.

In your researches into the laws of nature, begin always with the most common and obvious phænomena; accustoming your pupil to look upon them always as mere facts.

.   .   .   .   .

As soon as we are so far advanced as to give our pupil an idea of the word *useful,* we have attained a considerable influence over his future conduct; this term being very striking, provided the sense annexed to it be adapted to his years, and he see clearly its relation to his present welfare. Ordinary children are not affected by this term, because no care has been taken to affix to it an idea conformable to their understandings, and because others taking upon them to provide for them what is useful, they have no need to think of it themselves, and therefore remain ignorant of the meaning of utility.

What is the use of that? shall, for the future, be the determinate question between my pupil and me, on all occasions. On my part, I shall infallibly make use of it in answer to all his interrogatories; which may serve as a check to that multiplicity of silly, troublesome questions, with which children are incessantly teazing those about them, more for the sake of indulging themselves in a kind of

411

imperiousness, than out of a desire of information. The child who is taught, as the most important lesson, to know nothing but what is useful to him, will interrogate with the views of a Socrates: he will not put a question, without having an answer ready to that which he knows will be put to him before his own is resolved.

.   .   .   .   .

Never point out any thing to a child which is beyond his views. While he is a stranger to the relations and duties of humanity, as you cannot raise his comprehension to the state of manhood, you should bring down the state of manhood to a level with his capacity. In projecting what may be useful to him hereafter, speak to him directly only of what is apparently useful to him at present. Beware, also, in general, of making comparisons between your pupil and other children; let him have no rival, no competitor, not even in his corporeal exercises, as soon as he begins to reason. I had much rather he should not learn at all whatever must be taught him by means of vanity or jealousy. I would content myself, in this respect, with remarking his annual progress, and comparing his situation and exploits in the present year with those of the past. I would say to him, You are grown so much since such a time; here is the ditch you leaped, the weight you lifted, the distance you threw a stone, so far you run without fetching breath; let us see what you can do more at present. Thus would I excite him to emulation, without making him jealous or envious of a rival: he would be desirous indeed to excel himself, and so he ought to be; I see no inconvenience in this kind of emulation.

I hate books; they only teach people to talk about what they do not understand. It is said that Hermes engraved the elements of the sciences on columns, to secure his discoveries from being lost in the time of a general deluge. Had he imprinted them on the minds of men, they had been better preservd by tradition. The organs of the memory, duly prepared, are the monuments on which human science would be most indelibly engraven.

Is there no expedient to be thought of, to collect the various instructions, scattered up and down in so many voluminous tomes? to unite them under one general head, which may be easy to comprehend, interesting to pursue, and which may serve as a *stimulus* even to children of this age? If one could but conceive a situation, in which all the natural wants of man would be displayed in a manner adapted to the understanding of a child, and wherein the means of satisfying those wants are gradually discovered with the same

412

ease and simplicity, it would be in a just and lively description of such a state that we should first exercise his imagination.

I see the imagination of the philosopher already take fire. Impetuous genius! give yourself no trouble; such a situation is already discovered; it is already described, and I may say, without any impeachment to your talents, much better than you could describe it yourself; at least with more exactness and simplicity. Since we must have books, there is one already, which, in my opinion, affords a complete treatise on natural education. This book shall be the first Émile shall read. In this, indeed, will, for a long time, consist his whole library, and it will always hold a distinguished place among others. It will afford us the text, to which all our conversations on the objects of natural science will serve only as a comment. It will serve as our guide during our progress to a state of reason; and will even afterwards give us constant pleasure, unless our taste be totally vitiated. You ask impatiently, what is the title of this wonderful book? Is it Aristotle, Pliny, or Buffon? No. It is Robinson Crusoe.

Robinson Crusoe, cast ashore on a desolate island, destitute of human assistance, and of mechanical implements, providing, nevertheless, for his subsistence, for self-preservation, and even procuring for himself a kind of competency. In these circumstances, I say, there cannot be an object more interesting to persons of every age; and there are a thousand ways to render it agreeable to children. Thus, you see, I have realized that desert island, which I at first made use of only by way of comparison. Such a situation, I confess, is very different from that of man in a state of society. Very probably it will never be that of Émile; but it is from such a state he ought to learn to estimate others. The most certain method for him to raise himself above vulgar prejudices, and to form his judgment on the actual relations of things, is to take on himself the character of such a solitary adventurer, and to judge of every thing about him, as a man in such circumstances would, by its real utility. This romance, beginning with his shipwreck on the island, and ending with the arrival of the vessel that brought him away, would, if cleared of its rubbish, afford Émile, during the period we are now treating of, at once both instruction and amusement. I would have him indeed personate the hero of the tale, and be entirely taken up with his castle, his goats, and his plantations; he should make himself minutely acquainted, not from books, but circumstances, with every thing requisite for a man in such a situation. He should affect even his dress, wear a coat of skins, a great hat, a large hanger; in short, he should be entirely equipped in his grotesque manner, even with his umbrello, though he would have no occasion for it. I would have him, when at a loss about the measures necessary to be taken for his provision or security upon this or the other occasion, examine the conduct of his hero; he should see if he omitted nothing, or if any thing better could be substituted in the room of what was actually done; and, on the discovery of any mistake in Robinson, should amend it in a similar case himself: for I doubt not but he will form a project of going to make a like settlement. Not unlike to this were those ancient castles in Spain, in that happy age, when the height of human felicity consisted in the enjoyment of liberty and the necessaries of life.

What opportunities of instruction would such an amusement afford an able preceptor, who should project it only with a view to that end? The pupil, eager to furnish a magazine for his island, would be more ready to learn than his tutor to teach him. He would be solicitous to know every thing that is useful, and nothing else: you would in such a case have no more occasion to direct, but only to restrain him. Let us hasten, therefore, to establish him in this imaginary isle, since to this he confines his present happiness: for the time will now soon come, in which, if he is desirous of life, it is not to live alone; and in which even a man *Friday*, the want of whom does not now affect him, would not be long satisfactory.

The practice of simple manual arts, to the exercise of which the abilities of the individual are equal, leads to the invention of the arts of industry, the exercise of which requires the concurrence of many. The former may be practised by hermits and savages; but the latter can be exercised only in a state of society, and render that state necessary. While man is subject only to the calls of physical necessity, he is capable of satisfying them himself; but, by the introduction of superfluous wants, the joint concern and distribution of labour become indispensable: for though a man by his own labour, when alone, procures only subsistence for an individual; yet an hundred men working in concert, will easily procure, in the same time, subsistence for double the number. As soon, therefore, as one part of mankind take upon themselves to live idle, it becomes necessary that the concurrent labour of numbers should supply the place of those who live without work.

Your greatest care should be, to keep from your pupil the notions of those social relations which he is not in a capacity to comprehend; but when the connection of his ideas obliges you to speak of the mutual dependence of mankind, instead of presenting him at first the moral side of the question, divert his attention as much as

414

possible to industry and the mechanic arts, which render men useful to one another. In going about with him to the workshops of various artisans, never let him see any thing performed without lending a hand to the work, nor come out of the shop without perfectly understanding the reason of what he observes there. To this end you should work yourself, and in every thing set him an example. To make him a master, be you in every thing the apprentice; and reflect that he will learn more by one hour of manual labour, than he will retain from a whole day's verbal instructions.

The different arts are entitled to various proportions of public esteem, and that in an inverse ratio to their real use. This esteem is directly as their inutility, and so it politically ought to be. The most useful arts are those which are the worst paid for, or least rewarded; because the number of workmen is proportioned to the wants of the whole society, and the labour the poor must purchase must necessarily be at a low price. On the contrary, those important artisans, who, by way of distinction, are termed artists, and are employed only in the service of the rich and idle, set an arbitrary price on their workmanship; and as the excellence of their baubles is mere matter of opinion, their high price constitutes great part of their merit, and they are esteemed in proportion to what they cost. The value thus set upon them is not on account of any use they are of to the rich, but because they are too costly to be purchased by the poor. *Nolo habere bona nisi quibus populus inviderit* (Petron).

What will become of your pupils, if you permit them to adopt this ridiculous prejudice, if you encourage it yourself, or see them, for example, enter with more respect the shop of a jeweller than that of a locksmith? What a judgement will they form of the real merit of the arts, and the intrinsic value of things, when they see whim and caprice universally opposed to real utility, and find the more a thing costs, the less it is worth? If ever such ideas as these take root in their minds, you as well give up at once the remaining part of their education; they will, in spite of all you can do, be educated like the rest of the world, and you will have taken, for fourteen years past, all your trouble for nothing.

.   .   .   .   .

My child learn a trade! make my son a mechanic! consider, Sir, what you advise.—I do, Madam, I consider this matter better than you, who would reduce your child to the necessity of being a lord, a marquis, or a prince, or perhaps one day or other to be less than

415

nothing. I am desirous of investing him with a title that cannot be taken from him, that will in all times and places command respect; and, I can tell you, whatever you may think of it, he will have fewer equals in this rank than in that he may derive from you.

The letter destroys, and the spirit maketh alive. I would not have him learn a trade, merely for the sake of knowing how to exercise it, but that he may overcome the prejudices usually conceived against it. You will never be reduced, you say, to work for your bread. So much the worse for you; I say, so much the worse. But, no matter; if you labour not through necessity, do it for reputation. Stoop to the situation of an artisan, that you may raise yourself above your own. To make fortune subservient to your will, you must begin by rendering yourself independent. To triumph in the opinion of the world, you must begin by despising that opinion.

Remember, I do not advise you to acquire a talent, but a trade; a mechanical art, in the exercise of which the hands are more employed than the head; an art by which you will never get a fortune, but may be enabled to live without one.

· · · ·

All things duly considered, the trade I should like best my pupil should have a taste for, is that of a joiner. This is neat, useful, and may be carried on within doors: it is sufficiently laborious to keep the body in exercise, and requires both diligence and dexterity: at the same time, taste and elegance are not excluded from being displayed on the form and contrivance of the work.

If it should so happen, indeed, that your pupil has a natural turn for the speculative sciences, I should not blame you for teaching him a mechanic art conformable to his inclinations; let him learn, for example, to design and construct mathematical instruments, quadrants, telescopes, and the like.

When Émile learns a trade, I also will learn it with him; for I am convinced he will never learn, as should be, what we do not learn together. We will, therefore, both serve an apprenticeship; not affecting to be treated as gentlemen, but as real apprentices who are not trifling with a profession: nay, why should we not be so in reality? Czar Peter worked as a common ship-carpenter in the yard, and served as a drummer in his own troops: do you think that prince was not your equal, at least either in birth or merit? The reader will observe, I do not ask Émile this question, but put it to every one, of whatever rank he may happen to be.

416

If I have hitherto made myself understood, the reader will perceive, that, while I have accustomed my pupil to corporeal exercise and manual labour, I have given him insensibly a taste for reflection and meditation; in order to counterbalance that indolence which would be the natural result of his indifference for the opinions of mankind and the tranquility of his passions, it is necessary that he work like a peasant, and think like a philosopher, lest he become as idle as a savage. The great secret of education is, to make the exercises of the body and the mind serve as a relaxation to each other.

. . . . . .

BOOK IV

. . . Our passions are the principal instruments of our preservation: therefore, to endeavour to destroy them is equally vain and absurd; it is to find fault with nature, to attempt to reform the works of God. Should the Almighty require man to annihilate those passions which he had given him, he would not know his own mind, he would contradict himself: but the Almighty never gave such a ridiculous command; the heart of man has received no such injunction; and whatever is required of him, is not made known to him by the mouth of another, God himself imprints it on his heart.

To suppress the passions, in my opinion, is almost as absurd as entirely to destroy them; whoever imagines this to have been my intention, has grossly mistaken my meaning.

But because it is in the nature of man to have passions, is it therefore rational to conclude, that all the passions which we feel within ourselves, and which we perceive in others, are natural? Their source indeed is natural, but that source is increased by a thousand adventitious streams; it is a great river continually augmenting, in which it would be very difficult to find one drop of the original spring. Our natural passions are extremely limited; they are, however, the instruments of our liberty, and tend to our preservation. Such passions as are prejudicial, and by which our reason is subdued, spring from some other source; nature does not give them to us, we adopt them to the prejudice of nature.

. . . . . .

If the period when man becomes conscious of his sex is as much determined by education as by nature, consequently this period

417

may be accelerated or retarded: and if the body gains or loses solidity, in proportion as this progress is forwarded or delayed, it follows, that the longer it is retarded the stronger we grow. I am now speaking of mere physical effects; we shall soon perceive that there are other consequences.

By these reflections I am enabled to solve this question, so frequently the subject of debate, Whether it would be proper to gratify the curiosity of children betimes, or to put them off with some little piece of modest deceit? In my opinion, both should be avoided. First, as we ourselves are the cause of this curiosity, we should endeavour to prevent it; and secondly, when there is no necessity for resolving their questions, you are not obliged to deceive them. You had much better impose silence, than answer a child with a lie: he will not be surprised at such a command, if he has been used to submit in matters of indifference. In short, if you chuse to reply, let your answer be plain, without mystery, without embarrassment, and without a smile. There is much less danger in satisfying, than in exciting the curiosity of children.

Let your answers be always concise, serious, and determined, without seeming to hesitate. It is needless to add, that they should be strictly true; one cannot teach children the danger of telling lies to men, without perceiving the greater danger of deceiving children. A single falsehood averred by the master to his pupil, will for ever destroy the fruits of education.

A total ignorance of certain things were perhaps the most to be wished; but they should learn betimes what it is impossible always to conceal from them. Either their curiosity should not be at all excited, or it should be satisfied before the time of danger. Your conduct with regard to your pupil greatly depends on his particular situation, the people by whom he is surrounded, and many other circumstances. It is of importance to leave nothing to chance; and if you are not positively certain that you can keep him ignorant of the difference of sex till the age of sixteen, be careful to let him know it before the age of ten.

I cannot approve of speaking to children in a language too refined, nor of palpable circumlocution only to avoid calling things by their proper names. Virtuous innocence knows no disguise; but an imagination polluted by vice, renders the ear delicate, and obliges us to a continual refinement of expression. Mere words can be of no consequence; lascivious ideas are what we should guard against.

Though modesty is natural to the human species, yet children have it not from nature. A sense of shame proceeds only from the

418

knowledge of evil; and how can children who neither have, nor ought to have this knowledge, shew its effects? To read them lectures on shame and decency, is to teach them that there are things shameful and immodest; it is inspiring them with a secret desire of knowing these things. Sooner or later they arrive at this knowledge; and the first spark which catches the imagination, is sure to set the passions in a flame. Whoever blushes, is already culpable; real innocence can never be ashamed.

. . . . .

The first sentiment of which a youth, carefully educated, is susceptible, is not love, but friendship. The first act of his youthful imagination is to inform him that there are beings similar to himself, and the species affects him before the sex. Another advantage arising from prolonging his innocence is, that it enables us, by means of his growing sensibility, to sow the first seeds of humanity in his heart: an advantage of infinite importance, because it is the only time of his life when this care will be attended with equal success.

. . . . .

Émile, having bestowed little reflection on sensible beings, will be some time before he has my idea of suffering and death. Lamentation and cries will gradually begin to excite his compassion; he will turn away his eyes at the sight of blood; the convulsions of an expiring animal will create in him a kind of agony, before he is sensible whence these emotions proceed. Had he continued indeed in a state of barbarity, totally uncultivated, he would have known no such feelings; if he had been farther instructed, he would have known their source; he has compared ideas too often to have no feelings, but not sufficiently to conceive what they are.

Hence proceeds compassion, the first relative sentiment which touches the human heart, according to the order of nature. A child, before he can be sensible of pity, must know that there are beings like himself who are capable of feeling the same pain which he has already experienced. In short, how should we feel compassion, if not by being transported out of ourselves, and uniting our own persons, in imagination, to that of the suffering animal, by quitting, if I may so say, our own being for his? We suffer only in proportion as we think he suffers; it is not in ourselves, but in him that we suffer: therefore our sensibility does not commence till the imagination warms, and begins to carry us out of ourselves.

419

Our instructors complain, that the natural fire of this age renders youth ungovernable. Very true; but is it not entirely their own fault? Can they be ignorant, that when they have once suffered this fire to make its way through the senses, it is not in their power to divert its course? Will the tedious, frigid sermons of a pedant, efface from the mind of his pupil the idea of pleasure which he has conceived? Will they banish from his heart the desires which torment him? Will they quench the ardor of a flame of which he already knows the use? Will he not be enraged at those obstacles which oppose the only happiness of which he has any idea? and in the severe law prescribed without explanation, what can he discover except the caprice and hatred of a man who chuses to torment him? Is it therefore wonderful that he should oppose and hate the pedagogue in his turn?

It is easy to conceive, that, by relaxing his severity, a tutor may render himself less disagreeable to his pupil, and yet preserve an apparent authority: but I cannot perceive the use of that authority which serves only to foment the vices which it ought to repress; it is much the same as if a rider, in order to tame an unruly horse, were to leap him down a precipice.

This fire of youth, so far from being an obstacle in his education, is the proper instrument of its accomplishment; it is that which gives you an advantage over the heart of your pupil, when he ceases to be less powerful than yourself. His first affections are the reigns with which you should direct all his motions. He was before at liberty; but now he is enslaved. Whilst he was incapable of affection, he was dependent only on himself and his necessities; but the moment he loves, he depends on his attachments. Thus are formed the first bonds which unite him to his species; but we are not to suppose that his new born sensibility will be universal, or that he will conceive any meaning in the word *mankind*. No; that sensibility will be first confined to his equals; and his equals are those only with whom he is acquainted; those whom custom has rendered dear to him, or useful; those in whom he perceives a similitude of ideas and sensation; those who are exposed to the pains, and are sensible of the pleasures, which he has experienced; in a word, those in whom the manifest identity of nature increases his disposition to self-love. It is not till after having cultivated his disposition in a thousand forms, after much reflection on his own sentiments as well as those of others, that he will be able to generalize his notions under the abstract idea of humanity, and add to his particular affections those which are to unite him to the whole species.

420

In becoming capable of attachment, he becomes sensible of it in others,[5] and therefore attentive to the signs of this attachment. Thus you see what a new empire you acquire over him; you enslave his heart before he is aware of it. What must be his sensations, when, turning his eyes upon himself, he discovers the services you have done for him; when he compares himself with other young people of his own age, and you with other tutors? I say, when he discovers, for let it never be urged: if you once hint the obligation, from that instant he will cease to perceive it. If you exact obedience in return for your services, he will suspect that he has been deceived; he will conclude, that, under pretence of serving him, you have bound him in a contract to which he never consented. In vain you will urge, that what you exact is entirely for his own good; it is sufficient that it is exacted, and that in return for what was done without his consent.

When an unhappy wretch accepts a shilling, supposing it to be a gift, and afterwards finds himself to be enlisted, do we not exclaim against the injustice? And are you not equally unjust to demand a return for obligations which your pupil never accepted?

Ingratitude would be more rare, if benefits upon usury were less common. Nothing can be more natural than to love those who do us service. The heart of man is self-interested, but never ungrateful; and the obliged are less to be charged with ingratitude than their benefactors with self-interest. If you sell me your favours, let us settle the price; but if you pretend to give, and afterwards expect to make terms with me, you are guilty of fraud; it is their being given *gratis* which renders them inestimable. The heart will receive laws only from itself; by endeavouring to enslave it you give it liberty, and by leaving it at liberty it becomes your slave.

. . . . .

History is generally defective in recording only those facts which are rendered conspicuous by name, place, or date; but the slow progressive causes of those facts, not being thus distinguished, remain for ever unknown. How frequently do we find a battle lost or won, mentioned as the cause of a revolution which was become inevitable before the battle was fought? War is generally nothing

---

[5] Attachment may exist without a return, but friendship cannot; the latter is an exchange, a contract, like any other only more sacred. The word *friendship* has no *correlative*. Every man who is not the friend of his friend, is doubtless a cheat; for friendship can only be obtained by friendship, either real or apparent.

more than a manifestation of events already determined by moral causes, of which historians are ignorant.

The spirit of philosophy has, in like manner, infected many of the writers in this age; but I am in doubt whether truth gains any thing by their labours. A madness for system having got possession of them all, they never endeavour to see things as they really are, but as they best agree with their favourite hypotheses.

To these reflections we may add, that history is a representation of actions rather than of men, who are shown only at certain intervals, in their vestments of parade: we see man only in public life, after he has put himself in a proper position for being viewed. History follows him not into his house, into his closet, among his family and friends: it paints him only when he makes his appearance; it exhibits his dress, and not his person.

I should rather chuse to begin the study of the human heart by reading the lives of particular men; for there it is impossible for the hero to conceal himself a moment. The biographer pursues him into his most secret recesses, and exposes him to the piercing eye of the spectator; he is best known when he believes himself most concealed. "I like," says Montaigne, "those biographers who give us "the history of counsels, rather than events; who shew us what "passes within, rather than without: therefore Plutarch is the writer "after my own heart."

. . . . .

I foresee how much my readers will be surprised to find I have attended my pupil throughout the whole first age of life, without once speaking to him of religion. He hardly knows at fifteen years of age whether or not he hath a soul, and perhaps it will not be time to inform him of it when he is eighteen; for, if he learns it too soon, he runs a risk of never knowing it at all.

If I were to design a picture of the most deplorable stupidity, I would draw a pedant teaching children their catechism: and were I resolved to crack the brain of a child, I would oblige him to explain what he said when he repeated his catechism. It may be objected, that the greater part of the dogmas of Christianity being mysterious, to expect the human mind should be capable of conceiving them, is not so much to expect children should be men, but that man should be something more. To this I answer, in the first place, that there are mysteries, which it is not only impossible for man to comprehend, but also to believe; and I do not see what we get by teaching them to children, unless it be to learn them betimes to tell lies. I will say farther, that before we admit of mysteries, it is necessary for us to comprehend, at least, that they are incomprehensible, and children are not even capable of this. At an age when every thing is mysterious, there are no such things, properly speaking, as mysteries.

Believe in God, and thou shalt be saved. This dogma, misunderstood, is the principle of sanguinary persecution, and the cause of all those futile instructions which have given a mortal blow to human reason, by accustoming it to be satisfied with words. Doubtless not a moment is to be lost when we are running the race of eternal salvation; but if, to obtain this important prize, it be sufficient to learn to repeat a set form of words, I do not see what should hinder us from peopling heaven with magpies and parroquets, as well as with children.

To impose an obligation of believing, supposes the possibility of it. The philosopher who does not believe, is certainly in the wrong; because he misuses the understanding he has cultivated, and is capacitated to comprehend the sublime truths he rejects. But though a child should profess the Christian religion, what can he believe? He can believe only what he conceives, and he conceives so little of what is said to him, that if you tell him directly the contrary, he adopts the latter dogma as readily as he did the former. The faith of children, and indeed of many grown persons, is merely an affair of geography. Are they to be rewarded in heaven, because they were born at Rome, and not at Mecca? One man is told that Mahomet was a prophet sent by God, and he accordingly says that Mahomet was a prophet sent by God; the other is told that Mahomet was an impostor, and he also in like manner says Mahomet was an impostor. Had these two persons only changed places, each would also have changed his tone, and affirmed what he now denies. Can we infer from two dispositions so much alike, that one will go to heaven, and the other to hell? When a child says he believes in God, it is not in God he believes, but in Peter or James, who tells him there is something which is called God: thus he believes in the manner of Euripides, when Jupiter was thus addressed in one of his tragedies;[6]

O Jupiter! Though nothing I know of thee but thy name,——

We protestants hold, that no child who dies before he arrives at

[6] The tragedy of Menalippus, which at first began with this line; but the clamours of the Athenians obliged Euripides afterwards to alter it. *Plutarch.*

the age of reason is deprived of salvation; the Roman Catholics believe the same of every child that is baptized, though it should
never once have heard the name of God. There are some cases
therefore in which men may be saved without believing in God, as
in infancy or imbecillity of mind, as in idiots and madmen, where
the understanding is incapable of the operations requisite to infer
an acknowledgment of the Deity. All the difference that I see here
between me and my readers is, that you think children of seven
years of age capacitated to believe in God, and I do not think them
capable of it even at fifteen. Whether I am right or wrong in this
particular, it is not in itself an article of faith, but only a simple
observation in natural history.

On the same principles, it is evident, that if a man should arrive
at old age without believing in God, he would not be deprived of
his presence in the other world, provided his infidelity was not
wilful; and this I say may sometimes happen. You will admit, that
with respect to madmen, a malady deprives them of their intellectual faculties, but not of their condition as men, nor of course of
their claim to be beneficence of their Creator. Why then will you
not admit the same claim in those who, sequestered in their infancy
from all society, have lived the real life of a savage, deprived of
that information which is to be acquired only by conversation with
mankind?[7] for it is a demonstrable impossibility that such a savage
should ever raise his ideas to the knowledge of the true God.
Reason tells us, that man is punishable only for his wilful errors, and
that invincible ignorance can never be imputed to him as a crime.
Hence it should follow, that in the eyes of Eternal Justice every
man who would have believed had he had the opportunities of information, will appear as a believer; and that none will be punished
for infidelity but those whose hearts refuse to admit the truth.

Let us beware of divulging the truth to those who are incapable
of understanding it: for this is the way to substitute error in the
room of it. It were better to have no idea of God at all, than to
entertain those which are mean, fantastical, injurious, and unworthy
a divine object; it is a less crime to be ignorant of, than insult, him.

. . . . .

Custom and prejudice triumph particularly in matters of religion.
But how shall we, who on all occasions pretend to shake off its
yoke; we, who pay no regard to the authority of opinion; who would

[7] See the first part of my discourse on the Inequality of mankind, wherein I
treat of the natural state of the human mind, and the slowness of its progress.

424

teach our pupil nothing but what he might have learned himself, in any country; in what religion shall we educate Émile? To what sect shall we unite the man of nature? The answer appears to me very simple; we shall unite him neither to one nor another; but place him in a proper situation, and qualify him to make choice of that which the best use of his reason may induce him to adopt.

FRANKLIN 1706–1790

EVEN in his life-time Benjamin Franklin represented the best of the "New World" to both his compatriots and the nations abroad. He was the living embodiment of the idea of democratic progress, the man who through self-education had become one of the leading citizens of his country and who, in his *Poor Richard's Almanac*, spoke as a friend and guide to the common man. But he understood also how to speak the language of the scientists and to parry the feints of the diplomats of Paris. He believed in freedom, but he knew how easily it was abused by its own prophets; he was the passionate man who nevertheless forced himself through all his life to stick to the idea of tolerance and objectivity. And because he believed in freedom and tolerance and knew the perils by which they are constantly surrounded, he was one of the ardent advocates of education for the young and for adults.

Although he had no prejudice against the value of ancient languages for those who could profit from them he wished the American school to be a more integral part of the country's culture than the typical Latin School of his time. But, like Jefferson, he experienced that even in a politically progressive population such as that of the United States at the end of the 18th century, traditionalism can be stronger than cultural realism.

The following selections are taken from Franklin's *Autobiography and Other Writings,* reprinted from Mott and Jorgenson's *Representative Selections,* published in New York by the American Book Company in 1936.

AUTOBIOGRAPHY

. . . My elder Brothers were all put Apprentices to different Trades. I was put to the Grammar School at Eight Years of Age, my Father intending to devote me as the Tithe of his Sons to the Service of the Church. My early Readiness in learning to read (which must have been very early, as I do not remember when I could not read) and the Opinion of all his Friends that I should certainly make a good Scholar, encourag'd him in this Purpose of his. My Uncle Benjamin too approv'd of it, and propos'd to give me all his Shorthand Volumes of Sermons I suppose as a Stock to set up with, if I would learn his Character. I continu'd however at the Grammar School

426

not quite one Year, tho' in that time I had risen gradually from the Middle of the Class of that Year to be the Head of it, and farther was remov'd into the next Class above it, in order to go with that into the third at the End of the Year. But my Father in the mean time, from a View of the Expence of a College Education which, having so large a Family, he could not well afford, and the mean Living many so educated were afterwards able to obtain, Reasons that he gave to his Friends in my Hearing, altered his first Intention, took me from the Grammar School, and sent me to a School for Writing and Arithmetic kept by a then famous Man, Mr. Geo. Brownell, very successful in his Profession generally, and that by mild encouraging Methods. Under him I acquired fair Writing pretty soon, but I fail'd in the Arithmetic, and made no Progress in it.—At Ten Years old, I was taken home to assist my Father in his Business, which was that of a Tallow Chandler and Sope Boiler. A Business he was not bred to, but had assumed on his Arrival in New England and on finding his Dying Trade would not maintain his Family, being in little Request. Accordingly I was employed in cutting Wick for the Candles, filling the Dipping Mold, and the Molds for cast Candles, attending the Shop, going of Errands, etc.—I dislik'd the Trade and had a strong Inclination for the Sea; but my Father declar'd against it; however, living near the Water, I was much in and about it, learnt early to swim well, and to manage Boats, and when in a Boat or Canoe with other Boys I was commonly allow'd to govern, especially in any case of Difficulty; and upon other Occasions I was generally a Leader among the Boys, and sometimes led them into Scrapes, of wch I will mention one Instance, as it shows an early projecting public Spirit, tho' not then justly conducted. There was a salt Marsh that bounded part of the Mill Pond, on the Edge of which at Highwater, we us'd to stand to fish for Min[n]ows. By much Trampling, we had made it a mere Quagmire. My Proposal was to build a Wharf there fit for us to stand upon, and I show'd my Comrades a large Heap of Stones which were intended for a new House near the Marsh, and which would very well suit our Purpose. Accordingly in the Evening when the Workmen were gone, I assembled a Number of my Playfellows; and working with them diligently like so many Emmets, sometimes two or three to a Stone, we brought them all away and built our little Wharff.—The next Morning the Workmen were surpriz'd at Missing the Stones; which were found in our Wharff; Enquiry was made after the Removers; we were discovered and complain'd of; several of us were corrected by our Fathers; and tho' I pleaded the

Usefulness of the Work, mine convinc'd me that nothing was useful which was not honest.

. . . . .

I continu'd thus employ'd in my Father's Business for two Years, that is till I was 12 Years old; and my Brother John, who was bred to that Business having left my Father, married and set up for himself at Rhodeisland, there was all Appearance that I was destin'd to supply his Place and be a Tallow Chandler. But my Dislike to the Trade continuing, my Father was under Apprehensions that if he did not find one for me more agreable, I should break away and get to Sea, as his Son Josiah had done to his great Vexation. He therefore sometimes took me to walk with him, and see Joiners, Bricklayers, Turners, Braziers, etc. at their Work, that he might observe my Inclination, and endeavour to fix it on some Trade or other on Land. It has ever since been a Pleasure to me to see good Workmen handle their Tools; and it has been useful to me, having learnt so much by it, as to be able to do little Jobs myself in my House, when a Workman could not readily be got; and to construct little Machines for my Experiments while the Intention of making the Experiment was fresh and warm in my Mind. My Father at last fix'd upon the Cutler's Trade, and my Uncle Benjamin's Son Samuel who was bred to that Business in London[,] being about that time establish'd in Boston, I was sent to be with him some time on liking. But his Expectations of a Fee with me displeasing my Father, I was taken home again.—

From a Child I was fond of Reading, and all the little Money that came into my Hands was ever laid out in Books. Pleas'd with the Pilgrim's Progress, my first Collection was of John Bunyan's Works, in separate little Volumes. I afterwards sold them to enable me to buy R. Burton's Historical Collections; they were small Chapmen's Books and cheap, 40 or 50 in all.—My Father's little Library consisted chiefly of Books in polemic Divinity, most of which I read, and have since often regretted, that at a time when I had such a Thirst for Knowledge, more proper Books had not fallen in my Way, since it was now resolv'd I should not be a Clergyman. Plutarch's Lives there was, in which I read abundantly, and I still think that time spent to great ["Great" seems to have been deleted.] Advantage. There was also a Book of Defoe's, called an Essay on Projects, and another of Dr. Mather's, called Essays to do Good which perhaps gave me a Turn of thinking that had an influence on some of the principal future Events of my Life.

428

This Bookish inclination at length determin'd my Father to make me a Printer, tho' he had already one Son (James) of that Profession. In 1717 my Brother James return'd from England with a Press and Letters to set up his Business in Boston. I lik'd it much better than that of my Father, but still had a Hankering for the Sea.—To prevent the apprehended Effect of such an Inclination, my Father was impatient to have me bound to my Brother. I stood out some time, but at last was persuaded and signed the Indentures, when I was yet but 12 Years old.—I was to serve as an Apprentice till I was 21 Years of Age, only I was to be allow'd Journeyman's Wages during the last Year. In a little time I made great Proficiency in the Business, and became a useful Hand to my Brother. I now had Access to better Books. An Acquaintance with the Apprentices of Booksellers, enabled me sometimes to borrow a small one, which I was careful to return soon and clean. Often I sat up in my Room reading the greatest Part of the Night, when the Book was borrow'd in the Evening and to be return'd early in the Morning[,] lest it should be miss'd or wanted. And after some time an ingenious Tradesman Mr. Matthew Adams who had a pretty Collection of Books, and who frequented our Printing House, took Notice of me, invited me to his Library, and very kindly lent me such Books as I chose to read. I now took a Fancy to Poetry, and made some little Pieces. My Brother, thinking it might turn to account encourag'd me, and put me on composing two occasional Ballads. One was called The *Lighthouse Tragedy*, and contained an Acc^t of the drowning of Capt. Worthilake with his Two Daughters; the other was a Sailor Song on the Taking of *Teach* or Blackbeard the Pirate. They were wretched Stuff, in the Grub-street Ballad Stile, and when they were printed he sent me about the Town to sell them. The first sold wonderfully, the Event being recent, having made a great Noise. This flatter'd my Vanity. But my Father discourag'd me, by ridiculing my Performances, and telling me Verse-makers were generally Beggars; so I escap'd being a Poet, most probably a very bad one. . . .

. . . . .

Before I enter upon my public Appearance in Business it may be well to let you know the then State of my Mind, with regard to my Principles and Morals, that you may see how far those influenc'd the future Events of my Life. My Parent's [sic] had early given me religious Impressions, and brought me through my Childhood piously in the Dissenting Way. But I was scarce 15 when, after

429

doubting by turns of several Points as I found them disputed in the different Books I read, I began to doubt of Revelation it self. Some Books against Deism fell into my Hands; they were said to be the Substance of Sermons preached at Boyle's Lectures. It happened that they wrought an Effect on me quite contrary to what was intended by them: For the Arguments of the Deists which were quoted to be refuted, appeared to me much Stronger than the Refutations. In short I soon became a thorough Deist. My Arguments perverted some others, particularly Collins and Ralph: but each of them having afterwards wrong'd me greatly without the least Compunction and recollecting Keith's Conduct towards me, (who was another Freethinker) and my own towards Vernon and Miss Read, which at Times gave me great Trouble, I began to suspect that this Doctrine tho' it might be true, was not very useful.—My London Pamphlet, which had for its Motto these Lines of Dryden

> Whatever is, is right. Tho' purblind Man
> Sees but a Part of the Chain, the nearest Link,
> His Eyes not carrying to the equal Beam,
> That poises all, above.

And from the Attributes of God, his infinite Wisdom, Goodness and Power concluded that nothing could possibly be wrong in the World, and that Vice and Virtue were empty Distinctions, no such Things existing: appear'd now not so clever a Performance as I once thought it; and I doubted whether some Error had not insinuated itself unperceiv'd, into my Argument, so as to infect all that follow'd, as is common in metaphysical Reasonings.—I grew convinc'd that *Truth, Sincerity* and *Integrity* in Dealings between Man and Man, were of the utmost Importance to the Felicity of Life, and I form'd written Resolutions, (wch still remain in my Journal Book) to practice them everwhile I lived. Revelation had indeed no weight with me as such; but I entertain'd an Opinion, that tho' certain Actions might not be bad *because* they were forbidden by it, or good *because* it commanded them; yet probably those Actions might be forbidden *because* they were bad for us, or commanded *because* they were beneficial to us, in their own Natures, all the Circumstances of things considered. And this Persuasion, with the kind hand of Providence, or some guardian Angel, or accidental favourable Circumstances and Situations, or all together, preserved me (thro' this dangerous Time of Youth and the hazardous Situations I was sometimes in among Strangers, remote from the Eye and Advice of my Father) without any *wilful* gross Immorality or

430

Injustice that might have been expected from my Want of Religion. I say *wilful*, because the Instances I have mentioned, had something of *Necessity* in them, from my Youth, Inexperience, and the Knavery of others. I had therefore a tolerable Character to begin the World with, I valued it properly, and determin'd to preserve it.—

I should have mentioned before, that in the Autumn of the preceeding Year I had formed most of my ingenious Acquaintance into a Club of mutual Improvement, which we called the Junto. We met on Friday Evenings. The Rules I drew up required that every Member in his Turn should produce one or more Queries on any Point of Morals, Politics or Natural Philosophy, to be discussed by the Company, and once in three Months produce and read an Essay of his own Writing on any Subject he pleased. Our Debates were to be under the Direction of a President and to be conducted in the sincere Spirit of Enquiry after Truth, without Fondness for Dispute, or Desire of Victory; and to prevent Warmth all Expressions of Positiveness in Opinions or direct Contradiction, were after some time made contraband and prohibited under small pecuniary Penalties.—. . . And the club continu'd almost as long [40 years][,] and was the best School of Philosophy, and Politics that then existed in the Province; for our Queries which were read the Week preceding their Discussion, put us on reading with Attention upon the several Subjects, that we might speak more to the purpose: and here too we acquired better Habits of Conversation, every thing being studied in our Rules which might prevent our disgusting each other. From hence the long Continuance of the Club, which I shall have frequent Occasion to speak farther of hereafter; . . .

And now I sent on foot my first Project of a public Nature, [th]at for a Subscription Library. [I] drew up the Proposals, got them put into Form by our great Scrivener Brockden, and by the help of my Friends in the Junto, procur'd Fifty Subscribers of 40/ each to begin with and 10/ a Year for 50 Years, the Term our Company was to continue. We afterwards obtain'd a Charter, the Company being increas'd to 100. This was the Mother of all the N American Subscription Libraries now so numerous, is become a great thing itself, and continually increasing.—These Libraries have improv'd the general Conversation of the Americans, made the common Tradesmen and Farmers as intelligent as most Gentlemen from other Countries, and perhaps have contributed in some degree to the Stand so generally made throughout the Colonies in Defence of their Privileges.—

431

This library afforded me the means of improvement by constant study, for which I set apart an hour or two each day, and thus repair'd in some degree the loss of the learned education my father once intended for me. Reading was the only amusement I allow'd myself. I spent no time in taverns, games, or frolicks of any kind; and my industry in my business continu'd as indefatigable as it was necessary. I was indebted for my printing-house; I had a young family coming on to be educated, and I had to contend with for business two printers, who were established in the place before me. My circumstances, however, grew daily easier. My original habits of frugality continuing, and my father having, among his instructions to me when a boy, frequently repeated a proverb of Solomon, "Seest thou a man diligent in his calling, he shall stand before kings, he shall not stand before mean men," I from thence considered industry as a means of obtaining wealth and distinction, which encourag'd me, tho' I did not think that I should ever literally *stand before kings*, which, however, has since happened; for I have stood before *five*, and even had the honour of sitting down with one, the King of Denmark, to dinner.

· · · · ·

I had been religiously educated as a Presbyterian; and tho' some of the dogmas of that persuasion, such as *the eternal decrees of God, election, reprobation, etc.,* appeared to me unintelligible, others doubtful, and I early absented myself from the public assemblies of the sect, Sunday being my studying day, I never was without some religious principles. I never doubted, for instance, the existence of the Deity; that he made the world, and govern'd it by his Providence; that the most acceptable service of God was the doing good to man; that our souls are immortal; and that all crime will be punished, and virtue rewarded, either here or hereafter. These I esteem'd the essentials of every religion; and, being to be found in all the religions we had in our country, I respected them all, tho' with different degrees of respect, as I found them more or less mix'd with other articles, which, without any tendency to inspire, promote, or confirm morality, serv'd principally to divide us, and make us unfriendly to one another. This respect to all, with an opinion that the worst had some good effects, induc'd me to avoid all discourse that might tend to lessen the good opinion another might have of his own religion; and as our province increas'd in people, and new places of worship were continually wanted, and

432

generally erected by voluntary contribution, my mite for such purpose, whatever might be the sect, was never refused.

Tho' I seldom attended any public worship, I had still an opinion of its propriety, and of its utility when rightly conducted, and I regularly paid my annual subscription for the support of the only Presbyterian minister or meeting we had in Philadelphia. He us'd to visit me sometimes as a friend, and admonish me to attend his administrations, and I was now and then prevail'd on to do so, once for five Sundays successively. Had he been in my opinion a good preacher, perhaps I might have continued, notwithstanding the occasion I had for the Sunday's leisure in my course of study; but his discourses were chiefly either polemic arguments, or explications of the peculiar doctrines of our sect, and were all to me very dry, uninteresting, and unedifying, since not a single moral principle was inculcated or enforc'd, their aim seeming to be rather to make us Presbyterians than good citizens.

At length he took for his text that verse of the fourth chapter of Philippians, *"Finally, brethren, whatsoever things are true, honest, just, pure, lovely, or of good report, if there be any virtue, or any praise, think on these things."* And I imagin'd, in a sermon on such a text, we could not miss of having some morality. But he confin'd himself to five points only, as meant by the apostle, viz.: 1. Keeping holy the Sabbath day. 2. Being diligent in reading the holy Scriptures. 3. Attending duly the publick worship. 4. Partaking of the Sacrament. 5. Paying a due respect to God's ministers. These might be all good things; but, as they were not the kind of good things that I expected from that text, I despaired of ever meeting with them from any other, was disgusted, and attended his preaching no more. I had some years before compos'd a little Liturgy, or form of prayer, for my own private use (viz., in 1728), entitled *Articles of Belief and Acts of Religion.* I return'd to the use of this, and went no more to the public assemblies. My conduct might be blameable, but I leave it, without attempting further to excuse it; my present purpose being to relate facts, and not to make apologies for them.

It was about this time I conceiv'd the bold and arduous project of arriving at moral perfection. I wish'd to live without committing any fault at any time; I would conquer all that either natural inclination, custom, or company might lead me into. As I knew, or thought I knew, what was right and wrong, I did not see why I might not always do the one and avoid the other. But I soon found

I had undertaken a task of more difficulty than I had imagined. While my care was employ'd in guarding against one fault, I was often surprised by another; habit took the advantage of inattention; inclination was sometimes too strong for reason. I concluded, at length, that the mere speculative conviction that it was our interest to be completely virtuous, was not sufficient to prevent our slipping; and that the contrary habits must be broken, and good ones acquired and established, before we can have any dependence on a steady, uniform rectitude of conduct. For this purpose I therefore contrived the following method.

In the various enumerations of the moral virtues I had met with in my reading, I found the catalogue more or less numerous, as different writers included more or fewer ideas under the same name. Temperance, for example, was by some confined to eating and drinking, while by others it was extended to mean the moderating every other pleasure, appetite, inclination, or passion, bodily or mental, even to our avarice and ambition. I propos'd to myself, for the sake of clearness, to use rather more names, with fewer ideas annex'd to each, than a few names with more ideas; and I included under thirteen names of virtues all that at that time occurr'd to me as necessary or desirable, and annexed to each a short precept, which fully express'd the extent I gave to its meaning.

These names of virtues, with their precepts, were:

1. TEMPERANCE

Eat not to dullness; drink not to elevation.

2. SILENCE

Speak not but what may benefit others or yourself; avoid trifling conversation.

3. ORDER

Let all your things have their places; let each part of your business have its time.

4. RESOLUTION

Resolve to perform what you ought; perform without fail what you resolve.

5. FRUGALITY

Make no expense but to do good to others or yourself; *i. e.*, waste nothing.

434

6. INDUSTRY

Lose no time; be always employ'd in something useful; cut off all unnecessary actions.

7. SINCERITY

Use no hurtful deceit; think innocently and justly, and, if you speak, speak accordingly.

8. JUSTICE

Wrong none by doing injuries, or omitting the benefits that are your duty.

9. MODERATION

Avoid extreams; forbear resenting injuries so much as you think they deserve.

10. CLEANLINESS

Tolerate no uncleanliness in body, cloaths, or habitation.

11. TRANQUILLITY

Be not disturbed at trifles, or at accidents common or unavoidable.

12. CHASTITY

Rarely use venery but for health or offspring, never to dulness, weakness, or the injury of your own or another's peace or reputation.

13. HUMILITY

Imitate Jesus and Socrates.

My intention being to acquire the *habitude* of all these virtues, I judg'd it would be well not to distract my attention by attempting the whole at once, but to fix it on one of them at a time; and, when I should be master of that, then to proceed to another, and so on, till I should have gone thro' the thirteen; and, as the previous acquisition of some might facilitate the acquisition of certain others, I arrang'd them with that view, as they stand above. Temperance first, as it tends to procure that coolness and clearness of head, which is so necessary where constant vigilance was to be kept up, and guard maintained against the unremitting attraction of ancient habits, and the force of perpetual temptations. This being acquir'd and establish'd, Silence would be more easy; and my desire being to gain knowledge at the same time that I improv'd in virtue, and considering that in conversation it was obtain'd rather by the use of

435

the ears than of the tongue, and therefore wishing to break a habit I was getting into of prattling, punning, and joking, which only made me acceptable to trifling company, I gave *Silence* the second place. This and the next, *Order,* I expected would allow me more time for attending to my project and my studies. *Resolution,* once become habitual, would keep me firm in my endeavours to obtain all the subsequent virtues; *Frugality* and Industry freeing me from my remaining debt, and producing affluence and independence, would make more easy the practice of Sincerity and Justice, etc., etc. Conceiving then, that, agreeably to the advice of Pythagoras in his *Golden Verses,* daily examination would be necessary, I contrived the following method for conducting that examination.

I made a little book, in which I allotted a page for each of the virtues. I rul'd each page with red ink, so as to have seven columns, one for each day of the week, marking each column with a letter for the day. I cross'd these columns with thirteen red lines, marking the beginning of each line with the first letter of one of the virtues, on which line, and in its proper column, I might mark, by a little black spot, every fault I found upon examination to have been committed respecting that virtue upon that day.

Form of the Pages

TEMPERANCE.						
EAT NOT TO DULNESS. DRINK NOT TO ELEVATION.						
	S.	M.	T.	W.	T.	F.	S.
T.							
S.	*	*		*		*	
O.	* *	*	*		*	*	*
R.			*			*	
F.		*	*				
I.			*				
S.							
J.							
M.							
C.							
T.							
C.							
H.							

I determined to give a week's strict attention to each of the virtues successively. Thus, in the first week, my great guard was to

FRANKLIN

avoid every the least offence against *Temperance,* leaving the other virtues to their ordinary chance, only marking every evening the faults of the day. Thus, if in the first week I could keep my first line, marked T, clear of spots, I suppos'd the habit of that virtue so much strengthen'd, and its opposite weaken'd, that I might venture extending my attention to include the next, and for the following week keep both lines clear of spots. Proceeding thus to the last, I could go thro' a course compleat in thirteen weeks, and four courses in a year. And like him who, having a garden to weed, does not attempt to eradicate all the bad herbs at once, which would exceed his reach and his strength, but works on one of the beds at a time, and, having accomplish'd the first, proceeds to a second, so I should have, I hoped, the encouraging pleasure of seeing on my pages the progress I made in virtue, by clearing successively my lines of their spots, till in the end, by a number of courses, I should be happy in viewing a clean book, after a thirteen weeks' daily examination.

This my little book had for its motto these lines from Addison's *Cato:*

> Here will I hold. If there's a power above us
> (And that there is, all nature cries aloud
> Thro' all her works), He must delight in virtue;
> And that which he delights in must be happy.

Another from Cicero,

O vitæ Philosophia dux! O virtutum indagatrix expultrixque vitiorum! Unus dies, bene et ex præceptis tuis actus, peccanti immortalitati est anteponendus.

Another from the Proverbs of Solomon, speaking of wisdom or virtue:

Length of days is in her right hand, and in her left hand riches and honour. Her ways are ways of pleasantness, and all her paths are peace. —iii. 16, 17.

And conceiving God to be the fountain of wisdom, I thought it right and necessary to solicit his assistance for obtaining it; to this end I formed the following little prayer, which was prefix'd to my tables of examination, for daily use.

O powerful Goodness! bountiful Father! merciful Guide! Increase in me that wisdom which discovers my truest interest. Strengthen my resolutions to perform what that wisdom dictates. Accept my kind offices to thy other children as the only return in my power for thy continual favours to me.

I used also sometimes a little prayer which I took from Thomson's *Poems,* viz.:

> Father of light and life, thou Good Supreme!
> O teach me what is good; teach me Thyself!
> Save me from folly, vanity, and vice,
> From every low pursuit; and fill my soul
> With knowledge, conscious peace, and virtue pure;
> Sacred, substantial, never-fading bliss!

.   .   .   .   .

A PROPOSAL—FOR PROMOTING USEFUL KNOWLEDGE AMONG THE BRITISH PLANTATIONS IN AMERICA

Philadelphia, May 14, 1743.

The English are possessed of a long tract of continent, from Nova Scotia to Georgia, extending north and south through different climates, having different soils, producing different plants, mines, and minerals, and capable of different improvements, manufactures, &c.

The first drudgery of settling new colonies, which confines the attention of people to mere necessaries, is now pretty well over; and there are many in every province in circumstances that set them at ease, and afford leisure to cultivate the finer arts and improve the common stock of knowledge. To such of these who are men of speculation, many hints must from time to time arise, many observations occur, which if well examined, pursued, and improved, might produce discoveries to the advantage of some or all of the British plantations, or to the benefit of mankind in general.

But as from the extent of the country such persons are widely separated, and seldom can see and converse or be acquainted with each other, so that many useful particulars remain uncommunicated, die with the discoverers, and are lost to mankind; it is, to remedy this inconvenience for the future, proposed,

That one society be formed of *virtuosi* or ingenious men, residing in the several colonies, to be called *The American Philosophical Society,* who are to maintain a constant correspondence.

That Philadelphia, being the city nearest the centre of the continent colonies, communicating with all of them northward and southward by post, and with all the islands by sea, and having the advantage of a good growing library, be the centre of the Society.

438

That at Philadelphia there be always at least seven members, viz. a physician, a botanist, a mathematician, a chemist, a mechanician, a geographer, and a general natural philosopher, besides a president, treasurer, and secretary.

That these members meet once a month, or oftener, at their own expense, to communicate to each other their observations and experiments, to receive, read, and consider such letters, communications, or queries as shall be sent from distant members; to direct the dispersing of copies of such communications as are valuable, to other distant members, in order to procure their sentiments thereupon.

That the subjects of the correspondence be: all new-discovered plants, herbs, trees, roots, their virtues, uses, &c.; methods of propagating them, and making such as are useful, but particular to some plantations, more general; improvements of vegetable juices, as ciders, wines, &c.; new methods of curing or preventing diseases; all new-discovered fossils in different countries, as mines, minerals, and quarries; new and useful improvements in any branch of mathematics; new discoveries in chemistry, such as improvements in distillation, brewing, and assaying of ores; new mechanical inventions for saving labour, as mills and carriages, and for raising and conveying of water, draining of meadows, &c.; all new arts, trades, and manufactures, that may be proposed or thought of; surveys, maps, and charts of particular parts of the sea-coasts or inland countries; course and junction of rivers and great roads, situation of lakes and mountains, nature of the soil and productions; new methods of improving the breed of useful animals; introducing other sorts from foreign countries; new improvements in planting, gardening, and clearing land; and all philosophical experiments that let light into the nature of things, tend to increase the power of man over matter, and multiply the conveniences or pleasures of life.

That a correspondence, already begun by some intended members, shall be kept up by this Society with the ROYAL SOCIETY of London, and with the DUBLIN SOCIETY.

That every member shall have abstracts sent him quarterly, of every thing valuable communicated to the Society's Secretary at Philadelphia; free of all charge except the yearly payment hereafter mentioned.

That, by permission of the postmaster-general, such communications pass between the Secretary of the Society and the members, postage-free.

That, for defraying the expense of such experiments as the Society shall judge proper to cause to be made, and other contingent charges for the common good, every member send a piece of eight per annum to the treasurer, at Philadelphia, to form a common stock, to be disbursed by order of the President with the consent of the majority of the members that can conveniently be consulted thereupon, to such persons and places where and by whom the experiments are to be made, and otherwise as there shall be occasion; of which disbursements an exact account shall be kept, and communicated yearly to every member.

That, at the first meetings of the members at Philadelphia, such rules be formed for regulating their meetings and transactions for the general benefit, as shall be convenient and necessary; to be afterwards changed and improved as there shall be occasion, wherein due regard is to be had to the advice of distant members.

That, at the end of every year, collections be made and printed, of such experiments, discoveries, and improvements, as may be thought of public advantage; and that every member have a copy sent him.

That the business and duty of the Secretary be to receive all letters intended for the Society, and lay them before the President and members at their meetings; to abstract, correct, and methodize such papers as require it, and as he shall be directed to do by the President, after they have been considered, debated, and digested in the Society; to enter copies thereof in the Society's books, and make out copies for distant members; to answer their letters by direction of the President, and keep records of all material transactions of the Society.

Benjamin Franklin, the writer of this Proposal, offers himself to serve the Society as their secretary, till they shall be provided with one more capable.

ADVICE TO A YOUNG TRADESMAN [1748]

TO MY FRIEND, A. B.: As you have desired it of me, I write the following hints, which have been of service to me, and may, if observed, be so to you.

Remember, that *time* is money. He that can earn ten shillings a day by his labour, and goes abroad, or sits idle, one half of that day, though he spends but sixpence during his diversion or idleness, ought not to reckon *that* the only expense; he has really spent, or rather thrown away, five shillings besides.

Remember, that *credit* is money. If a man lets his money lie in my hands after it is due, he gives me the interest, or so much as I can make of it during that time. This amounts to a considerable sum where a man has good and large credit, and makes good use of it.

Remember, that money is of the prolific, generating nature. Money can beget money, and its offspring can beget more, and so on. Five shillings turned is six, turned again it is seven and three-pence, and so on till it becomes an hundred pounds. The more there is of it, the more it produces every turning, so that the profits rise quicker and quicker. He that kills a breeding sow, destroys all her offspring to the thousandth generation. He that murders a crown, destroys all that it might have produced, even scores of pounds.

Remember, that six pounds a year is but a groat a day. For this little sum (which may be daily wasted either in time or expense unperceived) a man of credit may, on his own security, have the constant possession and use of an hundred pounds. So much in stock, briskly turned by an industrious man, produces great advantage.

Remember this saying, *The good paymaster is lord of another man's purse.* He that is known to pay punctually and exactly to the time he promises, may at any time, and on any occasion, raise all the money his friends can spare. This is sometimes of great use. After industry and frugality, nothing contributes more to the raising of a young man in the world than punctuality and justice in all his dealings; therefore never keep borrowed money an hour beyond the time you promised, lest a disappointment shut up your friend's purse for ever.

The most trifling actions that affect a man's credit are to be regarded. The sound of your hammer at five in the morning, or nine at night, heard by a creditor, makes him easy six months longer; but, if he sees you at a billiard-table, or hears your voice at a tavern, when you should be at work, he sends for his money the next day; demands it, before he can receive it, in a lump.

It shows, besides, that you are mindful of what you owe; it makes you appear a careful as well as an honest man, and that still increases your credit.

Beware of thinking all your own that you possess, and of living accordingly. It is a mistake that many people who have credit fall into. To prevent this, keep an exact account for some time, both of your expenses and your income. If you take the pains at first to mention particulars, it will have this good effect: you will discover how wonderfully small, trifling expenses mount up to large sums, and will discern what might have been, and may for the future be saved, without occasioning any great inconvenience.

In short, the way to wealth, if you desire it, is as plain as the way to market. It depends chiefly on two words, *industry* and *frugality;* that is, waste neither *time* nor *money,* but make the best use of both. Without industry and frugality nothing will do, and with them every thing. He that gets all he can honestly, and saves all he gets (necessary expenses excepted), will certainly become *rich,* if that Being who governs the world, to whom all should look for a blessing on their honest endeavours, doth not, in his wise providence, otherwise determine.

AN OLD TRADESMAN.

PROPOSALS RELATING TO THE EDUCATION OF YOUTH IN PENSILVANIA—PHILADELPHIA: PRINTED IN THE YEAR, MDCCXLIX

ADVERTISEMENT TO THE READER.

It has long been regretted as a Misfortune to the Youth of this Province, that we have no ACADEMY, in which they might receive the Accomplishments of a regular Education. The following Paper of Hints towards forming a Plan for that Purpose, is so far approv'd by some publick-spirited Gentlemen, to whom it has been privately communicated, that they have directed a Number of Copies to be made by the Press, and properly distributed, in order to obtain the Sentiments and Advice of Men of Learning, Understanding, and Experience in these Matters; and have determined to use their Interest and best Endeavours, to have the Scheme, when compleated, carried gradually into Execution; in which they have Reason to believe they shall have the hearty Concurrence and Assistance of many who are Wellwishers to their Country. Those who incline to favour the Design with their Advice, either as to the Parts of Learning to be taught, the Order of Study, the Method of Teaching, the Œconomy of the School, or any other Matter of Importance to the Success of the Undertaking, are desired to communicate their Sentiments as soon as may be, by Letter directed to B. FRANKLIN, *Printer,* in PHILADELPHIA."

PROPOSALS

The good Education of Youth has been esteemed by wise Men in all Ages, as the surest Foundation of the Happiness both of private

442

Families and of Commonwealths. Almost all Governments have therefore made it a principal Object of their Attention, to establish and endow with proper Revenues, such Seminaries of Learning, as might supply the succeeding Age with Men qualified to serve the Publick with Honour to themselves, and to their Country.

Many of the first Settlers of these Provinces were Men who had received a good Education in *Europe*, and to their Wisdom and good Management we owe much of our present Prosperity. But their Hands were full, and they could not do all Things. The present Race are not thought to be generally of equal Ability: For though the *American* Youth are allow'd not to want Capacity; yet the best Capacities require Cultivation, it being truly with them, as with the best Ground, which unless well tilled and sowed with profitable Seed, produces only ranker Weeds.

That we may obtain the Advantages arising from an Increase of Knowledge, and prevent as much as may be the mischievous Consequences that would attend a general Ignorance among us, the following *Hints* are offered towards forming a Plan for the Education of the Youth of *Pennsylvania*, viz.

It is propos'd,

That some Persons of Leisure and publick Spirit apply for a CHARTER, by which they may be incorporated, with Power to erect an ACADEMY for the Education of Youth, to govern the same, provide Masters, make Rules, receive Donations, purchase Lands, etc., and to add to their Number, from Time to Time such other Persons as they shall judge suitable.

That the Members of the Corporation make it their Pleasure, and in some Degree their Business, to visit the Academy often, encourage and countenance the Youth, countenance and assist the Masters, and by all Means in their Power advance the Usefulness and Reputation of the Design; that they look on the Students as in some Sort their Children, treat them with Familiarity and Affection, and, when they have behav'd well, and gone through their Studies, and are to enter the World, zealously unite, and make all the Interest that can be made to establish them, whether in Business, Offices, Marriages, or any other Thing for their Advantage, preferably to all other Persons whatsoever even of equal Merit.

And if Men may, and frequently do, catch such a Taste for cultivating Flowers, for Planting, Grafting, Inoculating, and the like, as to despise all other Amusements for their Sake, why may not we expect they should acquire a Relish for that *more useful* Culture of young Minds. *Thompson* says,

" 'Tis Joy to see the human Blossoms blow,
When infant Reason grows apace, and calls
For the kind Hand of an assiduous Care.
Delightful Task! to rear the tender Thought,
To teach the young Idea how to shoot;
To pour the fresh Instruction o'er the Mind,
To breathe th' enliv'ning Spirit, and to fix
The generous Purpose in the glowing Breast."

That a House be provided for the ACADEMY, if not in the Town, not many Miles from it; the Situation high and dry, and if it may be, not far from a River, having a Garden, Orchard, Meadow, and a Field or two.

That the House be furnished with a Library (if in the Country, if in the Town, the Town Libraries may serve) with Maps of all Countries, Globes, some mathematical Instruments, an Apparatus for Experiments in Natural Philosophy, and for Mechanics; Prints, of all Kinds, Prospects, Buildings, Machines, &c.

That the Rector be a Man of good Understanding, good Morals, diligent and patient, learn'd in the Languages and Sciences, and a correct pure Speaker and Writer of the *English* Tongue; to have such Tutors under him as shall be necessary.

That the boarding Scholars diet together, plainly, temperately, and frugally.

That, to keep them in Health, and to strengthen and render active their Bodies, they be frequently exercis'd in Running, Leaping, Wrestling, and Swimming, &c.

That they have peculiar Habits to distinguish them from other Youth, if the Academy be in or near the Town; for this, among other Reasons, that their Behaviour may be the better observed.

As to their STUDIES, it would be well if they could be taught *every Thing* that is useful, and *every Thing* that is ornamental: But Art is long, and their Time is short. It is therefore propos'd that they learn those Things that are likely to be *most useful* and *most ornamental*. Regard being had to the several Professions for which they are intended.

All should be taught to write a *fair Hand*, and swift, as that is useful to All. And with it may be learnt something of *Drawing*, by Imitation of Prints, and some of the first Principles of Perspective.

Arithmetick, Accounts, and some of the first Principles of *Geometry* and *Astronomy*.

The *English* Language might be taught by Grammar; in which some of our best Writers, as *Tillotson, Addison, Pope, Algernoon*

444

Sidney, Cato's Letters, &c., should be Classicks: the *Stiles* principally to be cultivated, being the *clear* and the *concise.* Reading should also be taught, and pronouncing, properly, distinctly, emphatically; not with an even Tone, which *under-does,* nor a theatrical, which *over-does* Nature.

To form their Stile they should be put on Writing Letters to each other, making Abstracts of what they read; or writing the same Things in their own Words; telling or writing Stories lately read, in their own Expressions. All to be revis'd and corrected by the Tutor, who should give his Reasons, and explain the Force and Import of Words, &c.

To form their Pronunciation, they may be put on making Declamations, repeating Speeches, delivering Orations, &c.; The Tutor assisting at the Rehearsals, teaching, advising, correcting their Accent, &c.

But if History be made a constant Part of their Reading, such as the Translations of the *Greek* and *Roman* Historians, and the modern Histories of ancient *Greece* and *Rome,* &c. may not almost all Kinds of useful Knowledge be that Way introduc'd to Advantage, and with Pleasure to the Student? As

Geography, by reading with Maps, and being required to point out the Places *where* the greatest Actions were done, to give their old and new Names, with the Bounds, Situation, Extent of the Countries concern'd, &c.

Chronology, by the Help of *Helvicus* or some other Writer of the Kind, who will enable them to tell *when* those Events happened; what Princes were Cotemporaries, what States or famous Men flourish'd about that Time, &c. The several principal Epochas to be first well fix'd in their Memories.

Antient Customs, religious and civil, being frequently mentioned in History, will give Occasion for explaining them; in which the Prints of Medals, Basso-Relievos, and antient Monuments will greatly assist.

Morality, by descanting and making continual Observations on the Causes of the Rise or Fall of any Man's Character, Fortune, Power &c. mention'd in History; the Advantages of Temperance, Order, Frugality, Industry, Perseverance &c. &c. Indeed the general natural Tendency of Reading good History must be, to fix in the Minds of Youth deep Impressions of the Beauty and Usefulness of Virtue of all Kinds, Publick Spirit, Fortitude, &c.

History will show the wonderful Effects of Oratory, in governing, turning and leading great Bodies of Mankind, Armies, Cities,

Nations. When the Minds of Youth are struck with Admiration at this, then is the Time to give them the Principles of that Art, which they will study with Taste and Application. Then they may be made acquainted with the best Models among the antients, their Beauties being particularly pointed out to them. Modern Political Oratory being chiefly performed by the Pen and Press, its Advantages over the Antient in some Respects are to be shown; as that its Effects are more extensive, more lasting, &c.

History will also afford frequent Opportunities of showing the Necessity of a *Publick Religion,* from its Usefulness to the Publick; the Advantage of a Religious Character among private Persons; the Mischiefs of Superstition, &c. and the Excellency of the CHRISTIAN RELIGION above all others antient or modern.

History will also give Occasion to expatiate on the Advantage of Civil Orders and Constitutions; how Men and their Properties are protected by joining in Societies and establishing Government; their Industry encouraged and rewarded, Arts invented, and Life made more comfortable: The Advantages of *Liberty,* Mischiefs of *Licentiousness,* Benefits arising from good Laws and a due Execution of Justice, &c. Thus may the first Principles of sound *Politicks* be fix'd in the Minds of Youth.

On *Historical* Occasions, Questions of Right and Wrong, Justice and Injustice, will naturally arise, and may be put to Youth, which they may debate in Conversation and in Writing. When they ardently desire Victory, for the Sake of the Praise attending it, they will begin to feel the Want, and be sensible of the Use of *Logic,* or the Art of Reasoning to *discover* Truth, and of Arguing to *defend* it, and *convince* Adversaries. This would be the Time to acquaint them with the Principles of that Art. Grotius, Puffendorff, and some other Writers of the same Kind, may be used on these Occasions to decide their Disputes. Publick Disputes warm the Imagination, whet the Industry, and strengthen the natural Abilities.

When Youth are told, that the Great Men whose Lives and Actions they read in History, spoke two of the best Languages that ever were, the most expressive, copious, beautiful; and that the finest Writings, the most correct Compositions, the most perfect Productions of human Wit and Wisdom, are in those Languages, which have endured Ages, and will endure while there are Men; that no Translation can do them Justice, or give the Pleasure found in Reading the Originals; that those Languages contain all Science; that one of them is become almost universal, being the Language of Learned Men in all Countries; that to understand them is a distin-

446

guishing Ornament, &c. they may be thereby made desirous of learning those Languages, and their Industry sharpen'd in the Acquisition of them. All intended for Divinity, should be taught the *Latin* and *Greek;* for Physick, the *Latin, Greek,* and *French;* for Law, the *Latin* and *French;* Merchants, the *French, German,* and *Spanish:* And though all should not be compell'd to learn *Latin, Greek,* or the modern foreign Languages; yet none that have an ardent Desire to learn them should be refused; their *English,* Arithmetick and other Studies absolutely necessary, being at the same Time not neglected.

If the new *Universal History* were also read, it would give a *connected* Idea of human Affairs, so far as it goes, which should be follow'd by the best modern Histories, particularly of our Mother Country; then of these Colonies; which should be accompanied with Observations on their Rise, Encrease, Use to *Great Britain,* Encouragements, Discouragements, etc. the Means to make them flourish, secure their Liberties, &c.

With the History of Men, Times, and Nations, should be read at proper Hours or Days, some of the best *Histories of Nature,* which would not only be delightful to Youth, and furnish them with Matter for their Letters, &c. as well as other History; but afterwards of great Use to them, whether they are Merchants, Handicrafts, or Divines; enabling the first the better to understand many Commodities, Drugs, &c; the second to improve his Trade or Handicraft by new Mixtures, Materials, &c., and the last to adorn his Discourses by beautiful Comparisons, and strengthen them by new Proofs of Divine Providence. The Conversation of all will be improved by it, as Occasions frequently occur of making Natural Observations, which are instructive, agreeable, and entertaining in almost all Companies. *Natural History* will also afford Opportuities of introducing many Observations, relating to the Preservation of Health, which may be afterwards of great Use. *Arbuthnot* on Air and *Aliment, Sanctorius* on Perspiration, *Lemery* on Foods, and some others, may now be read, and a very little Explanation will make them sufficiently intelligible to Youth.

While they are reading Natural History, might not a little *Gardening, Planting, Grafting, Inoculating,* etc., be taught and practised; and now and then Excursions made to the neighbouring Plantations of the best Farmers, their Methods observ'd and reason'd upon for the Information of Youth? The Improvement of Agriculture being useful to all, and Skill in it no Disparagement to any.

The History of *Commerce,* of the Invention of Arts, Rise of Man-

447

ufactures, Progress of Trade, Change of its Seats, with the Reasons, Causes, &c., may also be made entertaining to Youth, and will be useful to all. And this, with the Accounts in other History of the prodigious Force and Effect of Engines and Machines used in War, will naturally introduce a Desire to be instructed in *Mechanicks,* and to be inform'd of the Principles of that Art by which weak Men perform such Wonders, Labour is sav'd, Manufactures expedited, &c. This will be the Time to show them Prints of antient and modern Machines, to explain them, to let them be copied, and to give Lectures in Mechanical Philosophy.

With the whole should be constantly inculcated and cultivated, that *Benignity of Mind,* which shows itself in *searching for* and *seizing* every Opportunity *to serve* and *to oblige;* and is the Foundation of what is called GOOD BREEDING; highly useful to the Possessor, and most agreeable to all.

The Idea of what is *true Merit* should also be often presented to Youth, explain'd and impress'd on their Minds, as consisting in an *Inclination* join'd with an *Ability* to serve Mankind, one's Country, Friends and Family; which *Ability* is (with the blessing of God) to be acquir'd or greatly encreas'd by *true Learning;* and should indeed be the great *Aim* and *End* of all Learning.

IDEA OF THE ENGLISH SCHOOL

SKETCH'D OUT FOR THE CONSIDERATION OF THE TRUSTEES OF THE PHILADELPHIA ACADEMY [1751]. It is expected that every Scholar to be admitted into this School, be at least able to pronounce and divide the Syllables in Reading, and to write a legible Hand. None to be receiv'd that are under   Years of Age.

FIRST OR LOWEST CLASS

Let the first Class learn the *English Grammar* Rules, and at the same time let particlar Care be taken to improve them in *Orthography.* Perhaps the latter is best done by *Pairing* the Scholars, two of those nearest equal in their Spelling to be put together; let these strive for Victory, each propounding Ten Words every Day to the other to be spelt. He that spells truly most of the other's Words, is Victor for that Day; he that is Victor most Days in a Month, to obtain a Prize, a pretty neat Book of some Kind useful in their future Studies. This Method fixes the Attention of Children extreamly to the Orthography of Words, and makes them good Spellers very

448

early. 'Tis a Shame for a Man to be so ignorant of this little Art, in his own Language, as to be perpetually confounding Words of like Sound and different Significations; the Consciousness of which Defect, makes some Men, otherwise of good Learning and Understanding, averse to Writing even a common Letter.

Let the Pieces read by the Scholars in this Class be short, such as *Croxall's* Fables, and little Stories. In giving the Lesson, let it be read to them; let the Meaning of the difficult Words in it be explained to them, and let them con it over by themselves before they are called to read to the Master, or Usher; who is to take particular Care that they do not read too fast, and that they duly observe the Stops and Pauses. A Vocabulary of the most usual difficult Words might be formed for their Use, with Explanations; and they might daily get a few of those Words and Explanations by Heart, which would a little exercise their Memories; or at least they might write a Number of them in a small Book for the Purpose, which would help to fix the Meaning of those Words in their Minds, and at the same Time furnish every one with a little Dictionary for his future Use.

THE SECOND CLASS

to be taught Reading with Attention, and with proper Modulations of the Voice, according to the Sentiments and Subject.

Some short Pieces, not exceeding the Length of a *Spectator*, to be given this Class as Lessons (and some of the easier *Spectators* would be very suitable for the Purpose.) These Lessons might be given over Night as Tasks, the Scholars to study them against the Morning. Let it then be required of them to give an Account, first of the Parts of Speech, and Construction of one or two Sentences; this will oblige them to recur frequently to their Grammar, and fix its principal Rules in their Memory. Next of the *Intention* of the Writer, or the *Scope* of the Piece; the Meaning of each Sentence, and of every uncommon Word. This would early acquaint them with the Meaning and Force of Words, and give them that most necessary Habit, of Reading with Attention.

The Master then to read the Piece with the proper Modulations of Voice, due Emphasis, and suitable Action, where Action is required; and put the Youth on imitating his Manner.

Where the Author has us'd an Expression not the best, let it be pointed out; and let his Beauties be particularly remarked to the Youth.

Let the Lessons for Reading be varied, that the Youth may be made acquainted with good Stiles of all Kinds in Prose and Verse, and the proper Manner of reading each Kind. Sometimes a well-told Story, a Piece of a Sermon, a General's Speech to his Soldiers, a Speech in a Tragedy, some Part of a Comedy, an Ode, a Satyr, a Letter, Blank Verse, Hudibrastick, Heroic, &c. But let such Lessons for Reading be chosen, as contain some useful Instruction, whereby the Understandings or Morals of the Youth, may at the same Time be improv'd.

It is requir'd that they should first study and understand the Lessons, before they are put upon reading them properly, to which End each Boy should have an *English* Dictionary, to help him over Difficulties. When our Boys read *English* to us, we are apt to imagine *they* understand what *they* read, because *we* do, and because 'tis their Mother Tongue. But they often read as Parrots speak, knowing little or nothing of the Meaning. And it is impossible a Reader should give the due Modulation to his Voice, and pronounce properly, unless his Understanding goes before his Tongue, and makes him Master of the Sentiment. Accustoming Boys to read aloud what they do not first understand, is the Cause of those even set Tones so common among Readers, which when they have once got a Habit of using, they find so difficult to correct: By which Means, among Fifty Readers, we scarcely find a good One. For want of good Reading, Pieces publish'd with a View to influence the Minds of Men for their own or the publick Benefit, lose Half their Force. Were there but one good Reader in a Neighbourhood, a publick Orator might be heard throughout a Nation with the same Advantages, and have the same Effect on his Audience, as if they stood within the Reach of his Voice.

THE THIRD CLASS

to be taught Speaking properly and gracefully, which is near of Kin to good Reading, and naturally follows it in the Studies of Youth. Let the Scholars of this Class begin with learning the Elements of Rhetoric from some short System, so as to be able to give an Account of the most usual Tropes and Figures. Let all their bad Habits of Speaking, all Offences against good Grammar, all corrupt or foreign Accents, and all improper Phrases, be pointed out to them. Short Speeches from the *Roman,* or other History, or from our *Parliamentary Debates,* might be got by heart, and deliver'd with the proper Action, &c. Speeches and Scenes in our best Tragedies and Comedies (avoiding every Thing that could injure the

450

Morals of Youth) might likewise be got by Rote, and the Boys exercis'd in delivering or acting them; great Care being taken to form their Manner after the truest Models.

For their farther Improvement, and a little to vary their Studies, let them now begin to read *History*, after having got by Heart a short Table of the principal Epochas in Chronology. They may begin with *Rollin's Antient and Roman Histories*, and proceed at proper Hours as they go thro' the subsequent Classes, with the best Histories of our own Nation and Colonies. Let Emulation be excited among the Boys by giving, Weekly, little Prizes, or other small Encouragements to those who are able to give the best Account of what they have read, as to Times, Places, Names of Persons, &c. This will make them read with Attention, and imprint the History well in their Memories. In remarking on the History, the Master will have fine Opportunities of instilling Instruction of various Kinds, and improving the Morals as well as the Understandings of Youth.

The Natural and Mechanic History contain'd in the *Spectacle de la Nature*, might also be begun in this Class, and continued thro' the subsequent Classes by other Books of the same Kind: For next to the Knowledge of *Duty*, this Kind of Knowledge is certainly the most useful, as well as the most entertaining. The Merchant may thereby be enabled better to understand many Commodities in Trade; the Handicraftsman to improve his Business by new Instruments, Mixtures and Materials; and frequently Hints are given of new Manufactures, or new Methods of improving Land, that may be set on foot greatly to the Advantage of a Country.

THE FOURTH CLASS

to be taught Composition. Writing one's own Language well, is the next necessary Accomplishment after good Speaking. 'Tis the Writing-Master's Business to take Care that the Boys make fair Characters, and place them straight and even in the Lines: But to *form their Stile*, and even to take Care that the Stops and Capitals are properly disposed, is the Part of the *English* Master. The Boys should be put on Writing Letters to each other on any common Occurrences, and on various Subjects, imaginary Business, &c., containing little Stories, Accounts of their late Reading, what Parts of Authors please them, and why; Letters of Congratulation, of Compliment, of Request, of Thanks, of Recommendation, of Admonition, of Consolation, of Expostulation, Excuse, &c. In these they

451

should be taught to express themselves clearly, concisely, and naturally, without affected Words or high-flown Phrases. All their Letters to pass through the Master's Hand, who is to point out the Faults, advise the Corrections, and commend what he finds right. Some of the best Letters published in our own Language, as *Sir William Temple's,* those of *Pope,* and his Friends, and some others, might be set before the Youth as Models, their Beauties pointed out and explained by the Master, the Letters themselves transcrib'd by the Scholar.

Dr. Johnson's *Ethices Elementa,* or First Principles of Morality, may now be read by the Scholars, and explain'd by the Master, to lay a solid Foundation of Virtue and Piety in their Minds. And as this Class continues the Reading of History, let them now at proper Hours receive some farther Instruction in Chronology, and in that Part of Geography (from the Mathematical Master), which is necessary to understand the Maps and Globes. They should also be acquainted with the modern Names of the Places they find mention'd in antient Writers. The Exercises of good Reading, and proper Speaking, still continued at suitable Times.

FIFTH CLASS

To improve the Youth in *Composition,* they may now, besides continuing to write Letters, begin to write little Essays in Prose, and sometimes in Verse, not to make them Poets, but for this Reason, that nothing acquaints a Lad so speedily with Variety of Expression, as the Necessity of finding such Words and Phrases as will suit with the Measure, Sound, and Rhime of Verse, and at the same time well express the Sentiment. These Essays should all pass under the Master's Eye, who will point out their Faults, and put the Writer on correcting them. Where the Judgment is not ripe enough for forming new Essays, let the Sentiments of a *Spectator* be given, and requir'd to be cloath'd in a Scholar's own Words; or the Circumstances of some good Story, the Scholar to find Expression. Let them be put sometimes on abridging a Paragraph of a diffuse Author, sometimes on dilating or amplifying what is wrote more closely. And now let Dr. Johnson's *Noetica,* or First Principles of Human Knowledge, containing a Logic, or Art of Reasoning, &c. be read by the Youth, and the Difficulties that may occur to them be explained by the Master. The Reading of History, and the Exercises of good Reading and just Speaking, still continued.

In this Class, besides continuing the Studies of the preceding, in History, Rhetoric, Logic, Moral and Natural Philosophy, the best *English* Authors may be read and explain'd; as *Tillotson, Milton, Locke, Addison, Pope, Swift,* the higher Papers in the *Spectator* and *Guardian,* the best Translations of *Homer, Virgil,* and *Horace,* of *Telemachus, Travels of Cyrus,* &c.

Once a Year let there be publick Exercises in the Hall, the Trustees and Citizens present. Then let fine gilt Books be given as Prizes to such Boys as distinguish themselves and excel the others in any Branch of Learning, making three Degrees of Comparison; giving the best Prize to him that performs best; a less valuable One to him that comes up next to the best; and another to the third. Commendations, Encouragement and Advice to the rest; keeping up their Hopes, that by Industry they may excel another Time. The Names of those that obtain the Prizes to be yearly printed in a List.

The Hours of each Day are to be divided and dispos'd in such a Manner, as that some Classes may be with the Writing-Master, improving their Hands, others with the Mathematical Master, learning Arithmetick, Accompts, Geography, Use of the Globes, Drawing, Mechanicks, &c.; while the rest are in the *English* School, under the *English* Master's Care.

Thus instructed, Youth will come out of this School fitted for learning any Business, Calling or Profession, except such wherein Languages are required; and tho' unacquainted with any antient or foreign Tongue, they will be Masters of their own, which is of more immediate and general Use; and withal will have attain'd many other valuable Accomplishments; the Time usually spent in acquiring those Languages, often without Success, being here employ'd in laying such a Foundation of Knowledge and Ability, as, properly improv'd, may qualify them to pass thro' and execute the several Offices of civil Life, with Advantage and Reputation to themselves and Country.

B. F.

THE WAY TO WEALTH

PREFACE TO *POOR RICHARD IMPROVED:* 1758.

COURTEOUS READER, I have heard that nothing gives an Author so great Pleasure, as to find his Works respectfully quoted by other learned Authors. This Pleasure I have seldom enjoyed; for tho' I have been, if I may say it without Vanity, an *eminent Author* of Almanacks annually now a full Quarter of a Century, my Brother Authors in the same Way, for what Reason I know not, have ever been very sparing in their Applauses; and no other Author has taken the least Notice of me, so that did not my Writings produce me some solid *Pudding*, the great Deficiency of *Praise* would have quite discouraged me.

I concluded at length, that the People were the best Judges of my Merit; for they buy my Works; and besides, in my Rambles, where I am not personally known, I have frequently heard one or other of my Adages repeated, with, *as Poor Richard says,* at the End on't; this gave me some Satisfaction, as it showed not only that my Instructions were regarded, but discovered likewise some Respect for my Authority; and I own, that to encourage the Practice of remembering and repeating those wise Sentences, I have sometimes *quoted myself* with great Gravity.

Judge then how much I must have been gratified by an Incident I am going to relate to you. I stopt my Horse lately where a great Number of People were collected at a Vendue of Merchant Goods. The Hour of Sale not being come, they were conversing on the Badness of the Times, and one of the Company call'd to a plain clean old Man, with white Locks, *Pray, Father* Abraham, *what think you of the Times? Won't these heavy Taxes quite ruin the Country? How shall we ever be able to pay them? What would you advise us to?*——Father *Abraham* stood up, and reply'd, If you'd have my Advice, I'll give it you in short, for a *Word to the Wise is enough,* and *many Words won't fill a Bushel,* as *Poor Richard says.* They join'd in desiring him to speak his Mind, and gathering round him, he proceeded as follows;

"Friends, says he, and Neighbours, the Taxes are indeed very heavy, and if those laid on by the Government were the only Ones we had to pay, we might more easily discharge them; but we have many others, and much more grievous to some of us. We are taxed twice as much by our *Idleness,* three times as much by our *Pride,* and four times as much by our *Folly,* and from these Taxes the Commissioners cannot ease or deliver us by allowing an Abatement. However let us hearken to good Advice, and something may be done for us; *God helps them that help themselves,* as *Poor Richard* says, in his Almanack of 1733.

It would be thought a hard Government that should tax its People one tenth Part of their *Time,* to be employed in its Service.

454

But *Idleness* taxes many of us much more, if we reckon all that is spent in absolute *Sloth*, or doing of nothing, with that which is spent in idle Employments or Amusements, that amount to nothing. *Sloth*, by bringing on Diseases, absolutely shortens Life. *Sloth, like Rust, consumes faster than Labour wears, while the used Key is always bright,* as *Poor Richard* says. But *dost thou love Life, then do not squander Time, for that's the Stuff Life is made of,* as *Poor Richard* says.—How much more than is necessary do we spend in Sleep! forgetting that *The sleeping Fox catches no Poultry,* and that *there will be sleeping enough in the Grave,* as *Poor Richard* says. If Time be of all Things the most precious, *wasting Time* must be, as *Poor Richard* says, *the greatest Prodigality,* since, as he elsewhere tells us, *Lost Time is never found again;* and what we call *Time-enough, always proves little enough:* Let us then up and be doing, and doing to the Purpose; so by Diligence shall we do more with less Perplexity. *Sloth makes all Things difficult, but Industry all easy,* as *Poor Richard* says; and *He that riseth late, must trot all Day, and shall scarce overtake his Business at Night.* While *Laziness travels so slowly, that Poverty soon overtakes him,* as we read in *Poor Richard,* who adds, *Drive thy Business, let not that drive thee;* and *Early to Bed, and early to rise, makes a Man healthy, wealthy and wise.*

. . . . . .

Methinks I hear some of you say, *Must a Man afford himself no Leisure?*—I will tell thee, my Friend, what *Poor Richard* says, *Employ thy Time well if thou meanest to gain Leisure;* and *since thou art not sure of a Minute, throw not away an Hour.* Leisure, is Time for doing something useful; this Leisure the diligent Man will obtain, but the lazy Man never; so that, as *Poor Richard* says, a *Life of Leisure and a Life of Laziness are two Things.* Do you imagine that Sloth will afford you more Comfort than Labour? No, for as *Poor Richard* says, *Trouble springs from Idleness, and grievous Toil from needless Ease. Many without Labour, would live by their* Wits *only, but they break for want of Stock.* Whereas Industry gives Comfort, and Plenty, and Respect: *Fly Pleasures, and they'll follow you. The diligent Spinner has a large Shift;* and *now I have a Sheep and a Cow, every Body bids me Good morrow;* all which is well said by *Poor Richard.*

But with our Industry, we must likewise be *steady, settled* and *careful,* and oversee our own Affairs *with our own Eyes,* and not trust too much to others; for, as *Poor Richard* says,

455

I never saw an oft removed Tree,
Nor yet an oft removed Family,
That throve so well as those that settled be.

And again, *Three Removes is as bad as a Fire;* and again, *Keep thy Shop, and thy Shop will keep thee;* and again, *If you would have your Business done, go; If not, send.* And again,

He that by the Plough would thrive,
Himself must either hold or drive.

. . . . .

So much for Industry, my Friends, and Attention to one's own Business; but to these we must add *Frugality*, if we would make our *Industry* more certainly successful. A Man may, if he knows not how to save as he gets, *keep his Nose all his Life to the Grindstone,* and die not worth a *Groat* at last. *A fat Kitchen makes a lean Will,* as *Poor Richard* says; and,

Many Estates are spent in the Getting,
Since Women for Tea forsook Spinning and Knitting,
And Men for Punch forsook Hewing and Splitting.

If you would be wealthy, says he, in another Almanack, *think of Saving as well as of Getting: The* Indies *have not made* Spain *rich, because her* Outgoes *are greater than her* Incomes. Away then with your expensive Follies, and you will not have so much Cause to complain of hard Times, heavy Taxes, and chargeable Families; for, as *Poor Dick* says,

Women and Wine, Game and Deceit,
Make the Wealth small, and the Wants great.

And farther, *What maintains one Vice, would bring up two Children.* You may think perhaps, That a *little* Tea, or a *little* Punch now and then, Diet a *little* more costly, Clothes a *little* finer, and a *little* Entertainment now and then, can be no *great* Matter; but remember what *Poor Richard* says, *Many* a Little *makes a Mickle;* and farther, *Beware of* little *Expences; a small Leak will sink a great Ship;* and again, *Who Dainties love, shall Beggars prove;* and moreover, *Fools make Feasts, and wise Men eat them.*

Here you are all got together at this Vendue of *Fineries* and *Knicknacks.* You call them *Goods,* but if you do not take Care, they will prove *Evils* to some of you. You expect they will be sold *cheap,*

456

and perhaps they may for less than they cost; but if you have no Occasion for them, they must be *dear* to you. Remember what *Poor Richard* says, *Buy what thou hast no Need of, and ere long thou shalt sell thy Necessaries.* And again, *At a great Pennyworth pause a while:* He means, that perhaps the Cheapness is *apparent* only, and not *real;* or the Bargain, by straitning thee in thy Business, may do thee more Harm than Good. For in another Place he says, *Many have been ruined by buying good Pennyworths.* Again, *Poor Richard* says, *'Tis foolish to lay out Money in a Purchase of Repentance;* and yet this Folly is practised every Day at Vendues, for want of minding the Almanack. *Wise Men,* as *Poor Dick* says, *learn by others Harms, Fools scarcely by their own;* but *Felix quem faciunt aliena Pericula cautum.* Many a one, for the Sake of Finery on the Back, have gone with a hungry Belly, and half starved their Families; *Silks and Sattins, Scarlet and Velvets,* as *Poor Richard* says, *put out the Kitchen Fire.* These are not the *Necessaries* of Life; they can scarcely be called the *Conveniencies,* and yet only because they look pretty, how many *want* to *have* them. The *artificial* Wants of Mankind thus become more numerous than the *natural;* and, as *Poor Dick* says, *For one* poor *Person, there are an hundred* indigent. By these, and other Extravagancies, the Genteel are reduced to Poverty, and forced to borrow of those whom they formerly despised, but who through *Industry* and *Frugality* have maintained their Standing; in which Case it appears plainly, that a *Ploughman on his Legs is higher than a Gentleman on his Knees,* as *Poor Richard* says. . . .

> *Fond* Pride of Dress *is sure a very Curse;*
> *E'er* Fancy *you consult, consult your Purse.*

And again, *Pride is as loud a Beggar as Want, and a great deal more saucy.* When you have bought one fine Thing you must buy ten more, that your Appearance may be all of a Piece; but *Poor Dick* says, *'Tis easier to* suppress *the first Desire, than to* satisfy *all that follow it.* And 'tis as truly Folly for the Poor to ape the Rich, as for the Frog to swell, in order to equal the Ox.

> *Great Estates may venture more,*
> *But little Boats should keep near Shore.*

'Tis however a Folly soon punished; for *Pride that dines on Vanity sups on Contempt,* as *Poor Richard* says. And in another Place, *Pride breakfasted with Plenty, dined with Poverty, and supped with*

457

Infamy. And after all, of what Use is this *Pride of Appearance,* for which so much is risked, so much is suffered? It cannot promote Health, or ease Pain; it makes no Increase of Merit in the Person, it creates Envy, it hastens Misfortune.

> *What is a Butterfly? At best*
> *He's but a Caterpillar drest.*
> *The gaudy Fop's his Picture just,*

as *Poor Richard* says.

But what Madness must it be to *run in Debt* for these Superfluities! We are offered, by the Terms of this Vendue, *Six Months Credit;* and that perhaps has induced some of us to attend it, because we cannot spare the ready Money, and hope now to be fine without it. But, ah, think what you do when you run in Debt; *You give to another, Power over your Liberty.* If you cannot pay at the Time, you will be ashamed to see your Creditor; you will be in Fear when you speak to him; you will make poor pitiful sneaking Excuses, and by Degrees come to lose your Veracity, and sink into base downright lying; for, as *Poor Richard* says, *The second Vice is Lying, the first is running in Debt.* And again, to the same Purpose, *Lying rides upon Debt's Back.* Whereas a freeborn *Englishman* ought not to be ashamed or afraid to see or speak to any Man living. But Poverty often deprives a Man of all Spirit and Virtue: *'Tis hard for an empty Bag to stand upright,* as *Poor Richard* truly says.

· · · · ·

This Doctrine, my Friends, is *Reason* and *Wisdom;* but after all, do not depend too much upon your own *Industry,* and *Frugality,* and *Prudence,* though excellent Things, for they may all be blasted without the Blessing of Heaven; and therefore ask that Blessing humbly, and be not uncharitable to those that at present seem to want it, but comfort and help them. Remember *Job* suffered, and was afterwards prosperous.

And now to conclude, *Experience keeps a dear School, but Fools will learn in no other, and scarce in that;* for it is true, *we may give Advice, but we cannot give Conduct,* as *Poor Richard* says: However, remember this, *They that won't be counselled, can't be helped,* as *Poor Richard* says: And farther, That *if you will not hear Reason, she'll surely rap your Knuckles.*

Thus the old Gentleman ended his Harangue. The People heard it, and approved the Doctrine and immediately practised the contrary, just as if it had been a common Sermon; for the Vendue

458

FRANKLIN

opened, and they began to buy extravagantly, notwithstanding all his Cautions, and their own Fear of Taxes.—I found the good Man had thoroughly studied my Almanacks, and digested all I had dropt on those Topicks during the Course of Five-and-twenty Years. The frequent Mention he made of me must have tired any one else, but my Vanity was wonderfully delighted with it, though I was conscious that not a tenth Part of the Wisdom was my own which he ascribed to me, but rather the *Gleanings* I had made of the Sense of all Ages and Nations. However, I resolved to be the better for the Echo of it; and though I had at first determined to buy Stuff for a new Coat, I went away resolved to wear my old One a little longer. *Reader,* if thou wilt do the same, thy Profit will be as great as mine.

I am, as ever,

Thine to serve thee,

July 7, 1757.   RICHARD SAUNDERS.

SPEECH IN THE CONVENTION

At the Conclusion of its Deliberations [September 17, 1787]

MR. PRESIDENT, I confess, that I do not entirely approve of this Constitution at present; but, Sir, I am not sure I shall never approve it; for, having lived long, I have experienced many instances of being obliged, by better information or fuller consideration, to change my opinions even on important subjects, which I once thought right, but found to be otherwise. It is therefore that, the older I grow, the more apt I am to doubt my own judgment of others. Most men, indeed, as well as most sects in religion, think themselves in possession of all truth, and that wherever others differ from them, it is so far error. Steele, a Protestant, in a dedication, tells the Pope, that the only difference between our two churches in their opinions of the certainty of their doctrine, is, the Romish Church is *infallible,* and the Church of England is *never in the wrong.* But, though many private Persons think almost as highly of their own infallibility as of that of their Sect, few express it so naturally as a certain French Lady, who, in a little dispute with her sister, said, "But I meet with nobody but myself that is *always* in the right." *"Je ne trouve que moi qui aie toujours raison."*

In these sentiments, Sir, I agree to this Constitution, with all its faults,—if they are such; because I think a general Government necessary for us, and there is no *form* of government but what may be a blessing to the people, if well administered; and I believe, farther, that this is likely to be well administered for a course of years, and can only end in despotism, as other forms have done before it, when the people shall become so corrupted as to need despotic government, being incapable of any other. I doubt, too, whether any other Convention we can obtain, may be able to make a better constitution; for, when you assemble a number of men, to have the advantage of their joint wisdom, you inevitably assemble with those men all their prejudices, their passions, their errors of opinion, their local interests, and their selfish views. From such an assembly can a *perfect* production be expected? It therefore astonishes me, Sir, to find this system approaching so near to perfection as it does; and I think it will astonish our enemies, who are waiting with confidence to hear, that our councils are confounded like those of the builders of Babel, and that our States are on the point of separation, only to meet hereafter for the purpose of cutting one another's throats. Thus I consent, Sir, to this Constitution, because I expect no better, and because I am not sure that it is not the best. The opinions I have had of its *errors* I sacrifice to the public good. I have never whispered a syllable of them abroad. Within these walls they were born, and here they shall die. If every one of us, in returning to our Constituents, were to report the objections he has had to it, and endeavour to gain Partisans in support of them, we might prevent its being generally received, and thereby lose all the salutary effects and great advantages resulting naturally in our favour among foreign nations, as well as among ourselves, from our real or apparent unanimity. Much of the strength and efficiency of any government, in procuring and securing happiness to the people, depends on *opinion*, on the general opinion of the goodness of that government, as well as of the wisdom and integrity of its governors. I hope, therefore, for our own sakes, as a part of the people, and for the sake of our posterity, that we shall act heartily and unanimously in recommending this Constitution, wherever our Influence may extend, and turn our future thoughts and endeavours to the means of having it *well administered.*

On the whole, Sir, I cannot help expressing a wish, that every member of the Convention who may still have objections to it, would with me on this occasion doubt a little of his own infallibility, and, to make *manifest* our *unanimity*, put his name to this Instrument.

[Then the motion was made for adding the last formula, viz.

460

FRANKLIN

"Done in convention by the Unanimous Consent," &c.; which was agreed to and added accordingly.]

TO EZRA STILES

Philad[a], March 9, 1790.

. . . You desire to know something of my Religion. It is the first time I have been questioned upon it. But I cannot take your Curiosity amiss, and shall endeavour in a few Words to gratify it. Here is my Creed. I believe in one God, Creator of the Universe. That he governs it by his Providence. That he ought to be worshipped. That the most acceptable Service we render to him is doing good to his other Children. That the soul of Man is immortal, and will be treated with Justice in another Life respecting its Conduct in this. These I take to be the fundamental Principles of all sound Religion, and I regard them as you do in whatever Sect I meet with them.

As to Jesus of Nazareth, my Opinion of whom you particularly desire, I think the System of Morals and his Religion, as he left them to us, the best the World ever saw or is likely to see; but I apprehend it has received various corrupting Changes, and I have, with most of the present Dissenters in England, some Doubts as to his Divinity; tho' it is a question I do not dogmatize upon, having never studied it, and think it needless to busy myself with it now, when I expect soon an Opportunity of knowing the Truth with less Trouble. I see no harm, however, in its being believed, if that Belief has the good Consequence, as probably it has, of making his Doctrines more respected and better observed; especially as I do not perceive, that the Supreme takes it amiss, by distinguishing the Unbelievers in his Government of the World with any peculiar Marks of his Displeasure.

I shall only add, respecting myself, that, having experienced the Goodness of that Being in conducting me prosperously thro' a long life, I have no doubt of its Continuance in the next, though without the smallest Conceit of meriting such Goodness. My Sentiments on this Head you will see in the Copy of an old Letter enclosed, which I wrote in answer to one from a zealous Religionist, whom I had relieved in a paralytic case by electricity, and who, being afraid I should grow proud upon it, sent me his serious though rather impertinent Caution. I send you also the Copy of another Letter, which will shew something of my Disposition relating to Religion. With great and sincere Esteem and Affection, I am, Your obliged old Friend and most obedient humble Servant

B. FRANKLIN.

P. S. Had not your College some Present of Books from the King of France? Please to let me know, if you had an Expectation given you of more, and the Nature of that Expectation? I have a Reason for the Enquiry.

I confide, that you will not expose me to Criticism and censure by publishing any part of this Communication to you. I have ever let others enjoy their religious Sentiments, without reflecting on them for those that appeared to me unsupportable and even absurd. All Sects here, and we have a great Variety, have experienced my good will in assisting them with Subscriptions for building their new Places of Worship; and, as I have never opposed any of their Doctrines, I hope to go out of the World in Peace with them all.

462

JEFFERSON 1743–1826

JEFFERSON, the democratic aristocrat, realized that a free society must be able to encompass both the vision of equality and the vision of excellence. Equality without excellence degenerates into mediocrity; excellence without equality becomes privilege.

For the cause of equality Jefferson tried to impose on his fellow citizens of Virginia a universal and free public school. For the idea of excellence he wished this school to be the broad basis for a selective process culminating in the University of Virginia.

Jefferson could not achieve the synthesis of which he dreamed even in his relatively uncomplicated community. However, the truth remains that only with the productive tension between spurring opposites such as equality and excellence, or freedom and discipline, can a society retain its vitality. If this tension disappears or becomes too fervid to be mastered, then it is easily replaced by the destructive fight between the tyranny of a few and the tyranny of the masses.

The following selections from Thomas Jefferson's *Notes on Virginia and Other Writings* are from Prescotts *Alexander Hamilton and Thomas Jefferson*, published in New York by the American Book Company, in 1937.

NOTES ON VIRGINIA AND OTHER WRITINGS

QUERY XIV.—*The administration of justice and the description of the laws?* . . . Another object of the revisal is to diffuse knowledge more generally through the mass of the people. This bill proposes to lay off every county into small districts of five or six miles square, called hundreds, and in each of them to establish a school for teaching reading, writing, and arithmetic. The tutor to be supported by the hundred, and every person in it entitled to send their children three years gratis, and as much longer as they please, paying for it. These schools to be under a visitor who is annually to choose the boy of best genius in the school, of those whose parents are too poor to give them further education, and to send him forward to one of the grammar schools, of which twenty are proposed to be erected in different parts of the country, for teaching Greek, Latin, geography, and the higher branches of numerical arithmetic.

463

Of the boys thus sent in any one year, trial is to be made at the grammar schools one or two years, and the best genius of the whole selected, and continued six years, and the residue dismissed. By this means twenty of the best geniuses will be raked from the rubbish annually, and be instructed, at the public expense, so far as the grammar schools go. At the end of six years' instruction, one-half are to be discontinued (from among whom the grammar schools will probably be supplied with future masters); and the other half, who are to be chosen for the superiority of their parts and disposition, are to be sent and continued three years in the study of such sciences as they shall choose, at William and Mary College, the plan of which is proposed to be enlarged, as will be hereafter explained, and extended to all the useful sciences. The ultimate result of the whole scheme of education would be the teaching all the children of the State reading, writing, and common arithmetic; turning out ten annually, of superior genius, well taught in Greek, Latin, geography, and the higher branches of arithmetic; turning out ten others annually, of still superior parts, who, to those branches of learning, shall have added such of the sciences as their genius shall have led them to; the furnishing to the wealthier part of the people convenient schools at which their children may be educated at their own expense. The general objects of this law are to provide an education adapted to the years, to the capacity, and the condition of every one, and directed to their freedom and happiness. Specific details were not proper for the law. These must be the business of the visitors entrusted with its execution. The first stage of this education being the schools of the hundreds, wherein the great mass of the people will receive their instruction, the principal foundations of future order will be laid here. Instead, therefore, of putting the Bible and Testament into the hands of the children at an age when their judgments are not sufficiently matured for religious inquiries, their memories may here be stored with the most useful facts from Grecian, Roman, European and American history. The first elements of morality too may be instilled into their minds; such as, when further developed as their judgments advance in strength, may teach them how to work out their own greatest happiness, by showing them that it does not depend on the condition of life in which chance has placed them, but is always the result of a good conscience, good health, occupation, and freedom in all just pursuits. Those whom either the wealth of their parents or the adoption of the State shall destine to higher degrees of learning, will go on to the grammar schools, which constitute the next

464

stage, there to be instructed in the languages. The learning Greek and Latin, I am told, is going into disuse in Europe. I know not what their manners and occupations may call for; but it would be very ill-judged in us to follow their example in this instance. There is a certain period of life, say from eight to fifteen or sixteen years of age, when the mind like the body is not yet firm enough for laborious and close operations. If applied to such, it falls an early victim to premature exertion; exhibiting, indeed, at first, in these young and tender subjects, the flattering appearance of their being men while they are yet children, but ending in reducing them to be children when they should be men. The memory is then most susceptible and tenacious of impressions; and the learning of languages being chiefly a work of memory, it seems precisely fitted to the powers of this period, which is long enough, too, for acquiring the most useful languages, ancient and modern. I do not pretend that language is science. It is only an instrument for the attainment of science. But that time is not lost which is employed in providing tools for future operation; more especially as in this case the books put into the hands of the youth for this purpose may be such as will at the same time impress their minds with useful facts and good principles. If this period be suffered to pass in idleness, the mind becomes lethargic and impotent, as would the body it inhabits if unexercised during the same time. The sympathy between body and mind during their rise, progress and decline, is too strict and obvious to endanger our being misled while we reason from the one to the other. As soon as they are of sufficient age, it is supposed they will be sent on from the grammar schools to the university, which constitutes our third and last stage, there to study those sciences which may be adapted to their views. By that part of our plan which prescribes the selection of the youths of genius from among the classes of the poor, we hope to avail the State of those talents which nature has sown as liberally among the poor as the rich, but which perish without use, if not sought for and cultivated. But of all the views of this law none is more important, none more legitimate, than that of rendering the people the safe, as they are the ultimate, guardians of their own liberty. For this purpose the reading in the first stage, where *they* will receive their whole education, is proposed, as has been said, to be chiefly historical. History, by apprising them of the past, will enable them to judge of the future; it will avail them of the experience of other times and other nations; it will qualify them as judges of the actions and designs of men; it will enable them to know ambition under every disguise it may assume; and knowing it, to defeat its views. In every government on earth is some trace of human weakness, some germ of corruption and degeneracy, which cunning will discover, and wickedness insensibly open, cultivate, and improve. Every government degenerates when trusted to the rulers of the people alone. The people themselves, therefore, are its only safe depositories. And to render even them safe, their minds must be improved to a certain degree. This indeed is not all that is necessary, though it be essentially necessary. An amendment of our constitution must here come in aid of the public education. The influence over government must be shared among all the people. If every individual which composes their mass participates of the ultimate authority, the government will be safe; because the corrupting the whole mass will exceed any private resources of wealth; and public ones cannot be provided but by levies on the people. In this case every man would have to pay his own price. The government of Great Britain has been corrupted, because but one man in ten has a right to vote for members of parliament. The sellers of the government, therefore, get nine-tenths of their price clear. It has been thought that corruption is restrained by confining the right of suffrage to a few of the wealthier of the people; but it would be more effectually restrained by an extension of that right to such members as would bid defiance to the means of corruption.

Lastly, it is proposed, by a bill in this revisal, to begin a public library and gallery, by laying out a certain sum annually in books, paintings, and statues.

QUERY XVII.—*The different religions received into that state?* . . . The present state of our laws on the subject of religion is this. The convention of May, 1776, in their declaration of rights, declared it to be a truth, and a natural right, that the exercise of religion should be free; but when they proceeded to form on that declaration the ordinance of government, instead of taking up every principle declared in the bill of rights, and guarding it by legislative sanction, they passed over that which asserted our religious rights, leaving them as they found them. The same convention, however, when they met as a member of the general assembly in October, 1776, repealed all *acts of Parliament* which had rendered criminal the maintaining any opinions in matters of religion, the forbearing to repair to church, and the exercising any mode of worship; and suspended the laws giving salaries to the clergy, which suspension was made perpetual in October, 1779. Statutory oppressions in religion being thus wiped away, we remain at present under those only imposed by the common law, or by our own acts of assembly. At the common law, *heresy* was a capital offence, punishable by burning. Its definition was left to the ecclesiastical judges, before whom the conviction was, till the statute of the 1 El. c. 1 circumscribed it, by declaring, that nothing should be deemed heresy, but what had been so determined by authority of the canonical scriptures, or by one of the four first general councils, or by some other council, having for the grounds of their declaration the express and plain words of the scriptures. Heresy, thus circumscribed, being an offence at the common law, our act of assembly of October, 1777, c. 17, gives cognizance of it to the general court, by declaring that the jurisdiction of that court shall be general in all matters at the common law. The execution is by the writ *De hæretico comburendo*. By our own act of assembly of 1705, c. 30, if a person brought up in the Christian religion denies the being of a God, or the Trinity, or asserts there are more gods than one, or denies the Christian religion to be true, or the scriptures to be of divine authority, he is punishable on the first offence by incapacity to hold any office or employment ecclesiastical, civil, or military; on the second by disability to sue, to take any gift or legacy, to be guardian, executor, or administrator, and by three years' imprisonment without bail. A father's right to the custody of his own children being founded in law on his right of guardianship, this being taken away, they may of course be severed from him, and put by the authority of a court into more orthodox hands. This is a summary view of that religious slavery under which a people have been willing to remain, who have lavished their lives and fortunes for the establishment of their civil freedom. The error seems not sufficiently eradicated, that the operations of the mind, as well as the acts of the body, are subject to the coercion of the laws.[1] But our rulers can have authority over such natural rights, only as we have submitted to them. The rights of conscience we never submitted, we could not submit. We are answerable for them to our God. The legitimate powers of government extend to such acts only as are injurious to others. But it does me no injury for my neighbor to say there are twenty gods, or no god. It neither picks my pocket nor breaks my leg. If it be said, his testimony in a court of justice cannot be relied on, reject it then, and be the stigma on him. Constraint may make him worse by making him a hypocrite, but it will never make him a truer man. It may fix him obstinately in his errors, but will not cure them. Reason and free inquiry are

[1] Furneaux passim.

467

the only effectual agents against error. Give a loose to them, they will support the true religion by bringing every false one to their tribunal, to the test of their investigation. They are the natural enemies of error, and of error only. Had not the Roman government permitted free inquiry, Christianity could never have been introduced. Had not free inquiry been indulged, at the era of the Reformation, the corruptions of Christianity could not have been purged away. If it be restrained now, the present corruptions will be protected, and new ones encouraged. Was the government to prescribe to us our medicine and diet, our bodies would be in such keeping as our souls are now. Thus in France the emetic was once forbidden as a medicine, and the potato as an article of food. Government is just as infallible, too, when it fixes systems in physics. Galileo was sent to the Inquisition for affirming that the earth was a sphere; the government had declared it to be as flat as a trencher, and Galileo was obliged to abjure his error. This error, however, at length prevailed, the earth became a globe, and Descartes declared it was whirled round its axis by a vortex. The government in which he lived was wise enough to see that this was no question of civil jurisdiction, or we should all have been involved by authority in vortices. In fact, the vortices have been exploded, and the Newtonian principle of gravitation is now more firmly established, on the basis of reason, than it would be were the government to step in, and to make it an article of necessary faith. Reason and experiment have been indulged, and error has fled before them. It is error alone which needs the support of government. Truth can stand by itself. Subject opinion to coercion: whom will you make your inquisitors? Fallible men; men governed by bad passions, by private as well as public reasons. And why subject it to coercion? To produce uniformity. But is uniformity of opinion desirable? No more than of face and stature. Introduce the bed of Procrustes then, and as there is danger that the large men may beat the small, make us all of a size, by lopping the former and stretching the latter. Difference of opinion is advantageous in religion. The several sects perform the office of a *censor morum* over each other. Is uniformity attainable? Millions of innocent men, women, and children, since the introduction of Christianity, have been burnt, tortured, fined, imprisoned; yet we have not advanced one inch towards uniformity. What has been the effect of coercion? To make one-half the world fools, and the other half hypocrites. To support roguery and error all over the earth. Let us reflect that it is inhabited by a thousand millions of people. That these profess probably a thou-

468

sand different systems of religion. That ours is but one of that thousand. That if there be but one right, and ours that one, we should wish to see the nine hundred and ninety-nine wandering sects gathered into the fold of truth. But against such a majority we cannot effect this by force. Reason and persuasion are the only practicable instruments. To make way for these, free inquiry must be indulged; and how can we wish others to indulge it while we refuse it ourselves. But every state, says an inquisitor, has established some religion. No two, say I, have established the same. Is this a proof of the infallibility of establishments? Our sister States of Pennsylvania and New York, however, have long subsisted without any establishment at all. The experiment was new and doubtful when they made it. It has answered beyond conception. They flourish infinitely. Religion is well supported; of various kinds, indeed, but all good enough; all sufficient to preserve peace and order; or if a sect arises, whose tenets would subvert morals, good sense has fair play, and reasons and laughs it out of doors, without suffering the State to be troubled with it. They do not hang more malefactors than we do. They are not more disturbed with religious dissensions. On the contrary, their harmony is unparalleled, and can be ascribed to nothing but their unbounded tolerance, because there is no other circumstance in which they differ from every nation on earth. They have made the happy discovery, that the way to silence religious disputes, is to take no notice of them. Let us too give this experiment fair play, and get rid, while we may, of those tyrannical laws. It is true, we are as yet secured against them by the spirit of the times. I doubt whether the people of this country would suffer an execution for heresy, or a three years' imprisonment for not comprehending the mysteries of the Trinity. But is the spirit of the people an infallible, a permanent reliance? Is it government? Is this the kind of protection we receive in return for the rights we give up? Besides, the spirit of the times may alter, will alter. Our rulers will become corrupt, our people careless. A single zealot may commence persecutor, and better men be his victims. It can never be too often repeated, that the time for fixing every essential right on a legal basis is while our rulers are honest, and ourselves united. From the conclusion of this war we shall be going down hill. It will not then be necessary to resort every moment to the people for support. They will be forgotten, therefore, and their rights disregarded. They will forget themselves, but in the sole faculty of making money, and will never think of uniting to effect a due respect for their rights. The shackles, therefore, which shall not be knocked off at the conclusion of this war will remain on us long, will be made heavier and heavier, till our rights shall revive or expire in a convulsion.

QUERY XVIII.—*The particular customs and manners that may happen to be received in that State?* It is difficult to determine on the standard by which the manners of a nation may be tried, whether *catholic* or *particular*. It is more difficult for a native to bring to that standard the manners of his own nation, familiarized to him by habit. There must doubtless be an unhappy influence on the manners of our people produced by the existence of slavery among us. The whole commerce between master and slave is a perpetual exercise of the most boisterous passions, the most unremitting despotism on the one part, and degrading submissions on the other. Our children see this, and learn to imitate it; for man is an imitative animal. This quality is the germ of all education in him. From his cradle to his grave he is learning to do what he sees others do. If a parent could find no motive either in his philanthropy or his self-love, for restraining the intemperance of passion towards his slave, it should always be a sufficient one that his child is present. But generally it is not sufficient. The parent storms, the child looks on, catches the lineaments of wrath, puts on the same airs in the circle of smaller slaves, gives a loose to the worst of passions, and thus nursed, educated, and daily exercised in tyranny, cannot but be stamped by it with odious peculiarities. The man must be a prodigy who can retain his manners and morals undepraved by such circumstances. And with what execration should the statesman be loaded, who, permitting one-half the citizens thus to trample on the rights of the other, transforms those into despots, and these into enemies, destroys the morals of the one part, and the *amor patriæ* of the other. For if a slave can have a country in this world, it must be any other in preference to that in which he is born to live and labor for another; in which he must lock up the faculties of his nature, contribute as far as depends on his individual endeavors to the evanishment of the human race, or entail his own miserable condition on the endless generations proceeding from him. With the morals of the people, their industry also is destroyed. For in a warm climate, no man will labor for himself who can make another labor for him. This is so true, that of the proprietors of slaves a very small proportion indeed are ever seen to labor. And can the liberties of a nation be thought secure when we have removed their only firm basis, a conviction in the minds of the people that these liberties are of the gift of God? That they are

470

not to be violated but with His wrath? Indeed I tremble for my country when I reflect that God is just; that his justice cannot sleep forever; that considering numbers, nature and natural means only, a revolution of the wheel of fortune, an exchange of situation is among possible events; that it may become probable by super-natural interference! The Almighty has no attribute which can take side with us in such a contest. But it is impossible to be temperate and to pursue this subject through the various considerations of policy, of morals, of history natural and civil. We must be con-tented to hope they will force their way into every one's mind. I think a change already perceptible, since the origin of the present revolution. The spirit of the master is abating, that of the slave ris-ing from the dust, his condition mollifying, the way I hope pre-paring, under the auspices of heaven, for a total emancipation, and that this is disposed, in the order of events, to be with the consent of the masters, rather than by their extirpation.

13. AN ACT FOR ESTABLISHING RELIGIOUS FREEDOM.— Passed in the Assembly of Virginia in the beginning of the year 1786. Well aware that Almighty God hath created the mind free; that all attempts to influence it by temporal punishments or bur-dens, or by civil incapacitations, tend only to beget habits of hypoc-risy and meanness, and are a departure from the plan of the Holy Author of our religion, who being Lord both of body and mind, yet chose not to propagate it by coercions on either, as was in his Almighty power to do; that the impious presumption of legislators and rulers, civil as well as ecclesiastical, who, being themselves but fallible and uninspired men, have assumed dominion over the faith of others, setting up their own opinions and modes of thinking as the only true and infallible, and as such endeavoring to impose them on others, hath established and maintained false religions over the greatest part of the world, and through all time; that to compel a man to furnish contributions of money for the propaga-tion of opinions which he disbelieves, is sinful and tyrannical; that even the forcing him to support this or that teacher of his own re-ligious persuasion, is depriving him of the comfortable liberty of giving his contributions to the particular pastor whose morals he would make his pattern, and whose powers he feels most persuasive to righteousness, and is withdrawing from the ministry those tem-poral rewards, which, proceeding from an approbation of their personal conduct, are an additional incitement to earnest and un-remitting labors for the instruction of mankind; that our civil rights

have no dependence on our religious opinions, more than our opinions in physics or geometry; that, therefore, the proscribing any citizen as unworthy the public confidence by laying upon him an incapacity of being called to the offices of trust and emolument, unless he profess or renounce this or that religious opinion, is depriving him injuriously of those privileges and advantages to which in common with his fellow citizens he has a natural right; that it tends also to corrupt the principles of that very religion it is meant to encourage, by bribing, with a monopoly of worldly honors and emoluments, those who will externally profess and conform to it; that though indeed these are criminal who do not withstand such temptation, yet neither are those innocent who lay the bait in their way; that to suffer the civil magistrate to intrude his powers into the field of opinion and to restrain the profession or propagation of principles, on the supposition of their ill tendency, is a dangerous fallacy, which at once destroys all religious liberty, because he being of course judge of that tendency, will make his opinions the rule of judgment, and approve or condemn the sentiments of others only as they shall square with or differ from his own; that it is time enough for the rightful purposes of civil government, for its officers to interfere when principles break out into overt acts against peace and good order; and finally, that truth is great and will prevail if left to herself, that she is the proper and sufficient antagonist to error, and has nothing to fear from the conflict, unless by human interposition disarmed of her natural weapons, free argument and debate, errors ceasing to be dangerous when it is permitted freely to contradict them.

Be it therefore enacted by the General Assembly, That no man shall be compelled to frequent or support any religious worship, place, or ministry whatsoever, nor shall be enforced, restrained, molested, or burdened in his body or goods, nor shall otherwise suffer on account of his religious opinions or belief; but that all men shall be free to profess, and by argument to maintain, their opinions in matters of religion, and that the same shall in nowise diminish, enlarge, or affect their civil capacities.

And though we well know this Assembly, elected by the people for the ordinary purposes of legislation only, have no power to restrain the acts of succeeding assemblies, constituted with the powers equal to our own, and that therefore to declare this act irrevocable would be of no effect in law, yet we are free to declare, and do declare, that the rights hereby asserted are of the natural rights of mankind, and that if any act shall be hereafter passed to

472

repeal the present or to narrow its operation, such act will be an infringement of natural right.

43. TO JOHN ADAMS [ARISTOCRACY, NATURAL AND ARTIFICIAL]

Monticello, October 28, 1813.

DEAR SIR,—

According to the reservation between us, of taking up one of the subjects of our correspondence at a time, I turn to your letters of August the 16th and September the 2d.

The passage you quote from Theognis, I think has an ethical rather than a political object. The whole piece is a moral *exhortation*, παραίνεσις, and this passage particularly seems to be a reproof to man, who, while with his domestic animals he is curious to improve the race, by employing always the finest male, pays no attention to the improvement of his own race, but intermarries with the vicious, the ugly, or the old, for considerations of wealth or ambition. It is in conformity with the principle adopted afterwards by the Pythagoreans, and expressed by Ocellus in another form; περὶ δὲ τῆς ἐξ τῶν ἀλλήλων ἀνθρώπων γενέσεως etc.,—οὐχ ἡδονῆς ἕνεκα ἡ μῖξις· which, as literally as intelligibility will admit, may be thus translated: "Concerning the interprocreation of men, how, and of whom it shall be, in a perfect manner, and according to the laws of modesty and sanctity, conjointly, this is what I think right. First to lay it down that we do not commix for the sake of pleasure, but of the procreation of children. For the powers, the organs and desires for coition have not been given by God to man for the sake of pleasure, but for the procreation of the race. For as it were incongruous for a mortal born to partake of divine life, the immortality of the race being taken away, God fulfilled the purpose by making the generations uninterrupted and continuous. This, therefore, we are especially to lay down as a principle, that coition is not for the sake of pleasure." But nature, not trusting to this moral and abstract motive, seems to have provided more securely for the perpetuation of the species, by making it the effect of the *œstrum* implanted in the constitution of both sexes. And not only has the commerce of love been indulged on this unhallowed impulse, but made subservient also to wealth and ambition by marriage, without regard to the beauty, the healthiness, the understanding, or virtue of the subject from which we are to breed. The selecting the best male for a harem of well-chosen females also, which Theognis seems to recommend from the example of our sheep and asses, would doubtless improve the human, as it does the brute animal, and produce a race of veritable ἄριστοι. For experience proves that the moral and physical qualities of man, whether good or evil, are transmissible in a certain degree from father to son. But I suspect that the equal rights of men will rise up against this privileged Solomon and his harem, and oblige us to continue acquiescence under the "ἀμαύρωσις γένεος ἀστῶν" which Theognis complains of, and to content ourselves with the accidental *aristoi* produced by the fortuitous concourse of breeders. For I agree with you that there is a natural aristocracy among men. The grounds of this are virtue and talents. Formerly, bodily powers gave place among the *aristoi*. But since the invention of gunpowder has armed the weak as well as the strong with missile death, bodily strength, like beauty, good humor, politeness, and other accomplishments, has become but an auxiliary ground of distinction. There is also an artificial aristocracy, founded on wealth and birth, without either virtue or talents; for with these it would belong to the first class. The natural aristocracy I consider as the most precious gift of nature, for the instruction, the trusts, and government of society. And indeed, it would have been inconsistent in creation to have formed man for the social state, and not to have provided virtue and wisdom enough to manage the concerns of the society. May we not even say, that that form of government is the best, which provides the most effectually for a pure selection of these natural *aristoi* into the offices of government? The artificial aristocracy is a mischievous ingredient in government, and provision should be made to prevent its ascendency. On the question, what is the best provision, you and I differ; but we differ as rational friends, using the free exercise of our own reason, and mutually indulging its errors. You think it best to put the *pseudo-aristoi* into a separate chamber of legislation, where they may be hindered from doing mischief by their co-ordinate branches, and where, also, they may be a protection to wealth against the agrarian and plundering enterprises of the majority of the people. I think that to give them power in order to prevent them from doing mischief, is arming them for it, and increasing instead of remedying the evil. For if the co-ordinate branches can arrest their action, so may they that of the co-ordinates. Mischief may be done negatively as well as positively. Of this, a cabal in the Senate of the United States has furnished many proofs. Nor do I believe them necessary to protect the wealthy; because enough of these will find their way into every branch of the legislation, to protect themselves. From fifteen to twenty legislatures of our own, in

474

action for thirty years past, have proved that no fears of an equalization of property are to be apprehended from them. I think the best remedy is exactly that provided by all our constitutions, to leave to the citizens the free election and separation of the *aristoi* from the *pseudo-aristoi,* of the wheat from the chaff. In general they will elect the really good and wise. In some instances, wealth may corrupt, and birth blind them; but not in sufficient degree to endanger the society.

It is probable that our difference of opinion may, in some measure, be produced by a difference of character in those among whom we live. From what I have seen of Massachusetts and Connecticut myself, and still more from what I have heard, and the character given of the former by yourself, who know them so much better, there seems to be in those two States a traditionary reverence for certain families; which has rendered the offices of the government nearly hereditary in those families. I presume that from an early period of your history, members of those families happening to possess virtue and talents, have honestly exercised them for the good of the people, and by their services have endeared their names to them. In coupling Connecticut with you, I mean it politically only, not morally. For having made the Bible the common law of their land, they seem to have modeled their morality on the story of Jacob and Laban. But although this hereditary succession to office with you, may, in some degree, be founded in real family merit, yet in a much higher degree, it has proceeded from your strict alliance of Church and State. These families are canonized in the eyes of the people on common principles, "you tickle me, and I will tickle you." In Virginia we have nothing of this. Our clergy, before the Revolution, having been secured against rivalship by fixed salaries, did not give themselves the trouble of acquiring influence over the people. Of wealth, there were great accumulations in particular families, handed down from generation to generation, under the English law of entails. But the only object of ambition for the wealthy was a seat in the King's Council. All their court then was paid to the crown and its creatures; and they Philipized in all collisions between the King and the people. Hence they were unpopular; and that unpopularity continues attached to their names. A Randolph, a Carter, or a Burwell must have great personal superiority over a common competitor to be elected by the people even at this day. At the first session of our legislature after the Declaration of Independence, we passed a law abolishing entails. And this was followed by one abolishing the privilege of primogeniture, and dividing the lands of intestates equally among all their children, or other representatives. These laws, drawn by myself, laid the axe to the foot of pseudo-aristocracy. And had another which I prepared been adopted by the legislature, our work would have been complete. It was a bill for the more general diffusion of learning. This proposed to divide every county into wards of five or six miles square, like your townships; to establish in each ward a free school for reading, writing, and common arith- metic; to provide for the annual selection of the best subjects from these schools, who might receive, at the public expense, a higher degree of education at a district school; and from these district schools to select a certain number of the most promising subjects, to be completed at an university, where all the useful sciences should be taught. Worth and genius would thus have been sought out from every condition of life, and completely prepared by education for defeating the competition of wealth and birth for public trusts. My proposition had, for a further object, to impart to these wards those portions of self-government for which they are best qualified, by confiding to them the care of their poor, their roads, police, elections, the nomination of jurors, administration of justice in small cases, elementary exercises of militia; in short, to have made them little republics, with a warden at the head of each, for all those concerns which, being under their eye, they would better manage than the larger republics of the county or State. A general call of ward meetings by their wardens on the same day through the State would at any time produce the genuine sense of the people on any required point, and would enable the State to act in mass, as your people have so often done, and with so much effect by their town meetings. The law for religious freedom, which made a part of this system, having put down the aristocracy of the clergy, and restored to the citizen the freedom of the mind, and those of entails and descents nurturing an equality of condition among them, this on education would have raised the mass of the people to the high ground of moral respectability necessary to their own safety, and to orderly government; and would have completed the great object of qualifying them to select the veritable *aristoi*, for the trusts of gov- ernment, to the exclusion of the pseudalists; and the same Theognis who has furnished the epigraphs of your two letters, assures us that "Οὐδεμίαν πω, Κύρν', ἀγαθοὶ πόλιν ὤλεσαν ἄνδρες." Although this law has not yet been acted on but in a small and inefficient degree, it is still considered as before the legislature, with other bills of the revised code, not yet taken up, and I have great hope that some patriotic spirit will, at a favorable moment, call it up, and make it the keystone of the arch of our government.

With respect to aristocracy, we should further consider, that before the establishment of the American States, nothing was known to history but the man of the old world, crowded within limits either small or overcharged, and steeped in the vices which that situation generates. A government adapted to such men would be one thing; but a very different one, that for the man of these States. Here every one may have land to labor for himself, if he chooses; or, preferring the exercise of any other industry, may exact for it such compensation as not only to afford a comfortable subsistence, but wherewith to provide for a cessation from labor in old age. Every one, by his property, or by his satisfactory situation, is interested in the support of law and order. And such men may safely and advantageously reserve to themselves a wholesome control over their public affairs, and a degree of freedom, which, in the hands of the *canaille* of the cities of Europe, would be instantly perverted to the demolition and destruction of everything public and private. The history of the last twenty-five years of France, and of the last forty years in America, nay of its last two hundred years, proves the truth of both parts of this observation.

But even in Europe a change has sensibly taken place in the mind of man. Science had liberated the ideas of those who read and reflect, and the American example had kindled feelings of right in the people. An insurrection has consequently begun, of science, talents, and courage, against rank and birth, which have fallen into contempt. It has failed in its first effort, because the mobs of the cities, the instrument used for its accomplishment, debased by ignorance, poverty, and vice, could not be restrained to rational action. But the world will recover from the panic of this first catastrophe. Science is progressive, and talents and enterprise on the alert. Resort may be had to the people of the country, a more governable power from their principles and subordination; and rank, and birth, and tinsel-aristocracy will finally shrink into insignificance, even there. This, however, we have no right to meddle with. It suffices for us, if the moral and physical condition of our own citizens qualifies them to select the able and good for the direction of their government, with a recurrence of elections at such short periods as will enable them to displace an unfaithful servant, before the mischief he meditates may be irremediable.

I have thus stated my opinion on a point on which we differ, not with a view to controversy, for we are both too old to change opin-

477

ions which are the result of a long life of inquiry and reflection; but on the suggestions of a former letter of yours, that we ought not to die before we have explained ourselves to each other. We acted in perfect harmony, through a long and perilous contest for our liberty and independence. A Constitution has been acquired, which, though neither of us thinks perfect, yet both consider as competent to render our fellow citizens the happiest and the securest on whom the sun has ever shone. If we do not think exactly alike as to its imperfections, it matters little to our country, which, after devoting to it long lives of disinterested labor, we have delivered over to our successors in life, who will be able to take care of it and of themselves.

Of the pamphlet on aristocracy which has been sent to you, or who may be its author, I have heard nothing but through your letter. If the person you suspect, it may be known from the quaint, mystical, and hyperbolical ideas, involved in affected, new-fangled, and pedantic terms which stamp his writings. Whatever it be, I hope your quiet is not to be affected at this day by the rudeness or intemperance of scribblers; but that you may continue in tranquility to live and to rejoice in the prosperity of our country, until it shall be your own wish to take your seat among the *aristoi* who have gone before you. Ever and affectionately yours.

53. TO ROGER C. WEIGHTMAN [THE RIGHTS OF MAN]
Monticello, June 24, 1826.

RESPECTED SIR,—

The kind invitation I receive from you, on the part of the citizens of the city of Washington, to be present with them at their celebration on the fiftieth anniversary of American Independence, as one of the surviving signers of an instrument pregnant with our own, and the fate of the world, is most flattering to myself, and heightened by the honorable accompaniment proposed for the comfort of such a journey. It adds sensibly to the sufferings of sickness, to be deprived by it of a personal participation in the rejoicings of that day. But acquiescence is a duty, under circumstances not placed among those we are permitted to control. I should, indeed, with peculiar delight, have met and exchanged there congratulations personally with the small band, the remnant of that host of worthies, who joined with us on that day, in the bold and doubtful election we were to make for our country, between submission or the sword; and to have enjoyed with them the consolatory fact, that our fellow citizens, after half a century of experience and

478

prosperity, continue to approve the choice we made. May it be to the world, what I believe it will be, (to some parts sooner, to others later, but finally to all), the signal of arousing men to burst the chains under which monkish ignorance and superstition had persuaded them to bind themselves, and to assume the blessings and security of self-government. That form which we have substituted, restores the free right to the unbounded exercise of reason and freedom of opinion. All eyes are opened, or opening, to the rights of man. The general spread of the light of science has already laid open to every view the palpable truth, that the mass of mankind has not been born with saddles on their backs, nor a favored few booted and spurred, ready to ride them legitimately, by the grace of God. These are grounds of hope for others. For ourselves, let the annual return of this day forever refresh our recollections of these rights, and an undiminished devotion to them.

I will ask permission here to express the pleasure with which I should have met my ancient neighbors of the city of Washington and its vicinities, with whom I passed so many years of a pleasing social intercourse; an intercourse which so much relieved the anxieties of the public cares, and left impressions so deeply engraved in my affections, as never to be forgotten. With my regret that ill health forbids me the gratification of an acceptance, be pleased to receive for yourself, and those for whom you write, the assurance of my highest respect and friendly attachments.

PESTALOZZI 1746–1827

JOHANN HEINRICH PESTALOZZI is one of those authors whose thoughts are forced out into the open only by crucial personal experiences. When he endeavours to be "scientific" he repeats his intuitions, only in an artificial language.

With men such as these it sometimes happens that they vision the essence of their work in an hour of almost trancelike insight, just as we all, in hours of extreme joy or danger, may see the whole of our life concentrated in a flash.

The result of such an hour of intense concentration is Pestalozzi's *Evening Hour of a Hermit*. Its aphorisms, jotted down after the failure of his first educational experiment, anticipate—without the use of a special technical jargon—many of the best insights of modern psychology, and they say deeper things about the character of values, about liberal and vocational education, and about the relation between "individual" and "general" truth than are contained in many voluminous reports of our time.

Whereas the *Evening Hour* remained almost unknown—in spite of Pestalozzi's fame during the later years of his life—his *Leonard and Gertrude* was widely read. But, to his disappointment, it was understood more as an idyllic novel on village life than as a social essay artistically treated. As a matter of fact, like the *Evening Hour*, it also contains ideas not yet realized in our time, namely, that education of both young and adults is ineffective unless it grows out of the initiative of the people themselves, unless it speaks their language, and unless it influences not only isolated individuals but the life of the whole community.

In the following translation, by the editor, large parts of the second half of Pestalozzi's *Evening Hour of a Hermit* have been omitted. They contain applications of the general philosophy of this essay to social and moral problems of society. *Leonard and Gertrude,* translated and abridged by Eva Channing, from which selections were taken, was published in 1901 by D. C. Heath and Company, of Boston, New York, and Chicago, in Heath's Pedagogical Library.

THE EVENING HOUR OF A HERMIT

MAN who is the same whether in the palace or in a hut, what is he in his innermost nature? Why do not the wise tell us? Why are the

480

greatest of our thinkers not concerned with knowing what their race is? Does a peasant use his ox without knowing it? Does not a shepherd care for the nature of his sheep?

And you who use man and profess that you guard and nurture him, do you care for him as the peasant cares for his ox? Do you tend him as the shepherd tends his sheep? Does your wisdom help you to understand truly your race and is your goodness the goodness of enlightened guardians of the people?

What man is, what his needs are, what elevates and humiliates him, what strengthens and what weakens him ought to be the most important knowledge for the rulers as well as for the humblest.

Mankind feels this need everywhere; everywhere man is struggling upward with pain, labor, and passion. Generations after generations fade away with their lives unfulfilled, and the end of their days tells them that they completed their careers without achieving their goal. Their end is not like the end of ripe fruits which have fulfilled their task before the sleep of the winter.

Why does man seek truth without method and scope? Why does he not search for the necessities of his nature that he may build upon them the enjoyment and happiness of his life? Why does he not seek such truth as gives him peace and enjoyment, which makes him content, which develops his strength, brightens his days and brings blessings upon his years?

Man, driven by his needs can find the road to this truth nowhere but in his own nature.

The nursling, his hunger satisfied, learns in this way what his mother is to him; she develops in him love, the essence of gratitude, before the infant is able to utter the words 'duty' and 'thank'; in the same natural way the son finds his happiness in the duties towards his father who gives him bread and a hearth to warm himself.

Man, if you seek truth in this way of Nature you will find it as you need it according to your station and your career.

Obedience to your nature is essential for your rest and your peace; it is your guiding star in your personal matters; it is the foundation on which your life ought to rest, and it is the spring of your happiness.

Following the path of your nature you cannot make use of all truths. The sphere of knowledge from which man in his individual station can receive happiness is limited; its sphere begins closely around him, around his own self and his nearest relationships, from there his knowledge will expand, and while expanding it must regulate itself according to this firm centre of all the powers of truth.

The pure feeling for truth is formed in limited circles and pure human wisdom rests upon the firm basis of man's knowledge of his closest relationships and upon his maturity in handling his own personal matters.

Power, strong and clear sentiments and a sense for right application is its expression.

Sublime road of Nature, the truth to which thou leadest is power and action and source of culture, enrichment and harmony of humankind.

Yet thou permittest not man to grow hastily and superficially and thy son, o Nature, cannot escape his natural limits, his speech cannot be more than the expression and the result of his knowledge. If men exceed the sequence of thy order, they destroy their inner power and disturb their peace and harmony.

They do so if they immerse themselves in the thousandfold confusion of verbal instruction and opinions, before having trained their minds for truth and wisdom through firsthand knowledge, or if they make sound, speech and words instead of truth derived from reality the basis of their mental development and of the growth of their capacities.

This artificial method of schooling, forging ahead of the free, slow and patient course of Nature and preferring words to things, gives man an artificial polish which conceals his lack of inherent natural power. Such a method can satisfy only times like our century.

.   .   .   .   .

The wretched and exhausting pursuit of the mere shadow of truth, the pursuit of tone and sound and words about truth, where no interest inspires and where no application is possible, the direction of all powers of growing youth toward the doctrines of harsh and onesided schoolmasters, the thousandfold arts of juggling words and the latest fashion in teaching, supposed to be the true foundation of human education, all this serves only to lead youth away from the road of Nature.

He, who flutters around all kinds of knowledge and who does not train himself through steady and firm application, he too loses the road of Nature, the clear, serene and attentive glance, and the quiet and undisturbed sense of deep and true gladness.

482

PESTALOZZI

Where art thou, Nature, true teacher of man? When also those condemned to travel through the dead and dreary deserts of ignorance, lose their natural simplicity?

Lack of knowledge of your own nature, o man, curbs your wisdom still more than all external restrictions forced upon you. Perversion of the first fundamental relations to your environment, murderous and oppressive power of tyranny, privation of all enjoyments of truth and happiness, unnatural absence of general national enlightenment concerning the fundamental interests and conditions of man, how your heavy shadow darkens the world!

Therefore the desire for full development of the capacities of man, this source of powerful actions and of peaceful enjoyments, is no imaginary impulse and no delusive error.

Realization of our selves, pure force in our nature, thou blessing of our existence, thou art no dream. To seek and strive for thee is the scope and destiny of man and I feel it also as my deepest urge; to search for thee is my innermost wish as well as the aim and destiny of mankind.

Where and how shall I find thee, truth, who art my salvation and who elevates me to the perfection of my nature?

My innermost nature discloses this truth. All men are fundamentally alike and there is only one road which leads to their happiness. Hence the truth which springs from our nature will be the universal truth of all mankind; it will be the truth that will unify the thousands who quarrel over its mere external form.

. . . . .

Hence it is the man with a simple and clear soul whom Nature allows to arrive at true human wisdom, for it is he who applies his knowledge humbly and skillfully and uses all his talents modestly and diligently; whereas the man who destroys this order of Nature and the harmony of his knowledge, will never enjoy the blessings of truth.

Actions which do not conform to the order of our nature undermine our capacity to perceive the truth; they confuse the noble and sublime simplicity of our natural and basic concepts and feelings.

Therefore all human wisdom is founded on the strength of a good and truthful heart and all human happiness on simplicity and purity.

. . . . .

483

Practice, application and use of power and of wisdom in specific situations and conditions is the proper goal of vocational and class-education. But this must always be subordinated to the aim of general education.

.   .   .   .   .

Certainly there are chasms between the humble father of a family and a prince, between the poor man toiling for his daily bread and the rich man harassed by still greater anxieties, between the idle dreamers and the genius, whose eagle-flight amazes the world.

Yet if the one on his heights is lacking in pure humanity dark clouds will amass around him; whereas humanity born in the lowest hut will radiate the pure light of human greatness.

.   .   .   .   .

Without it the most enlightened laws will be but words about brotherly love in the mouth of unfeeling men.

.   .   .   .   .

Man, though your self and the consciousness of your personality and powers is the first object of creative Nature, you do not live for yourself alone. Therefore Nature forms you also for living within human relationships, and it forms you through them.

In proportion as these relationships are close to you, they will educate you for fulfilling your destiny.

The power formed through mastering our nearest relationships is the source of our capacity to master the more remote.

A fatherly spirit makes a good governor—a brotherly spirit a good citizen; both create order at home and in the state.

Man's domestic relationships are the first and foremost ones of Nature.

Man toils in his vocation and bears the burden of communal duties in order to enjoy his home in harmony and peace.

To this peaceful enjoyment man's education for his vocation and for his social rank must be subordinated.

Hence the home is the foundation of a pure and natural education of mankind.

Hence the home is the school of morality and of the state.

Respect first the child in man and then think of him as an apprentice in his vocation.

A healthy childhood benefits the years of apprenticeship and is the foundation of all future happiness.

484

PESTALOZZI

Whoever departs from this natural order and lays artificial emphasis on class and vocational education, or training for rule or for service, leads man aside from the enjoyment of the most natural blessings to a sea of hidden dangers.

    •   •   ,   •   •   •

Do you not see, men, do you not feel it, sons of the earth, how their education causes the ruling classes to lose the pith and marrow of their strength? Do you not see it, men, how their departure from the wise order of Nature brings shallowness and misery to them and descends from them to the people? Do you not feel how everywhere men forget the beneficent intimacy of their homes and stream toward the glittering stages of life to brag their learning and to gratify their ambitions?

Erring mankind drifts towards a future of darkness!

God is the nearest relationship of man!

Even though you may deeply enjoy your home, it cannot always give you peace.

Your tender, kind and feeling nature is not strong enough to suffer force and death without God.

The faith in God, the father of your house and the source of your welfare, the faith in God's fatherhood, this faith gives you solace, strength and wisdom which neither force nor death can take from you.

Faith in God is the highest accord of man's feelings; in this faith man the child faces God the father.

From this faith springs the peace of life—from this peace of life springs our security—from our security springs the firm use of our talents, our growth and our wisdom—from wisdom springs all human welfare.

    •   •   •   •   •

Want of faith is immodesty, feeling ourselves as children of God creates sublime modesty in whatever we are and do.

    •   •   •   •   •

LEONARD AND GERTRUDE

CHAPTER I.—A WEAK MAN, A BRAVE WOMAN, AND A FATHERLY RULER. In the village of Bonnal there lived a mason named Leonard. His trade would have enabled him to support

485

his family of a wife and seven children, if he could have resisted the temptation to frequent the tavern, where there were always enough idle loafers to entice him in, and induce the good-natured, easy-going man to squander his earnings in drink and gambling. Leonard always repented his weakness when he saw his children want for bread, yet was not strong enough to reform. He was blest with a good, pious wife, who was overwhelmed with sorrow at the ruin which seemed to stare them in the face.

.　.　.　.　.

"Take courage, dear," she repeated, "and trust in your Father in heaven. I would not willingly grieve you, and you well know that I do not ask for more than bread and water at your side; and that I often work uncomplainingly till long past midnight for you and the children. But, husband, I should not feel I was true to you or our dear ones if I concealed my cares from you. Our children are loving and dutiful now; but they will not remain so if we do not fulfil our obligation as parents. Think how you would feel if all our little ones should lose their gratitude and respect for us through our fault! And could you bear to see your Nicholas, your Jonas, your Lizzie and Annie, homeless and forced to seek their bread among strangers? It would kill me!" and her tears flowed as she spoke.

Leonard wept also. "O Gertrude, what shall I do? It breaks my heart to make you miserable, but I cannot help it. I owe the Bailiff Hummel thirty florins, and if I stay away from his tavern, he threatens me with the law; yet if I go, he gets possession of all my wages."

"Can you not go to Arner, the people's father? All the widows and orphans praise him, and I think he would give you advice and protection."

"Gertrude, I dare not! How could I, a poor miserable drunkard, complain of the Bailiff, who has a thousand ways of blackening me in the eyes of his superior? And think how he would revenge himself if I should try it and fail!"

"But he will ruin you in any case. Leonard, think of your children, and go. If you do not, I shall!"

"I dare not! But, Gertrude, if you have the courage, go to Arner in Heaven's name, and tell him all."

"I will!" she answered. She prayed throughout the sleepless night, and the next morning took her blooming baby and walked two long hours to the Castle.

PESTALOZZI

The nobleman was sitting under a linden-tree at the gate, and saw her as she approached, with tears in her eyes and the infant on her arm. "Who are you, my daughter, and what do you wish?" he asked, in so kind a tone that she took heart to answer: "I am Gertrude, wife of the mason Leonard in Bonnal."

"You are a good woman," said Arner. "I have noticed that your children behave better than all the others in the village, and they seem better fed, although I hear you are very poor. What can I do for you, my daughter?"

"O gracious Sir, for a long time my husband has owed thirty florins to the Bailiff Hummel, a hard man, who leads him into all sorts of temptation. Leonard is in his power: so he dares not keep away from the tavern, where day after day he spends the wages which ought to buy bread for his family. We have seven little children, Sir, and unless something is done we shall all be beggars. I ventured to come to you for help, because I know that you have compassion for the widowed and fatherless. I have brought the money I have laid aside for my children, to deposit with you, if you will be so good as to make some arrangement so that the Bailiff shall not torment my husband any more until he is paid."

Arner took up a cup which stood near, and said to Gertrude: "Drink this tea, and give your pretty baby some of this milk." She blushed, and was moved even to tears by his fatherly kindness.

The nobleman now requested her to relate her causes of complaint against the Bailiff, and listened attentively to her story of the cares and troubles of many years. Suddenly he asked her how it had been possible to lay aside money for her children in the midst of her distress.

"It was very hard, gracious Sir; yet I could not help feeling as if the money were not mine, but had been given me by a dying man on his death-bed, in trust for his children. So when in the hardest times I had to borrow from it to buy bread for the family, I gave myself no rest till by working late and early I had paid it back again."

Gertrude laid seven neat packages on the table, each of which had a ticket attached, saying whose it was; and if she had taken anything from it, the fact was noted, and likewise when she had replaced it. She saw him read these tickets through attentively, and said blushing: "I ought to have taken those papers away, gracious Sir."

Arner only smiled, and admired the modesty which shrank from even merited praise. He added something to each parcel, saying:

487

"Carry back your children's money, Gertrude; I will lay aside thirty florins until the Bailiff is paid. Now go home; I shall be in the village to-morrow, at all events, and will settle the matter with Hummel."

"God reward you, gracious Sir!" she faltered; and started joyfully with her baby on the long homeward way. Leonard saw her as she approached the house. "Already back again?" he cried. "You have been successful with Arner."

"How do you know?"

"I can see it in your face, my dear wife,—you cannot deceive me."

From this time forward, when the mason's children said their prayers at morning and evening, they prayed not only for their father and mother, but also for Arner, the people's father.

. . . . .

CHAPTER VIII.—A GOOD MOTHER'S SATURDAY EVE-NING. Gertrude, meanwhile, was at home alone with her children. Thoughtful and silent, she prepared the supper, and then took from the chest the Sunday clothes of all the family, so that on the morrow no petty cares might distract her thoughts from better things. When all was ready, she gathered the children about her, for it was her custom every Saturday to call their attention to their faults, and inculcate any lessons which the events of the week might bring home to their minds. To-day she was especially anxious to impress their young hearts with a sense of the goodness of God, as manifested during the past week; and when the little hands were all folded, Gertrude thus spoke: "Children, I have something joyful to tell you. Your dear father has the promise of such good work that he will be able to earn much more than before, and we may hope in future to have less trouble and anxiety about getting our daily bread. Thank the dear God, my children, for being so good to us, and do not forget the time when every mouthful of bread had to be counted! Think always of those who suffer from hunger and want, as you did once, and if you have a trifle more than you really need, do not grudge giving it to them. Will you do this, children?"

"Oh, yes indeed, mother!" they all cried with one voice. Gertrude now asked the children whether they would not sometimes like to give away their afternoon bread to those poorer than themselves, and on meeting with an eager response, she told each one to think of some hungry child who might be gladdened by the gift. Nicholas mentioned their neighbor. little Rudy; Lizzie spoke of

488

Marx's daughter Betty; and so with the others in turn. They were all so full of the idea that they resolved, with one accord, to carry out the plan on the following day.

Then Gertrude spoke of Arner's presents to the children, and promising to show them the money after their evening prayer, she began: "Well, my dears, how has it been about doing right this week?" The children looked at each other, and were silent. "Annie, have you been good this week?"

Casting down her eyes in shame, the child replied: "No, mother; you know how it was with my little brother"—

"Annie, something might have happened to the child,—and just think how *you* would like it, if you should be shut up in a room all alone without food or amusement! Little children who are left alone in that way sometimes scream so that they injure themselves for life. Why, Annie, I could never feel easy about going away from home, if I thought you would not take good care of the child."

"Indeed, mother, I will never leave him alone again!"

"And, Nicholas," said Gertrude, turning to her oldest son; "how is it with you this week?"

"I don't remember anything wrong."

"Have you forgotten that you knocked down little Peggy on Monday?"

"I didn't mean to, mother."

"I should hope not, Nicholas! Aren't you ashamed of talking so? If you grow up without considering the comfort of those about you, you will have to learn the lesson through bitter experience. Remember that, and be careful, my dear boy.—And Lizzie, how have you behaved this week?"

"I can't think of anything out of the way this week, mother."

"Are you sure?"

"I really can't, mother, think as hard as I can; if I could, I would willingly tell you of it, mother."

"How you do manage to use as many words, even when you have nothing to say, as any one else who says a great déal!"

"What did I say now, mother?"

"Nothing at all, and yet a great deal. It is just what we have told you a thousand times,—you never think beforehand of what you are going to say, and yet must be always talking. What business was it of yours to tell the Bailiff, day before yesterday, that you knew Arner would come soon? Suppose your father had not wished him to know that he knew it, and your chattering had brought him into trouble?"

"I should be very sorry, mother. But neither of you said a word about its being a secret."

"Very well, I will tell your father when he comes home, that, whenever we are talking together, we must take care to add after each sentence: 'Lizzie may tell that to the neighbors, and talk about it at the well; but this she must not mention outside the house.' So then you will know precisely what you may chatter about."

"O mother, forgive me! That was not what I meant."

Gertrude talked similarly with all the other children about their faults, even saying to little Peggy: "You mustn't be so impatient for your soup, or I shall make you wait longer another time, and give it to one of the others."

After this was over, the children folded their hands and said their usual evening prayer, followed by a special prayer for Saturday night, which Gertrude had taught them. When the mother had uttered a final benediction, all sat quiet for a little while, until Lizzie broke the silence. "Now will you show us the new money, mother?"

"Yes. But, Lizzie, you are always the first to speak!"

Nicholas sprang from his seat, and in pressing forward to the light, gave little Peggy such a violent push that she cried aloud.

"Nicholas!" said his mother, "that is not right. It is not a quarter of an hour since you promised to be more careful. You are not in earnest."

"O mother, I never will do so again as long as I live! I am really in earnest, and very sorry."

"So am I, dear boy; but you will forget it all unless I punish you. You must go to bed without your supper."

She led the boy to his room, while the other children stood sadly by. "Do let him out again, just this once!" they entreated.

"No, my dears; he must be cured of his carelessness."

"Then we'll not look at our money till to-morrow, so that he can see it with us," proposed Annie.

"That is right, Annie!"—and after giving the children their supper, Gertrude went with them to the bedroom, where Nicholas was still crying. "My dear, dear boy," she said, "do be careful another time!"

"Forgive me, dear mother!" he cried, throwing his arms about her neck. "Only forgive me and kiss me, and I don't mind losing my supper at all."

Gertrude kissed him, and a warm tear fell upon his face. She

490

blessed the other children, and returned alone to the dimly lighted room. A solemn stillness filled her heart; she was penetrated with a consciousness of God's goodness, and the happiness of those who place their trust in him. She was so deeply moved that she sank upon her knees and wept. Her eyes were still moist when her husband returned home. "Why are you weeping, Gertrude?" he inquired.

"My dear husband, these are no tears of sorrow; I wanted to thank God for the blessings of this week, but my heart was so full that I could not speak for weeping."

Leonard leaned his head upon her breast, and his eyes were also filled with tears. Neither spoke for a short time; but at last Gertrude asked if he did not wish any supper. "No," he replied; "my heart is too full; I cannot eat."

"Neither can I, dear. But I will tell you what we will do. We will carry our supper to poor Rudy, whose mother died to-day."

When they reached the house, Rudy was sitting weeping beside the corpse, and his little boy called from the adjoining room, begging for bread, or raw roots, or anything to eat. "Alas! I have nothing," answered the father. "For Heaven's sake, be quiet till morning!"

"But I am so hungry, father!" moaned the child. "I am so hungry I cannot sleep."

Leonard and Gertrude heard the words, and opening the door, set down the food, and bade them eat quickly, before it was cold. Deeply affected, the mourner called to the boy: "Rudy, these are the people from whom you stole potatoes,—and alas! I too, have eaten some!"

"Say no more about that," said Gertrude, "but eat."

"Do let us eat, father!" begged the child.

"Well, then, say your grace."

The boy obeyed, then took up the spoon, trembled, wept and ate. They put aside a part of the food for the sleeping children, and the afflicted father attempted once more to thank his benefactors. As he did so, a sigh escaped him.

"Is anything the matter, Rudy? Is there anything we can do for you?" asked Leonard and Gertrude.

"No, nothing, thank you," he replied, with difficulty repressing another deep sigh.

The two looked at him compassionately. "But you sigh; you certainly have some trouble at heart."

"Do tell them, father, they are so good!" besought little Rudy.

491

"May I?" said the poor man reluctantly. "I have neither shoes nor stockings, and to-morrow I must follow my mother to the grave, and the day after go to the Castle."

"The idea of tormenting yourself so about that!" cried Leonard. "Why didn't you say so at first? I shall be very glad to provide you with them."

"And can you believe," said Rudy humbly, "that, after all that has happened, I will return them to you uninjured and with thanks?"

"Hush, Rudy! I would trust you yet further than that. Your poverty and distress have made you too distrustful."

As Gertrude expressed a wish to look upon the dead, they all went with a feeble light to the bedside, and stood with tears in their eyes, gazing down upon the peaceful face. Then they covered up the lifeless form, and took leave of each other warmly, although without words.

. . . . .

CHAPTER X.—SUNDAY JOYS AND CHILDISH CHARACTER.

Meanwhile, the Sunday had been very differently spent in the humble dwelling of the mason. While Leonard and Gertrude were at church, the children prayed, sang, and reviewed what they had learned during the week, so as to be ready to repeat it to their mother in the evening. Lizzie, the oldest, had the care of baby Peggy during Gertrude's absence, and it was her greatest delight to dress, feed, and tend the little one. It was pretty to see her motherly airs as she dandled and kissed and played with her charge. How pleased she was when the baby laughed back at her with outstretched arms, and kicked with its tiny feet! Then it would grasp Lizzie's cap, or her pig-tails, or her nose, and crow over her bright Sunday neckerchief, until Nicholas and Annie would come up behind and crow in imitation; then the little one would turn at the sound, and laugh at the merry Nicholas, who would spring forward to kiss his baby sister. This would arouse Lizzie's jealousy, and she would exert herself to the utmost to make the little darling laugh at her. She devoted herself to the amusement of her charge, lifting the child in her arms almost to the ceiling, and then letting it down carefully to the very ground, until it screamed aloud with delight. Then she would hold it close to the looking-glass, so that it laughed at the baby within; but the most joyful moment of all was when the little one espied its mother far down the street, crowed, stretched out its tiny hands, and nearly sprang out of Lizzie's arms.

PESTALOZZI

Gertrude was satisfied with her children to-day, for they had done everything as she had told them. They now had their reward in a frolic with their parents, for climbing joyfully into the laps of father and mother, the children possessed themselves of their hands, and clasped their necks tightly with small arms. Ever since Gertrude had been a mother, this was her Sunday delight; but to-day Leonard's eyes filled with tears at the thought that he had often deprived himself of these home joys. The happy parents talked with the children of their Father in heaven, and the sufferings of their Saviour, while the little ones listened attentively. The noon hour passed as swiftly and happily as a wedding feast, and the peal of bells again summoned Leonard and Gertrude to church.

When they returned home in the afternoon, the children ran down the steps to meet them, crying: "Oh, do hurry, mother! We want to repeat what we have learned this week, and get through as soon as possible."

"Why are you in such desperate haste, my dears?" asked Gertrude smiling.

"Why, when we are through, mother, you know what you promised us yesterday about the bread. We may, mother, mayn't we?"

"First I will see how well you know what you have learned," was the reply.

The lesson was soon satisfactorily concluded, whereupon Gertrude brought out the bread, and two dishes of milk from which she had not removed the cream, because it was a holiday. Not one of the children touched the bread, but each rejoiced over his or her piece, maintaining that it was the largest. When the milk had disappeared, Nicholas crept up to his mother's side, and taking her hand, whispered: "You will give me just one mouthful of bread for myself, will you not, mother?"

"You have your piece, Nicholas."

"But I must give it to Rudy."

"I haven't told you to give it to him," said his mother. "You can eat it if you like."

"I don't want to eat it; but you will give me just one mouthful?"

"Certainly not, my boy."

"Why not?"

"So that you needn't imagine we are only to think of the poor after our own hunger is satisfied. And now will you give him the whole of it?"

"Yes, mother, every bit. I know he is frightfully hungry, and we have supper at six."

"Yes, Nicholas, and I hardly think he will have anything to eat then."

The mother now turned to the other children, and asked if they, too, had quite decided to give their bread away, receiving in each case an affirmative answer. "That is right, children," she said. "But now, how will you set about it?—Nicholas, how are you going to manage with your bread?"

"I'll run as fast as I can, and call Rudy. I shall not put it in my pocket, so that he may have it all the quicker. Let me go, mother!"

"Stop a minute, Nicholas!—Lizzie, what are you going to do?"

"I am not going to do like Nicholas. I shall call Betty into a corner, and hide the bread under my apron, so that nobody will see it, not even her father."

"And Annie?"

"I can't tell where I shall find Harry—I shall give it to him just as it happens."

"And Jonas, you little rogue, you have some mischief in your head; how are you planning to do it?"

"I shall stick my bread into his mouth, mother, as you do to me in fun. 'Open your mouth and shut your eyes,' I shall say, and then put it between his teeth. Don't you think he'll laugh?"

"That is all very well, children," said Gertrude. "But I must tell you one thing: you must give away the bread quietly, so no one may see, that people needn't think you want to show off your generosity."

"Whew! mother," cried Nicholas; "then I must put my bread in my pocket?"

"Of course, Nicholas."

"That is just what occurred to me, mother," said Lizzie. "You know I said just now that I wouldn't do like him."

"You are always the wisest, Lizzie. I forgot to praise you for it, and you do well to remind me of it yourself." Lizzie colored, and was silent.

The children departed on their several missions.

.   .   .   .   .

The mason's children were all at their spinning-wheels, and although they greeted their guests joyfully, they did not stop working for a moment. "Hurry and get through, and then you can play with your little friends till six o'clock," said Gertrude. Rudy's children stood in open-mouthed wonder at the beautiful work and the cheerful aspect of the room. "Can you spin?" she asked.

494

"No," they answered.

"Then you must learn, my dears. My children wouldn't sell their knowledge of it at any price, and are happy enough on Saturday, when they each get their few kreutzers. The year is long, my dears, and if we earn something every week, at the end of the year there is a lot of money, without our knowing how we came by it."

"Oh, please teach us!" implored the children, nestling close to the good woman.

"Willingly," Gertrude replied; "come every day, if you like, and you will soon learn."

Meanwhile, the others had finished their work, and put away their yarn and wheels; they took their visitors by the hand, and all the children sprang merrily about in the meadow under the trees. Gertrude's children were more careful than their companions to avoid the mud and the thorns, and took heed to their clothes. They tied up their stockings and shoes when they became undone, and would often say to Rudy's children: "You are losing your garter," or "You are getting dirty," or "You will tear your dress on the thorns." Their playfellows took it all in good part, for they saw that the mason's children did everything themselves which they prescribed, and were not putting on airs.

On the stroke of six, Gertrude's children ran into the house, like birds to their nests at sundown. "Will you come with us? We are going to pray now," they said to their visitors; and as they were playing the game called "cat's tail," they led the long procession through the meadow, up the steps, and to the very table where they seated themselves. "Must you not go home to prayers, my dears?" inquired Gertrude of the little strangers.

"We don't pray till we go to bed," replied the eldest.

"And when must you go to bed?"

"How do I know?" said the child; and another answered: "When it begins to grow dark."

"Well, then, you can pray with us, and then it will be time for you to go home." Gertrude heard her own children pray in turn, and then, after letting Rudy's children repeat the prayers they knew, she accompanied them to the corner of the house with a cheery parting, bidding them come again soon.

.   .   .   .   .

CHAPTER XXII.—PLANS OF REGENERATION IN BONNAL.
As the Sunday approached when Arner had decreed that Hummel should be exposed to the view of the whole congregation, while the

pastor held up his previous life as a warning to those present, the prisoner expressed the utmost horror of this penalty, declaring that he would rather have his punishment at the gallows repeated, than stand under the pulpit to be the laughing-stock of the town. He represented that such a ceremony could neither dispose him to thoughts of repentance, nor have a beneficial effect upon the spectators. The pastor was finally so moved by his entreaties, as well as convinced of the reasonableness of his plea, that he interceded with Arner, and induced him to remit the sentence.[1] Accordingly, the clergyman merely took Hummel's life as a text, preaching a stirring sermon against the wickedness and corruption which had been fostered so long in their midst, and which were still rife, in almost equal measure, in the hearts of many of his listeners.

This discourse everywhere made a profound impression; the peasants could talk of nothing else on the way home, and Arner, pressing the good pastor's hand, thanked him heartily for his edifying words. He expressed, at the same time, an earnest desire to labor for the improvement of the village, and asked the clergyman if he could recommend an upright, able man from among the people, who could help him in furthering his designs. The parson mentioned at once the spinner known as Cotton Meyer, and proposed they should visit him and his sister that afternoon. They were accompanied by the Lieutenant Glülphi, one of Arner's aids in regulating the economic conditions of his government.

Cotton Meyer was sitting at his door with a child in his lap, when the three gentlemen approached, and had no suspicion that they were seeking him, until they paused before his garden gate. Then he went to meet them with so calm and dignified a bearing that Glülphi did not give him his hand, as he usually did to the peasants, and Arner addressed him less familiarly than was his wont when speaking to his dependents.

The visitors were about to seat themselves on the bench under the apple-tree; but Meyer led them into the parlor, where his sister was sitting by the table, nodding over the open Bible, as was her custom on Sunday afternoons. She started up with a cry as the door opened, and straightening her cap, closed the Bible; then, taking a sponge, she moistened it in a tin hand-basin which shone like silver, and erased the chalk figures with which her brother had covered the table, despite the remonstrance of the strangers, who feared that

---

[1] In the earlier editions of this work, the original plan of the Bailiff's punishment was adhered to. It is a sign of advancing civilization that in the edition of 1819 Arner's sentence was revoked as above.

496

Meyer might have further use for his reckoning. After wiping the table carefully, she brought a large fine linen table-cloth, and laid new tin plates, with knives, forks and heavy silver spoons upon it.

"What are you doing?" inquired her guests; "we have already dined."

"I suppose so," answered Maria; "but since you have come into a peasant's house, you must take kindly to our peasant ways." Running into the kitchen, she returned with two plates of little cakes and a fine large ham, and Arner, Glülphi and the pastor seated themselves good-naturedly before the shining dishes.

When the visitors began to praise the house, the garden and the whole establishment, Maria remarked that twenty years ago they had been among the poorest in the village. "I know it," said Arner, "and I wonder at your prosperity the more, as the weavers and spinners have usually turned out the most good-for-nothing people in the country."

Meyer was forced to admit that this was true, but denied that the cause lay in the industry itself. The trouble was, he said, that these poor people were not in the habit of laying up anything from their earnings, and led wretched, aimless lives. He felt sure that Arner might find many ways of winning the hearts of the people, so as to lead them into better paths, and suggested, as one expedient, that he should promise to every child, which up to its twentieth year should annually lay aside ten florins from its earnings, a field free from tithes. "But," went on Meyer, "after all, we can do very little with the people, unless the next generation is to have a very different training from that our schools furnish. The school ought really to stand in the closest connection with the life of the home, instead of, as now, in strong contradiction to it."

Glülphi joined in the conversation with eagerness, and argued that a true school should develop to the fullest extent all the faculties of the child's nature. The question next arose, how such a school could be established in Bonnal. Cotton Meyer, when appealed to, rejoined: "I know a spinning-woman in the village who understands it far better than I"; and he went on to tell the others such things of Gertrude's little school and its effects upon her children, that they resolved to visit her and examine her method for themselves. They also spoke of the corruption prevailing in the village, and discussed the best method of choosing a good bailiff. Cotton Meyer showed himself through it all a man of such clear judgment and practical common sense, that his guests left him with a feeling of respect almost approaching veneration.

497

CHAPTER XXV.—GERTRUDE'S METHOD OF INSTRUC-
TION. It was quite early in the morning when Arner, Glülphi and
the pastor went to the mason's cottage. The room was not in order
when they entered, for the family had just finished breakfast, and
the dirty plates and spoons still lay upon the table. Gertrude was
at first somewhat disconcerted, but the visitors reässured her, saying
kindly: "This is as it should be; it is impossible to clear the table
before breakfast is eaten!"

The children all helped wash the dishes, and then seated themselves in their customary places before their work. The gentlemen
begged Gertrude to let everything go on as usual, and after the first
half hour, during which she was a little embarrassed, all proceeded
as if no stranger were present. First the children sang their morning hymns, and then Gertrude read a chapter of the Bible aloud,
which they repeated after her while they were spinning, rehearsing
the most instructive passages until they knew them by heart. In the
mean time, the oldest girl had been making the children's beds in
the adjoining room, and the visitors noticed through the open door
that she silently repeated what the others were reciting. When this
task was completed, she went into the garden and returned with
vegetables for dinner, which she cleaned while repeating Bible-
verses with the rest.

It was something new for the children to see three gentlemen in
the room, and they often looked up from their spinning toward the
corner where the strangers sat. Gertrude noticed this, and said to
them: "Seems to me you look more at these gentlemen than at your
yarn." But Harry answered: "No, indeed! We are working hard,
and you'll have finer yarn to-day than usual."

Whenever Gertrude saw that anything was amiss with the wheels
or cotton, she rose from her work, and put it in order. The smallest
children, who were not old enough to spin, picked over the cotton
for carding, with a skill which excited the admiration of the visitors.

Although Gertrude thus exerted herself to develop very early the
manual dexterity of her children, she was in no haste for them to
learn to read and write. But she took pains to teach them early how
to speak; for, as she said, "Of what use is it for a person to be able
to read and write, if he cannot speak?—since reading and writing
are only an artificial sort of speech." To this end she used to make
the children pronounce syllables after her in regular succession, taking them from an old A-B-C book she had. This exercise in correct
and distinct articulation was, however, only a subordinate object
in her whole scheme of education, which embraced a true com-

prehension of life itself. Yet she never adopted the tone of instructor toward her children; she did not say to them: "Child, this is your head, your nose, your hand, your finger"; or: "Where is your eye, your ear?"—but instead, she would say: "Come here, child, I will wash your little hands," "I will comb your hair," or: "I will cut your finger-nails." Her verbal instruction seemed to vanish in the spirit of her real activity, in which it always had its source. The result of her system was that each child was skilful, intelligent and active to the full extent that its age and development allowed.

The instruction she gave them in the rudiments of arithmetic was intimately connected with the realities of life. She taught them to count the number of steps from one end of the room to the other, and two of the rows of five panes each, in one of the windows, gave her an opportunity to unfold the decimal relations of numbers. She also made them count their threads while spinning, and the number of turns on the reel, when they wound the yarn into skeins. Above all, in every occupation of life she taught them an accurate and intelligent observation of common objects and the forces of nature.

All that Gertrude's children knew, they knew so thoroughly that they were able to teach it to the younger ones; and this they often begged permission to do. On this day, while the visitors were present, Jonas sat with each arm around the neck of a smaller child, and made the little ones pronounce the syllables of the A-B-C book after him; while Lizzie placed herself with her wheel between two of the others, and while all three spun, taught them the words of a hymn with the utmost patience.

When the guests took their departure, they told Gertrude they would come again on the morrow. "Why?" she returned; "You will only see the same thing over again." But Glülphi said: "That is the best praise you could possibly give yourself." Gertrude blushed at this compliment, and stood confused when the gentlemen kindly pressed her hand in taking leave.

The three could not sufficiently admire what they had seen at the mason's house, and Glülphi was so overcome by the powerful impression made upon him, that he longed to be alone and seek counsel of his own thoughts. He hastened to his room, and as he crossed the threshold, the words broke from his lips: "*I* must be schoolmaster in Bonnal!" All night visions of Gertrude's schoolroom floated through his mind, and he only fell asleep toward morning. Before his eyes were fairly open, he murmured: "I will be schoolmaster!"—and hastened to Arner to acquaint him with his resolution.

CHAPTER XXVI.—MATCH-MAKING AND SCHOOL-MAK-ING. Arner rejoiced greatly over Glülphi's determination, and calling for the good pastor on their way, the two friends turned their steps for the second time to Gertrude's door. She had expected them, but had made no change in her usual programme. As they entered, at the close of the Bible reading, the morning sun shone brightly into the room, and the children, of their own accord, struck up the song beginning:

> "With what a fair and radiant gleam
> The sun's mild rays upon us beam,
> Bringing refreshment to the eye,
> And filling all our souls with joy!"

When they were all seated at their work, little Harry whispered in his mother's ear, to ask if the children might not thank Arner for the money he had given them, and on receiving permission, he noiselessly crept about between the wheels, bearing the message to his brothers and sisters. The little band came forth and stood shyly before the nobleman, no one daring to speak, until at a question from Arner, Harry plucked up courage to stammer out their errand. Arner lifted the boy kindly upon his knee, where he was soon as much at home as if it had been his own father.

Rudy's children now held a consultation, and came forward, black-eyed Nanny ahead, to thank their benefactor for the cow and the meadow. Arner set Harry down and took the little girl in his lap, where she was soon as much at her ease as the boy had been. In a minute she asked: "Have you much more of that beautiful money you gave the other children?"

"For shame!" cried all the rest in chorus.

"No, let her speak," said Arner. "Would you like some too?"

"Yes, if you please."

"But I have none with me at present."

"Don't you always have it with you?"

"No, but I shall have some when I come again."

. . . . . .

Glülphi had been waiting impatiently to speak to Gertrude of his own plans, and he now asked her whether she thought it would be possible to introduce into a regular school the same method she pursued at home with her children. "I am not sure," she replied; "although I am inclined to think that what is possible with ten children would be possible with forty. But it would be difficult to find a schoolmaster who would tolerate such an arrangement in his school."

"But supposing one could be found," said the lieutenant, "who would be willing to introduce it, would you help him?"

"To be sure,—*if* one could be found," she returned with a laugh.

"And if I were he?"

"Were *who?*"

"The man who is ready to establish such a school as you have in your room."

"You are no schoolmaster!"

"But I will be."

"Yes, in some great city, perhaps, and in things village people know nothing about!"

"No, in a village, and in things all village people ought to understand."

"That must be a queer sort of village, where a gentleman like you wants to be schoolmaster! Such a gentleman as you doesn't take a fancy to teach children like these here."

"That you don't know."

"But I have an idea that it is so."

"So I perceive. But if I really wanted to be such a schoolmaster, what then? Would you help me?"

"To be sure," said Gertrude again, still under the impression he was joking; "I will help you all I can."

Glülphi turned to Arner and the pastor, saying: "You have heard, she has promised twice to help me."

"That's fine!" they said laughing.

Gertrude began to be confused, and when she found they were actually in earnest, she stoutly declared herself incapable of showing the lieutenant the least thing in the world, although she would gladly send her children to school to him, and come herself if she were only younger. But they answered that her help would be indispensable, and when she pleaded her lack of time and the cares of her household, and named another excellent housekeeper whose aid might be of service, Glülphi replied: "She will doubtless be useful, too, but there can be no substitute for your mother's heart, which I must have for my school."

"My mother's heart is hardly large enough for my own room," said Gertrude; "and if you are really to be our schoolmaster, I know you will bring a father's heart and a father's strength into the work, such as will make my little mother's heart quite superfluous."

"It is very true," remarked the other gentlemen, "that our lieu-

501

tenant will bring a great father's heart with him; but that will not render the coöperation of your mother's heart unnecessary." Then they explained to her that they regarded the proper education of the youthful population as the only means of elevating the condition of the corrupt village; and full of emotion, Gertrude promised them she would do anything in her power to forward the good cause.

CHAPTER XXVIII.—HOW SLANDER IS PUNISHED AND THE COMMON DIVIDED. After his visit to Gertrude's school, Arner sat down and wrote a long letter to his intimate friend Bylifsky, now minister of the Duke, describing the impression made upon him by what he had just seen, and stating the views of Cotton Meyer with regard to the means of bettering the condition of the corrupt village. "These views," he concluded, "can be summed up under the following heads:

1. A school shall be organized which can be brought into harmony with the developing influence of domestic life, as is the case with that in Gertrude's house.

2. The better portion of the people of Bonnal shall unite with the Castle and the parsonage, for the purpose of gaining a sure and active influence over the various households of the village.

3. A new method of choosing the overseers shall be adopted, whereby the evil influence exerted by bad overseers may in future be removed."

.　.　.　.　.

CHAPTER XXXI.—THE ORGANIZATION OF A NEW SCHOOL. Glülphi was full of the idea of his school, and could speak of nothing else with Arner and the pastor. He used all his spare time in visiting Gertrude, in order to talk it over with her; but she seemed quite unable to explain her method in words, and usually deprecated the idea of her advice being necessary. Occasionally, however, she would let drop some significant remark which the lieutenant felt went to the root of the whole matter of education. For example, she said to him one day: "You should do for your children what their parents fail to do for them. The reading, writing and arithmetic are not, after all, what they most need; it is all well and good for them to learn something, but the really important thing is for them to *be* something,—for them to become what they are meant to be, and in becoming which they so often have no guidance or help at home."

Finally, the day arrived on which the new schoolmaster was to be formally presented to the village. Arner and the pastor led him

502

solemnly between them to the church, which was crowded with the inhabitants of Bonnal. The good clergyman preached a sermon on the ideal function of the school in its relation to the home, and to the moral development of the community; after which Arner led Glülphi forward to the railing of the choir, and introducing him to the people, made a short but earnest plea in his behalf. The lieutenant was much affected, but mastered his emotion sufficiently to express in a few words his sense of the responsibility conferred upon him, and his hope that the parents would coöperate with him in his undertaking.

Arner was anxious to make the occasion of Glülphi's installation a festival for the school-children, so after the services at the church, he invited all the little folks to the parsonage, where, with the help of the pastor's wife, preparations had been made to receive them. It was a time-honored custom that every year, at Christmas and Easter, eggs and rolls should be distributed among the children of Bonnal. On this day, on entering the parsonage, the young people beheld even more beautifully painted eggs than they had seen at Easter; and beside each child's portion lay a bright nosegay.

The lieutenant, who knew nothing of the whole matter, was in an adjoining room, when suddenly the door was thrown open, and the children, at a sign from Theresa, struck up with one accord their prettiest song, and Glülphi found himself surrounded by the lively throng of his future charges. He was much moved, and when the song was concluded, he greeted them kindly, shaking many of them by the hand, and chatting pleasantly with them. Arner ordered some of his own wine to be brought, and the children drank the health of their new schoolmaster.

On the following morning the lieutenant began his school, and Gertrude helped him in the arrangement of it. They examined the children with regard to their previous studies, and seated those together who were equally advanced. First there were those who had not learned their letters, then those who could read separate words, and finally, those who already knew how to read. Beside reading, all were to learn writing and arithmetic, which previously had only been taught to the more wealthy, in private lessons.

At first Glülphi found it harder than he had expected; but every day, as he gained in experience, his task became easier and more delightful. A good and capable woman, named Margaret, who came to take charge of the sewing, spinning etc., proved a most valuable and conscientious helper in the work. Whenever a child's hand or wheel stopped, she would step up and restore things to their former condition. If the children's hair was in disorder, she would braid it up while they studied and worked; if there was a hole in their clothes, she would take a needle and thread, and mend it; and she showed them how to fasten their shoes and stockings properly, beside many other things they did not understand.

The new master was anxious, above all, to accustom his charges to strict order, and thus lead them to the true wisdom of life. He began school punctually on the stroke of the clock, and did not allow any one to come in late. He also laid great stress on good habits and behavior. The children were obliged to come to school clean in person and apparel, and with their hair combed. While standing, sitting, writing and working, they always were taught to keep the body erect as a candle. Glülphi's schoolroom must be clean as a church, and he would not suffer a pane of glass to be missing from the window, or a nail to be driven crooked in the floor. Still less did he allow the children to throw the smallest thing upon the floor, or to eat while they were studying; and it was even arranged that in getting up and sitting down they should not hit against each other.

Before school began, the children came up to their teacher one by one, and said: "God be with you!" He looked them over from head to foot, so that they knew by his eye if anything was wrong. If this glance was not sufficient, he spoke to them, or sent a message to their parents. A child would not infrequently come home with the word: "The schoolmaster sends greetings, and wants to know whether you have no needles and thread," or "whether water is dear," etc. At the close of school, those who had done well went up to him first, and said: "God be with you!" He held out his hand to each one, replying: "God be with you, my dear child!" Then came those who had only done partly well, and to these he merely said: "God be with you!" without giving them his hand. Finally, those who had not done well at all had to leave the room without even going to him.

The lieutenant's punishments were designed to remedy the faults for which they were inflicted. An idle scholar was made to cut firewood, or to carry stones for the wall which some of the older boys were constructing under the master's charge; a forgetful child was made school-messenger, and for several days was obliged to take charge of all the teacher's business in the village. Disobedience and impertinence he punished by not speaking publicly to the child in question for a number of days, talking with him only in private, after school. Wickedness and lying were punished with the rod,

504

and any child thus chastised was not allowed to play with the others for a whole week; his name was registered in a special record-book of offences, from which it was not erased until plain evidence of improvement was given. The schoolmaster was kind to the children while punishing them, talking with them more then than at any other time, and trying to help them correct their faults.

CHAPTER XXXII.—A GOOD PASTOR AND SCHOOLMASTER; THE OPENING OF A NEW ERA. In his instruction, Glülphi constantly sought to lay the foundation of that equanimity and repose which man can possess in all circumstances of life, provided the hardships of his lot have early become a second nature to him. The success of this attempt soon convinced the pastor that all verbal instruction, in so far as it aims at true human wisdom, and at the highest goal of this wisdom, true religion, ought to be subordinated to a constant training in practical domestic labor. The good man, at the same time, became aware that a single word of the lieutenant's could accomplish more than hours of his preaching. With true humility, he profited by the superior wisdom of the schoolmaster, and remodelled his method of religious instruction. He united his efforts to those of Glülphi and Margaret, striving to lead the children, without many words, to a quiet, industrious life, and thus to lay the foundations of a silent worship of God and love of humanity. To this end, he connected every word of his brief religious teachings with their actual, every-day experience, so that when he spoke of God and eternity, it seemed to them as if he were speaking of father and mother, house and home, in short, of the things with which they were most familiar. He pointed out to them in their books the few wise and pious passages which he still desired them to learn by heart, and completely ignored all questions involving doctrinal differences. He no longer allowed the children to learn any long prayers by rote, saying that this was contrary to the spirit of Christianity, and the express injunctions of their Saviour.

The lieutenant often declared that the pastor was quite unable to make a lasting impression on men, because he spoiled them by his kindness. Glülphi's own principles in regard to education were very strict, and were founded on an accurate knowledge of the world. He maintained that love was only useful in the education of men when in conjunction with fear; for they must learn to root out thorns and thistles, which they never do of their own accord, but only under compulsion, and in consequence of training.

He knew his children better in eight days than their parents did in eight years, and employed this knowledge to render deception difficult, and to keep their hearts open before his eyes. He cared for their heads as he did for their hearts, demanding that whatever entered them should be plain and clear as the silent moon in the sky. To insure this, he taught them to see and hear with accuracy, and cultivated their powers of attention. Above all, he sought to give them a thorough training in arithmetic; for he was convinced that arithmetic is the natural safeguard against error in the pursuit of truth.

Despite the children's rapid progress in their school, the lieutenant did not please everybody in the village, and a rumor soon spread abroad that he was too proud for a schoolmaster. It was in vain that the children contradicted this report; their parents only answered: "Even if he is good to you, he may be proud all the same." It was not until three weeks after the beginning of the school, that an event occurred which accomplished for him what the children's defence had been unable to do.

For the last twenty years the old rotten foot-bridge opposite the schoolhouse had been out of repair, so that in a rainy season the children must get wet above their ankles in crossing the lane to school. The first time the road was in this condition, Glülphi planted himself in the middle of the street in all the rain, and as the children came, lifted them, one after the other, across the brook. Now it happened that some of the very persons who had complained most of the lieutenant's pride, lived just across the way. It amused them greatly to see him get wet through and through in his red coat, and they fancied it would not be many minutes before he would call to them for help. When, however, he kept on patiently lifting the children over, until his hair and clothes were dripping wet, they began to say behind the window-panes: "He must be a good-natured fool, and we were certainly mistaken; if he were proud, he would have given it up long ago." Finally, they came out, and offered to relieve him from his task, while he went home and dried himself. But this was not all; when school was out that day, the children found a foot-bridge built, over which they could go home dry-shod. And from that day forth, not a word more was heard of the schoolmaster's pride.

The school was still not without enemies, the bitterest among them being the old schoolmaster, whose envy and rage at its success would have known no bounds, had he not feared to lose the pension which had been granted him by Arner, on condition that he should not set himself against the new order of things. But the schoolmaster was not the only man in the village who looked back

506

with regret to bygone days. Half of the villagers had been accustomed to spend their evenings at the tavern, and the bitterest complaints were heard on all sides, because, after the affair with Hummel, Arner had caused this house to be closed. As soon as he learned the state of things, and found that many of the former loafers were making their homes miserable by their idle discontent, Arner opened the peat swamps in the vicinity of Bonnal, and at once supplied more than fifty men with good employment.

The condition of the poor people of the village was much improved in various ways. The prospect of tithe-free land brought order and thrift into the houses of many of the spinners, and the poor in general were no longer so servile in their obedience to the whims and exactions of the rich. Renold's wife, who had always been noted for her charity, began to see that more good could be done by leading the people to help themselves, than by all her almsgiving; and now, whenever her aid was asked, her first answer was: "I must go home with you, and see what you really need, and how I can best help you."

Every evening the lieutenant had a half dozen young people at his house, to whom he talked for hours of what Arner and the pastor intended, and showed how their designs had been misunderstood.

.   .   .   .   .

HERBART 1776–1841

Johann Friedrich Herbart represents the systematically trained and critical philosopher among the educators. His style is pedestrian, his thinking sometimes pedantic. But it was this very insistence on accuracy that allowed him to accomplish what men such as Comenius and Pestalozzi had aimed at, namely, to change education from a primarily intuitional kind of thought and practice into a scholarly discipline. He developed a theory of mental processes which, though one-sidedly intellectual, nevertheless served as a basis for a systematic educational methodology. Not only in Germany, but also in this country the Herbartians provided the textbooks for the training of elementary school teachers and also improved the textbooks for the children. That the school of Herbart often fell into the traps of formalism is not his fault, just as it is not Rousseau's fault that there were too many vague enthusiasts among his followers.

If the professors in the seminaries for teachers had read Herbart thoroughly they would have seen that in spite of the great merits in his analysis of the learning process, he never deviated from the great cultural tradition according to which instruction is only one part—and not even the most important part—of education. Again and again Herbart emphasized that the goal of education is the development of a person with character and humane convictions who understands the great art of constructive and harmonious living.

Selections from Herbart's *Brief Encyclopaedia of Practical Philosophy* are translations by the editor from *Kurze Encyklopädie der Philosophie aus praktischen Gesichtspuncten entworfen,* in Johann Friedrich Herbart's Sämmtliche Werke, . . . herausgegeben von G. Hartenstein, Band II, Leipzig, L. Voss, 1850-1852. The selections from Herbart's *Science of Education* are taken from the translation from the German with a biographical introduction by Henry M. and Emmie Felken and a preface by Oscar Browning, published in Boston in 1902, in Heath's Pedagogical Library. This translation has been revised by the editor after comparison with the original: *Allgemeine Pädagogik aus dem Zweck der Erziehung abgeleitet,* published in 1806, in Herbart's Sämmtliche Werke, Band X, Leipzig, 1851.

BRIEF ENCYCLOPAEDIA OF PRACTICAL PHILOSOPHY

CHAPTER XII.—ON EDUCATION. 103. . . . Even for an adult it is not always easy to acquire and maintain a desirable attitude

508

toward the problems of life. All the more one has to refrain from demanding indiscriminatingly that the teacher impart to his pupil the right attitude for the rest of his life. . . .

The simple duty of the teacher at any moment of his work is to preserve his pupil's natural vigor. To create or transform the personality is beyond the teacher's power; but what he can do and what we may demand from him is to ward off dangers from his pupil and to abstain from ill-handling him.

104. To this vigor belongs particularly the natural cheerfulness of youth; but man from his youth onward must voluntarily accept restrictions, particularly as he has to live a communal life. Hence, first: Children must learn to obey. Their natural exuberance must meet enough resistance to avert offense.

Immediately we meet a new difficulty. The easy means for a child not to offend his parents or teachers is concealment and lying!

To cut the knot some teachers assume at once that children always lie if they can. Hence they have to be so closely supervised and watched, and kept so busy from morning to evening that they have no time for trickery. There is some truth in this, but if it is carried out with too much harshness and exactness one may fail in the first fundamental postulate we have set up, that children's vigor must be preserved! For this they need freedom! Those teachers who restrict freedom to such a degree that all the children's actions are calculated to please the observer, educate babies. Such creatures will have to learn how to use their powers when they are grown up,—and in spite of all their endeavors they will remain timid, helpless, and inferior to free personalities, until eventually they will try to compensate in whatever way they can.

Consequently, as such a restricting form of education is dangerous something better must be combined with supervision and occupation.

One says rightly that well bred children have not the heart to deceive their father and mother. Why not? They are used to rely on truth and confidence. This, then becomes the key-note of their lives. Thus we have the third pedagogical postulate. Children must be accustomed to satisfy the need for confidential communication not only among themselves but also in relation to their teacher. Otherwise they will never learn to detest lying. If this attitude is deeply rooted then they will betray occasional lies immediately by showing shame. Only if such conditions prevail the teacher may demand complete sincerity, otherwise this demand only enhances the child's disposition to lie.

105. All this can be summarized in the following words: in spite of a certain severity in your guidance, lead the children into a situation which they like and which invites them to be free and confident.

This is the supreme demand in education; all the rest, whatever one may call it, is only of secondary and tertiary importance; all instruction from the elements of learning to the highest level of scholarship should tend to this. Hence those schools, whose main function is merely teaching and learning cannot be considered as serving education in the deepest sense of the word. They are only of assisting value, and this only for such families as have already fulfilled the educational postulates mentioned above. . . .

. . . . .

It follows that education in order to have a permanent effect must try to use instruction not only for mere information but also for the formation of character.

. . . . .

But the hope which some educators base on instruction has not much more chance to be realized than the hope based on government. It requires a great deal to raise knowledge to the level of erudition: it is a still more difficult task to combine the imparting of knowledge with the formation of character. To achieve this purpose knowledge must be deeply felt and experienced; in other words the mere quantity of knowledge and the logical and practical training in notions, maxims and principles must affect the whole emotional attitude of a person. One may show how instruction has to proceed to produce such an effect. (I have shown this in my *Science of Education*.) The degree of success, however, depends largely on the pupil's individuality.

Only teachers of much experience can imagine how rapidly even carefully implanted and cultivated knowledge vanishes under new conditions. They only can believe how easily new opinions and ambitions emerge and how irresistibly a person is attracted by temptations which appeal to his nature—in spite of all previous precautions. Even superficial experience teaches us that the results of an examination are valid only for the day when it is held. . . . Such facts, however, are easily explained through reference to the continual flow of ideas (apperceptive masses) in our mind. Those, who consider the human soul as a fixed and concrete object, will never understand the mutability of the human character; they will easily resort to false remedies which only aggravate the evil.

510 .

106. These facts would reduce to naught the educational value of instruction . . . if we had not to consider an additional factor. Most people are not independent enough to set their own standards; living among their friends and their occupation they need and meet natural leaders whose standards they accept. Thus there emerge in society certain dominant opinions and codes of honor and each individual tries to live up to them, according to his abilities.

Now it is exactly schooling which decides to what level of society an individual belongs. . . . Thus the character of social more than the character of individual life explains the decisive influence and role of knowledge, and the evil or good, confusing or unifying effects of schools and authors.

107. Those, however, who have no true psychological insight, rarely understand anything of education. They may cherish the obsolete opinion that there reside in the human soul certain powers or faculties which have to be trained in one way or another. These people seemingly have in mind gymnastic exercises which strengthen the muscles, for man has only one kind of muscles. Indeed in each single apperceptive mass (mass or group of ideas) are contained so-called fantasy, memory and intelligence, but they are not equally distributed. Rather in one and the same person a certain mass of apperceptions may be of more intellectual, imaginative or of reproductive character; one mass may be penetrated with profound feeling, another with an atmosphere of coolness etc. Therefore what educators call formal discipline (Formelle Bildung) would be an absurdity if it meant the training of isolated mental faculties which exist only in some people's imagination.[1] But often one mass of ideas supports another one according to the general laws of reproduction.

.   .   .   .   .

[After Latin has been taught] the general rule in our schools is to teach French or Greek. This sequence is supposed to be the easiest, since Latin—so one boasts—has already provided the neces-

[1] In paragraphs 112 and 113 of the same work Herbart states expressly that the value of the ancient languages cannot be found in the acquisition of formal discipline. Their value lies, according to him, in the preparation for certain professions and particularly in the obligation of our civilization to preserve among the educated adequate awareness of its cultural roots. "No doubt our knowledge would soon lose its foundations and we should lose all criteria of good style in the rhetorical arts if ever the learning of ancient languages should be given up. Furthermore we have to preserve carefully all the historical threads which enable us to trace backward the origin of our culture, otherwise we may lose it."

sary formal discipline. But what would have happened if first French and Greek had been taught and Latin afterwards? Then, so it is said, the formal discipline would have started with French or Greek and then carried over to Latin. And this way, one asserts would have been neither better nor worse than beginning with Latin, since the main purpose is to arouse the mental power. Why then quarrel about the way toward that end? The customary way is the best, simply by virtue of tradition; in a new way one could go astray without need or profit.

This may be true in that the philologist, if forced to begin with another language than Latin, would first have to make some effort to familiarize himself thoroughly with the method of teaching the new language, whereas the method of teaching Latin is already nicely prescribed for every level. But the opinion that it does not matter whether the faculties of the mind are awakened by Greek, French or Latin is a barrier to careful observation. For what is at stake and what must be trained are not abstract powers or faculties but masses of ideas and their gradual formation. . . . The masses of ideas which enter the pupil's mind with French, Latin or Greek are not at all the same. Consequently the sequence with which they are acquired is not unimportant. Rather it is exactly this sequence on which depends the structure and efficacy of the acquired ideas, and that so-called mental power, which is to be aroused, becomes something essentially different if the sequence in the connection of ideas is altered.

A French, a German and an English scholar are three different individuals, who may endeavor a lifetime to become as much alike as is their learning. But they will have to go different ways and will never succeed completely because their mother-tongues and their characteristic modes of thinking were different. . . .

A German, French or English scholar may debate which one of them may most easily attain that degree of scholarship, which is above all national differences. An impartial judge would tell them that each is in possession of what they are looking for, while he remains in his native country. . . . Certainly such a statement would not deviate from the truth.

. . . . .

108. Another instance of erroneous ideas about formal discipline is the frequent recommendation of mathematics as a special instrument for intellectual training. No wonder that most educators try to attain this end by a shorter method. Why all these figures and

formulas if the ancient languages which have to be learned anyway, serve the same purpose? Just study grammar; this will sharpen the intellect even more than mathematics, because as some people believe, they have discovered that even poor intellects can acquire skill in figuring.

But it is better not to ask whether the grammarians surpass the mathematicians and excel as great statesmen or generals or in other arenas.

Grammatical thinking remains within grammar; and mathematical thinking remains within mathematics; the reasoning within each discipline of thought forms itself in accordance with the discipline. But if grammatical or mathematical notions enter by any chance and even through distant channels into the sphere of activity of a general or a statesman, he will reproduce what he once learnt and it will assist him in his actions.

Hence grammar and mathematics cannot be substituted for one another, but each holds its value in its own sphere. Nor can grammar be used as a pattern for learning logic, though there exists some relationship, consequently also some educational interaction. The same holds true for logic and mathematics. But alas, if somebody who needs logic to master the higher spheres of philosophy relied on his previous studies in grammar and mathematics! Neither grammar, nor mathematics, nor logic makes the metaphysician, although he cannot make any progress without logic and mathematics.

One might better use geography as the example of a science for which training in other branches of learning is useful, for in geography, mathematics, the natural sciences, and history are combined. Unfortunately, geography enjoys least of all the reputation of requiring particular intellectual training, probably because this science, as it is usually taught in our schools, has never effectively combined mathematical, physical and social sciences.

109. If then the teacher cannot put his trust in formal discipline and if the mere bulk of memorized knowledge does not provide individual character and culture, on what can he rely?

First, in regard to subject-matter: synthesis and analysis.

Second, in regard to the pupil: on interest, in so far as it expands and deepens.

1. Synthesis and analysis refer immediately to the sequence of ideas inherent in specific subject-matter.[2] Whatever is possible must be done to build verbal instruction on a basis of experience,

[2] See *Science of Education,* Book II, Chapters 4 and 5.

be it natural or artificial. Children who have not seen or observed anything cannot be taught. But after experience is provided it has to be analyzed and conceptualized in order to be fitted for scientific understanding. Thus analysis prepares a great number of associations for all the new notions which afterwards arise from synthesis. The teacher is, from the psychologist's point of view, always on the right track if he considers the texture and the growth of the apperceptive masses occurring during instruction from both the analytical and synthetical point of view, provided his pupils can follow him without exhaustion and without confusion of their ideas from too much pressure.

2. As to interest, it is difficult to make general statements with respect to degrees of deepening. We probably do best to refer to the example of great poets who show the most astounding skill in capturing and increasing the interest of their readers.

On the other hand the expansion of interest can be described and subdivided into [6] different classes, as I have done above.[3]

110. The division of interest into six main classes can be useful to the teacher in the following respects. It can serve him as a criterion as to what and how much he can combine in his instruction in order to keep up the necessary equilibrium of interest. It can serve as a criterion for avoiding the useless and distracting variety of subjects; often the concentration on one subject can better serve the purpose of stimulating and maintaining manifold interests. Finally this division may be particularly useful for judging with some probability whether a pupil can profit from intellectual instruction. Often all classes of interest occurring in expanding instruction are feeble and transitory; in this case they are incapable of producing the necessary intellectual energy. Often just one or the other kind of interest emerges, but in a degree of isolation which characterizes more the onesided artist than a person of well rounded education. But in all cases in which neither curiosity, nor taste, nor patriotism, nor piety can be appealed to and in which neither careful instruction nor impressive presentation nor deliberate discipline show any effect—in such cases the teacher is unable to arouse in the pupil that degree of intellectual energy which could give promise for his future conduct. Then of course, the question arises how

---

[3] In paragraph 83 of the same work Herbart subdivides interest as expressing itself in the acquisition of *knowledge* (empirical, speculative and aesthetic) and in interest as expressing itself in form of *sympathy* (sympathy with the individual; sympathy with the welfare of society; religious feeling of the exposure and dependence of the human race).

much there is reason for serious anxiety, and what further resources the teacher has.

In this context, besides man's well known sensuality and its dangers, one has to consider the motives of human conduct as mentioned in the beginning of this book (paragraph 7).[4] If a person in his youth has failed to develop spontaneous manifold, and culturally rich interests it will show its effect on his later life in that he will be unable to enjoy enriching forms of recreation. But the other motives and modes of life which we have mentioned will still be valid. Industriousness, or a desire for work, is possible as a result of habituation, even without a developed empirical, speculative or aesthetic interest. Relaxation can alternate with work in a blameless, though not particularly commendable way, even if a person shows no outspoken sympathy for individuals, or society, or for religious life. In every-day social routine many a man succeeds who does not set an example but who understands how to keep the middle of the road. Respect for people with superior character, love for their fellows, attachment to their families and finally the severity of service carry many tolerably through their lives, without obvious absence of a good education. Hence, if the teacher has no opportunity for devoting himself to higher tasks, if he is hampered by the feeble disposition of his pupil, there still remains for him to adjust his work to such hopes, though they may not be particularly enchanting. But even for the realization of these hopes certain conditions are necessary which one cannot find or foresee in young men, particularly if they are unprotected by society. But in every case the educated man always appears tolerably refined and has a chance to become current coin, whereas the uneducated offends and repels, and if he falls he will mostly find himself deserted. We all shall agree that avoidance of gross ignorance helps to start and polish a person, though such ignorance cannot be completely avoided even by relatively good instruction which does not meet any interest.

[4] In paragraph 7 Herbart says the conduct of man's life is determined by the following motives:

1. *Occupation:*
   work
   enriching recreation
   relaxation.

2. *Disposition:*
   social intercourse ⎫
   approval   ⎬ and the reverse
   love   ⎭

3. *Family-relationships:*
   the spouse
   the parents
   the rest of the family.

4. *Service:*
   compulsory
   paid
   honorary.

111. If on the other hand the teacher succeeds in developing in the pupil manifold interest, then the education becomes a noble task in that it helps mankind to realize the great practical ethical ideas.[5] These ideas will become the more self-evident to the pupil the less it is necessary to teach him merely to swim on the waves of society as was the case with the unsusceptible type. On the other hand it is necessary to combine exact methods of thinking and self-criticism with the enthusiasm which can be imparted to the susceptible pupil by such means as religion and history. Of particular use for such an examining attitude is the capacity of clear ethical discrimination. For by its own nature the human mind is not so well disposed as to apprehend clearly the ideas of justice, equity, perfection and sympathy and to act accordingly. In addition a person with the capacity for inner freedom not rarely abandons traditional ideals and inclines towards eccentric claims and opinions for which, so he thinks, he has to fight and to bring sacrifices in order to carry off the crown of martyrdom. The striving for the unusual and the exceptional is in the spirit of the time, but it does not fit our country. Hence what education has to do is to preserve in talented youth their natural courage and openmindedness but not to inspire them with burning ambition.

．　．　．　．　．

114. Altogether there ought to be more diversity in our school-system than exists to-day. Each school receives a certain character from its teachers and this is generally desirable. In addition not all children are fitted for the same school.

Some are longing for knowledge to such a degree that they are never satisfied. For them a rich storehouse of intellectual goods is desirable.

Other children need much supervision. For them a school with severe discipline will be best fitted.

Still other children need friendly attachment, it would be a pity if they could not find teachers who understand them.

[5] These practical ideas, explained in paragraph 27 are:

Original ideas:	Derived ideas:
inner freedom (Innere Freiheit)	inspired society (Beseel te Gesellschaft)
striving for perfection (Vollkommenheit)	culture (Cultursystem)
sympathy (Wohlwollen)	commonweal (Verwaltungssystem)
justice	lawful government (Rechtsgesellschaft)
equity	just reward (Lohnsystem).

Some are lazy in scholarly studies, but talented for business; for them a brilliant academic institution is not the right place but only a modest secondary school which does not seek its merits in a high standard of scholarship, but in a steady implanting of useful knowledge.

But especially in the more elementary forms of training uniformity is less desirable than variety. For there the diversity of dispositions and needs is extremely great and so far this variety has been not sufficiently explored, nor sufficiently utilized.

.   .   .   .   .   .

GENERAL PRINCIPLES OF THE SCIENCE OF EDUCATION PSYCHOLOGICALLY DEDUCED FROM ITS AIM

INTRODUCTION. The aim of all those who educate and demand education is determined by the views they bring to the subject.

The majority of those who teach have entirely neglected to build up a proper view of their work; such a view opens out gradually as the work progresses, and is formed partly by the teacher's individuality, partly by the individuality and environment of the pupil. If the teachers possess originality, they will utilize all that comes to hand to provide stimulus and occupation for the objects of their care; if they have foresight, they exclude all which may be harmful to health, disposition, or manners. Thus a boy grows up, who has tested himself in everything that is not dangerous, who has experience in considering and treating the common things of daily life, and who has developed all the emotions which his environment could arouse in him. If he has really grown up thus, he may be congratulated on the result. But educators complain unceasingly of the harmful influence of surrounding circumstances—of servants, relatives, playmates, the sexual instincts and the university. No wonder that such an education does not always produce a strong character which can bid defiance to unfavorable influences, how could it be otherwise if the meagre mental diet is determined more by chance than by human skill.

Rousseau desired to *harden* his pupil. He defined for himself his own view of the subject, and remained true to it. He follows nature. All the processes of animal development in man are, by means of education, to be assured a free, happy growth from the mother's breast to the marriage bed. To live is the business which he teaches.

517

Yet, he evidently sympathizes with our poet's dictum, "Life is not the highest of all goods," for he sacrifices the whole individual life of the teacher, whom he makes the boy's constant companion. This education costs too dear. The companion's life is in any case worth more than the boy's, even if we go no further than mortality tables; for the probability of being able to live is greater for the man than the child. But is mere existence then, so difficult to man? We thought human *plants* were like the rose; that just as the queen of flowers give the gardener least trouble of all, so human beings thrive in every climate, are nourished by every species of food, learn most easily to accommodate themselves to all circumstances, and to turn everything to advantage. Still it is as difficult for the teacher to educate a "nature man" among cultivated men as it will be later for the pupil to live in the midst of so heterogeneous a society.

How to behave in society, is what *Locke's* pupil will know best. The principal thing for him is conventionality. For fathers who destine their sons for the world, no book of education need be written after Locke; anything added would degenerate into artificiality. Secure at any price a trustworthy man of refined habits, who "himself knows the rules of courtesy and good society with all the varieties arising from difference of persons, times and places, and who will then assiduously direct his pupil as suits his age to the observation of these things." [6] One can say nothing against this. It would be vain to dissuade men of the world from educating their sons to become men of the world. For this desire arises from the impressions of actual life, and is constantly confirmed and increased by new impressions. Preachers, poets, philosophers, may be all unction, all gaiety, all gravity in prose or verse, but one glance at the world around destroys all their effect, and they seem to the men of the world mere actors or visionaries. Why after all should a worldly education not succeed, for with the men of the world, the world is in league.

But I could tell of men who know the world without loving it; who while they will not withdraw their sons from the world, will still less allow them to be lost in it, and who assume that a clear headed person will find in his own consciousness, sympathy, and tastes, the best teachers, to guide him as far into the conventionalities of society as he is willing to go. Such men allow their sons

[6] Locke, *Some Thoughts concerning Education,* par. 93: "To form a young gentleman as he should be, 'tis fit his governor should himself be wellbred, understand the ways of carriage, and measures of civility in all the variety of persons, times, and places, and help his pupil, as much as his age requires, constantly to the observation of them."

to gain a knowledge of mankind among their comrades; they know that one studies Nature best in Nature, provided the home has already sufficiently sharpened, exercised and directed the power of observation. They desire that their children grow up in the midst of the generation with which they will live. Is this compatible with good education? Perfectly, so long as during the hours of instruction, when the teacher is occupied seriously and systematically with the pupil, such mental activity is pursued as will so arouse the pupil's interest that compared with these hours all boy's play will gradually become trifling, and of little account even to the boy himself.

But such an attitude will never be achieved, if the teacher leaves his pupil for some hours of the day to his natural life and forces him, during other hours, to learn from abstract books. Such an attitude can be created only if natural child-life and learning are interconnected. Therefore a teacher, inspired by ideals, with the idea of education in all its beauty and greatness, can understand the task of training a boy in the midst of his natural environment to a nobler life, if he has enough intelligence and knowledge to understand and represent natural life and actuality as a fragment of a great whole. He will then say of his own accord, that not he, but the whole power of what humanity has felt, experienced and thought, is the true teacher, to which the boy is entitled, and that the teacher is merely to help him by intelligent interpretation and elevating companionship. Thus to present to youth the whole fund of accumulated experience in a concentrated form is the highest service which mankind can render to its successors, be it as teaching or as warning.

Conventional education [as advocated by Locke] tends to prolong existing evils; whereas a merely natural education [in the sense of Rousseau] would force us to overcome in each pupil evils already overcome by the race. A teacher of limited outlook, who neither knows what is beyond, nor understands how to teach it, will narrow the sphere of teaching and warning to the immediate environment. One ought not to excuse this narrow concept of education by referring to the inefficiency of pedantic teachers, nor to the difficulties of children to grasp things beyond their immediate environment; for pedantry can be avoided and the difficulties don't exist.

How far, however, this may, or may not be true, each man decides from his own experience—I from mine, others from theirs. Only let us all consider the proposition—*each but experiences what he attempts.* A nonogenarian village schoolmaster has the experience

519

of his ninety years dull routine. He may rest on the consciousness of his long toils, but has he also the criticism of his work and his methods? Much that is new has prospered with our modern educators; they have found their reward in the gratitude of men, and they can rejoice over it. But it is another question whether they have a right to determine from their experience for ever all that can be attained by means of education, and all that can be done with children.

．　　．　　．　　．　　．

I have required scientific knowledge and intelligence from the teacher. . . .

The first, though by no means the only complete science of the teacher, would be a psychology in which all human activities were sketched *a priori*. I think I recognize the possibility as well as the difficulty of such a science. Long will it be before we have it, longer still before we can expect it from teachers. Never, however, can it be a substitute for observation of the pupil; the individual can only be discovered, not deduced. The construction of the pupil on *a priori* principles is therefore a misleading expression in itself, and an empty idea which the science of education cannot handle for a long time.

BOOK I, CHAPTER II.—I. IS THE AIM OF EDUCATION SINGLE OR MANIFOLD? . . . If one considers the nature of education he will recognize that unity of aim is an ideal which cannot be realized, because *the teacher must foresee the future man in the boy. Consequently the teacher must try to envisage the purposes which the pupil will pursue after he has grown up. It is the teacher's task to prepare beforehand in his pupil the desirable facility for achieving his goals.* He ought not to stunt the activity of the future man; consequently he ought neither to confine it to single points, nor weaken it by too much diversity. He ought to allow nothing to be lost either in *Intension* or *Extension*, which his pupil might afterwards demand back from him. Great as the difficulties may be, thus much is clear—*since human aims are manifold, the teacher's cares must be manifold also.*

The multiplicity of education can easily be classified under a few categories. The pupil's future aims may be divided into his merely possible aims, which he might perhaps take up at one time or another and pursue to a greater or less degree, and into the *necessary aims* which he could never forgive himself for having neglected. In other words, the aims of education can be subdivided according

520

to aims of *choice* (not of the teacher, nor the boy, but of the future man) and the aims of *morality*. Those two main headings are at once clear to every one who bears in mind the most generally recognized fundamentals of ethics.

II. MANY-SIDEDNESS OF INTEREST.—STRENGTH OF MORAL CHARACTER. (1) How can the teacher assume responsibility for those aims of the pupil which we designated as *merely possible?*

As these aims will be chosen by the pupil after he has grown up and become independent their factual content is beyond the competence of the teacher, who can seek only to form will and tendencies, and also the demands which the future man will make upon himself. The power, the initiative, and the activity wherewith the future man may meet those demands can be prepared and cultivated by the teacher according to the ideas he has about a mature person. Thus it is not a certain number of separate aims that we, as teachers, ought to have in mind (for how can we foresee them,) but the potential activity of the growing man, the quantum of his personal vitality and spontaneity. The greater and more harmonious this quantum, the greater will be the man's maturity and perfection, and the greater the effect of the teacher's care.

Only the flower must not burst its calyx—abundance must not become weakness through losing direction because of too many distractions. Human society has long found division of labor necessary, that every one may make perfect what he attempts. But the more sub-divided, the greater is that which each later receives from all the rest. Now, since intellectual receptivity rests on affinity of mind, and this on similar activities of mind, it follows that in the higher realm of human achievement, labor ought not to be divided to the point where each man is ignorant of his neighbour's work. Every man must love all activities and be a virtuoso in one. The particular virtuosity is a matter of choice; but manifold receptivity is a matter of education for it grows out of manifold beginnings of a pupil's own efforts. Therefore we call the first part of the educational aim—*many-sidedness of interest,* which must be distinguished from its exaggeration—dabbling in many things. And since no one object of will, nor its direction, interests us more than any other, we must assure a *well-balanced* many-sidedness. We shall thus get at the meaning of the common expression, "harmonious cultivation of all powers." But we must define what we mean when we speak of a "multiplicity and harmony of mental powers."

521

(2) How can the teacher assume responsibility for the *necessary* aims of the pupil?

Since morality has its place only in the individual's will, founded on right insight, it follows, first, that the work of education is not to develop in the pupil a certain external mode of action, but rather ethical insight with a corresponding will power.

I leave here untouched the metaphysical questions inherent in the problem of the genesis of morality. He who understands how to educate can forget them; he who cannot needs metaphysics before a science of education, and the outcome of his speculations will prove to him whether the idea of education is, or is not, a possible one for him.

I look at life, and find many upon whom morality is a stunted growth, few with whom it is the principle of life itself. Most men possess a character which has not much to do with real goodness, and a plan of life formed only according to their own inclination. They do the good when convenient and they avoid the evil gladly —provided the better leads to the same goal. Moral principles are wearisome to them, because for them nothing follows from these principles except now and then some limitation of their ideas. They rather welcome everything which prevents such limitations; the young rascal, if he sins with some boldness, can be sure of their sympathy, and sure that what is neither ridiculous nor malicious, will be forgiven. If it be the object of moral education to lead the pupil into the rank of these men, we have an easy task; we need only take care that he grows up in the self-consciousness without being teased or insulted, and that he receive certain principles of honor. These principles are easily inculcated because they treat of honor not as a wearisome acquisition, but as a possession given by nature which must be protected and put in force on certain occasions, according to conventional forms. But who will warrant us that the future man will not himself search out the real good, to make it the object of his willing, the aim of his life, the standard of his self-criticism? Who will protect us against the severe judgment which will then overtake us?

· · · · ·

FROEBEL 1782–1852

FRIEDRICH WILHELM FROEBEL is known to most laymen as the founder of the Kindergarten, but he is also the thinker who had the great Romantic vision of education's role as a part in the process of evolution.

His own experience, as well as his acquaintance with Schelling's philosophy of identity between mind and nature, led him toward a profound feeling of unity in all life: the fertilization of plants, love among animals and humans, and finally all loving creation being the expression of a spirit of infinite productivity. All individual existence—so Froebel thought—is but a link in the chain of total life; but as the single is contained in the total, so a reflection, or potentiality, of the total can be found in the single.

Therefore childhood is not just a transition toward adulthood, and child's play not just a preparation for the activities of a mature person, but are in themselves something complete and organic. As long as humanity has not acquired this deeper conception of childhood, it corrupts the springs of its own development.

Out of such reasoning, not just out of a charitable heart, Froebel worked for the foundation of the Kindergarten and contemplated methods of occupying the child in such a way that in each phase of his activity he would become more adult, but at the same time be fully himself.

The following selections are from Froebel's *Autobiography*, translated and annotated by Emilie Michaelis and Keatley Moore, published by C. W. Bardeen in Syracuse, New York, in 1890, and from Froebel's *The Education of Man*, translated by W. N. Hailmann, published by D. Appleton and Company, New York and London, in 1912 in the International Education Series.

AUTOBIOGRAPHY

A LETTER TO THE DUKE OF MEININGEN. I was born at Oberweissbach, a village in the Thuringian Forest, in the small principality of Schwarzburg-Rudolfstadt, on the 21 st April, 1782. My father was the principal clergyman, or pastor, there. (He died in 1802.) I was early initiated into the conflict of life amidst painful and narrowing circumstances; and ignorance of child-nature and insufficient education wrought their influence upon me. Soon after my birth my mother's health began to fail, and after nursing me nine months she died. This loss, a hard blow to me, influenced the whole environment and development of my being: I consider that

523

my mother's death decided more or less the external circumstances of my whole life.

The cure of five thousand souls, scattered over six or seven villages, devolved solely on my father. This work, even to a man so active as my father, who was very conscientious in the fulfilment of his duty as minister, was all-absorbing; the more so since the custom of frequent services still prevailed. Besides all this, my father had undertaken to superintend the building of a large new church, which drew him more and more from his home and from his children.

I was left to the care of the servants; but they, profiting by my father's absorption in his work, left me, fortunately for me, to my brothers, who were somewhat older than myself.

. . . . .

. . . my life was early brought under the influence of nature, of useful handiwork, and of religious feelings; or, as I prefer to say, the primitive and natural inclinations of every human being were even in my case also tenderly fostered in the germ. I must mention here, with reference to my ideas regarding the nature of man, to be treated of later, and as throwing light upon my professional and individual work, that at this time I used repeatedly, and with deep emotion, to resolve to try and be a good and brave man. As I have heard since, this firm inward resolution of mine was in flagrant contrast with my outward life. I was full of youthful energy and in high spirits, and did not always know how properly to moderate my vivacity. Through my want of restraint I got into all kinds of scrapes. Often, in my thoughtlessness, I would destroy the things I saw around me, in the endeavour to investigate and understand them.

My father was prevented by his manifold occupations from himself instructing me. Besides, he lost all further inclination to teach me, after the great trouble he found in teaching me to read—an art which came to me with great difficulty. As soon as I could read, therefore, I was sent to the public village school.

The position in which my father stood to the village schoolmasters, that is to say, to the Cantor,[1] and to the master of the girls' school, and his judgment of the value of their respective teaching,

[1] The Cantor would combine the duties of precentor (whence his title), leading the church singing and training the choristers, with those of the schoolmaster of the village boys' school. In large church-schools the Cantor is simply the choir-master. The great Bach was Cantor of the Thomas-Schule, Leipzig.

decided him to send me to the latter. This choice had a remarkable influence on the development of my inner nature, on account of the perfect neatness, quiet, intelligence, and order which reigned in the school; nay, I may go further, and say the school was exactly suitable for such a child as I was. . . . At that time church and school generally stood in strict mutual relationship, and so it was in our case. The school children had their special places in church; and not only were they obliged to attend church, but each child had to repeat to the teacher, at a special class held for the purpose every Monday, some passage of Scripture used by the minister in his sermon of the day before, as a proof of attention to the service From these passages that one which seemed most suitable to children was then chosen for the little ones to master or to learn by heart, and for that purpose one of the bigger children had during the whole week, at certain times each day, to repeat the passage to the little children, sentence by sentence. The little ones, all standing up, had then to repeat the text sentence by sentence in like manner, until it was thoroughly imprinted on their memories.

. . . . .

The surroundings amidst which I had grown up, especially those in which my first childhood was passed, had caused my senses to be much and early exercised. The pleasures of the senses were from the first, therefore, an object for the closest consideration with me. The results of this analysing and questioning habit of my early boyhood were perfectly clear and decisive, and, if not rendered into words, were yet firmly settled in my mind. I recognised that the transitory pleasures of the senses were without enduring and satisfying influence on man, and that they were therefore on no account to be pursued with too great eagerness. This conviction stamped and determined my whole being, just as my questioning examination and comparison of the inner with the outer world, and my study of their interconnection, is now the basis of my whole future life. Unceasing self-contemplation, self-analysis, and self-education have been the fundamental characteristics of my life from the very first, and have remained so until these latest days.

To stir up, to animate, to awaken, and to strengthen, the pleasure and power of the human being to labour uninterruptedly at his own education, has become and always remained the fundamental principle and aim of my educational work.

Great was my joy when I believed I had proved completely to my own satisfaction that I was not destined to go to hell. The stony,

525

oppressive dogmas of orthodox theology I very early explained away, perhaps assisted in this by two circumstances. Firstly, I heard these expressions used over and over again, from my habit of being present at the lessons given by my father in our own house, in preparation for confirmation. I heard them used also in all sorts of ways, so that my mind almost unconsciously constructed some sort of explanation of them. Secondly, I was often a mute witness of the strict way in which my father performed his pastoral duties, and of the frequent scenes between him and the many people who came to the parsonage to seek advice and consolation. I was thus again constantly attracted from the outer to the inner aspects of life. Life, with its inmost motives laid bare, passed before my eyes, with my father's comments pronounced upon it; and thing and word, act and symbol were thus perceived by me in their most vivid relationship. I saw the disjointed, heavy-laden, torn, inharmonious life of man as it appeared in this community of five thousand souls, before the watchful eyes of its earnest, severe pastor. Matrimonial and sexual circumstances especially were often the objects of my father's gravest condemnation and rebuke. The way in which he spoke about these matters showed me that they formed one of the most oppressive and difficult parts of human conduct; and, in my youth and innocence, I felt a deep pain and sorrow that man alone, among all creatures, should be doomed to these separations of sex, whereby the right path was made so difficult for him to find. I felt it a real necessity for the satisfaction of my heart and mind to reconcile this difficulty, and yet could find no way to do so. How could I at that age, and in my position? But my eldest brother, who, like all my elder brothers, lived away from home, came to stay with us for a time; and one day, when I expressed my delight at seeing the purple threads of the hazel buds, he made me aware of a similar sexual difference in plants. Now was my spirit at rest. I recognised that what had so weighed upon me was an institution spread over all nature, to which even the silent, beautiful race of flowers was submitted. From that time humanity and nature, the life of the soul and the life of the flower, were closely knit together in my mind; and I can still see my hazel buds, like angels, opening for me the great God's temple of Nature.

I now had what I needed: to the Church was added the Nature-Temple; to the religious Christian life, the life of Nature; to the passionate discord of human life the tranquil peace of the life of plants. From that time it was as if I held the clue of Ariadne to guide me through the labyrinth of life. An intimate communion

526

with Nature for more than thirty years (although, indeed, often interrupted, sometimes for long intervals) has taught me that plants, especially trees, are a mirror, or rather a symbol, of human life in its highest spiritual relations; and I think one of the grandest and deepest fore-feelings that have ever emanated from the human soul, is before us when we read, in the Holy Scriptures, of a tree of knowledge of good and evil; even the world of crystals and stones—though not so vividly, calmly, clearly, and manifestly as the world of plants and flowers. I said my hazel buds gave me the clue of Ariadne. Many things grew clear to me: for instance, the earliest life and actions of our first parents in Paradise, and much connected therewith.

`      .    .    .    .    .`

Towards the end of this epoch, my eldest brother, already spoken of, was at the university, and studied theology. Philosophic criticism was then beginning to elucidate certain Church dogmas. It was therefore not very surprising that father and son often differed in opinion. I remember that one day they had a violent dispute about religion and Church matters. My father stormed, and absolutely declined to yield; my brother, though naturally of mild disposition, flushed deep-red with excitement; and he, too, could not abandon what he had recognised as true. I was present also on this as on many other occasions, an unobserved witness, and can still see father and son standing face to face in the conflict of opinion. I almost thought I understood something of the subject in dispute; I felt as if I must side with my brother, but there seemed at the same time something in my father's view which indicated the possibility of a mutual understanding. Already I felt in a dim way that every illusion has a true side, which often leads men to cling to it with a desperate firmness. This conviction has become more and more confirmed in me the longer I have lived; and when at any time I have heard two men disputing for the truth's sake, I have found that the truth is usually to be learnt from both sides. Therefore I have never liked to take sides; a fortunate thing for me.

`          .    .    .    .    .`

The misapprehension, the oppression under which I suffered in my early years, prepared me to bear similar evils later on, and especially those which weigh upon me in the present circumstances of my life. And as I see my present private and public life and my destiny reflected in a part of my former life, just so do I read and

527

trace the present universal life in my former individual life. More-over, in the same way as I tried as child or boy to educate myself to be a worthy man according to those laws which God had implanted, unknown to me, within my nature, so now do I strive in the same way, according to the same laws, and by the same method, to edu-cate the children of my country. That for which I strove as a boy, not yet conscious of any purpose, the human race now strived for with equal unconsciousness of purpose, but for all that none the less truly. The race is, however, surrounded by less favourable circum-stances than those which influenced me in my boyhood.

Life in its great as well as in its small aspects, in humanity and the human race as well as in the individual (even though the individual man often wilfully mars his own existence)—life, in the present, the past, and the future, has always appeared to me as a great un-divided whole, in which one thing is explained, is justified, is con-ditioned and urged forward by the other.

·   ·   ·   ·   ·

A new existence now began for me, entirely opposed to that which I had hitherto led. An uncle on my mother's side came to visit us in this year; he was a gentle, affectionate man. His appear-ance among us made a most agreeable impression upon me. This uncle, being a man of experience, may have noticed the adverse influences which surrounded me; for soon after his departure he begged my father by letter to turn me over to him entirely. My father readily consented, and toward the end of the year 1792 I went to him. He had early lost his wife and child, and only his aged mother-in-law lived in his house with him. In my father's house severity reigned supreme; here, on the contrary, mildness and kindness held sway. There I encountered mistrust; here I was trusted. There I was under restraint; here I had liberty. Hitherto I had hardly ever been with boys of my own age; here I found forty schoolfellows, for I joined the upper class of the town school.[2]

·   ·   ·   ·   ·

The clergyman who taught us never interfered with our games, played at certain appointed playgrounds, and always with great fun and spirit. Deeply humiliating to me were the frequent slights I received in our play, arising from my being behind boys of my age in bodily strength, and more especially in agility; and all my dash

[2] Equal to an English middle-class school.

528

and daring could not replace the robust, steady strength, and the confident sureness of aim which my companions possessed. Happy fellows! they had grown up in continual exercise of their youthful boyish strength. I felt myself exceedingly fortunate when I had at length got so far that my schoolfellows could tolerate me as a companion in their games. But whatever I accomplished in this respect by practice, by continual effort of will, and by the natural course of life, I always felt myself physically deficient in contrast with their uncramped boyish powers. Setting aside that which I had been robbed of by my previous education, my new life was vigorous and unfettered by external restraint; and they tell me I made good use of my opportunity. The world lay open before me, as far as I could grasp it. It may indeed be because my present life was as free and constrained as my former life had been cramped and constrained, anyhow the companions of my youth have reminded me of several incidents of that time which make me think that my good spirits led me to the borders of wildness and extravagance; although as a boy I considered my demeanour quieter by far than that of my companions of my own age. My communion with Nature, silent hitherto, now became freer and more animated. And as, at the same time, my uncle's house was full of peace and quiet contemplation, I was able as I grew up to develop that side of my character also; thus on every side my life became harmoniously balanced.

. . . . .

The subjects best taught in the school of Stadt-Ilm were reading, writing, arithmetic, and religion. Latin was miserably taught, and still worse learnt. Here, as in so many similar schools, the teaching utterly lacked the elucidation of first principles. The time spent on Latin was therefore not wasted upon me, in so far that I learnt from it that such a method of teaching could bear no fruit among the scholars. Arithmetic was a very favourite study of mine; and as I also received private tuition in this subject, my progress was so rapid that I came to equal my teacher both in theory and practice, although his attainments were by no means despicable. But how astonished was I when, in my twenty-third year, I first went to Yverdon, and found I could not solve the questions there being set to the scholars! This was one of the experiences which prepossessed me so keenly in favour of Pestalozzi's method of teaching, and decided me to begin arithmetic myself from the very beginning over again, according to his system. But more of this later.

In physical geography we repeated our tasks parrot-wise, speaking much and knowing nothing; for the teaching on this subject had not the very least connection with real life, nor had it any actuality for us, although at the same time we could rightly name our little specks and patches of colour on the map. I received private tuition in this subject also. My teacher wished to advance further with me; he took me to England. I could find no connection between that country and the place and country in which I dwelt myself, so that of this instruction also I retained but little. As for actual instruction in German, it was not to be thought of; but we received directions in letter-writing and in spelling. I do not know with what study the teaching of spelling was connected, but I think it was not connected with any; it hovered in the air. I had lessons, furthermore, in singing and in pianoforte playing, but without result.

. . . . .

Here I am obliged to mention something which as an educationist I can by no means pass lightly by. We received instruction from two schoolmasters: one was pedantic and rigid; the other, more especially our class-teacher (*conrector*), was large-hearted and free. The first never had any influence over his class; the second could do whatever he pleased with us, and if he had but set his mind to it, or perhaps if he had been aware of his power, he might have done some thoroughly good sound work with his class.

. . . . .

. . . From my own experience it was . . . shown to me how eminently injurious it is in education and in instruction to consider only a certain circle of future activities or a certain rank in life. The wearisome old-fashioned education *ad hoc* (that is, for some one special purpose) has always left many a noble power of man's nature unawakened.

A career in our country frequently chosen by the worthiest and most anxious parents for their sons is that of a post in the Treasury and Exchequer. Aspirants to such a post have two means of entering and two starting-points in this career; either they become a clerk to one of the minor officials in the Treasury or Exchequer, or the personal servant of one of the highest officials. As my knowledge of writing and figures seemed to my father satisfactory and sufficient for such a post, and as he knew well that it might lead, not merely to a life free from pecuniary cares, but even to wealth and fortune, he chose this career as mine. But the minor Treasury official who might have found employment for such a young man, showed

530

various reasons why he could not or would not as yet receive me as
a clerk. There was something in my nature which revolted against
the second mode I have mentioned of entering this career; something which I never afterwards experienced, but which at the time
absolutely prevented me from choosing such a mode of starting in
my future profession, and that in spite of the most alluring hopes
that were held out to me. My father meant well and honestly by
me, but fate ruled it against him.

.   .   .   .   .

My own desires and inclinations were now at last consulted. I
wanted to be an agriculturist in the full meaning of the word; for
I loved mountain, field, and forest; and I heard also that to learn
anything solid in this occupation one must be well acquainted with
geometry and land-surveying. From what I had learnt of the latter
by snatches now and then, the prospect of knowing more about it
delighted me much; and I cared not whether I began with forestry,
with farming, or with geometry and land-surveying. My father tried
to find a position for me; but the farmer asked too high a premium.
Just at this time he became acquainted with a forester who had also
a considerable reputation as land-surveyor and valuer. They soon
came to terms, and I was apprenticed to this man for two years, to
learn forestry, valuing, geometry, and land-surveying. I was fifteen
years and a half old when I became an apprentice to the forester,
on Midsummer Day 1797.

.   .   .   .   .

. . . My life as forester's apprentice was a four-fold one: firstly,
there was the homelier and more practical side of life; then the life
spent with Nature, especially forest-nature; then also a life of the
study, devoted to work at mathematics and languages; and lastly,
the time spent in gaining a knowledge of plants. My chosen profession and the other circumstances of my position might have brought
me into contact with many kinds of men; but nevertheless my life
remained retired and solitary. My religious church life now changed
to a religious communion with Nature, and in the last half-year I
lived entirely amongst and with my plants, which drew me towards
them with fascination, notwithstanding that as yet I had no sense
of the inner life of the plant world. Collecting and drying specimens of plants was a work I prosecuted with the greatest care.
Altogether this time of my life was devoted in many various ways to
self-education, self-instruction, and moral advancement. Especially

531

did I love to indulge my old habit of self-observation and introspection.

.　.　.　.　.

On Midsummer Day 1799 my apprenticeship came to an end. The forester, who could now have made my practical knowledge of service to himself, wished to keep me another year. But I had by this time acquired higher views; I wished to study mathematics and botany more thoroughly, and I was not to be kept back from my purpose. When my apprenticeship was over I left him, and returned to my father's house.

.　.　.　.　.

. . . I went as a student to Jena, in 1799. I was then seventeen years and a half old.

.　.　.　.　.

The lectures of my excellent teacher were not so useful to me as they might have been, if I could have seen in the course of instruction and in its progress somewhat more of necessary connection and less of arbitrary arrangement. This want of necessary connection was the reason of the immediate dislike I always took to every course of instruction. I felt it even in pure mathematics, still more was it the case in applied mathematics, and most of all in experimental physics. Here it seemed to me as if everything were arranged in arbitrary series, so that from the very first I found this study a fatigue. The experiments failed to arrest my attention. I desired and sought after some inner connection between the phenomena, deduced from and explained by some simple root principles. But that was the very point withheld from me. Mathematical demonstrations came like halting messengers; they only became clear to the mind's eye when the truth to be demonstrated lay before me already in all its living strength. On the other hand, my attention was riveted by the study of gravitation, of force, of weight, which were living things to me, because of their evident relation to actual facts.

In mechanics (natural philosophy) I could not understand why so many of the so-called "mechanical powers" were assumed, and why several of them were not reduced to cases of the inclined plane.

In mineralogy my previous education had left many gaps unfilled, especially as regards the powers of observation. I was fond of min-

532

eral specimens, and gave myself much trouble to comprehend their several properties; but in consequence of my defective preparation I found insuperable difficulties in my way, and perceived thereby that neglect is neither quickly nor lightly to be repaired. The most assiduous practice in observation failed to make my sight so quick and so accurate as it ought to have been for my purpose. At that time I failed to apprehend the fact of my deficient quickness of sight; it ought to have taught me much, but I was not prepared to learn the lesson.

Chemistry fascinated me. The excellent teacher (Göttling) always demonstrated the true connection of the phenomena under consideration; and the theory of chemical affinity took strong hold upon me.

Note-taking at these lectures was a thing I never thought of doing; for that which I understood forthwith became a part of me, and that which I failed to understand seemed to me not worth writing down. I have often felt sorry for it since. But as regards this point, I have always had through my whole life the perfectly clear conviction that when I had mastered a whole subject in its intimate relations I could go back upon, and then understand, details which at the time of hearing had been unintelligible to me.

In botany I had a clear-sighted, kind-hearted teacher (Batsch). His natural system of botany[3] gave me great satisfaction, although I had always a painful perception of how much still remained for him to classify. However, my view of Nature as one whole became by his means substantially clearer, and my love for the observation of Nature in detail became more animated. I shall always think of him with gratitude. He was also my teacher in natural history. Two principles that he enunciated seized upon me with special force, and seemed to me valid. The first was the conception of the mutual relationship of all animals, extending like a network in all directions; and the second was that the skeleton or bony framework of fishes, birds, and men was one and the same in plan, and that the skeleton of man should be considered as the fundamental type which Nature strove to produce even in the lower forms of crea-

[3] Jussieu's natural system of botany may possibly be here alluded to. The celebrated "Genera Plantarum" appeared in 1798, and Froebel was at Jena in 1799. On the other hand, A. J. G. Batsch, Froebel's teacher, professor at the university since 1789, had published in 1787-8 his "Anleitung zur Kentniss und Geschichte der Pflanzen," 2 vols. We have not seen this work. Batsch also published an "Introduction to the Study of Natural History," which reached a second edition in 1805.

tion.[4] I was always highly delighted with his expositions, for they suggested ideas to me which bore fruit both in my intelligence and in my emotional nature. Invariably, whenever I grasped the interconnection and unity of phenomena, I felt the longings of my spirit and of my soul were fulfilled.

I easily understood the other courses I attended, and was able to take a comprehensive glance over the subjects of which they treated. I had seen building going on, and had myself assisted in building, in planting, etc.; here, therefore, I could take notes, and write complete and satisfactory memoranda of the lectures.

My stay in Jena had taught me much; by no means so much as it ought to have taught me, but yet I had won for myself a standpoint, both subjective and objective. I could already perceive unity in diversity, the correlation of forces, the interconnection of all living things, life in matter, and the principles of physics and biology.

. . . . .

Shortly before Midsummer Day, as I had arranged with my friend, I reached Frankfurt. During my many weeks' journey in the lovely springtime, my thoughts had had time to grow calm and collected. My friend, too, was true to his word; and we at once set to work together to prepare a prosperous future for me. The plan of seeking a situation with an architect was still firmly held to, and circumstances seemed favourable for its realisation; but my friend at last advised me to secure a livelihood by giving lessons for a time, until we should find something more definite than had yet appeared. Every prospect of a speedy fulfilment of my wishes seemed to offer, and yet in proportion as my hopes grew more clear, a certain feeling of oppression manifested itself more and more within me. I soon began seriously to ask myself, therefore:—

"How is this? Canst thou do work in architecture worthy of a man's life? Canst thou use it to the culture and the ennoblement of mankind?"

I answered my own question to my satisfaction. Yet I could not conceal from myself that it would be difficult to follow this profession conformably with the ideal I had now set before me. Notwithstanding this, I still remained faithful to my original scheme, and soon began to study under an architect with a view to fitting myself for my new profession.

[4] In justice to Froebel and his teacher, it must be remembered that the theory of evolution was not as yet formed, and that those who dimly sought after some explanation of the uniformity of the vertebrate plan, which they observed, were but all too likely to be led astray.

534

FROEBEL

My friend, unceasingly working towards the accomplishment of my views, introduced me to a friend of his, Herr Gruner, the headmaster at that time of the Frankfurt Model School,[5] which had not long been established. Here I found open-minded young people who met me readily and ingenuously, and our conversation soon ranged freely over life and its many-sided aspects. My own life and its object were also brought forward and talked over. I spoke openly, manifesting myself just as I was, saying what I knew and what I did not know about myself.

"Oh," said Gruner, turning to me, "give up architecture; it is not your vocation at all. Become a teacher. We want a teacher in our own school. Say you agree, and the place shall be yours."

My friend was for accepting Gruner's proposal, and I began to hesitate. Added to this, an external circumstance now came to my knowledge which hastened my decision. I received the news namely, that the whole of my testimonials, and particularly those that I had received in Jena, which were amongst them, had been lost. They had been sent to a gentleman who took a lively interest in my affairs, and I never found out through what mischance they were lost. I now read this to mean that Providence itself had thus broken up the bridge behind me, and cut off all return. I deliberated no longer, but eagerly and joyfully seized the hand held out to me, and quickly became a teacher in the Model School of Frankfurt-on-the-Main.[6]

The watchword of teaching and of education was at this time the name of PESTALOZZI. It soon became evident to me that Pestalozzi was to be the watchword of my life also; for not only Gruner, but also a second teacher at the school, were pupils of Pestalozzi, and the first-named had even written a book on his method of teaching. The name had a magnetic effect upon me, the more so as during my self-development and self-education it had seemed to me an aspiration—a something perhaps never to be familiarly known, yet distinct enough, and at all events inspiriting. And now I recalled how in my early boyhood, in my father's house, I had got a certain piece of news out of some newspaper or another, or at least that is how the matter stood in my memory. I gathered that in Switzerland a man of forty, who lived retired from the world,—Pestalozzi by name,—

[5] This school, still in existence up to 1865 and later, but now no longer in being, had been founded under Gruner, a pupil of Pestalozzi, to embody and carry out the educational principles of the latter.

[6] There is a smaller town called Frankfurt, on the Oder. "Am Main," or "An der Oder," is, therefore, added to the greater or the smaller Frankfurt respectively, for distinction's sake.

had taught himself, alone and unaided, reading, writing, and arithmetic. Just at that time I was feeling the slowness and insufficiency of my own development, and this news quieted me, and filled me with the hope and trust that I, too, might, through my own endeavour, repair the deficiencies of my bringing-up. As I have grown older I have also found it consolatory to remark how the culture of vigorous, capable men has not seldom been acquired remarkably late in life. And in general I must acknowledge it as part of the groundwork underlying my life and the evolution of my character, that the contemplation of the actual existences of real men always wrought upon my soul, as it were, by a fruitful rain and the genial warmth of sunshine; while the isolated truths these lives enshrined, the principles those who lived them had thought out and embodied in some phrase or another, fell as precious seed-corn, as it were, or as solvent salt crystals upon my thirsty spirit. And while on this head I cannot help especially calling to mind how deep and lasting was the impression made upon me in my last year at school by the accounts in the Holy Scriptures of the lives of earnestly striving youths and men. I mention it here, but I shall have to return to the subject later on.[7]

Now to return to the new life which I had begun. It was only to be expected that each thing and all things I heard of Pestalozzi seized powerfully upon me; and this more especially applies to a sketchy narrative of his life, his aims, and his struggles, which I found in a literary newspaper, where also was stated Pestalozzi's well-known desire and endeavour—namely, in some nook or corner of the world, no matter where, to build up an institution for the education of the poor, after his own heart. This narrative, especially the last point of it, was to my heart like oil poured on fire. There and then the resolution was taken to go and look upon this man who could so think and so endeavour to act, and to study his life and its work.

Three days afterwards (it was towards the end of August 1805) I was already on the road to Yverdon,[8] where Pestalozzi had not long before established himself. Once arrived there, and having met with the friendliest reception by Pestalozzi and his teachers, because of my introductions from Gruner and his colleagues, I was taken, like every other visitor, to the class-rooms, and there left more or less to my own devices. I was still very inexperienced, both

---

[7] He never does, for this interesting record remains a fragment.

[8] Situated at the head of the lake of Neuchatel, but in the canton of Vaud, in Switzerland.

in the theory and practice of teaching, relying chiefly in such things upon my memory of my own school-time, and I was therefore very little fitted for a rigorous examination into details of method and into the way they were connected to form a whole system. The latter point, indeed, was neither clearly thought out, nor was it worked out in practice. What I saw was to me at once elevating and depressing, arousing and also bewildering. My visit lasted only a fortnight. I worked away and tried to take in as much as I could; especially as, to help me in the duties I had undertaken, I felt impelled to give a faithful account in writing of my views on the whole system, and the effect it had produced upon me. With this idea I tried to hold fast in my memory all I heard. Nevertheless I soon felt that heart and mind would alike come to grief in a man of my disposition if I were to stay longer with Pestalozzi, much as I desired to do so. At that time the life there was especially vigorous; internally and externally it was a living, moving, stirring existence, for Prince Hardenberg, commissioned by the Austrian Government, had come to examine thoroughly into Pestalozzi's work.[9]

The fruits of my short stay with Pestalozzi were as follows:—

In the first place, I saw the whole training of a great educational institution, worked upon a clear and firmly-settled plan of teaching. I still possess the "teaching-plan" of Pestalozzi's institution in use at that time. This teaching-plan contains, in my opinion, much that is excellent, somewhat also that is prejudicial. Excellent, I thought, was the contrivance of the so-called "exchange classes." [10] In each subject the instruction was always given through the entire establishment at the same time. Thus the subjects for teaching were settled for every class, but the pupils were distributed amongst the various classes according to their proficiency in the subject in hand, so that the whole body of pupils was redistributed in quite a distinct division for each subject. The advantage of this contrivance struck me as so undeniable and so forcible that I have never since relinquished it in my educational work, nor could I now bring myself to do so. The prejudicial side of the teaching-plan, against which I intuitively rebelled, although my own tendencies on the subject were as yet so vague and dim, lay, in my opinion, in its incompleteness and its onesidedness. Several subjects of teaching

[9] Austria was not the only country alive to the importance of this new teaching. Prussia and Holland also sent commissioners to study Pestalozzi's system, and so did many other smaller states. The Czar (Alexander I.) sent for Pestalozzi to a personal interview at Basel.

[10] *Wandernde Classen.* Some of our later English schools have adopted a similar plan.

and education highly important to the all-round harmonious development of a man seemed to me thrust far too much into the background, treated in step-motherly fashion, and superficially worked out.

The results of the arithmetical teaching astounded me, yet I could not follow it into its larger applications and wider extent. The mechanical rules of this branch of instruction seemed to whirl me round and round as in a whirlpool. The teacher was Krüsi. The teaching, in spite of the brilliant results within its own circle, and in spite of the sharpness of the quickened powers of perception and comprehension in the children by which it attained those results, yet, to my personal taste, had something too positive in its setting forth, too mechanical in its reception. And Josias Schmid [11] had already, even at that time, felt the imperfection of this branch of instruction. He imparted to me the first ground-principles of his later work on the subject, and his ideas at once commanded my approval, for I saw they possessed two important properties, many-sidedness and an exhaustive scientific basis.

The teaching of drawing was also very incomplete, especially in its first commencement; but drawing from right-angled prisms with equal sides, in various lengths, which was one of the exercises required at a later stage, and drawing other mathematical figures by means of which the comprehension of the forms of actual objects of every-day life might be facilitated were much more to my mind. Schmid's method of drawing had not yet appeared.

In physical geography, the usual school course, with its many-coloured maps, had been left far behind. Tobler, an active young man, was the principal teacher in this section. Still, even this branch had far too much positive instruction[12] for me. Particularly unpleasant to me was the commencement of the course, which began with an account of the bottom of the sea, although the pupils could have no conception of their own as to its nature or dimensions. Nevertheless the teaching aroused astonishment, and carried one involuntarily along with it through the impression made by the lightning-quickness of the answers of the children.

In natural history I heard only the botany. The principal teacher, who had also prepared the plan of instruction in this subject for all the school, was Hopf, like the rest an active young man. The school

[11] One of Pestalozzi's teachers, to whom especially was confided the arrangement of the arithmetical studies.

[12] By positive instruction Froebel means learning by heart, or by being told results; as distinguished from actual education or development of the faculties, and the working out of results by pupils for themselves.

538

course arranged and carried out by him had much that was excellent. In each separate instance—for example, the shape and position of leaves, flowers, etc.—he would first obtain all the possible varieties of form by question and answer between the class and himself, and then he would select from the results the form which was before them in nature. These lessons, which were in this way made so attractive, and whose merits spoke for themselves, showed, however, when it came to practical application, an unpractical, I had almost said, a self-contradictory aspect.

(When, afterwards, in 1808, I visited Yverdon for the second time, I found to my regret neither Tobler nor Hopf there.)

With the method used for the German language I could not at all bring myself into sympathy, although it has been introduced into later school books elsewhere. Here also the arbitrary and non-productive style of teaching ran strongly counter to me at every step.

Singing was taught from figures.[13] Reading was taught from Pestalozzi's well-known "A.B.C."

[Memorandum.—All this lay dark within me, its value unrecognised even by myself. But my intellectual position tended to become more settled by passing through these experiences. As to my state at the time, I have, as accurately as may be, described it above, as at once exalted and depressed, animated and dull. That Pestalozzi himself was carried away and bewildered by this great intellectual machine of his appears from the fact that he could never give any definite account of his idea, his plan, his intention. He always said, "Go and see for yourself" (very good for him who knew *how* to look, how to hear, how to perceive); "it works splendidly!"[14] It was at that time, indeed, surprising and inexplicable to me that Pestalozzi's loving character did not win every one's heart as it won mine, and compel the staff of teachers to draw together into a connected whole, penetrated with life and intellectual strength in every part. His morning and evening addresses were deeply touching in their simplicity; and yet I remarked in them even already at that time some slight traces of the unhappy dissensions afterwards to arise.[15]]

[13] This must mean the system invented by Rousseau, a modern development of which is the Chevé system now widely used on the Continent. In England the tonic-sol-fa notation, which uses syllables instead of figures, but which rests fundamentally on the same principles, is much more familiar.

[14] *"Geht und schaut, es geht ungehür (ungeheuer)."*

[15] The miserable quarrels between Niederer and Schmid, which so distressed the later years of Pestalozzi, are here referred to.

I left Yverdon in mid-October (1805) with a settled resolution to return thither as soon as possible for a longer stay. As soon as I got back to Frankfurt, I received my definite appointment from the Consistorium.[16] The work that awaited me upon my arrival from Switzerland at the Model School (which was, in fact, properly two schools, one for boys and one for girls) was a share in the arrangement of an entirely new educational course and teaching-plan for the whole establishment. The school contained four or five classes of boys and two or three of girls; altogether about two hundred children. The staff consisted of four permanent masters and nine visiting masters.

. . . . .

Owing to the position and surroundings of the school buildings, which, though not apparently extensive as seen from the street, contained a considerable courtyard and a spacious garden, the scholars enjoyed perfect freedom of exercise, and could play just as they liked in courtyard or garden; with the result, moreover, of thereby affording a most important opportunity to the various teachers of becoming really intimate with the characters of the boys they taught. And there grew up out of all this a voluntary resolution on the part of the teachers that every teacher should take his boys for a walk once a week. Each adopted the method he liked best; some preferred to occupy the time of the walk over a permanent subject; others preferred leaving the subject to chance. I usually occupied my class with botanising; and also as geographical master, I turned these occasions to profit by leading on my boys to think for themselves and to apprehend the relations of various parts of the earth's surface: on these and other perceptions gained in this way I based my instruction in physiography, making them my point of departure.

The town was at once my starting-place and my centre. From it I extended our observations to the right and to the left, on this side and on that. I took the river Main as a base line, just as it lay; or I used the line of hills or the distant mountains. I settled firmly the direction of the four quarters of the compass. In everything I followed the leading of Nature herself, and with the data so obtained I worked out a representation of the place from direct observation,

[16] A Consistorium in Germany is a sort of clerical council or convocation, made up of the whole of the Established clergy of a province, and supervising Church and school matters throughout that province, under the control of the Ministry of Religion and Education. No educator could establish a school or take a post in a school without the approval of this body.

and on a reduced scale, in some level spot of ground or sandy tract carefully chosen for the purpose. When my representation (or map) was thoroughly understood and well impressed on every one's mind, then we reconstructed it in school on a black board placed horizontally. The map was first sketched by teachers and pupils between them, and then each pupil had to do it by himself as an exercise. These representations of the earth's surface of ours had a round contour, resembling the circular outline of the visible horizon.

At the next public examination of the school, I was fortunate enough, although this first attempt was full of imperfections, to win the unanimous approval of the parents present; and not only that, but the especial commendation of my superiors. Every one said, "That is how physiography[17] should be taught. A boy must first learn all about his home before he goes further afield." My boys were as well acquainted with the surroundings of the town as with their own rooms at home; and gave rapid and striking answers as to all the natural peculiarities of the neighbourhood. This course was the fountain-head of the teaching method which I afterwards thoroughly worked out, and which has now been in use for many years.

In arithmetic I did not take the lower, but the middle classes; and here also my teaching received cheering encomiums.

In drawing I also taught the middle classes. My method in this subject was to work at the thorough comprehension and the representation of planes and solids in outline, rising from the simplest forms to complex combinations. I not only had the gratification of obtaining good results, which thoroughly satisfied those who tested them, but also of seeing my pupils work with pleasure, with ardour, and with individuality.

In the girls' school I had to teach orthography[18] in one of the elementary classes. This lesson, ordinarily standing by itself, disconnected with anything, I based upon correct pronunciation.[19] The teaching was imperfect, certainly; but it nevertheless gained an unmistakable charm for both teacher and pupils; and, finally, its results were very satisfactory.

In one of the other classes of the girls' school I taught preparatory drawing. I took this by combinations of single lines; but the method was wanting in a logically necessary connection, so that it

[17] *Erdkunde.*
[18] *Recht schreiben.*
[19] *Recht sprechen.*

did not satisfy me. I cannot remember whether the results of this teaching were brought to the test or not.

Such was the outcome of my first attempts as a teacher. The kind indulgence and approval granted to me, more because of my good intentions and the fire of my zeal than for my actual performance, spurred me on to plunge deeper into the inquiry as to the nature of true teaching. But the whole system of a large school must have its settled form, with its previously-appointed teaching-course arranged as to times and subjects; and everything must fit in like a piece of clockwork. My system, on the other hand, called only for ready senses and awakened intellect. Set forms could only tolerate this view of education so far as it served to enliven and quicken them. But I have unfortunately again and again observed during my career, that even the most active life, if its activity and its vitality be not properly understood and urged ever onward, easily stiffens into bony rigidity. Enough, my mind, now fully awakened, could not suffer these set forms, necessary though they were; and I felt that I must seek out some position in which my nature could unfold itself freely according to the needs of the development of my life and of my mind.

This longing endeavour of life and mind, which could not submit to the fetters of external limitations, may have been the more exaggerated at the time by my becoming acquainted with Arndt's "Fragments on Human Culture," [20] which I had purchased. This book satisfied at once my character, my resolves, and my aspirations; and what hitherto lay isolated within me was brought into ordered connection through its pages, while ideas which possessed me without my perceiving them took definite form and expression as the book brought them to light. Indeed, I thought then that Arndt's book was the bible of education.

In those days I spoke of my life and my aims in the following words: "I desire to educate men whose feet shall stand on God's earth, rooted fast in Nature, while their head towers up to heaven, and reads its secrets with steady gaze, whose heart shall embrace both earth and heaven, shall enjoy the life of earth and nature with all its wealth of forms, and at the same time shall recognise the purity and peace of heaven, that unites in its love God's earth with God's heaven." In these phrases I now see my former life and aims vividly brought before me as in a picture.

[20] One of Arndt's pamphlets, then quite new.

My departure from the school was now arranged, and I could let my mind pursue its development free and unshackled. As heretofore, so now also, my kindly fate came lovingly to my help: I can never speak of it with sufficient thankfulness. The three lads to whom I had hitherto given private instruction in arithmetic and language now needed a tutor, as their former tutor was leaving them. The confidential charge was laid upon me, because I of all men best knew their nature and its needs, of seeking out some fit teacher and educator for them from amongst my acquaintance.

.   .   .   .   .

I began to apply my thoughts vigorously to the subjects of education and instruction. The first thing that absorbed me was the clear conviction that to educate properly one must share the life of one's pupil. Then came the question, "What is elementary education? and of what value are the educational methods advocated by Pestalozzi? Above all, what is the purpose of education?"

In answering the question, "What is the purpose of education?" I relied at that time upon the following observations: Man lives in a world of objects, which influence him, and which he desires to influence; therefore he ought to know these objects in their nature, in their conditions, and in their relations with each other and with mankind. Objects have form, measurement, and number.

By the expression, "the external world," at this time I meant only Nature; my life was so bound up in natural objects that I altogether passed by the productions of man's art or manufacture. Therefore for a long time it was an effort to me to regard man's handiwork, with Pestalozzi's scholars, Tobler and Hopf, as a proper subject for elementary culture, and it broadened my inward and outward glance considerably when I was able to look upon the world of the works of man as also part of the "external world." In this way I sought, to the extent of such powers as I consciously possessed at that time, to make clear the meaning of all things through man, his relations with himself, and with the external world.

The most pregnant thought which arose in me at this period was this: All is unity, all rests in unity, all springs from unity, strives for and leads up to unity, and returns to unity at last. This striving in unity and after unity is the cause of the several aspects of human life. But between my inner vision and my outer perception, presentation, and action was a great gulf fixed. Therefore it seemed to

543

me that everything which should or could be required for human education and instruction must be necessarily conditioned and given, by virtue of the very nature of the necessary course of his development, in man's own being, and in the relationship amidst which he is set. A man, it seemed to me, would be well educated, when he had been trained to care for these relationships and to acknowledge them, to master them and to survey them.

I worked hard, severely hard, during this period, but both the methods and the aims of education came before me in such an incoherent heap, so split up into little fragments, and so entirely without any kind of order, that during several years I did not make much progress towards my constant purpose of bringing all educational methods into an orderly sequence and a living unity. As my habitual and therefore characteristic expression of my desires then ran, I longed to see, to know, and to show forth, all things in inter-connection.

.   .   .   .   .

The demand of my pupils set me upon the following question: "What did you do as a boy? What happened to you to satisfy that need of yours for something to do and to express? By what, at the same period of your life, was this need most fully met, or what did you then most desire for this purpose?" Then there came to me a memory from out my earliest boyhood, which yielded me all I wanted in my emergency. It was the easy art of impressing figures and forms by properly arranged simple strokes on smooth paper.[21] I have often made use of this simple art in my later life, and have never found it fail in its object; and on this occasion, too, it faithfully served my pupils and me, for our skill, at first weak both on the part of the teacher and pupil, grew rapidly greater with use.

From these forms impressed upon paper we rose to making forms out of paper itself, and then to producing forms in pasteboard, and finally in wood. My later experience has taught me much more as to the best shapes and materials for the study of forms,[22] of which I shall speak in its proper place.

I must, however, permit myself to dwell a little upon this extremely simple occupation of impressing forms on paper, because at the proper age it quite absorbs a boy, and completely fills and contents the demands of his faculties. Why is this? It gives the

[21] Probably done with the point of a knitting needle, etc. The design is then visible on the other side of the paper in an embossed form.

[22] This account is dated 1827, it is always necessary to remember.

544

boy, easily and spontaneously, and yet at the same time imperceptibly, precise, clear, and many-sided results due to his own creative power.

Man is compelled not only to recognise Nature in her manifold forms and appearances, but also to understand her in the unity of her inner working, of her effective force. Therefore he himself follows Nature's methods in the course of his own development and culture, and in his games he imitates Nature at her work of creation. The earliest natural formations, the fixed forms of crystals, seem as if driven together by some secret power external to themselves; and the boy in his first games gladly imitates these first activities of nature, so that by the one he may learn to comprehend the other. Does not the boy take pleasure in building, and what else are the earliest forms of Nature but built-up forms? However, this indication that a higher meaning underlies the occupation and games which children choose out for themselves must for the present suffice. And since these spontaneous activities of children have not yet been thoroughly thought out from a high point of view, and have not yet been regarded from what I might almost call their cosmical and anthropological side, we may from day to day expect some philosopher to write a comprehensive and important book about them.[23] From the love, the attention, the continued interest and the cheerfulness with which these occupations are plied by children other important considerations also arise, of quite a different character.

A boy's game necessarily brings him into some wider or fuller relationship, into relationship with some more elevated group of ideas. Is he building a house?—he builds it so that he may dwell in it like grown-up people do, and have just such another cupboard, and so forth, as they have, and be able to give people things out of it just as they do. And one must always take care of this: that the child who receives a present shall not have his nature cramped and stunted thereby; according to the measure of how much he receives, so much must he be able to give away. In fact, this is a necessity for a simple-

---

[23] After all, the work was left to Froebel himself to do. These words were written in 1827. The "Menschen Erziehung" of Froebel ("Education of Man"), which appeared the year before, had also touched upon the subject. It was further developed in his "Mutter und Koselieder" ("Mother's Songs and Games"), in which his first wife assisted him. That appeared in 1838. In the same year was also founded the *Sonntags-Blatt* (*Sunday Journal*), to which many essays and articles on this subject were contributed by Froebel. The third volume ("Pädagogik") of Dr. Wichard Lange's complete edition of Froebel's works is largely made up of these *Sonntags-Blatt* articles. The whole Kindergarten system rests mainly on this higher view of children's play.

hearted child. Happy is that little one who understands how to satisfy this need of his nature, to give by producing various gifts of his own creation! As a perfect child of humanity, a boy ought to desire to enjoy and to bestow to the very utmost, for he dimly feels already that he belongs to the whole, to the universal, to the comprehensive in Nature, and it is as part of this that he lives; therefore, as such would he accordingly be considered and so treated. When he has felt this, the most important means of development available for a human being at this stage has been discovered. With a well-disposed child at such a time nothing has any value except as it may serve for a common possession, for a bond of union between him and his beloved ones. This aspect of the child's character must be carefully noticed by parents and by teachers, and used by them as a means of awakening and developing the active and presentative side of his nature; wherefore none, not even the simplest gifts from a child, should ever be suffered to be neglected.

To sketch my first attempt as an educator in one phrase, I sought with all my powers to give my pupils the best possible instruction, and the best possible training and culture, but I was unable to fulfil my intentions, to attain my end, in the position I then occupied, and with the degree of culture to which I had myself attained.

As soon as this had become fully evident to me, it occurred to my mind that nothing else could be so serviceable to me as a sojourn for a time with Pestalozzi. I expressed my views on this head very decidedly, and accordingly, in the summer of 1808, it was agreed that I should take my three pupils with me to Yverdon.

So it soon afterwards came about I was teacher and scholar, educator and pupil, all at the same time.

If I were to attempt to put into one sentence all I expected to find at Yverdon, I should say it was a vigorous inner life amongst the boys and youths, quickening, manifesting itself in all kinds of creative activity, satisfying the manysidedness of man, meeting all his necessities, and occupying all his powers both mental and bodily. Pestalozzi, so I imagined, must be the heart, the life-source, the spiritual guide of this life and work; from his central point he must watch over the boy's life in all its bearings, see it in all its stages of development, or at all events sympathise with it and feel with it, whether as the life of the individual, of the family, of the community, of the nation, of mankind at large.

With such expectations I arrived at Yverdon. There was no educational problem whose resolution I did not firmly expect to find there.

546

The forcible, comprehensive, stimulating life stimulated me too, and seized upon me with all its comprehensiveness and all its force. It is true it could not blind me to many imperfections and deficiencies, but these were retrieved by the general tendency and endeavour of the whole system; for this, though containing several absolute contradictions, manifest even at that time, yet vindicated on a general view its inner connection and hidden unity. The powerful, indefinable, stirring, and uplifting effect produced by Pestalozzi when he spoke, set one's soul on fire for a higher nobler life, although he had not made clear or sure the exact way towards it, nor indicated the means whereby to attain it. Thus did the power and manysidedness of the educational effort make up for deficiency in unity and comprehensiveness; and the love, the warmth, the stir of the whole, the human kindness and benevolence of it replaced the want of clearness, depth, thoroughness, extent, perserverance, and steadiness. In this way each separate branch of education was in such a condition as to powerfully interest, but never wholly to content the observer, since it prepared only further division and separation and did not tend towards unity.

The want of unity of effort, both as to means and aims, I soon felt; I recognised it in the inadequacy, the incompleteness, and the unlikeness of the ways in which the various subjects were taught. Therefore I endeavoured to gain the greatest possible insight into all, and became a scholar in all subjects—arithmetic, form, singing, reading, drawing, language, physical geography, the natural sciences, etc.

. . . . .

I also studied the boy's play, the whole series of games in the open air, and learned to recognise their mighty power to awake and to strengthen the intelligence and the soul as well as the body. In these games and what was connected with them I detected the mainspring of the moral strength which animated the pupils and the young people in the institution. The games, as I am now fervently assured, formed a mental bath of extraordinary strengthening power;[24] and although the sense of the higher symbolic meaning of games had not yet dawned upon me, I was nevertheless able to perceive in each boy genuinely at play a moral strength governing both mind and body which won my highest esteem.

[24] That the boys' characters were immersed in an element of strengthening and developing games as the body is immersed in the water of strengthening bath, seems to be Froebel's idea.

To obtain the means of a satisfactory judgment upon the best method of teaching the classical tongues, I took Greek and Latin under a young German, who was staying there at that time; but I was constructing a method of my own all the while, by observing all the points which seemed valuable, as they occurred in actual teaching. But the want of a satisfactory presentation of the classical tongues as part of the general means of education and culture of mankind, especially when added to the want of a consideration of natural history as a comprehensive and necessary means of education, and above all the uncertain wavering of the ground-principles on which the whole education and teaching rested at Yverdon, decided me not only to take my pupils back to their parents' house, but to abandon altogether my present educational work, in order to equip myself, by renewed study at some German university, with that due knowledge of natural science which now seemed to me quite indispensable for an educator.

In the year 1810 I returned from Yverdon by Bern, Schaffhausen, and Stuttgart to Frankfurt.

I should have prepared to go to the university at once, but found myself obliged to remain at my post till the July of the following year. The piece-meal condition of the methods of teaching and of education which surrounded me hung heavy on my mind, so that I was extremely glad when at last I was able to shake myself free from my position.

In the beginning of July 1811 I went to Göttingen. I went up at once, although it was in the middle of the session, because I felt that I should require several months to see my way towards harmonising my inward with my outward life, and reconciling my thoughts with my actions. And it was in truth several months before I gained peace within myself, and before I arrived at that unity which was so necessary to me, between my inward and my outward life, and at the equally necessary harmony between aim, career, and method.

Mankind as a whole, as one great unity, had now become my quickening thought. I kept this conception continually before my mind. I sought after proofs of it in my little world within, and in the great world without me; I desired by many a struggle to win it, and then to set it worthily forth. And thus I was led back to the first appearance of man upon our earth, to the land which first saw man, and to the first manifestation of mankind, his speech.

Linguistic studies, the learning of languages, philology, etc., now formed the object of my attack. The study of Oriental tongues

548

seemed to me the central point, the fountain head, whither my search was leading me; and at once I began upon them with Hebrew and Arabic. I had a dim idea of opening up a path through them to other Asiatic tongues, particularly those of India[25] and Persia. I was powerfully stimulated and attracted by what I had heard about the study of these languages, then in its early youth—namely, the acknowledgment of a relationship between Persian and German. Greek also attracted me in quite a special way on account of its inner fulness, organisation, and regularity. My whole time and energy were devoted to the two languages I have named.[26] But I did not get far with Hebrew in spite of my genuine zeal and my strict way with myself, because between the manner of looking at a language congenial to my mind and the manner in which the elementary lesson book presented it to me, lay a vast chasm which I could find no means to bridge over. In the form in which language was offered to me, I could find and see no means of making it a living study; and yet, nevertheless, nothing would have drawn me from my linguistic studies had I not been assured by educated men that these studies, especially my work on Indian and Persian tongues, were in reality quite beside the mark at which I aimed. Hebrew also was abandoned; but, on the other hand, Greek irresistibly enthralled me, and nearly all my time and energy were finally given to its study, with the help of the best books.

.   .   .   .   .

Through my work at the dynamical, chemical, and mathematical aspects of Nature I came once more upon the consideration of the laws of number, particularly as manifested through figures; and this led me to a perfectly fresh general view of the subject—namely, that number should be regarded as horizontally related.[27] That way of considering the subject leads one to very simple fundamental conceptions of arithmetic, which, when applied in practice, prove to be as accurate as they are clear. The connection of these (dynamical and arithmetical) phenomena was demonstrably ap-

[25] Sanskrit is here probably meant.

[26] Hebrew and Arabic.

[27] It is to be regretted that Froebel has not developed this point more fully. He speaks of "die Betrachtung des Zahlensinnes in horizontaler oder Seiten-Richtung," and one would be glad of further details of this view of number. We think that the full expression of the thought here shadowed out, is to be found in the Kindergarten occupations of mat-weaving, stick-laying, etc., in their arithmetical aspect. Certainly in these occupations, instead of number being built up as with bricks, etc., it is laid along horizontally.

parent to me; since arithmetic may be considered, firstly, as the outward expression of the manifestation of force, secondly (in its relationship to man), as an example of the laws of human thought.

On all sides, through nature as well as through history, through life as well as through science (and as regards the latter through pure science as well as through the applied branches), I was thus encountered and appealed to by the unity, the simplicity, and the unalterably necessary course, of human development and human education. I became impelled by an irresistible impulse towards the setting forth of that unity and simplicity, with all the force, both of my pen and of my life, in the shape of an educational system. I felt that education as well as science would gain by what I may call a more human, related, affiliated, connected treatment and consideration of the subjects of education.

. . . . .

THE EDUCATION OF MAN

I.—GROUNDWORK OF THE WHOLE. § 1. In all things there lives and reigns an eternal law. To him whose mind, through disposition and faith, is filled, penetrated, and quickened with the necessity that this can not possibly be otherwise, as well as to him whose clear, calm mental vision beholds the inner in the outer and through the outer, and sees the outer proceeding with logical necessity from the essence of the inner, this law has been and is enounced with equal clearness and distinctness in nature (the external), in the spirit (the internal), and in life which unites the two. This all-controlling law is necessarily based on an all-pervading, energetic, living, self-conscious, and hence eternal Unity. This fact, as well as the Unity itself, is again vividly recognized, either through faith or through insight, with equal clearness and comprehensiveness; therefore, a quietly observant human mind, a thoughtful, clear human intellect, has never failed, and will never fail, to recognize this Unity.

This Unity is God. All things have come from the Divine Unity, from God, and have their origin in the Divine Unity, in God alone. God is the sole source of all things. In all things there lives and reigns the Divine Unity, God. All things live and have their being in and through the Divine Unity, in and through God. All things are only through the divine effluence that lives in them. The divine effluence that lives in each thing is the essence of each thing.

§ 2. It is the destiny and life-work of all things to unfold their

550

essence, hence their divine being, and, therefore, the Divine Unity itself—to reveal God in their external and transient being. It is the special destiny and life-work of man, as an intelligent and rational being, to become fully, vividly, and clearly conscious of his essence, of the divine effluence in him, and, therefore, of God; to become fully, vividly, and clearly conscious of his destiny and life-work; and to accomplish this, to render it (his essence) active, to reveal it in his own life with self-determination and freedom.

Education consists in leading man, as a thinking, intelligent being, growing into self-consciousness, to a pure and unsullied, conscious and free representation of the inner law of Divine Unity, and in teaching him ways and means thereto.

[In his educational work this principle of life-unity was ever uppermost in Froebel's mind. The full, clear, consistent translation of this principle into life, and into work of education, constitutes the chief characteristic, as well as the chief merit, of his work. Viewed in its light, education becomes a process of unification; therefore, Froebel frequently called his educational method "developing, or human culture for all-sided unification of life." In his letter to the Duke of Meiningen he characterizes his tendency in these words: "I would educate human beings who with their feet stand rooted in God's earth, in nature, whose heads reach even into heaven and there behold truth, in whose hearts are united both earth and heaven, the varied life of earth and nature, and the glory and peace of heaven, God's earth and God's heaven." Still later he said, in the same vein: "There is no other power but that of the idea; the identity of the cosmic laws with the laws of our mind must be recognized, all things must be seen as the embodiments of *one* idea." With reference to the individual human being, this *unification of life* means to Froebel harmony in feeling, thinking, willing, and doing; with reference to humanity, it means subordination of self to the common welfare and to the progressive development of mankind; with reference to nature, it means a thoughtful subordination to her laws of development; with reference to God, it means perfect faith as Froebel finds it realized in Christianity.

It may not be amiss to point out at the very start the essential agreement between Froebel and Herbert Spencer in this fundamental principle of unification. Of course, it will be necessary in this comparison to keep in mind that Froebel applies the principle to education in its practical bearings as an interpretation of thought in life, whereas Spencer applies it to philosophy, as the interpretation of life in thought. To Spencer "knowledge of the lowest kind is *ununified* knowledge; science is *partially-unified* knowledge; philosophy is *completely-unified* knowledge." In the concluding paragraphs of "First Principles" he sets forth the "power of which no limit in time or space can be conceived" as the "inexpugnable consciousness in which religion and philosophy are at one with common sense," and as "likewise that on which all exact science is based." He designates "unification" as the "characteristic of developing thought," just as Froebel finds in it the characteristic of developing life; and Spencer's faith in the

551

"eventual arrival at unity" in thought is as firm as Froebel's faith in the eventual arrival at unity in life.—*Translator.*]

§ 3. The knowledge of that eternal law, the insight into its origin, into its essence, into the totality, the connection, and intensity of its effects, the knowledge of life in its totality, constitute *science, the science of life;* and, referred by the self-conscious, thinking, intelligent being to representation and practice through and in himself, this becomes *science of education.*

The system of directions, derived from the knowledge and study of that law, to guide thinking, intelligent beings in the apprehension of their life-work and in the accomplishment of their destiny, is *the theory of education.*

The self-active application of this knowledge in the direct development and cultivation of rational beings toward the attainment of their destiny, is *the practice of education.*

The object of education is the realization of a faithful, pure, inviolate, and hence holy life.

Knowledge and application, consciousness and realization in life, united in the service of a faithful, pure, holy life, constitute the *wisdom of life,* pure wisdom.

§ 4. *To be wise is the highest aim of man,* is the most exalted achievement of human self-determination.

To educate one's self and others, with consciousness, freedom, and self-determination, is a twofold achievement of wisdom: it *began* with the first appearance of man upon the earth; it *was manifest* with the first appearance of full self-consciousness in man; it *begins now* to proclaim itself as a necessary, universal requirement of humanity, and to be heard and heeded as such. With this achievement man enters upon the path which alone leads to life; which surely tends to the fulfillment of the inner, and thereby also to the fulfillment of the outer, requirement of humanity; which, through a faithful, pure, holy life, attains beatitude.

§ 5. By education, then, the divine essence of man should be unfolded, brought out, lifted into consciousness, and man himself raised into free, conscious obedience to the divine principle that lives in him, and to a free representation of this principle in his life.

Education, in instruction, should lead man to see and know the divine, spiritual, and eternal principle which animates surrounding nature, constitutes the essence of nature, and is permanently manifested in nature; and, in living reciprocity and united with training, it should express and demonstrate the fact that the same

552

law rules both (the divine principle and nature), as it does nature and man.

Education as a whole, by means of instruction and training, should bring to man's consciousness, and render efficient in his life, the fact that man and nature proceed from God and are conditioned by him—that both have their being in God.

Education should lead and guide man to clearness concerning himself and in himself, to peace with nature, and to unity with God; hence, it should lift him to a knowledge of himself and of mankind, to a knowledge of God and of nature, and to the pure and holy life to which such knowledge leads.

§ 6. In all these requirements, however, education is based on considerations of the innermost.

The inner essence of things is recognized by the innermost spirit (of man) in the outer and through outward manifestations. The inner being, the spirit, the divine essence of things and of man, is known by its outward manifestations. In accordance with this, all education, all instruction and training, all life as a free growth, start from the outer manifestations of man and things, and, proceeding from the outer, act upon the inner, and form its judgments concerning the inner. Nevertheless, education should not draw its inferences concerning the inner from the outer directly, for it lies in the nature of things that always in some relation inferences should be drawn inversely. Thus, the diversity and multiplicity in nature do not warrant the inference of multiplicity in the ultimate cause—a multiplicity of gods—nor does the unity of God warrant the inference of finality in nature; but, in both cases, the inference lies conversely from the diversity in nature to the oneness of its ultimate cause, and from the unity of God to an eternally progressing diversity in natural developments.

The failure to apply this truth, or rather the continual sinning against it, the drawing of direct inferences concerning the inner life of childhood and youth from certain external manifestations of life, is the chief cause of antagonism and contention, of the frequent mistakes in life and education. This furnishes constant occasion for innumerable false judgments concerning the motives of the young, for numberless failures in the education of children, for endless misunderstanding between parent and child, for so much needless complaint and unseemly arraignment of children, for so many unreasonable demands made upon them. Therefore, this truth, in its application to parents, educators, and teachers, is of such great importance that they should strive to render themselves familiar with its application in its smallest details. This would bring into the relations between parents and children, pupils and educators, teacher and taught, a clearness, a constancy, a serenity which are now sought in vain: for the child that seems good outwardly often is not good inwardly, i. e., does not desire the good spontaneously, or from love, respect, and appreciation; similarly, the outwardly rough, stubborn, self-willed child that seems outwardly not good, frequently is filled with the liveliest, most eager, strongest desire for spontaneous goodness in his actions; and the apparently inattentive boy frequently follows a certain fixed line of thought that withholds his attention from all external things.

§ 7. Therefore, education in instruction and training, originally and in its first principles, should necessarily be *passive, following* (only guarding and protecting), *not prescriptive, categorical, interfering.*

[This should in no way be interpreted as a pretext for letting the child alone, giving him up wholly to his own so-called self-direction, allowing him possibly to drift into vicious lawlessness instead of training him upward into free obedience to law. Froebel, indeed, sees in the child a fresh, tender bud of progressing humanity, and it is with reference to the divinity that to him lies in the child thus viewed that he calls for passive following and vigilant protection. He would have the educator study the child as a struggling expression of an inner divine law; and it is this he would have us obey and follow, guard and protect, in our educational work. It is evident that this involves constant activity in judicious adjustment of surroundings, so that the child may be free from temptation and from the growth of unhealthy whims and pernicious tendencies; while, on the other hand, he may be supplied with ample incentives and opportunities to unfold aright.

Spencer says, with the same thought: "A higher knowledge tends continually to limit our interference with the processes of life. As in medicine, etc., . . . so in education, we are finding that success is to be achieved only by rendering our measures subservient to that spontaneous unfolding which all minds go through in their progress to maturity."—*Tr.*]

§ 8. Indeed, in its very essence, education should have these characteristics; for the undisturbed operation of the Divine Unity is necessarily good—can not be otherwise than good. This necessity implies that the young human being—as it were, still in process of creation—would seek, although still unconsciously, as a product of nature, yet decidedly and surely, that which is in itself best; and, moreover, in a form wholly adapted to his condition, as well as to his disposition, his powers, and means. Thus the duckling hastens to the pond and into the water, while the young chicken scratches

554

the ground, and the young swallow catches its food upon the wing and scarcely ever touches the ground. Now, whatever may be said against the previously enounced law of converse inference, and against this other law of close sequence, as well as against their application to and in education, they will be fully vindicated in their simplicity and truth among the generations that trust in them fully and obey them.

We grant space and time to young plants and animals because we know that, in accordance with the laws that live in them, they will develop properly and grow well; young animals and plants are given rest, and arbitrary interference with their growth is avoided, because it is known that the opposite practice would disturb their pure unfolding and sound development; but the young human being is looked upon as a piece of wax, a lump of clay, which man can mold into what he pleases. O man, who roamest through garden and field, through meadow and grove, why dost thou close thy mind to the silent teaching of nature? Behold even the weed, which, grown up amid hindrances and constraint, scarcely yields an indication of inner law; behold it in nature, in field or garden, and see how perfectly it conforms to law—what a pure inner life it shows, harmonious in all parts and features: a beautiful sun, a radiant star, it has burst from the earth! Thus, O parents, could your children, on whom you force in tender years forms and aims against their nature, and who, therefore, walk with you in morbid and unnatural deformity—thus could your children, too, unfold in beauty and develop in all-sided harmony!

In accordance with the laws of divine influence, and in view of the original soundness and wholeness of man, all arbitrary (active), prescriptive and categorical, interfering education in instruction and training must, of necessity, annihilate, hinder, and destroy. Thus—to take another lesson from nature—the grape-vine must, indeed, be trimmed; but this trimming as such does not insure wine. On the other hand, the trimming, although done with the best intention, may wholly destroy the vine, or at least impair its fertility and productiveness, if the gardener fail in his work passively and attentively to follow the nature of the plant. In the treatment of the things of nature we very often take the right road, whereas in the treatment of man we go astray; and yet the forces that act in both proceed from the same source and obey the same law. Hence, from this point of view, too, it is so important that man should consider and observe nature.

Nature, it is true, rarely shows us that unmarred original state, especially in man; but it is for this reason only the more necessary to assume its existence in every human being, until the opposite has been clearly shown; otherwise that unmarred original state, where it might exist contrary to our expectation, might be easily impaired. If, however, there is unmistakable proof from his entire inner and outer bearing that the original wholeness of the human being to be educated has been marred, then directly categorical, mandatory education in its full severity is demanded.

On the other hand, however, it is not always possible, and often difficult, to prove with certainty that the inner being is marred; at least, this applies to the point, the source in which the marring originates and whence it derives its tendency. Again, the last essentially infallible criterion of this lies only in the human being himself. Hence, from this point of view, too, education in training and in all instruction should be by far more passive and following than categorical and prescriptive; for, by the full application of the latter mode of education, we should wholly lose the pure, the sure and steady progressive development of mankind—i. e., the free and spontaneous representation of the divine in man, and through the life of man, which, as we have seen, is the ultimate aim and object of all education, as well as the ultimate destiny of man.

Therefore, the purely categorical, mandatory, and prescriptive education of man is not in place before the advent of intelligent self-consciousness, of unity in life between God and man, of established harmony and community of life between father and son, disciple and master; for then only can truth be deduced and known from insight into the essential being of the whole and into the nature of the individual.

Before any disturbance and marring in the original wholeness of the pupil has been shown and fully determined in its origin and tendency, nothing, therefore, is left for us to do but to bring him into relations and surroundings in all respects adapted to him, reflecting his conduct as in a mirror, easily and promptly revealing to him its effects and consequences, readily disclosing to him and others his true condition, and affording a minimum of opportunities for injury from the outbreaks and consequences of his inner failings.

§ 9. The prescriptive, interfering education, indeed, can be justified only on two grounds: either because it teaches the clear, living thought, self-evident truth, or because it holds up a life whose ideal value has been established in experience. But, where self-evident, living, absolute truth rules, the eternal principle itself reigns, as it were, and will on this account maintain a passive, following char-

556

acter. For the living thought, the eternal divine principle as such demands and requires free self-activity and self-determination on the part of man, the being created for freedom in the image of God.

[Self-activity, in Froebel's sense of the word, implies not merely that the learner shall do all himself, not merely that he will be benefitted only by what he himself does: it implies that at all times *his whole self shall be active,* that the activity should enlist his entire self in all the phases of being. The law of self-activity demands not activity alone, but all-sided activity of the whole being, the whole self.

There is much difference between the self-activity of Pestalozzi and that of Froebel. The former has reference more to acquisitive or learning processes that fill the memory with little that bears directly on mental expansion; it is much concerned with long lists of names, verbal facts and formulas, recitation, and with imitation even in reading, writing, singing, and drawing. Froebel's self-activity applies to the whole being; it would have all that is in the child self-actively growing, simultaneously and continuously. He looks upon the child as an individuality distinctly separated from all other individualities that make up the universe, but with an all-sided instinctive yearning for unification with these, with points eager for contact in all directions of being, and his self-activity applies to these outward tendencies, to *doing* in its widest sense, as much as it does to the inward tendencies, or to *seeing* in its widest sense.

Froebel, consequently, lays more stress than Pestalozzi on spontaneity of action, on the adaptation of all activities to the child's power, and on the full, whole-hearted, sympathetic, active co-operation of the teacher, whom he urges "to live (to learn and do) with the children."

Froebel's self-activity is necessarily coupled with joy on the part of the child. To him joy is the inward reaction of self-activity. Here, too, he is closely followed by Spencer, who asks that "throughout youth, as in early childhood and maturity, the process (of intellectual education) shall be one of self-instruction"; and "that the mental action induced by this process shall be throughout intrinsically grateful."

It is a matter of great regret that Spencer, who seems to be quite familiar with Pestalozzi, was unacquainted with Froebel's work. What a weapon of strength Froebel's thoughts and suggestions would have proved in Spencer's hands!—*Tr.*]

§ 10. Again, a life whose ideal value has been perfectly established in experience never aims to serve as model in its form, but only in its essence, in its spirit. It is the greatest mistake to suppose that spiritual, human perfection can serve as a model in its form. This accounts for the common experience that the taking of such external manifestations of perfection as examples, instead of elevating mankind, checks, nay, represses, its development.

§ 11. Jesus himself, therefore, in his life and in his teachings, constantly opposed the imitation of external perfection. Only spiritual, striving, living perfection is to be held fast as an ideal; its external manifestation—on the other hand—its form should not be limited. The highest and most perfect life which we, as Christians, behold in Jesus—the highest known to mankind—is a life which found the primordial and ultimate reason of its existence clearly and distinctly in its own being; a life which, in accordance with the eternal law, came from the eternally creating All-Life, self-acting and self-poised. This highest eternally perfect life itself would have each human being again become a similar image of the eternal ideal, so that each again might become a similar ideal for himself and others; it would have each human being develop from within, self-active and free, in accordance with the eternal law. This is, indeed, the problem and the aim of all education in instruction and training; there can and should be no other. We see, then, that even the eternal ideal is following, passive, in its requirements concerning the form of being.

§ 12. Nevertheless, in its inner essence (and we see this in experience), the living thought, the eternal spiritual ideal, ought to be and is categorical and mandatory in its manifestations: and we see it, indeed, sternly mandatory, inexorable, and inflexible, but only when the requirement appears as a pronounced necessity in the essence of the whole, as well as in the nature of the individual, and can be recognized as such in him to whom it is addressed; only where the ideal speaks as the organ of necessity, and, therefore, always relatively. The ideal becomes mandatory only where it supposes that the person addressed enters into the reason of the requirement with serene, child-like faith, or with clear, manly insight. It is true, in word or example, the ideal is mandatory in all these cases, but always only with reference to the spirit and inner life, never with reference to outer form.

In good education, then, in genuine instruction, in true training, necessity should call forth freedom; law, self-determination; external compulsion, inner free-will; external hate, inner love. Where hatred brings forth hatred; law, dishonesty and crime; compulsion, slavery; necessity, servitude; where oppression destroys and debases; where severity and harshness give rise to stubbornness and deceit—all education is abortive. In order to avoid the latter and to secure the former, all prescription should be adapted to the pupil's nature and needs, and secure his co-operation. This is the case when all education in instruction and training, in spite of its necessarily categorical character, bears in all details and ramifications the irrefutable and irresistible impress that the one who makes the demand is himself strictly and unavoidably subject to an eternally ruling law, to an unavoidable eternal necessity, and that, therefore, all despotism is banished.

§ 13. All true education in training and instruction should, therefore, at every moment, in every demand and regulation, be simultaneously double-sided—giving and taking, uniting and dividing, prescribing and following, active and passive, positive yet giving scope, firm and yielding; and the pupil should be similarly conditioned: but between the two, between educator and pupil, between request and obedience, there should invisibly rule a third something, to which educator and pupil are equally subject. This third something is the *right*, the *best*, necessarily conditioned and expressed without arbitrariness in the circumstances. The calm recognition, the clear knowledge, and the serene, cheerful obedience to the rule of this third something is the particular feature that should be constantly and clearly manifest in the bearing and conduct of the educator and teacher, and often firmly and sternly emphasized by him. The child, the pupil, has a very keen feeling, a very clear apprehension, and rarely fails to distinguish, whether what the educator, the teacher, or the father says or requests is personal or arbitrary, or whether it is expressed by him as a general law and necessity.

§ 14. This obedience, this trustful yielding to an unchangeable third principle to which pupil and teacher are equally subject, should appear even in the smallest details of every demand of the educator and teacher. Hence, the general formula of instruction is: *Do this and observe what follows in this particular case from thy action, and to what knowledge it leads thee.* Similarly, the precept for life in general and for every one is: *Exhibit only thy spiritual essence, thy life, in the external, and by means of the external in thy actions, and observe the requirements of thy inner being and its nature.*

Jesus himself charges man in and with this precept to acknowledge the divinity of his mission and of his inner life, as well as the truth of his teaching; and this is, therefore, the precept that opens the way to the knowledge of all life in its origin and nature, as well as of all truth.

This explains and justifies, too, the next requirement, and indicates, at the same time, the manner of its fulfillment: *The educator, the teacher, should make the individual and particular general, the general particular and individual, and elucidate both in life; he should make the external internal, and the internal external, and indicate the necessary unity of both; he should consider the finite in the light of the infinite, and the infinite in the light of the finite, and harmonize both in life; he should see and perceive the divine essence in whatever is human, trace the nature of man to God, and seek to exhibit both within one another in life.*

This appears from the nature of man the more clearly and definitely, the more distinctly and unmistakably, the more man studies himself in himself, in the growing human being, and in the history of human development.

§ 15. Now, the representation of the infinite in the finite, of the eternal in the temporal, of the celestial in the terrestrial, of the divine in and through man, in the life of man by the *nursing* of his originally divine nature, confronts us unmistakably on every side as the only object, the only aim of all education, in all instruction and training. Therefore man should be viewed from this only true standpoint immediately with his appearance on earth; nay, as in the case of Mary, immediately with his annunciation, and he should be thus heeded and nursed while yet invisible, unborn.

With reference to his eternal immortal soul, every human being should be viewed and treated as a manifestation of the Divine Spirit in human form, as a pledge of the love, the nearness, the grace of God, as a gift of God. Indeed, the early Christians viewed their children in this light, as is shown by the names they gave them.

Even as a child, every human being should be viewed and treated as a necessary essential member of humanity; and therefore, as guardians, parents are responsible to God, to the child, and to humanity.

Similarly, parents should view their child in his necessary connection, in his obvious and living relations to the present, past, and future development of humanity, in order to bring the education of the child into harmony with the past, present, and future requirements of the development of humanity and of the race. For *man, as such, gifted with divine, earthly, and human attributes, should be viewed and treated as related to God, to nature, and to humanity; as comprehending within himself unity* (God), *diversity* (nature), *and individuality* (humanity), *as well as also the present, past, and future.*

§ 16. Man, humanity in man, as an external manifestation, should, therefore, be looked upon not as perfectly developed, not as fixed and stationary, but as steadily and progressively growing, in a state of ever-living development, ever ascending from one stage of culture to another toward its aim which partakes of the infinite and eternal.

It is unspeakably pernicious to look upon the development of humanity as stationary and completed, and to see in its present phases simply repetitions and greater generalizations of itself. For the child, as well as every successive generation, becomes thereby exclusively imitative, an external dead copy—as it were, a cast of the preceding one—and not a living ideal for its stage of development which it had attained in human development considered as a whole, to serve future generations in all time to come. Indeed, each successive generation and each successive individual human being, inasmuch as he would understand the past and present, must pass through all preceding phases of human development and culture, and this should not be done in the way of dead imitation or mere copying, but in the way of living, spontaneous self-activity (see § 24). Every human being should represent these phases spontaneously and freely as a type for himself and others. For in every human being, as a member of humanity and as a child of God, there lies and lives humanity as a whole; but in each one it is realized and expressed in a wholly particular, peculiar, personal, unique manner; and it should be exhibited in each individual human being in this wholly peculiar, unique manner, so that the spirit of humanity and of God may be recognized ever more clearly and felt ever more vividly and distinctly in its infinity, eternity, and as comprehending all existing diversity.

Only this exhaustive, adequate, and comprehensive knowledge of man and of the nature of man, from which diligent search derives spontaneously, as it were, all other knowledge needful in the care and education of man—only this view of man, from the moment of his conception, can enable true, genuine education to thrive, blossom, bear fruit, and ripen.

[Herbert Spencer, in his "Education," states this less broadly in these words: "The education of the child must accord both in mode and arrangement with the education of mankind as considered historically; or, in other words, the genesis of knowledge in the individual must follow the same course as the genesis of knowledge in the race." He attributes the enunciation of this doctrine to M. Comte. Inasmuch as M. Comte published the first volume of his "Positive Philosophy" in 1830, and Froebel issued his "Education of Man" in 1826, the question of priority is easily settled. However, the thought was in the atmosphere of that period. It would be easy to show traces of it in Pestalozzi, in Richter and Goethe, in Kant and Hegel, and certainly in Herbart; Froebel himself clearly foreshadows it in writings from the years 1821 and 1822.—*Tr.*]

561

§ 17. From this all that parents should do before and after the annunciation follows readily, clearly, and unmistakably—to be pure and true in word and deed, to be filled and penetrated with the worth and dignity of man, to look upon themselves as the keepers and guardians of a gift of God, to inform themselves concerning the mission and destiny of man as well as concerning the ways and means for their fulfillment. Now, the destiny of the *child as such* is to harmonize in his development and culture the nature of his parents, the fatherly and motherly character, their intellectual and emotional drift, which, indeed, may lie as yet dormant in both of them, as mere tendencies and energies. Thus, too, the destiny of *man as a child of God and of nature* is to represent in harmony and unison the spirit of God and of nature, the natural and the divine, the terrestrial and the celestial, the finite and the infinite. Again, the destiny of the child as *a member of the family* is to unfold and represent the nature of the family, its spiritual tendencies and forces, in their harmony, all-sidedness, and purity; and, similarly, it is the destiny and mission of man as a *member of humanity* to unfold and represent the nature, the tendencies and forces, of humanity as a whole.

§ 18. Now, although the nature of the parents and of the family as a whole may still lie concealed in them, unrecognized even in its dimmest foreshadowings, it will be developed and represented most purely and perfectly by the children, if each unfolds and represents his own being, as perfectly, purely, and universally as possible; and, on the other hand, as much as possible in accordance with his own individuality and personality. Thus, too, the spirit of God and of humanity—although as yet concealed and unrecognized—is revealed most purely and perfectly by man as a child of God and of humanity as a whole, if he unfolds and represents his own being as much as possible in accordance with his individuality and personality. This is done if man develops and perfects himself in *that* manner and according to *that* law by which all things are developed and perfected, have been developed and perfected and which is supreme wherever Creator and creature, God and nature, are found; if man in his life reveals his being in inner and outer *unity;* in *individuality,* pure and perfect, in all individual outward reactions; in *diversity* so far as all he does and all that proceeds from him has diverse relations. Only and alone in this threefold, yet in itself *one* and *united,* representation, is the inner being perfectly shown, manifested, and revealed. Wherever one phase of this threefold representation is really lacking, or, indeed, only imperfectly known

562

or understood, we find imperfect, incomplete representation—imperfect, hindering insight. Only in this way each thing is manifested and revealed in its unity, all-sidedly, and in accordance with its nature; only by the recognition and application of this triune representation of each thing whose nature is to be completely manifested and revealed, can a true knowledge of each thing, a true understanding of its nature, be reached.

§ 19. Therefore the child should, from the very time of his birth, be viewed in accordance with his nature, treated correctly, and given the free, all-sided use of his powers. By no means should the use of certain powers and members be enhanced at the expense of others, and these hindered in their development; the child should neither be partly chained, fettered, nor swathed; nor, later on, spoiled by too much assistance. The child should learn early how to find in himself the center and fulcrum of all his powers and members, to seek his support in this, and, resting therein, to move freely and be active, to grasp and hold with his own hands. to stand and walk on his own feet, to find and observe with his own eyes, to use his members symmetrically and equally. At an early period the child should learn, apply, and practice the most difficult of all arts— to hold fast the center and fulcrum of his life in spite of all digressions, disturbances, and hindrances.

§ 20. The *child's first utterance is that of force.* The operation of force, of the forceful, calls forth counter-force; hence the first crying of the child, his pushing with his feet against whatever resists them, the holding fast of whatever touches his little hands.

Soon after, and together with this, there is developed in the child sympathy. Hence his *smile,* his enjoyment, his delight, his vivacity in comfortable warmth, in clear light, in pure, fresh air. This is the beginning of self-consciousness in its very first germs.

Thus the first utterances of the child—of *human* life—are rest and unrest, joy and sorrow, smiles and tears.

Rest, joy, and smiles indicate whatever in the child's feeling is adapted to the pure, undisturbed development of his nature, of his human nature, to the child's life, to human life in the child. To foster and guard these should be the first concern of all educating influences, of life-development, life-elevation, and life-representation.

Unrest, sorrow, tears, indicate in their first appearance whatever is opposed to the development of the child, of the human being. These, too, should be considered in education; it should strive and labor to find their cause or causes, and to remove them.

In the very first—but generally only in the very first—manifestations of fretting, restlessness, and crying, the child is unquestionably wholly free from stubbornness and willfulness; but, as soon as the little one feels—we know not how and in what degree—that he is left arbitrarily or from negligence or indolence to whatever may give him discomfort or pain, these faults begin to germinate.

Whenever this unfortunate feeling has been, as it were, inoculated, willfulness, the first and most hideous of all faults, has been begotten—nay, is born—a fault that threatens to destroy the child and his surroundings, and which can scarcely be banished without injury to some trait of his better nature; a fault that soon becomes the mother of deceit, of falsehood, defiance, obstinacy, and a host of subsequent sad and hideous faults.

However, in choosing the right way, too, we may err in the manner and form of proceeding.

In accordance with the spirit and destiny of humanity, man should be trained to learn, by the endurance of small, insignificant suffering, how to bear heavy suffering and burdens that threaten destruction. If, then, parents or attendants are firmly and surely convinced that all the fretting, restless child may need at the time has been supplied—that all that is or can be injurious has been removed—they should calmly and quietly leave the fretting, restless, or crying child to himself; calmly give him time *to find himself*. For, if the little one has once or repeatedly compelled sympathy and help from others in illusory suffering or slight discomfort, parents and attendants have lost much, almost all, and can scarcely retrieve their loss by force; for the little ones have so keen a sense, so correct a feeling for the weaknesses of attendants, that they would rather put forth their native energy in the easier way of control of others— for which the weakness of attendants gives them the opportunity— than to exercise and cultivate it in themselves, in patience, endurance, and activity.

At this stage of development the young and growing human being is called *Säugling* (suckling), and this he is in the fullest sense of the word; for *sucking in* (absorbing) is as yet the almost exclusive activity of the child. Does he not, indeed, *suck in* (absorb) the condition of surrounding human beings?

For this reason even this first stage of development is of the utmost importance for the present and later life of the human being. It is highly important for man's present and later life that at this stage he absorb nothing morbid, low, mean; nothing ambiguous, nothing bad. The looks, the countenances of attendants should,

564

therefore, be pure; indeed, every phase of the surroundings should be firm and sure, arousing and stimulating confidence, pure and clear: pure air, clear light, a clean room, however needy it may be in other respects. For, alas! often the whole life of man is not sufficient to efface what he has absorbed in childhood, the impressions of early youth, simply because his whole being, like a large eye, as it were, was opened to them and wholly given up to them. Often the hardest struggles of man *with himself,* and even the later most adverse and oppressive events in his life, have their origin in this stage of development; for this reason the care of the infant is so important.

Positive testimony to this can be borne by mothers who have nursed some of their children themselves, have relegated the nursing of others to attendants, and have observed both in later life. Similarly, mothers also know that the first smile of the child marks a very definite epoch in the child's life and development; that it is the expression, at least, of the first physical finding-of-self (*Sich-Selbst-findens*), and may be much more. For that first smile originates not only in the physical feeling of his individuality, but in a still higher physical feeling of community between mother and child; then with father and brothers and sisters; and, later, between these and humanity on the one hand and the child on the other.

§ 21. This feeling of community, first uniting the child with mother, father, brothers, and sisters, and resting on a higher spiritual unity, to which, later on, is added the unmistakable discovery that father, mother, brothers, sisters, human beings in general, feel and know themselves to be in community and unity with a higher principle—with humanity, with God—this feeling of community is the very first germ, the very first beginning of all true religious spirit, of all genuine yearning for unhindered unification with the Eternal, with God. Genuine and true, living religion, reliable in danger and struggles, in times of oppression and need, in joy and pleasure, must come to man in his infancy; for the Divine Spirit that lives and is manifest in the finite, in man, has an early though dim feeling of its divine origin; and this vague·sentiment, this exceedingly misty feeling, should be fostered, strengthened, nurtured, and, later on, raised into full consciousness, into clear apprehension.

.   .   .   .   .

§ 22. Not only in regard to the cultivation of the divine and religious elements in man, but in his entire cultivation, it is highly important that his development should proceed continuously from *one* point, and that this *continuous* progress be seen and ever guarded. Sharp limits and definite subdivisions within the continuous series of the years of development, withdrawing from attention the permanent continuity, the living connection, the inner living essence, are therefore highly pernicious, and even destructive in their influence. Thus, it is highly pernicious to consider the stages of human development—infant, child, boy or girl, youth or maiden, man or woman, old man or matron—as really distinct, and not, as life shows them, as continuous in themselves, in unbroken transitions; highly pernicious to consider the child or boy as something wholly different from the youth or man, and as something so distinct that the common foundation (human being) is seen but vaguely in the idea and word, and scarcely at all considered in life and for life.

.   .   .   .   .

How different could this be in every respect, if parents were to view and treat the child with reference to all stages of development and age, without breaks and omissions; if, particularly, they were to consider the fact that the vigorous and complete development and cultivation of each successive stage depends on the vigorous, complete, and characteristic development of each and all preceding stages of life! Parents are especially prone to overlook and disregard this. When the human being has reached the age of boyhood, they look upon him as a boy; when he has reached the age of youth or manhood, they take him to be a youth or a man. Yet the boy has not become a boy, nor has the youth become a youth, by reaching a certain age, but only by having lived through childhood, and, further on, through boyhood, true to the requirements of his mind, his feelings, and his body; similarly, adult man has not become an adult man by reaching a certain age, but only by faithfully satisfying the requirements of his childhood, boyhood, and youth. Parents and fathers, in other respects quite sensible and efficient, expect not only that the child should begin to show himself a boy or a youth, but, more particularly, that the boy, at least, should show himself a man, that in all his conduct he should be a man, thus jumping the stages of boyhood and youth. To see and respect *in* the child and boy the germ and promise of the coming youth and man is very different from considering and treating him as if he were already a man; very different from asking the child or boy to show himself a youth or man; to feel, to think, and to conduct himself as a youth or a man. Parents who ask this overlook and forget

566

that they themselves became mature and efficient only in so far as they lived through the various stages in natural succession and in certain relationships which they would have their child to forego.

This disregard of the value of earlier, and particularly of the earliest, stages of development with reference to later ones, prepares for the future teacher and educator of the boy difficulties which it will be scarcely possible to overcome. In the first place, the boy so conditioned has also a notion that it is possible for him to do wholly without the instruction and training of the preceding stage of development; in the second place, he is much injured and weakened by having placed before himself, at an early period, an extraneous aim for imitation and exertion, such as preparation for a certain calling or sphere of activity. *The child, the boy, man, indeed, should know no other endeavor but to be at every stage of development wholly what this stage calls for.* Then will each successive stage spring like a new shoot from a healthy bud; and, at each successive stage, he will with the same endeavor again accomplish the requirements of this stage: for only the adequate development of man at each preceding stage can effect and bring about adequate development at each succeeding later stage.

§ 23. It is especially needful to consider this in the development and cultivation of human activity for the pursuits of practical industry.

At present the popular notions of work and the pursuits of practical industry are wholly false, superficial, untenable, oppressive, debasing, devoid of all elements of life.

God creates and works productively in uninterrupted continuity. Each thought of God is a work, a deed, a product; and each thought of God continues to work with creative power in endless productive activity to all eternity. Let him who has not seen this behold Jesus in his life and works; let him behold genuine life and work in man; let him, if he truly lives, behold his own life and work.

The Spirit of God hovered over chaos, and moved it; and stones and plants, beasts and man took form and separate being and life. *God created man in his own image; therefore, man should create and bring forth like God.* His spirit, the spirit of man, should hover over the shapeless, and move it that it may take shape and form, a distinct being and life of its own. This is the high meaning, the deep significance, the great purpose of work and industry, of productive and creative activity. We become truly godlike in diligence and industry, in working and doing, which are accompanied by the clear perception or even by the vaguest feeling that thereby we represent the inner in the outer; that we give body to spirit, and form to thought; that we render visible the invisible; that we impart an outward, finite, transient being to life in the spirit. Through this godlikeness we rise more and more to a true knowledge of God, to insight into his Spirit; and thus, inwardly and outwardly, God comes ever nearer to us. Therefore, Jesus so truly says in this connection of the poor, "Theirs is the kingdom of heaven," if they could but see and know it and practice it in diligence and industry, in productive and creative work. Of children, too, is the kingdom of heaven; for, unchecked by the presumption and conceit of adults, they yield themselves in childlike trust and cheerfulness to their formative and creative instinct.

[How deeply Froebel valued the creative activity, and how constantly he studied to keep it from degenerating into destructiveness, appears from the account of "a visit to Froebel," by Bormann. He writes, in speaking of the building-games: "Two things seemed to me particularly interesting and significant. Froebel never permitted the children to destroy an old form built by them for the sake of building a new one with the same material, but insisted that the new formations should be made (by suitable changes) from the old ones. Thus he avoids haste, and awakens thoughtfulness and patience, and, on the other hand, inspires respect for existing things, and teaches at an early period not to build from the ruins of destroyed things, but to build up in an orderly manner from the things that are."—*Tr.*]

The debasing illusion that man works, produces, creates only in order to preserve his body, in order to secure food, clothing, and shelter, may have to be endured, but should not be diffused and propagated. Primarily and in truth man works only that his spiritual, divine essence may assume outward form, and that thus he may be enabled to recognize his own spiritual, divine nature and the innermost being of God. Whatever food, clothing, and shelter he obtains thereby comes to him as an insignificant surplus. Therefore Jesus says, "Seek ye first the kingdom of heaven," i.e., the realization of the divine spirit in your life and through your life, and whatever else your finite life may require will be added unto you.

Again, Jesus says, "My meat is to do the will of him who sent me," to work and accomplish whatever God has enjoined me to do and as he has enjoined me to do.

Thus the lilies of the field—which, in the ordinary human sense, do not toil—are clothed by God more splendidly than Solomon in all his glory. But does not the lily put forth leaves and blossoms; does it not in its whole outward being reveal the inner being of God?

568

Now, all spiritual effects as finite manifestations suppose a succession of time and events. If, therefore, at any time in his life man has neglected to respect in the use of his powers their divine nature and to exalt them to work, or, at least, to develop them for work, he will necessarily and unavoidably be overtaken by want in proportion to his neglect. At least, he will not, at some time, reap what he could have reaped, had he, in the use of his powers, in his calling, always respected their divine nature; for, in accordance with the earthly and universal laws under which we live, the results of that neglected activity would have appeared at some time. Now, if the activity was neglected, how can its results appear? If, then, at any time such want overtake him, man has no other alternative than to let the second side of his spiritual power, renunciation and endurance, come into play in order to allay the want, and to labor most diligently in order to avoid all similar want for the future.

The young, growing human being should, therefore, be trained early for outer work, for creative and productive activity. For this there exists a double reason, an inner and an outer requirement; and the former, inasmuch as it includes the latter, is of the greatest importance and eternal. The requirement is supported, too, by the nature of man as such.

The activity of the senses and limbs of the infant is the first germ, the first bodily activity, the bud, the first formative impulse; play, building, modeling are the first tender blossoms of youth (see § 30); and this is the period when man is to be prepared for future industry, diligence, and productive activity. Every child, boy, and youth, whatever his condition or position in life, should devote daily at least one or two hours to some serious activity in the production of some definite external piece of work. Lessons through and by work, through and from life, are by far the most impressive and intelligible, and most continuously and intensely progressive both in themselves and in their effect on the learner. Notwithstanding this, children—mankind, indeed—are at present too much and too variously concerned with aimless and purposeless pursuits, and too little with work. Children and parents consider the activity of actual work as much to their disadvantage, and so unimportant for their future conditions in life, that educational institutions should make it one of their most constant endeavors to dispel this delusion. The domestic and scholastic education of our time leads children to indolence and laziness; a vast amount of human power thereby remains undeveloped and is lost. It would be a most wholesome arrangement in schools to establish actual working hours similar to the existing study hours; and it will surely come to this. By the current practice of using his powers so sparingly and in reference only to outer requirements, man has lost their inner and outer measure, and, therefore, fails adequately to know, appreciate, respect, and faithfully guard them.

As for religion, so, too, for *industry*, early cultivation is highly important. Early work, guided in accordance with its inner meaning, confirms and elevates religion. Religion without industry, without work, is liable to be lost in empty dreams, worthless visions, idle fancies. Similarly, work or industry without religion degrades man into a beast of burden, a machine. Work and religion must be simultaneous; for God, the Eternal, has been creating from all eternity. Were this fully recognized, were men thoroughly impressed with this truth, were they to act and work in conformity to it in life, what a height could mankind soon attain!

Yet human power should be developed, cultivated, and manifested, not only in inner repose, as religion and religious spirit; not only in outward efficiency, as work and industry; but also—withdrawing upon itself and its own resources—in abstinence, temperance, and frugality. Is it needful to do more than indicate this to a human being not wholly at variance with himself? Where *religion, industry,* and *temperance,* the truly undivided trinity, rule in harmony, in true pristine unity, there, indeed, is heaven upon earth —peace, joy, salvation, grace, blessedness.

Thus is seen in the child man as a whole; thus the unity of humanity and of man appears in childhood; thus the whole future activity of man has its germs in the child. And it can not be otherwise. If we would develop man and in him humanity as a whole, we must view him even in the child as a unit and in all his earthly relations. Now, since unity in the finite manifestations implies diversity, and since all all-sidedness in the finite manifestations implies a succession in time, the world and life are unfolded for the child and in the child in diversity and succession. Similarly, powers and tendencies, the activities of the senses and limbs, should be developed in the order in which they appear in the child.

. . . . .

§ 27. With the advancing development of the senses, there is developed in the child, simultaneously and symmetrically, the use of the body, of the limbs; and this, too, in a succession determined by their nature and the properties of corporeal objects.

External objects are themselves near, at rest, and invite rest; or

570

they are in motion, moving away, and invite seizure, grasping, holding fast; or they are fixed in distant places or spaces, and thus invite him who would bring them nearer to move toward them.

Thus is developed the use of the limbs in sitting and lying, in grasping and holding, in walking and running.

Standing represents the use of the body and limbs in their most complete totality; it is the finding of the center of gravity of the body.

This bodily standing is as significant for this stage as the first smile, the physical finding of self, was for the preceding stage, and as moral and religious equipoise is for the highest stage of human development.

At this stage of development the young, growing human being cares for the use of his body, his senses, his limbs, merely for the sake of their use and practice, but not for the sake of the results of this use. He is wholly indifferent to this; or, rather, he has as yet no idea whatever of this. For this reason the child at this stage begins to *play* with his limbs—his hands, his fingers, his lips, his tongue, his feet, as well as with the expression of his eyes and face.

Now, as has been just indicated, these movements of the face and body are, at first, in no way representations of the internal in the external; indeed, this is reserved for the next stage of development. Yet these plays, as the first utterances of the child, should be carefully observed and watched, lest the child contract habitual bodily and, particularly, *facial* movements that have no inner meaning (e. g., distortions of the eyes and face), thus inducing at an early period a separation between gestures and feelings, between body and mind, between the inner and the outer. This separation, in its turn, might lead either to hypocrisy or to the formation of habitual movements and manners which refuse obedience to the will and accompany man like a mask through all his life.

From a very early period, therefore, children should never be left too long to themselves on beds or in cradles without some external object to occupy them. This precaution is needful, too, in order to avoid bodily enervation, which necessarily gives rise to mental enervation and weakness.

In order to avoid this enervation, the bed of children should from the beginning, from the very first moment, not be too soft. It should consist of pillows of hay, sea-grass, fine straw, chaff, or possibly, horse-hair, but never of feathers. So, too, the child should be but lightly covered while asleep, securing for it the influence of fresh air.

In order to avoid leaving the child on its bed mentally unoccupied while going to sleep, and, still more, just after waking, it is advisable to suspend in a line with the child's natural vision, a swinging cage with a lively bird.[28] This secures occupation for the senses and the mind, profitable in many directions.

§ 28. As soon as the activity of the senses, of the body and the limbs is developed to such a degree that the child begins self-actively to represent the internal outwardly, the stage of infancy in human development ceases, and the stage of *childhood* begins.

Up to this stage the inner being of man is still unorganized, undifferentiated.

With language, the expression and representation of the internal begin; with language, organization, or a differentiation with reference to ends and means, sets in. The inner being is organized, differentiated, and strives to make itself known (*hund tun*), to announce itself (*verkündigen*) externally.

.   .   .   .   .

But man and his education are, at this stage, wholly intrusted to the mother, the father, the family, who, together with the child, constitute a complete, unbroken unity. For language—the medium of representation—audible speaking is at this stage in no way differentiated from the human being. He does not, as yet, know or view it as having a being of its own. Like his arms, his eye, his tongue, it is one with him, and he is unconscious of its existence.

.   .   .   .   .

§ 28 . . . Now, since this stage of human development requires that the child should learn to designate all things rightly, clearly, and distinctly, it is essentially needful that all things should be brought before him rightly, clearly, and distinctly, so that he may see and know them rightly, clearly, and distinctly. These things are inseparable and reciprocally dependent (see § 33).

However, inasmuch as at this stage language is still undifferentiated or one with the speaking human being, names are for the speaking child still one (united) with the things—i.e., he can not as yet separate the name and the thing, as he can not separate matter and spirit, soul and body. To him they are still one and the same. This is seen particularly in the play of children at this time;

---

[28] The women of Appenzell, naturally great lovers of liberty, substituted for this an artificial bird cut from bright-colored paper. Froebel himself, at a later period, proposed the substitution of the balls of the first gift.—*Tr.*

572

how eagerly and (if he can do so) how much the child speaks during his play.

Play and speech constitute the element in which the child lives. Therefore, the child at this stage imparts to each thing the faculties of life, feeling, and speech. Of everything he imagines that it can hear. Because the child himself begins to represent his inner being outwardly, he imputes the same activity to all about him, to the pebble and chip of wood, to the plant, the flower, and the animal.

And thus there is developed in the child at this stage his own life, his life with parents and family, his life with a higher invisible spirit, common to both, and particularly his life in and with nature, as if this held life like that which he feels within himself. Indeed, life in and with nature and with the fair, silent things of nature should be fostered at this time by parents and other members of the family as a chief fulcrum of child-life; and this is accomplished chiefly in play, in the cultivation of the child's play, which at first is simply natural life.

§ 30. *Play.*—*Play* is the highest phase of child-development— of human development at this period; for *it is self-active representation of the inner—representation of the inner from inner necessity and impulse* (see § 27).

Play is the purest, most spiritual activity of man at this stage, and, at the same time, typical of human life as a whole—of the inner hidden natural life in man and all things. It gives, therefore, joy, freedom, contentment, inner and outer rest, peace with the world. It holds the sources of all that is good. A child that plays thoroughly, with self-active determination, perseveringly until physical fatigue forbids, will surely be a thorough, determined man, capable of self-sacrifice for the promotion of the welfare of himself and others. Is not the most beautiful expression of child-life at this time a playing child?—a child wholly absorbed in his play?—a child that has fallen asleep while so absorbed?

As already indicated, play at this time is not trivial, it is highly serious and of deep significance. Cultivate and foster it, O mother; protect and guard it, O father! To the calm, keen vision of one who truly knows human nature, the spontaneous play of the child discloses the future inner life of the man.

The plays of childhood are the germinal leaves of all later life; for the whole man is developed and shown in these, in his tenderest dispositions, in his innermost tendencies. The whole later life of man, even to the moment when he shall leave it again, has its source in the period of childhood—be this later life pure or impure, gentle

573

or violent, quiet or impulsive, industrious or indolent, rich or poor
in deeds, passed in dull stupor or in keen creativeness, in stupid
wonder or intelligent insight, producing or destroying, the bringer
of harmony or discord, of war or peace. His future relations to
father and mother, to the members of the family, to society and
mankind, to nature and God—in accordance with the natural and
individual disposition and tendencies of the child—depend chiefly
upon his mode of life at this period; for the child's life in and with
himself, his family, nature, and God, is as yet a unit. Thus, at this
age, the child can scarcely tell which is to him dearer—the flowers,
or his joy about them, or the joy he gives to the mother when he
brings or shows them to her, or the vague presentiment of the dear
Giver of them.

Who can analyze these joys in which this period is so rich?

If the child is injured at this period, if the germinal leaves of the
future tree of his life are marred at this time, he will only with the
greatest difficulty and the utmost effort grow into strong manhood;
he will only with the greatest difficulty escape in his further development the stunting effects of the injury or the one-sidedness it
entails.

. . . . . .

§ 35 . . . Rich indeed, is the life of the child ripening into boyhood; but we see it not. Real is his life, but we feel it not. His life
accords with the destiny and mission of humanity, but we know it
not. We not only fail to guard, nurse, and develop the inner germ
of his life, but we allow it to be stifled and crushed by the weight
of his own instincts, or to find vent on some weaker side in unnat-
uralness. We then see the same phenomenon which, in the plant,
we call wild-shoot, or water-shoot, a misdirection of the energies,
of the desires and instincts in the child (the human plant).

Now, at last, we would fain give another direction to the energies,
desires, and instincts of the child growing into boyhood; but it is
too late. For the deep meaning of child-life passing into boyhood
we not only failed to appreciate, but we misjudged it; we not only
failed to nurse it, but we misdirected and crushed it.

. . . . . .

§ 40 . . . The child—your child, ye fathers—feels this so intensely, so vividly, that he follows you wherever you are, wherever
you go, in whatever you do. Do not harshly repel him; show no impatience about his ever-recurring questions. Every harshly repel-

574

ling word crushes a bud or shoot of his tree of life. Do not, however, tell him in words much more than he could find himself without your words. For it is, of course, easier to hear the answer from another, perhaps to only half hear and understand it, than it is to seek and discover it himself. To have found one fourth of the answer by his own effort is of more value and importance to the child than it is to half hear and half understand it in the words of another; for this causes mental indolence. Do not, therefore, always answer your children's questions at once and directly; but, *as soon as they have gathered sufficient strength and experience,* furnish them with the means to find the answers in the sphere of their own knowledge.

Let parents—more particularly fathers (for to their special care and guidance the child ripening into boyhood is confided)—let fathers contemplate what the fulfillment of their paternal duties in child-guidance yields to them; let them feel the joys it brings. It is not possible to gain from anything higher joy, higher enjoyment, than we do from the guidance of our children, from living with and for our children. It is inconceivable how we can seek and expect to find anywhere higher joy, higher enjoyment, fuller gratification of our best desires than we can find in intercourse with our children; more recreation than we can find in the family circle, where we can create joy for ourselves in so many respects.

We should be deeply impressed with the truth of these statements could we but see in his plain homesurroundings, in his happy, joyous family, the father who, from his own resources, has created what here has been but partially described: "To lead children early to think, this I consider the first and foremost object of child-training."

To give them early habits of work and industry seemed to him so natural and obvious a course as to need no statement in words. Besides, the child that has been led to think will thereby, at the same time, be led to industry, diligence—to all domestic and civic virtues.

Those words are a seed from which springs a shady, evergreen tree of life, full of fragrant blossoms and sound, ripe fruit. May those of us who allow our children to grow up thoughtless and idle, and therefore dull and dead, hear and heed this!

§ 41. But—it is hard to say it, yet its truth will appear if, in our intercourse and life with our children, we cast a searching glance upon the condition of our minds and hearts—we are dull, our surroundings are dull to us. With all our knowledge, we are empty for

575

our children. Almost all we say is hollow and empty, without meaning and without life. Only in the few rare cases, when our discourse rests on intercourse with life and nature, we enjoy its life.

Let us hasten, then! Let us impart life to ourselves, to our children; let us through them give meaning to our speech and life to the things about us! Let us live with them, and let them live with us; thus shall we obtain through them what we all need.

Our words, our discourses in social life, are dull, are empty husks, lifeless puppets, worthless chips; they are devoid of inner life and meaning; they are evil spirits, for they have neither body nor substance.

Our surroundings are dead and dull. Objects are matter. They crush, instead of lifting us, for they lack the quickening word that gives them significance and meaning.

We do not feel the meaning of what we say, for our speech is made up of memorized ideas, based neither on perception nor on productive effort. Therefore, it does not lead to perception, production, life; it has not proceeded, it does not proceed, from life.

Our speech is like the book out of which we have learned it, at third or fourth hand. We do not ourselves see what we say, we can not give outer form to what we say. Therefore, our speech is so empty and meaningless. For this reason, and only for this, our inward and outward life, as well as the life of our children, is so poor, because our speech is not born from a life, rich inwardly and outwardly, in seeing and doing; because our speech, our word, is not based on the perception of the thing it designates. Therefore, we hear the sound, it is true, but we fail to get the image; we hear the noise, but see no movement.

§ 42. Fathers, parents, let us see that our children may not suffer from similar deficiencies. What we no longer possess—the all-quickening, creative power of child-life—let it again be translated from their life into ours.

Let us learn from our children, let us give heed to the gentle admonitions of their life, to the silent demands of their minds.

Let us live with our children: then will the life of our children bring us peace and joy, then shall we begin to grow wise, to be wise.

.   .   .   .   .

EMERSON 1803–1882

ALL ESSAYS written by Ralph Waldo Emerson are educational in the broadest sense of the word. Whether he writes on nature or on culture, he always addresses the creative powers in man and relates them to the deeper powers in the universe. His essays are, as it were, transparent; behind each of them stands something like the Platonic Idea, the Plotinian One and All, the Schellingian concept of life.

The ultimate source of Life is, by necessity, dynamic. Wherever there is crystallization, Life suffers or disappears. Therefore all institutions, from Emerson's point of view, are dangerous; they lead toward formalism and mechanization. Real Life is only in individuals. Emerson is an optimist with respect to individuals, a pessimist with respect to organizations.

Therefore he is suspicious also about organized education. See how much life, how much curiosity, how much initiative there is in children. Use all these wonderful energies, unfold them, make them creative. Do not even create a children's world for the children, let them create their own world. Change the usual education from outside into an education from inside. This does not mean formlessness, or lack of discipline. On the contrary, the creative process, once awakened in the child, will seek form, guidance, discipline, and loyalties. But they will then be organic results of development, not obligations, imposed from outside.

Emerson closes the circle of the great idealists Rousseau, Pestalozzi, and Froebel, on whom all the essential concepts of modern, or progressive education are based. What we have had since then are explanations, applications, variations in detail, and attempts to substitute the originally idealist background of progressive education with a more "naturalist" or "pragmatic" philosophy. These attempts, of course, reflect the aversion of many of us to any kind of metaphysics.

But who knows whether the loss of a metaphysics in the various approaches to the problems of humanity does not lead—or has not already led—to mere conventionalism and legality which are bound to break down in any real crisis? For if conformity is used to replace man's creative consciousness of values, he may not be able to bring to realization the great laws of existence on which human evolution depends.

Education is reprinted from *The Works of Ralph Waldo Emerson,* Centenary Edition, Volume X, published by Houghton Mifflin Company, Boston and New York. *Self-Reliance* is reprinted from Carpenter's *Representative Selections,* published in New York by the American Book Com-Company in 1934.

V. EDUCATION

With the key of the secret he marches faster
From strength to strength, and for night brings day,
While classes or tribes too weak to master
The flowing conditions of life, give way.

A new degree of intellectual power seems cheap at any price. The use of the world is that man may learn its laws. And the human race have wisely signified their sense of this, by calling wealth, means,—Man being the end. Language is always wise.

Therefore I praise New England because it is the country in the world where is the freest expenditure for education. We have already taken, at the planting of the Colonies (for aught I know for the first time in the world), the initial step, which for its importance might have been resisted as the most radical of revolutions, thus deciding at the start the destiny of this country,—this, namely, that the poor man, whom the law does not allow to take an ear of corn when starving, nor a pair of shoes for his freezing feet, is allowed to put his hand into the pocket of the rich, and say, You shall educate me, not as you will, but as I will: not alone in the elements, but, by further provision, in the languages, in sciences, in the useful and in elegant arts. The child shall be taken up by the State, and taught, at the public cost, the rudiments of knowledge, and at last, the ripest results of art and science.

Humanly speaking, the school, the college, society, make the difference between men. All the fairy tales of Aladdin or the invisible Gyges or the talisman that opens kings' palaces or the enchanted halls underground or in the sea, are only fictions to indicate the one miracle of intellectual enlargement. When a man stupid becomes a man inspired, when one and the same man passes out of the torpid into the perceiving state, leaves the din of trifles, the stupor of the senses, to enter into the quasi-omniscience of high thought,—up and down, around, all limits disappear. No horizon shuts down. He sees things in their causes, all facts in their connection.

One of the problems of history is the beginning of civilization. The animals that accompany and serve man make no progress as races. Those called domestic are capable of learning of man a few tricks of utility or amusement, but they cannot communicate the skill to their race. Each individual must be taught anew. The trained dog cannot train another dog. And Man himself in many races retains almost the unteachableness of the beast. For a thousand years the islands and forests of a great part of the world have been filled with savages who made no steps of advance in art or skill beyond the necessity of being fed and warmed. Certain nations, with a better brain and usually in more temperate climates, have made such progress as to compare with these as these compare with the bear and the wolf.

Victory over things is the office of man. Of course, until it is accomplished, it is the war and insult of things over him. His continual tendency, his great danger, is to overlook the fact that the world is only his teacher, and the nature of sun and moon, plant and animal only means of arousing his interior activity. Enamoured of their beauty, comforted by their convenience, he seeks them as ends, and fast loses sight of the fact that they have worse than no values, that they become noxious, when he becomes their slave.

This apparatus of wants and faculties, this craving body, whose organs ask all the elements and all the functions of Nature for their satisfaction, educate the wondrous creature which they satisfy with light, with heat, with water, with wood, with bread, with wool. The necessities imposed by this most irritable and all-related texture have taught Man hunting, pasturage, agriculture, commerce, weaving, joining, masonry, geometry, astronomy. Here is a world pierced and belted with natural laws, and fenced and planted with civil partitions and properties, which all put new restraints on the young inhabitant. He too must come into this magic circle of relations, and know health and sickness, the fear of injury, the desire of external good, the charm of riches, the charm of power. The household is a school of power. There, within the door, learn the tragi-comedy of human life. Here is the sincere thing, the wondrous composition for which day and night go round. In that routine are the sacred relations, the passions that bind and sever. Here is poverty and all the wisdom its hated necessities can teach, here labor drudges, here affections glow, here the secrets of character are told, the guards of man, the guards of woman, the compensations which, like angels of justice, pay every debt: the opium of custom, whereof all drink and many go mad. Here is Economy, and Glee, and Hospitality, and Ceremony, and Frankness, and Calamity, and Death, and Hope.

Every one has a trust of power,—every man, every boy a jurisdiction, whether it be over a cow or a rood of a potato-field, or a fleet of ships, or the laws of a state. And what activity the desire of power inspires! What toils it sustains! How it sharpens the perceptions and stores the memory with facts. Thus a man may well spend many years of life in trade. It is a constant teaching of the laws of matter and of mind. No dollar of property can be created without some direct communication with Nature, and of course some acquisition of knowledge and practical force. It is a constant contest with the active faculties of men, a study of the issues of one and another course of action, an accumulation of power, and, if the higher faculties of the individual be from time to time quickened, he will gain wisdom and virtue from his business.

As every wind draws music out of the Æolian harp, so doth every object in Nature draw music out of his mind. Is it not true that every landscape I behold, every friend I meet, every act I perform, every pain I suffer, leaves me a different being from that they found me? That poverty, love, authority, anger, sickness, sorrow, success, all work actively upon our being and unlock for us the concealed faculties of the mind? Whatever private or petty ends are frustrated, this end is always answered. Whatever the man does, or whatever befalls him, opens another chamber in his soul,—that is, he has got a new feeling, a new thought, a new organ. Do we not see how amazingly for this end man is fitted to the world?

What leads him to science? Why does he track in the midnight heaven a pure spark, a luminous patch wandering from age to age, but because he acquires thereby a majestic sense of power; learning that in his own constitution he can set the shining maze in order, and finding and carrying their law in his mind, can, as it were, see his simple idea realized up yonder in giddy distances and frightful periods of duration. If Newton come and first of men perceive that not alone certain bodies fall to the ground at a certain rate, but that all bodies in the Universe, the universe of bodies, fall always, and at one rate; that every atom in Nature draws to every other atom,— he extends the power of his mind not only over every cubic atom of his native planet, but he reports the condition of millions of worlds which his eye never saw. And what is the charm which every ore, every new plant, every new fact touching winds, clouds, ocean currents, the secrets of chemical composition and decomposition possess for Humboldt? What but that much revolving of similar facts in his mind has shown him that always the mind contains in its transparent chambers the means of classifying the most refractory phenomena, of depriving them of all casual and chaotic aspect, and subordinating them to a bright reason of its own, and so giving to man a sort of property,—yea, the very highest property in every district and particle of the globe.

By the permanence of Nature, minds are trained alike, and made

580

intelligible to each other. In our condition are the roots of language and communication, and these instructions we never exhaust.

In some sort the end of life is that the man should take up the universe into himself, or out of that quarry leave nothing unrepresented. Yonder mountain must migrate into his mind. Yonder magnificent astronomy he is at last to import, fetching away moon, and planet, solstice, period, comet and binal star, by comprehending their relation and law. Instead of the timid stripling he was, he is to be the stalwart Archimedes, Pythagoras, Columbus, Newton, of the physic, metaphysic and ethics of the design of the world.

For truly the population of the globe has its origin in the aims which their existence is to serve; and so with every portion of them. The truth takes flesh in forms that can express it; and thus in history an idea always overhangs, like the moon, and rules the tide which rises simultaneously in all the souls of a generation.

Whilst thus the world exists for the mind; whilst thus the man is ever invited inward into shining realms of knowledge and power by the shows of the world, which interpret to him the infinitude of his own consciousness,—it becomes the office of a just education to awaken him to the knowledge of this fact.

We learn nothing rightly until we learn the symbolical character of life. Day creeps after day, each full of facts, dull, strange, despised things, that we cannot enough despise,—call heavy, prosaic and desert. The time we seek to kill: the attention it is elegant to divert from things around us. And presently the aroused intellect finds gold and gems in one of these scorned facts,—then finds that the day of facts is a rock of diamonds; that a fact is an Epiphany of God.

We have our theory of life, our religion, our philosophy; and the event of each moment, the shower, the steamboat disaster, the passing of a beautiful face, the apoplexy of our neighbor, are all tests to try our theory, the approximate result we call truth, and reveal its defects. If I have renounced the search of truth, if I have come into the port of some pretending dogmatism, some new church or old church, some Schelling or Cousin, I have died to all use of these new events that are born out of prolific time into multitude of life every hour. I am as a bankrupt to whom brilliant opportunities offer in vain. He has just foreclosed his freedom, tied his hands, locked himself up and given the key to another to keep.

When I see the doors by which God enters into the mind; that there is no sot or fop, ruffian or pedant into whom thoughts do not enter by passages which the individual never left open, I can expect any revolution in character. "I have hope," said the great Leibnitz, "that society may be reformed, when I see how much education may be reformed."

It is ominous, a presumption of crime, that this word Education has so cold, so hopeless a sound. A treatise on education, a convention for education, a lecture, a system, affects us with slight paralysis and a certain yawning of the jaws. We are not encouraged when the law touches it with its fingers. Education should be as broad as man. Whatever elements are in him that should foster and demonstrate. If he be dexterous, his tuition should make it appear; if he be capable of dividing men by the trenchant sword of his thought, education should unsheathe and sharpen it; if he is one to cement society by his all-reconciling affinities, oh! hasten their action! If he is jovial, if he is mercurial, if he is great-hearted, a cunning artificer, a strong commander, a potent ally, ingenious, useful, elegant, witty, prophet, diviner,—society has need of all these. The imagination must be addressed. Why always coast on the surface and never open the interior of Nature, not by science, which is surface still, but by poetry? Is not the Vast an element of the mind? Yet what teaching, what book of this day appeals to the Vast?

Our culture has truckled to the times,—to the senses. It is not manworthy. If the vast and the spiritual are omitted, so are the practical and the moral. It does not make us brave or free. We teach boys to be such men as we are. We do not teach them to aspire to be all they can. We do not give them a training as if we believed in their noble nature. We scarce educate their bodies. We do not train the eye and the hand. We exercise their understandings to the apprehension and comparison of some facts, to a skill in numbers, in words; we aim to make accountants, attorneys, engineers; but not to make able, earnest, great-hearted men. The great object of Education should be commensurate with the object of life. It should be a moral one; to teach self-trust: to inspire the youthful man with an interest in himself; with a curiosity touching his own nature; to acquaint him with the resources of his mind, and to teach him that there is all his strength, and to inflame him with a piety towards the Grand Mind in which he lives. Thus would education conspire with the Divine Providence. A man is a little thing whilst he works by and for himself, but, when he gives voice to the rules of love and justice, is godlike, his word is current in all countries; and all men, though his enemies, are made his friends and obey it as their own.

In affirming that the moral nature of man is the predominant ele-

582

ment and should therefore be mainly consulted in the arrangements of a school, I am very far from wishing that it should swallow up all the other instincts and faculties of man. It should be enthroned in his mind, but if it monopolize the man he is not yet sound, he does not yet know his wealth. He is in danger of becoming merely devout, and wearisome through the monotony of his thought. It is not less necessary that the intellectual and the active faculties should be nourished and matured. Let us apply to this subject the light of the same torch by which we have looked at all the phenomena of the time; the infinitude, namely, of every man. Everything teaches that.

One fact constitutes all my satisfaction, inspires all my trust, viz., this perpetual youth, which, as long as there is any good in us, we cannot get rid of. It is very certain that the coming age and the departing age seldom understand each other. The old man thinks the young man has no distinct purpose, for he could never get anything intelligible and earnest out of him. Perhaps the young man does not think it worth his while to explain himself to so hard and inapprehensive a confessor. Let him be led up with a long-sighted forbearance, and let not the sallies of his petulance or folly be checked with disgust or indignation or despair.

I call our system a system of despair, and I find all the correction, all the revolution that is needed and that the best spirits of this age promise, in one word, in Hope. Nature, when she sends a new mind into the world, fills it beforehand with a desire for that which she wishes it to know and do. Let us wait and see what is this new creation, of what new organ the great Spirit had need when it incarnated this new Will. A new Adam in the garden, he is to name all the beasts in the field, all the gods in the sky. And jealous provision seems to have been made in his constitution that you shall not invade and contaminate him with the worn weeds of your language and opinions. The charm of life is this variety of genius, these contrasts and flavors by which Heaven has modulated the identity of truth, and there is a perpetual hankering to violate this individuality, to warp his ways of thinking and behavior to resemble or reflect your thinking and behavior. A low self-love in the parent desires that his child should repeat his character and fortune; an expectation which the child, if justice is done him, will nobly disappoint. By working on the theory that this resemblance exists, we shall do what in us lies to defeat his proper promise and produce the ordinary and mediocre. I suffer whenever I see that common sight of a parent or senior imposing his opinion and way

of thinking and being on a young soul to which they are totally unfit. Cannot we let people be themselves, and enjoy life in their own
way? You are trying to make that man another *you*. One's enough.

Or we sacrifice the genius of the pupil, the unknown possibilities
of his nature, to a neat and safe uniformity, as the Turks whitewash
the costly mosaics of ancient art which the Greeks left on their
temple walls. Rather let us have men whose manhood is only the
continuation of their boyhood, natural characters still; such are able
and fertile for heroic action; and not that sad spectacle with which
we are too familiar, educated eyes in uneducated bodies.

I like boys, the masters of the playground and of the street,—
boys, who have the same liberal ticket of admission to all shops,
factories, armories, town-meetings, caucuses, mobs, target-shoot-
ings, as flies have; quite unsuspected, coming in as naturally as the
janitor,—known to have no money in their pockets, and themselves
not suspecting the value of this poverty; putting nobody on his
guard, but seeing the inside of the show,—hearing all the asides.
There are no secrets from them, they know everything that befalls
in the fire-company, the merits of every engine and of every man
at the brakes, how to work it, and are swift to try their hand at
every part; so too the merits of every locomotive on the rails, and
will coax the engineer to let them ride with him and pull the handles when it goes to the engine-house. They are there only for fun,
and not knowing that they are at school, in the court-house, or the
cattle-show, quite as much and more than they were, an hour ago,
in the arithmetic class.

They know truth from counterfeit as quick as the chemist does.
They detect weakness in your eye and behavior a week before you
open your mouth, and have given you the benefit of their opinion
quick as a wink. They make no mistakes, have no pedantry, but
entire belief on experience. Their elections at baseball or cricket
are founded on merit, and are right. They don't pass for swimmers
until they can swim, nor for stroke-oar until they can row: and I
desire to be saved from their contempt. If I can pass with them, I
can manage well enough with their fathers.

Everybody delights in the energy with which boys deal and talk
with each other; the mixture of fun and earnest, reproach and coaxing, love and wrath, with which the game is played;—the good-
natured yet defiant independence of a leading boy's behavior in the
school-yard. How we envy in later life the happy youths to whom
their boisterous games and rough exercise furnish the precise element which frames and sets off their school and college tasks, and

584

teaches them, when least they think it, the use and meaning of these. In their fun and extreme freak they hit on the topmost sense of Horace. The young giant, brown from his hunting-tramp, tells his story well, interlarded with lucky allusions to Homer, to Virgil, to college-songs, to Walter Scott; and Jove and Achilles, partridge and trout, opera and binomial theorem, Cæsar in Gaul, Sherman in Savannah, and hazing in Holworthy, dance through the narrative in merry confusion, yet the logic is good. If he can turn his books to such picturesque account in his fishing and hunting, it is easy to see how his reading and experience, as he has more of both, will interpenetrate each other. And every one desires that this pure vigor of action and wealth of narrative, cheered with so much humor and street rhetoric, should be carried into the habit of the young man, purged of its uproar and rudeness, but with all its vivacity entire. His hunting and campings-out have given him an indispensable base: I wish to add a taste for good company through his impatience of bad. That stormy genius of his needs a little direction to games, charades, verses of society, song, and a correspondence year by year with his wisest and best friends. Friendship is an order of nobility; from its revelations we come more worthily into nature. Society he must have or he is poor indeed; he gladly enters a school which forbids conceit, affectation, emphasis and dulness, and requires of each only the flower of his nature and experience; requires good will, beauty, wit and select information; teaches by practice the law of conversation, namely, to hear as well as to speak.

Meantime, if circumstances do not permit the high social advantages, solitude has also its lessons. The obscure youth learns there the practice instead of the literature of his virtues; and, because of the disturbing effect of passion and sense, which by a multitude of trifles impede the mind's eye from the quiet search of that fine horizon-line which truth keeps,—the way to knowledge and power has ever been an escape from too much engagement with affairs and possessions; a way, not through plenty and superfluity, but by denial and renunciation, into solitude and privation; and, the more is taken away, the more real and inevitable wealth of being is made known to us. The solitary knows the essence of the thought, the scholar in society only its fair face. There is no want of example of great men, great benefactors, who have been monks and hermits in habit. The bias of mind is sometimes irresistible in that direction. The man is, as it were, born deaf and dumb, and dedicated to a narrow and lonely life. Let him study the art of solitude, yield as gracefully as he can to his destiny. Why cannot he get the good of his doom, and if it is from eternity a settled fact that he and society shall be nothing to each other, why need he blush so, and make wry faces to keep up a freshman's seat in the fine world? Heaven often protects valuable souls charged with great secrets, great ideas, by long shutting them up with their own thoughts. And the most genial and amiable of men must alternate society with solitude, and learn its severe lessons.

There comes the period of the imagination to each, a later youth; the power of beauty, the power of books, of poetry. Culture makes his books realities to him, their characters more brilliant, more effective on his mind, than his actual mates. Do not spare to put novels into the hands of young people as an occasional holiday and experiment; but, above all, good poetry in all kinds, epic, tragedy, lyric. If we can touch the imagination, we serve them, they will never forget it. Let him read Tom Brown at Rugby, read Tom Brown at Oxford,—better yet, read Hodson's Life—Hodson who took prisoner the king of Delhi. They teach the same truth,—a trust, against all appearances, against all privations, in your own worth, and not in tricks, plotting, or patronage.

I believe that our own experience instructs us that the secret of Education lies in respecting the pupil. It is not for you to choose what he shall know, what he shall do. It is chosen and foreordained, and he only holds the key to his own secret. By your tampering and thwarting and too much governing he may be hindered from his end and kept out of his own. Respect the child. Wait and see the new product of Nature. Nature loves analogies, but not repetitions. Respect the child. Be not too much his parent. Trespass not on his solitude.

But I hear the outcry which replies to this suggestion:—Would you verily throw up the reins of public and private discipline; would you leave the young child to the mad career of his own passions and whimsies, and call this anarchy a respect for the child's nature? I answer,—Respect the child, respect him to the end, but also respect yourself. Be the companion of his thought, the friend of his friendship, the lover of his virtue,—but no kinsman of his sin. Let him find you so true to yourself that you are the irreconcilable hater of his vice and the imperturbable slighter of his trifling.

The two points in a boy's training are, to keep his *naturel* and train off all but that:—to keep his *naturel,* but stop off his uproar, fooling and horse-play;—keep his nature and arm it with knowl-

586

edge in the very direction in which it points. Here are the two capital facts, Genius and Drill. The first is the inspiration in the well-born healthy child, the new perception he has of nature. Somewhat he sees in forms or hears in music or apprehends in mathematics, or believes practicable in mechanics or possible in political society, which no one else sees or hears or believes. This is the perpetual romance of new life, the invasion of God into the old dead world, when he sends into quiet houses a young soul with a thought which is not met, looking for something which is not there, but which ought to be there: the thought is dim but it is sure, and he casts about restless for means and masters to verify it; he makes wild attempts to explain himself and invoke the aid and consent of the bystanders. Baffled for want of language and methods to convey his meaning, not yet clear to himself, he conceives that though not in this house or town, yet in some other house or town is the wise master who can put him in possession of the rules and instruments to execute his will. Happy this child with a bias, with a thought which entrances him, leads him, now into deserts now into cities, the fool of an idea. Let him follow it in good and in evil report, in good or bad company; it will justify itself; it will lead him at last into the illustrious society of the lovers of truth.

In London, in a private company, I became acquainted with a gentleman, Sir Charles Fellowes, who, being at Xanthus, in the Ægean Sea, had seen a Turk point with his staff to some carved work on the corner of a stone almost buried in the soil. Fellowes scraped away the dirt, was struck with the beauty of the sculptured ornaments, and, looking about him, observed more blocks and fragments like this. He returned to the spot, procured laborers and uncovered many blocks. He went back to England, bought a Greek grammar and learned the language; he read history and studied ancient art to explain his stones; he interested Gibson the sculptor; he invoked the assistance of the English Government; he called in the succor of Sir Humphry Davy to analyze the pigments; of experts in coins, of scholars and connoisseurs; and at last in his third visit brought home to England such statues and marble reliefs and such careful plans that he was able to reconstruct, in the British Museum, where it now stands, the perfect model of the Ionic trophy-monument, fifty years older than the Parthenon of Athens, and which had been destroyed by earthquakes, then by iconoclast Christians, then by savage Turks. But mark that in the task he had achieved an excellent education, and become associated with distinguished scholars whom he had interested in his pursuit; in short, had formed a college for himself; the enthusiast had found the master, the masters, whom he sought. Always genius seeks genius, desires nothing so much as to be a pupil and to find those who can lend it aid to perfect itself.

Nor are the two elements, enthusiasm and drill, incompatible. Accuracy is essential to beauty. The very definition of the intellect is Aristotle's: "that by which we know terms or boundaries." Give a boy accurate perceptions. Teach him the difference between the similar and the same. Make him call things by their right names. Pardon in him no blunder. Then he will give you solid satisfaction as long as he lives. It is better to teach the child arithmetic and Latin grammar than rhetoric or moral philosophy, because they require exactitude of performance; it is made certain that the lesson is mastered, and that power of performance is worth more than the knowledge. He can learn anything which is important to him now that the power to learn is secured: as mechanics say, when one has learned the use of tools, it is easy to work at a new craft.

Letter by letter, syllable by syllable, the child learns to read, and in good time can convey to all the domestic circle the sense of Shakspeare. By many steps each just as short, the stammering boy and the hesitating collegian, in the school debate, in college clubs, in mock court, comes at last to full, secure, triumphant unfolding of his thought in the popular assembly, with a fulnèss of power that makes all the steps forgotten.

But this function of opening and feeding the human mind is not to be fulfilled by any mechanical or military method; is not to be trusted to any skill less large than Nature itself. You must not neglect the form, but you must secure the essentials. It is curious how perverse and intermeddling we are, and what vast pains and cost we incur to do wrong. Whilst we all know in our own experience and apply natural methods in our own business,—in education our common sense fails us, and we are continually trying costly machinery against nature, in patent schools and academies and in great colleges and universities.

The natural method forever confutes our experiments, and we must still come back to it. The whole theory of the school is on the nurse's or mother's knee. The child is as hot to learn as the mother is to impart. There is mutual delight. The joy of our childhood in hearing beautiful stories from some skilful aunt who loves to tell them, must be repeated in youth. The boy wishes to learn to skate, to coast, to catch a fish in the brook, to hit a mark with a snowball or a stone; and a boy a little older is just as well pleased

588

to teach him these sciences. Not less delightful is the mutual pleasure of teaching and learning the secret of algebra, or of chemistry, or of good reading and good recitation of poetry or of prose, or of chosen facts in history or in biography.

Nature provided for the communication of thought, by planting with it in the receiving mind a fury to impart it. 'Tis so in every art, in every science. One burns to tell the new fact, the other burns to hear it. See how far a young doctor will ride or walk to witness a new surgical operation. I have seen a carriage-maker's shop emptied of all its workmen into the street, to scrutinize a new pattern from New York. So in literature, the young man who has taste for poetry, for fine images, for noble thoughts, is insatiable for this nourishment, and forgets all the world for the more learned friend, —who finds equal joy in dealing out his treasures.

Happy the natural college thus self-instituted around every natural teacher; the young men of Athens around Socrates; of Alexandria around Plotinus; of Paris around Abelard; of Germany around Fichte, or Niebuhr, or Goethe: in short the natural sphere of every leading mind. But the moment this is organized, difficulties begin. The college was to be the nurse and home of genius; but, though every young man is born with some determination in his nature, and is a potential genius; is at last to be one; it is, in the most, obstructed and delayed, and, whatever they may hereafter be, their senses are now opened in advance of their minds. They are more sensual than intellectual. Appetite and indolence they have, but no enthusiasm. These come in numbers to the college: few geniuses: and the teaching comes to be arranged for these many, and not for those few. Hence the instruction seems to require skilful tutors, of accurate and systematic mind, rather than ardent and inventive masters. Besides, the youth of genius are eccentric, won't drill, are irritable, uncertain, explosive, solitary, not men of the world, not good for every-day association. You have to work for large classes instead of individuals; you must lower your flag and reef your sails to wait for the dull sailors; you grow departmental, routinary, military almost with your discipline and college police. But what doth such a school to form a great and heroic character? What abiding Hope can it inspire? What Reformer will it nurse? What poet will it breed to sing to the human race? What discoverer of Nature's laws will it prompt to enrich us by disclosing in the mind the statute which all matter must obey? What fiery soul will it send out to warm a nation with his charity? What tranquil mind will it have fortified to walk with meekness in private and obscure duties, to wait and to suffer? Is it not manifest that our academic institutions should have a wider scope; that they should not be timid and keep the ruts of the last generation, but that wise men thinking for themselves and heartily seeking the good of mankind, and counting the cost of innovation, should dare to arouse the young to a just and heroic life; that the moral nature should be addressed in the school-room, and children should be treated as the high-born candidates of truth and virtue?

So to regard the young child, the young man, requires, no doubt, rare patience: a patience that nothing but faith in the remedial forces of the soul can give. You see his sensualism; you see his want of those tastes and perceptions which make the power and safety of your character. Very likely. But he has something else. If he has his own vice, he has its correlative virtue. Every mind should be allowed to make its own statement in action, and its balance will appear. In these judgments one needs that foresight which was attributed to an eminent reformer, of whom it was said "his patience could see in the bud of the aloe the blossom at the end of a hundred years." Alas for the cripple Practice when it seeks to come up with the bird Theory, which flies before it. Try your design on the best school. The scholars are of all ages and temperaments and capacities. It is difficult to class them, some are too young, some are slow, some perverse. Each requires so much consideration, that the morning hope of the teacher, of a day of love and progress, is often closed at evening by despair. Each single case, the more it is considered, shows more to be done; and the strict conditions of the hours, on one side, and the number of tasks, on the other. Whatever becomes of our method, the conditions stand fast,—six hours, and thirty, fifty, or a hundred and fifty pupils. Something must be done, and done speedily, and in this distress the wisest are tempted to adopt violent means, to proclaim martial law, corporal punishment, mechanical arrangement, bribes, spies, wrath, main strength and ignorance, in lieu of that wise genial providential influence they had hoped, and yet hope at some future day to adopt. Of course the devotion to details reacts injuriously on the teacher. He cannot indulge his genius, he cannot delight in personal relations with young friends, when his eye is always on the clock, and twenty classes are to be dealt with before the day is done. Besides, how can he please himself with genius, and foster modest virtue? A sure proportion of rogue and dunce finds its way into every school and requires a cruel share of time, and the gentle teacher, who wished to be a Providence to youth, is grown a martinet, sore with sus-

590

picions; knows as much vice as the judge of a police court, and his love of learning is lost in the routine of grammars and books of elements.

A rule is so easy that it does not need a man to apply it; an automaton, a machine, can be made to keep a school so. It facilitates labor and thought so much that there is always the temptation in large schools to omit the endless task of meeting the wants of each single mind, and to govern by steam. But it is at frightful cost. Our modes of Education aim to expedite, to save labor; to do for masses what cannot be done for masses, what must be done reverently, one by one: say rather, the whole world is needed for the tuition of each pupil. The advantages of this system of emulation and display are so prompt and obvious, it is such a timesaver, it is so energetic on slow and on bad natures, and is of so easy application, needing no sage or poet, but any tutor or schoolmaster in his first term can apply it,—that it is not strange that this calomel of culture should be a popular medicine. On the other hand, total abstinence from this drug, and the adoption of simple discipline and the following of nature, involves at once immense claims on the time, the thoughts, on the life of the teacher. It requires time, use, insight, event, all the great lessons and assistances of God; and only to think of using it implies character and profoundness; to enter on this course of discipline is to be good and great. It is precisely analogous to the difference between the use of corporal punishment and the methods of love. It is so easy to bestow on a bad boy a blow, overpower him, and get obedience without words, that in this world of hurry and distraction, who can wait for the returns of reason and the conquest of self; in the uncertainty too whether that will ever come? And yet the familiar observation of the universal compensations might suggest the fear that so summary a stop of a bad humor was more jeopardous than its continuance.

Now the correction of this quack practice is to import into Education the wisdom of life. Leave this military hurry and adopt the pace of Nature. Her secret is patience. Do you know how the naturalist learns all the secrets of the forest, of plants, of birds, of beasts, of reptiles, of fishes, of the rivers and the sea? When he goes into the woods the birds fly before him and he finds none; when he goes to the river-bank, the fish and the reptile swim away and leave him alone. His secret is patience; he sits down, and sits still; he is a statue; he is a log. These creatures have no value for their time, and he must put as low a rate on his. By dint of obstinate sitting still, reptile, fish, bird and beast, which all wish to return to their

591

haunts, begin to return. He sits still; if they approach, he remains passive as the stone he sits upon. They lose their fear. They have curiosity too about him. By and by the curiosity masters the fear, and they come swimming, creeping and flying towards him; and as he is still immovable, they not only resume their haunts and their ordinary labors and manners, show themselves to him in their work-day trim, but also volunteer some degree of advances towards fellowship and good understanding with a biped who behaves so civilly and well. Can you not baffle the impatience and passion of the child by your tranquillity? Can you not wait for him, as Nature and Providence do? Can you not keep for his mind and ways, for his secret, the same curiosity you give to the squirrel, snake, rabbit, and the sheldrake and the deer? He has a secret; wonderful methods in him; he is,—every child,—a new style of man; give him time and opportunity. Talk of Columbus and Newton! I tell you the child just born in yonder hovel is the beginning of a revolution as great as theirs. But you must have the believing and prophetic eye. Have the self-command you wish to inspire. Your teaching and discipline must have the reserve and taciturnity of Nature. Teach them to hold their tongues by holding your own. Say little; do not snarl; do not chide; but govern by the eye. See what they need, and that the right thing is done.

I confess myself utterly at a loss in suggesting particular reforms in our ways of teaching. No discretion that can be lodged with a school-committee, with the overseers or visitors of an academy, of a college, can at all avail to reach these difficulties and perplexities, but they solve themselves when we leave institutions and address individuals. The will, the male power, organizes, imposes its own thought and wish on others, and makes that military eye which controls boys as it controls men; admirable in its results, a fortune to him who has it, and only dangerous when it leads the workman to overvalue and overuse it and precludes him from finer means. Sympathy, the female force,—which they must use who have not the first,—deficient in instant control and the breaking down of resistance, is more subtle and lasting and creative. I advise teachers to cherish mother-wit. I assume that you will keep the grammar, reading, writing and arithmetic in order; 'tis easy and of course you will. But smuggle in a little contraband wit, fancy, imagination, thought. If you have a taste which you have suppressed because it is not shared by those about you, tell them that. Set this law up, whatever becomes of the rules of the school: they must not whisper, much less talk; but if one of the young people says a wise thing,

592

greet it, and let all the children clap their hands. They shall have no book but schoolbooks in the room; but if one has brought in a Plutarch or Shakspeare or Don Quixote or Goldsmith or any other good book, and understands what he reads, put him at once at the head of the class. Nobody shall be disorderly, or leave his desk without permission, but if a boy runs from his bench, or a girl, because the fire falls, or to check some injury that a little dastard is inflicting behind his desk on some helpless sufferer, take away the medal from the head of the class and give it on the instant to the brave rescuer. If a child happens to show that he knows any fact about astronomy, or plants, or birds, or rocks, or history, that interests him and you, hush all the classes and encourage him to tell it so that all may hear. Then you have made your school-room like the world. Of course you will insist on modesty in the children, and respect to their teachers, but if the boy stops you in your speech, cries out that you are wrong and sets you right, hug him!

To whatsoever upright mind, to whatsoever beating heart I speak, to you it is committed to educate men. By simple living, by an illimitable soul, you inspire, you correct, you instruct, you raise, you embellish all. By your own act you teach the beholder how to do the practicable. According to the depth from which you draw your life, such is the depth not only of your strenuous effort, but of your manners and presence.

The beautiful nature of the world has here blended your happiness with your power. Work straight on in absolute duty, and you lend an arm and an encouragement to all the youth of the universe. Consent yourself to be an organ of your highest thought, and lo! suddenly you put all men in your debt, and are the fountain of an energy that goes pulsing on with waves of benefit to the borders of society, to the circumference of things.

SELF-RELIANCE

"Ne te quæsiveris extra."

"Man is his own star; and the soul that can
Render an honest and a perfect man
Commands all light, all influence, all fate;
Nothing to him falls early or too late.
Our acts our angels are, or good or ill,
Our fatal shadows that walk by us still."

Epilogue to Beaumont and
Fletcher's *Honest Man's Fortune*

Cast the bantling on the rocks,
Suckle him with the she-wolf's teat,
Wintered with the hawk and fox,
Power and speed be hands and feet.

I read the other day some verses written by an eminent painter
which were original and not conventional. The soul always hears
an admonition in such lines, let the subject be what it may. The
sentiment they instil is of more value than any thought they may
contain. To believe your own thought, to believe that what is true
for you in your private heart is true for all men,—that is genius.
Speak your latent conviction, and it shall be the universal sense;
for the inmost in due time becomes the outmost, and our first
thought is rendered back to us by the trumpets of the Last Judgment. Familiar as the voice of the mind is to each, the highest merit
we ascribe to Moses, Plato and Milton is that they set at naught
books and traditions, and spoke not what men, but what *they*
thought. A man should learn to detect and watch that gleam of
light which flashes across his mind from within, more than the
lustre of the firmament of bards and sages. Yet he dismisses without notice his thought, because it is his. In every work of genius we
recognize our own rejected thoughts; they come back to us with a
certain alienated majesty. Great works of art have no more affecting lesson for us than this. They teach us to abide by our spontaneous impression with good-humored inflexibility then most when the
whole cry of voices is on the other side. Else to-morrow a stranger
will say with masterly good sense precisely what we have thought
and felt all the time, and we shall be forced to take with shame our
own opinion from another.

There is a time in every man's education when he arrives at the
conviction that envy is ignorance; that imitation is suicide; that he
must take himself for better for worse as his portion; that though
the wide universe is full of good, no kernel of nourishing corn can
come to him but through his toil bestowed on that plot of ground
which is given to him to till. The power which resides in him is
new in nature, and none but he knows what that is which he can
do, nor does he know until he has tried. Not for nothing one face,
one character, one fact, makes much impression on him, and another none. This sculpture in the memory is not without preëstab-
lished harmony. The eye was placed where one ray should fall,
that it might testify of that particular ray. We but half express ourselves, and are ashamed of that divine idea which each of us repre-

594

sents. It may be safely trusted as proportionate and of good issues, so it be faithfully imparted, but God will not have his work made manifest by cowards. A man is relieved and gay when he has put his heart into his work and done his best; but what he has said or done otherwise shall give him no peace. It is a deliverance which does not deliver. In the attempt his genius deserts him; no muse befriends; no invention, no hope.

Trust thyself: every heart vibrates to that iron string. Accept the place the divine providence has found for you, the society of your contemporaries, the connection of events. Great men have always done so, and confided themselves childlike to the genius of their age, betraying their perception that the absolutely trustworthy was seated at their heart, working through their hands, predominating in all their being. And we are now men, and must accept in the highest mind the same transcendent destiny; and not minors and invalids in a protected corner, not cowards fleeing before a revolution, but guides, redeemers and benefactors, obeying the Almighty effort and advancing on Chaos and the Dark.

What pretty oracles nature yields us on this text in the face and behavior of children, babes, and even brutes! That divided and rebel mind, that distrust of a sentiment because our arithmetic has computed the strength and means opposed to our purpose, these have not. Their mind being whole, their eye is as yet unconquered, and when we look in their faces we are disconcerted. Infancy conforms to nobody; all conform to it; so that one babe commonly makes four or five out of the adults who prattle and play to it. So God has armed youth and puberty and manhood no less with its own piquancy and charm, and made it enviable and gracious and its claims not to be put by, if it will stand by itself. Do not think the youth has no force, because he cannot speak to you and me. Hark! in the next room his voice is sufficiently clear and emphatic. It seems he knows how to speak to his contemporaries. Bashful or bold then, he will know how to make us seniors very unnecessary.

The nonchalance of boys who are sure of a dinner, and would disdain as much as a lord to do or say aught to conciliate one, is the healthy attitude of human nature. A boy is in the parlor what the pit is in the playhouse; independent, irresponsible, looking out from his corner on such people and facts as pass by, he tries and sentences them on their merits, in the swift, summary way of boys, as good, bad, interesting, silly, eloquent, troublesome. He cumbers himself never about consequences, about interests; he gives an independent, genuine verdict. You must court him; he does not court you. But the man is as it were clapped into jail by his consciousness. As soon as he has once acted or spoken with *éclat* he is a committed person, watched by the sympathy or the hatred of hundreds, whose affections must now enter into his account. There is no Lethe for this. Ah, that he could pass again into his neutrality! Who can thus avoid all pledges and, having observed, observe again from the same unaffected, unbiased, unbribable, unaffrighted innocence,—must always be formidable. He would utter opinions on all passing affairs, which being seen to be not private but necessary, would sink like darts into the ear of men and put them in fear.

These are the voices which we hear in solitude, but they grow faint and inaudible as we enter into the world. Society everywhere is in conspiracy against the manhood of every one of its members. Society is a joint-stock company, in which the members agree, for the better securing of his bread to each shareholder, to surrender the liberty and culture of the eater. The virtue in most request is conformity. Self-reliance is its aversion. It loves not realities and creators, but names and customs.

Whoso would be a man, must be a nonconformist. He who would gather immortal palms must not be hindered by the name of goodness, but must explore if it be goodness. Nothing is at last sacred but the integrity of your own mind. Absolve you to yourself, and you shall have the suffrage of the world. I remember an answer which when quite young I was prompted to make to a valued adviser who was wont to importune me with the dear old doctrines of the church. On my saying, "What have I to do with the sacredness of traditions, if I live wholly from within?" my friend suggested,— "But these impulses may be from below, not from above." I replied, "They do not seem to me to be such; but if I am the Devil's child, I will live then from the Devil." No law can be sacred to me but that of my nature. Good and bad are but names very readily transferable to that or this; the only right is what is after my constitution; the only wrong what is against it. A man is to carry himself in the presence of all opposition as if every thing were titular and ephemeral but he. I am ashamed to think how easily we capitulate to badges and names, to large societies and dead institutions. Every decent and well-spoken individual affects and sways me more than is right. I ought to go upright and vital, and speak the rude truth in all ways. If malice and vanity wear the coat of philanthropy, shall that pass? If an angry bigot assumes this bountiful cause of Abolition, and comes to me with his last news from Barbadoes, why should I not say to him, "Go love thy infant; love

596

thy wood-chopper; be good-natured and modest; have that grace; and never varnish your hard, uncharitable ambition with this incredible tenderness for black folk a thousand miles off. Thy love afar is spite at home." Rough and graceless would be such greeting, but truth is handsomer than the affectation of love. Your goodness must have some edge to it,—else it is none. The doctrine of hatred must be preached, as the counteraction of the doctrine of love, when that pules and whines. I shun father and mother and wife and brother when my genius calls me. I would write on the lintels of the door-post, *Whim.* I hope it is somewhat better than whim at last, but we cannot spend the day in explanation. Expect me not to show cause why I seek or why I exclude company. Then again, do not tell me, as a good man did to-day, of my obligation to put all poor men in good situations. Are they *my* poor? I tell thee, thou foolish philanthropist, that I grudge the dollar, the dime, the cent I give to such men as do not belong to me and to whom I do not belong. There is a class of persons to whom by all spiritual affinity I am bought and sold; for them I will go to prison if need be; but your miscellaneous popular charities; the education at college of fools; the building of meeting-houses to the vain end to which many now stand; alms to sots, and the thousand-fold Relief Societies;— though I confess with shame I sometimes succumb and give the dollar, it is a wicked dollar, which by and by I shall have the manhood to withhold.

Virtues are, in the popular estimate, rather the exception than the rule. There is the man *and* his virtues. Men do what is called a good action, as some piece of courage or charity, much as they would pay a fine in expiation of daily non-appearance on parade. Their works are done as an apology or extenuation of their living in the world,—as invalids and the insane pay a high board. Their virtues are penances. I do not wish to expiate, but to live. My life is for itself and not for a spectacle. I much prefer that it should be of a lower strain, so it be genuine and equal, than that it should be glittering and unsteady. I wish it to be sound and sweet, and not to need diet and bleeding. I ask primary evidence that you are a man, and refuse this appeal from the man to his actions. I know that for myself it makes no difference whether I do or forbear those actions which are reckoned excellent. I cannot consent to pay for a privilege where I have intrinsic right. Few and mean as my gifts may be, I actually am, and do not need for my own assurance or the assurance of my fellows any secondary testimony.

What I must do is all that concerns me, not what the people

597

think. This rule, equally arduous in actual and in intellectual life, may serve for the whole distinction between greatness and meanness. It is the harder because you will always find those who think they know what is your duty better than you know it. It is easy in the world to live after the world's opinion; it is easy in solitude to live after our own; but the great man is he who in the midst of the crowd keeps with perfect sweetness the independence of solitude.

The objection to conforming to usages that have become dead to you is that it scatters your force. It loses your time and blurs the impression of your character. If you maintain a dead church, contribute to a dead Bible-society, vote with a great party either for the government or against it, spread your table like base housekeepers, under all these screens I have difficulty to detect the precise man you are: and of course so much force is withdrawn from your proper life. But do your work, and I shall know you. Do your work, and you shall reinforce yourself. A man must consider what a blind-man's-buff is this game of conformity. If I know your sect I anticipate your argument. I hear a preacher announce for his text and topic the expediency of one of the institutions of his church. Do I not know beforehand that not possibly can he say a new and spontaneous word? Do I not know that with all this ostentation of examining the grounds of the institution he will do no such thing? Do I not know that he is pledged to himself not to look but at one side, the permitted side, not as a man, but as a parish minister? He is a retained attorney, and these airs of the bench are the emptiest affectation. Well, most men have bound their eyes with one or another handkerchief, and attached themselves to some one of these communities of opinion. This conformity makes them not false in a few particulars, authors of a few lies, but false in all particulars. Their every truth is not quite true. Their two is not the real two, their four not the real four; so that every word they say chagrins us and we know not where to begin to set them right. Meantime nature is not slow to equip us in the prison-uniform of the party to which we adhere. We come to wear one cut of face and figure, and acquire by degrees the gentlest asinine expression. There is a mortifying experience in particular, which does not fail to wreak itself also in the general history; I mean "the foolish face of praise," the forced smile which we put on in company where we do not feel at ease, in answer to conversation which does not interest us. The muscles, not spontaneously moved but moved by a low usurping wilfulness, grow tight about the outline of the face, with the most disagreeable sensation.

598

EMERSON

For nonconformity the world whips you with its displeasure. And therefore a man must know how to estimate a sour face. The bystanders look askance on him in the public street or in the friend's parlor. If this aversion had its origin in contempt and resistance like his own he might well go home with a sad countenance; but the sour faces of the multitude, like their sweet faces, have no deep cause, but are put on and off as the wind blows and a newspaper directs. Yet is the discontent of the multitude more formidable than that of the senate and the college. It is easy enough for a firm man who knows the world to brook the rage of the cultivated classes. Their rage is decorous and prudent, for they are timid, as being very vulnerable themselves. But when to their feminine rage the indignation of the people is added, when the ignorant and the poor are aroused, when the unintelligent brute force that lies at the bottom of society is made to growl and mow, it needs the habit of magnanimity and religion to treat it godlike as a trifle of no concernment.

The other terror that scares us from self-trust is our consistency; a reverence for our past act or word because the eyes of others have no other data for computing our orbit than our past acts, and we are loth to disappoint them.

But why should you keep your head over your shoulder? Why drag about this corpse of your memory, lest you contradict somewhat you have stated in this or that public place? Suppose you should contradict yourself; what then? It seems to be a rule of wisdom never to rely on your memory alone, scarcely even in acts of pure memory, but to bring the past for judgment into the thousand-eyed present, and live ever in a new day. In your metaphysics you have denied personality to the Deity, yet when the devout motions of the soul come, yield to them heart and life, though they should clothe God with shape and color. Leave your theory, as Joseph his coat in the hand of the harlot, and flee.

A foolish consistency is the hobgoblin of little minds, adored by little statesmen and philosophers and divines. With consistency a great soul has simply nothing to do. He may as well concern himself with his shadow on the wall. Speak what you think now in hard words and to-morrow speak what to-morrow thinks in hard words again, though it contradict every thing you said to-day.— "Ah, so you shall be sure to be misunderstood."—Is it so bad then to be misunderstood? Pythagoras was misunderstood, and Socrates, and Jesus, and Luther, and Copernicus, and Galileo, and Newton, and every pure and wise spirit that ever took flesh. To be great is to be misunderstood.

I suppose no man can violate his nature. All the sallies of his will are rounded in by the law of his being, as the inequalities of Andes and Himmaleh are insignificant in the curve of the sphere. Nor does it matter how you gauge and try him. A character is like an acrostic or Alexandrian stanza;—read it forward, backward, or across, it spells the same thing. In this pleasing contrite wood-life which God allows me, let me record day by day my honest thought without prospect or retrospect, and, I cannot doubt, it will be found symmetrical, though I mean it not and see it not. My book should smell of pines and resound with the hum of insects. The swallow over my window should interweave that thread or straw he carries in his bill into my web also. We pass for what we are. Character teaches above our wills. Men imagine that they communicate their virtue or vice only by overt actions, and do not see that virtue or vice emit a breath every moment.

There will be an agreement in whatever variety of actions, so they be each honest and natural in their hour. For of one will, the actions will be harmonious, however unlike they seem. These varieties are lost sight of at a little distance, at a little height of thought. One tendency unites them all. The voyage of the best ship is a zigzag line of a hundred tacks. See the line from a sufficient distance, and it strengthens itself to the average tendency. Your genuine action will explain itself and will explain your other genuine actions. Your conformity explains nothing. Act singly, and what you have already done singly will justify you now. Greatness appeals to the future. If I can be firm enough to-day to do right and scorn eyes, I must have done so much right before as to defend me now. Be it how it will, do right now. Always scorn appearances and you always may. The force of character is cumulative. All the fore-gone days of virtue work their health into this. What makes the majesty of the heroes of the senate and the field, which so fills the imagination? The consciousness of a train of great days and victories behind. They shed a united light on the advancing actor. He is attended as by a visible escort of angels. That is it which throws thunder into Chatham's voice, and dignity into Washington's port, and America into Adams's eye. Honor is venerable to us because it is no ephemera. It is always ancient virtue. We worship it to-day because it is not of to-day. We love it and pay it homage because it is not a trap for our love and homage, but is self-depend-

600

ent, self-derived, and therefore of an old immaculate pedigree, even if shown in a young person.

I hope in these days we have heard the last of conformity and consistency. Let the words be gazetted and ridiculous henceforward. Instead of the gong for dinner, let us hear a whistle from the Spartan fife. Let us never bow and apologize more. A great man is coming to eat at my house. I do not wish to please him; I wish that he should wish to please me. I will stand here for humanity, and though I would make it kind, I would make it true. Let us affront and reprimand the smooth mediocrity and squalid contentment of the times, and hurl in the face of custom and trade and office, the fact which is the upshot of all history, that there is a great responsible Thinker and Actor working wherever a man works; that a true man belongs to no other time or place, but is the centre of things. Where he is, there is nature. He measures you and all men and all events. Ordinarily, every body in society reminds us of somewhat else, or of some other person. Character, reality, reminds you of nothing else; it takes place of the whole creation. The man must be so much that he must make all circumstances indifferent. Every true man is a cause, a country, and an age; requires infinite spaces and numbers and time fully to accomplish his design;—and posterity seem to follow his steps as a train of clients. A man Cæsar is born, and for ages after we have a Roman Empire. Christ is born, and millions of minds so grow and cleave to his genius that he is confounded with virtue and the possible of man. An institution is the lengthened shadow of one man; as, Monachism, of the Hermit Antony; the Reformation, of Luther; Quakerism, of Fox; Methodism, of Wesley; Abolition, of Clarkson. Scipio, Milton called "the height of Rome;" and all history resolves itself very easily into the biography of a few stout and earnest persons.

Let a man then know his worth, and keep things under his feet. Let him not peep or steal, or skulk up and down with the air of a charity-boy, a bastard, or an interloper in the world which exists for him. But the man in the street, finding no worth in himself which corresponds to the force which built a tower or sculptured a marble god, feels poor when he looks on these. To him a palace, a statue, or a costly book have an alien and forbidding air, much like a gay equipage, and seem to say like that, "Who are you, Sir?" Yet they all are his, suitors for his notice, petitioners to his faculties that they will come out and take possession. The picture waits for my verdict; it is not to command me, but I am to settle its claims to praise. That popular fable of the sot who was picked up dead-drunk in the street, carried to the duke's house, washed and dressed and laid in the duke's bed, and, on his waking, treated with all obsequious ceremony like the duke, and assured that he had been insane, owes its popularity to the fact that it symbolizes so well the state of man, who is in the world a sort of sot, but now and then wakes up, exercises his reason and finds himself a true prince.

Our reading is mendicant and sycophantic. In history our imagination plays us false. Kingdom and lordship, power and estate, are a gaudier vocabulary than private John and Edward in a small house and common day's work; but the things of life are the same to both; the sum total of both is the same. Why all this deference to Alfred and Scanderberg and Gustavus? Suppose they were virtuous; did they wear out virtue? As great a stake depends on your private act to-day as followed their public and renowned steps. When private men shall act with original views, the lustre will be transferred from the actions of kings to those of gentlemen.

The world has been instructed by its kings, who have so magnetized the eyes of nations. It has been taught by this colossal symbol the mutual reverence that is due from man to man. The joyful loyalty with which men have everywhere suffered the king, the noble, or the great proprietor to walk among them by a law of his own, make his own scale of men and things and reverse theirs, pay for benefits not with money but with honor, and represent the law in his person, was the hieroglyphic by which they obscurely signified their consciousness of their own right and comeliness, the right of every man.

The magnetism which all original action exerts is explained when we inquire the reason of self-trust. Who is the Trustee? What is the aboriginal Self, on which a universal reliance may be grounded? What is the nature and power of that science-baffling star, without parallax, without calculable elements, which shoots a ray of beauty even into trivial and impure actions, if the least mark of independence appear? The inquiry leads us to that source, at once the essence of genius, of virtue, and of life, which we call Spontaneity or Instinct. We denote this primary wisdom as Intuition, whilst all later teachings are tuitions. In that deep force, the last fact behind which analysis cannot go, all things find their common origin. For the sense of being which in calm hours arises, we know not how, in the soul, is not diverse from things, from space, from light, from time, from man, but one with them and proceeds obviously from the

602

same source whence their life and being also proceed. We first share the life by which things exist and afterwards see them as appearances in nature and forget that we have shared their cause. Here is the fountain of action and of thought. Here are the lungs of that inspiration which giveth man wisdom and which cannot be denied without impiety and atheism. We lie in the lap of immense intelligence, which makes us receivers of its truth and organs of its activity. When we discern justice, when we discern truth, we do nothing of ourselves, but allow a passage to its beams. If we ask whence this comes, if we seek to pry into the soul that causes, all philosophy is at fault. Its presence or its absence is all we can affirm. Every man discriminates between the voluntary acts of his mind and his involuntary perceptions, and knows that to his involuntary perceptions a perfect faith is due. He may err in the expression of them, but he knows that these things are so, like day and night, not to be disputed. My wilful actions and acquisitions are but roving;—the idlest reverie, the faintest native emotion, command my curiosity and respect. Thoughtless people contradict as readily the statement of perceptions as of opinions, or rather much more readily; for they do not distinguish between perception and notion. They fancy that I choose to see this or that thing. But perception is not whimsical, but fatal. If I see a trait, my children will see it after me, and in course of time all mankind,—although it may chance that no one has seen it before me. For my perception of it is as much a fact as the sun.

The relations of the soul to the divine spirit are so pure that it is profane to seek to interpose helps. It must be that when God speaketh he should communicate, not one thing, but all things; should fill the world with his voice; should scatter forth light, nature, time, souls, from the centre of the present thought; and new date and new create the whole. Whenever a mind is simple and receives a divine wisdom, old things pass away,—means, teachers, texts, temples fall; it lives now, and absorbs past and future into the present hour. All things are made sacred by relation to it,—one as much as another. All things are dissolved to their centre by their cause, and in the universal miracle petty and particular miracles disappear. If therefore a man claims to know and speak of God and carries you backward to the phraseology of some old mouldered nation in another country, in another world, believe him not. Is the acorn better than the oak which is its fulness and completion? Is the parent better than the child into whom he has cast his ripened being? Whence then this worship of the past? The centuries are conspirators against the sanity and authority of the soul. Time and space are but physiological colors which the eye makes, but the soul is light: where it is, is day; where it was, is night; and history is an impertinence and an injury if it be any thing more than a cheerful apologue or parable of my being and becoming.

Man is timid and apologetic; he is no longer upright; he dares not say "I think," "I am," but quotes some saint or sage. He is ashamed before the blade of grass or the blowing rose. These roses under my window make no reference to former roses or to better ones; they are for what they are; they exist with God to-day. There is no time to them. There is simply the rose; it is perfect in every moment of its existence. Before a leaf-bud has burst, its whole life acts; in the full-blown flower there is no more; in the leafless root there is no less. Its nature is satisfied and it satisfies nature in all moments alike. But man postpones or remembers; he does not live in the present, but with reverted eye laments the past, or, heedless of the riches that surround him, stands on tiptoe to foresee the future. He cannot be happy and strong until he too lives with nature in the present, above time.

This should be plain enough. Yet see what strong intellects dare not yet hear God himself unless he speak the phraseology of I know not what David, or Jeremiah, or Paul. We shall not always set so great a price on a few texts, on a few lives. We are like children who repeat by rote the sentences of grandames and tutors, and, as they grow older, of the men of talents and character they chance to see,—painfully recollecting the exact words they spoke; afterwards, when they come into the point of view which those had who uttered these sayings, they understand them and are willing to let the words go; for at any time they can use words as good when occasion comes. If we live truly, we shall see truly. It is as easy for the strong man to be strong, as it is for the weak to be weak. When we have new perception, we shall gladly disburden the memory of its hoarded treasures as old rubbish. When a man lives with God, his voice shall be as sweet as the murmur of the brook and the rustle of the corn.

And now at last the highest truth on this subject remains unsaid; probably cannot be said; for all that we say is the far-off remembering of the intuition. That thought by what I can now nearest approach to say it, is this. When good is near you, when you have life in yourself, it.is not by any known or accustomed way; you shall not discern the footprints of any other; you shall not see the face of man; you shall not hear any name;—the way, the thought, the good, shall

604

be wholly strange and new. It shall exclude example and experience. You take the way from man, not to man. All persons that ever existed are its forgotten ministers. Fear and hope are alike beneath it. There is somewhat low even in hope. In the hour of vision there is nothing that can be called gratitude, nor properly joy. The soul raised over passion beholds identity and eternal causation, perceives the self-existence of Truth and Right, and calms itself with knowing that all things go well. Vast spaces of nature, the Atlantic Ocean, the South Sea; long intervals of time, years, centuries, are of no account. This which I think and feel underlay every former state of life and circumstances, as it does underlie my present, and what is called life and what is called death.

Life only avails, not the having lived. Power ceases in the instant of repose; it resides in the moment of transition from a past to a new state, in the shooting of the gulf, in the darting to an aim. This one fact the world hates; that the soul *becomes;* for that forever degrades the past, turns all riches to poverty, all reputation to a shame, confounds the saint with the rogue, shoves Jesus and Judas equally aside. Why then do we prate of self-reliance? Inasmuch as the soul is present there will be power not confident but agent. To talk of reliance is a poor external way of speaking. Speak rather of that which relies because it works and is. Who has more obedience than I masters me, though he should not raise his finger. Round him I must revolve by the gravitation of spirits. We fancy it rhetoric when we speak of eminent virtue. We do not yet see that virtue is Height, and that a man or a company of men, plastic and permeable to principles, by the law of nature must overpower and ride all cities, nations, kings, rich men, poets, who are not.

This is the ultimate fact which we so quickly reach on this, as on every topic, the resolution of all into the ever-blessed ONE. Self-existence is the attribute of the Supreme Cause, and it constitutes the measure of good by the degree in which it enters into all lower forms. All things real are so by so much virtue as they contain. Commerce, husbandry, hunting, whaling, war, eloquence, personal weight, are somewhat, and engage my respect as examples of its presence and impure action. I see the same law working in nature for conservation and growth. Power is, in nature, the essential measure of right. Nature suffers nothing to remain in her kingdoms which cannot help itself. The genesis and maturation of a planet, its poise and orbit, the bended tree recovering itself from the strong wind, the vital resources of every animal and vegetable, are demonstrations of the self-sufficing and therefore self-relying soul.

605

Thus all concentrates: let us not rove; let us sit at home with the cause. Let us stun and astonish the intruding rabble of men and books and institutions by a simple declaration of the divine fact. Bid the invaders take the shoes from off their feet, for God is here within. Let our simplicity judge them, and our docility to our own law demonstrate the poverty of nature and fortune beside our native riches.

But now we are a mob. Man does not stand in awe of man, nor is his genius admonished to stay at home, to put itself in communication with the internal ocean, but it goes abroad to beg a cup of water of the urns of other men. We must go alone. I like the silent church before the service begins, better than any preaching. How far off, how cool, how chaste the persons look, begirt each one with a precinct or sanctuary! So let us always sit. Why should we assume the faults of our friend, or wife, or father, or child, because they sit around our hearth, or are said to have the same blood? All men have my blood and I all men's. Not for that will I adopt their petulance or folly, even to the extent of being ashamed of it. But your isolation must not be mechanical, but spiritual, that is, must be elevation. At times the whole world seems to be in conspiracy to importune you with emphatic trifles. Friend, client, child, sickness, fear, want, charity, all knock at once at thy closet door and say,— "Come out unto us." But keep thy state; come not into their confusion. The power men possess to annoy me I give them by a weak curiosity. No man can come near me but through my act. "What we love that we have, but by desire we bereave ourselves of the love."

If we cannot at once rise to the sanctities of obedience and faith, let us at least resist our temptations; let us enter into the state of war and wake Thor and Woden, courage and constancy, in our Saxon breasts. This is to be done in our smooth times by speaking the truth. Check this lying hospitality and lying affection. Live no longer to the expectation of these deceived and deceiving people with whom we converse. Say to them, "O father, O mother, O wife, O brother, O friend, I have lived with you after appearances hitherto. Henceforward I am the truth's. Be it known unto you that henceforward I obey no law less than the eternal law. I will have no covenants but proximities. I shall endeavor to nourish my parents, to support my family, to be the chaste husband of one wife, —but these relations I must fill after a new and unprecedented way. I appeal from your customs. I must be myself. I cannot break myself any longer for you, or you. If you can love me for what I am, we shall be the happier. If you cannot, I will still seek to deserve that you should. I will not hide my tastes or aversions. I will so trust that what is deep is holy, that I will do strongly before the sun and moon whatever inly rejoices me and the heart appoints. If you are noble, I will love you; if you are not, I will not hurt you and myself by hypocritical attentions. If you are true, but not in the same truth with me, cleave to your companions; I will seek my own. I do this not selfishly but humbly and truly. It is alike your interest, and mine, and all men's, however long we have dwelt in lies, to live in truth. Does this sound harsh to-day? You will soon love what is dictated by your nature as well as mine, and if we follow the truth it will bring us out safe at last."—But so may you give these friends pain. Yes, but I cannot sell my liberty and my power, to save their sensibility. Besides, all persons have their moments of reason, when they look out into the region of absolute truth; then will they justify me and do the same thing.

The populace think that your rejection of popular standards is a rejection of all standard, and mere antinomianism; and the bold sensualist will use the name of philosophy to gild his crimes. But the law of consciousness abides. There are two confessionals, in one or the other of which we must be shriven. You may fulfil your round of duties by clearing yourself in the *direct,* or in the *reflex* way. Consider whether you have satisfied your relations to father, mother, cousin, neighbor, town, cat and dog—whether any of these can upbraid you. But I may also neglect this reflex standard and absolve me to myself. I have my own stern claims and perfect circle. It denies the name of duty to many offices that are called duties. But if I can discharge its debts it enables me to dispense with the popular code. If any one imagines that this law is lax, let him keep its commandment one day.

And truly it demands something godlike in him who has cast off the common motives of humanity and has ventured to trust himself for a taskmaster. High be his heart, faithful his will, clear his sight, that he may in good earnest be doctrine, society, law, to himself, that a simple purpose may be to him as strong as iron necessity is to others!

If any man consider the present aspects of what is called by distinction *society,* he will see the need of these ethics. The sinew and heart of man seem to be drawn out, and we are become timorous, desponding whimperers. We are afraid of truth, afraid of fortune, afraid of death, and afraid of each other. Our age yields no great and perfect persons. We want men and women who shall renovate

607

life and our social state, but we see that most natures are insolvent, cannot satisfy their own wants, have an ambition out of all proportion to their practical force and do lean and beg day and night continually. Our housekeeping is mendicant, our arts, our occupations, our marriages, our religion we have not chosen, but society has chosen for us. We are parlor soldiers. We shun the rugged battle of fate, where strength is born.

If our young men miscarry in their first enterprises they lose all heart. If the young merchant fails, men say he is *ruined.* If the finest genius studies at one of our colleges and is not installed in an office within one year afterwards in the cities or suburbs of Boston or New York, it seems to his friends and to himself that he is right in being disheartened and in complaining the rest of his life. A sturdy lad from New Hampshire or Vermont, who in turn tries all the professions, who *teams it, farms it, peddles,* keeps a school, preaches, edits a newspaper, goes to Congress, buys a township, and so forth, in successive years, and always like a cat falls on his feet, is worth a hundred of these city dolls. He walks abreast with his days and feels no shame in not "studying a profession," for he does not postpone his life, but lives already. He has not one chance, but a hundred chances. Let a Stoic open the resources of man and tell men they are not leaning willows, but can and must detach themselves; that with the exercise of self-trust, new powers shall appear; that a man is the word made flesh, born to shed healing to the nations; that he should be ashamed of our compassion, and that the moment he acts from himself, tossing the laws, the books, idolatries and customs out of the window, we pity him no more but thank and revere him;—and that teacher shall restore the life of man to splendor and make his name dear to all history.

It is easy to see that a greater self-reliance must work a revolution in all the offices and relations of men; in their religion; in their education; in their pursuits; their modes of living; their association; in their property; in their speculative views.

1. In what prayers do men allow themselves! That which they call a holy office is not so much as brave and manly. Prayer looks abroad and asks for some foreign addition to come through some foreign virtue, and loses itself in endless mazes of natural and supernatural, and mediatorial and miraculous. Prayer that craves a particular commodity, anything less than all good, is vicious. Prayer is the contemplation of the facts of life from the highest point of view. It is the soliloquy of a beholding and jubilant soul. It is the spirit of God pronouncing his works good. But prayer as a means to

effect a private end is meanness and theft. It supposes dualism and not unity in nature and consciousness. As soon as the man is at one with God, he will not beg. He will then see prayer in all action. The prayer of the farmer kneeling in his field to weed it, the prayer of the rower kneeling with the stroke of his oar, are true prayers heard throughout nature, though for cheap ends. Caratach, in Fletcher's "Bonduca," when admonished to inquire the mind of the god Audate, replies,—

> "His hidden meaning lies in our endeavors;
> Our valors are our best gods."

Another sort of false prayers are our regrets. Discontent is the want of self-reliance: it is infirmity of will. Regret calamities if you can thereby help the sufferer; if not, attend your own work and already the evil begins to be repaired. Our sympathy is just as base. We come to them who weep foolishly and sit down and cry for company, instead of imparting to them truth and health in rough electric shocks, putting them once more in communication with their own reason. The secret of fortune is joy in our hands. Welcome evermore to gods and men is the self-helping man. For him all doors are flung wide; him all tongues greet, all honors crown, all eyes follow with desire. Our love goes out to him and embraces him because he did not need it. We solicitously and apologetically caress and celebrate him because he held on his way and scorned our disapprobation. The gods love him because men hated him. "To the persevering mortal," said Zoroaster, "the blessed Immortals are swift."

As men's prayers are a disease of the will, so are their creeds a disease of the intellect. They say with those foolish Israelites, "Let not God speak to us, lest we die. Speak thou, speak any man with us, and we will obey." Everywhere I am hindered of meeting God in my brother, because he has shut his own temple doors and recites fables merely of his brother's, or his brother's brother's God. Every new mind is a new classification. If it prove a mind of uncommon activity and power, a Locke, a Lavoisier, a Hutton, a Bentham, a Fourier, it imposes its classification on other men, and lo! a new system. In proportion to the depth of the thought, and so to the number of the objects it touches and brings within reach of the pupil, is his complacency. But chiefly is this apparent in creeds and churches, which are also classifications of some powerful mind acting on the elemental thought of duty and man's relation to the Highest. Such is Calvinism, Quakerism, Swedenborgism. The pupil takes the same delight in subordinating every thing to the new terminology as a girl who has just learned botany in seeing a new earth and new seasons thereby. It will happen for a time that the pupil will find his intellectual power has grown by the study of his master's mind. But in all unbalanced minds the classification is idolized, passes for the end and not for a speedily exhaustible means, so that the walls of the system blend to their eye in the remote horizon with the walls of the universe; the luminaries of heaven seem to them hung on the arch their master built. They cannot imagine how you aliens have any right to see,—how you can see; "It must be somehow that you stole the light from us." They do not yet perceive that light, unsystematic, indomitable, will break into any cabin, even into theirs. Let them chirp awhile and call it their own. If they are honest and do well, presently their neat new pinfold will be too strait and low, will crack, will lean, will rot and vanish, and the immortal light, all young and joyful, million-orbed, million-colored, will beam over the universe as on the first morning.

2. It is for want of self-culture that the superstition of Travelling, whose idols are Italy, England, Egypt, retains its fascination for all educated Americans. They who made England, Italy, or Greece venerable in the imagination, did so by sticking fast where they were, like an axis of the earth. In manly hours we feel that duty is our place. The soul is no traveller; the wise man stays at home, and when his necessities, his duties, on any occasion call him from his house, or into foreign lands, he is at home still and shall make men sensible by the expression of his countenance that he goes, the missionary of wisdom and virtue, and visits cities and men like a sovereign and not like an interloper or a valet.

I have no churlish objection to the circumnavigation of the globe for the purposes of art, of study, and benevolence, so that the man is first domesticated, or does not go abroad with the hope of finding somewhat greater than he knows. He who travels to be amused, or to get somewhat which he does not carry, travels away from himself, and grows old even in youth among old things. In Thebes, in Palmyra, his will and mind have become old and dilapidated as they. He carries ruins to ruins.

Travelling is a fool's paradise. Our first journeys discover to us the indifference of places. At home I dream that at Naples, at Rome, I can be intoxicated with beauty and lose my sadness. I pack my trunk, embrace my friends, embark on the sea and at last wake up in Naples, and there beside me is the stern fact, the sad self, unrelenting, identical, that I fled from. I seek the Vatican and the palaces. I affect to be intoxicated with sights and suggestions, but I am not intoxicated. My giant goes with me wherever I go.

3. But the rage of travelling is a symptom of a deeper unsoundness affecting the whole intellectual action. The intellect is vagabond, and our system of education fosters restlessness. Our minds travel when our bodies are forced to stay at home. We imitate; and what is imitation but the travelling of the mind? Our houses are built with foreign taste; our shelves are garnished with foreign ornaments; our opinions, our tastes, our faculties lean, and follow the Past and the Distant. The soul created the arts wherever they have flourished. It was in his own mind that the artist sought his model. It was an application of his own thought to the thing to be done and the conditions to be observed. And why need we copy the Doric or the Gothic model? Beauty, convenience, grandeur of thought and quaint expression are as near to us as to any, and if the American artist will study with hope and love the precise thing to be done by him, considering the climate, the soil, the length of the day, the wants of the people, the habit and form of the government, he will create a house in which all these will find themselves fitted, and taste and sentiment will be satisfied also.

Insist on yourself; never imitate. Your own gift you can present every moment with the cumulative force of a whole life's cultivation; but of the adopted talent of another you have only an extemporaneous half possession. That which each can do best, none but his Maker can teach him. No man yet knows what it is, nor can, till that person has exhibited it. Where is the master who could have taught Shakspeare? Where is the master who could have instructed Franklin, or Washington, or Bacon, or Newton? Every great man is a unique. The Scipionism of Scipio is precisely that part he could not borrow. Shakspeare will never be made by the study of Shakspeare. Do that which is assigned you, and you cannot hope too much or dare too much. There is at this moment for you an utterance brave and grand as that of the colossal chisel of Phidias, or trowel of the Egyptians, or the pen of Moses or Dante, but different from all these. Not possibly will the soul, all rich, all eloquent, with thousand-cloven tongue, deign to repeat itself; but if you can hear what these patriarchs say, surely you can reply to them in the same pitch of voice; for the ear and the tongue are two organs of one nature. Abide in the simple and noble regions of thy life, obey thy heart, and thou shalt reproduce the Foreworld again.

4. As our Religion, our Education, our Art look abroad, so does our spirit of society. All men plume themselves on the improvement of society, and no man improves.

Society never advances. It recedes as fast on one side as it gains on the other. It undergoes continual changes; it is barbarous, it is civilized, it is christianized, it is rich, it is scientific; but this change is not amelioration. For every thing that is given something is taken. Society acquires new arts and loses old instincts. What a contrast between the well-clad, reading, writing, thinking American, with a watch, a pencil and a bill of exchange in his pocket, and the naked New Zealander, whose property is a club, a spear, a mat and an undivided twentieth of a shed to sleep under! But compare the health of the two men and you shall see that the white man has lost his aboriginal strength. If the traveller tell us truly, strike the savage with a broad-axe and in a day or two the flesh shall unite and heal as if you struck the blow into soft pitch, and the same blow shall send the white to his grave.

The civilized man has built a coach, but has lost the use of his feet. He is supported on crutches, but lacks so much support of muscle. He has a fine Geneva watch, but he fails of the skill to tell the hour by the sun. A Greenwich nautical almanac he has, and so being sure of the information when he wants it, the man in the street does not know a star in the sky. The solstice he does not observe; the equinox he knows as little; and the whole bright calendar of the year is without a dial in his mind. His note-books impair his memory; his libraries overload his wit; the insurance-office increases the number of accidents; and it may be a question whether machinery does not encumber; whether we have not lost by refinement some energy, by a Christianity, entrenched in establishments and forms, some vigor of wild virtue. For every Stoic was a Stoic; but in Christendom where is the Christian?

There is no more deviation in the moral standard than in the standard of height or bulk. No greater men are now than ever were. A singular equality may be observed between the great men of the first and of the last ages; nor can all the science, art, religion, and philosophy of the nineteenth century avail to educate greater men than Plutarch's heroes, three or four and twenty centuries ago. Not in time is the race progressive. Phocion, Socrates, Anaxagoras, Diogenes, are great men, but they leave no class. He who is really of their class will not be called by their name, but will be his own man, and in his turn the founder of a sect. The arts and inventions of each period are only its costume and do not invigorate men. The

612

harm of the improved machinery may compensate its good. Hudson and Behring accomplished so much in their fishing-boats as to astonish Parry and Franklin, whose equipment exhausted the resources of science and art. Galileo, with an opera-glass, discovered a more splendid series of celestial phenomena than any one since. Columbus found the New World in an undecked boat. It is curious to see the periodical disuse and perishing of means and machinery which were introduced with loud laudation a few years or centuries before. The great genius returns to essential man. We reckoned the improvements of the art of war among the triumphs of science, and yet Napoleon conquered Europe by the bivouac, which consisted of falling back on naked valor and disencumbering it of all aids. The Emperor held it impossible to make a perfect army, says Las Cases, "without abolishing our arms, magazines, commissaries and carriages, until, in imitation of the Roman custom, the soldier should receive his supply of corn, grind it in his hand-mill and bake his bread himself."

Society is a wave. The wave moves onward, but the water of which it is composed does not. The same particle does not rise from the valley to the ridge. Its unity is only phenomenal. The persons who make up a nation to-day, next year die, and their experience dies with them.

And so the reliance on Property, including the reliance on governments which protect it, is the want of self-reliance. Men have looked away from themselves and at things so long that they have come to esteem the religious, learned and civil institutions as guards of property, and they deprecate assaults on these, because they feel them to be assaults on property. They measure their esteem of each other by what each has, and not by what each is. But a cultivated man becomes ashamed of his property, out of new respect for his nature. Especially he hates what he has if he see that it is accidental,—came to him by inheritance, or gift, or crime; then he feels that it is not having; it does not belong to him, has no root in him and merely lies there because no revolution or no robber takes it away. But that which a man is, does always by necessity acquire; and what the man acquires, is living property, which does not wait the beck of rulers, or mobs, or revolutions, or fire, or storm, or bankruptcies, but perpetually renews itself wherever the man breathes. "Thy lot or portion of life," said the Caliph Ali, "is seeking after thee; therefore be at rest from seeking after it." Our dependence on these foreign goods leads us to our slavish respect for numbers. The political parties meet in numerous conventions; the greater the concourse and with each new uproar of announcement, The delegation from Essex! The Democrats from New Hampshire! The Whigs of Maine! the young patriot feels himself stronger than before by a new thousand of eyes and arms. In like manner the reformers summon conventions and vote and resolve in multitude. Not so, O friends! will the God deign to enter and inhabit you, but by a method precisely the reverse. It is only as a man puts off all foreign support and stands alone that I see him to be strong and to prevail. He is weaker by every recruit to his banner. Is not a man better than a town? Ask nothing of men, and, in the endless mutation, thou only firm column must presently appear the upholder of all that surrounds thee. He who knows that power is inborn, that he is weak because he has looked for good out of him and elsewhere, and, so perceiving, throws himself unhesitatingly on his thought, instantly rights himself, stands in the erect position, commands his limbs, works miracles; just as a man who stands on his feet is stronger than a man who stands on his head.

So use all that is called Fortune. Most men gamble with her, and gain all, and lose all, as her wheel rolls. But do thou leave as unlawful these winnings, and deal with Cause and Effect, the chancellors of God. In the Will work and acquire, and thou hast chained the wheel of Chance, and shall sit hereafter out of fear from her rotations. A political victory, a rise of rents, the recovery of your sick or the return of your absent friend, or some other favorable event raises your spirits, and you think good days are preparing for you. Do not believe it. Nothing can bring you peace but yourself. Nothing can bring you peace but the triumph of principles.

1841

DEWEY 1859–1952

THERE ARE two reasons for the unique influence of John Dewey on modern American education and on certain groups of teachers in other countries.

First, like Herbart, he was one of the few modern systematic philosophers concerned with the application of theory to the work of the school and the classroom.

Second, his philosophy of pragmatism gathered in itself the rays of the movements of thought that formed the mentality of the last decades of the nineteenth and first decades of the twentieth century. From Hegel and Marx, Dewey received the incentive to investigate the impact of organizations and institutions on the history of man; from Darwin the evolutionary-progressive interpretation of life; from the great educators the conviction of the significance of systematically pursued public education; from science in general the faith in the experimental method not only in relation to matter, but also in relation to the great issues of humanity—a faith that made him suspicious of "supernatural" traditions and metaphysical a prioris.

Yet, it would be wrong to describe Dewey as a mere eclectic and compiler. There is in his work a fusion between ideas and personality, method and ethos, as well as of individuality and social consciousness that has made him for many the symbol of American democracy—this not rarely to such a degree that they are satisfied with using him as a reference without a serious study of his more difficult books. In their insistence on pragmatism as the "typical American," and the only really important, school of philosophy they also forget Dewey's own background. In his intellectual autobiography of the year 1930, "From Absolutism to Experimentalism," reproduced in this volume, he refers to the metaphysical idealist Hegel as "that acquaintance" which "has left a permanent deposit in my thinking . . ." "Were it possible for me to be the devotee of any system, I still should believe that there is greater richness and greater variety of insight in Hegel than in any other single systematic philosopher—though when I say this I exclude Plato, who still provides my favorite philosophical reading."

The historian of philosophy—despite all differences in detail and even controversy—will place Dewey near to Charles S. Peirce, William James, and Bertrand Russell. Russell is quoted as writing:

"To my mind, the best work that has been done anywhere in philosophy and psychology during the present century has been done in America. Its merit is due not so much to the individual ability of the

615

men concerned as to their freedom from certain hampering traditions which the European man of learning inherits from the Middle Ages . . .

". . . The philosophy of an industrial world cannot be materialism, for materialism, just as much as theism, worships the power which it believes to exist outside Man. Pious Russia, barely emerging from Byzantine ecclesiasticism, has become officially materialistic; probably the more pious portions of the American population will have to pass through this same phase. But sophisticated America, wherever it has succeeded in shaking off slavery to Europe (which is too common among the sophisticated) has already developed a new outlook, mainly as a result of the work of James and Dewey. This new outlook, embodied in the so-called instrumental theory of knowledge, constitutes the philosophy appropriate to industrialism, which is science in the sphere of practice." [1]

This statement of Bertrand Russell is now severely challenged by many Americans themselves, who often without a thorough reading of Dewey's works, in this respect resembling some of his disciples, blame him for his "relativism" and "neglect of spiritual values," for having fostered an "anti-traditional progressivism" and for having lowered the respect for duty and discipline in education. New philosophical concerns are arising out of the depressive influence of the last two World Wars and out of the uncertainty as to the blessings of science. There is increasing doubt in the validity of scientific methods in regard to human values. Dewey himself, so one reads, has not sufficiently delved into the metaphysical premises of his experimentalist pragmatism. Nor has he gone deep enough into the spiritual and moral roots of democracy itself.

The author of these lines—despite his profound respect for Dewey's work and personality—has expressed himself critically.[2] Yet, this does not make him inclined to condone a certain type of obscurantist irrationalism that has arisen from the anguish of our present world conflicts and likes to choose Dewey and modern education as its target. Certainly, there are omissions in Dewey's philosophy which, in the minds of some, may be so severe as to offset his contributions. But much as man may need the profoundly mystical aspect of life—as to be found in the thoughts of a Pascal, an Amiel, or a Kierkegaard—advancing civilization needs also the mixture of critical insight and intellectual courage of a Locke, a Voltaire, a Diderot, and a John Dewey. And though Dewey's most well known work *Democracy and Education* can in regard to beauty of style not compete with Alfred N. Whitehead's *Aims of Education,* it is nevertheless one of the important documents of modern educational philosophy.

"From Absolutism to Experimentalism" is from *Contemporary American Philosophy,* edited by George P. Adams and William P. Montague (New York: The Macmillan Company, 1930), I, 13-27. *My Pedagogic Creed* is from the first edition, 1897. "Evolution and Ethics" is from the essay by that name in *The Monist. A Quarterly Magazine Devoted to*

[1] *Whither Mankind?* Edited by Charles A. Beard, chap. iii, pp. 66-67.
[2] See Robert Ulich, "John Dewey," *History of Educational Thought* (New York: American Book Co., Second Edition, 1950), pp. 315 ff.

616

JOHN DEWEY

the Philosophy of Science, VIII (Chicago: The Open Court Publishing Company, 1898), 339-341.

FROM ABSOLUTISM TO EXPERIMENTALISM

In the late 'seventies, when I was an undergraduate, "electives" were still unknown in the smaller New England colleges. But in the one I attended, the University of Vermont, the tradition of a "senior-year course" still subsisted. This course was regarded as a kind of intellectual coping to the structure erected in earlier years, or, at least, as an insertion of the key-stone of the arch. It included courses in political economy, international law, history of civilization (Guizot), psychology, ethics, philosophy of religion (Butler's *Analogy*), logic, etc., not history of philosophy, save incidentally. The enumeration of these titles may not serve the purpose for which it is made; but the idea was that after three years of somewhat specialized study in languages and sciences, the last year was reserved for an introduction into serious intellectual topics of wide and deep significance—an introduction into the world of ideas. I doubt if in many cases it served its alleged end; however, it fell in with my own inclinations, and I have always been grateful for that year of my schooling. There was, however, one course in the previous year that had excited a taste that in retrospect may be called philosophical. That was a rather short course, without laboratory work, in Physiology, a book of Huxley's being the text. It is difficult to speak with exactitude about what happened to me intellectually so many years ago, but I have an impression that there was derived from that study a sense of interdependence and interrelated unity that gave form to intellectual stirrings that had been previously inchoate, and created a kind of type or model of a view of things to which material in any field ought to conform. Subconsciously, at least, I was led to desire a world and a life that would have the same properties as had the human organism in the picture of it derived from study of Huxley's treatment. At all events, I got great stimulation from the study, more than from anything I had had contact with before; and as no desire was awakened in me to continue that particular branch of learning, I date from this time the awakening of a distinctive philosophic interest.

The University of Vermont rather prided itself upon its tradition in philosophy. One of its earlier teachers, Dr. Marsh, was almost the first person in the United States to venture upon the specula-

617

tive and dubiously orthodox seas of German thinking—that of Kant, Schelling, and Hegel. The venture, to be sure, was made largely by way of Coleridge; Marsh edited an American edition of Coleridge's *Aids to Reflection*. Even this degree of speculative generalization, in its somewhat obvious tendency to rationalize the body of Christian theological doctrines, created a flutter in ecclesiastical dovecots. In particular, a controversy was carried on between the Germanizing rationalizers and the orthodox representatives of the Scottish school of thought through the representatives of the latter at Princeton. I imagine—although it is a very long time since I have had any contact with this material—that the controversy still provides data for a section, if not a chapter in the history of thought in this country.

Although the University retained pride in its pioneer work, and its atmosphere was for those days theologically "liberal"—of the Congregational type—the teaching of philosophy had become more restrained in tone, more influenced by the still dominant Scotch school. Its professor, M. H. A. P. Torrey, was a man of genuinely sensitive and cultivated mind, with marked esthetic interest and taste, which, in a more congenial atmosphere than that of northern New England in those days, would have achieved something significant. He was, however, constitutionally timid, and never really let his mind go. I recall that, in a conversation I had with him a few years after graduation, he said: "Undoubtedly pantheism is the most satisfactory form of metaphysics intellectually, but it goes counter to religious faith." I fancy that remark told of an inner conflict that prevented his native capacity from coming to full fruition. His interest in philosophy, however, was genuine, not perfunctory; he was an excellent teacher, and I owe to him a double debt, that of turning my thoughts definitely to the study of philosophy as a life-pursuit, and of a generous gift of time to me during a year devoted privately under his direction to a reading of classics in the history of philosophy and learning to read philosophic German. In our walks and talks during this year, after three years on my part of high-school teaching, he let his mind go much more freely than in the class-room, and revealed potentialities that might have placed him among the leaders in the development of a freer American philosophy—but the time for the latter had not yet come.

Teachers of philosophy were at that time, almost to a man, clergymen; the supposed requirements of religion, or theology, dominated the teaching of philosophy in most colleges. Just how and why Scotch philosophy lent itself so well to the exigencies of

618

religion I cannot say; probably the causes were more extrinsic than intrinsic; but at all events there was a firm alliance established between religion and the cause of "intuition." It is probably impossible to recover at this date the almost sacrosanct air that enveloped the idea of intuitions; but somehow the cause of all holy and valuable things was supposed to stand or fall with the validity of intuitionalism; the only vital issue was that between intuitionalism and a sensational empiricism that explained away the reality of all higher objects. The story of this almost forgotten debate, once so urgent, is probably a factor in developing in me a certain scepticism about the depth and range of purely contemporary issues; it is likely that many of those which seem highly important today will also in a generation have receded to the status of the local and provincial. It also aided in generating a sense of the value of the history of philosophy; some of the claims made for this as a sole avenue of approach to the study of philosophic problems seem to me misdirected and injurious. But its value in giving perspective and a sense of proportion in relation to immediate contemporary issues can hardly be over-estimated.

I do not mention this theological and intuitional phase because it had any lasting influence upon my own development, except negatively. I learned the terminology of an intuitional philosophy, but it did not go deep, and in no way did it satisfy what I was dimly reaching for. I was brought up in a conventionally evangelical atmosphere of the more "liberal" sort; and the struggles that later arose between acceptance of that faith and the discarding of traditional and institutional creeds came from personal experiences and not from the effects of philosophical teaching. It was not, in others words, in this respect that philosophy either appealed to me or influenced me—though I am not sure that Butler's *Analogy*, with its cold logic and acute analysis, was not, in a reversed way, a factor in developing "scepticism."

During the year of private study, of which mention has been made, I decided to make philosophy my life-study, and accordingly went to Johns Hopkins the next year (1884) to enter upon that new thing, "graduate work." It was something of a risk; the work offered there was almost the only indication that there were likely to be any self-supporting jobs in the field of philosophy for others than clergymen. Aside from the effect of my study with Professor Torrey, another influence moved me to undertake the risk. During the years after graduation I had kept up philosophical readings and I had even written a few articles which I sent to Dr. W. T. Harris,

619

the well-known Hegelian, and the editor of the *Journal of Speculative Philosophy,* the only philosophic journal in the country at that time, as he and his group formed almost the only group of laymen devoted to philosophy for non-theological reasons. In sending an article I asked Dr. Harris for advice as to the possibility of my successfully prosecuting philosophic studies. His reply was so encouraging that it was a distinct factor in deciding me to try philosophy as a professional career.

The articles sent were, as I recall them, highly schematic and formal; they were couched in the language of intuitionalism; of Hegel I was then ignorant. My deeper interests had not as yet been met, and in the absence of subject-matter that would correspond to them, the only topics at my command were such as were capable of a merely formal treatment. I imagine that my development has been controlled largely by a struggle between a native inclination toward the schematic and formally logical, and these incidents of personal experience that compelled me to take account of actual material. Probably there is in the consciously articulated ideas of every thinker an over-weighting of just those things that are contrary to his natural tendencies, an emphasis upon those things that are contrary to his intrinsic bent, and which, therefore, he has to struggle to bring to expression, while the native bent, on the other hand, can take care of itself. Anyway, a case might be made out for the proposition that the emphasis upon the concrete, empirical, and "practical" in my later writings is partly due to considerations of this nature. It was a reaction against what was more natural, and it served as a protest and protection against something in myself which, in the pressure of the weight of actual experiences, I knew to be a weakness. It is, I suppose, becoming a commonplace that when anyone is unduly concerned with controversy, the remarks that seem to be directed against others are really concerned with a struggle that is going on inside himself. The marks, the stigmata, of the struggle to weld together the characteristics of a formal, theoretic interest and the material of a maturing experience of contacts with realities also showed themselves, naturally, in style of writing and manner or presentation. During the time when the schematic interest predominated, writing was comparatively easy; there were even compliments upon the clearness of my style. Since then thinking and writing have been hard work. It is easy to give way to the dialectic development of a theme; the pressure of concrete experiences was, however, sufficiently heavy, so that a sense of intellectual honesty prevented a surrender to that course. But,

620

on the other hand, the formal interest persisted, so that there was an inner demand for an intellectual technique that would be consistent and yet capable of flexible adaptation to the concrete diversity of experienced things. It is hardly necessary to say that I have not been among those to whom the union of abilities to satisfy these two opposed requirements, the formal and the material, came easily. For that very reason I have been acutely aware, too much so, doubtless, of a tendency of other thinkers and writers to achieve a specious lucidity and simplicity by the mere process of ignoring considerations which a greater respect for concrete materials of experience would have forced upon them.

It is a commonplace of educational history that the opening of Johns Hopkins University marked a new epoch in higher education in the United States. We are probably not in a condition as yet to estimate the extent to which its foundation and the development of graduate schools in other universities, following its example, mark a turn in our American culture. The 'eighties and 'nineties seem to mark the definitive close of our pioneer period, and the turn from the Civil War era into the new industrialized and commercial age. In philosophy, at least, the influence of Johns Hopkins was not due to the size of the provision that was made. There was a half-year of lecturing and seminar work given by Professor George Sylvester Morris, of the University of Michigan; belief in the "demonstrated" (a favourite word of his) truth of the substance of German idealism, and of belief in its competency to give direction to a life of aspiring thought, emotion, and action. I have never known a more single-hearted and whole-souled man—a man of a single piece all the way through; while I long since deviated from his philosophic faith, I should be happy to believe that the influence of the spirit of his teaching has been an enduring influence.

While it was impossible that a young and impressionable student, unacquainted with any system of thought that satisfied his head and heart, should not have been deeply affected, to the point of at least a temporary conversion, by the enthusiastic and scholarly devotion of Mr. Morris, this effect was far from being the only source of my own "Hegelianism." The 'eighties and 'nineties were a time of new ferment in English thought; the reaction against atomic individualism and sensationalistic empiricism was in full swing. It was the time of Thomas Hill Green, of the two Cairds, of Wallace, of the appearance of the *Essays in Philosophical Criticism*, co-operatively produced by a younger group under the leadership of the late Lord Haldane. This movement was at the time the vital

621

and constructive one in philosophy. Naturally its influence fell in with and reinforced that of Professor Morris. There was but one marked difference, and that, I think, was in favour of Mr. Morris. He came to Kant through Hegel instead of to Hegel by way of Kant, so that his attitude toward Kant was the critical one expressed by Hegel himself. Moreover, he retained something of his early Scotch philosophical training in a common-sense belief in the existence of the external world. He used to make merry over those who thought the existence of this world and of matter were things to be proved by philosophy. To him the only philosophical question was as to the meaning of this existence; his idealism was wholly of the objective type. Like his contemporary, Professor John Watson, of Kingston, he combined a logical and idealistic metaphysics with a realistic epistemology. Through his teacher at Berlin, Trendelenburg, he had acquired a great reverence for Aristotle, and he had no difficulty in uniting Aristotelianism with Hegelianism.

There were, however, also "subjective" reasons for the appeal that Hegel's thought made to me; it supplied a demand for unification that was doubtless an intense emotional craving, and yet was a hunger that only an intellectualized subject-matter could satisfy. It is more than difficult, it is impossible, to recover that early mood. But the sense of divisions and separations that were, I suppose, borne in upon me as a consequence of a heritage of New England culture, divisions by way of isolation of self from the world, of soul from body, of nature from God, brought a painful oppression—or, rather, they were an inward laceration. My earlier philosophic study had been an intellectual gymnastic. Hegel's synthesis of subject and object, matter and spirit, the divine and the human, was, however, no mere intellectual formula; it operated as an immense release, a liberation. Hegel's treatment of human culture, of institutions and the arts, involved the same dissolution of hard-and-fast dividing walls, and had a special attraction for me.

As I have already intimated, while the conflict of traditional religious beliefs with opinions that I could myself honestly entertain was the source of a trying personal crisis, it did not at any time constitute a leading philosophical problem. This might look as if the two things were kept apart; in reality it was due to a feeling that any genuinely sound religious experience could and should adapt itself to whatever beliefs one found oneself intellectually entitled to hold—a half unconscious sense at first, but one which ensuing years have deepened into a fundamental conviction. In

622

JOHN DEWEY

consequence, while I have, I hope, a due degree of personal sympathy with individuals who are undergoing the throes of a personal change of attitude, I have not been able to attach much importance to religion as a philosophic problem; for the effect of that attachment seems to be in the end a subornation of candid philosophic thinking to the alleged but factitious needs of some special set of convictions. I have enough faith in the depth of the religious tendencies of men to believe that they will adapt themselves to any required intellectual change, and that it is futile (and likely to be dishonest) to forecast prematurely just what forms the religious interest will take as a final consequence of the great intellectual transformation that is going on. As I have been frequently criticized for undue reticence about the problems of religion, I insert this explanation: it seems to me that the great solicitude of many persons, professing belief in the universality of the need for religion, about the present and future of religion proves that in fact they are moved more by partisan interest in a particular religion than by interest in religious experience.

The chief reason, however, for inserting these remarks at this point is to bring out a contrast effect. Social interests and problems from an early period had to me the intellectual appeal and provided the intellectual sustenance that many seem to have found primarily in religious questions. In undergraduate days I had run across, in the college library, Harriet Martineau's exposition of Comte. I cannot remember that his law of "the three stages" affected me particularly; but his idea of the disorganized character of Western modern culture, due to a disintegrative "individualism," and his idea of a synthesis of science that should be a regulative method of an organized social life, impressed me deeply. I found, as I thought, the same criticisms combined with a deeper and more far-reaching integration in Hegel. I did not, in those days when I read Francis Bacon, detect the origin of the Comtean idea in him, and I had not made acquaintance with Condorcet, the connecting link.

I drifted away from Hegelianism in the next fifteen years; and the word "drifting" expresses the slow and, for a long time, imperceptible character of the movement, though it does not convey the impression that there was an adequate cause for the change. Nevertheless I should never think of ignoring, much less denying, what an astute critic occasionally refers to as a novel discovery—that acquaintance with Hegel has left a permanent deposit in my thinking. The form, the schematism, of his system now seems to me

623

artificial to the last degree. But in the content of his ideas there is often an extraordinary depth; in many of his analyses, taken out of their mechanical dialectical setting, an extraordinary acuteness. Were it possible for me to be a devotee of any system, I still should believe that there is greater richness and greater variety of insight in Hegel than in any other single systematic philosopher— though when I say this I exclude Plato, who still provides my favourite philosophic reading. For I am unable to find in him that all-comprehensive and overriding system which later interpretation has, as it seems to me, conferred upon him as a dubious boon. The ancient sceptics overworked another aspect of Plato's thought when they treated him as their spiritual father, but they were nearer the truth, I think, than those who force him into the frame of a rigidly systematized doctrine. Although I have not the aversion to system as such that is sometimes attributed to me, I am dubious of my own ability to reach inclusive systematic unity, and in consequence, perhaps, of that fact also dubious about my contemporaries. Nothing could be more helpful to present philosophizing than a "Back to Plato" movement; but it would have to be back to the dramatic, restless, co-operatively inquiring Plato of the Dialogues, trying one mode of attack after another to see what it might yield; back to the Plato whose highest flight of metaphysics always terminated with a social and practical turn, and not to the artificial Plato constructed by unimaginative commentators who treat him as the original university professor.

The rest of the story of my intellectual development I am unable to record without more faking than I care to indulge in. What I have so far related is so far removed in time that I can talk about myself as another person; and much has faded, so that a few points stand out without my having to force them into the foreground. The philosopher, if I may apply that word to myself, that I became as I moved away from German idealism, is too much the self that I still am and is still too much in process of change to lend itself to record. I envy, up to a certain point, those who can write their intellectual biography in a unified pattern, woven out of a few distinctly discernible strands of interest and influence. By contrast, I seem to be unstable, chameleon-like, yielding one after another to many diverse and even incompatible influences; struggling to assimilate something from each and yet striving to carry it forward in a way that is logically consistent with what has been learned from its predecessors. Upon the whole, the forces that have influenced me have come from persons and from situations more than

624

from books—not that I have not, I hope, learned a great deal from philosophical writings, but that what I have learned from them has been technical in comparison with what I have been forced to think upon and about because of some experience in which I found myself entangled. It is for this reason that I cannot say with candour that I envy completely, or envy beyond a certain point, those to whom I have referred. I like to think, though it may be a defence reaction, that with all the inconveniences of the road I have been forced to travel, it has the compensatory advantage of not inducing an immunity of thought to experiences—which perhaps, after all should not be treated even by a philosopher as the germ of a disease to which he needs to develop resistance.

While I cannot write an account of intellectual development without giving it the semblance of a continuity that it does not in fact own, there are four special points that seem to stand out. One is the importance that the practice and theory of education have had for me: especially the education of the young, for I have never been able to feel much optimism regarding the possibilities of "higher" education when it is built upon warped and weak foundations. This interest fused with and brought together what might otherwise have been separate interests—that in psychology and that in social institutions and social life. I can recall but one critic who has suggested that my thinking has been too much permeated by interest in education. Although a book called *Democracy and Education* was for many years that in which my philosophy, such as it is, was most fully expounded, I do not know that philosophic critics, as distinct from teachers, have ever had recourse to it. I have wondered whether such facts signified that philosophers in general, although they are themselves usually teachers, have not taken education with sufficient seriousness for it to occur to them that any rational person could actually think it possible that philosophizing should focus about education as the supreme human interest in which, moreover, other problems, cosmological, moral, logical, come to a head. At all events, this handle is offered to any subsequent critic who may wish to lay hold of it.

A second point is that as my study and thinking progressed, I became more and more troubled by the intellectual scandal that seemed to me involved in the current (and traditional) dualism in logical standpoint and method between something called "science" on the one hand and something called "morals" on the other. I have long felt that the construction of a logic, that is, a method of effective inquiry, which would apply without abrupt breach of con-

625

tinuity to the fields designated by both of these words, is at once our needed theoretical solvent and the supply of our greatest practical want. This belief has had much more to do with the development of what I termed, for lack of a better word, "instrumentalism," than have most of the reasons that have been assigned.

The third point forms the great exception to what was said about no very fundamental vital influence issuing from books; it concerns the influence of William James. As far as I can discover, one specifiable philosophic factor which entered into my thinking so as to give it a new direction and quality, it is this one. To say that it proceeded from his *Psychology* rather than from the essays collected in the volume called *Will to Believe*, his *Pluralistic Universe*, or *Pragmatism*, is to say something that needs explanation. For there are, I think, two unreconciled strains in the *Psychology*. One is found in the adoption of the subjective tenor of prior psychological tradition; even when the special tenets of that tradition are radically criticized, an underlying subjectivism is retained, at least in vocabulary—and the difficulty in finding a vocabulary which will intelligibly convey a genuinely new idea is perhaps the obstacle that most retards the easy progress of philosophy. I may cite as an illustration the substitution of the "stream of consciousness" for discrete elementary states: the advance made was enormous. Nevertheless the point of view remained that of a realm of consciousness set off by itself. The other strain is objective, having its roots in a return to the earlier biological conception of the psyche, but a return possessed of a new force and value due to the immense progress made by biology since the time of Aristotle. I doubt if we have as yet begun to realize all that is due to William James for the introduction and use of this idea; as I have already intimated, I do not think that he fully and consistently realized it himself. Anyway, it worked its way more and more into all my ideas and acted as a ferment to transform old beliefs.

If this biological conception and mode of approach had been prematurely hardened by James, its effect might have been merely to substitute one schematism for another. But it is not tautology to say that James's sense of life was itself vital. He had a profound sense, in origin artistic and moral, perhaps, rather than "scientific," of the difference between the categories of the living and of the mechanical; some time, I think, someone may write an essay that will show how the most distinctive factors in his general philosophic view, pluralism, novelty, freedom, individuality, are all con-

626

nected with his feeling for the qualities and traits of that which lives. Many philosophers have had much to say about the idea of organism; but they have taken it structurally and hence statically. It was reserved for James to think of life in terms of life in action. This point, and that about the objective biological factor in James's conception of thought (discrimination, abstraction, conception, generalization), is fundamental when the role of psychology in philosophy comes under consideration. It is true that the effect of its introduction into philosophy has often, usually, been to dilute and distort the latter. But that is because the psychology was bad psychology.

I do not mean that I think that in the end the connection of psychology with philosophy is, in the abstract, closer than is that of other branches of science. Logically it stands on the same plane with them. But historically and at the present juncture the revolution introduced by James had, and still has, a peculiar significance. On the negative side it is as important, for it is indispensable as a purge of the heavy charge of bad psychology that is so embedded in the philosophical tradition that is not generally recognized to be psychology at all. As an example, I would say that the problem of "sense data," which occupies such a great bulk in recent British thinking, has to my mind no significance other than as a survival of an old and outworn psychological doctrine—although those who deal with the problem are for the most part among those who stoutly assert the complete irrelevance of psychology to philosophy. On the positive side we have the obverse of this situation. The newer objective psychology supplies the easiest way, pedagogically if not in the abstract, by which to reach a fruitful conception of thought and its work, and thus to better our logical theories— provided thought and logic have anything to do with one another. And in the present state of men's minds the linking of philosophy to the significant issues of actual experience is facilitated by constant interaction with the methods and conclusions of psychology. The more abstract sciences, mathematics and physics, for example, have left their impress deep upon traditional philosophy. The former, in connection with an exaggerated anxiety about formal certainty, has more than once operated to divorce philosophic thinking from connection with questions that have a source in existence. The remoteness of psychology from such abstractions, its nearness to what is distinctively human, gives it an emphatic claim for a sympathetic hearing at the present time.

In connection with an increasing recognition of this human aspect, there developed the influence which forms the fourth heading of this recital. The objective biological approach of the Jamesian psychology led straight to the perception of the importance of distinctive social categories, especially communication and participation. It is my conviction that a great deal of our philosophizing needs to be done over again from this point of view, and that there will ultimately result an integrated synthesis in a philosophy congruous with modern science and related to actual needs in education, morals, and religion. One has to take a broad survey in detachment from immediate prepossessions to realize the extent to which the characteristic traits of the science of today are connected with the development of social subjects—anthropology, history, politics, economics, language and literature, social and abnormal psychology, and so on. The movement is both so new, in an intellectual sense, and we are so much of it and it so much of us, that it escapes definite notice. Technically the influence of mathematics upon philosophy is more obvious; the great change that has taken place in recent years in the ruling ideas and methods of the physical sciences attracts attention much more easily than does the growth of the social subjects, just because it is farther away from impact upon us. Intellectual prophecy is dangerous; but if I read the cultural signs of the times aright, the next synthetic movement in philosophy will emerge when the significance of the social sciences and arts has become an object of reflective attention in the same way that mathematical and physical sciences have been made the objects of thought in the past, and when their full import is grasped. If I read these signs wrongly, nevertheless the statement may stand as a token of a factor significant in my own intellectual development.

In any case, I think it shows a deplorable deadness of imagination to suppose that philosophy will indefinitely revolve within the scope of the problems and systems that two thousand years of European history have bequeathed to us. Seen in the long perspective of the future, the whole of western European history is a provincial episode. I do not expect to see in my day a genuine as distinct from a forced and artificial, integration of thought. But a mind that is not too egotistically impatient can have faith that this unification will issue in its season. Meantime a chief task of those who call themselves philosophers is to help get rid of the useless lumber that blocks our highways of thought, and strive to make straight and open the paths that lead to the future. Forty years spent in

628

wandering in a wilderness like that of the present is not a sad fate
—unless one attempts to make himself believe that the wilderness
is after all itself the promised land.

MY PEDAGOGIC CREED

ARTICLE ONE—WHAT EDUCATION IS

I BELIEVE THAT

All education proceeds by the participation of the individual in
the social consciousness of the race. This process begins unconsciously almost at birth, and is continually shaping the individual's
powers, saturating his consciousness, forming his habits, training his
ideas, and arousing his feelings and emotions. Through this unconscious education the individual gradually comes to share in the
intellectual and moral resources which humanity has succeeded in
getting together. He becomes an inheritor of the funded capital
of civilization. The most formal and technical education in the
world cannot safely depart from this general process. It can only
organize it or differentiate it in some particular direction.

The only true education comes through the stimulation of the child's
powers by the demands of the social situations in which he finds
himself. Through these demands he is stimulated to act as a member
of a unity, to emerge from his original narrowness of action and
feeling, and to conceive of himself from the standpoint of the welfare of the group to which he belongs. Through the responses which
others make to his own activities he comes to know what these
mean in social terms. The value which they have is reflected back
into them. For instance, through the response which is made to the
child's instinctive babblings the child comes to know what those
babblings mean; they are transformed into articulate language,
and thus the child is introduced into the consolidated wealth of
ideas and emotions which are now summed up in language.

This educational process has two sides—one psychological and
one sociological—and that neither can be subordinated to the
other, or neglected, without evil results following. Of these two
sides, the psychological is the basis. The child's own instincts and
powers furnish the material and give the starting-point for all education. Save as the efforts of the educator connect with some
activity which the child is carrying on of his own initiative independent of the educator, education becomes reduced to a pressure

from without. It may, indeed, give certain external results, but cannot truly be called educative. Without insight into the psychological structure and activities of the individual, the educative process will, therefore, be haphazard and arbitrary. If it chances to coincide with the child's activity it will get a leverage; if it does not, it will result in friction, or disintegration, or arrest of the child-nature.

Knowledge of social conditions, of the present state of civilization, is necessary in order properly to interpret the child's powers. The child has his own instincts and tendencies, but we do not know what these mean until we can translate them into their social equivalents. We must be able to carry them back into a social past and see them as the inheritance of previous race activities. We must also be able to project them into the future to see what their outcome and end will be. In the illustration just used, it is the ability to see in the child's babblings the promise and potency of a future social intercourse and conversation which enables one to deal in the proper way with that instinct.

The psychological and social sides are organically related, and that education cannot be regarded as a compromise between the two, or a superimposition of one upon the other. We are told that the psychological definition of education is barren and formal —that it gives us only the idea of a development of all the mental powers without giving us any idea of the use to which these powers are put. On the other hand, it is urged that the social definition of education, as getting adjusted to civilization, makes of it a forced and external process, and results in subordinating the freedom of the individual to a preconceived social and political status.

Each of these objections is true when urged against one side isolated from the other. In order to know what a power really is we must know what its end, use, or function is, and this we cannot know save as we conceive of the individual as active in social relationships. But, on the other hand, the only possible adjustment which we can give to the child under existing conditions is that which arises through putting him in complete possession of all his powers. With the advent of democracy and modern industrial conditions, it is impossible to foretell definitely just what civilization will be twenty years from now. Hence it is impossible to prepare the child for any precise set of conditions. To prepare him for the future life means to give him command of himself; it means so to train him that he will have the full and ready use of

630

JOHN DEWEY

all his capacities; that his eye and ear and hand may be tools ready to command, that his judgment may be capable of grasping the conditions under which it has to work, and the executive forces be trained to act economically and efficiently. It is impossible to reach this sort of adjustment save as constant regard is had to the individual's own powers, tastes, and interests—that is, as education is continually converted into psychological terms.

In sum, I believe that the individual who is to be educated is a social individual, and that society is an organic union of individuals. If we eliminate the social factor from the child we are left only with an abstraction; if we eliminate the individual factor from society, we are left only with an inert and lifeless mass. Education, therefore, must begin with a psychological insight into the child's capacities, interests, and habits. It must be controlled at every point by reference to these same considerations. These powers, interests, and habits must be continually interpreted—we must know what they mean. They must be translated into terms of their social equivalents—into terms of what they are capable of in the way of social service.

ARTICLE TWO—WHAT THE SCHOOL IS

I BELIEVE THAT

The school is primarily a social institution. Education being a social process, the school is simply that form of community life in which all those agencies are concentrated that will be most effective in bringing the child to share in the inherited resources of the race, and to use his own powers for social ends.

Education, therefore, is a process of living and not a preparation for future living.

The school must represent life, life as real and vital to the child as that which he carries on in the home, in the neighborhood, or on the playground.

That education which does not occur through forms of life, forms that are worth living for their own sake, is always a poor substitute for the genuine reality, and tends to cramp and to deaden.

The school, as an institution, should simplify existing social life; should reduce it, as it were, to an embryonic form. Existing life is so complex that the child cannot be brought into contact with it without either confusion or distraction; he is either overwhelmed by the multiplicity of activities which are going on, so that he loses

631

his own power of orderly reaction, or he is so stimulated by these various activities that his powers are prematurely called into play and he becomes either unduly specialized or else disintegrated.

As such simplified social life, the school should grow gradually out of the home life; that it should take up and continue the activities with which the child is already familiar in the home.

It should exhibit these activities to the child, and reproduce them in such ways that the child will gradually learn the meaning of them, and be capable of playing his own part in relation to them.

This is a psychological necessity, because it is the only way of securing continuity in the child's growth, the only way of giving a background of past experience to the new ideas given in school.

It is also a social necessity because the home is the form of social life in which the child has been nurtured and in connection with which he has had his moral training. It is the business of the school to deepen and extend his sense of the values bound up in his home life.

Much of present education fails because it neglects this fundamental principle of the school as a form of community life. It conceives the school as a place where certain information is to be given, where certain lessons are to be learned, or where certain habits are to be formed. The value of these is conceived as lying largely in the remote future; the child must do these things for the sake of something else he is to do; they are mere preparations. As a result they do not become a part of the life experience of the child and so are not truly educative.

The moral education centers upon this conception of the school as a mode of social life, that the best and deepest moral training is precisely that which one gets through having to enter into proper relations with others in a unity of work and thought. The present educational systems, so far as they destroy or neglect this unity, render it difficult or impossible to get any genuine, regular moral training.

The child should be stimulated and controlled in his work through the life of the community.

Under existing conditions far too much of the stimulus and control proceeds from the teacher, because of neglect of the idea of the school as a form of social life.

The teacher's place and work in the school is to be interpreted from this same basis. The teacher is not in the school to impose certain ideas or to form certain habits in the child, but is there as

632

JOHN DEWEY

a member of the community to select the influences which shall affect the child and to assist him in properly responding to these influences.

The discipline of the school should proceed from the life of the school as a whole and not directly from the teacher.

The teacher's business is simply to determine, on the basis of larger experience and riper wisdom, how the discipline of life shall come to the child.

All questions of the grading of the child and his promotion should be determined by reference to the same standard. Examinations are of use only so far as they test the child's fitness for social life and reveal the place in which he can be of the most service and where he can receive the most help.

ARTICLE THREE—THE SUBJECTMATTER OF EDUCATION

I BELIEVE THAT

The social life of the child is the basis of concentration, or correlation, in all his training or growth. The social life gives the unconscious unity and the background of all his efforts and of all his attainments.

The subjectmatter of the school curriculum should mark a gradual differentiation out of the primitive unconscious unity of social life.

We violate the child's nature and render difficult the best ethical results by introducing the child too abruptly to a number of special studies, of reading, writing, geography, etc., out of relation to this social life.

The true center of correlation on the school subjects is not science, nor literature, nor history, nor geography, but the child's own social activities.

Education cannot be unified in the study of science, or socalled nature study, because apart from human activity, nature itself is not a unity; nature in itself is a number of diverse objects in space and time, and to attempt to make it the center of work by itself is to introduce a principle of radiation rather than one of concentration.

Literature is the reflex expression and interpretation of social experience; that hence it must follow upon and not precede such experience. It, therefore, cannot be made the basis, although it may be made the summary of unification.

Once more that history is of educative value in so far as it presents phases of social life and growth. It must be controlled by

633

reference to social life. When taken simply as history it is thrown into the distant past and becomes dead and inert. Taken as the record of man's social life and progress it becomes full of meaning. I believe, however, that it cannot be so taken excepting as the child is also introduced directly into social life.

The primary basis of education is in the child's powers at work along the same general constructive lines as those which have brought civilizaton into being.

The only way to make the child conscious of his social heritage is to enable him to perform those fundamental types of activity which make civilization what it is.

In the socalled expressive or constructive activities is the center of correlation.

This gives the standard for the place of cooking, sewing, manual training, etc., in the school.

They are not special studies which are to be introduced over and above a lot of others in the way of relaxation or relief, or as additional accomplishments. I believe rather that they represent, as types, fundamental forms of social activity; and that it is possible and desirable that the child's introduction into the more formal subjects of the curriculum be through the medium of these constructive activities.

The study of science is educational in so far as it brings out the materials and processes which make social life what it is.

One of the greatest difficulties in the present teaching of science is that the material is presented in purely objective form, or is treated as a new peculiar kind of experience which the child can add to that which he has already had. In reality, science is of value because it gives the ability to interpret and control the experience already had. It should be introduced, not as so much new subjectmatter, but as showing the factors already involved in previous experience and as furnishing tools by which that experience can be more easily and effectively regulated.

At present we lose much of the value of literature and language studies because of our elimination of the social element. Language is almost always treated in the books of pedagogy simply as the expression of thought. It is true that language is a logical instrument, but it is fundamentally and primarily a social instrument. Language is the device for communication; it is the tool through which one individual comes to share the ideas and feelings of others. When treated simply as a way of getting individual information, or

634

JOHN DEWEY

as a means of showing off what one has learned, it loses its social motive and end.

There is, therefore, no succession of studies in the ideal school curriculum. If education is life, all life has, from the outset, a scientific aspect, an aspect of art and culture, and an aspect of communication. It cannot, therefore, be true that the proper studies for one grade are mere reading and writing, and that at a later grade, reading, or literature, or science, may be introduced. The progress is not in the succession of studies, but in the development of new attitudes towards, and new interests in, experience.

Education must be conceived as a continuing reconstruction of experience; that the process and the goal of education are one and the same thing.

To set up any end outside of education, as furnishing its goal and standard, is to deprive the educational process of much of its meaning, and tends to make us rely upon false and external stimuli in dealing with the child.

ARTICLE FOUR—THE NATURE OF METHOD

I BELIEVE THAT

The question of method is ultimately reducible to the question of the order of development of the child's powers and interests. The law for presenting and treating material is the law implicit within the child's own nature. Because this is so I believe the following statements are of supreme importance as determining the spirit in which education is carried on.

The active side precedes the passive in the development of the child-nature; that expression comes before conscious impression; that the muscular development precedes the sensory; that movements come before conscious sensations; I believe that consciousness is essentially motor or impulsive; that conscious states tend to project themselves in action.

The neglect of this principle is the cause of a large part of the waste of time and strength in school work. The child is thrown into a passive, receptive, or absorbing attitude. The conditions are such that he is not permitted to follow the law of his nature; the result is friction and waste.

Ideas [intellectual and rational processes] also result from action and devolve for the sake of the better control of action. What we term reason is primarily the law of order or effective action. To

635

attempt to develop the reasoning powers, the powers of judgment, without reference to the selection and arrangement of means in action, is the fundamental fallacy in our present methods of dealing with this matter. As a result we present the child with arbitrary symbols. Symbols are a necessity in mental development, but they have their place as tools for economizing effort; presented by themselves they are a mass of meaningless and arbitrary ideas imposed from without.

The image is the great instrument of instruction. What a child gets out of any subject presented to him is simply the images which he himself forms with regard to it.

If nine-tenths of the energy at present directed towards making the child learn certain things were spent in seeing to it that the child was forming proper images, the work of instruction would be indefinitely facilitated.

Much of the time and attention now given to the preparation and presentation of lessons might be more wisely and profitably expended in training the child's power of imagery and in seeing to it that he was continually forming definite vivid and growing images of the various subjects with which he comes in contact in his experience.

Interests are the signs and symptoms of growing power. I believe that they represent dawning capacities. Accordingly the constant and careful observation of interests is of the utmost importance for the educator.

These interests are to be observed as showing the state of development which the child has reached.

They prophesy the stage upon which he is about to enter.

Only through the continual and sympathetic observation of childhood's interests can the adult enter into the child's life and see what it is ready for, and upon what material it could work most readily and fruitfully.

These interests are neither to be humored nor repressed. To repress interest is to substitute the adult for the child, and so to weaken intellectual curiosity and alertness, to suppress initiative, and to deaden interest. To humor the interests is to substitute the transient for the permanent. The interest is always the sign of some power below; the important thing is to discover this power. To humor the interest is to fail to penetrate below the surface, and its sure result is to substitute caprice and whim for genuine interest.

The emotions are the reflex of actions.

636

JOHN DEWEY

To endeavor to stimulate or arouse the emotions apart from their corresponding activities is to introduce an unhealthy and morbid state of mind.

If we can only secure right habits of action and thought, with reference to the good, the true, and the beautiful, the emotions will for the most part take care of themselves.

Next to deadness and dullness, formalism and routine, our education is threatened with no greater evil than sentimentalism.

This sentimentalism is the necessary result of the attempt to divorce feeling from action.

ARTICLE FIVE—THE SCHOOL AND SOCIAL PROGRESS

I BELIEVE THAT

Education is the fundamental method of social progress and reform.

All reforms which rest simply upon the enactment of law, or the threatening of certain penalties, or upon changes in mechanical or outward arrangements, are transitory and futile.

Education is a regulation of the process of coming to share in the social consciousness; and that the adjustment of individual activity on the basis of this social consciousness is the only sure method of social reconstruction.

This conception has due regard for both the individualistic and socialistic ideals. It is duly individual because it recognizes the formation of a certain character as the only genuine basis of right living. It is socialistic because it recognizes that this right character is not to be formed by merely individual precept, example, or exhortation, but rather by the influence of a certain form of institutional or community life upon the individual, and that the social organism through the school, as its organ, may determine ethical results.

In the ideal school we have the reconciliation of the individualistic and the institutional ideals.

The community's duty to education is, therefore, its paramount moral duty. By law and punishment, by social agitation and discussion, society can regulate and form itself in a more or less haphazard and chance way. But through education society can formulate its own purposes, can organize its own means and resources, and thus shape itself with definiteness and economy in the direction in which it wishes to move.

When society once recognizes the possibilities in this direction,

637

and the obligations which these possibilities impose, it is impossible to conceive of the resources of time, attention, and money which will be put at the disposal of the educator.

It is the business of everyone interested in education to insist upon the school as the primary and most effective interest of social progress and reform in order that society may be awakened to realize what the school stands for, and arouse to the necessity of endowing the educator with sufficient equipment properly to perform his task.

Education thus conceived marks the most perfect and intimate union of science and art conceivable in human experience.

The art of thus giving shape to human powers and adapting them to social service is the supreme art; one calling into its service the best of artists; that no insight, sympathy, tact, executive power, is too great for such service.

With the growth of psychological service, giving added insight into individual structure and laws of growth; and with growth of social science, adding to our knowledge of the right organization of individuals, all scientific resources can be utilized for the purposes of education.

When science and art thus join hands the most commanding motive for human action will be reached, the most genuine springs of human conduct aroused, and the best service that human nature is capable of guaranteed.

The teacher is engaged, not simply in the training of individuals, but in the formation of the proper social life.

Every teacher should realize the dignity of his calling; that he is a social servant set apart for the maintenance of proper social order and the securing of the right social growth.

In this way the teacher always is the prophet of the true God and the usherer in of the true kingdom of God.

EVOLUTION AND ETHICS

Evolution is a continued development of new conditions which are better suited to the needs of organisms than the old. The unwritten chapter in natural selection is that of the evolution of environments.

Now, in man we have this power of variation and consequent discovery and constitution of new environments set free. All biological process has been effected through this, and so every tendency which forms this power is selected; in man it reaches its climax.

638

JOHN DEWEY

So far as the individual is concerned, the environment (the specific conditions which relate to his life) is highly variable at present. The growth of science, its application in invention to industrial life, the multiplication and acceleration of means of transportation and intercommunication, have created a peculiarly unstable environment. It shifts constantly within itself, or qualitatively, and as to its range, or quantitatively. Simply as an affair of nature, not of art (using these terms in Mr. Huxley's sense[1]) it is a profitable, and advantageous thing that structural changes, if any occur, should not get too set. They would limit unduly the possibility of change in adaptation. In the present environment, flexibility of function, the enlargement of the range of uses to which one and the same organ, grossly considered, may be put, as a great, almost the supreme, condition of success. As such, any change in that direction is a favorable variation which must be selected. In a word, the difference between man and animal is not that selection has ceased, but that selection along the line of variations which enlarge and intensify the environment is active as never before.

We reach precisely the same conclusion with respect to "selection" that we have reached with reference to the cognate ideas—"fit" and "struggle for existence." It is found in the ethical process as it is in the cosmic, and it operates in the same way. So far as conditions have changed, so far as the environment is indefinitely more complex, wider, and more variable, so far of necessity and as a biological and cosmic matter, not merely an ethical one, the functions selected differ.

There are no doubt sufficiently profound distinctions between the ethical process and the cosmic process as it existed prior to man and to the formation of human society. So far as I know, however, all of these differences are summed up in the fact that the process and the forces bound up with the cosmic have come to consciousness in man. That which was instinct in the animal is conscious impulse in man. That which was "tendency to vary" in the animal is conscious foresight in man. That which was unconscious adaptation and survival in the animal, taking place by the "cut and try" method until it worked itself out, is with man conscious deliberation and experimentation. That this transfer from unconsciousness to consciousness has immense importance, need hardly be argued. It is enough to say that it means the whole distinction of the moral from the unmoral. We have, however, no reason to suppose that the cosmic process has become arrested or

[1] T. H. Huxley. "Evolution and Ethics," Romanes Lecture for 1893.

639

that some new force has supervened to struggle against the cosmic. Some theologians and moralists, to be sure, welcomed Huxley's apparent return to the idea of a dualism between the cosmic and the ethical as likely to inure favorably to the spiritual life. But I question whether the spiritual life does not get its surest and most ample guarantees when it is learned that the laws and conditions of righteousness are implicated in the working processes of the universe; when it is found that man in his conscious struggles, in his doubts, temptations, and defeats, in his aspirations and successes, is moved on and buoyed up by the forces which have developed nature; and that in this moral struggle he acts not as a mere individual but as an organ in maintaining and carrying forward the universal process.

THE JUDAIC TRADITION

THE JUDAIC TRADITION

JUDAISM is not only in itself one of the greatest expressions of mankind's religious spirit; from it also two other great world religions have derived their faith, namely the Christian and the Moslem. The Ten Commandments are the foundation of our moral tradition; the Covenant that Jehovah concluded with His people was a reality not only for the Jews, but also the source of courage and conviction for many Christian generations, among them the early settlers of this continent.

After the sword of Rome had brought to an end the political aspirations of the ancient Jews, the transcendental kingdom accompanied them into the diaspora, as it had gone with them into Egypt and Babylon. This kingdom was kept alive through the synagogue. Wherever Jews settled on the tortuous path of migration and martyrdom, there was the reminiscence of the destroyed temple of Jerusalem.

The synagogue, besides the home, was the center of worship. A great tradition of learned interpreters of the sacred texts grew up, and during the first centuries after Christ, about the time when the Christian Church formed its dogma, there was reduced to writing the *Talmud* which is the Hebrew rendering of "teaching" and "learning." The *Talmud* is the collection of the religious-legal opinions of the wise, the canon for moral behavior of the pious, and at the same time the source of a highly developed theological casuistry.

As in all institutions of historical vigor and continuity, the belief in the sacredness of a central and divine revelation did not prevent adjustment to the various environmental and cultural influences to which the people of Israel were exposed during their wanderings. While the Law remained the same, its execution in daily life, its form of transmission to the young, as well as its philosophical interpretation were subject to continual scrutiny, always with the aim of harmonizing new impressions with sacred traditions.

Thus, Philo Judaeus of Alexandria, at the time of Christ, proved the comparableness, and in certain aspects even the compatibility of essential tenets of Judaism with Greek philosophy, exercising thereby a decisive influence on the Christian Church fathers. Another important merging of Greek and Rabbinical philosophies occurred at the twelfth century when the Spanish Jew Maimonides—to mention only one of several great thinkers of the period—tried to incorporate the Aristotelian-

643

Arabic into the Jewish tradition. Like Philo's, so also the ideas of Maimonides reached far into the Christian camp which then started on a similar enterprise, for also Albert the Great of Cologne and Thomas Aquinas were engaged in blending the thought of Aristotle with a supranatural revelation.

The history of Israel is the history of the relation of a people to its God—a God for Whom "the burnt offerings of rams, and the fat of fed beasts," "vain oblations" and "incense" were "an abomination," but who told them: "Learn to do well; seek judgment, relieve the oppressed, judge the fatherless, plead for the widow. Come now and let us reason together." (Isaiah i, 10-18.)

In this kind of religion in which the practical and the theoretical elements were so closely fused with each other, instruction was not, as it often is with us, a matter of individual promotion, but a sacred duty.

In Deuteronomy (xi, 18 ff.) the Jews read: "Therefore shall ye lay up these my words in your heart and in your soul . . . And ye shall teach them your children, speaking of them when thou sittest in thine house, and when thou walkest by the way, when thou liest down, and when thou risest up." And Philo added to the Platonic virtues of wisdom, prudence, courage, and temperance among others the virtue of study.[1]

All the more for a people in the state of dispersion the uninterrupted transmission of its spiritual values and the acquisition of the language of the scriptures became a matter of self-preservation. Thus the literature of Judaism is replete not only with profound contemplations and practical proverbial wisdom, but also with suggestions about the best methods of teaching, some of them obsolete from our point of view, others of surprising insight into the nature of human learning.

[1] See H. A. Wolfson, *Philo, Foundations of Religious Philosophy in Judaism, Christianity, and Islam,* II (Harvard University Press, 1948), 237 ff.

THE BIBLE

THE following selections are from the Old Testament in the King James Version.

The Second Book of Moses Called EXODUS

CHAPTER XXIII

Thou shalt not raise a false report: put not thine hand with the wicked to be an unrighteous witness.

2. Thou shalt not follow a multitude to *do* evil; neither shalt thou speak in a cause to decline after many to wrest *judgment*.

3. Neither shalt thou countenance a poor man in his cause.

4. If thou meet thine enemy's ox or his ass going astray, thou shalt surely bring it back to him again.

5. If thou see the ass of him that hateth thee lying under his burden, and wouldest forbear to help him, thou shalt surely help with him.

6. Thou shalt not wrest the judgment of thy poor in his cause.

7. Keep thee far from a false matter; and the innocent and righteous slay thou not: for I will not justify the wicked.

8. And thou shalt take no gift: for the gift blindeth the wise, and perveteth the words of the righteous.

9. Also thou shalt not oppress a stranger: for ye know the heart of a stranger, seeing ye were strangers in the land of Egypt.

10. And six years thou shalt sow they land, and shalt gather in the fruits thereof:

11. But the seventh *year* thou shalt let it rest and lie still; that the poor of thy people may eat: and what they leave the beasts of the field shall eat. In like manner thou shalt deal with thy vineyard, *and* with thy oliveyard.

12. Six days thou shalt do thy work, and on the seventh day thou shalt rest: that thine ox and thine ass may rest, and the son of thy handmaid, and the stranger, may be refreshed.

.   .   .   .   .

The Third Book of Moses, Called LEVITICUS

CHAPTER XIX

And the Lord spake unto Moses, saying,

2. Speak unto all the congregation of the children of Israel, and say unto them, Ye shall be holy: for I the LORD your GOD *am* holy.

3. Ye shall fear every man his mother, and his father, and keep my sabbaths: I *am* the LORD your God.

.   .   .   .   .

9. And when ye reap the harvest of your land, thou shalt not wholly reap the corners of thy field, neither shalt thou gather the gleanings of thy harvest.

10. And thou shalt not glean thy vineyard, neither shalt thou gather *every* grape of thy vineyard; thou shalt leave them for the poor and stranger: I am the LORD your God.

11. Ye shall not steal, neither deal falsely, neither lie one to another.

12. And ye shall not swear by my name falsely, neither shalt thou profane the name of thy God: I *am* the LORD.

13. Thou shalt not defraud thy neighbour, neither rob *him:* the wages of him that is hired shall not abide with thee all night until the morning.

14. Thou shalt not curse the deaf, nor put a stumblingblock before the blind, but shalt fear thy God: I *am* the LORD.

15. Ye shall do no unrighteousness in judgment: thou shalt not respect the person of the poor, nor honour the person of the mighty: *but* in righteousness shalt thou judge thy neighbour.

16. Thou shalt not go up and down *as* a talebearer among thy people: neither shalt thou stand against the blood of thy neighbour: I *am* the LORD.

17. Thou shalt not hate thy brother in thine heart: thou shalt in any wise rebuke thy neighbour, and not suffer sin upon him.

18. Thou shalt not avenge, nor bear any grudge against the children of thy people, but thou shalt love thy neighbour as thyself: I *am* the LORD.

.   .   .   .   .

THE BIBLE

The Fifth Book of Moses, Called DEUTERONOMY

CHAPTER V

And Moses called all Israel, and said unto them, Hear, O Israel, the statutes and judgments which I speak in your ears this day, that ye may learn them, and keep, and do them.

2. The Lord our God made a covenant with us in Hôr'-ĕb.

. . . . .

6. I *am* the Lord thy God, which brought thee out of the land of Egypt, from the house of bondage.

7. Thou shalt have none other gods before me.

8. Thou shalt not make thee *any* graven image, *or* any likeness *of any thing* that *is* in heaven above, or that *is* in the earth beneath, or that *is* in the waters beneath the earth:

9. Thou shalt not bow down thyself unto them, nor serve them: for I the Lord thy God *am* a jealous God, visiting the iniquity of the fathers upon the children unto the third and fourth *generation* of them that hate me.

10. And shewing mercy unto thousands of them that love me and keep my commandments.

11. Thou shalt not take the name of the Lord thy God in vain: for the Lord will not hold *him* guiltless that taketh his name in vain.

12. Keep the sabbath day to sanctify it, as the Lord thy God hath commanded thee.

13. Six days thou shalt labour, and do all thy work:

14. But the seventh day *is* the sabbath of the Lord thy God: *in it* thou shalt not do any work, thou, nor thy son, nor thy daughter, nor thy manservant, nor thy maidservant, nor thine ox, nor thine ass, nor any of thy cattle, nor thy stranger that *is* within thy gates; that thy manservant and thy maidservant may rest as well as thou.

15. And remember that thou wast a servant in the land of Egypt, and *that* the Lord thy God brought thee out thence through a mighty hand and by a stretched out arm: therefore the Lord thy God commanded thee to keep the sabbath day.

16. Honour thy father and thy mother, as the Lord thy God hath commanded thee; that thy days may be prolonged, and that it may go well with thee, in the land which the Lord thy God giveth thee.

17. Thou shalt not kill.

18. Neither shalt thou commit adultery.

19. Neither shalt thou steal.

20. Neither shalt thou bear false witness against thy neighbour.

21. Neither shalt thou desire thy neighbour's wife neither shalt thou covet thy neighbour's house, his field, or his manservant, or his maidservant, his ox, or his ass, or any *thing* that *is* thy neighbour's.

22. These words the LORD spake unto all your assembly in the mount out of the midst of the fire, of the cloud, and of the thick darkness, with a great voice: and he added no more. And he wrote them in two tables of stone, and delivered them unto me.

    .   .   .   .   .

BABA BATHRA

THE following selections are from *Baba Bathra*, translated into English with Notes, Glossary, and Indices, Chapters I-IV by Maurice Simon; Chapters V and VI by Israel Slotki. (*The Babylonian Talmud, Seder Nezikin*, under the Editorship of Rabbi Dr. I. Epstein, in two volumes, London, the Soncino Press, 1935, I, 105-107.)

BABA BATHRA, 21a

GEMARA . . . Verily the name of that man is to be blessed, to wit Joshua ben Gamala, [officiated about 64 A.D.] for but him the Torah would have been forgotten from Israel. For at first if a child had a father, his father taught him, and if he had no father he did not learn at all. By what [verse of the Scripture] did they guide themselves?—By the verse, *And ye shall teach them to your children* [Deut. xi, 19], laying the emphasis on the word '*ye.*' They then made an ordinance that teachers of children should be appointed in Jerusalem. By what verse did they guide themselves?—By the verse, *For from Zion shall the Torah go forth* [Isa. ii, 3]. Even so, however, if a child had a father, the father would take him up to Jerusalem and have him taught there, and if not, he would not go up to learn there. They therefore ordained that teachers should be appointed in each prefecture [the district under an '*Eparchus,*' which might be either a town or a province], and that boys should enter school at the age of sixteen or seventeen, [They did so] and if the teacher punished them they used to rebel and leave the school. At length Joshua b. Gamala came and ordained that teachers of young children should be appointed in each district and each town, and that children should enter school at the age of six or seven.

Rab said to R. Samuel b. Shilath: Before the age of six do not accept pupils; from that age you can accept them, and stuff them with Torah like an ox. Rab also said to R. Samuel b. Shilath: When you punish a pupil, only hit him with a shoe latchet. The

649

attentive one will read [of himself], and if one is inattentive, put him next to a diligent one.

. . . . . .

Raba further said: The number of pupils to be assigned to each teacher is twenty-five. If there are fifty, we appoint two teachers. If there are forty, we appoint an assistant, at the expense of the town.

Raba also said: If we have a teacher who gets on with the children and there is another who can get on better, we do not replace the first by the second, for fear that the second when appointed will become indolent [Having no competitor to fear]. R. Dimi from Nehardea, however, held that he would exert himself still more if appointed: 'the jealousy of scribes increaseth wisdom.'

Raba further said: If there are two teachers of whom one gets on fast but with mistakes and the other slowly but without mistakes, we appoint the one who gets on fast and makes mistakes, since the mistakes correct themselves in time. R. Dimi from Nehardea on the other hand said that we appoint the one who goes slowly but makes no mistakes, for once a mistake is implanted it cannot be eradicated.

MAIMONIDES 1135–1204

Moses ben Maimon, born in Cordoba, Spain, in 1135, received a thorough Talmudic education from his father and studied Arabic philosophy under the Arabic philosophers of Spain. He taught philosophy and practiced medicine in Fez, North Africa, and died at Fostat, Egypt, in 1204, after a life of many persecutions. The following selections are taken from the *Book of Mishnah Torah Yod Ha-Hazakah*, with Rabd's Criticism and References. Translated by Rabbi Simon Glazer (New York; Hebrew Publishing Co., 1927), I, 236, 237, and from Maimonides' main philosophical work, *The Guide for the Perplexed*, originally written in Arabic, translated by M. Friedländer (New York: Pardes Publishing House, 1946), pp. 2, 4, 42-49, 394-397.

THE TREATISE CONCERNING
THE STUDY OF THE TORAH

BOOK III, CHAPTER 1

8. Every man in Israel is obliged to study the Torah, whether he be poor or rich, whether he be physically healthy or ailing, whether he be in full vigor of youth or of great age and weakened vitality; even if he be dependent upon alms for his livelihood, or going around from door to door begging his daily bread, yea, even he who has a wife and children to support is obliged to have an appointed time for the study of the Torah, both during the day and at night, for it is said: "But thou shalt meditate therein day and night." (Joshua, i, 8.) [Talmud: Yoma, 35a; Menahot 99b G.G.]

9. Some of the great scholars in Israel were hewers of wood, some of them drawers of water, and some of them blind: nevertheless they engaged themselves in the study of the Torah by day and by night. Moreover, they are included among those who translated the tradition as it was transmitted from mouth of man to mouth of man, even from the mouth of Moses our Master.

10. Until what age in life is one obliged to study the Torah?

Even until the day of one's demise; for it is said: "And lest they depart from thy heart all the days of thy life" (Deut. iv, 9). Forsooth, as long as one will not occupy himself with study he forgets what he did study. [Talmud: Kiddushin, 28 b.G.]

11. One is obliged to divide his time of study by three; one third for the study of Holy Writ, one third for the study of the Oral Torah, and one third for thinking and reflecting so that he may understand the end of a thing from its beginning, and deduct one matter from another, and compare one matter to another, and reason out by the hermeneutical rules in which the Torah is expounded to the end that he may know which are the principal rules and how to deduct therefrom that which is forbidden and that which is permitted, and other like matters which he studied from oral tradition. This subject of study is called Gemara. [Talmud: Kiddushin, 30a; Abodah Zarah, 19 b C.]

GUIDE FOR THE PERPLEXED

INTRODUCTION

The object of this treatise is to enlighten a religious man who has been trained to believe in the truth of our holy Law, who conscientiously fulfils his moral and religious duties, and at the same time has been successful in his philosophical studies. Human reason has attracted him to abide within its sphere; and he finds it difficult to accept as correct the teaching based on the literal interpretation of the Law, and especially that which he himself or others derived from those homonymous, metaphorical, or hybrid expressions. Hence he is lost in perplexity and anxiety. If he be guided solely by reason, and renounce his previous views which are based on those expressions, he would consider that he had rejected the fundamental principles of the Law; and even if he retain the opinions which were derived from those expressions, and if, instead of following his reason, he abandon its guidance altogether, it would still appear that his religious convictions had suffered loss and injury. For he would then be left with those errors which give rise to fear and anxiety, constant grief and great perplexity.

This work has also a second object in view. It seeks to explain certain obscure figures which occur in the Prophets, and are not distinctly characterized as being figures. Ignorant and superficial readers take them in a literal, not in a figurative sense. Even well-

652

informed persons are bewildered if they understand these passages in their literal signification, but they are entirely relieved of their perplexity when we explain the figure, or merely suggest that the terms are figurative. For this reason I have called this book *Guide for the Perplexed.*

. . . . . .

You must know that if a person, who has attained a certain degree of perfection, wishes to impart to others, either orally or in writing, any portion of the knowledge which he has acquired of these subjects, he is utterly unable to be as systematic and explicit as he could be in a science of which the method is well known. The same difficulties which he encountered when investigating the subject for himself will attend him when endeavouring to instruct others; viz., at one time the explanation will appear lucid, at another time, obscure; this property of the subject appears to remain the same both to the advanced scholar and to the beginner. For this reason, great theological scholars gave instruction in all such matters only by means of metaphors and allegories. They frequently employed them in forms varying more or less essentially. . . .

If we were to teach in these disciplines, without the use of parables and figures, we should be compelled to resort to expressions both profound and transcendental, and by no means more intelligible than metaphors and similes; as though the wise and learned were drawn into this course by the Divine Will, in the same way as they are compelled to follow the laws of nature in matters relating to the body. You are no doubt aware that the Almighty, desiring to lead us to perfection and to improve our state of society, has revealed to us laws which are to regulate our actions. These laws, however, presuppose an advanced state of intellectual culture. We must first form a conception of the Existence of the Creator according to our capabilities; that is, we must have a knowledge of Metaphysics. But this discipline can only be approached after the study of Physics; for the science of Physics borders on Metaphysics, and must even precede it in the course of our studies, as is clear to all who are familiar with these questions. Therefore the Almighty commenced Holy Writ with the description of the Creation, that is, with Physical Science; the subject being on the one hand most weighty and important, and on the other hand our means of fully comprehending those great problems being limited. He described those profound truths, which His Divine Wisdom found it neces-

sary to communicate to us, in allegorical, figurative, and metaphorical language . . . It has been treated in metaphors in order
that the uneducated may comprehend it according to the measure
of their faculties and the feebleness of their apprehension, while
educated persons may take it in a different sense.

.   .   .   .   .

ON THE STUDY OF METAPHYSICS

CHAPTER XXXII

You must consider, when reading this treatise, that mental perception, because connected with matter, is subject to conditions
similar to those to which physical perception is subject. That is
to say, if your eye looks around, you can perceive all that is within
the range of our vision; if, however, you overstrain your eye, exerting it too much by attempting to see an object which is too distant
for your eye, or to examine writings or engravings too small for
your sight, and forcing it to obtain a correct perception of them,
you will not only weaken your sight with regard to that special
object, but also for those things which you otherwise are able to
perceive: your eye will have become too weak to perceive what
you were able to see before you exerted yourself and exceeded the
limits of your vision.

The same is the case with the speculative faculties of one who
devotes himself to the study of any science. If a person studies
too much and exhausts his reflective powers, he will be confused,
and will not be able to apprehend even that which had been within
the power of his apprehension. For the powers of the body are all
alike in this respect.

The mental perceptions are not exempt from a similar condition.
If you admit the doubt, and do not persuade yourself to believe
that there is a proof for things which cannot be demonstrated, or to
try at once to reject and positively to deny an assertion the opposite
of which has never been proved, or attempt to perceive things
which are beyond your perception, then you have attained the
highest degree of human perfection, . . . If, on the other hand, you
attempt to exceed the limit of your intellectual power, or at once
to reject things as impossible which have never been proved to be
impossible, or which are in fact possible, though their possibility be
very remote, then . . . you will not only fail to become perfect,
but you will become exceedingly imperfect. Ideas founded on mere

654

imagination will prevail over you, you will incline towards defects, and towards base and degraded habits, on account of the confusion which troubles the mind, and of the dimness of its light, just as weakness of sight causes invalids to see many kinds of unreal images, especially when they have looked for a long time at dazzling or at very minute objects.

Respecting this it has been said, "Hast thou found honey? eat so much as is sufficient for thee, lest thou be filled therewith, and vomit it" (Prov. xxv, 16) . . .

It was not the object of the Prophets and our Sages in these utterances to close the gate of investigation entirely, and to prevent the mind from comprehending what is within its reach, as is imagined by simple and idle people, whom it suits better to put forth their ignorance and incapacity as wisdom and perfection, and to regard the distinction and wisdom of others as irreligion and imperfection, thus taking darkness for light and light for darkness. The whole object of the Prophets and Sages was to declare that a limit is set to human reason where it must halt. Do not criticise the words used in this chapter and in others in reference to the mind, for we only intended to give some idea of the subject in view, not to describe the essence of the intellect; . . .

CHAPTER XXXIII

You must know that it is very injurious to begin with this branch of philosophy, viz., Metaphysics; or to explain [at first] the sense of the similes occurring in prophecies, and interpret the metaphors which are employed in historical accounts and which abound in the writings of the Prophets. On the contrary, it is necessary to initiate the young and to instruct the less intelligent according to their comprehension; those who appear to be talented and to have capacity for the higher method of study, i.e., that based on proof and on true logical argument, should be gradually advanced towards perfection, either by tuition or by self-instruction. He, however, who begins with Metaphysics, will not only become confused in matters of religion, but will fall into complete infidelity. I compare such a person to an infant fed with wheaten bread, meat and wine; it will undoubtedly die, not because such food is naturally unfit for the human body, but because of the weakness of the child, who is unable to digest the food, and cannot derive benefit from it. The same is the case with the true principles of science. They were presented in enigmas, clad in riddles, and taught by all wise

655

men in the most mysterious way that could be devised, not because they contain some secret evil, or are contrary to the fundamental principles of the Law (as fools think who are only philosophers in their own eyes), but because of the incapacity of man to comprehend them at the beginning of his studies: only slight allusions have been made to them to serve for the guidance of those who are capable of understanding them. These sciences were, therefore, called Mysteries (*sodoth*) and Secrets of the Law (*sitre torah*), . . .

CHAPTER XXXIV

There are five reasons why instruction should not begin with metaphysics, but should at first be restricted to pointing out what is fitted for notice and what may be made manifest to the multitude.

First Reason.—The subject itself is difficult, subtle and profound, . . . Instruction should not begin with abstruse and difficult subjects. In one of the similes contained in the Bible, wisdom is compared to water, and amongst other interpretations given by our Sages of this simile, occurs the following: He who can swim may bring up pearls from the depth of the sea, he who is unable to swim will be drowned, therefore only such persons as have had proper instruction should expose themselves to the risk.

Second Reason.—The intelligence of man is at first insufficient; for he is not endowed with perfection at the beginning, but at first possesses perfection only *in potentiâ*, not in fact . . . If a man possesses a certain faculty *in potentiâ*, it does not follow that it must become in him a reality. He may possibly remain deficient either on account of some obstacle, or from want of training in practices which would turn the possibility into a reality . . . There are many things which obstruct the path to perfection, and which keep man away from it. Where can he find sufficient preparation and leisure to learn all that is necessary in order to develop that perfection which he has *in potentiâ?*

Third Reason.—The preparatory studies are of long duration, and man, in his natural desire to reach the goal, finds them frequently too wearisome, and does not wish to be troubled by them. Be convinced that, if man were able to reach the end without preparatory studies, such studies would not be preparatory but tiresome and utterly superfluous. Suppose you awaken any person, even the most simple, as if from sleep, and you say to him, Do you not desire to know what the heavens are, what is their number and their

656

form; what beings are contained in them; what the angels are; how the creation of the whole world took place; what is its purpose, and what is the relation of its various parts to each other; what is the nature of the soul; how it enters the body; whether it has an independent existence, and if so, how it can exist independently of the body; by what means and to what purpose, and similar problems. He would undoubtedly say "Yes," and show a natural desire for the true knowledge of these things; but he will wish to satisfy that desire and to attain to that knowledge by listening to a few words from you. Ask him to interrupt his usual pursuits for a week, till he learn all this, he would not do it, and would be satisfied and contented with imaginary and misleading notions; he would refuse to believe that there is anything which requires preparatory studies and persevering research.

You, however, know how all these subjects are connected together; for there is nothing else in existence but God and His works, the latter including all existing things besides Him; we can only obtain a knowledge of Him through His works; His works give evidence of His existence, and show what must be assumed concerning Him, that is to say, what must be attributed to Him either affirmatively or negatively. It is thus necessary to examine all things according to their essence, to infer from every species such true and well-established propositions as may assist us in the solution of metaphysical problems. Again, many propositions based on the nature of numbers and the properties of geometrical figures, are useful in examining things which must be negatived in reference to God, and these negations will lead us to further inferences. You will certainly not doubt the necessity of studying astronomy and physics, if you are desirous of comprehending the relation between the world and Providence as it is in reality, and not according to imagination. There are also many subjects of speculation, which, though not preparing the way for metaphysics, help to train the reasoning power, enabling it to understand the nature of a proof, and to test truth by characteristics essential to it. They remove the confusion arising in the minds of most thinkers, who confound accidental with essential properties, and likewise the wrong opinions resulting therefrom. We may add, that although they do not form the basis for metaphysical research, they assist in forming a correct notion of these things, and are certainly useful in many other things connected with that discipline. Consequently he who wishes to attain to human perfection, must therefore first study Logic, next the various branches of Mathematics in their proper order, then Physics, and lastly Metaphysics. We find that many who have advanced to a certain point in the study of these disciplines become weary, and stop; that others, who are endowed with sufficient capacity, are interrupted in their studies by death, which surprises them while still engaged with the preliminary course. Now, if no knowledge whatever had been given to us by means of tradition, and if we had not been brought to the belief in a thing through the medium of similes, we would have been bound to form a perfect notion of things with their essential characteristics, and to believe only what we could prove; a goal which could only be attained by long preparation. In such a case most people would die, without having known whether there was a God or not, much less that certain things must be asserted about Him, and other things denied as defects. From such a fate not even "one of a city or two of a family" (Jer. iii, 14) would have escaped.

As regards the privileged few, "the remnant whom the Lord calls" (Joel iii, 5), they only attain the perfection at which they aim after due preparatory labour. The necessity of such a preparation and the need of such a training for the acquisition of real knowledge, has been plainly stated by King Solomon in the following words: "If the iron be blunt, and he do not whet the edge, then must he put to more strength; and it is profitable to prepare for wisdom" (Eccles. x, 10); "Hear counsel, and receive instruction, that thou mayest be wise in thy latter end" (Prov. xix, 20) . . .

The majority of scholars, that is to say, the most famous in science, are afflicted with this failing, viz., that of hurrying at once to the final results and of speaking about them, without treating of the preliminary disciplines. Led by folly or ambition to disregard those preparatory studies, for the attainment of which they are either incapable or too idle, some scholars endeavour to prove that these are injurious or superfluous. On reflection the truth will became obvious.

The Fourth Reason is taken from the physical constitution of man. It has been proved that moral conduct is a preparation for intellectual progress, and that only a man whose character is pure, calm and steadfast, can attain to intellectual perfection; that is, acquire correct conceptions. Many men are naturally so constituted that all perfection is impossible; e.g., he whose heart is very warm and is himself very powerful, is sure to be passionate, though he tries to counteract that disposition by training; he whose testicles are warm, humid, and vigorous, and the organs connected therewith are surcharged, will not easily refrain from sin, even if he makes

658

great efforts to restrain himself. You also find persons of great levity and rashness, whose excited manners and wild gestures prove that their constitution is in disorder, and their temperament so bad that it cannot be cured. Such persons can never attain to perfection; it is utterly useless to occupy oneself with them on such a subject [as Metaphysics]. Medicine and of Geometry, and, from the reason already mentioned, it is not every person who is capable of approaching it. It is impossible for a man to study it successfully without moral preparation; he must acquire the highest degree of uprightness and integrity, "for the froward is an abomination to the Lord, but His secret is with the righteous" (Prov. iii, 32). Therefore it was considered inadvisable to teach it to the young men; nay, it is impossible for them to comprehend it, on account of the heat of their blood and the flame of youth, which confuses their minds; that heat, which causes all the disorder, must first disappear; they must have become moderate and settled, humble in their hearts, and subdued in their temperament; only then will they be able to arrive at the highest degree of the perception of God, i.e., the study of Metaphysics, . . .

Fifth Reason.—Man is disturbed in his intellectual occupation by the necessity of looking after the material wants of the body, especially if providing for wife and children be superadded; much more so if he seeks superfluities in addition to his ordinary wants, for by custom and bad habits these become a powerful motive. Even the perfect man to whom we have referred, if too busy with these necessary things, much more so if busy with unnecessary things, and filled with a great desire for them—must weaken or altogether lose his desire for study, to which he will apply himself with interruption, lassitude, and want of attention. He will not attain to that for which he is fitted by his abilities, or he will acquire imperfect knowledge, a confused mass of true and false ideas. For these reasons it was proper that the study of Metaphysics should have been exclusively cultivated by privileged persons, and not entrusted to the common people. It is not for the beginner, and he should abstain from it, as the little child has to abstain from taking solid food and from carrying heavy weight.

· · · · ·

ON TRUE WISDOM

CHAPTER LIV

The ancient and the modern philosophers have shown that man can acquire four kinds of perfection. The first kind, the lowest, in the acquisition of which people spend their days, is perfection as regards property; the possession of money, garments, furniture, servants, land, and the like; the possession of the title of a great king belongs to this class. There is no close connexion between this possession and its possessor; it is a perfectly imaginary relation when on account of the great advantage a person derives from these possessions, he says, This is my house, this is my servant, this is my money, and these are my hosts and armies. For when he examines himself he will find that all these things are external, and their qualities are entirely independent of the possessor. When, therefore, that relation ceases, he that has been a great king may one morning find that there is no difference between him and the lowest person, and yet no change has taken place in the things which were ascribed to him. The philosophers have shown that he whose sole aim in all his exertions and endeavours is the possession of this kind of perfection, only seeks perfectly imaginary and transient things; and even if these remain his property all his lifetime, they do not give him any perfection.

The second kind is more closely related to man's body than the first. It includes the perfection of the shape, constitution, and form of man's body; the utmost evenness of temperaments, and the proper order and strength of his limbs. This kind of perfection must likewise be excluded from forming our chief aim; because it is a perfection of the body, and man does not possess it as man, but as a living being; he has this property besides in common with the lowest animal; and even if a person possesses the greatest possible strength, he could not be as strong as a mule, much less can he be as strong as a lion or an elephant; he, therefore, can at the utmost have strength that might enable him to carry a heavy burden, or break a thick substance, or do similar things, in which there is no great profit for the body. The soul derives no profit whatever from this kind of perfection.

The third kind of perfection is more closely connected with man himself than the second perfection. It includes moral perfection, the highest degree of excellency in man's character. Most of the

660

precepts aim at producing this perfection; but even this kind is only a preparation for another perfection, and is not sought for its own sake. For all moral principles concern the relation of man to his neighbour; the perfection of man's moral principles is, as it were, given to man for the benefit of mankind. Imagine a person being alone, and having no connexion whatever with any other person, all his good moral principles are at rest, they are not required, and give man no perfection whatever. These principles are only necessary and useful when man comes in contact with others.

The fourth kind of perfection is the true perfection of man; the possession of the highest intellectual faculties; the possession of such notions which lead to true metaphysical opinions as regards God. With this perfection man has obtained his final object; it gives him true human perfection; it remains to him alone; it gives him immortality, and on its account he is called man. Examine the first three kinds of perfection, you will find that, if you possess them, they are not your property, but the property of others; according to the ordinary view, however, they belong to you and to others. But the last kind of perfection is exclusively yours; no one else owns any part of it, "They shall be only thine own, and not strangers, with thee" (Prov. v, 17). Your aim must therefore be to attain this [fourth] perfection that is exclusively yours, and you ought not to continue to work and weary yourself for that which belongs to others, whilst neglecting your soul till it has lost entirely its original purity through the dominion of the bodily powers over it. The same idea is expressed in the beginning of those poems, which allegorically represent the state of our soul. "My mother's children were angry with me; they made me the keeper of the vineyards; but mine own vineyard have I not kept" (Song i, 6). Also the following passage refers to the same subject, "Lest thou give thine honour unto others, and thy years unto the cruel" (Prov. v, 9).

. . . . . .

This is all that I thought proper to discuss in this treatise, and which I considered useful for men like you. I hope that, by the help of God, you will after due reflection, comprehend all the things which I have treated here. May He grant us and all Israel with us to attain what He promised us, "Then the eyes of the blind shall be opened, and the ears of the deaf shall be unstopped" (Isa. xxxv, 5); "The people that walked in darkness have seen a great light; they that dwell in the shadow of death upon them hath the light shined" (*Ibid.* ix, 1).

God is near to all who call Him, if they call Him in truth, and turn to Him. He is found by every one who seeks Him, if he always goes towards Him, and never goes astray. AMEN.

GLÜCKEL VON HAMELN 1644–1724

GLÜCKEL VON HAMELN was born in Hamburg and died at Metz. Her diary, originally written in Yiddish, relates many noteworthy events of the time, as well as the experiences of her life as wife, mother, and, after her husband's death, as businesswoman. The following is taken from *The Memoirs,* translated with Introduction and Notes by Marvin Lowenthal, pp. 1-5. It is reprinted by permission of Behrman House, Inc., 1261 Broadway, New York 1, N. Y.

THE MEMOIRS

In my great grief and for my heart's ease I begin this book the year of Creation 5451/1690-91/—God soon rejoice us and send us His redeemer!

I began writing it, dear children, upon the death of your good father, in the hope of distracting my soul from the burdens laid upon it, and the bitter thought that we have lost our faithful shepherd. In this way I have managed to live through many wakeful nights, and springing from my bed shortened the sleepless hours.

This, dear children, will be no book of morals. Such I could not write, and our sages have already written many. Moreover, we have our holy Torah in which we may find and learn all that we need for our journey through this world to the world to come. It is like a rope which the great and gracious God has thrown to us as we drown in the stormy sea of life, that we may seize hold of it and be saved.

The kernel of the Torah is, Thou shalt love thy neighbour as thyself. But in our days we seldom find it so, and few are they who love their fellowmen with all their heart—on the contrary, if a man can contrive to ruin his neighbour, nothing pleases him more.

The best thing for you, my children, is to serve God from your heart, without falsehood or sham, not giving out to people that you

663

are one thing while, God forbid, in your heart you are another. Say your prayers with awe and devotion. During the time for prayers, do not stand about and talk of other things. While prayers are being offered to the Creator of the world, hold it a great sin to engage another man in talk about an entirely different matter— shall God Almighty be kept waiting until you have finished your business?

Moreover, put aside a fixed time for the study of the Torah, as best you know how. Then diligently go about your business, for providing your wife and children a decent livelihood is likewise a *mitzwah*—the command of God and the duty of man. We should, I say, put ourselves to great pains for our children, for on this the world is built, yet we must understand that if children did as much for their parents, the children would quickly tire of it.

A bird once set out to cross a windy sea with its three fledglings. The sea was so wide and the wind so strong, the father bird was forced to carry his young, one by one, in his strong claws. When he was half-way across with the first fledgling the wind turned to a gale, and he said, "My child, look how I am struggling and risking my life in your behalf. When you are grown up, will you do as much for me and provide for my old age?" The fledgling replied, "Only bring me to safety, and when you are old I shall do everything you ask of me." Whereas the father bird dropped his child into the sea, and it drowned, and he said, "So shall it be done to such a liar as you." Then the father bird returned to shore, set forth with his second fledgling, asked the same question, and receiving the same answer, drowned the second child with the cry, "You, too, are a liar!" Finally he set out with the third fledgling, and when he asked the same question, the third and last fledgling replied, "My dear father, it is true you are struggling mightily and risking your life in my behalf, and I shall be wrong not to repay you when you are old, but I cannot bind myself. This though I can promise: when I am grown up and have children of my own, I shall do as much for them as you have done for me." Whereupon the father bird said, "Well spoken, my child, and wisely; your life I will spare and I will carry you to shore in safety."

Above all, my children, be honest in money matters, with both Jews and Gentiles, lest the name of Heaven be profaned. If you have in hand money or goods belonging to other people, give more care to them than if they were your own, so that, please God, you do no one a wrong. The first question put to a man in the next world is, whether he was faithful in his business dealings. Let a

664

man work ever so hard amassing great wealth dishonestly, let him during his lifetime provide his children fat dowries and upon his death a rich heritage—yet woe, I say, and woe again to the wicked who for the sake of enriching his children has lost his share in the world to come! For the fleeting moment he has sold Eternity.

When God send evil days upon us, we shall do well to remember the remedy contrived by the physician in the story told by Rabbi Abraham ben Sabbatai Levi. A great king, he tells us, once imprisoned his physician, and had him bound hand and foot with chains, and fed on a small dole of barley-bread and water. After months of this treatment, the king despatched relatives of the physician to visit the prison and learn what the unhappy man had to say. To their astonishment he looked as hale and hearty as the day he entered his cell. He told his relatives he owed his strength and wellbeing to a brew of seven herbs he had taken the precaution to prepare before he went to prison, and of which he drank a few drops every day. "What magic herbs are these?" they asked; and he answered: "The first is trust in God, the second is hope, and the others are patience, recognition of my sins, joy that in suffering now I shall not suffer in the world to come, contentment that my punishment is not worse, as well it could be, and lastly, knowledge that God who thrust me into prison can, if He will, at any moment set me free."

However, I am not writing this book in order to preach to you, but, as I have already said, to drive away the melancholy that comes with the long nights. So far as my memory and the subject permit, I shall try to tell everything that has happened to me from my youth upward. Not that I wish to put on airs or pose as a good and pious woman. No, dear children, I am a sinner. Every day, every hour, and every moment of my life I have sinned, nearly all manner of sins. God grant I may find the means and occasion for repentance. But, alas, the care of providing for my orphaned children, and the ways of the world, have kept me far from that state.

· · · · ·

MOSES HAYYIM LUZZATTO 1707–1747

Moses Hayyim Luzzatto, a Jewish mystic writer, was born in Padua in 1707 and died at Acre, Palestine in 1747. His best known work is the *Path of the Upright* of which the concluding paragraph is here reproduced. (*Mesillat Yesharim. The Path of the Upright.* A Critical Edition provided with a Translation and Notes by Mordecai M. Kaplan. Philadelphia, The Jewish Publication Society of America, 1936, pages 229–230.)

THE PATH OF THE UPRIGHT

It is evident that every man has to be led and guided according to the calling which he pursues, or the business in which he is engaged. The method of attaining saintliness which applies to one whose calling is the study of the Torah does not apply to the manual laborer, and neither method applies to one who is engaged in business. Each man must be shown a method which fits his occupation. Not that there are different kinds of saintliness, since saintliness must consist for all alike in doing that which is pleasing to the Creator, but as there are different kinds of men, the means of accomplishing that purpose are bound to vary. The man who is compelled to labor at the meanest work is as capable of being a perfect saint as one who never leaves off the study of Torah; as it is written, "The Lord hath made all things for Himself" (Prov. 16.4); and, elsewhere, "In all thy ways acknowledge Him, and He shall direct thy paths" (Prov. 3.6). God, blessed be His name, will, in His mercy, open our eyes to His Torah, teach us His ways, and guide us in His paths, and we shall be privileged to honor His name and to afford Him delight.

> The glory of the Lord shall endure for ever:
> The Lord shall rejoice in His works. (Ps. 104.31)

> Let Israel rejoice in Him that made him;
> Let the children of Zion be joyful in their King. (Ps. 149.2)

666

MEMORIAL OF
THE DEPARTED

Service of the Synagogue. Day of Atonement. A New Edition of the Festival Prayers with an English Translation in Prose and Verse. Reprinted from the Latest and Best London Edition. New York, Jewish Premium Publishing Co. [1915], Part II, pp. 118, 119.

Lord, what is man, that thou regardest him? or the son of man, that thou takest account of him?

Man is like to vanity: his days are as a shadow that passeth away.

In the morning he bloometh and sprouteth afresh; in the evening he is cut down and withereth.

So teach us to number our days that we may get us a heart of wisdom.

Mark the innocent man, and behold the upright: for the latter end of that man is peace.

But God will redeem my soul from the grasp of the grave: for he will receive me. Selah.

My flesh and my heart faileth: but God is the strength of my heart and my portion for ever.

And the dust returneth to the earth as it was, but the spirit returneth unto God who gave it.

I shall behold thy face in righteousness; I shall be satisfied when I awake with thy likeness.

Father of mercy! In thy hand are the souls of the living and the dead. May thy comforts soothe our hearts as we remember on this sacred day our revered and beloved kinsfolk who have gone to their eternal rest, and as we think of our dear parents, the crown of our heads and our glory, whose desire it was to train us in the way of virtue and righteousness, to teach us thy statutes and precepts, and to instruct us to do justice and to love mercy. We beseech thee, O Lord! grant us strength to remain faithful to their teachings, while the breath given of thee is within us. And may their souls repose

667

in the land of life, beholding thy majesty and delighting in thy reward.

And now, O good and beneficent God! what shall we say, what shall we speak unto thee? Our needs are so manifold; we cannot declare them. We are filled with shame as we think of all the goodness thou hast dealt unto us. O turn thou in mercy and loving-kindness unto the supplications of thy servants who now pour out their souls before thee. May thy loving kindness not depart from us. Give us our daily sustenance, and let us not be in need of the gifts of flesh and blood. Remove from us care and sorrow, distress and fear, shame and contempt. Strengthen us in our reverence for thee, and fortify us to keep thy perfect law. Vouchsafe unto us the joy of training our sons and daughters to keep thy commandments and to perform thy will all the days of their life. O God, take us not hence in the midst of our days. Let us complete in peace the number of our years. Verily we know that our life is frail, that our days are as an hand-breadth. Therefore help us, O God of our salvation, to live before thee in truth and uprighteousness during the years of our pilgrimage. And when it will please thee to take us from earth, be thou with us; and may our souls be bound up in the bond of life with the souls of our parents and of the righteous who stand before thee in heaven. AMEN. AMEN.